Klaus von Heusinger, Claudia Maienborn and Paul Portner (Eds.)
Semantics – Typology, Diachrony and Processing

This volume is part of a larger set of handbooks to Semantics

1	**Semantics: Foundations, History and Methods**
	Klaus von Heusinger, Claudia Maienborn, Paul Portner (eds.)

2	**Semantics: Lexical Structures and Adjectives**
	Claudia Maienborn, Klaus von Heusinger, Paul Portner (eds.)

3	**Semantics: Theories**
	Claudia Maienborn, Klaus von Heusinger, Paul Portner (eds.)

4	**Semantics: Noun Phrases and Verb Phrases**
	Paul Portner, Klaus von Heusinger, Claudia Maienborn (eds.)

5	**Semantics: Sentence and Information Structure**
	Paul Portner, Claudia Maienborn, Klaus von Heusinger (eds.)

6	**Semantics: Interfaces**
	Claudia Maienborn, Klaus von Heusinger, Paul Portner (eds.)

7	**Semantics: Typology, Diachrony and Processing**
	Klaus von Heusinger, Claudia Maienborn, Paul Portner (eds.)

Semantics
Typology, Diachrony and Processing

Edited by
Klaus von Heusinger
Claudia Maienborn
Paul Portner

DE GRUYTER
MOUTON

ISBN 978-3-11-058724-1
e-ISBN (PDF) 978-3-11-058982-5
e-ISBN (EPUB) 978-3-11-058732-6

Library of Congress Cataloging-in-Publication Data
Names: Heusinger, Klaus von, editor. | Maienborn, Claudia, editor. | Portner,
   Paul, editor.
Title: Semantics : typology, diachrony and processing / edited by Klaus von Heusinger,
   Claudia Maienborn, Paul Portner.
Description: Berlin ; Boston : De Gruyter, [2019] | Series: Mouton reader |
   Includes bibliographical references and index.
Identifiers: LCCN 2018031263 (print) | LCCN 2018047130 (ebook) | ISBN
   9783110589825 (electronic Portable Document Format (pdf) | ISBN
   9783110587241 (paperback) | ISBN 9783110589825 (e-book pdf) | ISBN
   9783110587326 (e-book epub)
Subjects: LCSH: Semantics. | BISAC: LANGUAGE ARTS & DISCIPLINES / Linguistics
   / Semantics.
Classification: LCC P325 (ebook) | LCC P325 .S37999 2019 (print) | DDC
   401/.43--dc23
LC record available at https://lccn.loc.gov/2018031263

Bibliographic information published by the Deutsche Nationalbibliothek
The Deutsche Nationalbibliothek lists this publication in the Deutsche Nationalbibliografie;
detailed bibliographic data are available in the Internet at http://dnb.dnb.de.

© 2019 Walter de Gruyter GmbH, Berlin/Boston
Cover image: skyNext/iStock / Getty Images Plus
Typesetting: Integra Software Services Pvt. Ltd.
Printing and Binding: CPI books GmbH, Leck

www.degruyter.com

Contents

	Emmon Bach and Wynn Chao	
1	**Semantic types across languages** —— 1	

    Jenny Doetjes
2   **Count/mass distinctions across languages** —— 29

    Carlota S. Smith
3   **Tense and aspect: Time across languages** —— 57

    Eric Pederson
4   **The expression of space across languages** —— 92

    Gerd Fritz
5   **Theories of meaning change: An overview** —— 113

    Dirk Geeraerts
6   **Cognitive approaches to diachronic semantics** —— 147

    Regine Eckardt
7   **Grammaticalization and semantic reanalysis** —— 177

    Lyn Frazier
8   **Meaning in psycholinguistics** —— 210

    Stephen Crain
9   **Meaning in first language acquisition** —— 237

    Roumyana Slabakova
10   **Meaning in second language acquisition** —— 274

    Stephanie Kelter and Barbara Kaup
11   **Conceptual knowledge, categorization and meaning** —— 303

    Barbara Landau
12   **Space in semantics and cognition** —— 341

Manfred Pinkal and Alexander Koller
13 **Semantic research in computational linguistics** —— 366

Graham Katz
14 **Semantics in corpus linguistics** —— 409

Anette Frank and Sebastian Padó
15 **Semantics in computational lexicons** —— 444

Paul Buitelaar
16 **Web Semantics** —— 482

Kurt Eberle
17 **Semantic issues in machine translation** —— 499

Index —— 536

Emmon Bach and Wynn Chao
1 Semantic types across languages

1 Introduction —— 1
2 Universals and universals —— 4
3 Model-theoretic semantics —— 5
4 Universal types: Model structures for natural languages —— 6
5 Types and categories —— 7
6 From types to categories —— 11
7 From categories to types —— 21
8 Lexical semantics —— 23
9 Conclusions —— 24
10 References —— 25

Abstract: A semantic perspective on language universals deals with absolute universals of meaning and the semantic import of syntactic and inflectional categories, and lexical items. This paper takes a model-theoretical basis as primary and looks both at the independent semantics and at the mappings from syntax to semantics and from semantics to syntax. Denotational semantics is contrasted with conceptual semantics. The grammatical side of the discussion works mainly with categorial and cartographic approaches. The general approach is hypothetico-deductive and at every point in a description it is necessary to ask whether we are dealing with a universal property of human language or with a property or distinction that is limited to one or several languages. In the latter case we need to ask about the space of variation and about dependencies across such spaces. Looking from grammar to meaning, the paper takes up nominal, verbal, and clausal constructions as well as sub-topics: mass and count nouns, numbers and number, adjectival modification, kinds of verbs and verbal complexes.

1 Introduction

Languages can be compared as to the semantic types they invoke *per se* and as to the reflections of these types in other aspects of language, for example, syntactic

---

Emmon Bach and Wynn Chao, London, United Kingdom

https://doi.org/10.1515/9783110589825-001

categories, syntactic and morphological features, word-building, and so on. We are interested in universals in both perspectives.

There are two main approaches to semantics, sometimes placed in opposition: (i) Denotational semantics and (ii) Conceptual semantics. The two may, however, be considered complementary: Denotational semantics assigns denotations "in the world" to the expressions of the language being interpreted. Conceptual semantics links expressions of the language to concepts considered as psychological entities "in the head". In practice, people who follow the two modes or traditions mostly do so independently of each other. In this sketch, we will mainly follow the first approach. In both approaches questions about universals loom large. At every point when we investigate a particular language or build and test a general theory about human languages we face this question: *Is this piece of our description something that is limited to a single language, or is it something that is common to many or all languages?*

Two moves are possible and both have been and still are popular:

A. Assume parochial until licensed to say otherwise!
B. Assume universal unless forced to say otherwise!

Here we find in practice a parting of the ways on methodological grounds. On the one side we have the empiricist stance epitomized by Leonard Bloomfield's dictum: "The only useful generalizations about language are inductive generalizations" (Bloomfield 1933: 20); on the other, we have the hypothetico-deductive procedure of most generative linguists. With these two approaches, the notion of a universal takes on quite different meanings. For one side, saying that something is a universal means that you have investigated all languages and found that every language instantiates the universal. Of course no one has done or ever will investigate all languages, so we must be content with looking at representative samples. On the other side, a universal is just an element in a theoretical structure that can be supported by looking at the consequences of the general theory. (Lewis 1972 is a classic defense of the denotational view. Ray Jackendoff (in many writings, for example 1972 is a prominent advocate of the conceptual position. Zwarts & Verkuyl 1994 is a valuable study, which in effect provides a model-theoretic interpretation for one version of conceptual semantics.)

The first approach was characterized like this by William Croft:

> One of the features that distinguishes the typological method of discovering constraints on possible language type is the empirical method applied to the problem. If a typologist wants to find restrictions on possible relative clause structures, for example, he or she

gathers a large sample of languages and simply observes which of the possible relative clause types are present and which are absent. That is, the restrictions on logically possible language types are motivated by the actually attested language types. If there is a gap in the attested language types, then it is provisionally assumed that the gap represents a constraint on what is a possible language, and explanations are sought for the gap. This is the inductive method, which must be used in constructing generalizations from empirical data. (Croft 2003: 49)

Here is a representative defense of the second position by Guglielmo Cinque, writing about the cartographic approach to syntactic structures (see section 6.2.2 below):

What makes the enterprise all the more interesting is the mounting evidence of the last several years that the distinct hierarchies of functional projections may be universal in the inventory of the heads they involve, in their number, and in their relative order (despite certain appearances). This is, at any rate, the strongest position to take, as it is compatible with only one state of affairs. It is the most exposed to refutation, and, hence, more likely to be correct, if unrefuted.

In front of recalcitrant facts we might be led to a weaker position—one that allows languages to vary either in the inventory, or the number, or the order of the functional heads that they admit (or any combination thereof). Even if this position should eventually turn out to be right, methodologically it would be wrong to start with it, discarding the stronger position. That would only make us less demanding with respect to the facts and could lead us to miss more subtle evidence supporting the stronger position (a risk not present under the other option). (Cinque 2002: 3–4)

Typological questions arise immediately when you try to advance along either route.

In our research, we follow generally the second mode. Why? Perhaps surprisingly, in part because it leads to better empirical coverage. The main reason is that recording what is can tell you what is possible but never tell you for sure what isn't possible. Of course, there are dangers, but you have to do good linguistics no matter how you operate. Elicitation has its pitfalls but so also does the online search!

Take the NP-Quantifier universal of Barwise & Cooper (1981):

NP-QUANTIFIER UNIVERSAL: *Every natural language has syntactic constituents (called noun-phrases) whose semantic function is to express generalized quantifiers over the domain of discourse.*

Since it was put forward as a hypothesis, there have been many studies of particular languages intended to test the hypothesis, and arguing that is wrong, right, in need of refinement, and so on, and questions about quantification have been routinely put into the task book for investigators of "new" languages. Alleged counterexamples have made the public press (cf. the *New Yorker* article featuring Dan Everett and the Amazonian language Pirahã: Colapinto 2007).

We take the thesis of *effability* as a general guide or heuristic which puts conditions of adequacy on the general framework within which languages can vary (von Fintel & Matthewson 2008, Katz 1976: 37):

> EFFABILITY: *Languages are by and large equivalent in their expressive power.*

To give some content to this claim we need to spell out what "by and large" is supposed to allow. We can move toward this by making claims about meanings that must be expressible in every language. We say "meaning" because we want to leave open for now specific questions about whether a particular aspect of meaning is to be attributed to semantics in the narrow sense, to pragmatics and theories of conventional and conversational implicature, or the like. Here are some examples.

> ABSOLUTE UNIVERSALS OF MEANING: *Every language has expressions that can*
> i. *refer to individuals,*
> ii. *make assertions,*
> iii. *express questions,*
> iv. *express commands and suggestions,*
> v. *make particular assertions (questions, etc.),*
> vi. *make general assertions (questions, etc.)*
> *and so on...*

We take up a number of such universals in section 6.

Let us be careful about what is claimed here: the mode or place of expressing these meanings is kept completely open. In particular, we do not claim that the distinctions implicit in the list are necessarily directly reflected in the grammar of any particular language. For example, right or wrong, it allows Everett's claims that Pirahã (Everett 2005) does not overtly distinguish between particular and general assertions in its grammar.

2 Universals and universals

There are several kinds of universals:
i. *Every language shows property P.*
ii. *There is a universal set of properties Π from which languages choose.*
iii. *If L has property P, then it has property Q.*

(i) and (ii) are *absolute* universals. (iii) is an *implicational* universal.

An example of an absolute universal was the one proposed by Barwise & Cooper (1981), repeated here:

> NP-QUANTIFIER UNIVERSAL: *Every natural language has syntactic constituents (called noun-phrases) whose semantic function is to express generalized quantifiers over the domain of discourse.* [NP here corresponds to what is now usually called DP, following Abney 1987.]

Note that this claim is about syntax and semantics: a particular syntactic category and its interpretation is claimed to be universal. (On the fate of this proposed universal, see Bach et al. 1995.)

Examples of absolute semantic universals might be various proposals about the model structures used for model-theoretic interpretation, if it is claimed that they are necessary or adequate for the interpretation of every natural language. We will deal with such questions directly.

A purely semantic universal might be this:

> *Every natural language has expressions that are interpreted as denoting individuals in the domain A of entities* (see section 3 below on model structures for this kind of differentiation).

A claim about grammar and interpretation might be one (like the Barwise-Cooper NP-Universal) that claimed that every language had particular categories—say proper names and pronouns—for this universal semantic type. Here again there could be a stronger claim: there is a particular category which is the category for individual names. (We return to this question below in section 6.1.1.)

An example of the second sort of absolute universals might be an enumeration of the sorts that are used to interpret various kinds of nominal expressions, as in Greg Carlson's (1977) hypotheses about kinds, individuals, and stages. Obviously, the strongest hypothesis would be that all languages make use of all of these semantic distinctions and the posited relations among them. A weaker hypothesis would relegate the distinctions to membership in a tool-box of distinctions that a language might or might not choose. A more realistic example might be the various distinctions of verbal meanings usually discussed under the rubric of *Aktionsarten* or aspectual categories.

3 Model-theoretic semantics

As we noted above, we will follow in the first instance the route of a denotational semantics, which is committed to associating things, relations, and the like—that is things that are not language—with linguistic expressions. This approach acknowledges the claim that when someone talks about some object, they are in general not just talking about a concept. *My cat is hungry* does not mean that the concept of my cat is hungry or falls under the concept of being hungry.

We should stress that model-theoretic semantics is not the same as possible-world semantics, which is just one choice among many about appropriate models. Moreover, the approach must necessarily proceed by making something like mockups or models of the space of denotations, since we cannot put real dogs, houses, much less whole worlds into our accounts (compare article 7 [Semantics: Theories] (Zimmerman) *Model-theoretic semantics*). The important contrast here is this: denotations are not just expressions in some other language: logical form, the Language of Thought, or the like.

4 Universal types: Model structures for natural languages

Here is a typical minimal model structure of the sort that has figured in formal semantic treatments of English and other languages (for example, by Montague 1973, henceforth PTQ):

MODEL STRUCTURE M_1:
i. *A: a set of entities*
ii. *BOOL: two truth values {1, 0} (True, False)*
iii. *S: a set of situations including worlds as maximal situations*
iv. *F: set of all functions constructed (recursively) from the above*

In addition, we suppose that there are various relations defined on the above sets, such as ordering, accessibility, and inclusion relations for S (on situations, see Bach 1986; Kratzer 1989, 2007; cf. also article 9 [Semantics: Theories] (Ginzburg) *Situation Semantics and NL ontology*). This model structure forms the basis for a hierarchy of semantic *types* (see below).

We believe that most model-theoretic semanticists who discuss various model structures construe them as universal. For example, the standard model structure M_1 just given builds on basic set theory. One might build a model using not set theory but mereology (theory of part-whole relations). Or one might have one which exploits both set-theory and mereology. But one could also suppose that some language uses one of these options and another language chooses another. This approach might underlie or be associated with claims like those made by Whorf about the different understandings of time and space as between Hopi (Uto-Aztecan) and Standard Average European, for example. In Bach (1981, 1986) the argument is made that such choices should not be made at the level of general model-structures and that the (universal) model-structure should be set up in ways that are not too specific. One such area is that of temporal relations. We believe that claims about the basic structure of time of the sort that Whorf made should not be reconstructed in the general model structure. They are probably best thought of as reflections of cultural lore. Intuitively, this means that the general structure of the semantics in the narrow sense should leave room for disagreements among users of the language. In the case of temporal structures, this view leads to taking a relatively simple setup with events as constitutive elements and allowing for "local" relations of overlap and precedence among these events (see van Lambalgen & Hamm 2005).

The type theory and concomitant model structure just sketched can be considered universal in one of the senses we mentioned above: a set of semantic distinctions from which languages may choose. As a metatheory the model structure might need to be widened to allow n-ary functional types. For illustrative purposes, we have set the limit on n at two.

Most discussion of semantic universals is, however, not about the space of semantic models in and of themselves, but rather about the semantics *of* various linguistic elements, categories, features. The remainder of this chapter will deal with a selection of such issues.

5 Types and categories

We follow standard usage in distinguishing *semantic types* and *syntactic categories*. In a narrow sense, categories are taken to be labels for syntactic structures like *S, DP, VP*, and the like. In an extended sense we can include any kind of distinctive element of the grammatical description, including features and feature values.

There are various possibilities for the relationships between the syntactic items and the semantic values. Looking in one direction, from grammar to interpretation, the strongest hypothesis would be to require a functional mapping: for every syntactic category there is a unique semantic type for the interpretation of the expressions in that category. This is the requirement of classical Montague grammar.

This functional mapping has been relaxed in work that seeks to accommodate the various kinds of interpretations that seem to be required for some syntactic categories, notably nominal structures (discussion below in section 7).

One might consider a functional relation in the other direction. Take the two together and you will have a one-to-one correspondence between categories and types. As far as we know, no semanticist has proposed such a stringent requirement (sometimes people have claimed that Montague grammar requires such a one-to-one mapping, but this is wrong).

We can actually derive a prediction from the functional mapping from syntax to semantics:

> There can be semantically identical categories that are associated with syntactically distinct expressions. This happens in Montague's analysis of English in PTQ: common nouns and intransitive verbs are both interpreted as predicates, functions from individuals to truth values. (More on this below, section 7.)

In the following discussion, we will start from the category-type scheme of Montague Grammar. The system of semantic types used by Montague in PTQ goes like this (compare the scheme for model structure M_i above):

i. e is the type of entities
ii. t is the type for truth values
iii. s is the type for situations (or worlds)
iv. $<a, b>$ is the type for functions from things of type a to things of type b

This setup departs from Montague's in respect of the treatment of situations (worlds in Montague) in that there is an explicit type here, while Montague provides a separate rule that builds functions for *senses* by a separate clause making types $<s, a>$ for every type. We believe this is a technical detail that has no importance. Moreover, as indicated above, PTQ works with sets of worlds and times.

Here are some type assignments for some categories of English (we ignore intensional types for simplicity):
– common nouns and intransitive verbs are both modeled by type $<e, t>$, characteristic functions for entities, understood equivalently as sets
– transitive verbs are functions from entities to sets: $<e, <e, t>>$
– sentences are interpreted as of type t or $<s, t>$, the latter is Montague's modeling of propositions as sets of worlds
– Term phrases (DPs or in older syntaxes NPs) were modeled as generalized quantifiers, that is sets of sets: $<<e, t>, t>$ (or properties if we bring in intensional entities).

In PTQ there are no expressions directly interpreted as denoting individuals (entities). The relaxing of the category-type mapping mentioned above (Partee & Rooth 1983; Partee 1987) allowed Term phrases to have three systematically related types of denotations: individuals *e*, predicates or properties <*e, t*> (like common nouns), as well as the generalized quantifier type of PTQ.

A recurrent question about syntactic categories has been this:

> Do all lan guages share the same syntactic categories, and if so in the first or second sense of absolute universals distinguished above: that is does every language instantiate the same set, or is there a universal set from which languages draw?

Given either view or indeed any view that identifies syntactic categories across languages, we are led to the parallel semantic question:

> Are syntactic categories given the same semantic interpretation across languages?

This is just the question raised above for an individual language but taken up here about categories across languages.

It should be noted that none of the questions raised in this section makes any sense unless it is possible to identify or relate syntactic categories across different languages. It is instructive to compare the situation in syntactic typology: claims about basic clause structures as verb-initial and so on (VSO vs. SVO vs. SOV) presuppose that there is some definite way to relate the syntactic categories or relations that are appealed to for the comparisons.

5.1 A universal schema: Fregean functions and arguments

Frege's view of the semantics of language was built squarely on the relation of functions and arguments. Montague's PTQ takes over this view: the default interpretation of a construction of two expressions was to take one as a function from the intension of the other to some—possibly higher order—type (see Heim & Kratzer 1998). If we mirror the function-argument semantic interpretation in the syntax, we have a *categorial grammar* (Oehrle, Bach & Wheeler 1988; Wood 1993; Steedman 2000).

We now turn to a discussion of particular syntactic categories and questions about universals in their interpretation. Given limitations of space, we have to concentrate on a few areas and issues, with only brief mention or references for others.

5.2 Cross-categorial classifications

X-BAR SCHEMES

So called X̄ (X-Bar) theory (Chomsky 1970; Jackendoff 1977) was set up to express cross-categorial regularities within various major categories. Skipping details, a uniform scheme was posited that looked like this:

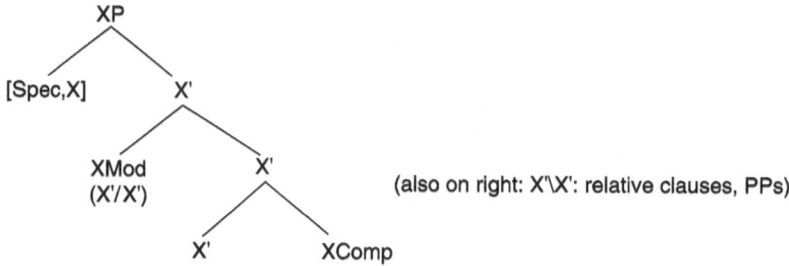

(also on right: X'\X': relative clauses, PPs)

MODIFIERS

Free modifiers or adjuncts are in bad shape in many recent theories. An adjunct is an expression which goes together with an expression of a certain category X to yield an expression of that very same category X. In a categorial view, then, an expression of category X/X or $X\backslash X$. In traditional terms, these are the true endocentric constructions. Typical examples have been attributive adjectives, relative clauses, and some kinds of adverbs.

If we eliminate the possibility of adjunct phrases, we get this kind of basic structure:

In place of XMod   X':   [Spec' X']   X'

Direct immediate recursion is carried by endocentric modifiers, traditionally and in earliest generative grammars. Such modification by free adjuncts leads to predictions that a sequence of free adjuncts can occur in any order. Many recent writers have questioned or limited severely the postulation of such adjuncts, replacing them with stacked functional categories (Cinque 1999; Chao, Mui & Scott 2001; Scott 2002, 2003), as suggested by the structures mentioned just above.

Functional categories

Kayne (2005: 12–14) lists some forty (kinds of) functional elements relevant to syntax. An important issue we do not have space to enter into here is whether to choose entirely separate categories or the same categories with different featural content? Above and beyond that are questions about the formal and semantic import of features and feature systems.

5.3 Configurational vs rule-to-rule relations

In mainstream generative grammar (to borrow a term from Culicover & Jackendoff 2005), the relation between syntax and semantics is mediated by defining mappings from structures of some sort: phrase-markers or tree structures or so called logical forms. There are several other alternatives. The main method of mainstream formal semantics stemming from Montague uses a rule-to-rule relation: every formation rule in the grammar (usually just syntax) is matched by a unique semantic rule specifying how to combine the interpretations of the input expressions into the interpretation of the resulting expressions (Bach 1976). Something like this setup is compatible with multidimensional systems (Sadock 1991; Oehrle 1988) and has been widely assumed in a number of different frameworks, especially in those derived from Categorial Grammar (for example Jacobson 1996; Steedman 2000). One way to think about such systems is as grammars that recursively specify *k*-tuples or *signs* in the Saussurean sense including at least a phonological, a syntactic, and a semantic object. We can then compare different general theories by looking at the nature of these various objects, and the operations that are allowed in the recursion. These basically Saussurean views of linguistic objects as multidimensional signs has been emphasized especially in HPSG and related frameworks.

6 From types to categories

In this section we will look from semantics to syntax and discuss a number of central domains and their expression in syntax(es). We take off in each instance from one or another absolute semantic universal of the sort illustrated above in section 1. We believe much of what we say here is completely uncontroversial.

6.1 Individuals

UNIVERSAL I. *Every language has expressions that refer to individuals.*

In the type theory sketched, there are two options: denotations of types e and $<s, e>$. The latter type is for what Montague calls individual concepts: functions from contexts (in this paper: situations, in Montague: world-time pairs) to individuals. This distinction is seen in the differing interpretations of an expression like *the president*.

In the context of our model structures, this means that every language has expressions that refer to individual members of the domain A, that is, things of type *e*. They can do this directly as in the primary use of proper names, personal pronouns, or deictics, definite descriptions, or indirectly, when we bring in intensional contexts. It is a matter of convention or culture just what kinds of things receive names in a language: people, places, times, memorable events. It is a matter of analysis or hypothesis what kinds of things are interpreted as being of type *e*: objects, stages of objects, kinds, groups, sets, have all been included in this type in various proposals (Carlson 1977 is a *locus classicus* for investigations in this area, a somewhat later reference Carlson & Pelletier 1995). The point here is that a particular member of the set of entities can be singled out and referred to with a proper name.

The grammatical locus of individual reference is in the nominal domain with categories like N, Det, DP, NP and the like, with variations in various frameworks and theories and possibly languages. Early generative studies of English assumed that names were a subspecies of nouns, characterized (in English) as not going with determiners, except in special circumstances.

(1) Mary is here.
(2) *The Mary is here.
(3) The Mary that I knew is no longer.
(4) Die Maria ist da.
    The Maria is here.

But the last example shows that in German proper names can go with definite determiners, and in some language they must do so. The whole grammar of proper names is fraught with details. In German, names of countries do not usually take determiners unless they are feminine or plural, and so on:

(5) ... in Amerika 'in America'
(6) ... in der Schweiz 'in Switzerland'
(7) ... in den Vereinigten Staaten 'in the United States'

Many languages treat proper names in special ways, either as a subspecies of definite expressions or in their own right. Place names are a special case, combining the category of places with the category of names, sometimes with special selectional requirements or possibilities.

Personal pronouns like *she, he, I, you, they* form another major class of expressions referring directly to individuals. It is a matter of analysis and a certain amount of controversy where pronouns are to be placed in the syntax: as determiners (Postal 1969) or as a type of noun.

We see in the details of the grammar of names instantiations of a general principle of the semantics-grammar relation: THE YOU-DO-OR-YOU-DON'T PRINCIPLE (YDYD):

> Suppose a language encodes in its grammar a particular semantic distinction and suppose there is a class of expressions that as a matter of semantics express this distinction. Then the language will either require that that class of expressions conform to the grammatical marking or prohibit it.

Here the principle shows itself in the domain of definiteness and proper names. Assuming that definite articles like English *the* are direct expressions of definiteness and that proper names are definite the collocation of the two is often either prohibited or required. Another instantiation of the principle is in the realm of numerals in construction with nominals. If a noun is construed with a number and the language has a grammatical distinction of number in its nouns, do you use the plural with a cardinal number (Corbett 2000)? Details of this kind of situation can be found in reference grammars of many languages.

The principle is a kind of reflex of the tension between the forces of redundancy and economy. Perhaps, Optimality Theory would provide a fruitful way to think about this situation. But the rankings between redundancy and economy cannot be global for a language, rather being tied to very particular parts of the language.

6.1.1 The nominal domain: NPs and DPs, Det, QP

Informally, the various categories that are associated with the label N include these: pronouns, common nouns, determiners, demonstratives, expressions of quantity. In addition, modifiers of various sorts come in here, we defer discussion to the section on adjectives (section 6.3.1) below.

The whole domain is clustered around individuals, up to generalized quantifiers, The NP-Universal of Barwise & Cooper falls under this rubric (above section 1, Barwise & Cooper 1981; Bach et al. 1995) and has been the locus of intense research and debate. One thread of this research goes to the heart of the constraints on category to type matches. In several papers, Partee and Rooth have argued for a systematic ambiguity in the interpretation of term phrases (DPs and the like) as denoting individuals (*e*), generalized quantifiers (<<e,t>,t>), and (nominal) predicates (<*e, t*>) (and corresponding intensional types, Partee & Rooth 1983; Partee 1987).

6.1.2 Number

The semantic domain of number enters into general theories of language in several places. At the level of lexical semantics there is the question of whether all languages have words for numbers, with widespread claims that some do not (Everett 2005 and subsequent debates such as Nevins, Pesetsky & Rodrigues 2007; Everett 2007).

In grammar, number enters into several different axes: numeral expressions in the nominal domain, inflections of nominal, adjectival, and verbal categories, connections to classifiers or counter expressions, and the like. We cannot go into these various areas here. As far as universality goes, the question of numbers and related categories was a prime example for Ken Hale (1975) in his important paper on "gaps in culture and grammar". Hale argues for a kind of universality of potential, both in the domain of counting and in the grammar of relative clauses. Note that the potential for counting is present in the basic model structure we have posited as long as the domain of individuals is interpreted as containing discrete entities, and the functional types include types for sets.

As mentioned above, the realm of grammatical number offers another good example of what we have called the YDYD (say "YD-squared") principle. In expressions of number plus nominal, if the languages have grammatical number they generally differ on whether the nominals may, may not, or must not express number in the nominal in concord with the number expression.

6.1.3 Nominal sorts

As we mentioned above, the nominal domain has been the locus for a lot of discussion of sorts, considered as subsets of the set of individuals. We have no space to enter into an extended discussion of the issues here. We simply mention two big areas of discussion: one is the discussion of generics with kinds, objects, stages and relations among them, introduced by Greg Carlson (Carlson 1977; Carlson & Pelletier 1995; Kratzer 1995; ct. also article 8 [Semantics: Noun Phrases and Verb Phrases] (Carlson) *Genericity*), the other is the set of distinctions between Mass and Count expressions and Plurality (Link 1983; Landman 1996; cf. also articles 7 [Semantics: Noun Phrases and Verb Phrases] (Lasersohn) *Mass nouns and plurals* and 3 [this volume] (Doetjes) *Count/mass distinctions*). Some of the distinctions reflected in Carlson's original analysis have been widely reformulated and modified in approaches that bring in *events* or *eventualities* either in the semantics or in the syntax or both (Parsons 1990, Tenny & Pustejovsky 2000).

6.2 Propositions

> UNIVERSAL II. *Every language has expressions that denote truth values and expressions that denote propositions.*

6.2.1 Clausal categories

The first generative grammars for natural languages (of all stripes) identified S as the highest category. Similarly, PTQ has *t* as the highest category, identified at the top level with the type *t* for truth value, or interpreted according to the general pattern as the intension of that type, that is, a proposition, when occurring as the argument of some function, such as a verb of propositional attitude like *believe* (propositions are of type: <s, t>).

In subsequent developments of the transformational-generative tradition, the category S was decomposed into more and more layers. Early on, something like Montague's distinction came in with S and S̄(S'). Within S, another conceptual split came with the CASE grammar of Charles Fillmore (1968), subsequently followed up in the UCLA grammar (Stockwell, Schachter & Partee 1973). Fillmore's CASE grammar posited underlying flat structures, but conceptually and on the way to surface structure there was a sharp split between the constituent M (think Mood) and the core verb and arguments (somewhat more comprehensive than later argument structures plus verb). M continued the tradition of Aux but in Fillmore's scheme there was a more intimate connection between the main verb and its arguments than was expressed in the earliest phrase-structure rules of Chomsky:

S → NP AUX VP

Explosions of cascading structures happened at various stages of generative theory: in Generative Semantics with a meager set of categories: Verbs, NPs, S's; in more recent generative theories with an apparently open-ended set of functional categories (compare Culicover & Jackendoff 2005: 98–103). The first steps in this development came with CP (complementizer phrase), IP (inflectional phrase) as reinterpretations of earlier S and S̄. In an influential paper, Jean-Yves Pollock posited a split of IP into two further layers, on the basis of comparisons of French and English (Pollock 1989).

Some of the phrase types based on functional categories that have been proposed in recent times are these (we take up some of them in particular below):

- TnsP: tense phrase
- AspP: aspect phrase
- VoiceP: voice phrase
- AgrP1: subject agreement phrase
- AgrP2: object agreement phrase
- NegP: negative phrase
- FocusP: focus phrase

sometimes more than one of these, as for Hungarian, where several elements can come into focus, and so on.

We are concerned here only with the semantic side of these proposals. In view of what was said above about the syntax-semantics mapping, it is possible that all of these categories could be of the same semantic type, differing only in their syntactic categorization. Again, we cannot pursue the questions raised here in detail, but make a small choice from the extensive literature on these topics.

6.2.2 Cinque's cartography

Guglielmo Cinque has consistently pursued a research programme for mapping out a "cartography" of functional categories and related adverbial expressions with a wide cross-linguistic base (Cinque 1999, 2002). We do not have space to discuss the very rich set of categories and predictions that he and other "cartographers" have studied. We will take up just a few of the areas that have been studied from this point of view (see also sections 7 and 9 below). Here is an example of the kinds of data and arguments involved.

Two classes of clause-level adverbials—examples:

(8) Unfortunately, it is raining.
(9) It is unfortunately raining.
(10) Probably, it is raining.
(11) It is probably raining.
(12) Unfortunately, it is probably raining.
(13) *Probably it is unfortunately raining.
(14) It is unfortunate that it is probable that it is raining.
(15) It is probable that it is unfortunate that it is raining.

(16) It is raining, probably
(17) It is raining, unfortunately.

With questions:

(18) Is it probably raining?
(19) *Is it unfortunately raining?

With imperatives:

(20) You will unfortunately go home.
(21) You will certainly go home.
(22) *Go home unfortunately.
(23) *Go home certainly! *Certainly go home!
(24) *Go certainly home!

and so on.

These two classes of adverbial expressions differ semantically. The type of *unfortunately* is called "evaluative", they typically express something about the speakers feelings about the content of the sentence. The second type illustrated by *certainly* and *probably* are aptly called "modal", having to do with judgments about the certainty, likelihood, probability of the truth of the remaining content of the sentence.

Cinque entertains briefly and dismisses the possibility that the ordering characteristics can be explained on a semantic basis and hence need not be directly reflected in the syntax (Cinque 1999: 134–136). It needs to be registered that possible paraphrases of the kinds of sentences under discussion have different properties, as shown by the contrast between examples (13) and (15) above. But in any case, careful consideration of meanings is required. There is a subtle shift in the sense of the words and their import in the examples above.

6.2.3 Tense

English and many other languages have sentential expressions which differ minimally in the presence or absence of tense, or some other nontense item like *to*:

(25) Andy leaves.
(26) (I saw) Andy leave.
(27) (I want) Andy to leave.
(28) (I am anxious for) Andy to leave.

In standard tense logics, tense is generally treated as a sentence operator. This view is compatible with the earliest generative treatments of English, which usually start with something like this rule:

S → NP AUX VP

Since there are three constituents, it is possible to interpret the tense (and aspect) part of the AUX constituent as having highest scope. Montague's PTQ treats tenses and negation syncategorematically built into the rules for putting together tenseless Intransitive Verb Phrases. In the Montague tradition, Bach (1980) argued for an analysis in which tensed verb phrases are built as constituents that take subjects as arguments to make sentences with a corresponding semantic value: that is the basic structure would be something like NP tVP where tVP stands for tensed verb-phrase and includes the auxiliary elements.

6.3 Properties and predicatives

> UNIVERSAL III. *Every language has expressions which denote functions from (possibly sequences of) individuals (or other semantic objects) to truth values or propositions. Some examples are types: <e, t>, <<s, e>, t>.*

In laying out the type theory above, we have followed a kind of binarism in the definition of the functional types. Because the functional theory in and of itself allows for restructuring of n-ary functions to sequences of unary functions ("currying") this does not actually have any limiting effect. As we noted, a change in the definition of possible functional types would get back the possibility of direct interpretation of flat structures. It would take us too far afield to pursue this question here. The type theory as laid out here goes well with the kind of syntax favoured by many analysts (Montague 1973; Kayne 1984 and elsewhere).

In a sense, Universal III follows from the first two, as long as we make the (reasonable) assumption that languages can make composite truth-bearing expressions about individuals. What kinds of grammatical categories correspond to these semantic types is in general a matter of controversy. In the following sections, we take up the main categories, which by and large correspond to very traditional ones.

6.3.1 Adjectives and adjectives

Traditionally, two quite different kinds of expressions have been called adjectives, distinguished as attributive or predicative:

(29) Take the red box. (attributive)
(30) This box is red. (predicative)
(31) The former president spoke for his wife.
(32) *This president is former.
(33) Johnny is ill.
(34) *The ill child wept.

Siegel (1980) is the *locus classicus* for the first detailed studies of adjectives in the model-theoretic tradition of Montague Grammar. Cf. also article 12 [Semantics: Lexical Structures and Adjectives] (Demonte) *Adjectives*.

These examples show that the two classes of adjectives in English are not coextensive. Languages differ a good deal in the extent to which these two uses are possible, the membership of the two classes, and the amount of overlap (see Chao, Mui & Scott 2001, and literature cited there).

Adjectives have figured large in the debates about universality of syntactic categories (Baker 2003). Recent research in the spirit of Cinque's programme has classified attributive adjectives syntactically not as free endocentric modifiers but rather as specifiers for various functional categories (Chao, Mui & Scott 2001; Scott 2002, 2003).

As far as predicative adjectives are concerned, whether or not a language distinguishes verbs and adjectives seems to be largely a matter of grammar. Items which can stand by themselves (inflected) or with their arguments and modifiers to denote predicates are assigned to various classes of verbs, while those which require a copula to make such predicators are called (predicative) adjectives.

6.3.2 Common noun denotations

Traditionally and in Montague's analyses of English, common noun denotations are assigned the type $<e, t>$, or with intensional types $<<s,e>, t>$. These are the same types that are assigned to intransitive verbs and verb-phrases. Later, Muffy Siegel (1980 also assigned the same type to (predicative) adjectives. These assignments illustrate well the many-to-one relation between categories and types of Montague grammar and related theories, reflecting the fact that the syntax of these kinds of expressions is sharply different. Gupta (1980) argued strongly that common noun meanings in-cluded a component of "re-identification" (*the same squirrel*) and this point is taken up by Baker in his book on lexical categories (2003). This view would not necessarily lead to a new type, but presumably would be dealt with by meaning postulates or by sorting.

6.3.3 The verbal domain

The prime category at the basis of predication is the verb, and this fact has gone into the terminology of most modern theories of syntax. In dependency grammar, the verb is the main expression from which other elements of a sentence depend. Many languages can use verbs as full sentences, inflected or not.

The minimal potential truth-bearing expression of natural languages is the combination of a subject and a predicate. We include here ambience sentences with no overt subject or a dummy expletive:

(35) It's raining.
(36) Piove. (Italian)
 'It's raining.'
(37) Hot!

In English, as in many languages, such combinations require a finite form of the verb, here a present tense, registering also the singular agreement. As mentioned above this bit of the sentence is generally stripped out or off as an element *Aux*, *Infl*, or *M* (see section 6.2.1 on Fillmore's CASE Grammar).

6.4 Eventualities

The term "eventualities" (Bach 1981) has come to be used for the set of distinctions in meaning and grammar that comprise such items as *events*, *processes*, *states*, *accomplishements*, *achievements*, and so on and use descriptive terminology such as *telic*, *atelic*, and the like. Modeling such distinctions in semantics has made up an impor-tant part of the literature of model-theoretic semantics over the last few decades (Verkuyl 1972, Dowty 1977, 1979). Here are a few examples illustrating differences in interpretation and acceptability that seem to depend on these various types of verbs and verb-phrases.

Activities:

(38) John runs.
(39) John is running.

Statives:

(40) Sally knows the answer.

(41) ?Sally is knowing the answer.

Activity (→ accomplishment)

(42) John was running for an hour.

Accomplishment:

(43) Harry discovered the answer in an hour.
(44) ?Harry discovered the answer for an hour.

7 From categories to types

A good bit of our discussion in the previous sections has already dealt indirectly with the perspective of this section, looking from grammar to interpretation, so we can be brief.

As we noted at the outset, the classical view of the relation between syntactic categories and semantic types is that the relation is a many-to-one mapping. So several different syntactic categories could be assigned a single corresponding type. This situation is realized in Montague grammar and its conservative extensions in the example of common nouns, intransitive verb phrases, and predicative adjectives—other categories come to mind as well such as certain prepositional phrases. We also noted that departures from this functional relationship have been argued for, but in such a way that there is a systematic relation among the various options, as in the Partee-Rooth treatment of term-phrase interpretations (Partee & Rooth 1983; Partee 1987).

When we look cross-linguistically at this question, there are several positions to consider. The strongest hypothesis would be to claim that the relations between categories and types is functional, and fixed for every language. Even stronger would be the claim that the relation is one-to-one in every case. It seems that the last claim cannot be reasonably maintained. Some semanticists have argued for a parametric view of the options (Chierchia 1998): languages may differ in systematic ways in their assignments of semantic types to syntactic categories. As in all parametric approaches to language variation, this view is intended to explain clusterings of properties across languages. And the general problem of such a parametric view is the same in the realm of semantics as in other areas. The range of variation within a single language tends to approximate variation across languages. The observation or principle has been called "the congruence of intra- and interlinguistic diversity" (Bach 1974: 255).

A good example of the failure of a one-to-one mapping from grammar to semantics is the treatment of kinds as in generic sentences like these:

(45) Dinosaurs are extinct.
(46) The lion is a carnivore.
(47) Man is not grand.
(48) A cat is a curious beast.

Bare plurals—as in (45)—are perhaps the most usual or unmarked way of referring to kinds in English (and the starting point for Carlson's classic 1977 study; cf. also article 8 [Semantics: Noun Phrases and Verb Phrases] (Carlson) *Genericity*), but English includes all the other options illustrated in (46)–(48), some of which are the norm in other languages with comparable structures. There can be subtle differences among the various possible structures illustrated (Wilkinson 1991).

Similarly, some languages (Chinese, Japanese) have been called "classifier" languages since collocations of nouns and numbers are impossible without the help of counters or classifiers. But English has nouns which also require similar counter or measure expressions (cf. also article 3 [this volume] (Doetjes) *Count/mass distinctions*):

(49) three pieces of furniture
(50) *three furnitures
(51) three blobs of mud
(52) *three muds

7.1 Some many-to-one correspondences

We've already mentioned the three (or more) kinds of syntactic categories that map to the same type of $<e, t>$: common noun (phrases), intransitive verbs, predicative adjectives. There are two other places where we might consider such many-to-one correspondences: clausal or S level elements and nominal expressions with adjectival extensions.

7.1.1 Clausal categories again

Referring back to the discussion of clausal categories (sections 6.2.1, 6.2.2), we note that there are possibly a large number of categories that can plausibly be considered to map into the types of truth-values or propositions. We mention here only a few of the possible categories:

(53) NegP: Mary hasn't left.
(54) Modal$_{evaluative}$P: Mary unfortunately hasn't left.
(55) Modal$_{epistemic}$P: Mary has certainly left.
(56) ForceP: Leave! (= illocutionary force)

7.1.2 Nominals with adjectives

Here we pick up the discussion on attributive adjective constructions (section 6.3.1). Some examples from Scott (2002) (Scott's numbering in parentheses):

(57) He arrived in an ancient old car. (33a)
(58) *He arrived in an old ancient car. (33b)
(59) What a long cool red dress! (29a) (cool = not hot)
(60) What a cool long red drink! (29b) (cool = excellent)

(The point of the last two examples is that the two are judged ungrammatical if the interpretations of *cool* are switched.) Again, it is plausible that the semantic values of the adjectives are of the same type, perhaps the type of functions from <*e, t*> or <<*s, e*>, *t*> to the same types, but the constraints on order can be encoded in the syntax. It is likely that there are at least two levels of adjectival modifiers or specifiers that are different in type (compare Chao & Bach in preparation; Chao, Mui & Scott 2001).

8 Lexical semantics

We have concentrated in this paper on the semantics of grammar. There is a very rich tradition of (formal and informal) analyses of the meanings of words and other lexical items. Linguists differ a lot in the extent to which they try to tie together lexical and grammatical structures. Derivations of lexical items from syntactic structures has been a common thread in the generative tradition, especially in the so-called generative semantics tradition and more recently in some branches of the Chomskyan trend (Hale & Keyser 1993; for commentary compare Culicover & Jackendoff 2005: 53–56).

8.1 The syntax and semantics of lexical items

What is the semantic type of a lexical item as it comes from a lexical entry of some sort? A wide-spread assumption is that the category and the type of the item is just the same as that of the phrasal (syntactic) category into which it fits. In configurational terms, this is the question of the mapping that we assume given structures of this sort:

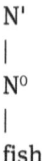

N'
|
N⁰
|
fish

In Montague grammar something like this assumption (without the structural guise) is explicit in the principle embodied in the distinction between basic categories and phrasal categories and the "rule":

For all A: $B_A \subseteq P_A$

That is, every member A of a Basic category B (more or less = lexical category) is a member of the corresponding Phrasal category P. This is shorthand for the more precise locution "every member of the basic—i.e. lexical—set indexed by the category A is a member of the phrasal set indexed by A."

Assumptions like these went very well with the X-bar theories of phrase structure, which assumed that the syntactic categories were projected from the lexicon. With the explosion of functional categories mentioned above (sections 6.2.1 and 6.2.2), this idea about syntactic categories was swept away. Borer (2005a,b) and others assume that crucial parts of the syntax and semantics of expressions are contributed from the functional categories themselves (Borer's "exoskeletal" theory). This approach is reminiscent of attempts to reduce lexical categories such as Noun, Verb, Adjective to a single category of Contentive or the like (Bach 1968). It is a task for semanticists to figure out how to deal with the semantics of the situation: just what is the semantic value of the "bare" lexical item, and how does the functional category contribute to the semantics of the item as it is used in a larger construction.

9 Conclusions

We hope to have shown here that the semantic perspective on language universals, both semantic universals *per se* and the semantics of syntax and lexicon, is and continues to be a vital part of the linguistic enterprise. In the last few years, there has been a considerable widening of the empirical base, as more and more languages—especially "under-represented" ones—are looked at with semantic questions in mind (compare the conferences of SULA: the Semantics of Under-represented Languages of the Americas.) In semantics too it seems that looking at "other languages" leads to new insights about the language from which one starts.

We have not said very much about the relation between the conceptual and the model-theoretic mode of thinking about semantic universals that we mentioned at the outset of this chapter. We believe that both approaches are valid and complementary. Does the structure of our semantic theories reflect the way the world is or the way we conceptualize it? Such a Kantian kind of question leads to looking at the enterprise at a higher level, where "Natural Language Metaphysics" (Bach 1981, 1986) verges into metaphysics proper.

10 References

Abney, Steven 1987. *The English Noun Phrase in its Sentential Aspect*. Ph.D. dissertation, MIT, Cambridge, MA.
Bach, Emmon 1968. Nouns and noun phrases. In: E. Bach & Robert T. Harms (eds.). *Universals in Linguistic Theory*. New York: Holt, Rinehart & Winston, 90–122.
Bach, Emmon 1974. *Syntactic Theory*. New York: Holt, Rinehart & Winston.
Bach, Emmon 1976. An extension of classical Transformational Grammar. In: *Problems of Linguistic Metatheory (Proceedings of the 1976 Conference)*. East Lansing, MI: Michigan State University, 183–224.
Bach, Emmon 1980. Tenses and aspects as functions on verb-phrases. In: C. Rohrer (ed.). *Time, Tense and Quantifiers: Proceedings of the Stuttgart Conference on the Logic of Tense and Quantification*. Tübingen: Niemeyer, 19–38.
Bach, Emmon 1981. On time, tense, and aspect: An essay in English metaphysics. In: P. Cole (ed.). *Radical Pragmatics*. New York: Academic Press, 63–81.
Bach, Emmon 1986. Natural language metaphysics. In: R. Barcan Marcus, G.J.W. Dorn & P. Weingartner (eds.). *Logic, Methodology, and Philosophy of Science VII*. Amsterdam: North Holland, 573–595.
Bach, Emmon & Wynn Chao 2009. On semantic universals and typology. In: C. Collins, M. Christiansen & S. Edelman (eds.). *Language Universals*. Oxford: Oxford University Press, 152–173.
Bach, Emmon, Eloise Jelinek, Angelika Kratzer & Barbara H. Partee (eds.) 1995. *Quantification in Natural Languages*. Dordrecht: Kluwer.
Baker, Mark C. 2003. *Lexical Categories: Verbs, Nouns, and Adjectives*. Cambridge: Cambridge University Press.
Barwise, Jon & Robin Cooper 1981. Generalized quantifiers and natural languages. *Linguistics & Philosophy* 4, 159–219.
Bloomfield, Leonhard 1933. *Language*. New York: Henry Holt and Co.
Borer, Hagit 2005a. *Structuring Sense Volume I: In Name Only*. Oxford: Oxford University Press.
Borer, Hagit 2005b. *Structuring Sense Volume II: The Normal Course of Events*. Oxford: Oxford University Press.

Carlson, Gregory N. 1977. *Reference to Kinds in English*. Ph.D. dissertation. University of Massachusetts, Amherst, MA.
Carlson, Gregory N. & Francis J. Pelletier (eds.) 1995. *The Generic Book*. Chicago, IL: The University of Chicago Press.
Chao, Wynn & Emmon Bach (in preparation). Mandarin nominals: Categories and types.
Chao, Wynn, Evelynne Mui & Gary-John Scott 2001. Adjectival modifications in Chinese: A cross-linguistic perspective. Paper presented at the *North American Conference on Chinese Linguistics (= NACCL) 13*. University of California, Irvine, CA.
Chierchia, Gennaro 1998. Plurality of mass nouns and the notion of 'semantic parameter'. In: S. Rothstein (ed.). *Events and Grammar*. Dordrecht: Kluwer, 53–103.
Chomsky, Noam 1970. Remarks on nominalization. In: R. A. Jacobs & P. S. Rosenbaum (eds.). *Readings in English Transformational Grammar*. The Hague: Mouton, 11–61.
Cinque, Guglielmo 1999. *Adverbs and Functional Heads: A Cross-Linguistic Perspective*. Oxford: Oxford University Press.
Cinque, Guglielmo (ed.) 2002. *Functional Structure in the DP and the IP: The Cartography of Syntactic Structures. Vol. I*. Oxford: Oxford University Press.
Colapinto, John 2007. The interpreter: Has a remote Amazonian tribe upended our understanding of language? *New Yorker*, April 16 issue.
Corbett, Greville G. 2000. *Number*. Cambridge: Cambridge University Press.
Croft, William 2003. *Typology and Universals*. 2nd ed. Cambridge: Cambridge University Press.
Culicover, Peter W. & Ray Jackendoff 2005. *Simpler Syntax*. Oxford: Oxford University Press.
Dowty, David R. 1977. Toward a semantic analysis of verb aspect and the English 'imperfective' progressive. *Linguistics & Philosophy* 1, 45–78.
Dowty, David R. 1979. *Word Meaning and Montague Grammar*. Dordrecht: Reidel.
Everett, Daniel L. 2005. Cultural constraints on grammar and cognition in Pirahã. *Current Anthropology* 46, 621–634.
Everett, Daniel L. 2007. *Cultural Constraints on Grammar in Pirahã: A Reply to Nevins, Pesetsky, and Rodrigues*. Ms. Normal, IL, Illinois State University. http://ling.auf.net/lingB.zz/000427, June 10, 2008.
Fillmore, Charles J. 1968. The case for case. In: E. Bach & R. T. Harms (eds.). *Universals in Linguistic Theory*. New York: Holt, Rinehart & Winston, 1–88.
von Fintel, Kai & Lisa Matthewson 2008. Universals in semantics. *The Linguistic Review* 25, 139–201.
Gupta, Anil 1980. *The Logic of Common Nouns*. New Haven, CT: Yale University Press.
Hale, Ken 1975. Gaps in grammar and culture. In: M. D. Kinkade, K. L. Hale & O. Werner (eds.). *Linguistics and Anthropology, in Honor of C. F. Voegelin*. Lisse: Peter de Ridder Press, 295–315.
Hale, Kenneth & Samuel Jay Keyser 1993. On argument structure and the lexical expression of syntactic relations. In: K. Hale & S. J. Keyser (eds.). *The View from Building 20: Essays in Linguistics in Honor of Sylvain Bromberger*. Cambridge, MA: The MIT Press, 53–109.
Heim, Irene & Angelika Kratzer 1998. *Semantics in Generative Grammar*. Oxford: Blackwell.
Jackendoff, Ray 1972. *Semantic Interpretation in Generative Grammar*. Cambridge, MA: The MIT Press.
Jackendoff, Ray S. 1977. *X'-Syntax: A Study of Phrase Structure*. Cambridge, MA: The MIT Press.
Jackendoff, Ray 1997. *The Architecture of the Language Faculty*. Cambridge, MA: The MIT Press.
Jacobson, Pauline 1996. The syntax/semantics interface in categorial grammar. In: S. Lappin (ed.). *The Handbook of Contemporary Semantic Theory*. Oxford: Blackwell, 89–116.

Katz, Jerrold 1976. A hypothesis about the uniqueness of human language. In: S. Harnad, H. Steklis & J. Lancaster (eds.). *Origins and Evolution of Language and Speech*. New York: New York Academy of Sciences, 33–41.
Kayne, Richard S. 1984. *Connectedness and Binary Branching*. Dordrecht: Foris.
Kayne, Richard S. 2005. Some notes on comparative syntax, with special reference to English and French. In: G. Cinque & R. S. Kayne (eds.). *The Oxford Handbook of Comparative Syntax*. Oxford: Oxford University Press, 3–69.
Kratzer, Angelika 1989. An investigation of the lumps of thought. *Linguistics & Philosophy* 12, 607–653.
Kratzer, Angelika 1995. Stage-level and individual-level predicates. In: G. N. Carlson & F. J. Pelletier (eds.). *The Generic Book*. Chicago, IL: The University of Chicago Press, 125–175.
Kratzer, Angelika 2007. Situations in natural language semantics. In: E.N. Zalta (ed.). *The Stanford Encyclopedia of Philosophy*. Spring 2007 Edition. http://plato.stanford.edu/entries/situations-semantics/, June 10, 2011.
van Lambalgen, Michiel & Fritz Hamm 2005. *The Proper Treatment of Events*. Oxford: Blackwell.
Landman, Fred 1996. Plurality. In: S. Lappin (ed.). *The Handbook of Contemporary Semantic Theory*. Oxford: Blackwell, 425–457.
Lewis, David 1972. General semantics. In: D. Davidson & G. Harman (eds.). *Semantics of Natural Language*. Dordrecht: Reidel, 169–218.
Link, Godehard 1983. The logical analysis of plurals and mass terms. In: R. Bäuerle, Ch. Schwarze & A. von Stechow (eds.). *Meaning, Use, and Interpretation of Language*. Berlin: de Gruyter, 302–323.
Montague, Richard 1973. The proper treatment of quantification in ordinary English. In: R. Thomason (ed.). *Formal Philosophy. Selected Papers of Richard Montague*. New Haven, CT: Yale University Press, 247–270.
Nevins, Andrew, David Pesetsky & Cilene Rodrigues 2007. *Pirahã Exceptionality: A Reassessment*. http://ling.auf.net/lingBuzz/000411, June 10, 2011.
Oehrle, Richard T. 1988. Multi-dimensional compositional functions as a basis for grammatical analysis. In: R. T. Oehrle, E. Bach & D. Wheeler (eds.). *Categorial Grammars and Natural Language Structures*. Dordrecht: Reidel, 349–389.
Oehrle, Richard T., Emmon Bach & Deirdre Wheeler (eds.) 1988. *Categorial Grammars and Natural Language Structures*. Dordrecht: Reidel.
Parsons, Terence 1990. *Events in the Semantics of English: A Study in Subatomic Semantics*. Cambridge, MA: The MIT Press.
Partee, Barbara 1987. Noun phrase interpretation and type-shifting principles. In: J. Groenendijk, D. de Jongh & M. Stokhof (eds.). *Studies in Discourse Representation Theory and the Theory of Generalized Quantifiers*. Dordrecht: Foris, 115–143.
Partee, Barbara & Mats Rooth 1983. Generalized conjunction and type ambiguity. In: R. Bäuerle, Ch. Schwarze & A. von Stechow (eds.). *Meaning, Use, and Interpretation of Language*. Berlin: de Gruyter, 361–383.
Pollock, Jean-Yves 1989. Verb movement, universal grammar and the structure of IP. *Linguistic Inquiry* 20, 365–424.
Postal, Paul 1969. On 'pronouns' in English. In: D. Reibel & S. Schane (eds.). *Modern Studies in English*. Englewood Cliffs, NJ: Prentice Hall, 201–224.
Sadock, Jerrold M. 1991. *Autolexical Syntax*. Chicago, IL: The University of Chicago Press.

Scott, Gary-John 2002. Stacked adjectival modification and the structure of nominal phrases. In: G. Cinque (ed.). *Functional Structure in the DP and the IP: The Cartography of Syntactic Structures. Vol. I.* Oxford: Oxford University Press, 91–120.
Scott, Gary-John 2003. *The Syntax and Semantics of Adjectives: A Cross-linguistic Study.* Ph.D. dissertation. SOAS, The University of London.
Siegel, Muffy E. A. 1980. *Capturing the Adjective.* New York: Garland.
Steedman, Mark 2000. *The Syntactic Process.* Cambridge, MA: The MIT Press.
Stockwell, Robert, Paul Schachter & Barbara Partee 1973. *The Major Syntactic Structures of English.* New York: Holt, Rinehart & Winston.
Tenny, Carol & James Pustejovsky (eds.) 2000. *Events as Grammatical Objects.* Stanford, CA: CSLI Publications.
Verkuyl, Henk J. 1972. *On the Compositional Nature of the Aspects.* Dordrecht: Reidel.
Wilkinson, Karina 1991. *Studies in the Semantics of Generic Noun Phrases.* Ph.D. dissertation. University of Massachusetts, Amherst, MA.
Wood, Mary McGee 1993. *Categorial Grammars.* London: Routledge.
Zwarts, Joost & Henk J. Verkuyl 1994. An algebra of conceptual structure: An investigation into Jackendoff's conceptual semantics. *Linguistics & Philosophy* 17, 1–28.

Jenny Doetjes
2 Count/mass distinctions across languages

1 Outline —— 29
2 Correlates of the count/mass distinction —— 30
3 The Sanches-Greenberg-Slobin generalization —— 38
4 Count versus mass in the lexicon —— 46
5 Concluding remarks: Count and mass across languages —— 53
6 References —— 54

Abstract: This article examines the opposition between count and mass in a variety of languages. It starts by an overview of correlates of the count/mass distinction, illustrated by data from three types of languages: languages with morphological number marking, languages with numeral classifiers and languages with neither of these. Despite the differences, the count/mass distinction can be shown to play a role in all three systems. The second part of the paper focuses on the Sanches-Greenberg-Slobin generalization, which states that numeral classifier languages do not have obligatory morphological number marking on nouns. Finally the paper discusses the relation between the count/mass distinction and the lexicon.

1 Outline

The first question to ask when looking at the count/mass distinction from a cross-linguistic point of view is whether this distinction plays a role in all languages, and if so, whether it plays a similar role. Obviously, all languages include means to refer both to individuals (in a broad sense) and to masses. However, it is a matter of debate whether the distinction between count and mass plays a role in the linguistic system of all languages, whether it should be made at a lexical level, and whether all languages are alike in this respect.

In English the count/mass distinction shows up in a number of contexts. Count nouns have a singular and a plural form while mass nouns cannot be pluralized unless they shift to a count interpretation. Numerals and certain other quantity expressions (*several, many*) can only be used with plural nouns, while

Jenny Doetjes, Leiden, The Netherlands

https://doi.org/10.1515/9783110589825-002

others need a singular count noun (*each*, *a*) or a mass noun (*a bit*). If a numeral combines with a mass term, one has to add a measure word, as in *two glasses of wine*. This strategy is similar to the way numerals combine with all nouns in so-called numeral classifier languages such as Mandarin Chinese. In Mandarin, the use of the numeral forces the presence of a so-called numeral classifier, that is, an expression that indicates a unit of counting or a measure:

(1) a. sān běn shū [Mandarin]
 three CL^{volume} book
 three books
 b. liǎng jīn mǐ
 two CL$^{1/2\ kilo}$ rice
 two half-kilos of rice

Yet another type of strategy can be found in Tagalog (Austronesian, Philippines, Schachter & Otanes 1972). This language lacks number morphology, on a par with Mandarin, but the use of a numeral does not trigger insertion of a classifier. A general overview of the main correlates of the count/mass distinction in these three types of languages will be given in section 2.

According to Greenberg (1972/1977: 286) languages that make use of numeral classifiers in their "basic mode of forming quantitative expressions" never have compulsory number marking on the noun (see also Sanches & Slobin 1973). It is important to realize that the implication goes only one way, as there are languages that have neither morphological number marking nor numeral classifiers, such as Tagalog. The Sanches-Greenberg-Slobin generalization and the relation between number and numeral classifiers will be the topic of section 3.

Section 4 focuses on the relation between the count/mass distinction and the lexicon. A central issue is the status of nouns such as *furniture*, which are in many respects similar to nouns that may be argued to have a "count" interpretation in numeral classifier languages.

2 Correlates of the count/mass distinction

2.1 Number morphology and the interpretation of count and mass terms

In many languages, including English, number marking is an important correlate of the count/mass distinction. For count expressions, both a singular and a plural can be formed, and sometimes also a dual or other number categories (trial, paucal). Mass terms may take number morphology only if they receive a count interpretation (see also section 4.1 below). For example, a noun like *gold* can be turned into the plural form *golds*, but then it gets a count interpretation such as 'types of gold' or 'gold medals'. Morphological number marking on the noun is only one of the many ways of marking plural. In several languages clitics are used, or number is morphologically marked on a determiner rather than on the noun (see Corbett 2000; Dryer 2005).

It has often been shown that number marking in English does not exactly correlate with mass and count concepts (see Pelletier & Schubert 1989). There are nouns with a count interpretation that are morphologically mass in the sense that they do not have a singular and a plural form. Examples are *furniture* and *cattle* in English (note that the noun *cattle* is used in some varieties of English as an invariable count noun such as *sheep* or *fish*). These nouns will be called collective mass nouns (cf. Krifka 1991).

Plurals and mass nouns have similar semantic properties (cf. article 7 [Semantics: Noun Phrases and Verb Phrases] (Lasersohn) *Mass nouns and plurals*). More in particular, they both have the property of cumulative reference. As argued by Quine (1960), if two items can be called *water*, the item they form when put together can be called *water* as well. Link (1983: 303) adds to this that the same is true for bare plurals, as illustrated by the following sentence: "If the animals in this camp are horses, and the animals in that camp are horses, then the animals in both camps are horses."

Singulars lack cumulative reference. The plural object formed of one teapot and another teapot should be called "teapots", not "a teapot". This can be accounted for in a model where singulars denote sets of atomic individuals, while plurals denote sets of individuals plus all possible sums of these individuals and mass nouns denote all possible sums of substance (cf. Link 1983; Krifka 1986, 1991; article 7 [Semantics: Noun Phrases and Verb Phrases] (Lasersohn) *Mass nouns and plurals*).

Even though mass nouns and plurals share the property of cumulative reference, it has been argued by a number of authors that they differ from each other with respect to their minimal parts. In the case of count nouns, it is in principle clear what units we are talking about (but see Pelletier & Schubert 1989: 342; Rothstein 2010; Nicolas 2004). Mass nouns, on the other hand, have been said to refer homogeneously. Homogeneous reference is defined as the combination of cumulative and divisive reference. Divisivity is the downward counterpart of cumulativity, and implies the absence of minimal parts: given a quantity of water, one can take a subpart of it, and that subpart will be water as well. Quine (1960) already pointed out that the concept of divisivity is problematic: there are parts of water that are too small to count as water, and this is even more clearly so in the case of furniture.

Authors who claim that mass nouns have homogeneous reference usually make a difference between linguistic properties of meaning and the real world: homogeneity is not a property of the substance water, but rather of the linguistic representation of water. According to Bunt (1985: 46) mass nouns do not single out any particular parts and as such do not make any commitments concerning the existence of minimal parts. In the same spirit, Lønning (1987: 8) claims that "it is not critical if mass terms really refer *homogeneously* [. . .]. Rather what is of importance is whether they behave as if they did and what it means to behave in such a way."

The claim of homogeneous reference has been challenged by Chierchia (1998a,b), who does take the real world properties of nouns such as *furniture* into account in his linguistic model. Chierchia argues that all mass nouns correspond to structures that have minimal parts, even though these minimal parts may be more or less vague. In this respect mass nouns are similar to plurals, which explains the existence of pairs such as *footwear* and *shoes*.

Chierchia argues that languages such as Mandarin lack true singulars: all nouns are mass nouns and as such they trigger insertion of a numeral classifier. As plural formation depends on the presence of nouns with a singular denotation and cannot apply to mass nouns, the language is predicted not to have plurals (for an extensive discussion of Chierchia's proposal and of the relation between kind denotations, the occurrence of bare argument nouns and numeral classifiers cf. article 5 [Semantics: Noun Phrases and Verb Phrases] (Dayal) *Bare noun phrases*, article 8 [Semantics: Noun Phrases and Verb Phrases] (Carlson) *Genericity* and article 2 [this volume] (Bach & Chao) *Semantic types across languages*).

In reaction to Chierchia's claims, it has been pointed out that some languages have plural count nouns even though they seem to lack real singulars. Brazilian Portuguese *criança* 'child/children' formally alternates with a plural form (*crianças* 'children'), but its meaning is number neutral rather than singular, that is, the use of this form does not imply singularity, but is neutral with respect to the singular/plural opposition. Within Chierchia's framework the number neutral interpretation is identical to a mass interpretation. Given that number neutral nouns do not have singular reference, they would be predicted not to pluralize, and to behave like mass nouns, contrary to fact (see Munn & Schmidt 2005 and article 5 [Semantics: Noun Phrases and Verb Phrases] (Dayal) *Bare noun phrases*).

2.2 Count environments

In certain environments count interpretations are forced. This is particularly clear for numerals, even though other expressions may impose similar requirements (see section 2.3). This section discusses three ways in which nouns can adapt to the presence of a numeral. Section 2.2.1 focuses on English and other languages in which numerals trigger the presence of number morphology. Section 2.2.2 discusses numeral classifiers. Finally, section 2.2.3 considers a system in which the numeral combines with number neutral nouns without any overt marking of countability.

2.2.1 Morphological number marking

In English, numerals typically combine with plural count nouns or, in the case of *one* with a singular count noun (e.g. *two books, one book*). If a mass term is used in this type of context, it either has to undergo a shift to a count interpretation and behave like a count noun (*two wines*), or a special structure has to be used that includes an expression indicating a unit of counting or a measure. This expression is usually a noun with number morphology, as in *two liters of water* or *three pots of honey*. The nouns that may be used in this position form an open class of items indicating for instance a conventional measure (*a kilo of sugar, a liter of wine*), containers or contained quantity (*a cup of coffee, a box of books*), shape (*a slice of bread*), collection (*a bunch of flowers*) and arrangement (*a pile of wood*) (cf. Allan 1977; Lehrer 1986). Following Grinevald (2004), these expressions will be referred to as measure terms. Measure terms are in many respects similar to classifiers, but do not form part of a general system of classification.

In English, where count and mass nouns are easily distinguished from one another by plural marking, measure terms are usually compatible with both mass nouns and plurals. In case they combine with a plural, they have scope over the pluralities: in *two boxes of books*, each box contains of a plurality of books. Some measure terms are even restricted to plurals; examples are *bunch, crowd* and *flock*.

There are no measure terms that combine with singular nouns in English. It will be argued below that this results from a cross-linguistic generalization that applies to both measure terms and numeral classifiers: all of these expressions combine with nouns that have cumulative reference. As English singulars lack cumulative reference, they cannot be used in this type of context. Note that measure terms differ in this respect from *type* and *kind*, as in *two types of car* (cf. article 8 [Semantics: Noun Phrases and Verb Phrases] (Carlson) *Genericity*).

Languages vary in the type of structures they use for measure terms (see for instance Koptjevskaja-Tamm 2001; Rothstein 2009). Even within Germanic two different types can be distinguished. Whereas English uses a pseudo-partitive construction (*two pots of honey*), Dutch and German use structures without a genitive preposition (*twee potten honing* lit. 'two pots honey'). Moreover, Dutch and German do not always require the presence of the plural morpheme on the measure term, as in *twee liter wijn* lit. 'two liter wine'. However, only a small number of measure terms can be used this way. In general non classifier languages tend to treat their measure terms as ordinary count nouns in the sense that they need to be marked for number.

2.2.2 Numeral classifiers

As already illustrated in (1), numerals in languages such as Mandarin trigger the insertion of a so-called numeral classifier. Numeral classifiers can be either mensural or sortal. Mensural classifiers are similar to the measure terms discussed in the previous section (Allan 1977; Grinevald 2004). Both Grinevald and Allan insist on the fact that measure terms and mensural classifiers should be distinguished from one another. Mensural classifiers are part of a larger system of classification as they co-exist with sortal classifiers. One can add to this that some classifier languages only have sortal classifiers. In the numeral classifier language Mokilese (Austronesian, Micronesia, Harrison 1976: 106), measure words behave as count nouns, and need classification themselves: *jilu-w poaun in koahpihen* lit. 'three-CL^{general} pound of coffee'/ 'three pounds of coffee' (morpheme boundary added, cf. (4) below).

Sortal classifiers specify units "in terms of which the referent of the head noun can be counted" (Grinevald 2004: 1020). Sortal classifiers may indicate shape (long object, round object, flat object), an essential property (woman, man, animal, plant) or function (drinkable, for transportation) (see also Allan 1977 and Aikhenvald 2000). Whereas mensural classifiers usually constitute a rather large set, the number of sortal classifiers varies from language to language. In Totzil (Mayan, Mexico, Grinevald 2004), several hundred numeral classifiers have been identified, only eight of which are sortal, while Mandarin has several dozen sortal classifiers (Li & Thompson 1981). Even though it is clear that English does not have sortal classifiers, expressions such as *head* and *piece* in *two head of cattle* and *three pieces of furniture* come rather close (cf. Greenberg 1972/1977; Allan 1977: 293).

According to Grinevald (2004), sortal classifiers indicate a unit of counting while appearing to be semantically redundant in the sense that they specify an inherent characteristic of the noun they modify. In many classifier languages there is one classifier that functions as a general classifier, which is semantically bleached and tends to combine with a large set of nouns in the language. An example is Mandarin *ge*, the classifier normally used with the noun *rén* 'person', which tends to replace more specialized ones (Li & Thompson 1981). There are also many languages in which the sortal classifier may be left out without a change in meaning (see for instance Jacob 1965 and Adams 1991 on Khmer, an Austro-Asiatic language spoken in Cambodia).

It is usually predictable which sortal classifier should be used, even though Becker (1975) shows that creative language users such as writers may use the same noun with different (sortal) classifiers, thus emphasizing different aspects of the meaning of the noun. Similarly, classifiers may trigger different meanings of a polysemous noun (cf. Zhang 2007).

Cheng & Sybesma (1998, 1999) show that syntactic structures containing sortal classifiers ("count-classifiers") differ from those containing mensural classifiers ("massifiers" or mass-classifiers in their terminology). Sortal classifiers, contrary to mensural ones, do not allow for the presence of *de*, a marker typically found at internal phrasal boundaries inside a noun phrase, and they cannot be modified by adjectives. This is illustrated for the sortal classifier *zhī* 'CL^{branch}' and the mensural classifier *xiāng* 'box' in (2):

(2) a. sān   (*xiǎo)   zhī   (*de)   bǐ   [Mandarin]
       three   small   CL^{branch} DE   pen
       'three pens'
    b. liǎng   (xiǎo)   xiāng   (de)   shū
       two   small   box   DE   book
       'two boxes of books'

Cheng & Sybesma argue that "massifiers" (mensural classifiers) are ordinary nouns that under specific conditions may fill a classifier slot.

Classifiers may have different relations to the noun and to the numeral (cf. Greenberg 1972/1977; Allan 1977; Aikhenvald 2000). In many languages, they are fused with the numeral (e.g. Nivkh (Nivkh, Siberia, Gruzdeva 1998), Japanese (Downing 1996) and Mokilese (Austronesian, Micronesia, Harrison 1976)). In other languages (e.g. Mandarin) they constitute a separate lexeme between the noun and the numeral and have been argued to form a constituent with the noun phrase first (cf. Cheng & Sybesma 1999). This pattern occurs in e.g. Thai (Tai-Kadai, Thailand), Tashkent Uzbek (Altaic, Uzbekistan) and Assamese (Indo-European, India) (cf. Aikhenvald 2000). The classifier and the numeral are always adjacent. It is possible, however, that the classifier forms a prosodic unit with the noun rather than with the numeral, as shown by Ikoro (1994) for Kana (Niger-Congo, Nigeria), but this is the exception rather than the rule (Aikhenvald 2000).

A classified noun is usually number neutral. When used as a bare noun, Mandarin *shū* 'book(s)' may be used to refer to one or several books (cf. among many others Krifka 1995; Rullmann & You 2006). The next section discusses a type of language with number neutral nouns that does not make use of numeral classifiers.

2.2.3 Number neutral nouns without numeral classifiers

In many languages of the world numerals combine directly with number neutral nouns (cf. Gil 2005). Even though this type of strategy is rarely taken into account in the literature on the count/mass distinction, the difference between count and mass does play a role in this type of languages as well (cf. Wilhelm 2008, who reached similar conclusions to the ones presented here on the basis of facts from Dëne Sųłiné, Athapaskan, Canada). The following examples from Tagalog (Austronesian, Philippines, Schachter & Otanes 1972: 143, 208) illustrate the use of numerals with count and mass nouns. In the latter case a measure term is inserted (a ganta corresponds to three liters):

(3) a. dalawang   mansanas   [Tagalog]
     two+LINKER apple
     'two apples'
   b. dalawang   salop na   bigas
     two+LINKER ganta LINKER rice
     'two gantas of rice'

Schachter & Otanes indicate that Tagalog nouns are number neutral, even though in many contexts the plural marker *mga* may be added (interestingly not with numerals, as they note on page 142). However, they insist on the fact that there is a count/mass distinction in the language: "Tagalog makes a distinction between pluralizable and unpluralizable nouns that is like a distinction made in English. [...] In general, Tagalog count nouns correspond to English count nouns and refer to items that are perceived as distinct units: e.g., *bahay* 'house', *baro* 'dress', *bata* 'child'." (Schachter & Otanes 1972: 112) As for mass nouns, Tagalog and English are similar as well, even though nouns such as *furniture* tend to be count nouns in Tagalog. One might speculate that collective mass nouns, which have a count meaning but the morphology of a mass noun, typically occur in languages with an obligatory system of singular/plural marking, as the lack of number marking distinguishes them from other nouns with count interpretations (cf. section 4 below).

2.3 Selectional properties of determiners

Numerals are not the only expressions that may trigger number morphology on nouns or insertion of a classifier. Quite in general, determiners impose restrictions on the nouns they combine with (the term determiner will be used in a very broad sense for quantifying expressions as well as definite and indefinite determiners).

In English, *several, few, many* and *different* only combine with plural nouns on a par with the numerals above *one*, while *a, every* and the numeral *one* select singular nouns. Interestingly, there do not seem to be any determiners that combine with all count nouns (singulars and plurals) and not with mass nouns. At least in English, determiners that combine with both singulars and plurals also combine with mass nouns (*some, any, the, no*), and as such they are not sensitive to the count/mass distinction.

A very large class of determiners combines with mass nouns and plurals. This class includes *a lot, more, less*. Most of these determiners can also be used as adverbs indicating the quantity corresponding to an event, as in *John slept a lot*. These "adverbial" determiners have been claimed to be sensitive to the property of cumulative reference (cf. Doetjes 1997, 2004). A small class of determiners is restricted to mass nouns, and these usually allow for adverbial use as well (*a bit, much, little*). In English these expressions are in complementary distribution with a plural selecting determiner (*much–many, little–few, a little/ a bit–a few*). One way of looking at these "mass only" determiners is to assume that their incompatibility with plurals is due to blocking by the plural selecting alternative.

Mandarin distinguishes between determiners that force insertion of a classifier, determiners that allow for the optional presence of a classifier and determiners that disallow classifiers. Not only numerals, but also demonstratives and certain quantificational determiners (e.g. *jǐ* 'how many', 'a few') require the presence of a numeral classifier. With certain other determiners the classifier is either absent or optional depending on the dialect (cf. *hěn duō (%wǎn) tāng* 'much soup' or 'many cups of soup', *hěn duō (%běn) shū* 'many/a lot of books'). Mandarin speakers from the North tend not to allow for a classifier at all (sortal or mensural), while speakers from the South optionally insert a classifier. Furthermore, some speakers reject the use of a sortal classifier (*běn*) while accepting the use of container words such as *wǎn* in their container reading, but not when used as a measure. Despite the dialectal differences, these determiners are similar to *a lot* and *more* in English in the sense that they combine directly with mass nouns and count nouns, and as such can be said to be insensitive to the count/mass distinction. Interestingly, Mandarin also has a counterpart of *a bit*. The form *yī diǎnr* 'a little' never allows for insertion of a classifier, and is typically used with nouns that have a mass or an abstract denotation (Iljic 1994). The form alternates with *jǐ* 'a few', which always triggers insertion of a classifier.

As for Tagalog, Schachter & Otanes (1972) state that expressions such as the cardinal numerals, *iilan* 'only a few', *ilan* 'a few' and *hindi iilan* 'not a few, quite a few' are used with count nouns, while for instance *kaunti* 'a little' and *hindi kaunti* 'not a little, quite a lot' typ-ically combine with mass nouns. Other expressions, such as *marami* 'a lot', are insensitive to the count/mass distinction, and combine with count nouns and mass nouns alike.

As shown in Tab. 2.1, determiners in all three languages may be sensitive to the count/mass distinction.

Tab. 2.1: Selectional properties of determiners (examples)

	count	mass	indifferent
English	*one* (singular noun), *a few* (plural noun)	*a little*	*a lot*
Mandarin	*yī* 'one', *jī* 'a few' (CL + number neutral noun)	*yī diǎnr* 'a little'	*hěn duō* 'a lot'
Tagalog	*isa* 'one', *ilan* 'a few' (number neutral noun)	*kaunti* 'a little'	*marami* 'a lot'

3 The Sanches-Greenberg-Slobin generalization

3.1 Number and classifiers

An important universal associated with the count/mass distinction concerns the relation between number and classifiers (for universals in general, cf. article 13 [Semantics: Foundations, History and Methods] (Matthewson) *Methods in cross-linguistic semantics* and article 2 [this volume] (Bach & Chao) *Semantic types across languages*). In 1972 Greenberg postulates that languages without compulsory number marking on the noun may have obligatory use of numeral classifiers, referring to an unpublished paper by Sanches from 1971, later published as Sanches & Slobin (1973). Sanches originally states the generalization as follows (Greenberg 1972/1977: 286): "If a language includes in its basic mode of forming quantitative expressions numeral classifiers, then [...] it will not have obligatory marking of the plural on nouns." Moreover, Sanches claims that classified nouns are normally singulars.

According to Greenberg, it rather seems to be the case that the classified noun is normally not marked for number. In what follows it will become clear that Greenberg's version of the observation is on the right track: classifiers are used predominantly with number neutral nouns. Greenberg argues that the loss of number marking on nouns in a language may lead to the emergence of a numeral classifier system, in which case the classifier construction is modelled after structures containing a measure term.

The Sanches-Greenberg-Slobin generalization seems to be quite robust. When examining this universal, two aspects of the generalization should be kept in mind. In the first place, the generalization is implicational and only holds one way. Thus, it is not the case that languages without obligatory number marking on the noun will have a general system of numeral classifiers. The examples of Tagalog in section 2.2.3 illustrate this point. In the second place, the generalization speaks about "marking of plural on nouns". As will become clear below, this should be taken literally in the sense of morphological number marking. Other types of number marking do not count (e.g. number morphology on a demonstrative or number marking by means of an independent morpheme cf. Dryer 2005). Moreover, the morphological number marking should be compulsory. Yucatec (Mayan, Mexico; Allan 1977: 294) is an example of a numeral classifier language with optional number morphology on the noun, which may be used even in the presence a classifier: *oš tul maak(oob)* lit. 'three CL[animate] person(s)'/ 'three persons'.

In the literature, several counter-examples to the Sanches-Greenberg-Slobin generalization have been mentioned, including for instance Nivkh (Nivkh, Siberia), Ejagham (Benue-Congo, Nigeria/ Cameroon) and Southern Dravidian languages (India) (cf. Aikhenvald 2000). However, none of them constitutes a clear case of a language with obligatory number marking on the noun and a general system of numeral classifiers. Nivkh does not have compulsory number marking (Gruzdeva 1998: 17) while Ejagham is not a numeral classifier language (see section 3.4 below). As for Southern Dravidian Languages, Haspelmath et al. (2005) provide information on a number of languages of this genus, but do not classify any of them as a numeral classifier language with obligatory morphological number. Further research, providing detailed information about the relevant facts in potentially problematic languages, is necessary. Given the accessible data so far, it seems that if counter-examples exist, they are typologically extremely rare.

Several types of languages are of special interest for gaining a better understanding of the generalization. Section 3.2 discusses languages that have both obligatory number marking and obligatory use of numeral classifiers. Section 3.3 investigates optional use of classifiers in languages with obligatory number marking on nouns. In section 3.4 a mixed system will be discussed in which classifiers and number seem to co-occur. Section 3.5 concludes and reconsiders the Sanches-Greenberg-Slobin generalization in the light of the presented data.

3.2 Obligatory plural marking and obligatory classifiers

An example of a language with obligatory number marking and obligatory use of numeral classifiers is Mokilese (Austronesian, Micronesia; Harrison 1976; in the cited examples relevant morpheme boundaries have been added). Mokilese makes use of a limited set of classifiers. Singular indefinites are marked by suffixation of the classifier. The general classifier -w is preceded by the numeral *oa-*'one', suggesting that this numeral may have been dropped in cases where it is absent: *pukk-oaw* (*puk + oa-w*) lit. 'book-one-CL^{general}'/ 'a book', *koaul-pas* lit. 'song-CL$^{long\ object}$'/ 'a song'. A plural indefinite is marked by a separate morpheme *-pwi*, which alternates with the classifiers (*woal-pwi* lit. 'man-PL'/ '(some) men'). In case a numeral is used, the numeral fuses with the appropriate classifier and the use of *-pwi* is excluded. This shows that *-pwi* is more similar to a plural indefinite determiner such as French *des* in *des livres* 'books', than to the English plural suffix *-s*.

(4) a. mwumw jilu-w/ jil-men [Mokilese]
    fish three-CL^{general} three-CL^{animate}
    'three fish'
  b. suhkoa rah-pas
    tree two-CL$^{long\ object}$
    'two trees'

The pattern found in Mokilese for indefinites is similar to the pattern found in Mandarin. The Mandarin numeral *yī* 'one' may be left out in direct object position, yielding a sequence of a classifier and a noun with a singular indefinite interpretation (cf. Cheng & Sybesma 1999). Mokilese *-pwi* resembles the element *xīe* in Mandarin, which is sometimes called a 'plural classifier' (but see Iljic 1994 for differences between *xīe* and classifiers). *Xīe* can be preceded by the numeral *yī* 'one' but it is incompatible with all other numerals: (*yī*)/ *sān xīe rén/bǐ* lit. '(one)/*three PL person/pen'/ 'some persons/pens'. This property is reminiscent of elements such as *few* in English, that do combine with the indefinite determiner *a* but not with numerals (*a few pens* vs. *two few(s) pens*).

However, Mokilese differs significantly from Mandarin with regard to the way in which demonstratives are used. Whereas Mandarin demonstratives trigger insertion of a classifier, demonstratives in Mokilese show up as suffixes and are obligatorily marked for number, as shown in *woall-o* (*woal + -o*) lit. 'man-that'/ 'that man', *woall-ok* (*woal + -ok*) lit. 'man-those'/ 'those men'. Thus, the singular/plural opposition in this language is marked obligatorily, but it is marked on the demonstrative rather than on the noun. Consequently, the Mokilese data are in accordance with the Sanches-Greenberg-Slobin generalization.

The Mokilese data illustrate that morphological number on a noun differs from morphological number marking on a demonstrative. One could argue that Mokilese nouns are always number neutral, as in the case of Mandarin. Number marking plays a role at a different level: the demonstrative determiner has a singular and a plural form, not the noun. The presence of number marking on the demonstrative should not be taken to be a reflection of agreement with an invisible category for singular or plural on the noun, as the comparison with other classifier languages strongly suggests that Mokilese bare nouns are semantically and morphologically number neutral.

3.3 Optional classifiers and obligatory number

The Sanches-Greenberg-Slobin generalization is about languages that make obligatory use of numeral classifiers. In order to find out why languages make use of classifiers, languages with optional use of numeral classifiers are also an important object of study. Optional classifiers are very frequent cross-linguistically. Haspelmath et al. (2005) list almost as many languages with optional classifiers as languages with obligatory ones. Some languages with optional classifiers have a set of sortal classifiers and thus resemble Mandarin and Mokilese (e.g. Khmer, Austro-Asiatic, Cambodia; Jacob 1965). Other languages have only one optional sortal classifier, which is sometimes also called an enumerator (e.g. Hausa, Chadic, Nigeria; Newman 2000).

This section focuses on languages with optional classifiers that also have morphological number marking which in some contexts is obligatorily present. The first language that will be considered is Armenian (Indo-European, Turkey/Armenia; Borer 2005; Bale & Khanjian 2008; Minassian 1980). Borer (2005: 94), citing Michelle Siegler (p.c.), gives the paradigm in (5) for Western Armenian (Turkey). Eastern Armenian (Armenia) is similar in the relevant respects.

(5) a. Yergu (had)   hovanoc uni-m   [Western Armenian]
       two   (CL)   umbrella have-1SG
    b. Yergu (*had) hovanoc-ner uni-m
       two   (*CL) umbrella-s have-1SG

The data in (5) show that the numeral combines with a non-plural noun, with a plural noun or with a classifier followed by a non-plural noun, while plural marking on the noun following the classifier is excluded. Note that even though the use of the plural is optional with numerals and in a number of other contexts, it is obligatory in non generic noun phrases containing the definite article (cf. Minassian, 1980: 81–82 for Eastern Armenian). However, Bale & Khanjian (2008) show that the non-plural form is not a singular but rather a number neutral noun, which means that it denotes an atomic join semi-lattice rather than a set of atoms. This is in accordance with the observation above that classifiers do not combine with real singulars, which lack cumulative reference. The data in (5) reflect the patterns discussed for Mandarin, Tagalog and English above. (5a) corresponds to the patterns found in Mandarin (classifier plus number neutral noun) and Tagalog (number neutral noun), while (5b) is similar to the pattern found in English.

Borer accounts for the data in (5) in a syntactic way. In her view, a count interpretation has to be syntactically licensed by the presence of a so-called "divider". Both classifiers and number may act as dividers, but as there is only one syntactic slot available, stacking of dividers is excluded, ruling out the combination of a classifier and a plural. In order to account for the optionality of the classifier in (5a), Borer assumes that numerals in this language may function as dividers (Borer 2005: 117–118). Contrary to Borer, Bale & Khanjian (2008) offer a semantic explanation for the impossibility of the use of a classifier (5b). They argue that plurals in this language are real plurals in the sense that their denotation excludes the atoms (cf. article 7 [Semantics: Noun Phrases and Verb Phrases] (Lasersohn) *Mass nouns and plurals*). Under the assumption that the classifier needs atoms in the denotation of the noun it combines with, it is incompatible with the plural form.

From the perspective of the Sanches-Greenberg-Slobin generalization, the Armenian facts are particularly interesting, as they show that (optional) classifiers are not impossible in a system in which number marking is in some cases obligatorily marked on the noun. Languages with obligatory plural marking tend to lack number neutral nouns, but in some linguistic systems the two may co-occur. Sortal classifiers are typically found with nouns that are neither singular nor plural, as indicated by Greenberg (cf. section 3.1).

However, it is not the case that combinations of classifiers and plural nouns are completely excluded, contrary to the predictions of Borer. There are also languages that present all four possibilities given in (5). An example of such a language is Hausa (Afro-Asiatic, Niger, Nigeria; Zimmermann 2008), as illustrated in *kujèeraa/kùjèeruu (gùdaa) hudù* lit.'chair.SG/PL (CL) four'/'four chairs'. According to Zimmermann, various facts indicate that Hausa non-plural nouns are number neutral rather than singular. Moreover, he argues that the plural in Hausa does not include the atoms. If this is right, the pattern is not only unexpected under Borer's syntactic account of the Armenian data in (5), but also under the semantic analysis of Bale & Khanjian.

The mixed properties of Armenian and Hausa seem to correlate with the existence of number neutral nouns in these languages. Hausa is of special interest, as this language uses the classifier also with plural nouns (cf. also the Yucatec example in section 3.1). It is unclear at this point under what conditions plural nouns can co-occur with sortal classifiers.

3.4 Mixed systems

It is clear from the preceding discussion that the distinction between languages such as English, Mandarin and Tagalog illustrated in section 2 is a very rough one, which does not account for the many existing intermediate cases. The patterns in Armenian and Hausa discussed in the previous section illustrate the fact that a numeral can be used in various ways with the same noun in a single language. There are also mixed systems where part of the lexicon has a singular/plural opposition, whereas a large class of other nouns with count interpretations need insertion of an expression that resembles a sortal classifier in order to be combined with a numeral.

This is the case in Ejagham (Niger-Congo, Cameroon, Nigeria; Watters 1981), which is taken to be a numeral classifier language by for instance Aikhenvald (2000). Ejagham uses a noun class system that encodes, among other things, the opposition between singular and plural, resulting in obligatory plural marking on the nouns that fall in these classes. Numerals agree in noun class with the noun they modify, as in *Ǹ-díg mɔ́-d* lit. '3-rope 3-one'/'one rope' and *à-ríg á-sá* lit. '6-rope 6-three'/'three ropes', where 3 and 6 refer to a singular and a corresponding plural noun class respectively (Watters 1981: 469, 471).

The language also has quite a large class of nouns with count interpretations that are members of a single noun class, which means that they do not introduce a singular-plural opposition. When these nouns are combined with numerals, a unit counter is used, which Watters calls a classifier (Watters 1981: 309–313). Many words for fruits, roots, trees, plants and vegetables are in this class, while most of their English counterparts are marked for number. The system strongly resembles a numeral classifier system. Watters distinguishes five different "classifiers", some of which can also be used as independent nouns. However, as noted by Aikhenvald (2000), the "classifiers" in this language are in a plural or a singular noun class, and the numeral agrees with the classifier in noun class. This is illustrated by (6). The classifier used in this example belongs to noun class 5 if it is singular and to noun class 9 if it is plural; GN is a (tonal) genitive linker:

(6) a. ɛ́-rɔ́m ́ í-čɔ́kùd jɔ́-d [Ejagham]
     5-CL^{fruit} GN 19-orange 5-one
     'one orange'
   b. Ǹ-dɔ́m ̀ í-čɔ́kùd ɛ́-bá'ɛ́
     9-CL^{fruit} GN 19-orange 9-two
     'two oranges'

The expression of singular and plural on the "classifiers" shows that they behave like ordinary count nouns in the language, and as such should not be considered to be sortal classifiers but rather count nouns that function as unit counters, on a par with *piece* in English (cf. the discussion in section 2.2 and Greenberg 1972/1977). Ejagham thus seems to have a large number of collective mass nouns, that is, nouns that are similar to *furniture* in English in the sense that they do not have a singular and a plural form, even though from a semantic point of view they have a count interpretation.

Ikoro (1994) argues that the unit counters used for part of the lexicon in Ejagham and the numeral classifiers generally used in the numeral classifier language Kana (Niger-Congo, Nigeria; Ikoro 1994) have a common origin, suggesting that collective mass nouns may well have played an important role in the genesis of the numeral classifier system of Kana (cf. Greenberg 1972/1977).

3.5 Consequences for the Sanches-Greenberg-Slobin generalization

In the preceding sections a number of languages have been looked at in view of the Sanches-Greenberg-Slobin generalization, which states that numeral classifier languages do not have obligatory marking of the plural on nouns. It has been argued in the preceding sections that the presence of number neutral nouns in a language seems to be the crucial factor for the presence of sortal classifiers, as illustrated in several ways.

In the first place, the generalization itself insists on the compulsory nature of number morphology: languages with optional number marking on the noun may have numeral classifiers (e.g. Yucatec, Mayan, Mexico; Allan 1977). If number is an optional category on the noun, the non-plural noun should have a number neutral denotation and cannot be a true singular, as it can also be used to denote pluralities.

In the second place, languages with number marking that is not realized as a morphological affix on the noun may have numeral classifiers. This possibility was illustrated on the basis of the numeral classifier language Mokilese (Austronesian, Micronesia; Harrison 1976), which marks number obligatorily on the demonstrative. At the level of the noun, number does not seem to play a role, and it makes sense to assume that bare nouns in this language are number neutral.

In the third place, a language may have obligatory number marking on nouns in certain contexts, while also having number neutral nouns. This seems to be the case in Armenian (Indo-European, Turkey/Armenia; Borer 2005; Bale & Khanjian 2008; Minassian 1980). The language has number neutral nouns, and optionally inserts a sortal classifier between a numeral and a number neutral noun.

The way the Sanches-Greenberg-Slobin generalization is formulated does not make reference to number neutral nouns, but rather to obligatory marking of plural on nouns. The case of Armenian shows that in some languages number neutral nouns may occur in a system with obligatory plural morphology on nouns. What does not seem to exist are languages with general use of numeral classifiers (i.e. sortal classifiers may or must occur with all nouns that have a count interpretation) and a systematic morphological singular-plural opposition, excluding number neutrality. This distinguishes between languages such as English, which has true singulars as well as obligatory plural marking on nouns, and languages such as Armenian where plural nouns alternate with number neutral forms rather than with (semantic) singulars.

Interestingly, one could say that number neutrality also plays a role in systems with a strict singular-plural opposition. In English *furniture*, *cattle* and *footwear* arguably have a number neutral interpretation, and the same is true for a large class of nouns in Ejagham (Niger-Congo, Cameroon/ Nigeria; Watters 1981). In order to use numerals with these nouns, one has to insert a count noun that functions as a unit counter.

At this point, a number of questions need further investigation. First, more languages need to be studied in order to see whether there are systematic differences between languages with obligatory use of numeral classifiers and languages with optional numeral classifiers. For instance, one may wonder whether there are obligatory numeral classifier languages with one single numeral classifier (cf. the systems of optional classifier insertion in Armenian and Hausa).

A second issue concerns the possibility of having numeral classifiers with nouns that are morphologically plural, as in Yucatec (section 3.1) and Hausa (section 3.3). Plural marking in combination with a classifier is the exception rather than the rule, and it is not clear at this point whether this pattern ever occurs in a language without number neutral nouns. More languages need to be studied in order to gain insight into this issue.

A further question that needs to be answered is why the generalization exists. Even though some proposals have been made in the literature, this is still an open question. In the syntactic literature, it has been argued that both classifiers and number may have a similar function in a language. As already indicated in section 3.3 above, Borer assumes that classifiers and number morphology function as so-called dividers. She claims that count interpretations need to be syntactically licensed by the presence of a divider. As there is a single syntactic slot for the divider, the classifier and number morphology compete for the same syntactic position, which predicts that they are mutually exclusive. Similarly, Doetjes (1997) argues that both classifiers and number morphology function as grammatical markers of countability. Numerals need the presence of a grammatical element that signals the presence of minimal parts in the denotation of the noun. In this view, classifiers and number morphology have the same syntactic function.

From a semantic point of view, plural morphology and classifiers do not seem to have the same function. If it is true that the classified noun is number neutral, the denotation of the number neutral noun in a numeral classifier language is very close if not identical to that of a plural noun in a language with a systematic distinction between singular and plural (cf. article 7 [Semantics: Noun Phrases and Verb Phrases] (Lasersohn) *Mass nouns and plurals* for arguments in favor of including the atoms in the denotation of plural nouns in English). Classifiers have been argued to be "singularizers", in the sense that they map an atomic semi-lattice into a set of atoms (Chierchia 1998b: 347; Cheng & Sybesma 1999: 521). This does not predict an alternation between classified nouns and plural nouns, unless one were to assign singular interpretation to plurals in the context of numerals, in which case the plural marker would reflect agreement rather than semantic plurality (cf. Ionin & Matushansky 2006, who argue in favor of such an approach). If one were to accept such a proposal, it would still not explain why, in the absence of classifiers, languages tend to use plural or number neutral nouns with numerals.

On the other hand, if mass nouns and count nouns have different reference properties, as proposed by Bunt (1985), one could say that numeral classifier languages lack a count-mass distinction: all nouns are mass, and as such, the classifiers are necessary in order to provide a measure or unit for counting. The next section will argue that such a view cannot be maintained. Both numeral classifier languages and languages with obligatory morphological number marking present evidence in favor of the idea that the count/mass distinction plays a role at a lexical level.

4 Count versus mass in the lexicon

In the literature on the count/mass distinction, a central question is to what extent the correlates of the count/mass distinction have to do with lexical properties of nouns. According to a lexicalist point of view (see among others Gillon 1992), there are count nouns and mass nouns in the lexicon of a language such as English. A different point of view, recently defended by Borer (2005), takes the count structures in syntax to be triggers for a count interpretation of nouns that are lexically mass (see also Sharvy 1978). The reason for the existence of "unitarian expression approaches", as Pelletier & Schubert (1989) call them, is the fact that most nouns can be either mass or count, depending on the context (e.g. *Kim put an apple in the salad* versus *Kim put apple in the salad*).

This section explores the semantic properties of count nouns and mass nouns, or rather, count meanings and mass meanings. Section 4.1 investigates meaning shifts from mass-to-count and vice versa and section 4.2 comes back to the status of count and mass in the lexicon in languages such as English. Section 4.3 extends the discussion to other types of languages, focusing specifically on numeral classifier languages, as these languages have been claimed not to have a lexical count/mass distinction (cf. Denny 1986, Lucy 1992 among others), while others refute this claim (cf. for instance Cheng & Sybesma 1998; Doetjes 1997).

4.1 Shifts

Nouns that one would like to call "count nouns", can easily be used with a mass interpretation. In order to illustrate this, Pelletier (1975/1979) introduces the concept of the "universal grinder", suggested to him by David Lewis:

> Consider a machine, the "universal grinder". This machine is rather like a meat grinder in that one introduces something into one end, the grinder chops and grinds it up into a homogeneous mass and spews it onto the floor from its other end. [...] Now if we put into one end of a meat grinder a steak, and ask what there is on the floor at the other end, the answer is 'There is steak all over the floor' (where steak has a mass sense). [...] The reader has doubtless guessed by now the purpose of our universal grinder: Take an object corresponding to any (apparent) count noun [...] (e.g., 'man'), put the object in one end of the grinder, and ask what is on the floor (answer: 'There is man all over the floor').
>
> (Pelletier 1975/1979: 6)

Pelletier concludes that basically any noun, provided the right context, may have a mass interpretation.

Nouns that one would like to call "mass nouns" frequently allow for a count interpretation as well. Most if not all mass nouns in English have a "type of" reading which is count. So, *two golds* may mean two types of gold and *two wines* two types of wine. Bunt (1985: 11) calls this the "universal sorter". Moreover, mass nouns can often be used to refer to a typical object made of the stuff the mass noun normally refers to, or a portion of N-mass. In the case of *gold* this can be for instance a gold medal, as in: *He won two Olympic golds*, while the noun *wine* can be used for a glass of wine.

One might conclude from this that basically all nouns can be used in mass and in count contexts, and that these contexts force a count or a mass interpretation. This in turn begs the question whether we want to have a distinction between mass nouns and count nouns in the first place. Before addressing this question, some more cases of count-to-mass shifts and mass-to-count shifts will be considered (cf. Doetjes 1997; Nicolas 2002).

Going back to Pelletier's universal grinder, it is clear that it grinds physical objects. However, there are also count nouns that refer to abstract objects. These usually do not allow for grinding. Take for instance the noun *aspect*. Can one put an aspect in the grinder? And if there is aspect all over the floor, what does that mean? The same is true for other abstract count nouns such as *characteristic* and measure nouns such as *mile* and *kilometer*.

As for mass-to-count shifts, the type reading and the portion reading seem to be rather common and productive. However, not all languages allow for these readings for all nouns. Take for instance the example of Dutch. In the first place, certain classes of mass nouns lack count readings all together. Dutch does not have a count noun *gold*: *twee gouden* 'two golds' being unacceptable. The same is true for other material nouns in Dutch, such as *hout* 'wood'. In the second place, there are nouns that do have a type reading, but lack a portion reading. In that case, the portion reading can usually be derived by adding the diminutive marker *-tje* (cf. *twee wijnen* lit. 'two wine+PL'/ 'two types of wine' vs. *twee wijntjes* lit. two wine+DIM+PL/ 'two glasses of wine').

Turning to other types of mass-to-count shifts, namely the ones that result in a reading of the kind *object made of N*, it is usually not predictable at all what the meaning of the count noun will be. Take again the English noun *gold*. Even though this word can refer to a gold medal, it is much harder if not impossible to use it in order to refer to a gold necklace.

4.2 The semantics of count nouns and mass nouns

The fact that nouns normally have both count and mass meanings led to question whether it is necessary to assume a distinction between mass nouns and count nouns in the lexicon.

Sharvy (1978) tentatively argues that English might be "like Chinese" and lack count nouns all together in the sense that all nouns need insertion of a classifier. The structure of *two beers* would be one with an empty classifier for *glass*, and the plural morphology on *beer* would originate from the covert classifier. Recently, Borer (2005) makes a similar claim, without assuming the presence of a covert classifier. In her view the presence of count syntax (as realized by number morphology and classifiers) triggers a count reading of a noun phrase: "all nouns are born unspecified for any properties, including count or mass, and [...] as a default, and unless more structure is provided, they will be interpreted as mass" (Borer 2005: 108).

Given the restrictions on the shifts discussed in the previous section, it is far from obvious that the count/mass distinction is absent at the level of the lexicon. In the first place, there are nouns that are always mass or always count. Moreover, when shifts take place, one often has the impression to be able to indicate a direction in which the meaning shifts. Another important question is what kind of object a given noun may refer to. Take the noun *chicken* and assume that this noun is lexically mass. The question is then how to predict what meaning one obtains if this noun is used with count syntax, as in *three chickens*. Why would this not mean, in a relevant context, *three drumsticks*? Under the assumption that the shifts discussed above represent lexical rules, lexical restrictions are expected, both on the possible interpretations of a noun and on the availability of count and mass readings.

The count/mass distinction can be implemented in the lexicon in different ways (cf. Pelletier & Schubert 1989). One could assume that the lexicon contains both a count noun *chicken* and a mass noun *chicken* which are [+count] and [−count] respectively. Alternatively, there might be a single noun with several senses that may introduce criteria for counting or not, but that are not marked syntactically by a feature [± count]. In the latter case, count syntax would force the choice of a sense of a word that introduces a criterion for counting. Mass syntax would be used in the absence of such a criterion.

A central point of discussion in this context is the status of collective mass nouns. As often noted in the literature on the mass count distinction, *shoes* and *footwear*, *coins* and *change* have very similar meanings. Given that collective nouns seem to provide a criterion for counting, what prevents them from being used in a count environment? In the spirit of Bunt and Lønning one could say that even though *footwear* and *shoes* are nouns that can be used to refer to the same objects, *footwear* represents this meaning as if it has homogeneous reference, while *shoes* provides a linguistically relevant criterion for counting.

However, there are reasons to assume that the nouns *footwear* and *furniture* provide a criterion for counting which is linguistically relevant (see for instance Chierchia 1998a,b; Doetjes 1997; Nicolas 2002; Chierchia 2010). For instance, *a pair of footwear* and *a pair of shoes* can be opposed to #*a pair of water*. The interpretation of this type of nouns in the context of degree words, and in particular comparative *more*, is even more telling. As shown in (7), the evaluation of the quantity of objects indicated by *more* depends on whether *more* is used with a mass noun or a plural (see Gathercole 1985; Doetjes 1997; Barner & Snedeker 2005):

(7) Peter ate more chocolates than John ↔
    Peter ate more chocolate than John

In order to evaluate a sentence with *more* one needs a criterion for evaluating the quantity. When the plural *chocolates* is used, this must be the number of separate chocolates. As for *more chocolate*, the global quantity is evaluated, probably in terms of weight or volume. Thus, if Peter has eaten 5 big chocolates and John 6 quite small ones, the first sentence in (7) is false and the second true.

Barner & Snedeker (2005) show on the basis of a psycholinguistic experiment that the following equivalence holds:

(8) Barbie has more pieces of furniture than us ↮
     Barbie has more furniture than us

The contrast between (7) and (8) indicates that collective mass nouns such as *furniture* impose a criterion for counting when combined with *more*, while non collective mass nouns do not, which demonstrates that not only count nouns but also collectives involve a criterion for counting.

This complicates a view according to which count and mass are not represented in the lexicon as features but rather as properties of meanings. It is clear that *furniture* behaves like a mass noun in the sense that it does not take number morphology and does not allow for direct modification by a numeral. If a count sense created by a mass-to-count shift in the lexicon automatically results in count syntax, it is strange to assume that *furniture* has count semantics and yet no access to count syntax.

One way to stick to a "senses approach" to the count/mass distinction, while taking into account the existence of count senses without count syntax (as in the case of *furniture*), is to assume that collective mass nouns enter the lexicon with a count meaning and lexical incompatibility with number (cf. Chierchia 2010 for a similar view). This might be related to the group interpretation associated with these nouns (cf. Borer 2005: 103, note 13). As such, they could be seen as the mass counterparts of group nouns such as *committee* (cf. Chierchia 1998a: 86). Assigning an exceptional status to these nouns makes it possible to assume that count meanings result by default in the obligatory use of number morphology in syntax, unless they are lexically specified as being incompatible with number. This correctly predicts that a collective meaning is always the core meaning of a noun, and cannot be obtained by a shifting process. Whenever the meaning of a noun shifts towards a count meaning in a language with obligatory morphological number marking on nouns, the noun will be marked for number.

The borderline between collective nouns and non collective ones is by no means a simple one to draw. Consider cases such as *a drop of water* and *a grain of sand*. One may wonder whether the criterion for counting introduced by *grain of sand* and *drop of water* is introduced by the noun or by *grain* and *drop*. The *more*-test might offer a way out: it does not seem to be possible to say: #*This small heap actually contains more sand than that big heap over there* implying that the small heap contains more grains of sand.

4.3 "Count nouns" in numeral classifier languages

A related question is whether nouns in numeral classifier languages can be lexically count. The idea that Mandarin would be a language without a lexical mass-count distinction has been made for different reasons. In what follows it will be shown that the arguments that are offered in the literature are not valid and that there is evidence in favor of a lexical count/mass distinction in a language such as Mandarin.

A first reason why it has been assumed that numeral classifier languages do not distinguish between count nouns and mass nouns is the obligatory presence of classifiers in the context of numerals with both mass and count nouns, which is reminiscent of the insertion of measure terms with mass nouns in languages such as English. However, as shown in section 2.2.2 above, it is not true that mass nouns and count nouns introduce exactly the same structures, as one has to distinguish between sortal and mensural classifiers. The former typically combine with nouns that have a count interpretation (cf. Cheng & Sybesma 1999; Grinevald 2004).

According to some authors, classifiers are responsible for the presence of atomic structure in a very concrete way. Denny (1986) and Lucy (1992) argue for instance, that languages such as English have a lexical count/mass distinction while classifier languages do not, assuming that number marking does not introduce units of counting while classifiers do introduce such units. Based on psycholinguistic experiments among speakers of the numeral classifier language Yucatec (Mayan, Mexico), Lucy claims that his Yucatec subjects have a substance oriented way of viewing the world as compared to speakers of English.

Even though such a "parametric" view may seem appealing at first sight, the evidence in favor of this type of approach is not very strong. As shown by Li, Dunham & Carey (2009), a new set of experiments sheds serious doubts on Lucy's interpretation of his results, and shows convincingly that being speaker of a numeral classifier language does not affect one's perspective on substances and objects in the world.

From a purely linguistic point of view, the parametric approach is problematic as well (cf. Doetjes 1997). Some classifiers provide no information about what the atoms would be, and in this respect they do not differ from number morphology. Many classifier languages have for instance a so-called general classifier, which may replace other sortal classifiers, and does not contain any information about the units that are to be counted (e.g. Mandarin *ge*). Yet, it always triggers a count interpretation of the noun (see also Adams 1991). Moreover, numeral classifier languages often do not use classifiers in combination with expressions corresponding to large numbers. Rather, these expressions behave like classifiers themselves and are similar to English nouns such as *pair* and *dozen*. Again, no criterion for counting is present, yet a count meaning of the noun is necessarily present.

This is not to deny that in certain cases the choice of classifier may decide which meaning to pick for a polysemous noun. Zhang (2007) cites for instance the example of the noun *kè*, which means either class or course depending on the context. In the first case, the classifier *táng* is selected and in the second case *mén*. Similar cases of polysemy exist in non classifier languages. The Dutch noun *college* 'course, class' can have the same two interpretations as Mandarin *kè*. It is to be expected that a numeral classifier language with a rather large collection of sortal classifiers may pick different classifiers for different meanings of a polysemous noun, and this type of data should not be mistaken for evidence in favor of a mass interpretation of the noun at a lexical level.

Finally, it has been claimed that classifiers need to be present in order to trigger a count meaning (see in particular Borer 2005). However, it turns out that count meanings may impose themselves in the absence of a classifier. This is particularly clear in the case of a grinding context. As shown by Cheng, Doetjes & Sybesma (2008), grinding is not possible in the following sentence:

(9) qiáng-shang dōu shì gǒu [Mandarin]
 wall-top all be dog
 'There are dogs all over the wall'
 NOT: 'There is dog all over the wall'

This type of data is hard to understand if one assumes that the noun *gǒu* does not provide a criterion for counting. The lack of grinding in Mandarin is quite interesting in view of the fact that numeral classifier languages have been a model to explain the fact that in languages such as English nouns may shift so easily from count to mass interpretations and vice versa, and confirms the idea that grinding should be seen as a lexical operation.

As a whole, it seems clear that there are reflections of the count/mass distinction in numeral classifier languages. They are not only present in syntax, but there are also reasons to assume that lexical entries of nouns may provide a criterion for counting or not depending on the meaning of the noun. What these languages lack is not nouns with count semantics, but rather nouns with a difference between a singular and a plural form. In this sense they resemble languages such as Tagalog, in which nouns are number neutral. If this is right, the difference between Mandarin and Tagalog is not a lexical difference but rather a difference in the type of requirements certain elements in the language (numerals, demonstratives) impose on the nouns they combine with.

5 Concluding remarks: Count and mass across languages

From the data discussed above it seems that languages do not differ in having count meanings and mass meanings at a lexical level. However, they differ in the type of syntax triggered by count and mass meanings, in particular with respect to numerals. Numerals need something to count. As such, in order to combine them with a noun that has a mass meaning, either a measure term or mensural classifier has to be used, or the noun must shift towards a (usually lexically determined) count meaning. In case a noun has a count meaning, several things may happen depending on the language. In a language such as Tagalog nothing happens: the numeral combines directly with the noun. In a language such as English, nouns with count meanings are usually marked for number. If so, number marking is necessary in combination with the numeral. Finally, in numeral classifier languages such as Mandarin, nouns with a count meaning are not marked for number, and in order to use such a noun with a numeral, a sortal classifier has to be inserted. Even though this basic classification is useful, it is important to realize that languages may have mixed properties.

Quite in general, the patterns that have been discussed are in accordance with the Sanches-Greenberg-Slobin generalization: the general use of classifiers is restricted to languages without compulsory number marking on the noun. This has been related to the fact that these languages normally do not have number neutral count nouns while classifiers combine predominantly with number neutral nouns. Nouns that are morphologically marked for plural are usually incompatible with classifiers, but some exceptions exist (Yucatec, Allan 1977; Hausa, Zimmermann 2008). In both languages, number marking on a classified noun is optional. What does not seem to exist is a language in which the use of a numeral triggers both obligatory insertion of a classifier and obligatory plural morphology on the noun.

The reasons behind the existence of the Sanches-Greenberg-Slobin generalization are not clear at this point, given that number neutral nouns and plurals are usually assumed to have very similar if not identical denotations. Somehow both plurals and classifiers seem to "foreground" the atoms, to use Chierchia's (1998a) terminology. Further research needs to make clear what this foregrounding is and under what conditions plural nouns may co-occur with sortal classifiers.

Acknowledgements: I would like to thank Willem Adelaar, Lisa Cheng, Camelia Constantinescu, Klaus von Heusinger, Theo van Lint, David Nicolas, Thilo Schadeberg, Kateřina Součková, Rint Sybesma, Roberto Zamparelli, the Netherlands Organisation for Scientific Re-search NWO (grant # 276-70-007) as well as the makers of the World Atlas of Language Structures (Haspelmath et al. 2005).

6 References

Adams, Karen L. 1991. *Systems of Numeral Classification in the Mon-Khmer, Nicobarese and Aslian Subfamilies of Austroasiatic*. Canberra: Pacific Linguistics.
Aikhenvald, Alexandra 2000. *Classifiers: A Typology of Noun Categorization Devices*. Oxford: Oxford University Press.
Allan, Keith 1977. Classifiers. *Language* 53, 277–311.
Barner, David & Jesse Snedeker 2005. Quantity judgments and individuation: Evidence that mass nouns count. *Cognition* 97, 41–46.
Bale, Alan & Hrayr Khanjian 2008. Classifiers and number marking. In: T. Friedman & S. Ito (eds.). *Proceedings of Semantics and Linguistic Theory (SALT) XVIII*. Ithaca, NY: Cornell University, 73–89.
Becker, Alton L. 1975. A linguistic image of nature: The Burmese numerative classifier system. *Linguistics* 165, 109–121.
Borer, Hagit 2005. *Structuring Sense*, part I. Oxford: Oxford University Press.
Bunt, Harry 1985. *Mass Terms and Model Theoretic Semantics*. Cambridge: Cambridge University Press.
Cheng, Lisa & Rint Sybesma 1998. *yi-wan tang, yi-ge Tang*: Classifiers and massifiers. *The Tsing Hua Journal of Chinese Studies* 28, 385–412.
Cheng, Lisa & Rint Sybesma 1999. Bare and not so bare nouns and the structure of NP. *Linguistic Inquiry* 30, 509–542.
Cheng, Lisa, Jenny Doetjes & Rint Sybesma 2008. How universal is the universal grinder? In: M. van Koppen & B. Botma (eds.). *Linguistics in the Netherlands 2008*. Amsterdam: Benjamins, 50–62.
Chierchia, Gennaro 1998a. Plurality of mass nouns and the notion of "Semantic Parameter". In: S. Rothstein (ed.). *Events and Grammar*. Dordrecht: Kluwer, 53–103.
Chierchia, Gennaro 1998b. Reference to kinds across languages. *Natural Language Semantics* 6, 339–405.
Chierchia, Gennaro 2010. Mass nouns, vagueness and semantic variation. *Synthese* 174, 99–149.
Corbett, Greville 2000. *Number*. Cambridge: Cambridge University Press.
Denny, J. Peter 1986. The semantic role of noun classifiers. In: C. Craig (ed.). *Noun Classes and Categorization*. Amsterdam: Benjamins, 279–308.

Doetjes, Jenny 1997. *Quantifiers and Selection. On the Distribution of Quantifying Expressions in French, Dutch and English*. The Hague: HAG.
Doetjes, Jenny 2004. Adverbs and quantification: Degrees versus frequency. *Lingua* 117, 685–720.
Downing, Pamela 1996. *Numeral Classifier Systems: The Case of Japanese*. Amsterdam: Benjamins.
Dryer, Matthew 2005. Coding of nominal plurality. In: M. Haspelmath et al. (eds.). *The World Atlas of Language Structures*. Oxford: Oxford University Press, 138–141.
Gathercole, Virginia 1985. More and more and more about more. *Journal of Experimental Child Psychology* 40, 72–104.
Gil, David 2005. Numeral classifiers. In: Haspelmath et al. (eds.). *The World Atlas of Language Structures*. Oxford: Oxford University Press, 226–229.
Gillon, Brendan 1992. English count nouns and mass nouns. *Linguistics & Philosophy* 15, 597–639.
Greenberg, Joseph 1972/1977. Numeral classifiers and substantival number: Problems in the genesis of a linguistic type. *Stanford Papers on Language Universals* 9, 1–39. Reprinted in: A. Makkai et al. (eds.). *Linguistics at the Crossroads*. Lake Bluff, IL: Jupiter Press, 1977, 276–300.
Grinevald, Colette 2004. Classifiers. In: C. Lehmann, G. Booij & J. Mugdan (eds.). *Morphology: A Handbook on Inflection and Word Formation*. Vol. 2. (HSK 17.2). Berlin: Walter de Gruyter, 1016–1031.
Gruzdeva, Ekaterina 1998. *Nivkh*. München: Lincom Europa.
Harrison, Sheldon 1976. *Mokilese Reference Grammar*. Honolulu, HI: University Press of Hawaii.
Haspelmath, Martin, Matthew S. Dryer, David Gil & Bernard Comrie (eds.) 2005. *World Atlas of Language Structures*. Oxford: Oxford University Press.
Ikoro, Suanu 1994. Numeral classifiers in Kana. *Journal of African Languages and Linguistics* 15, 7–28.
Iljic, Robert 1994. Quantification in Mandarin Chinese: Two markers of plurality. *Linguistics* 32, 91–116.
Ionin, Tania & Ora Matushansky 2006. The composition of complex cardinals. *Journal of Semantics* 23, 315–360.
Jacob, Judith 1965. Notes on the numerals and numerical coefficients in Old, Middle and Modern Khmer. *Lingua* 15, 143–162.
Koptjevskaja-Tamm, Maria 2001. "A piece of the cake" and "a cup of tea": Partitive and pseudo-partitive nominal constructions in the Circum-Baltic languages. In: Ö. Dahl & M. Koptjevskaja-Tamm (eds.). *The Circum-Baltic Languages. Typology and Contact*. Vol. 2. Amsterdam: Benjamins, 523–568.
Krifka, Manfred 1986. *Nominalreferenz und Zeitkonstitution. Zur Semantik von Massentermen, Pluraltermen und Aspektklassen*. Doctoral dissertation. Ludwig-Maximilians-Universität München.
Krifka, M. 1991. Massennomina. In: A. von Stechow & D. Wunderlich (eds). *Semantik—Semantics. Ein internationales Handbuch der zeitgenössischen Forschung—An International Handbook of Contemporary Research* (HSK 6). Berlin: de Gruyter, 399–417.
Krifka, Manfred 1995. Common nouns: A contrastive analysis of Chinese and English. In: G. Carlson & F. Pelletier (eds.). *The Generic Book*. Chicago, IL: The University of Chicago Press, 398–412.
Lehrer, Adrienne 1986. English classifier constructions. *Lingua* 68, 109–148.
Li, Peggy, Yarrow Dunham & Susan Carey 2009. Of substance: The nature of language effects on entity construal. *Cognitive Psychology* 58, 487–524.

Li, Charles N. & Sandra A. Thompson 1981. *Mandarin Chinese: A Functional Reference Grammar*. Berkeley, CA: University of California Press.
Link, Godehard 1983. The logical analysis of plurals and mass terms: A lattice-theoretical approach. In: R. Bäuerle, Ch. Schwarze & A. von Stechow (eds.). *Meaning, Use, and Interpretation of Language*. Berlin: de Gruyter, 302–323.
Lønning, Jan Tore 1987. Mass terms and quantification. *Linguistics & Philosophy* 10, 1–52.
Lucy, John A. 1992. *Grammatical Categories and Cognition*. Cambridge: Cambridge University Press..
Minassian, Martiros 1980. *Grammaire d'arménien oriental*. Delmar, NY: Caravan Books.
Munn, Allan & Cristina Schmitt 2005. Indefinites and number. *Lingua* 115, 821–855.
Newman, Paul 2000. *The Hausa Language: An Encyclopedic Reference Grammar*. New Haven, CT: Yale University Press.
Nicolas, David 2002. *La distinction entre noms massifs et noms comptables. Aspects linguistiques et conceptuels*. Louvain/Paris: Editions Peeters.
Nicolas, David 2004. Is there anything characteristic about the meaning of a count noun? *Revue de la Lexicologie*, 18–19.
Pelletier, Francis 1975/1979. Non-singular reference: Some preliminaries. *Philosophia* 5, 451–465. Reprinted in: F. Pelletier (ed.). *Mass Terms: Some Philosophical Problems*. Dordrecht: Reidel, 1979, 1–14.
Pelletier, Francis & Lenhart Schubert 1989. Mass expressions. In: D. Gabbay & F. Guenthner (eds.). *Handbook of Philosophical Logic. Volume IV: Topics in the Philosophy of Language*. Dordrecht: Reidel, 327–408.
Quine, Willard van Orman 1960. *Word and Object*. Cambridge, MA: The MIT Press.
Rothstein, Susan 2009. Individuating and measure readings of classifier constructions: Evidence from Modern Hebrew. *Brill's Annual of Afroasiatic Languages and Linguistics* 1, 106–145.
Rothstein, Susan 2010. The semantics of count nouns. In: M. Aloni et al. (eds.). *Logic, Language and Meaning*. Heidelberg: Springer, 395–404.
Rullmann, Hotze & Aili You 2006. General number and the semantics and pragmatics of indefinite bare nouns in Mandarin Chinese. In: K. von Heusinger & K. Turner (eds.). *Where Semantics Meets Pragmatics*. Amsterdam: Elsevier, 175–196.
Sanches, Mary & Linda Slobin 1973. Numeral classifiers and plural marking: An implicational universal. *Working Papers in Language Universals* 11, 1–22.
Schachter, Paul & Fe T. Otanes 1972. *Tagalog Reference Grammar*. Berkeley, CA: University of California Press.
Sharvy, Richard 1978. Maybe English has no count nouns: Notes on Chinese semantics. *Studies in Language* 2, 345–365.
Watters, John R. 1981. *A Phonology and Morphology of Ejagham, with Notes on Dialect Variation*. Ph.D. dissertation. University of California, Los Angeles, CA.
Wilhelm, Andrea. 2008. Bare nouns and number in Děne Sųłiné. *Natural Language Semantics* 16, 39–68.
Zhang, Hong 2007. Numeral classifiers in Mandarin Chinese. *Journal of East Asian Linguistics* 16, 43–59.
Zimmermann, Malte 2008. Quantification in Hausa. In: L. Matthewson (ed.). *Quantification: Universals and Variation*. Bingley: Emerald, 415–475.

Carlota S. Smith
3 Tense and aspect: Time across languages

1 Introduction —— 57
2 Aspectual systems —— 58
3 Tense —— 68
4 Tenseless languages —— 79
5 Tense and aspect in discourse —— 84
6 Conclusion —— 87
7 References —— 89

Abstract: This chapter discusses the cross-linguistic realization of temporal information. I introduce the notion of tense as the grammatical marking of location in time, and the notion of aspect through which the temporal structure of an eventuality (a state or event) is conveyed, this latter operating both through lexical meaning and through grammatical marking of the perspective or viewpoint from which an eventuality is seen. There is a complex interplay between tense and aspect across languages, and this is discussed with regard to the use of aspectual marking in tenseless languages.

1 Introduction

Information about time is conveyed in language primarily by tense and/or aspect, depending on the resources of a given language. Tense locates events and states in time; aspect classifies and presents them according to key temporal properties. A language has a tense or aspectual system if overt morphemes, possibly alternating with zero, convey the relevant information. Semantically, temporal information is essential: location in time is one of the coordinates of truth-conditional assessment. If a language lacks tense, aspectual information allows the inference of temporal location. Tense and aspect are complementary domains. Tense takes situations externally, aspect deals with their internal temporal properties (Comrie 1976). The terms 'situation' or 'eventuality' (Bach 1986) include both events and states. Adverbs, present in all languages, also convey relevant information. Adverbs are discussed here only in connection with other topics.

Carlota S. Smith (†), Austin, TX, USA

https://doi.org/10.1515/9783110589825-003

2 Aspectual systems

Aspect concerns the internal temporal structure of events and states. Every clause of a language introduces a situation into the universe of discourse; and makes visible all or part of that situation for semantic interpretation and inference. There are two kinds of aspectual information: the properties of the situation itself (event structure) and the aspectual viewpoint (perfective, imperfective, neutral) that makes it semantically visible. The two interact in sentences. In some approaches they are distinct, in others they are not. I will emphasize here the approach in which they are independent, the 'two component theory' (Smith 1991/1997). Aspectual information specifies the event argument associated with every predicate.

The element of choice is important in the aspectual domain. Speakers can talk about a situation in the world in more than one way: for instance, depending on the particulars and shared knowledge, an event may be presented as open, ongoing, or bounded. Moreover, a situation can be presented as a state or event, as part of a pattern or discrete; etc. Thus the categories conveyed by aspectual information are 'speaker-based'. The point will become clearer in the discussion that follows; it is one of the unique features of aspect.

2.1 Event structure: Situation type

Situation type indirectly classifies a sentence as expressing a situation or eventuality of a certain category. The categories are at once semantic and syntactic. As semantic concepts, they are idealizations of types of situations, differentiated by a cluster of temporal features. As realized linguistically, each category has unique distributional and interpretive properties; they are covert categories in the sense of Whorf (1956). There are five situation types: State, Accomplishment, Achievement, Activity, and Semelfactive. The two-valued temporal features Static-Dynamic, Telic-Atelic, and Punctual-Durative distinguish the situation type categories. (1) gives English examples of the situation types.

(1) Situation types
   States: static, unbounded
   a. Lee knows the answer. Sam is happy. We own the farm.
   b. Lions eat meat. John feeds the cat every day.
   Events: dynamic
   c. Emily drew a picture. (Accomplishment)
   d. They reached the top. (Achievement)

e. Jan slept. Lee pushed a cart. (Activity)
f. The bird flapped a wing. (Semelfactive)

The state category includes generic and generalizing/habitual sentences (1b). They express a pattern rather than a particular situation (Krifka et al. 1995). They often have the basic verb constellation of an event or a state, shifted by coercion; see below for discussion (cf. also article 10 [Semantics: Lexical Structures and Adjectives] (de Swart) *Mismatches and coercion*).

The five situation types that I have mentioned are the basic stock of situation types in language generally, though there is some variation. Situation type is conveyed by the verb and its arguments—that is, the basic verb constellation—and by adverbs and other information in a sentence. The verb contributes important information, but the composite must be considered (Verkuyl 1972). For instance, *He built a house* expresses an Accomplishment, because the event is discrete, limited. But *He built houses* expresses an Activity, because *houses* is unlimited. Again, *discover* is an Achievement verb at the basic level; but *Tourists have been discovering that quaint little village for years* expresses a generalizing state. The semantic properties of the situation type categories hold across languages.

Situations with the feature [dynamic] occur at successive stages, each of which takes time. Every stage of a dynamic situation involves a change. Dynamic situations without duration involve a single stage. With duration, they have an initial endpoint and a final endpoint. Situations with the feature [static] consist of an undifferentiated interval that does not go on in time.

The features [telic-atelic] pertain to the final endpoint of a situation. Telic situations have an intrinsic terminal point, or natural final endpoint. The final endpoint involves a change of state, a new state over and above the occurrence of the situation itself. When this new state is reached the situation is completed and cannot continue. Telic situations have a heterogeneous part structure: there is no entailment from part to whole (Vendler 1957; Kenny 1963; Krifka 1998). Atelic situations have an arbitrary final endpoint: they may terminate at any time. Atelic situations have a homogeneous part structure but, unlike states, only "down to a certain limit in size" (Dowty 1986: 42; also see Taylor 1977); there is an entailment from part to whole. Durative events occur over an interval; punctual events occur at an instant, in principle. Certain punctual events may have preliminary stages, as in *She was reaching the top*. Here the progressive focuses an interval preliminary to the actual event.

The distributional properties that distinguish each category depend partly on semantics and partly on the particulars of a given language. They must be determined for each language. Dynamic situations in English are compatible with the progressive viewpoint, and with pseudo-cleft *do*. They appear with forms of agency and volition; with verbs relating a situation to the passing of time (*spend*, *take*); with adverbials of motion (*slowly, quickly*); etc. There are also interpretive properties. In sentences about the present with the simple verb form, dynamic constellations have a habitual interpretation, whereas state constellations do not. Accomplishment, Achievement, Activity and Semelfactive verb constellations are all interpreted in terms of dynamic situations.

The feature of telicity has indirect linguistic correlates. Distributionally, telic verb constellations are compatible with expressions of completion, e.g. verbs like *finish* and *take*, as well as *in* adverbials. In contrast, atelic verb constellations are compatible with expressions of termination, e.g. verbs like *stop*, and of simple duration, e.g. *for* adverbials. These facts lead to a useful contrast between types of adverbials and categories of verb constellations. In (2) the completive adverb *in an hour* is good with an Accomplishment verb constellation, and odd with an Activity. The simple durative adverb *for an hour* is good with an Activity, and odd with an Accomplishment verb constellation.

(2) a. Lee repaired the machine in an hour. (Accomplishment)
  b. #Lee walked in the park in an hour.
  c. Lee walked in the park for an hour. (Activity)
  d. #Lee repaired the machine for an hour.

The odd sentences (here marked by the symbol #) trigger a special interpretation of coercion, in which the verb constellations are reinterpreted to be compatible with the adverbs. Thus (2b) is taken as an Accomplishment, (2d) as an Activity. This distinction between completive adverbials and verbs can be used as a test for situation type, if the language allows. Not all languages have forms that clearly distinguish completion and simple duration.

Durative telic sentences are ambiguous with *almost*, whereas atelic sentences are not. Compare (3a) and (3b):

(3) a. Pat almost sang in the rain.
  b. Pat almost opened the door.

(3a) is unambiguous; but (3b) can mean either that Pat almost began to open the door, or almost finished opening it. If a language allows *almost* to appear in a position where it can have either interpretation, *almost* can serve as a semantic test for telicity. The semantic difference between telic and atelic sentences comes out in different relations between progressive (or imperfective) and perfective sentences. With telic sentences there is no entailment from progressive to perfective sentences. Atelic situations are homogeneous, however, so that there is such an entailment. If *Mary was sleeping* it follows that *Mary slept*.

State verb constellations do not appear with forms characteristic of dynamic syntax, and they have contrasting interpretive properties. States are compatible with forms of simple duration. These and other features/tests for situation type are discussed in Vendler (1957), Dowty (1979), and Smith (1991/1997).

One of the key features of aspectual information is boundedness. Telic events (Achievements, Accomplishments), and instantaneous events (Semelfactives, Achievements), are intrinsically bounded; states and atelic, durative events (Activities) are unbounded. Aspectual viewpoint gives boundedness information for a given sentence; see below. Boundedness is important for temporal inference and narrative.

The situation type category labels (State, Accomplishment, etc.) are each shorthand for a cluster of defining temporal features. I will assume that the defining features are stated in a 'temporal schema' associated with each situation type. Compositional construction rules interpret the situation type of a verb constellation as an entity with the defining temporal schema, for instance in Discourse Representation Structure (Kamp & Reyle 1993).

2.2 Events

2.2.1 Incremental themes and telicity

Telicity involves a change to an affected or effected object, the theme argument. Accomplishments are durative and telic. In an Accomplishment, there is often a close relation between the gradual course of the event and its effect on a theme. As the event progresses, the theme object is gradually affected so that the event 'measures out' the change of state (Tenny 1987). This applies nicely to events such as eating a sandwich, drawing a circle: one begins, taking a bite of the sandwich, drawing a curve. As the eating and drawing progress, there is less and less of the sandwich, more and more of the circle. Finally the sandwich is no more, you have eaten the sandwich; and the circle is complete, you have drawn a circle.

In cases like this, there is a homomorphism between the event's progress and the effect on the theme argument, known as the 'incremental theme' (Krifka 1998). Incremental themes are delimited, with the key property of 'quantization'. Quantized predicates have no proper parts that are instances of the predicate: If X is quantized, then $\forall x,y[(X(x) \& X(y)) \rightarrow \neg(y < x)]$. The complementary property is 'cumulative'. For a cumulative predicate that does not denote a singleton set, given any two elements in X, their sum is also in X.

The theme argument of a clause appears canonically in object position. However, themes can also appear as subjects, e.g. *The ship/John slowly entered the freezing water* (Dowty 1991). The properties 'quantized' and 'cumulative' also apply to nominals; for example, *an apple* and *a glass of water* are quantized, whereas *apples* and *water* are cumulative. Not all Accomplishments fit this picture. Most serious among counter-examples are telic predicates for which "it makes no sense to see the extent of the event as determined by the extent of the theme" (Rothstein 2004: 98). Examples include *repair the computer, prove the theorem, wash the clothes*, etc. In these and other cases, the extent of the theme doesn't determine the final endpoint of the event. Certain resultatives are also counter-examples to the incremental theme account. In *John sang the baby asleep*, for instance, falling asleep does not affect the extent of the baby incrementally (not feet first, then legs, etc.). Again, some predicates with quantized objects need not be telic: *wipe the table* may also be atelic. One might also object that the theory makes too much difference between Accomplishments and Achievements since it doesn't apply to punctual telic events. The homomorphic theory of telicity holds for many but not all cases. Rothstein (2004) gives an extensive critique of the theory and proposes a general revision.

2.2.2 Events and states

The most far-reaching distinction among situation types is that between statives and non-statives, or states and events (cf. also article 8 [Semantics: Theories] (Maienborn) *Event semantics*). One way of understanding the difference is through mereology, or part structure. The mereological approach holds that mereological properties, or the relations between part and whole, are sufficient to distinguish states from events. Telic events are heterogenous: the whole is distinct from its parts. In contrast, statives are cumulative and homogenous, with uniform part structures. In this view only telic situations are events. Activities, which are homogenous, do not belong to the class of events. The class of Statives includes all unbounded situations, called imperfectives. Statives include State sentences, Activity sentences, and sentences with a progressive or other imperfective viewpoint (Herweg 1991). All are homogenous, and have the sub-interval property. The class is sometimes referred to as 'imperfective'. These global categories are superordinate to the categories of situation type and viewpoint. They are claimed to account for sentence interpretation and the contribution of sentences to discourse.

Another approach takes *energeia*, or dynamism, as an essential property of events. Events take place in time. They occur in successive stages which are located at different moments. In contrast, states consist of an undifferentiated period, and continue unless something happens to change them. Taylor comments that although states are in time, they do not take time (1977: 206). *Energeia* accords event status to all dynamic situations. In a sentence with the perfective viewpoint an Activity has a final endpoint, albeit an arbitrary one. Activities move narrative time in discourse, thus providing evidence that they should be considered events (Smith 1999). Thus the global category of Events consists of Accomplishments, Achievements, Activities, and Semelfactives. Events are bounded in different ways. Telic events have intrinsic final endpoints; Semelfactives are single-stage events, with an intrinsic endpoint; Activities have arbitrary final endpoints.

2.2.3 Coercion

Aspectual choice enables people to talk about situations in the world in more than one way. States may be presented as events, for instance in an inchoative like *Suddenly she understood the truth*, or with the progressive *I'm loving this walk*. Single-stage events may be presented as parts of multiple-stage events, as in *He knocked for five minutes*. Events may be presented as part of a pattern, a generalizing state, as in the habituals *We play a game of tennis every week*. Thus verb constellations do not always have their basic aspectual meaning.

'Coercion', or situation type shift, explains such cases (cf. also article 10 [Semantics: Lexical Structures and Adjectives] (de Swart) *Mismatches and coercion*). The basic-level situation type is coerced or shifted to another category. What triggers the shift is additional information. Moens & Steedman (1987) identified coercion patterns in an aspectual network; later work has elaborated on their insights. Coercion is due to a clash of temporal features between the simple verb constellation and another form; the clash triggers the derived-level reading. In (4) the verb constellation is Semelfactive at the basic level; the adverbial is durative.

(4) Mary coughed for an hour.   (Multiple-event Activity)

In the shift, the adverbial feature [-punctual] required for a situation which lasts an hour overrides the [+punctual] value of the basic verb constellation, which would otherwise pick out a single cough, which the aspectual system treats as instantaneous. The coerced sentence has the shifted situation type of Activity, a durative event.

The progressive viewpoint is associated with duration. It triggers a shift to a multiple-event Activity with a Semelfactive verb constellation [-durative], as in (5):

(5) a. Mary was coughing.   (Multiple-event Activity)
    b. Mary was knocking at the door.   (Multiple-event Activity)

These cases resolve a clash between feature values in a consistent, predictable way. Generalizing, the 'principle of external override' (Smith 1991/1997) holds for many instances of coercion. The principle holds for clashes between the temporal feature values of a verb constellation and the features of forms external to it. When there is such a clash, the temporal feature of the external form determines the shifted situation type. The principle can be stated in compositional rules.

Coercion explains the oddity—and the marked interpretations—of a sentence like *Lee ran in an hour*. The atelic verb constellation appears with the telic adverbial *in an hour*, and the whole is taken as telic—Lee has a certain amount of running to do. In *Lee read a book for an hour*, a telic verb constellation appears with an atelic adverbial, and the whole is atelic—Lee did some book-reading. Another type of example is the perfect, an aspectual operator that maps a situation onto a state. Coercion is stated as a group of "hidden operators" including grammaticalized aspectual operators like the Perfect or the Progressive (de Swart 1998). The coercion operators C are eventuality description modifiers, which map a set of eventualities onto another set of eventualities. The input and output types are represented as indices on the operator, e.g. C_{sd}, C_{he}, C_{eh}. The Progressive requires a mapping C_{sd}, from stative onto dynamic eventualities. Consider the highly marked sentence *Susan is liking this play*. The stative verb constellation is the input to the coercion operator, the progressive: [PRES [PROG [C_{sd} [Susan like this play]]]]. A dynamic interpretation is obtained by coercion; it is the right kind of input for the Progressive operator. These approaches provide that the interpretation of coercion is fully compositional.

2.3 Aspectual viewpoints

Aspectual viewpoints are salient in many languages of the world. They focus a situation like the lens of a camera. As the camera lens makes a scene available, so viewpoint makes semantically visible all or part of the situation expressed in a sentence. The visible information is available for pragmatic inference. (The terms 'grammatical aspect' or, in Wilhelm 2003, 'outer aspect' are also used in the literature.) Viewpoints are usually expressed by overt morphemes, for instance, the progressive auxiliary *be + ing* in English (*Joan is swimming*) or by inflections, such as the *imparfait* in French (*Joan nageait*). The key feature of an aspectual viewpoint is whether it makes visible an unbounded, ongoing situation or a closed, bounded one. Imperfective viewpoints are of the former category; perfective viewpoints of the latter. The neutral viewpoint allows either bounded or unbounded interpretation; this is the 'zero-marked' case, when no overt viewpoint morpheme appears.

Aspectual systems differ most in the viewpoint component. Languages may have one perfective and one imperfective viewpoint, like English; in contrast, Mandarin has two imperfective viewpoints and three perfectives. Viewpoints may be syntactically obligatory or optional. Linguistic expression of tense and aspectual viewpoint is distinct in some languages, intertwined in others. The two vary independently in English. In French and other Romance languages past tenses code different aspectual viewpoints: the *imparfait* is a past imperfective tense, the *passé composé* and *passé simple* are past perfectives. Finnish, Icelandic and German have only the neutral viewpoint; case-marking may convey boundedness information. In Chinese, Thai and some other languages aspectual viewpoint morphemes are optional and many clauses are zero-marked, with the neutral viewpoint.

2.3.1 Perfective viewpoints

Perfective viewpoints generally present situations as discrete, bounded. They vary across languages for Accomplishment sentences. In English, French, and Russian a perfective clause of a durative telic event expresses a completed event. The perfective is conveyed in English by the simple verb form (6a); in French and other Romance languages, by certain tenses (6b); and in Russian by prefix (6c). All three sentences have the same meaning.

(6) a. He wrote a letter.
    b. Il a ecrit une lettre. (French, *passé composé*)
    c. On napisal pis'mo. (Russian, *na-*, a perfective prefix)

The interpretation of completion can be demonstrated with conjunction. It is semantically contradictory to conjoin a perfective sentence with an assertion that the event continues:

(7) a. #Mary opened the door, but she didn't get it open.
    b. #Donald fixed the clock and he is still fixing it.

In Mandarin Chinese, however, a perfective clause of a telic event only implicates completion. For instance, the first clause of (8) has the perfective morpheme *-le*; the second clause cancels the implicature of completion, and is not contradictory.

(8) Wǒ   zuótiān   xiě-le   gěi Zhāngsān de-xìn,   kěshì   méi xiě wán
     I   yesterday write-LE   to Zhangsan DE-letter, but   not write-finish
     'I wrote a letter to Zhangsan yesterday but I didn't finish it.'

Completion is expressed directly in Mandarin by certain Resultative Verb Complements (RVC), which appear as verb suffixes with or without -*le*. RVCs contribute to situation type as well as viewpoint; similar morphemes are found in Russian and other languages.

Languages differ as to whether and how the perfective viewpoint applies to statives. Statives do not allow the perfective in Russian, Mandarin, and some other languages; although a stative verb constellation may be coerced to an inchoative. In French and other Romance languages, perfective viewpoints apply to statives, with a bounded meaning. The English perfective applies to states, focusing their complete temporal schema. Thus the English perfective, expressed by the simple verb form, presents statives as unbounded, shown by the felicity of *Mary knew the answer and she still knows it*. Formally, the perfective viewpoint can be stated in terms of endpoints: For an event e with the perfective morpheme P: P(e) holds of interval I, where t, t' $\subseteq$ I and there is no t" such that t"< t or > t'. This statement provides for termination.

2.3.2 Imperfective viewpoints

Imperfective viewpoints make part of a situation semantically visible, without information as to endpoints. In principle, imperfectives may focus an internal interval, a preliminary interval, or a resulting interval, depending on the situation. Imperfective viewpoints are conveyed by particular verb forms, e.g. the progressive auxiliary *be + ing* in English; by particular tenses, e.g. the *imparfait* in French; or by a preposition, prefix or suffix. Example (9) illustrates this; the three sentences all have the same meaning.

(9) a. They are playing ball.
 b. Tāmen zài dǎ qiú. (Mandarin: *zài*, the progressive form)
 c. Ils jouaient aux balles. (French: *imparfait* tense)

The focused interval has the sub-interval property. This is why imperfectives are stative in global super-categories of aspectual meaning. General imperfective viewpoints are available for all situations; the French and Russian viewpoints are of this type. The progressive is a kind of imperfective, available for non-statives only: *Mary is singing*, but **John is knowing the answer*. There are also stative imperfectives, such as the Mandarin -*zhe*.

Within situation types, languages differ. For instance, Achievements do not allow preliminary intervals to be focused with the progressive in Mandarin, but they may be in English. Again, the imperfective may focus either an internal interval or a resultant interval, giving rise to ambiguous sentences like (10) in Japanese:

(10) Yoshi-wa   atarasii   shatu-o   ki-te-ita
     Yoshio-NOM   new   shirt-ACC   put on/wear-IMPF-PAST
     a. 'Yoshio was putting on his new shirt.'
     b. 'Yoshio was wearing his new shirt.'

Similar ambiguities arise in other languages. The imperfective viewpoint may be used to convey that a situation is ongoing, and that an event is not completed. The latter is an implicature only. There are many language-particular conventions associated with the imperfective. Russian has a 'Statement of Fact' convention by which speakers use the imperfective viewpoint to talk about well-known, completed events such as Tolstoy's writing *War and Peace*; or to talk about recent events.

There is an intensional component to an imperfective of internal or preliminary interval. The imperfective makes visible stages of a process, which, if continued to its final endpoint, results in an event. The final outcome is unknown, so that one cannot infer from a progressive sentence, *They were building a house*, that the event was completed. Yet one interprets this sentence as expressing a telic event in some sense. This gap between knowledge of the type of situation and its outcome is known as the Imperfective Paradox (Dowty 1979). Dowty models the meaning of a progressive with a branching time model of the future; in at least one branch of the model the event in progress continues to its final endpoint, in others it does not. The approach is further developed in Landman (1992), with the notion of a continuation branch in which the event has a reasonable chance of continuing as expected.

Formal expression of the imperfective viewpoint can be stated for an interval that does not include endpoints; Init(e) and Fin(e) denote the endpoints of the event. For an Event e with an imperfective morpheme I: I(e) holds of interval I, where Init(e) holds at t and Fin(e) holds at t', and t, t' $\notin$ I.

2.3.3 The Neutral viewpoint

The Neutral viewpoint allows bounded and unbounded interpretations, depending on contextual information. It is more flexible than either perfective or imperfective viewpoints. The Neutral viewpoint arises in sentences with no viewpoint morpheme, zero-marked clauses. Therefore, it is not relevant to English or other languages in which a choice between overt aspectual viewpoints is obligatory.

The neutral viewpoint appears in such varied languages as German, Mandarin Chinese, and Navajo.

In the two-component approach to aspect, all sentences have an aspectual viewpoint. Viewpoints make all or part of a situation visible for semantic interpretation (Smith 1991/1997). The neutral viewpoint is weak, requiring only that part of a situation be visible. This accounts for the indeterminacy of zero-marked clauses: they can be taken as bounded or unbounded, depending on the context in which they appear. The two possibilities are mutually exclusive for other viewpoints. The formal statement: N(e) holds for times t of interval I, where $t \subseteq e$. There is a default pattern of pragmatic inference for the zero-marked clauses (see section 3 below).

3 Tense

Tense is a grammatical form with temporal meaning: it conveys "grammaticalized location in time" (Comrie 1985: 10). Tense forms are usually morphologically bound inflections on the verb. The category has a limited set of members, forming a closed system. Choice from within the category is obligatory, so that all main clauses of a tensed language carry temporal information. In another approach, Dahl proposes a general category of tense, aspect, and mood (1985, 2000). The building blocks for tense-aspect-mood are the individual tenses, aspects, and moods. They represent grams, on the cross-linguistic level a restricted set of gram types. We will not pursue this approach here. (Cf. also article 11 [Semantics: Noun Phrases and Verb Phrases] (Portner) *Verbal mood*.)

The dimension of time is single and unbounded, analogous to space but simpler. Like space, time requires an orientation point for location. The speaker is the canonical center of linguistic communication, so that the basic temporal orientation point in language is the time of speaking, Speech Time (*now*). 'Absolute tenses' are deictic: they are anchored to Speech Time (SpT). The present is simultaneous with SpT, the past precedes SpT, the future follows SpT. There are also 'relative tenses' such as the English past and future perfect, that have a flexible orientation point.

The grammatical domain of tense is the clause. Each tense assigns a temporal location to the situation talked about in its clause. Temporal adverbials, which are optional syntactically, affect the information conveyed by tense. In simple tenses they narrow down the time indicated by tense.

The temporal expressions of a language form a closed system, a limited domain. However neither the distribution nor the interpretation of tense is systematic in a combinatorial sense. Tenses do not combine nor embed freely, as would be expected in systems such as those of tense logic (Prior 1967). Tenses do not iterate (there is no *Kim had had left); complex tenses do not behave as nested operators, with one tense morpheme within the scope of another tense morpheme, so e.g. *Kim had left* is normally analyzed semantically as involving a single pluperfect temporal operator, rather than as a combination of separate past and participle operators. Nor is the relation of a temporal adverb to tense that of an operator: in *Mary left yesterday*, for instance, we don't interpret *yesterday* as prior to the time indicated by the past tense. Rather, the adverb further specifies that time.

3.1 Tense systems

Tense systems differ in the distinctions they mark. The basic possibilities for absolute tenses are past, present, and future. *The World Atlas of Linguistic Structures* (Haspelmath et al. 2005) presents a study of tense distinctions across languages and their geographical distribution. The *Atlas* is based on a sample of languages distributed as evenly as possible throughout the world. The maps show 75 languages with both inflectional past and future; 59 languages with inflectional past, no future; and 35 languages with inflectional future, no past. In a detailed discussion of tense in the *Atlas*, Dahl & Velupillai (2005: 268–270) consider 222 languages, drawing also on the typological surveys in Dahl (1985) and Bybee, Perkins & Pagliuca (1994). More languages in the sample have both past and future, or neither, than languages that have only one of the two categories. Tense distinctions may contrast a positive value with a negative one—e.g., past vs. no information about time; or they may contrast two positive values—e.g., past vs. nonpast.

The most common distinction is between past and nonpast. Of 222 languages, 138 have a past-nonpast distinction, 88 have no such distinction. Some languages mark degrees of remoteness from Speech Time. About one-fifth of languages with past tense mark one or more remoteness distinctions in the past. The most common distinguishes 'today' from 'before today'. There are some areal tendencies. The largest homogenous past-marking area extends from Iceland to the Horn of Africa to Bangladesh; other areas are Australia, northern South America, and central New Guinea.

Future distinctions, marked inflectionally, are made in about half of the language sample: 110 of 222 languages. There are some areal tendencies but no homogenous areas, unlike the past tense. Languages with inflectional futures tend to appear in North America, Australia, and New Guinea; on the South Asian continent; and in some European languages. South America and Africa are varied. In this study, irrealis categories that are not inflectional were not considered to be future tenses. Futures tend to be less bound morphologically then present or past tenses (Ultan 1978). In English, the future *will* patterns syntactically and semantically with modals rather than with tense. The special properties of *will*, often called *woll* in its abstract form (Ogihara 1996), are not discussed here. In other languages, including French, there is an inflectional future that patterns with the tenses (Smith 2006). The grammatical status of the future is evidently a language-particular matter.

Future tenses inevitably have a component of modality, or uncertainty. As Lyons (1977: 677) puts it: "Futurity is never a purely temporal concept; it necessarily includes an element of prediction or some related notion." The future is 'open': we cannot know what will happen but can only predict, with more or less certainty. Thus the categories of irrealis, modal, and future categories overlap. The close connection is often seen in historical development: future tenses tend to develop from modal categories (Ultan 1978). The component of modality makes the future more complex informationally than the past; this will be important in an account of temporal interpretation in tenseless languages, section 4 below.

Relative tenses are anchored not to Speech Time, but to another time in the linguistic or pragmatic context. The perfect, e.g. *Mary had already opened the package by then, Mary will have opened the package by then*, is the most common relative tense. The perfect conveys that a situation occurred anterior to a time specified in the context. Of the 222 languages examined by Dahl & Velupillai (2005), 108 or almost half, have a perfect construction. In the areas of Western Europe, South and Southeast Asia, languages tend to have them. Many languages in Africa, Mesoamerica, and the northwestern corner of South America also have perfects. The meanings of the perfect are discussed further below. The other relative tense is the future-in-past, which conveys that a situation occurs after a given reference time, as in the complement clause of *Gretchen said that she would leave soon*. Relative time reference is common in subordinate clauses.

Not all languages have tense. Of the 222 languages in the *Atlas* study, 53 languages have neither past or future tense. Temporal adverbs are not included in the categories discussed above; so far as I know they are optionally available in all languages. The temporal structure of certain language families is still unclear: for instance, whether Arabic, Korean, and certain Mayan languages have tense is in dispute. For Arabic, Brustad (2000) argues convincingly that the language is aspectual and tenseless.

3.2 Syntax

In tensed languages, tense is an obligatory bound morpheme that expresses temporal information. The tense morpheme is part of the grammatical 'spine' of a sentence. As such, tense has grammatical ramifications: it is involved in agreement, case, anaphora, and the finite/non-finite distinction. All main clauses have an obligatory tense morpheme, so that all main clauses convey temporal information. English, French, German, and Hindi are tensed languages.

The simplest syntactic assumption for a tensed language is that the basic phrase marker includes TensePhrase as a functional category. The tense morpheme has scope over an entire clause. In some accounts, e.g. Discourse Representation Theory, it is this structure that is then the input used to form a semantic representation. In a more syntactic approach, Stowell (1996) proposes that tense is a dyadic temporal ordering predicate. He posits a functional category ZP (for ZeitPhrase), the complement of tense; ZP is modeled on DP. The arguments of the tense head T represent times and situations. See also Giorgi & Pianesi (1997) and Demirdache & Uribe-Extebarria (2000).

Tenseless languages have a syntactic AspectPhrase category but no TensePhrase. These languages introduce some temporal information, but the information must be supplemented by pragmatic inference, as developed below. I do not posit syntactic structure that corresponds to the pragmatics of temporal inference. Thus although all languages convey information that allows temporal location, they do so with different syntactic structures and semantics.

3.3 Semantics

The semantics of tense deals with the times expressed by tense, and their relations; the notion of temporal standpoint, or temporal perspective, associated with tense; the interpretation of so-called 'sequence of tense'; and the problem of how temporal relations between situations are conveyed in tensed languages. Not all semantic theories address all these questions.

In traditional tense logic (Prior 1967), tense is an operator that existentially quantifies over times. Partee (1973) gives strong evidence against the treatment of tense as an operator. She shows that tenses have both deictic and anaphoric uses, somewhat like pronouns. One celebrated example of the latter is *I didn't turn off the stove*, uttered when driving down the road: here the past tense is "used to refer to an understood particular time not introduced by previous linguistic context" (Partee 1984: 244). Tenses should be represented as variables that bind the event argument of a predicate. The notion that tense operators existentially quantify over time is maintained in current theory. There is evidence that tense does not have the entire sentence in its scope, but that relative clauses and nominals are independent (see section 3.5 below).

The 'simple tenses' of past, present, and future require two times to represent their temporal meanings: the anchor of Speech Time (SpT) and the time of the situation expressed in a clause, Situation Time. Perfects and other relative tenses require three times. The past perfect, for instance, conveys that the situation talked about precedes another time that may or may not be specified:

(11) (Yesterday,) John had arrived.

John's arrival precedes another time, here 'yesterday'. Three times are required to account for the meaning of this construction: Speech Time, Situation Time (SitT), and another time, 'yesterday', known as 'Reference Time'. The perfect has an aspectual component: aspectually all perfects are stative. The notion of Reference Time (RT) was introduced by Hans Reichenbach (1947). His classic argument for RT contrasts a simple tense with the corresponding perfect: the two differ conceptually but not truth-conditionally. For instance:

(12) a. Mary arrived.
b. Mary has arrived.

The difference between (12a,b) is that of temporal standpoint or perspective. In (12a) the event is set squarely in the past: RT is the same as ET. (12b) presents the event from the standpoint of the present, so that RT is the same as SpT. Generalizing, all tenses are taken to involve RT. (13) states schematic meanings for three tenses:

(13) Present: $RT = SpT$, $SitT = RT$
Present Perfect: $RT = SpT$, $SitT < RT$
Past: $RT < SpT$, $SitT = RT$

If simple and perfect tenses are analyzed in this way we capture both conceptual and truth-conditional meanings.

A second argument, also due to Reichenbach, concerns the temporal relation between events and statives or progressives in multi-clause sentences. In (14a) the arrival occurs during the interval of the smile; in (14b) it precedes the smile.

(14) a. Mary was smiling when John arrived.
b. Mary smiled when John arrived.

The notion of RT provides a locus for relating the events in a principled manner. The same argument can be made for events expressed in independent sentences (Hinrichs 1986). Partee (1984) notes that Reichenbach's notion of Reference Time provides the antecedent needed for the anaphoric use of tense.

Another argument for RT concerns the phenomena of shifted deixis. Deictic adverbials such as *now, in three days*, etc., normally anchored to the moment of speech, can shift their anchor to a past (or future) time, as in (15):

(15) Mary sat down at the desk. Now she was ready to start work.

In such contexts the shifted *now* suggests Mary's perspective. The notion of RT is the anchoring point for this perspective. The approach of Reichenbach is widely accepted, although difficulties in his system have been pointed out and proposals made to improve it. The system as Reichenbach proposed it allows for too many relations between times; Comrie (1985) and Hornstein (1991) each have proposed changes to deal with this problem.

The boundedness of a situation determines the nature of its location at Situation Time. Bounded situations occur within the Situation Time interval; for instance, in *Mary walked to school* the event of walking occurs within the past interval talked about (see 16). Unbounded situations—ongoing events and states—overlap or surround the Situation Time interval; for instance, in *Mary was walking to school* the event extends beyond the interval talked about in the sentence (again see 16). These relations are part of the representation of tense meaning.

(16) Bounded events (E) are included in the SitT interval: *Leigh built a sandcastle*.
 SitT ⊆ E

 Unbounded events and states (S) overlap the SitT interval: *Leigh was working*.
 E/S O SitT

Tense meaning of the Reichenbach type has been implemented in Discourse Representation Theory (DRT) with full construction rules (Kamp & Reyle 1993, Smith 1991/1997; cf. also article 11 [Semantics: Theories] (Kamp & Reyle) *Discourse Representation Theory*). DRT develops a dynamic semantic representation, known as a Discourse Representation Structure (DRS), that encodes information from the surface structure of the successive clauses of a text. Times are introduced as discourse referents into the DRS by tenses, and their relations stated as conditions.

A neo-Reichenbach semantics has also been developed in the framework of semantically-based syntax. In this approach, tenses are dyadic predicates of spatiotemporal ordering: they establish a topological relation between two time-denoting arguments. The tense head may have an external and internal argument (Enç 1987; Stowell 1996; Giorgi & Pianesi 1997; Demirdache & Uribe-Extebarria 2000). Another theory, due to Klein (1994), also involves three times. Klein posits that tense meaning relates Topic Time and Speech Time, while aspect relates Topic Time and Situation Time. The notions of Topic Time and Reference Time are quite similar: Topic Time is 'the time for which a claim is made' in a given sentence (Klein 1994: 3).

Other dynamic semantic approaches to tense meanings involve two times. De Swart (1998), for instance, gives a DRT account of this kind. The past, present, and future tenses involve two times, Speech Time and Situation Time. The perfect introduces the consequent state of an event into the DRS. As a state, the temporal interval of the situation overlaps the time talked about. Presumably in a past or future perfect, not discussed directly by de Swart, the situation overlaps the past or future time introduced by the tense. A 'relational semantics' view of tense is developed by von Stechow (1995): he proposes a formal account with a distinguished variable that denotes speech time, or a different anchor time. Operators on this variable produce the additional tenses.

3.4 The present perfect

The present perfect has some special peculiarities. Like other perfects it conveys anteriority and stativity: the present perfect focuses a current state that results from a prior event. Reference Time is equal to Speech Time (*now*) and Situation Time is anterior to now; this is the neo-Reichenbach view sketched above. Under appropriate circumstances the present perfect may convey different meanings, notably the perfect of Continuing Result, the Experiential, the Recent Past, Current Relevance, Indefinite Past. We ask whether these interpretations are semantic, involving distinct meanings, or whether they are due to pragmatic factors. McCoard (1978) argues convincingly for the latter case: pragmatic, contextual factors are responsible for the different interpretations. Rather than recognize different perfects, McCoard suggests one general meaning that underlies them all: the notion of an 'extended now' period. The extended now is a period that ends at Speech Time and extends into the past, perhaps delimited by temporal information in the sentence or context. The speaker chooses to present a given situation as falling within the extended now period. The extended now (XN) approach has been widely accepted. However, there are some points about the present perfect that it does not explain.

Within the XN approach, two distinct semantic meanings for the present perfect are now recognized: the universal and the existential (Mittwoch 1988). Sentence (17) is ambiguous:

(17) Sam has been in Boston for 20 minutes.

On the existential reading there is a 20-minute period in the relevant XN interval in which Sam was in Boston; on the universal reading, the XN interval is a 20-minute period extending to the present, with the implication that Sam is in Boston now. Mittwoch explains the two readings in terms of scope. On the existential reading the adverb has wider scope than the perfect [Pres (w,i) [Have[for 20 minutes] (Sam be in Boston)]]; on the universal reading the perfect has wider scope than the adverb [Pres (w,i) [for 20 minutes [Have] (Sam be in Boston)]]. In confirmation of the scope hypothesis, note that when the adverb is preposed, as in *For 20 minutes Sam has been in Boston*, only the universal reading arises.

The properties of the XN interval itself have also been investigated, in an attempt to explain a strong constraint on the temporal adverbials and the present perfect in English. Adverbials that include Speech Time are good but past adverbials are not:

(18) a. Sam has arrived now.
  b. *Sam has been in Boston yesterday.
  c. *I have seen Dana last year.

This constraint does not hold for all languages: Norwegian, Icelandic, German, Dutch, and other languages allow past adverbials with the present perfect. Further, the constraint is limited to the present perfect: adverbs specifying Situation Time are good with past perfects, e.g. *Sam had been working in Boston on Tuesday*. Past adverbials may appear with *since* in the present perfect: *Sam has been in Boston since last year*. (See Mittwoch 1988 for discussion of *since*.)

The differences can be accounted for nicely by providing that the XN interval differs across languages. In English the XN interval includes Speech Time. This explains why past adverbials cannot appear in the present perfect (Klein 1992; Pancheva & von Stechow 2004). The system of German is different. In German (and some other languages), the XN interval does not necessarily include Speech Time.

3.5 Dependent clauses

Tenses in dependent clauses are governed by the verb of the matrix clause and do not always have their expected, consistent values. This phenomenon is known as 'sequence of tense' (SOT). Latin had an intricate set of rules for the sequence of tense in matrix and complement clauses, including the perfect, the subjunctive, the imperfective, and occasionally the infinitive (Binnick 1991).

In English, SOT rules apply most clearly to a sequence of past tenses in main and complement clauses. To convey that the complement situation occurs at the time of the main clause—the simultaneous reading—the past tense appears (19a,b). In such cases it does not have the standard relational value of anteriority. To convey that the complement event time is anterior to the matrix time, the past-of-past reading, either the past or the pluperfect is used (19c). Thus sentences like (19a,b) have an anterior and a simultaneous reading:

(19) a. Jones said that Mary won the race.
b. Jones thought that Mary was sick.
c. Jones said that Mary had won the race.

Special provision must be made for the simultaneous reading. The European languages have SOT rules with variation. In Russian and other Slavic languages, and in Amharic, the simultaneous reading of a stative complement clause is expressed with present tense. In such cases the present tense has its standard relational value of simultaneity, dependent on the main clause. German allows both the English and Russian patterns. In some West African languages, complement tense is 'neutralized'; in some languages, such as Imbabura Quechua, relative tenses appear in complement clauses (Comrie 1985: 61, 104).

The special interpretation of tense in these dependent contexts can be handled by rule or by semantic features (Enç 1987; von Stechow 1995). An interesting case is that of a present tense embedded under a past tense, which has a 'double access' reading:

(20) Mary said that Jones is sick.

The speaker is responsible for the truth of the complement both at the moment of speech, now; and for its truth at the past time of Mary's speaking (Abusch 1997).

Dependent tenses include the subjunctive, found in European languages. The subjunctive is sometimes called a 'mood', contrasting with the indicative (assertion) and possibly the optative (wish). The subjunctive appears with verbs of speaker attitude, especially those that express doubt or uncertainty; but in other cases it has a purely grammatical function. For instance, the French temporal conjunction *avant que* (before) requires the subjunctive. Infinitivals and other non-finite forms also appear in dependent contexts, and in such cases the licensing context provides the infinitival clause's temporal interpretation. For example, the infinitival *to win* is given a futurate interpretation in *Lee wants to win*, whereas *to lose* is given a past interpretation in *Lee was disappointed to lose*. Adverbial clauses in many languages require agreement with the tense of the main clause, sometimes expressed as zero tense.

3.6 Atemporal tense meaning

In certain contexts, tense has atemporal meaning. The past tense is often associated with non-actual, irrealis, and distanced meanings. The conditional is one such context: past tense frequently does not refer to time, but rather has a modal meaning. Consider these examples, based on Iatridou (2000):

(21) a. If Jack took his medicine, he would get better.
     b. If Jack had taken his medicine, he would have gotten better.

The past tense in both examples is atemporal. (21a) conveys that, if at some present or future time Jack takes his medicine, he can be expected to get better. There is an implicature that the medicine will not be taken. (21b) conveys that at some past time, if Jack took the medicine, he would get better; and there is an implicature that the medicine was not taken. In (21b), the pluperfect *had taken* is morphologically (past (past)); it conveys both past and the atemporal meaning. Cross-linguistic studies show that, in conditionals, non-present tenses often have atemporal meanings (Steele 1975). The counter-factual meaning is salient in these examples, but it is only an implicature: it can be cancelled. For instance, one can reply to (21b): *Fortunately, he did (take it) and he is (better)*. The counter-factual meaning is strong in the past examples because past events are often known to the speaker and hearer. But when the facts are not known, conditional predictions about the past are natural and, in context, need not implicate counter-factuality.

Iatridou (2000: 246) proposes an abstract account of the past tense morpheme in which it has a single meaning, yet operates in more than one domain (specifically, times or worlds). This meaning is stated with an 'exclusion feature'. Ranging over times, a past tense morpheme with the exclusion feature means that 'the topic time excludes the utterance time.' Ranging over worlds, it means that the world of the speaker, the actual world, is excluded—as in the conditionals discussed above. Verbs of wishing trigger, in their complements, the atemporal interpretation of the exclusion feature of the past tense morpheme. Other languages have additional contexts in which the exclusion feature comes into play.

3.7 Nominals and relative clauses

The temporal interpretation of noun phrases is independent of the main clause. For instance, consider the interpretation of *fugitives* in (22):

(22) Every fugitive was in jail.

The possible readings include individuals who are fugitives now, or were fugitives before they were in jail. Other examples include nouns that have a specific temporal modifier:

(23) a. The former president came to the party.
b. He met his future wife when they were 3 years old.

In the first example, the president was a 'former president' at the time of the party; in the second, the 'future wife' was a child at the time of the meeting. Such facts can be accounted for if nouns, like verbs, have temporal arguments whose values are supplied by the utterance context (Enç 1987).

In some languages nominals have been described as having a tense system independent of the main verb tense. Lecarme (2004) suggests that nominals in Somali, an African language, have a tense system. The past tense has a set of atemporal uses in contexts which involve a modal meaning. Lecarme suggests that an exclusion feature like that posited by Iatridou for main clause tenses can account for these cases. Many other cases where there is evidence for nominal tense systems, notably among South American languages, are discussed by Nordlinger & Sadler (2004). However, Tonhauser (2006) argues that at least one of these languages, Paraguayan Guaraní, is better described as having nominal aspect rather than a nominal tense system.

Relative clause tense is independent of the main clause tense. The tense of a relative clause is evaluated with respect to a contextually salient reference time.

(24) a. Lee married a man who would become President.
b. Sam talked to the person who will chair the meeting.
c. Sheila will read all about those islanders, who had a weird cargo cult.

The examples show that both restrictive and non-restrictive relative clauses are temporally independent.

3.8 Tense uses: Primary and secondary

The prototypical uses of tenses follow their labels: a present tense sentence talks about present time, past tense about past time, etc. In these uses a given tense is compatible with adverbials of the same type, for instance, present tense with present adverbials, *Cynthia is in town now*. There are other uses, however.

The present tense is quite flexible. In many languages, including English and Romance, the combination of present tense and past adverbial—known as the 'historical present'—can be used to talk about the past, typically in a narrative context. Such forms are often said to make narration vivid, by presenting past events as present, as in (25). The historical present can alternate with the past tense, or it can appear in sustained sequences.

(25) Yesterday something unexpected happened. This man walks up to me and he says . . .

The present tense can also be used to talk about the future, and can even appear with future adverbials, as in the use of the simple present in (26a), or in the construction known as the periphrastic future (26b), frequently found across languages. Yet another use of the present is to express general truths in sentence that are taken to be timeless (26c).

(26) a. The train leaves tomorrow at 2pm.
   b. Tomorrow the train is going to arrive.
   c. The Texas redbud blooms in the early spring.

This flexibility shows that the present tense has a relational value of simultaneity, allowing it to be simultaneous with an explicitly given time as well as SpT.

The past tense can be used to convey politeness, as in (27):

(27) I wanted to ask you a question.

Here the past tense sets up a distance between speaker and hearer, conveying respect for the hearer.

4 Tenseless languages

4.1 Temporal information in language: A classification

Languages can be classified according to how they convey temporal information. A three-way classification allows for the variation that we find: there are fully tensed languages, mixed-temporal languages, and tenseless languages. Tensed languages have been discussed above. Mixed-temporal languages have some of the characteristics of tensed languages. They have inflectional morphemes and/

or temporal particles and clitics that give direct temporal information. However, these forms are syntactically optional and do not participate in other grammatical processes. Thus a given sentence may or may not convey temporal information; Navajo and other Athabaskan languages are of this type. Finally, there are languages without temporal inflections or particles, such as Mandarin Chinese and Thai, some Mayan languages, and many others (Dahl & Velupillai 2005). I will refer to them as tenseless languages.

4.2 The inference of temporal location

The sentences of tenseless and mixed-temporal languages need not have direct temporal information—though temporal adverbs are always possible. Aspectual information enables inference about temporal location. The property of boundedness is the key to such inference. We find that Speech Time, Reference Time, and Situation Time, and their relations, are relevant to these languages. Aspectual viewpoints code the relation between Reference Time and Situation Time, while the relation between Speech Time and Reference Time is due to inference. This is the key difference between tensed languages and other languages. In the latter, grammatical forms do not relate Reference Time to Speech Time.

This discussion focuses on Mandarin Chinese; the findings apply, mutatis mutandis, to other tenseless languages (e.g. Thai, Yukatek Mayan) and to mixed-temporal languages (e.g. Navajo). There is evidence that the grammar of Mandarin Chinese must recognize Reference Time and Situation Time (Smith & Erbaugh 2005). Consider first the two perfective viewpoint suffixes -*le* and -*guo* (cf. Mangione & Dingxuan 1993). They convey different relations between Reference Time (RT) and Situation Time (SitT). The suffix -*le* conveys that the SitT interval is simultaneous with RT; -*guo* conveys that SitT precedes RT. The examples illustrate, from Chao (1968).

(28) a. Wǒ   shuāiduàn-le   tuǐ
     I   break-LE   leg
     'I broke my leg (it's still in a cast).'

   b. Wǒ   shuāiduàn-guo   tuǐ
     I   break-GUO   leg
     'I broke my leg (it has healed since).'

Reference Time explains the contrast: the viewpoints code different relations between SitT and RT. The -*guo* perfective conveys that SitT is prior to RT; it is a perfect (in that it also has additional properties). The approach holds for all aspectual viewpoints, including the neutral viewpoint; the default is that RT and SitT are simultaneous. Additional evidence for RT in Mandarin is similar to that for tensed languages: (i) there are adverbials *yijing* ('already') and *cai* ('only then') which require an RT different from SitT; (ii) there are occurrences of temporal deictic forms that have a shifted interpretation analogous to the use of the deictic *now* in *now it was quiet*; and (iii) situations in complex sentences and in discourse can stand in temporal relations that force some component sentences to be interpreted at RT.

Informal study of a variety of other languages that are mixed-temporal or tenseless (e.g. Thai, Navajo, Yukatek Mayan, Mam, ASL) suggests that the arguments for RT hold for them as well. The basic pattern of default temporal location holds quite generally for sentences without direct temporal information.

(29) Temporal location pattern—a default
 Unbounded situations, Present
 Bounded events, Past

Situations located in the future require explicit future information. This pattern can be explained by three pragmatic principles. Two are specifically linguistic, the third holds for information generally.

(30) Pragmatic principles of interpretation
 a. The Deictic Principle
   Speech Time is the central orientation point for language. The present is located at Speech Time; the past precedes it, the future follows.
 b. The Bounded Event Constraint
   Bounded situations may not be located in the present.
 c. The Simplicity Principle of Interpretation
   Choose the interpretation that requires least information added or inferred.

Since the speaker is the center of linguistic communication, Speech Time is the default orientation point. The Deictic Principle (30a) allows situations to be located in the past, present, or future. But we do not locate all situations freely. There is a constraint that blocks bounded situations from location in the present: the Bounded Event Constraint (30b). In taking the temporal perspective of the present, speakers obey a tacit convention that communication is instantaneous. A report of a bounded event is incompatible with a present interpretation, because the bounds would go beyond the present moment (Kamp & Reyle 1993: 536–537). There are some real and apparent exceptions, e.g. sports announcer narratives, performatives, and stage directions (Smith 2003). Situations located in the present are unbounded: they include ongoing events (*Mary is drawing a circle*); particular states (*Agnes is excited*); and general states (*Louis often feeds the cat*). The third principle is a general simplicity principle. People often utter sentences that underdetermine an interpretation, saying the minimum that is necessary. Receivers fill out what is said with additional information, making the simplest possible completion. This is a very general principle of information-processing (Kanisza 1976).

Clauses without explicit temporal information are incomplete as to temporal location. By inference, unbounded situations are located in the present, since, by the Deictic Principle and the Simplicity principle this is the simplest deictic interpretation. On the other hand, bounded events are located in the past. The explanation for this familiar observation appeals to all three principles. By the Deictic Principle and the Bounded Event Constraint, bounded events are oriented to Speech Time but cannot be located in the present. They might then be located in the past or the future. By the Simplicity Principle, they are located in the past. The past is simpler in terms of information conveyed than the future because the past doesn't have the element of uncertainty that is always part of the future.

4.3 Applying the principles

Sentences with overt aspectual viewpoints are interpreted by default following the pattern given above in (29). Sentences with the neutral viewpoint require another principle, the Temporal Schema Principle, to explain their temporal interpretation, and this is introduced below. Adverbial or other information in the context can override these defaults.

I continue with examples from Mandarin Chinese (Smith & Erbaugh 2005), but it should be noted that the principles also apply to languages like English. By the Bounded Event Constraint, bounded events are not located in the present; rather, simple present tense event sentences are taken as generalizing, or habitual, hence the interpretations available for a sentence like e.g. *she sings*.

4.3.1 Sentences with overt aspectual viewpoints

Imperfective viewpoints focus situations as unbounded, with no information as to endpoints. Mandarin has two imperfective viewpoints, a progressive (*zai*) as in (31), and a stative imperfective (*-zhe*). Imperfective sentences such as (31) are taken as located in the present. The Deictic and Simplicity Principles predict this interpretation.

(31) shìshí-shàng zhè-zhǒng   móshì shì zài   chāoxí zìrán   kēxué
     fact-on,   this-kind   model be ZAI   copy   natural science
     'In fact, this model is already copying the natural sciences.'

Perfective viewpoints focus events with bounds, located in the past by default. There are three perfectives: -*le*, -*guo*, and resultative verb complements (RVCs). (32) has an RVC suffix:

(32) ... zhè shì wǒ   hé   duō-wèi   niánqīng xuézhě   jiāo-tán   hòu
     ... this be I   and   many-CL   young   scholar exchange-talk after
     suǒ   dé-dào   de   jiélùn.
     SUO   reach-RVC   DE   conclusion
     'This is the conclusion which many young scholars and I reached after exchangingviews.'

As noted, perfectives cannot be located in the present, by the Deictic Principle and the Bounded Event Constraint. They are located in the past rather than the future by the Simplicity Principle.

4.3.2 Zero-marked sentences: The neutral viewpoint

There is a pragmatic pattern of interpretation for zero-marked clauses, based on event structure. One infers the boundedness of a clause from the temporal features of the situation expressed. Telic and single-stage events are intrinsically bounded, states and atelic events are unbounded.

(33) Temporal Schema Principle (a default):
     In a zero-marked clause, interpret boundedness according to the temporal features of the event or state entity.

This is a special case of the Simplicity Principle; it supplements the weak semantic information of the neutral viewpoint. In some languages, e.g. Thai, duration also plays a role in the temporal interpretation of zero-marked clauses (Smith 2008).

 The Temporal Schema Principle allows the inference of boundedness; armed with this information, the pragmatic principles lead to temporal interpretation. Sentences with intrinsically bounded situation entities are taken as past, others are taken as present. Thus the interpretation of zero-marked clauses has one inferential step more than that of sentences with overt aspectual viewpoints.

In another approach to zero-marked clauses, Bohnemeyer & Swift (2004) propose that they be interpreted in aspectual viewpoint terms. Telic events are perfective, unbounded and atelic situations are imperfective. The two approaches are similar in recognizing boundedness in event structure as the key property.

Decoupling the two RT relations is the key to temporal inference in tenseless and mixed-temporal languages. Overt aspectual viewpoints code the relation between RT and SitT; the relation between RT and SpT is inferred. In zero-marked clauses, both boundedness and temporal location are inferred. This account of temporal inference shows the close relation between aspect and temporal location.

5 Tense and aspect in discourse

While the syntactic domain of tense and aspect is the clause, they have important discourse effects as well. Tense and aspect contribute to the advancement of discourse, to point of view and to subtle effects of patterning. The main factors are the same across languages. In discourse of tenseless languages, aspect plays an important role.

Discourse can be considered at the global and local levels. Globally a discourse belongs to a genre, e.g. fiction, news article, courtroom interrogation. At the local level of the passage, five 'discourse modes' can be recognized: Narrative, Report, Description, Information, and Argument-Commentary; the list ignores conversation and procedural discourse (Smith 2003). The modes are characterized with two interpreted linguistic features, both relating to temporality. One is the type of situation entity the text introduces into the universe of discourse, the other the principle of advancement. For situation entities, we recognize the main classes of Eventualities (events and specific states), Generalizing Statives (generic and habitual or characterizing sentences), and Abstract Entities (embedded facts and propositions). Each class has distributional correlates, so that they are linguistically based. Different situation entities are predominant in each discourse mode.

5.1 Tense interpretation in discourse

Three patterns of tense interpretation are found in discourse, depending on the discourse mode of a clause. They are Continuity, Anaphora, and Deixis. All texts advance through a structured domain, but not in the same manner: texts of different modes have different principles of advancement. Advancement is a linguistic feature in the sense that information in the text gives rise to a given interpretation. There is also a literal sense of advancement, in which the receiver processes a text unit-by-unit. I discuss tense interpretation in this section; but note that the principles of interpretation hold for tenseless languages also.

Narrative is the most-studied type of discourse mode, and genre. In Narrative, situations are related to each other, and tense conveys Continuity; it does not involve time. The point is made emphatically by Weinrich (1973), who distinguishes text *commenté* and *raconté*, discursive and narrative. Tense is usually unchanging throughout a narrative; conventionally, past is the narrative tense although there are many narratives in the present, including the historical present. Within a given pattern of tense continuity, the perfect tenses allow reference to prior time; the prospective future-in-past allows reference to a subsequent time. Narrative introduces events and states into the universe of discourse. Aspect determines narrative advancement in tensed and tenseless languages; see below.

In Report, situations are related to Speech Time and tense is Deictic. The orientation center is usually Speech Time, in newspaper reports. But it may also be a past time. Time progresses forward and backward from that time. Report passages present situations from the temporal standpoint of the reporter. They are, like Narrative, mainly concerned with events and states. But in reports, the relation to Speech Time determines temporal advancement. This is due to the deictic pattern of tense interpretation. In (34) the adverb *here* in S1 reinforces the sense of the deictic center.

(34) S1 A week that began in violence ended violently here, with bloody clashes in the West Bank and Gaza and intensified fighting in Southern Lebanon. S2 Despite the violence, back-channel talks continued in Sweden. S3 Israeli, Palestinian and American officials have characterized them as a serious and constructive dialogue on the process itself and on the final status issues. S4 News accounts here say that Israel is offering as much as 90 percent of the West Bank to the Palestinians, although it is difficult to assess what is really happening by the bargaining moves that are leaked. (*New York Times*, 5/20/2000)

In this mode, tense often changes from past to present, or to future. Reports in tenseless languages also follow the deictic pattern, by the principles of inference given above.

In Description time is static, suspended: there are no significant changes or advancements. Tense is anaphoric to a previously established time, and the text progresses spatially through the scene described. Typically in Description there is a locative phrase with scope over the material that follows. Tenseless languages have passages of description, usually with time adverbials that establish a Reference Time and/or a relationship to a prior situation. The Informative and Argument modes have deictic tense interpretation, but are atemporal. They progress through metaphorical changes of location in the information space of the text. Information passages tend to have a preponderance of general statives; abstract entities predominate in argument passages.

5.2 Aspectual contribution to discourse

Aspectual information plays a key role in the narrative mode. The aspectual property of boundedness determines narrative advancement. We interpret the events of a narrative as advancing in sequence, one after another. Bounded events—event clauses with the perfective viewpoint—advance narrative time; unbounded events and states do not. This is the basic finding of discourse dynamics (Kamp & Rohrer 1983, Partee 1984, Hinrichs 1986). Temporal adverbials and inference also advance narrative time. When a narrative changes place, for instance, the reader often infers that there has been a change in time.

Imperfectives, progressives, and statives, including perfects, are taken as simultaneous to the previous Reference Time. The example illustrates:

(35) S1 She put on her apron, took a lump of clay from the bin and weighed off enough for a small vase. S2 The clay was wet. S3 Frowning, she cut the lump in half with a cheese-wire to check for air bubbles, then slammed the pieces together much harder than usual. S4 A fleck of clay spun off and hit her forehead, just above her right eye. (Peter Robinson, *A Necessary End*)

In this fragment, bounded events appear in sentences 1, 3, and 4; they advance the narrative. S2 expresses a state, which we interpret as simultaneous with the previous RT. I ignore flashbacks, changes of scale, etc., which require special treatment. Narrative advancement can be modeled as a succession of RTs, or as a succession of Temporal Perspective points (Kamp & Reyle 1993).

Unexpected aspectual choices are often found in Narrative. The imperfective or progressive may appear where one would expect a perfective, an "idiosyncratic" choice (Fleischman 1991); such choices are found in medieval and contemporary French texts, and in other Romance languages. Actually these choices are far from idiosyncratic: they are expressive, conveying point of view and/or foregrounding. The expressive uses of aspect are possible because it is a closed, obligatory sub-system, often redundant with other information in a text.

In tenseless languages, narrative advancement proceeds along the same lines. Situations are related to each other, and narrative time advances with bounded events. Boundedness is conveyed with aspectual viewpoint and, in zero-marked sentences, with events that are intrinsically bounded. By the Temporal Schema Principle (33), such sentences are interpreted as perfective. Expressive aspectual choices also appear in tenseless languages. They are especially common when aspectual viewpoints are obligatory. Progressives appear in contexts that move narrative time—for instance, in narrative texts of the Mayan language Mam. They are used in Navajo narratives to highlight key events.

The entities introduced in Descriptive passages are states, ongoing events, atelic events. One can also assume a tacit durative time adverbial for descriptive passages.

(36) S1 In the passenger car every window was propped open with a stick of kindling wood. S2 A breeze blew through, hot and then cool, fragrant of the woods and yellow flowers and of the train. S3 The yellow butterflies flew in at any window, out at any other. (Eudora Welty, *Delta Wedding*)

When telic events appear in description, they do not have their usual telic value. This is due to the implicit durative adverbial, which coerces the telic events, shifting them to atelic events. Thus the telic events in sentence 3 are coerced to stages of multiple-event activities. In descriptive passages of tenseless languages the situation entities are also unbounded. Thus Description passages tend not to have perfective sentences, although with coercion they are possible.

6 Conclusion

Aspectual systems provide event structure and aspectual viewpoints. The viewpoints focus events and states like the lens of a camera, making semantically visible all or part of the situation. Boundedness, a key feature in temporal interpretation, is conveyed by both the event structure and viewpoint components. Three times are needed, in tensed and tenseless languages, to account for temporal meanings. In tensed languages, tense codes times and their relations. Tenses introduce Speech Time, Reference Time, and Situation Time; tense also codes two relations, that between RT and SitT, and that between RT and SpT. This second relation determines temporal location. In tenseless languages, the two temporal relations are conveyed differently. Aspectual viewpoints introduce Reference Time and Situation Time and code their relation. The relation between Speech Time and Reference Time is not grammatically coded, but is inferred from aspectual information. The aspectual property of boundedness determines the inference of temporal location, guided by general pragmatic principles. Bounded events are located in the past, unbounded situations are located in the present. These are defaults: contextual information can override them, and can imply, for example, that an unbounded situation is located in the future.

This overview of time in language shows that the temporal sub-systems of tense and aspect are closely related. The similarities across languages are striking, although there are real differences. Yet, it is impossible to cover a wide range of languages in a single introductory article; I hope that the reader will be able to extend the approach to languages not discussed here.

A brief note from the final editors of the manuscript

Professor Carlota S. Smith died on May 24, 2007 at the age of 73 after a long battle with cancer. She taught at The University of Texas at Austin for 38 years, and was the Dallas TACA Centennial Professor in the Humanities. Professor Smith's work on tense and aspect, perhaps her most important line of research, began in the mid-1970s. In many papers and in a very influential book (*The Parameter of Aspect*, published in 1991 by Kluwer), she analyzed how languages encode time, and introduced her signature 'two-component' theory of aspect. Her work on temporal aspect is notable for its empirical foundation in her careful analyses of languages, including English, French, Russian, Mandarin, and Navajo. Through her many years of research on Navajo, she became a member of the Navajo Language Academy. In 2003, Cambridge University Press published Professor Smith's second book, *Modes of Discourse*. This book analyzes the grammatical properties that distinguish different genres of discourse, and brought the analytic tools of linguistics to the humanistic study of literature.

Much of Professor Smith's most fruitful work is available in the posthumous collection *Text, Time, and Context: Selected Papers by Carlota S. Smith* (Springer 2009, edited by Richard P. Meier, Helen Aristar-Dry, and Emilie Destruel). The current article is the final piece of work that Professor Smith completed; she submitted it to the editors just a month before her death. It will presumably be the final publication of a distinguished and productive scholar who has forever changed the way linguists think about time.—David I. Beaver & Richard P. Meier, Austin, April 9, 2011.

Acknowledgment: We wish to thank Yahui Huang for her assistance in checking the Mandarin data.

7 References

Abusch, Dorit 1997. Sequence of tense and temporal *de re*. *Linguistics & Philosophy* 20, 1–50.
Bach, Emmon 1986. The algebra of events. *Linguistics & Philosophy* 9, 5–16.
Binnick, Robert 1991. *Time and the Verb*. Oxford: Oxford University Press.
Bohnemeyer, Jürgen & Mary Swift 2004. Event realization and default aspect. *Linguistics & Philosophy* 27, 263–296.
Brustad, Kristen 2000. *The Syntax of Spoken Arabic: A Comparative Study of Moroccan, Egyptian, Syrian, and Kuwaiti Dialects*. Washington, DC: Georgetown University Press.
Bybee, Joan, Revere Perkins & William Pagliuca 1994. *The Evolution of Grammar*. Chicago, IL: The University of Chicago Press.
Chao, Yuen Ren 1968. *A Grammar of Spoken Chinese*. Berkeley, CA: University of California Press.
Comrie, Bernard 1976. *Aspect*. Cambridge: Cambridge University Press.
Comrie, Bernard 1985. *Tense*. Cambridge: Cambridge University Press.
Dahl, Östen 1985. *Tense and Aspect Systems*. New York: Blackwell.
Dahl, Östen 2000. *Tense and Aspect in the Languages of Europe*. Berlin: Walter de Gruyter.
Dahl, Östen & Viveka Velupillai 2005. Tense and aspect: Introduction. In: M. Haspelmath et al. (eds.). *World Atlas of Language Structures*. Oxford: Oxford University Press, 266–281.
Demirdache, Hamida & Myriam Uribe-Extebarria 2000. The primitives of temporal relations. In: R. Martin, D. Michaels & J. Uriagereka (eds.). *Step by Step: Essays on Minimalist Syntax in Honor of Howard Lasnik*. Cambridge, MA: The MIT Press, 157–186.
Dowty, David 1979. *Word Meaning and Montague Grammar*. Dordrecht: Kluwer.
Dowty, David 1986. The effects of aspectual class on the temporal structure of discourse: Semantics or pragmatics. *Linguistics & Philosophy* 9, 37–61.
Dowty, David 1991. Thematic proto-roles and argument selection. *Language* 67, 547–619.
Enç, Mürvet 1987. Anchoring conditions for tense. *Linguistic Inquiry* 18, 633–658.
Fleischman, Suzanne 1991. *Tense and Narrativity*. Austin, TX: University of Texas Press.
Giorgi, Alessandra & Fabio Pianesi 1997. *Tense and Aspect: From Semantics to Morphosyntax*. Oxford: Oxford University Press.
Haspelmath, Martin, Matthew S. Dryer, David Gil & Bernard Comrie (eds.) 2005. *The World Atlas of Language Structures*. Oxford: Oxford University Press.
Herweg, Michael 1991. Perfective and imperfective aspect and the theory of events and states. *Linguistics* 29, 969–1010.
Hinrichs, Erhard 1986. Temporal anaphora in discourses of English. *Linguistics & Philosophy* 9, 63–82.
Hornstein, Norbert 1991. *As Time Goes By*. Cambridge, MA: The MIT Press.
Iatridou, Sabine 2000. The grammatical ingredients of counterfactuality. *Linguistic Inquiry* 31, 231–270.
Kamp, Hans & Christian Rohrer 1983. Tense in texts. In: R. Bäuerle, Ch. Schwarze & A. von Stechow (eds.). *Meaning, Use and Interpretation of Language*. Berlin: de Gruyter, 250–269.
Kamp, Hans & Uwe Reyle 1993. *From Discourse to Logic*. Dordrecht: Kluwer.
Kanisza, Gaetano 1976. Subjective contours. *Scientific American* 234, 48–52.
Kenny, Anthony 1963. *Action, Emotion and Will*. London: Routledge & Kegan Paul.
Klein, Wolfgang 1992. The present perfect puzzle. *Language* 68, 525–552.

Klein, Wolfgang 1994. *Time in Language*. London: Routledge.
Krifka, Manfred 1998. The origins of telicity. In: S. Rothstein (ed.). *Events and Grammar*. Dordrecht: Kluwer, 197–235.
Krifka, Manfred, Francis J. Pelletier, Gregory Carlson, Alice ter Meulen, Gennaro Chierchia, & Godehard Link 1995. Genericity: An introduction. In: G. Carlson & F.J. Pelletier (eds.). *The Generic Book*. Chicago, IL: The University of Chicago Press, 1–124.
Landman, Fred 1992. The progressive. *Natural Language Semantics* 1, 1–32.
Lecarme, Jacqueline 2004. Tense in nominals. In: J. Guéron & J. Lecarme (eds.). *The Syntax of Time*. Cambridge, MA: The MIT Press, 440–475.
Lyons, John 1977. *Semantics*. Cambridge: Cambridge University Press.
Mangione, Louis & Dingxuan Li 1993. Compositional analysis of -*guo* and -*le*. *Journal of Chinese Linguistics* 21, 65–122.
McCoard, Robert 1978. *The English Perfect: Tense-Choice and Pragmatic Inference*. Amsterdam: North-Holland.
Mittwoch, Anita 1988. Aspects of English aspect: On the interaction of perfect, progressive and durational adverbials. *Linguistics & Philosophy* 11, 203–254.
Moens, Marc & Mark Steedman 1987. Temporal ontology in natural language. *Proceedings of the 25th Annual Conference of the Association for Computational Linguistics,* Stanford, CA: ACL, 1–7.
Nordlinger, Rachel & Louisa Sadler. 2004. Nominal tense in crosslinguistic perspective. *Language* 80, 776–806.
Ogihara, Toshiyuki 1996. *Tense, Attitudes and Scope*. Dordrecht: Kluwer.
Pancheva, Roumyana & Arnim von Stechow 2004. On the present perfect puzzle. In: K. Moulton & M. Wolf (eds.). *Proceedings of the North Eastern Linguistic Society (= NELS) 34*. Amherst, MA: GLSA, 469–484.
Partee, Barbara 1973. Some structural analogies between tenses and pronouns. *The Journal of Philosophy* 70, 601–609.
Partee, Barbara 1984. Nominal and temporal anaphora. *Linguistics & Philosophy* 7, 243–286.
Prior, Arthur 1967. *Past, Present and Future*. Oxford: Clarendon Press.
Reichenbach, Hans 1947. *Elements of Symbolic Logic*. London: Macmillan.
Rothstein, Susan 2004. *Structuring Events*. Oxford: Blackwell.
Smith, Carlota S. 1991/1997. *The Parameter of Aspect*. Dordrecht: Kluwer. 2nd edn. 1997.
Smith, Carlota S. 1996. Aspectual categories in Navajo. *International Journal of American Linguistics* 62, 227–263.
Smith, Carlota S. 1999. Activities: States or events. *Linguistics & Philosophy* 22, 479–508.
Smith, Carlota S. 2003. *Modes of Discourse*. Cambridge: Cambridge University Press.
Smith, Carlota S. 2006. Tense and context in French. In: E. Labeau, C. Vetters & P. Caudal (eds.). *Sémantique et diachronie du système verbal français*. Amsterdam: Rodopi, 1–21.
Smith, Carlota S. 2008. Time with and without tense. In: J. Guéron & J. Lecarme (eds.). *Time and Modality: Studies in Natural Language and Linguistic Theory*. Dordrecht: Kluwer, 227–250.
Smith, Carlota S. & Mary Erbaugh 2005. Temporal interpretation in Mandarin Chinese. *Linguistics* 43, 713–756.
von Stechow, Arnim 1995. On the proper treatment of tense. In: T. Galloway & M. Simons (eds.). *Proceedings of Semantics and Linguistic Theory (= SALT) V*. Ithaca, NY: Cornell University, 362–386.
Steele, Susan 1975. Past and irrealis. *International Journal of American Linguistics* 41, 200–217.

Stowell, Tim 1996. The phrase structure of tense. In: J. Rooryck & L. Zaring (eds.). *Phrase Structure and the Lexicon*. Dordrecht: Kluwer, 277–292.
de Swart, Henriëtte 1998. Aspect shift and coercion. *Natural Language and Linguistic Theory* 16, 347–385.
Taylor, Barry 1977. Tense and continuity. *Linguistics & Philosophy* 1, 199–220.
Tenny, Carol 1987. *Grammaticalizing Aspect and Affectness*. Ph.D. dissertation. MIT, Cambridge, MA.
Tonhauser, Judith 2006. *The Temporal Semantics of Noun Phrases: Evidence from Guarani (Paraguay)*. Ph.D. dissertation. Stanford University, Stanford, CA.
Ultan, Russell (1978). The nature of future tenses. In: J. Greenberg (ed.). *Universals of Human Language. Volume 3: Word Structure*. Stanford, CA: Stanford University Press, 83–123.
Vendler, Zeno 1957. Verbs and times. *Philosophical Review* 66, 143–160.
Verkuyl, Henk 1972. *On the Compositional Nature of the Aspects*. Dordrecht: Kluwer.
Weinrich, Harald 1973. *Le temps*. Paris: Éditions du Seuil.
Whorf, Benjamin Lee 1956. *Language, Thought, and Reality*. New York: Wiley.
Wilhelm, Andrea 2003. *The Grammatization of Telicity and Durativity in Dëne Suliné (Chipewyan) and German*. Ph.D. dissertation. University of Calgary, Calgary, AB.

Eric Pederson
4 The expression of space across languages

1. The importance of space —— 92
2. Localism —— 94
3. Formal marking of spatial expression —— 97
4. Dimensional expressions —— 100
5. Topology —— 100
6. Spatial deixis —— 103
7. Reference frames —— 104
8. Motion events (dynamic spatial relations) —— 107
9. Conclusion —— 108
10. References —— 109

Abstract: This chapter provides an overview of the expression of space in the semantics of natural language. Dimensionality and location in space are clearly among the most basic concerns for any mobile organism and language prominently provides a rich way to communicate about spatial information. After a brief discussion of the linguistic constructions which typically express spatial relationships, the major semantic subdivisions of space and spatial relationships are presented: dimensionality (of a single entity), topological relationships (e.g. containment), deixis (or the spatial relationship between an entity and a simple reference point), reference frames (the geometry of locating one entity in space), and motion events. Throughout the discussion, there is an emphasis on semantic typology and cross-linguistic variation.

1 The importance of space

The very essence of our existence is fundamentally spatial. We evolved in space, live in space, think about space, find things in space, and naturally we talk almost incessantly about space: the dimensionality of objects, location in space, change of spatial location, and the geometric relationship between objects situated in space. Given this fundamental nature of spatial locating and reckoning, space may be considered one of the most fundamental cognitive and semantic domains.

Spatial expression is often among the first elicited material in early language descriptions and accounts for a substantial portion of grammatical descriptions

Eric Pederson, Eugene, OR, USA

of well described languages. For example, spatial language constitutes a substantial portion of the use of adpositions, adverbial expressions, adjectives, and complex noun phrases.

Because space is understood as "concrete" (vs. abstract, figurative, or metaphorical) and because spatial relations are well describable in all languages, it provides an ideal and prevalent source domain (see article 11 [Semantics: Lexical Structures and Adjectives] (Tyler & Takahashi) *Metaphors and metonymies*) of vocabulary and grammatical constructions which can be used to describe non-spatial relations as well.

The various approaches which take spatial language and/or reasoning as fundamental to many or most other expressions are subsumed under the cover term "Localism". Localist approaches argue that space is the premier source for expressions which refer to more abstract non-spatial relations. (See section 2 below.)

However, because spatial expressions are so commonly extended to refer to non-spatial expressions, expressions which are wholly dedicated to spatial expression are relatively rare. For example, while the adposition systems of many languages seem to largely express spatial relations, they also commonly express argument structure, temporal, causal and other relations. As a result, this chapter is organized according to the ways different types of spatial relations are commonly expressed in natural language rather than according to typical grammatical classification.

In recent decades, the range of linguistic variation concerning spatial expression has been demonstrated to be far greater than had been widely assumed primarily on the basis of analyses of (Indo-)European languages. The implications for semantic theory of this broader variation are only now beginning to be explored. For instance, since around 1990, some of this cross-linguistic variation has led to testing of various versions of the *linguistic relativity hypothesis* (see, e.g., article 2 [this volume] (Bach & Chao) *Semantic types across languages*, or Pederson 2010).

There is a large and growing interest in the semantics of spatial language in various applied disciplines. For example, robotics and artificial intelligence are concerned with how to operationalize spatial representations and to implement human—machine interactions. Geographic Information Science has a fundamental concern with the language of space as the results of even a simple query will vary widely depending on the interpretation of the spatial terms used. More generally, spatial language and representation is a core concern of cognitive science, especially developmental psychology (see article 13 [this volume] (Landau) *Space in semantics and cognition*).

For some general references on space beyond this short chapter, a good starting point (in German) is Klein (1991). For more recent typological collections see Levinson & Wilkins (2006a) and Hickmann & Robert (2006). Many references to spatial language are in fact more specific to particular subdomains of space and will be referenced in the appropriate sections below.

2 Localism

Localism is generally defined as the hypothesis that spatial expressions (including direction) are more basic, grammatically and semantically, than various kinds of non-spatial expressions. Claims of Localism can be of various strengths, from relatively weak claims that selected non-spatial domains are understood in terms of space to stronger claims that virtually all "abstract" categories are structured with a spatial understanding.

Some of the more forceful proponents of localism within linguistics include John Anderson (Anderson 1973) and Jan van Voorst (van Voorst 1993). Localism is also implicit in much work within Cognitive Linguistics and other fields which give a prominent role to semantic mapping relations or metaphor, e.g., Lakoff & Johnson (1980). Within psychology, many since Miller & Johnson-Laird (1976) have argued that spatial organization is of central importance in human cognition.

Within semantics, localism has often structured the metalanguage. For example, Jackendoff (1983), following the line of work descending from Gruber (1965: 188) argued for the Thematic Relations Hypothesis: "In any semantic field of [EVENTS] and [STATES], the principal event-, state-, path-, and place-functions are a subset of those used for the analysis of spatial location and motion." Non-spatial expressions were understood to have a theme (akin to the located object), a reference object (akin to the Ground or Landmark), and a relationship which assumes the role played by location in the field of spatial expressions. (For an update on Jackendoff's Conceptual Semantics, see article 4 [Semantics: Theories] (Jackendoff) *Conceptual Semantics*.)

For example, Anderson (1973), Clark (1973) and others have long noted that temporal expressions follow the same form (or derive from) spatial expressions: *The future/building lies ahead of us, We meet at 10:00/the drugstore*, etc. The diachronic literature (see also articles 6 [this volume] (Fritz) *Theories of meaning change* and 7 [this volume] (Geeraerts) *Cognitive approaches to diachronic semantics*) often notes the development of temporal markers from spatial markers as well. For example, Traugott (1978) observes that "nearly every preposition or particle that is locative in English is also temporal" and all of these developed from initial spatial uses. The purely temporal *for, since, (un)til* were initially spatial terms as well. This is presumably motivated by the ready availability and conceptualizability of spatial relations together with a transparent mapping from the "here" to the "now". For example, any increase in travel distance from a present location correlates nearly perfectly with increasing time since being at that location. (However, for a challenge to the orthodox assumption that temporal markers inherently derive from spatial markers, see Tenbrink 2007.)

Tense markers commonly derive historically from deictic forms and motion verbs (e.g. English *gonna* and French *allez* + infinitive). Aspectual forms, especially progressives and statives, commonly derive from locative constructions (e.g. the English progressive: *is hunting* historically deriving from *is on/at/in hunting*). Similar observations of parallels between space and other non-spatiotemporal domains (possession, states, properties, etc.) argue for a generalized use of the metalanguage and analytical tools of spatial language for an understanding of non-spatial expressions.

2.1 Grammatical case

Various frameworks model grammatical case relations as largely spatially derived. For example, DeLancey (1991) argues that the traditional underlying cases need to be redefined in terms of AT or GOTO relations: the three basic case roles (Theme, Location, and Agent) boil down to "theme AT location", "theme GOTO location", and "Agent CAUSE theme GOTO location". In other words, states and events are essentially understood in terms of spatial relationships. Like DeLancey's, other case hierarchy theories essentially attribute a progression of force from an agent through the other mentioned participants but with varying degrees of spatial metalanguage, cf. the occasionally spatial descriptions of *action chains* in Langacker (1991), and the purely *energy transfer* model of transitivity in van Voorst (1996) which has no mention of spatial relations at all.

Of course, language with explicit case marking will typically indicate spatial relationships with at least one or two grammatical cases. Cases described as "locative", obviously tend to be spatial, but they may in fact vary considerably from language to language in their semantics. For example, the Lithuanian locative case *-ė* tends to represent containment relations, but not contact or support relationships. There may also be multiple "locative" cases. For example, in Tamil, there is a general locative *-il* (for general location, such as *a cat is on the mat*). However, Tamil also has a case marker *-iṭam* which refers to location with an agent capable of control over the located item (akin to English *having money on him*).

Dative case is commonly used to express direction as well as locations. It often alternates with a locative case in interesting ways. To continue the Tamil example, ownership would be marked with the dative *-ku* (1s-Dat money

Copula-Pr-3sn "I have money, [but not necessarily on my person]"). Replacing the dative case with the locative *-iTam* would indicate temporary control or possession, but not conclusive ownership. Compare with the English: *I have money* vs. *The money is with/on me.*

German famously has an Accusative/Dative distinction with many of its prepositions such that the Dative case indicates static location (e.g. *in dem* or *im* for static containment) while the Accusative indicates a change into that locative relationship (e.g. *in das* or *ins* for entering into containment). In contrast, French would use *dans* for both situations.

Instrumental/manner expressions and passive "by-phrases" are often marked with forms which historically derive from spatial path markers. For example, Dutch or German *door/durch* was a path marker which came to be used for marking a demoted agent via an instrumental use.

2.2 Fictive motion

Localism posits that spatial language is used to describe properties and relationships which are not literally construed as spatial. The idea of *fictive motion* (Talmy 1996) is that scenes or events which in terms of objective reality are not actually motion events are described or construed as though they were motion events. (The roots of this analysis are found in Talmy 1983.) For example, *This fence goes from the plateau to the valley* and *The scenery rushes past* are not referentially about motion even though they use motion verbs and path expressions. Indeed, most path expressions can be used for either dynamic or static spatial relations (*the man/the grass runs along the river*). Similarly, cases which express path (ablative, allative, inessive, etc.) typically have both dynamic and static uses as well.

These are not cases of metaphor, according to Talmy, as they are generally perceived as motion and therefore involve no mapping for literal source to metaphorical target. That said, the choice of verbs and other lexical items do seem to indicate that there are constraints on the ascription of motion. It is not an accident that one says *the highway runs through the mountains* rather than *the highway walks through the mountains*. English *run* has been conventionally understood to apply to cases other than actual motion events, whereas other motion verbs are prohibited from such uses.

Many of Talmy's examples of fictive motion involve fictive paths. For example, shadows are construed as cast by objects onto and along the Ground (in reality, shadows are just areas struck by and reflecting less light). Perspectives are also represented using path expressions: *The trees get shorter as you move down the road.*

Fictive motion is seen as less veridical with reality of motion (i.e. likely not actual physical motion) and *factive motion* is understood to be more veridical (and likely true). Events described as motion events must be understood as fictive as a matter of degree. There are clear parallels with the study of *perceived motion* in the visual system. For example, a linear flashing of a series of lights, when rapid and close enough, will be perceived as factive motion.

Parallel work on non-real, non-metaphorical motion has also been pursued by Matsumoto (Matsumoto 1996b) which explores language-specific patterns across English and Japanese. See also Matsumoto (1996a) which relates fictive motion to change of state expressions more generally. Earlier treatments relating non-actual motion in language and vision include Jackendoff (1987) and Langacker (1986).

3 Formal marking of spatial expression

As mentioned above, no single area in grammar is purely dedicated to spatial expression. Given the tendency of spatial forms to become conventionally used for non-spatial expressions, it seems that should a language have a dedicated spatial system at one point, it would rapidly expand to non-spatial uses as well.

Nonetheless, there is a predominant spatial use of adpositional expressions in many unrelated languages. These are especially commonly used for expressing *topological relations* (cf. section 5). This is perhaps the closest to a spatially dedicated form class commonly found across languages. Here too, however, non-spatial uses of adpositions are frequent. Landau & Jackendoff (1993) argue that the prepositions are the forms which answer the *Where?* questions in language. This work drew heavily from work on European languages and today alternatives to adpositional expression are better known.

The *Basic Locative Construction* (or BLC) is a term formalized from work at the Max Planck Institute for Psycholinguistics. The assumption is that each language will have a construction which is the simplest answer to a question "Where is X?". This is not to be confused with existential questions such as "Is something there?". Levinson & Wilkins (2006b) propose that cross-linguistic variation leads to a BLC hierarchy, such that if a BLC is used for certain spatial descriptions, one can predict that it will probably also be used for certain others. For example, if a BLC can represent a *Figure* (the located object, see section 5 below) which is a part of a *Ground* (the reference or landmark object), then it will probably be usable for adornment or clothing—at least if this latter use is not preempted by a more specialized construction.

There has been particular interest in the necessity and/or specificity of a verb in the BLC. This is most elaborated in Grinevald (2006) who proposes a range of verb specificity in the BLC as follows:
- No locative information (no verb or just an existential copula)
- A dedicated locative verb (e.g., "to be at")
- Postural verb (includes information about the disposition of the Figure, e.g. *sitting* vs. *standing*)
- Locative stems (e.g., classificatory verb stems as in Kwakwala: "bulky object is somewhere")
- Positional verbs (e.g., Tzotzil "seated on something elevated above the ground")

The specificity of the verbs through this list generally increases through an increasing specification of the Figure in the verb. As a partial exception to this trend, postural verbs can elaborate on the nature of the relationship between the Figure and the Ground e.g. *surround* rather than just on the disposition of the Figure in isolation.

Positional verbs are robustly exemplified by Mayan languages (see Brown 1994 for Tzeltal and Haviland 1992 for the closely related Tzotzil). For example Tzeltal *pachal* is a verb used of wide-mouthed containers canonically 'sitting'. In other words, positional verbs commonly have semantic elements typical of both postural and classificatory verbs.

One question regarding typical BLC constructions cross-linguistically asks how comparable they are in terms of information structure. Generally speaking, languages with extensive adposition systems have no obligatory use of an extensive set of verbs and vice versa. However, this is only an imperfect correlation. English generally does not require postural verbs in its BLC, though German with its comparable set of prepositions, generally does require postural verbs.

According to Kahr's survey (Kahr 1975), every language has at least one adposition or affix that can be used to indicate that a Figure is in a spatial relationship to a Ground (although this form is likely to have other grammatical functions as well). When the relationship is canonical, often nothing more is needed. But to pin down a spatial relationship more precisely speakers may add a *relational noun* that specifies a particular *region* in relation to the Ground object, such as its top or 'above' region, its bottom or 'below' region, its side, back, inside, or outside region as in the Japanese examples below.

(1) a. Neko ga matto no *ue* ni iru
    cat SUBJ mat GEN ABOVE LOC be
    'The cat is at the mat's above-region' (= the cat is on the mat)

b. Ringo ga   booru no   *naka*   ni   aru
   apple SUBJ bowl GEN   inside   LOC   be
   'The apple is at the bowl's inside-region' (= the apple is in the bowl)

To complicate matters, there is an unclear boundary between adpositions and relational nouns. Relational nouns are generally considered distinct from adpositions by virtue of still having formal properties of nouns (especially in taking articles or genitives) as in on the <u>top</u> of. (These typically derive from *part nouns*.) However, with time, relational nouns tend to lose their status as separate nouns and increasingly approximate adpositions or become part of compound adpositions, e.g. in English, *on top of, atop, across, between*. As mentioned in the previous section, grammatical case often expresses spatial relationships and there is a well-traveled diachronic pathway from adposition to case. There is also a strong tendency for adpositions and case to have complex semantic and constructional interactions. Note that adpositions often occur as compound adpositions, e.g. *in+to*, which raises the question of whether the forms should be treated as semantically compositional as well.

There is sometimes a broad discrepancy between how much information about the same scene speakers of two languages might provide. Languages such as English are *hyperspecifying* in their use of prepositions. For example, even if the containment of a book with respect to a drawer is completely expected, an English speaker will still specify that *the book is IN the drawer*. Other languages are more commonly *pragmatically inferencing* in that they will use a general locative form except when the location cannot be expected to be readily inferred or otherwise needs particular mention. For example, under most circumstances, a boat and a fish will both be described as "locative" with respect to the water. However, should the boat be sunk or the fish be floating, then they would probably be described as "in(side)" or "on (top of)" the water respectively. Of course, while a language may be hyperspecifying in one domain, it will probably be pragmatically inferencing in another domain. Indeed these differences across languages in their description of space give each language much of its character.

Speakers and languages also vary in whether or not a particular situation should be expressed as though it were spatial at all. For example, an English speaker would typically describe an apple as *(impaled)* <u>on</u> *a skewer*. Describing this as a fundamentally spatial scene seems next to impossible in other languages which must say some variant of *the apple has been speared by the skewer* which is essentially an agent or instrument expression with only an implicit locative relationship.

Path verbs also express a Figure-Ground relationship in what might otherwise be an agent-patient grammatical construction. For example, *the fence surrounds the house* is not grammatically distinct from *the man eats the apple* or for that matter from *the men surround the prisoner*. Occasional path verbs incorporate Ground information, e.g. English *deplane* or French *se terrer* 'to land', but all path verbs necessarily require spatially appropriate Grounds. For example, *enter* requires a Ground which can contain the Figure/subject. In many languages, simplex path verbs (most notably "go", "come", and "ascend") have become conventionalized to the point of being obligatory direction markers that attach to a main *manner of motion* verb. Without the direction marker, the motion is typically taken to be *non-translational*, e.g. "running (in place)" (see section 8).

4 Dimensional expressions

Dimensional expressions are those expressions which denote the spatial extent of an object. Dimensional expressions as usually discussed are the direct expressions of one or more dimensions of an object. Most common are expressions of breadth, depth, etc. As these are essentially the spatial properties of objects divorced from relational information, they are typically treated separately from spatial semantics and treated as object properties instead. There is an extensive typological summary by Lang (2001). See also the collection Bierwisch & Lang (1989) and a more recent theoretical overview by Tenbrink (2005).

In addition to direct expressions of dimensions, many languages make systematic use of classification systems which rely in large part on dimensional classification. For example, typical East and Southeast Asian nominal classifiers will include categories for long and thin objects, approximately round objects, and so on. Verbal classification systems, for example the classificatory verb stems of Navajo (see Young 2000), will have some stems specific to particular shapes, or dimensional configurations, such as *ł-tsooz* for flat and flexible items, though these forms seem to generally represent functional qualities rather than purely dimensional characteristics.

5 Topology

The relationship between *Figure* and *Ground* is generally taken to be asymmetric: most descriptions of Figure and Ground cannot reverse these two roles. Talmy's example is that a bicycle makes a reasonable Figure relative to a church as Ground, but it is not typically appropriate to locate a church with respect to a bicycle. Similar asymmetries are found in other domains such as comment/topic and assertion/presupposition suggesting that at least with respect to language behavior, such asymmetry is a fundamental pattern.

Most commonly associated with adpositions, the expression of *topological relations* between a Figure and a Ground encompasses concepts of containment, contact, and other *non-metrical* concepts. Talmy (1977) borrowed the term *topology* from mathematics where it refers to geometry in an infinitely stretchable space. However, in semantics the term tends to be used for notions beyond the few which are topological mathematically (e.g. partial containment, and adjacency). Further semantic topology notions which are recurrently invoked include verticality, support, attachment, and sometimes occlusion. Topological space distinctions are quite distinct from the projective coordinate systems of reference frames discussed below.

Importantly, topological relations are not by any means limited to adpositions. For example, Finnish distinguishes between contact (case), containment (case) and inferior vertical (adposition):

(2) a. The book is on/in/under the desk.   (M. Bowerman, p.c.)
    b. Kirja on kirioituspöydä-llä / kirioituspöydä-ssa / kirioituspöydä-n alla
       book is desk-on   / desk-in   / desk-GEN under

Herskovits (1986) presented an extensive examination of largely topological relations expressed by English adpositions which helped to popularize semantic analyses of adpositions more generally. She argues for larger categories of *use types* as a way of categorizing the apparently endless range of spatial uses of English prepositions into larger generalizations. Since this work, there has been a small industry of cross-linguistic research in the expression of topological space. Initial reports assumed prepositions were semantically similar cross-linguistically, but as surveys were completed, notable variations were reported. This variation should not have been surprising since many second language learners will attest that learning the nuances of a foreign adposition system is maddeningly difficult.

For example, Bowerman (1996) gives the simple example of four languages each with a dramatically different pattern. Of the five logically possible groupings of these three topological relations (a cup on a table, an apple in a bowl, and a handle attached to a door), only one has not been found (a grouping of support "on table" with containment "in bowl" but without attachment of "handle to door"), cf. Fig. 4.1. These cross-linguistic patterns are examined in Bowerman & Pederson (1992) and subsequent work by Feist (2000, 2004). One finds that within the considerable cross-linguistic variation, there are systematic cross-linguistic patterns. This suggests strong universalist factors driving and constraining

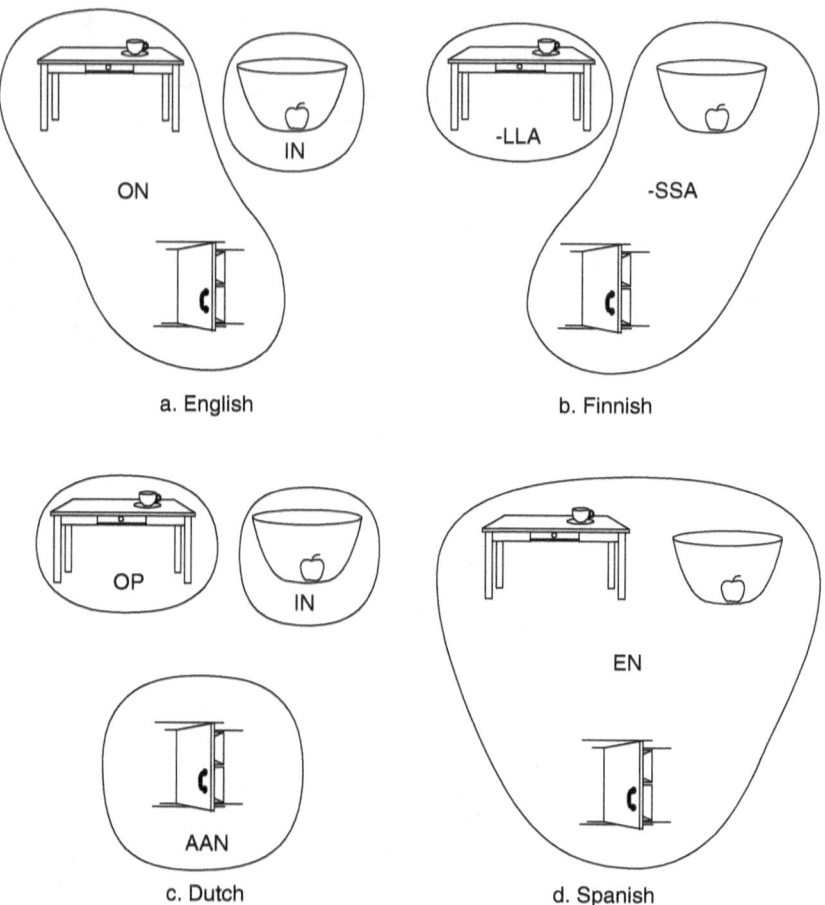

Fig. 4.1: *Classification of three static spatial situations in English, Finnish, Dutch and Spanish (from Bowerman 1996: 394)*

language particular patterns. That said, Choi & Bowerman (1991) demonstrate that even at early stages of spatial language acquisition, children more closely follow the adult pattern of their target language than they resemble children learning typologically different languages.

A recurrent problem for the semantic analysis of topological relationships is determining to what extent language variation represents different semantic patterns of the forms or differing construals of the reference. For example, English speakers say that freckles are found on the face (spots on a surface), whereas Swedish speakers say that the freckles lie in the face (points within a bound area). This difference is not attributable to differences between the forms for ON and

IN in English and Swedish, but to conventional construal of how to think about freckles. Similarly, Clark (1973) cites the example of British vs. American English collocation of the *house in the street* vs. *on the street* as indicating a different pattern of use rather than differing understandings of *in* and *on* across these two dialects. (Neither collocation is strictly geometrical as most houses lie alongside streets and neither "in" nor "on" them.)

However, the use of topological spatial expressions has also been demonstrated to be highly influenced by non-geometric factors. Specifically the role of the functional relationship between the Figure and Ground can profoundly affect whether or not a supposedly geometric term can be used. For an English example, if an apple is effectively prevented from rolling away because of its relationship to a bowl, then the apple can be said to be "in" the bowl even if it may lie atop a pile of apples such that it is geometrically far beyond the boundaries of the bowl. For research in functional determination, consult Carlson-Radvansky et al. (1999), Coventry et al. (2001), and Carlson & Kenny (2006).

6 Spatial deixis

There is a confusing array of uses of the term spatial deixis. Most generally it means any spatial reference which must be contextualized (typically relative to a speech event) for interpretation. Miller & Johnson-Laird (1976) is the standard reference for early modern work for deixis and spatial reference generally.

In this section, I briefly discuss spatial deixis as a class of spatial expressions distinct from topological relations (section 5) and reference frames (section 7). Specifically, these are the demonstrative expressions which rely on a spatial deictic center and indicate, e.g., *distal* (away from the deictic center) vs. *proximal* (near the deictic center) contrasts and other similar notions. For a comprehensive cross-linguistic overview of the semantics of demonstratives and spatial deixis, consult article 13 [Semantics: Interfaces] (Diessel) *Deixis and demonstratives* as well as Diessel (1999), Enfield (2003) and Imai (2003). There is also a typological overview in Haase (2001) and Klein (2001, section 44.6 Ortsdeixis).

While these contrasts may be expressed most commonly through a demonstrative pronoun system, some languages have developed further grammatical expressions for such contrasts. For example, Tamil has a prefix set (proximal, distal, and archaically medial) which can affix to different word classes and derive deictic demonstrative pronouns, determiners, and even some adverbs (e.g., *i-ppaṯi* "proximal: in this way", *a-ppaṯi* "distal: in that way").

Like topological relations, most deictic systems are metrically neutral in that a distal form may be used for a distance which might be used with a proximal form when the relevant scale differs. Generally speaking, most languages have two or three grammaticalized demonstratives indicating spatial deixis, though languages have been reported with as many as five purely spatial demonstratives.

Two term systems, unsurprisingly, indicate something like a proximal vs. distal distinction broadly applied. Some languages allow distal forms to be used for proximal locations when they are contrastive in some non-spatial way (e.g. referring to something less topical or less recently mentioned), whereas other languages prohibit this. For example, Arrernte speakers (Central Australian Pama-Nyungan) cannot refer to "this tooth" vs. "that tooth" when both are clearly proximal to the speaker (D. Wilkins, p.c.).

When there is a third demonstrative, interesting variation emerges. Essentially, one of the forms remains proximal, but there are multiple possible interpretations of what non-proximal might be. Some languages (e.g., Spanish and Japanese) use an addressee-based system in which the addressee by virtue of being a speech act participant is not distal, but is necessarily less proximal than the speaker. Alternatively, the notion of distal can be subdivided into nearer and farther, or visible and non-visible, relatively lower and higher, and so forth—presumably depending on the ecological needs of the community. For a study of demonstrative usage in interaction and an argument for minimal semantic description of the demonstrative forms, see Enfield (2003).

7 Reference frames

Reference frames are defined here as the system of locating one object relative to another using a co-ordinate system. As such, a reference frame is distinct from simple deictic location (here/there). Some deictic expressions clearly relate one item to another indirectly by virtue of expressing "by me"/"by you", though these can be understood as essentially indicating a search space without coordinates. A reference frame will narrow a search space by specifying some sort of co-ordinate system on which to locate an object. There are several ways to typologize reference frames, though the most widely followed today is the system most carefully presented in Levinson (2003). In this typology, there are exactly three frames of reference found in natural languages: the *intrinsic*, *relative*, and *absolute*. The intrinsic reference frame is presumed to be a linguistic universal (though languages may vary in how elaborately and when they use this system). Relative and absolute reference frames are taken to be optional alternatives.

As reference frames by definition rely on a co-ordinate system, there is a natural distinction between systems which derive the co-ordinates from features which are *intrinsic* to the Ground and those which derive their co-ordinates from features *extrinsic* to the Ground. Thus, examples of the former, such as "car in front of the store" or "stone to my right" are considered to be both examples of intrinsic reference frame use. Because the description of this Figure-Ground relationship remains constant even if the array of Figure and Ground are rotated relative to the world or an observer, these relationships have also been called "orientation-free" (Danziger 1994, 2001) whereas all other co-ordinate based depictions might be called "orientation-bound".

Alternatively, a major distinction can be drawn between reference frame depiction which relies on speech-act participants (the speaker, but occasionally the hearer) for the determination of the co-ordinates and those depictions which do not derive from speech act participants. That is, "stone to my/our/your right" might be grouped with "car to the (my/our/your) right of the sign". However, following Levinson, the former is intrinsic whereas the latter is *relative* because the latter's use of co-ordinates derive from a viewer who is distinct from the Ground object. That is, in a relative reference frame, the use of *left/right* for relations on a transverse axis and the use of *front/back* for the sagittal axis consist of a transposition of a co-ordinate system from the speech act participant onto a presumed co-ordinate neutral Ground object. Language communities which have been reported to not use the relative reference frame appear to seldom use left and right in their otherwise robust inventory of intrinsic expressions, though intrinsic uses may still occur. This suggests that the use of "left" and "right" terms cross-cuts the terminological distinction of intrinsic versus relative. Indeed, no language appears to have been described which uses one term for "intrinsically left" and another term for "relatively/extrinsically left".

Most discussions of relative reference frame implicitly assume an *egocentric* perspective or a reference frame based on the speaker as viewpoint. However, what we might term an *altercentric* perspective based on the hearer's potentially distinct perspective is frequently found as well, e.g., *place the box to your left of the mailbox*.

As an alternative to both an intrinsic co-ordinate system and a speech-act participant relative system, a co-ordinate system can be derived from the world beyond the Figure, Ground, and viewers more generally. These *absolute* co-ordinates may consist of relatively abstract notions such as "North", which may only be inferred from a landscape. Alternatively, they may be quite context-dependent, perhaps an impromptu use of a local, visible landmark in a direction extending beyond the Ground object (e.g. "toward the wall"). Accordingly, the classification of "absolute reference frame" comprises a considerable range of expressions and widely varying degrees of conventionalization and abstraction across linguistic communities. Note that whereas a relative reference frame is essentially defined as *viewpoint dependent* in that moving the speaker and or hearer inherently disrupts the orientation of the coordinates, absolute reference frames, like intrinsic reference frames, are *viewpoint independent*,.

Mühlhäusler (2001) provides an overview of the reference frame literature from the 1990's. Svorou (1994) examines the use and origins of terms for "before" and "after" (typical relative reference frame terms) across a carefully sampled set of the world's languages. Pederson (2003) argues speakers may not be consistently using coherent reference frames so much as ascribing ad hoc and conventional relationships using a number of cognitive operations. While it may be heuristically useful to have a three-way classification scheme, this may be an oversimplification of actual usage. Spatial terms in natural language seem to regularly extend from one reference frame to another suggesting at a minimum that there are rather porous boundaries between reference frames. For example, the term for "up(hill)" became associated with a particular cardinal direction in Tzeltal (Brown & Levinson 1993) and in Tamil (Pederson 2006).

Generally then, it can be a misleading simplification to describe a linguistic community as "relative-speaking" or "absolute-speaking" without defining the conditions of reference frame usage. The use of a particular reference frame (or a subtype such as a local landmark versus a cardinal direction system) typically varies with context. A New Yorker may speak of *uptown* vs. *downtown* when navigating Manhattan but not when arranging objects on a dinner table. For a discussion of scales in spatial reference see Montello (1993).

Additionally, as Levinson notes, speakers of presumably any language will use environmentally derived absolute co-ordinates when locating objects on a purely vertical dimension. Gravity has special salience and can almost always be referenced. However, even on the horizontal plane at the same scale, speakers will often use one co-ordinate system for transverse relations and another for sagittal relations. Even within a single reference frame, several languages have been reported as distinguishing directions along one axis of a reference frame (e.g. the sagittal or inland/seaward), but not differentiating direction on the other axis (e.g. the transverse or along the coast). See, e.g., Wassmann & Dasen (1998).

Indeed, the sagittal and transverse relationships have such perceptually distinctive properties it is remarkable that they are ever expressed using a single reference frame. As a simple example, English *left of the tree* and *in front of the tree* are both typically described as expressing the relative frame of reference. However, the assignment of "left" uses a transposition of the viewer's co-ordinates without any rotation as though the viewer were standing in the place of the tree facing the same direction. Hill (1974) describes rural Hausa speakers as using an *aligned* strategy in which the "front" of a tree is the side further from the speaker. However, to assign the "front" of the tree in French or English, the coordinates need to be rotated 180° form the left/right projection such that the front of the tree is treated as though it were facing the viewer. This *opposing* strategy is described in Vandeloise (1991). As a third variation, "front" may be used as an *ascribed intrinsic* use in which a Ground is treated as having a front by virtue of an ascribed path or direction rather than a current feature of the Ground. Someone standing at a speaker's back might nonetheless be "in front" of the speaker if that person is closer to the "head" of a queue.

There are relatively few studies that systematically explore how speakers assign reference frames when choices might be available, however Grabowski & Weiss (1996) survey experimental data from speakers of Western European languages. Anecdotal evidence suggests that, cross-linguistically, there is considerable variation in the extent to which different spatial terms can be used for contact and adjacency relations "(immediately) at my left" vs. projected far from a Ground or viewer.

Given the acute differences in the logical properties of each reference frame, speakers must make quite different calculations about the spatial properties of scenes in order to speak about them. Levinson (2003) argues that there is an inherent untranslatability (at least for some situations) between these reference frames. For example, knowing that a bottle is (intrinsically) in front of a chair does not allow one to infer whether that bottle is also to the north (absolute) or to the speaker's right (relative) of the chair. These logical differences which vary across linguistic communities, coupled with the foundational properties of space in cognition more generally, make investigations into reference frames ideal candidates for studies in linguistic relativity. See especially Pederson et al. (1998) and Levinson (2003). For an argument that perception need not be reference-frame dependent see Dokic & Pacherie (2006).

8 Motion events (dynamic spatial relations)

Thus far, we have focused on essentially static location. When there is a change of location, we refer to (translocational) *motion events*. Just as static locations are associated with stative expressions, motion events are associated with change of state expressions via metaphor, image schema, or simple analogy.

Talmy (1985) argues that there are certain recurrent elements to any motion event. The most fundamental of these is the fact of motion itself, such that static location can be treated as the limiting case of zero motion. There is also almost always expression of the Figure, the Ground, and a path. Beyond this, languages commonly express a manner of motion and sometimes a cause of motion. His approach groups languages in either of two ways. The first examines which semantic element is typically *conflated* in the meaning of the verb along with the fact of motion or location. For example, the path-conflation verb *ascend* describes both a fact of motion and an upward path. In contrast, a manner-conflating verb such as *crawl* conflates information about the particular manner of motion used by the Figure. Less common patterns exist, such as Figure-conflating: a verb like *rain* conflates the Figure (water drops) with motion (and perhaps direction of motion). Figure-conflation is an atypical pattern for English, but Talmy describes this as a common pattern in Atsugewi.

More widely cited is Talmy's second typological distinction which examines which grammatical element will express the path. In a language with path-conflating verbs, simple paths will typically be expressed by the verb (the "Romance language pattern"). In languages without common use of path-conflating verbs, path is expressed in *satellites*, elements such as verb particles that are peripheral to the verb root (the "Germanic pattern"). Languages are assumed to be typically dominated by one of these two patterns and this has led to a number of linguistic relativity studies arguing both for and against the relevance of this linguistic pattern to non-linguistic categorization (Finkbeiner et al. 2002; Gennari et al. 2002; Loucks & Pederson 2011; Papafragou et al. 2002).

Even with careful semantic analysis, it is not always clear whether a particular manner of motion verb is also a verb of translocational motion. Languages with obligatory path verbs typically are described as having manner verbs which in the absence of path verbs express manner without translational motion (e.g., a "flying" overhead without an entailment of motion across the sky), but the relation between what is semantically entailed and what is pragmatically implied is often not clear, especially for less extensively documented languages. Further complicating the semantics of motion verbs is the challenge of distinguishing between motion and fictive motion (see section 2.2. above).

9 Conclusion

Given the fundamental nature of spatial relations in human cognition, the extent to which expressions of space permeate language is scarcely surprising. While the semantics of spatial relations were once considered largely universal if not innate, in recent years, there has been a growing interest in exploring the range and depth of cross-linguistic variation. It has become clear that relying on simple translations of morphemes had overly biased analysts' perception toward universality. A form such as "on" may be used quite differently in different languages and a form like "right" may refer to critically different reference frames depending on the language and cultural context of use. In other words, careful semantic analysis proves critical even for the seemingly most fundamental expressions.

10 References

Anderson, John M. 1973. *An Essay Concerning Aspect. Some Considerations of a General Character Arising from the Abbe Darrigol's Analysis of the Basque Verb*. The Hague: Mouton.
Bierwisch, Manfred & Ewald Lang (eds.) 1989. *Dimensional Adjectives: Grammatical Structure and Conceptual Interpretation*. Berlin: Springer.
Bowerman, Melissa 1996. Learning how to structure space for language: A crosslinguistic perspective. In: P. Bloom et al. (eds.). *Language and Space*. Cambridge, MA: The MIT Press, 385–436.
Bowerman, Melissa & Eric Pederson 1992. Cross-linguistic perspectives on topological spatial relationships. Paper presented at the *91th Annual Meeting of the American Anthropological Association*, San Francisco, CA, December 2–6.
Brown, Penelope 1994. The INs and ONs of Tzeltal locative expressions: The semantics of static descriptions of location. *Linguistics* 32, 743–790.
Brown, Penelope & Stephen C. Levinson 1993. "Uphill" and "downhill" in Tzeltal. *Journal of Linguistic Anthropology* 3, 46–74.
Carlson, Laura A. & Ryan Kenny 2006. Interpreting spatial terms involves simulating interactions. *Psychonomic Bulletin & Review* 13, 682–88.
Carlson-Radvansky, Laura A., Eric S. Covey & Kathleen M. Lattanzi 1999. "What" effects on "where": Functional influences on spatial relations. *Psychological Science* 10, 516–521.
Choi, Soonja & Melissa Bowerman 1991. Learning to express motion events in English and Korean: The influence of language-specific lexicalization patterns. *Cognition* 41, 83–121.
Clark, Herbert H. 1973. Space, time, semantics, and the child. In: T.E. Moore (ed.). *Cognitive Development and the Acquisition of Language*. New York: Academic Press, 27–63.
Coventry, Kenny R., Merce Prat-Sala & Lynn Richards 2001. The interplay between geometry and function in the comprehension of 'over', 'under', 'above', and 'below'. *Journal of Memory and Language* 44, 376–398.
Danziger, Eve 1994. Out of sight, out of mind: Person, perception and function in Mopan Maya spatial deixis. *Linguistics* 32, 885–907.
Danziger, Eve 2001. *Relatively Speaking: Language, Thought, and Kinship among the Mopan Maya*. Oxford: Oxford University Press.
DeLancey, Scott 1991. Event construal and case role assignment. In: L.A. Sutton, C. Johnson & R. Shields (eds.). *Proceedings of the Annual Meeting of the Berkeley Linguistics Society (= BLS) 17*. Berkeley, CA: Berkeley Linguistics Society, 338–353.
Diessel, Holger 1999. *Demonstratives: Forms, Function, and Grammaticalization*. Amsterdam: Benjamins.

Dokic, Jérôme & Elisabeth Pacherie 2006. On the very idea of a frame of reference. In: M. Hickmann & S. Robert (eds.). *Space in Languages Linguistic Systems and Cognitive Categories*. Amsterdam: Benjamins, 259–280.

Enfield, Nick J. 2003. Demonstratives in space and interaction: Data from Lao speakers and implications for semantic analysis. *Language* 79, 82–117.

Feist, Michele I. 2000. *On 'in' and 'on': An Investigation into the Linguistic Encoding of Spatial Scenes*. Ph.D. dissertation. Northwestern University, Evanston, IL.

Feist, Michele I. 2004. Talking about space: A cross-linguistic perspective. Paper presented at the *26th Annual Meeting of the Cognitive Science Society*, Chicago, IL, August 5–7.

Finkbeiner, Matthew, Janet Nicol, Delia Greth & Kumiko Nakamura 2002. The role of language in memory for actions. *Journal of Psycholinguistic Research* 31, 447–457.

Gennari, Silvia P., Steven A. Sloman, Barbara C. Malt & W. Tecumseh Fitch 2002. Motion events in language and cognition. *Cognition* 83, 49–79.

Grabowski, Joachim & Petra Weiss 1996. Determinanten der Interpretation dimensionaler Lokalizationsäußerungen: Experimente in fünf Sprachen. *Sprache und Kognition* 15, 234–250.

Grinevald, Colette 2006. The expression of static location in a typological perspective. In: M. Hickmann & S. Robert (eds.). *Space in Languages: Linguistic Systems and Cognitive Categories*. Amsterdam: Benjamins, 29–58.

Gruber, Jeffrey S. 1965. *Studies in Lexical Relations*. Ph.D. dissertation. MIT, Cambridge, MA.

Haase, Martin 2001. Local deixis. In: M. Haspelmath et al. (eds.). *Sprachtypologie und sprachliche Universalien—Language Typology and Language Universals. Ein internationales Handbuch—An International Handbook* (HSK 20.1). Berlin: de Gruyter, 760–768.

Haviland, John B. 1992. Seated and settled: Tzotzil verbs of the body. *Zeitschrift für Phonetik, Sprachwissenschaft und Kommunikationsforschung* 45, 543–561.

Herskovits, Anette 1986. *Language and Spatial Cognition: An Interdisciplinary Study of the Prepositions in English*. Cambridge: Cambridge University Press.

Hickmann, Maya & Stéphane Robert (eds.) 2006. *Space in Languages Linguistic Systems and Cognitive Categories*. Amsterdam: Benjamins.

Hill, Clifford 1974. Spatial perception and linguistic encoding: A case study in Hausa and English. *Studies in African Linguistics* 5, 135–148.

Imai, Shingo 2003. *Spatial Deixis*. Ph.D. dissertation. State University of New York, Buffalo, NY.

Jackendoff, Ray 1983. *Semantics and Cognition*. Cambridge, MA: The MIT Press.

Jackendoff, Ray 1987. On beyond zebra: The relation of linguistic and visual information. *Cognition* 26, 89–114.

Kahr, Joan C. 1975. *Adpositions and Locationals: Typology and Diachronic Development* (Stanford University Working Papers on Language Universals 19). Stanford, CA: Stanford University.

Klein, Wolfgang 1991. Raumausdrücke. *Linguistische Berichte* 132, 77–114.

Klein, Wolfgang 2001. Deiktische Orientierung. In: M. Haspelmath et al. (eds.). *Sprachtypologie und sprachliche Universalien—Language Typology and Language Universals. Ein internationales Handbuch—An International Handbook* (HSK 20.1). Berlin: de Gruyter, 575–589.

Lakoff, George & Mark Johnson 1980. *Metaphors We Live By*. Chicago, IL: The University of Chicago Press.

Landau, Barbara & Ray Jackendoff. 1993. "What" and "where" in spatial language and spatial cognition. *Behavioral and Brain Sciences* 16, 217–238.

Lang, Ewald 2001. Spatial dimension terms. In: M. Haspelmath et al. (eds.). *Sprachtypologie und sprachliche Universalien—Language Typology and Language Universals. Ein internationales Handbuch—An International Handbook* (HSK 20.2). Berlin: de Gruyter, 1251–1275.

Langacker, Ronald W. 1986. Abstract motion. In: V. Nikiforidou et al. (eds.). *Proceedings of the Twelfth Annual Meeting of the Berkeley Linguistics Society.* Berkeley, CA: Berkeley Linguistics Society, 455–471.

Langacker, Ronald W. 1991. *Foundations of Cognitive Grammar. Vol. II: Descriptive Application.* Stanford, CA: Stanford University Press.

Levinson, Stephen C. 2003. *Space in Language and Cognition: Explorations in Cognitive Diversity.* Cambridge: Cambridge University Press.

Levinson, Stephen C. & David Wilkins (eds.) 2006a. *Grammars of Space: Explorations in Cognitive Diversity.* Cambridge: Cambridge University Press.

Levinson, Stephen & David Wilkins 2006b. Towards a semantic typology of spatial description. In: S. Levinson & D. Wilkins (eds.). *Grammars of Space: Explorations in Cognitive Diversity.* Cambridge: Cambridge University Press, 512–552.

Loucks, Jeff & Eric Pederson 2011. Linguistic and non-linguistic categorization of complex motion events. In: J. Bohnemeyer & E. Pederson (eds.). *Event Representation in Language.* Cambridge: Cambridge University Press, 108–133.

Matsumoto, Yo 1996a. Subjective-change expressions in Japanese and their cognitive and linguistic bases. In: G. Fauconnier & E. Sweetser (eds.). *Spaces, Worlds, and Grammar.* Chicago, IL: The Univerisity of Chicago Press, 124–156.

Matsumoto, Yo 1996b. Subjective motion and English and Japanese verbs. *Cognitive Linguistics* 7, 183–226.

Miller, George A. & Philip N. Johnson-Laird. 1976. *Language and Perception.* Cambridge, MA: The Belknap Press of Harvard University Press.

Montello, Daniel R. 1993. Scale and multiple psychologies of space. In: A.U. Frank & I. Campari (eds.). *Spatial Information Theory.* Heidelberg: Springer, 312–321.

Mühlhäusler, Peter 2001. Universals and typology of space. In: M. Haspelmath et al. (eds.). *Sprachtypologie und sprachliche Universalien—Language Typology and Language Universals. Ein internationales Handbuch—An International Handbook* (HSK 20.1). Berlin: de Gruyter, 568–574.

Papafragou, Anna, Chris Massey & Lila Gleitman 2002. Shake, rattle, 'n' roll: The representation of motion in language and cognition. *Cognition* 84, 189–219.

Pederson, Eric 1998. Spatial language, reasoning, and variation across Tamil communities. In: P. Zima & V. Tax (eds.). *Language and Location in Space and Time.* München: Lincom Europa, 111–119.

Pederson, Eric 2003. How many reference frames? In: C. Freksa et al. (eds). *Spatial Cognition III.* Heidelberg: Springer, 287–304.

Pederson, Eric 2006. Tamil spatial language. In: S. Levinson & D. Wilkins (eds.). *Grammars of Space: Explorations in Cognitive Diversity.* Cambridge: Cambridge University Press, 400–436.

Pederson, Eric 2010. Linguistic relativity. In: B. Heine & H. Narrog (eds.). *The Oxford Handbook of Linguistic Analysis.* Oxford: Oxford University Press, 663–677.

Svorou, Soteria 1994. *The Grammar of Space.* Amsterdam: Benjamins.

Talmy, Leonard 1977. Rubber-sheet cognition in language. In: W.A. Beach et al. (eds.). *Papers form the Regional Meeting of the Chicago Linguistic Society (= CLS) 13.* Chicago, IL: Chicago Linguistic Society, 612–628.

Talmy, Leonard 1983. How language structures space. In: H. Pick & L. Acredolo (eds.). *Spatial Orientation: Theory, Research, and Application*. New York: Plenum, 225–282.

Talmy, Leonard 1985. Lexicalization patterns: Semantic structure in lexical form. In: T. Shopen (ed.). *Language Typology and Syntactic Description. Vol. III: Grammatical Categories and the Lexicon*. Cambridge: Cambridge University Press, 57–149.

Talmy, Leonard 1996. Fictive motion in language and "ception". In: P. Bloom et al. (eds.). *Language and Space*. Cambridge, MA: The MIT Press, 211–276.

Tenbrink, Thora 2005. *Semantics and Application of Spatial Dimensional Terms in English and German* (Report Series of the Transregional Collaborative Research Center SFB/TR 8 Spatial Cognition Universität Bremen / Universität Freiburg, Report No. 004–03/2005). Bremen: University of Bremen.

Tenbrink, Thora 2007. *Space, Time, and the Use of Language: An Investigation of Relationships*. Berlin: Mouton de Gruyter.

Traugott, E. 1978. On the expression of spatiotemporal relations in language. In: J. Greenberg (ed.). *Universals of Human Language. Vol. 3: Word Structure*. Stanford, CA: Stanford University Press. 369–400.

Vandeloise, Claude 1991. *Spatial Prepositions: A Case Study from French*. Chicago, IL: The University of Chicago Press.

van Voorst, Jan 1993. A Localist model for event semantics. *Journal of Semantics* 10, 65–111.

van Voorst, Jan 1996. Some systematic differences between the Dutch, French and English transitive construction. *Language Sciences* 18, 227–245.

Wassmann, Jürg & Pierre R. Dasen 1998. Balinese spatial orientation: Some empirical evidence for moderate linguistic relativity. *Journal of the Royal Anthropological Institute (New Series)* 4, 689–711.

Young, Robert W. 2000. *The Navajo Verb System: An Overview*. Albuquerque, NM: University of New Mexico Press.

Gerd Fritz
5 Theories of meaning change: An overview

1   Basic issues of historical semantics —— 113
2   19th century historical semasiology and the ideational theory of meaning —— 115
3   Diachronic structural semantics —— 119
4   Cognitive semantics —— 123
5   Theories of grammaticalization —— 126
6   Meaning as use and pragmatic semantics —— 130
7   Formal semantics and pragmatics —— 135
8   Conclusion —— 138
9   References —— 141

Abstract: Semantics as a scientific study first arose in the context of 19th century historical linguistics, and also in 20th century semantics and especially since the 1980s many foundational issues of semantics have been discussed in connection with problems of meaning change, e.g. the problem of polysemy. The kinds of questions that can be asked concerning meaning change and the types of possible answers to these questions are determined to a large extent by the theories of meaning presupposed in formulating these questions. So the history of historical semantics is highly instructive for a study of the ways in which the development of lexical semantics was advanced by competing theoretical conceptions of word meaning. Therefore my discussion of important traditions of research in historical semantics will be linked to and partly organized in relation to the theories of meaning embraced by scholars in the respective research traditions, e.g. traditional semasiology and its present-day successor cognitive semantics, structural semantics, and pragmatic semantics. Part of this history of theories will be told as a history of controversies. Aspects of meaning and change of meaning that have been discussed in these traditions include the conditions of semantic variation and change, types and regularities of meaning change, polysemy and its relation to meaning change, diffusion of semantic innovations, and the connections between semantic change and changes in social and cultural traditions.

1 Basic issues of historical semantics

Theories of meaning change have to give answers at least to some of the following questions: (i) Under what conditions are semantic innovations possible? (ii) Are

Gerd Fritz, Gießen, Germany

https://doi.org/10.1515/9783110589825-005

there characteristic types and regularities of meaning change? (iii) How do universal constraints and cultural traditions interact in meaning change? (iv) How do innovations become routinized and conventionalized? (v) What are the paths and mechanisms of diffusion of semantic innovations? (vi) How does semantic innovation change the internal structure of a cluster of senses of a lexical item (the question of polysemy)? (vii) How does semantic innovation change the semantic relationships between different expressions (the question of meaning relations and semantic fields)? (viii) How are meaning changes related to changes in the history of mind, the history of society, the history of theories (changes of knowledge and changes of concepts) etc.? (ix) How do we interpret texts from earlier historical periods (the hermeneutical question)? (x) What counts as an explanation of a meaning change?

One of the aims of this article is to show which of these questions have been tackled so far in different research traditions, in which ways and with what amount of success. The kinds of detailed questions that can be asked concerning meaning change and the types of possible answers to these questions are determined to a large extent by the theories of meaning presupposed in formulating these questions. Therefore my discussion of important traditions of research in historical semantics will be linked to and partly organized in relation to the theories of meaning embraced by scholars in the respective research traditions.

The relationship between historical semantics and theoretical semantics is not a one-sided affair. Not only did semantics as a scientific study first arise in the context of 19th century historical linguistics, but also in 20th century semantics and especially since the 1980s many foundational issues of semantics have been discussed in connection with problems of meaning change, e.g. the problem of polysemy. What Blank & Koch wrote about cognitive semantics could be generalized to other approaches to semantics as well:

> In our opinion, investigation of diachronic problems can, in turn, sharpen our view for fundamental semantic processes and should therefore be able to advance theorizing in cognitive linguistics. In this sense, historical semantics is an ideal testing ground for semantic models and theories [...].
>
> (Blank & Koch 1999: 1)

This includes issues like the boundaries between semantics and pragmatics, and methodological questions like minimalism. A case could be made for the view that theories of meaning which contribute to our understanding of meaning change are not only wider in scope than those that do not, but that they are actually superior. It is therefore not surprising that recently even scholars in the field of formal semantics, a family of approaches to semantics originally not attracted to historical questions, have taken up matters of flexibility of meaning and meaning change (cf. Eckardt 2006, and article 8 [this volume] (Eckardt) *Grammaticalization and semantic reanalysis*). Generally speaking, the history of historical semantics is highly instructive for a study of the ways in which the development of lexical semantics was advanced by competing theoretical conceptions of word meaning. So part of this history of theories can be told as a history of controversies. In this context it is worth noting that the discussion of a rapprochement between competing schools of semantics (cognitive semantics, pragmatic semantics, formal semantics) which has been initiated in the last few years has also partly taken place in the context of historical semantics (cf. Geeraerts 2002; Eckardt, von Heusinger & Schwarze 2003; Fritz 2011; and article 7 [this volume] (Geeraerts) *Cognitive approaches to diachronic semantics*). From the point of view of empirical research in semantics, the history of word meanings in different languages is an invaluable repository of data for semantic analysis and a source of inspiration for the treatment of questions like what is universal and what is culturally determined in meaning and change of meaning.

The history of historical semantics is also highly instructive for a study of the ways in which the development of lexical semantics was advanced by competing theoretical conceptions of word meaning. Aspects of meaning and change of meaning that have been discussed in these traditions include the conditions of semantic variation and change, types and regularities of meaning change, polysemy and its relation to meaning change, diffusion of semantic innovations, and the connections between semantic change and changes in social and cultural traditions.

2 19th century historical semasiology and the ideational theory of meaning

Throughout the early development of historical semantics up to 1930 and in some cases much later (cf. Kronasser 1952) a view of meaning was taken for granted which has been called the ideational theory of meaning (cf. Alston 1964: 22–25). The classic statement of this theoretical view had been given by Locke as follows: „Words, in their primary or immediate signification, stand for nothing but the *Ideas* in the mind of him that uses them, how imperfectly soever, or carelessly [sic] those *Ideas* are collected from the Things, which they are supposed to represent" (Locke 1689/1975: 405). By the time historical semantics emerged as a scientific enterprise in the second half of the 19th century, this view was more or less the common-sense view of meaning (cf. article 9 [Semantics: Foundations, History and Methods] (Nerlich) *Emergence of semantics*). The fact that Frege and other contemporaries forcefully critized this view on the grounds that ideas ("Vorstellungen") were purely subjective, whereas meaning ("Sinn") ought to be in some sense intersubjective, was either not noticed or not considered a serious problem (cf. Frege 1892/1969: 43f; Frege 1918/1966: 40ff; cf. article 3 [Semantics: Foundations, History and Methods] (Textor) *Sense and reference*). (The problem of the subjectivity of ideas had of course been noticed by Locke.) One consequence of the ideational theory of meaning was that semantics was considered to be intimately related to matters of psychology, which was an unquestioned assumption for many linguists of the period. This attitude was, of course, also fostered by the fact that by the end of the 19th century psychology had become a highly successful and prestigious field of research. So at least paying lip-service to the psychological relevance of historical work was also a matter of scientific rhetoric for many linguists—very much like today. In the first paragraph of his classic "Meaning and change of meaning" Stern explicitly stated: "The study of meanings, as of all psychic phenomena, belongs to psychology" (Stern 1931: 1). It is therefore not surprising that the problem of lexical innovation was largely posed as a problem of individual psychology: How do new associations of ideas come about in the mind of an individual? To explain a change of meaning was to show how the mind could bridge the gap between a first cluster of ideas, the original meaning, and a second cluster, the new meaning. A case in point is the treatment of metaphor as a potentially innovative semantic technique. An explanation of a meaning change could be considered successful from this point of view if the gap between the original and the new set of ideas could be shown to be small, if the gap could be reduced by the introduction of plausible intermediary stages, or if it could be bridged with reference to general laws of association (cf. Wundt 1904: 623). This methodological principle, which one could call the principle of minimal steps, was based on a psychological hypothesis which was rarely made explicit as it was again firmly grounded in common-sense assumptions: The mind, like nature, does not take excessive leaps.

From this point of view three stages of a change of meaning could be differentiated: In the first stage a word is used in a certain context, in which a certain (additional) idea becomes connected to the word. In a second, transitory stage the new idea is more intimately connected to the word through continuous use, so that the additional idea is called up in the mind even outside the original specific context. Finally, in the last stage, the new idea becomes the central idea ("Hauptbedeutung") which again admits new combinations of ideas. So what happens is that a secondary idea which is originally only associated to the word in certain specific contexts gains in strength and becomes the primary idea (cf. Stöcklein 1898: 14f). This view anticipates both the recent emphasis on the importance of certain "critical contexts" of innovation (cf. Diewald 2002) and the cognitivist idea of shifts from peripheral uses to prototypical uses in meaning change and vice versa (cf. Geeraerts 1997).

In a classic of historical semantics, the chapter on meaning change in his book "Principien der Sprachgeschichte", Hermann Paul introduced a refinement of the ideational theory by distinguishing between established meaning ("usuelle Bedeutung") and contextual meaning ("occasionelle Bedeutung"), a distinction which plays a fundamental role in his theory of meaning change (Paul 1886: 66ff). He defined the established meaning as the total content of ideas which is associated with the word for the members of a community of speakers, whereas the "occasional" meaning is defined as the content of ideas which the individual speaker associates with the utterance of a word and which he expects the hearer to associate with this utterance as well. "Occasional" meaning is considered to be richer in content and narrower in range than conventional meaning, it is generally more specialized and monosemous, whereas conventional meaning is more general and may be polysemous. The latter explication shows that Paul did not have at his disposal the sharp distinction between sentence (or word) meaning and utterer's meaning which Grice introduced in his seminal article "Meaning" (Grice 1957) and which was also inherent in Wittgenstein's distinction between "bedeuten" and "meinen" (Wittgenstein 1953). The main tenet of Paul's theory is that every meaning change starts from an innovative occasional meaning. Such an innovative use may then be remembered by a speaker and thereby become a precedent for later uses. Through repeated application of the word in its occasional meaning the occasional meaning may become established in the community of speakers and thereby become "usual". The next generation of speakers will then learn the word in its new conventional meaning. As an important element in his theory of meaning change Paul assumed that the types of meaning change exactly correspond to the types of modification of occasional meaning. This assumption makes the essential theoretical link between synchronic meaning variation and change of meaning, which up to the present day connects pragmatics and historical semantics. Paul's theory of meaning change also comprises other elements which are familiar to modern historical semanticist, e.g. a version of the concept of common knowledge as a basis for semantic innovation and the idea that knowledge is socially distributed, which leads to semantic specialization in different social groups. The importance of context for the emergence of innovations was stressed by other authors of the semasiological tradition as well, e.g. by Wegener (1885) and Sperber (1923/1965), who explicitly differentiated between syntactic context and context of situation ("Situationszusammenhang") (Sperber 1923/1965: 25). The relevance of the syntactic context for the emergence of semantics innovations, which has also recently been emphasized again (cf. Eckardt 2006), was stressed by Paul as well as by other contemporaries (e.g. Stöcklein

1898) and later representatives of semasiological research (e.g. Wellander 1917). Another aspect of meaning change that was emphasized by several authors of this tradition was that, as mentioned before, in an early stage innovations are often restricted to a limited context from which they are then later generalized (cf. Stöcklein 1898: 13f; Sperber 1923/1965: 24).

One corollary of Paul's and others' view of meaning change was that meaning change leads to polysemy and that types of meaning change are reflected in types of polysemy, an idea that has recently been taken up again by various researchers (cf. Blank 1997; Fritz 1995; Geeraerts 1997). The most insightful early treatment of polysemy was due to Michel Bréal, who, in his "Essai de Sémantique" (1897), introduced the term *polysémie* and devoted a chapter to this phenomenon. Whereas polysemy was often thought of as a defect of language, Bréal pointed out the functional advantages of polysemy: "Une nouvelle acception équivaut à un mot nouveau" (Bréal 1897/1924: 146).

Outside the mainstream of traditional semasiology we find an important contribution to the theory of meaning change in a classic article by Antoine Meillet, "Comment les mots changent de sens", published in 1905 in "Année Sociologique" (Meillet 1905/1965). In this programmatic article, Meillet presented the outline of a sociolinguistic view of meaning change which consists in an integrated theory of innovation and diffusion. According to this theory, semantic changes arise mainly due to the fact that speech communities are heterogeneous and that they are organized into different social groups. In a rudimentary form Meillet's picture contains all the ingredients of later languages-in-contact theories of innovation and diffusion.

One of the main issues of late 19th and early 20th century historical semantics was the question of the regularity of meaning change. As the discovery of "sound laws" (e.g. Grimm's law) was the paradigm of successful linguistic research in the second half of the 19th century, one easily came to the conclusion that semantics should aim to find "semantic laws" on a par with sound laws. An important step in accounting for the variety of semantic innovation was to show how that innovation was guided. In remarkable unison the handbooks on historical semasiology which appeared from the 1870s onwards (Bréal 1897/1924; Darmesteter 1887; Nyrop 1903; Paul 1886; Whitney 1876) dealt with this question by giving a classification of types of semantic change. Seeking to impose order on the seeming chaos of semantic developments, they made use of categories well-known from classical logic and rhetoric: restriction of meaning, expansion of meaning, metaphor, metonymy, euphemism, and irony. The productive idea embodied in these classifications was the application of a methodological principle which had been forcefully proclaimed by the so-called Neogrammarians (Paul and others), the principle that the observation of present-day linguistic facts should serve as the basis for the explanation of the linguistic past. Following this principle, general knowledge about contemporary forms and conditions of referring uses, metaphorical and euphemistic speech etc. could be brought to bear on the explanation of historical changes. Of these categories of meaning change the first two (expansion and restriction of meaning) were often criticized as being non-explanatory, merely classificatory categories taken from logic, whereas a description of a semantic innovation as a case of metaphorical innovation was obviously accepted as explanatory. But, of course, the assertion that innovations of these types frequently occurred was no law statement, and therefore assigning an innovation to one of these types was, strictly speaking, no causal explanation. The same can be said for certain other generalizations that were formulated in this tradition and were called "laws", e.g. the generalization that semantically closely related expressions tend to show similar meaning changes (cf. Sperber 1923/1965: 67; Stern 1931: 185ff). In many cases the observation of parallel developments, which is of course a methodically important step, amounts to no more than the documentation of data which call for explanation. (For further examples and discussion of the question of "semantic laws" cf. Fritz 1998: 870ff.) Generally speaking, explicit reflection on what could count as an explanation of meaning change was fairly rare in this period, and it was only much later that basic questions concerning the concept of explanation in historical semantics were raised (cf. Coseriu 1974; Keller 1990). Overviews of semasiological research can be found in Jaberg (1901), Kronasser (1952), Ullmann (1957), and Nerlich (1992) (cf. also article 9 [Semantics: Foundations, History and Methods] (Nerlich) *Emergence of semantics*).

3 Diachronic structural semantics

In the late 1920s and early 1930s, structuralist methods, which had been particularly successful in phonology, began to become applied also to the field of semantics. Essentially, structural semantics is not a theory of meaning at all but rather a methodology for semantic analysis. The basic idea that semantic analysis of a linguistic item should not be restricted to individual words but should also take into consideration its neighbours, i.e. words with a similar meaning, and its opponents, i.e. words with antonymous meaning, had been well-known to late 19th century linguists before the advent of structuralism (e.g. Paul 1895). It is interesting to see that in describing parts of the vocabulary where the systematic character of groups of expressions is fairly obvious, pre-structuralist and non-structuralist authors often displayed a quasi-structuralist approach. This is true, for example, of descriptions of the history of kinship terms or forms of address.

In a more programmatic and theoretically explicit way this basic structuralist idea had been spelt out by Ferdinand de Saussure in his "Cours de linguistique générale" (1916). In Part 2, Chapter IV, § 2 of this groundbreaking book, which was compiled and edited by his pupils after his death, de Saussure discussed the difference between the meaning of a word and its "value" ("valeur"). He started out from the traditional definition of meaning as the idea conventionally connected to the sound pattern of an expression and then went on to argue that this definition captures only one aspect of meaning, which has to be complemented with a second aspect, the "value", i.e. the position which the respective word occupies in a system of lexical items. To illustrate this point he compared the meaning/value of the French word *mouton* and the English word *sheep*. The two words, so his argument goes, may have the same meaning, i.e. they evoke the same idea of a certain kind of animal, but they do not have the same value, as there is in English a second word in opposition to *sheep*, namely *mutton*, which is not the case with French *mouton*. Apart from the fact that this description could be improved upon, this theory obviously shows a certain tension between the two aspects that determine meaning, which was not clarified by de Saussure or his followers like Trier (1931). The question remained open in which way meaning as idea and meaning as value contribute to the overall meaning of an expression. This theoretical problem did however not interfere with the application of the basic methodological principle.

Starting from de Saussure's fundamental assumptions and applying his general methodological principles to the field of semantics, Jost Trier and some of his contemporaries (e.g. Weisgerber 1927) criticized the atomist views of traditional semasiology, as they saw it, and developed a type of structuralist semantics which in its early form was called the theory of *conceptual fields* ("Begriffsfelder", Trier 1931), sometimes also called *lexical fields* ("Wortfelder") or *semantic fields* ("Bedeutungsfelder"). The basic tenets of this theory have been described by Ullmann (1957), Gloning (2002) and others. Therefore I shall only point out those facets of the theory that are particulary interesting from the point of view of theories of meaning change. As mentioned before, words were no longer considered as isolated units but as elements of a lexical system. Their value was defined by their position in a system of lexical oppositions and could be described in terms of a network of semantic relations. Trier himself used the concepts of hyponymy ("Oberbegriff") and antonymy ("Gegensinn"), however, due to his informal style of presentation he did not attempt to make explicit these or other types of sense relations (cf. Lyons 1963), nor did he attempt the kind of componential analysis that later structuralist authors used (e.g. Bech 1951). Change of meaning, in Trier's view, consisted in the change of the structure of a lexical system from one synchronic stage of a language to the next.

Within the framework of this theory the task of historical semantics could no longer be the description and explanation of the historical fate of individual words ("Einzelwortschicksale") but rather the comparison of the structures of successive synchronic semantic fields along the time axis. Trier used his methods to analyze stages in the history of expressions of intellectual appraisal in German from Old High German to Middle High German, i.e. adjectives corresponding in meaning approximately to Latin words like *sapiens* and *prudens* or English words like *wise, intelligent, clever, cunning* etc. as well as the respective substantives. Starting by assuming a given conceptual field and then differentially analyzing the expressions allocated to this field, he used an onomasiological approach on a large corpus of medieval texts. Trier's pupils and followers applied this method to later historical developments in the intellectual field and to other fields like perception verbs (Seiffert 1968) or adjectives of quantification and dimensionality (Stanforth 1967). Whereas Trier's approach concentrated on the paradigmatic dimension, i.e. the dimension of items replaceable for each other in a certain position in the linear sequence, other authors dealt with the syntagmatic dimension, i.e. the co-occurrence of words in sentences. Again, this topic had also been dealt with by pre-structuralist authors like Sperber who, in his classic booklet (Sperber 1923/1965) analyzed the collocations ("Konsoziationen") of various expressions. A well-known early structuralist paper on this topic is Porzig (1934), where the co-occurrence of words like *blond* and *hair* or *to fell* and *trees* is described. Historical changes in this dimension could also be considered part of the change of meaning of a given expression. However, authors of this period did not do much to clarify in what sense co-occurrence relations could be considered to be an aspect of the meaning of a word. This was only later achieved in the development of distributional semantics (cf. Firth 1957), an approach which has recently gained renewed attraction due to new techniques of corpus analysis, which make it possible to analyze characteristic collocations and their historical change in great detail and with a view to quantitative data (cf. Heringer 1999).

Later versions of structural semantics, which were theoretically more ambitious and descriptively more precise, were developed and applied to historical material by scholars like Gunnar Bech (1951) and Eugenio Coseriu (1964). Bech (1951) used a system of semantic features to characterize the meaning of lexical items belonging to a closely-patterned domain of vocabulary, namely the modal verbs of German (e.g. *müssen, können, dürfen, mögen*). A similar method was applied to the history of English modals by Tellier (1962). When the semantics of modals and their history became a focus of semantic research some twenty years ago (cf. Fritz 1997a; Diewald 1999; Traugott & Dasher 2002: 105ff), these classical studies also received new interest.

From the point of view of the theory of meaning, the semantic features used by Bech involve problems concerning their status and their formal properties, which they share with other concepts of semantic features and which have been discussed by Lewis (1972: 169ff) and others. It is not clear whether the expressions used to indicate the features were considered to be simply descriptive natural language predicates or part of a special metalinguistic vocabulary or if they were even meant to indicate a universal store of concepts. And, of course, the feature language had no syntax, which considerably restricted its descriptive power.

Criticism of structuralist semantics, especially feature semantics (*Semantic Markerese*, as Lewis called it), has come from various quarters, from truth-functional theorists, as mentioned before, and more recently from cognitivist and "meaning-as-use" theorists. Among the properties and assumptions of structural semantics which make it less adequate for historical semantics than other present-day semantic theories, the following have frequently been mentioned:

i. Structuralist theory is strong on the aspects of the language system ("la langue"), but weak on the properties of speech ("la parole"), i.e. the use of language. As semantic innovation and diffusion are matters of language use, large portions of historical semantics cannot be adequately treated within the framework of structural semantics.
ii. As structuralist semantics is focussed on the analysis of language-internal relationships, it has to draw a strict boundary between semantic and encyclopaedic knowledge, which makes it difficult to explain how innovative patterns of use like metaphor or metonymy work.
iii. Due to its minimalist methodology, structuralist semantics is not well equipped to analyze cases of polysemy, which play a central role in semantic development.
iv. Semantic features tend to be viewed in terms of necessary and collectively sufficient conditions for the correct use of an expression. This view precludes a satisfactory analysis of cases of family resemblances and prototype effects of the kind that Wittgenstein and cognitivists influenced by Wittgenstein (e.g. Rosch & Mervis 1975; Lakoff 1987) described. It therefore makes it difficult to account for minimal shifts of meaning and semantic changes involving the shifting of prototypical uses within the polysemic structure of a word.

To conclude: As structural semantics is essentially a theory of the structure of vocabulary and not of the use of vocabulary, it does not provide a theoretical framework for a number of important problems in historical semantics. Generally speaking, it fails to give an integrative view of linguistic activity in its various contexts, i.e. the relationship between language structure and social practices as part of historical forms of life. It does not provide the theoretical means for taking into account either the knowledge used in semantic innovation or the communicative function of innovations, two aspects which, according to more recent views, play a fundamental role in the explanation of semantic innovation. A final limitation lies in the methodological requirement that lexical oppositions should only be sought within homogeneous systems, whereas semantic change is often due to the heterogeneity of linguistic traditions within one linguistic community. As a consequence of these limitations, structural semantics has not contributed much to recent developments in historical semantics. It is, however, interesting to see that the structuralist heritage has been absorbed by most later approaches, e.g. the principle that one should take into account the network of semantic relations between lexical units, both paradigmatic and syntagmatic (cf. Lehrer 1985; Heringer 1999).

4 Cognitive semantics

The rise of cognitive semantics in the 1980s was partly driven by a dissatisfaction with structuralist and "formalist" theories of meaning and language in general (e.g. structural semantics, truth-functional semantics, Chomskyan linguistics). Many of the basic ideas of the various strands of cognitive semantics were developed and presented rhetorically, sometimes polemically, in opposition to these approaches (cf. Lakoff 1987; Taylor 1999). The following points summarize some of the basic tenets of cognitive semantics, of which most are in direct contradiction to fundamental assumptions of structural semantics as mentioned in the preceding section:

i. Meanings are mental entities (e.g. concepts, conceptualizations or categories).
ii. Aspects of meaning are to be described with reference to cognitive processing.
iii. Concepts/categories exhibit an internal structure (clusters of subconcepts structured by different types of links, prototype structures, family resemblance structures etc.)
iv. Categories are often blurred at the edges.
v. Many categories cannot be defined by necessary and sufficient conditions.
vi. Linguistic meaning is essentially encyclopaedic. There may be central and peripheral aspects of lexical knowledge, but there is no dividing line between encyclopaedic and lexical knowledge.

vii. Metaphorical and metonymical models play a fundamental role for meaning.
viii. Cognitive Grammar does not draw a distinction in principle between "sentence meaning" and "utterance meaning" (cf. Taylor 1999: 20).

Whereas structural semantics and its successors did not have much to say about phenomena like metaphor and polysemy, it was exactly these topics that played a central role in the development of cognitive semantics and which triggered the popularity of cognitive linguistics in the in the 1980s and beyond (cf. Lakoff & Johnson 1980; Brugmann & Lakoff 1988; Taylor 2002). And it is also these topics which made historical semantics interesting for cognitive semantics and vice versa. Of course, the differences between broadly structuralist views and cognitive semantics are linked to fundamental differences in the goals pursued by these directions of research, especially the cognitive linguists' goal of using the study of linguistic meaning as a window on cognitive processes of conceptualization.

In certain respects, the cognitive view of semantics harks back to traditional semasiology, e.g. in its close relation to psychology, in its concept of meaning, its rejection of a clear distinction between sentence meaning (or word meaning) and utterance meaning, its pronounced interest in topics like polysemy and metaphor, and in its interest in semantic regularity and the "laws of thought". This connection has been acknowledged by several scholars (e.g. Lakoff 1987: 18; Geeraerts 1997: 26f), but, as Geeraerts hastened to add, cognitive semantics is not to be seen as a simple re-enactment of the approach of the older school. What puts present-day cognitive semantics in a different position seems to be not only the fact that there have been considerable advances in linguistic theory and semantic theory in particular, but also the availability of more sophisticated theories of categorization and conceptualization like the theory of prototypes and family resemblances developed by Rosch and others (e.g. Rosch & Mervis 1975), advanced psychological theories of metaphor (cf. Gibbs 1994), the theory of conceptual blending (Fauconnier & Turner 2002), and the conception of figure-ground organization from Gestalt psychology. Still, on account of the similarity in theoretical outlook it is not surprising that some of the objections to traditional "ideational" views (cf. section 2) have been raised also in relation to cognitive semantics. These objections include the problem of subjectivism (cf. Sinha 1999), the speculative character of the assumed conceptual structures and processes (cf. Taylor 2002: 64f) and, even more fundamentally, the question of circularity of (some) cognitivist explanations in (historical) semantics, which was raised by Lyons and others (e.g. Lyons 1991: 13) and has recently been brought up again by Keller (1998: 72). These objections are mostly not considered worth discussing at all by the practitioners of cognitive semantics or tend to be waved aside (e.g. Langacker 1988: 90), but there are exceptions, for instance John R. Taylor, who devotes a chapter of his book on cognitive grammar to these questions (cf. Taylor 2002, Ch. 4; cf. also Taylor 1999: 38). No doubt, these foundational questions should be given further reflection. There are also observations from historical semantics which could shed doubt on the advisability of the direct identification of meaning with concepts. In many cases of meaning change it is doubtful that one should describe the relevant developments as changes of concept. As for its contribution to historical semantics, it is particularly through research on metaphor, metonymy and polysemy in general that cognitive semantics has inspired historical work both theoretically and in its methodological outlook. Concerning relevant work in the field to date, we can discern two kinds of contributions. There is on the one hand programmatic work using synchronic data or well-known historical data for the purpose of demonstrating the feasibility and fruitfulness of a cognitive approach to problems of historical semantics (e.g. Sweetser 1990) and on the other hand genuinely data-driven empirical work, for instance by Geeraerts (e.g. Geeraerts 1997) or the Romance scholars Blank and Koch (e.g. Blank 1997; Koch 2001, 2003) both from an onomasiological and a semasiological perspective.

In addition to his empirical analyses, Geeraerts also focuses on theoretical matters of the explanation of change of meaning. He insists that one should not confuse mechanisms and causes of semantic change. The patterns of use he calls mechanisms (e.g. metaphor, metonymy, euphemisms etc.) "indicate the possible paths of change" (Geeraerts 1997: 103), whereas a cause "indicates why one of these possibilities is realized" by an individual speaker (Geeraerts 1997: 103). He further emphasizes that functional aspects should play a major role in the explanation of semantic changes. In his view, principles like the principle of expressivity or the principle of efficiency are causes in this sense (Geeraerts 1997: 120). As for these principles, expressivity concerns the communicative needs of the speakers, an aspect of meaning change that has always been emphasized in functional approaches (cf. section 6), whereas principles of efficiency include, amongst others, prototypicality as "a cognitive efficiency principle". So, the upshot seems to be that, strictly speaking, there are no causes at all at this level of analysis. There is no doubt that principles play an important role in the speakers' practice of finding new uses and accepting them. But they do not *cause* linguistic action, they *guide* linguistic action. At the level of the individual's activities there are no causes of semantic innovation.

Somewhat outside the mainstream of cognitive semantics we find a group of Romance scholars (Blank, Koch, and their collaborators) who have contributed extensively to historical semantics from a basically cognitivist viewpoint. A "summa" of this research programme is the comprehensive book on the principles of lexical meaning change by the late Andreas Blank (Blank 1997), in which he discusses basic questions of meaning change, drawing on a wealth of data from the Romance languages. What links him to the cognitivist movement is his view that meanings have Gestalt properties and that forms of meaning change are essentially based on conceptual associations of various types (Blank 1997: 137ff). However, he criticizes the identification of meaning and concept and suggests a semiological model which reintroduces the differentiation of encyclopedic knowledge ("Weltwissen") and language-specific semantic knowledge ("sememisches Wissen") including knowledge of the polysemous meaning structure of words (Blank 1997: 102). Central to this framework is his presentation of types of meaning change in terms of techniques (or devices) of semantic innovation. He aims to show that what was often subsumed under "causes of semantic change" has to be differentiated into techniques of innovation on the one hand (e.g. linguistic devices like metaphor and metonymy), including their cognitive prerequisites, and motives for innovation and for the uptake and lexicalization of innovations on the other. Such motives include the speakers' practice of observing communicative principles, a view which he shares with pragmatic theories of meaning change. On the cognitive plain, he characterizes metaphor and metonymy by the speakers' use of similarity associations and contiguity associations respectively, explicating the traditional contiguity relation in terms of concepts, frames and scenarios.

In various case studies Blank shows the interaction of culture-specific knowledge and general cognitive principles as resources for semantic innovation. It is, among other points, Blank's insistence on the importance of socio-cultural knowledge within historical traditions of discourse which shows a shift of emphasis in his view of semantic change as compared to the mainstream cognitivist focus on universal cognitive principles. This provides a fruitful tension between the historical and the universalist perspectives and "avoids prematurely treating the findings at the historical level as universal, especially making the characteristics of certain individual languages into the standard of an analysis of linguistic universals" (Koch 2003: 45).

5 Theories of grammaticalization

The term *grammaticalization* is generally used to refer to a type of historical change by which lexical items come to serve grammatical functions. In this process, the lexical items are said to become "semantically bleached" and they undergo syntactic restrictions and "phonetic erosion". A classic example is the development of the Old English main verb *willan* 'to want', which becomes an auxiliary verb used to refer to the future, like in *she'll come*. A similar type of development is the change from post-classical Latin *facere habeo* 'I have to do', 'I will do' to French *(je) ferai*, where the original Latin verb *habere* with the meaning 'to have' is grammaticalized into the future tense suffix *-ai*. This type of development was well known to 19th century linguists, who already used metaphors like *fading* or *bleaching* (German *Verblassen*) to describe the result of relevant semantic developments. In a much-quoted article, published in 1912, the French linguist Antoine Meillet introduced the term *grammaticalisation* to refer to this type of development and emphasized the "weakening" of both meaning and phonetic form ("l'affaiblissement du sens et l'affaiblissement de la forme"; Meillet 1912/1965: 139) as characteristic of this process. He also put forward the view that innovations like the post-classical Latin *facere habeo* (as opposed to classical *faciam*) had a particular expressive value at the time when they were first used, but lost this value in the course of the further process of grammaticalization. From the 1980s onwards there has been a "veritable flood of [. . .] scholarship on grammaticalization" (Campbell & Janda 2001), including detailed analyses of individual phenomena like the ones mentioned before (e.g. Aijmer 1985) and comprehensive overviews of cross-linguistic research (Bybee, Perkins & Pagliuca 1994; Heine & Kuteva 2002) as well as introductory texts (e.g. Hopper & Traugott 2003).

From the point of view of historical semantics, the interest of grammaticalization research lies mainly in its contribution to the description of paths of semantic change from a given "source", e.g. a lexical unit denoting movement (*to go*), to a "target" expression which is used to signal future events (*to be going to*), some of which seem to have a remarkable breadth of cross-linguistic distribution. It is the richness of data from both genetically related and unrelated languages that makes grammaticalization research such a useful heuristic instrument for questions of regularity in semantic change. On the strength of these cross-linguistic data some quite strong claims have been made concerning the regularity of relevant types of semantic change, including the assumption that there exist quasi-universal "cognitive and communicative patterns underlying the use of language" (Bybee, Perkins & Pagliuca 1994: 15) and "the hypothesis that semantic development is predictable" (Bybee, Perkins & Pagliuca 1994: 18). Other researchers have been somewhat more guarded in their claims, restricting themselves to the assertion that there are interesting cross-linguistic similarities in the recruitment of certain lexical sources for given grammatical targets. A further hypothesis, which has received a great deal of attention in the last few years, is the hypothesis of unidirectionality, i.e. the non-reversibility of the direction of change from less to more grammaticalized (cf. Campbell 2001: 124ff; Hopper & Traugott 2003, Ch. 5).

As for their background of semantic theory, scholars working on grammaticalization are frequently not very explicit as to the kind of semantic theory they embrace. From the fact that some authors at times use the expressions "meaning" and "concept" more or less interchangeably one might infer that they are of a basically cognitivist persuasion (e.g. Heine & Kuteva 2002), whereas others rely on pragmatic (Gricean or Neo-Gricean) concepts (e.g. Traugott & König 1991). Concerning its descriptive methodology, research on grammaticalization, especially in the case of cross-linguistic surveys, often tends to settle for relatively coarse-grained semantic descriptions, which usually serve the purposes of this work quite well, but which can sometimes also give a wrong picture of the actual types of semantic micro-development. This preference for a semantic macro-perspective is not really surprising, as the focus of much of this work is the origin and development of *grammatical* forms.

From a theoretical point of view, some of the semantic concepts used in grammaticalization research are both interesting and, in some respects, problematic. This is true, for instance, of the term *bleaching* mentioned above, which comes in handy as a metaphorical cover-all for various types of semantic development. One such type of change is the loss of expressive meaning of metaphors in the course of routinization. Another type, which is often mentioned in grammaticalization research, is explained as "loss of concrete and literal meanings" and the acquisition "of more abstract and general meanings" (cf. Bybee, Perkins & Pagliuca 1994: 5; Brinton & Traugott 2005: 100). This explanation presupposes that we know what an "abstract and general meaning" is, but a clarification of this concept, which again goes back at least to Meillet, is generally not attempted. As for the use of the *bleaching* metaphor, it seems that in many cases this may be quite harmless, but if used as a stand-in for more precise semantic descriptions, it might give an inaccurate view of the developments in question. For instance, calling the development of an additional epistemic use of the modal *may* (as in *He may have known*, as opposed to *You may go now*) a case of bleaching is downright misleading, as the epistemic use is in no way more "abstract" or the like and the non-epistemical sense normally remains being used alongside the epistemic one. The use of the term *bleaching* can be particularly problematic in those cases where the diagnosis of *bleaching* is based on a direct comparison of the source and the target use of an expression, leaving out several intermediate steps of development. As some authors have noticed, there is a tendency in grammaticalization research to reduce continuous, chainlike processes to two uses of forms, viz., source and target uses (cf. Heine & Kuteva 2002: 6), without paying attention to the complex development of systems of related uses of the expressions in question. In such cases the diagnosis of bleaching turns out to be an artefact of the descriptive methodology. These observations lead to the conclusion that the description of source-target-relations should be generally supplemented with detailed studies of the individual steps of semantic change in terms of the changing structure of clusters of uses. The importance of this methodological precept has also been acknowledged by scholars from the grammaticalization movement (Heine 2003: 83).

A closely connected conceptual question concerns the relation of "lexical meaning" to "grammatical meaning". Traditionally, the background for the classification of the meaning of an expression as a case of grammatical meaning is often the following: If what can be expressed by a certain expression (e.g. declaring one's future intentions by using a sentence with a modal verb) can also be expressed by a grammatical morpheme in the same or another language (e.g. by a future tense morpheme in Latin), then this expression has (a) grammatical meaning. This is somewhat doubtful reasoning, as one could easily turn the argument around and say that if a certain meaning can be expressed by non-grammatical means, then this is a case of non-grammatical meaning, which could be said for the expression of wishes or the expression of admonitions, which in Latin can be expressed by lexical means as well as by the use of the subjunctive mood ("coniunctivus optativus" and "coniunctivus adhortativus"). So, from the fact that Latin uses the subjunctive to express wishes it does not follow that 'expressing wishes' is a case of grammatical meaning. So there is a certain vagueness to the concept of grammatical meaning, which is sometimes acknowledged by the assertion that there is "no clear distinction between lexical and grammatical meaning" (cf. Taylor, Cuyckens & Dirven 2003: 1) or that there is a gradient from lexical to grammatical meaning.

A final point worth mentioning is the question of how the individual steps of a grammaticalization chain should be described and explained. Some researchers, mainly from the cognitivist camp, assumed that these individual steps were generally cases of metaphorical transfer, e.g. from the spatial to the temporal domain (from *going to* as a motion verb to *going to* as a future tense marker) or from the social to the cognitive domain in the case of the development of epistemic uses of modals from non-epistemic uses (e.g. the *may* of permission to the *may* of possibility, cf. Sweetser 1990: 58ff). However, recent more data-oriented research has shown that in many cases there is no evidence in the data of metaphorical transfer at all, but rather of the use of contextual and general knowledge for small metonymic steps (cf. Brinton & Traugott 2005: 28; Fritz 1991, 1997b; Traugott & Dasher 2002). Generally speaking, the upshot of these observations on meaning change in grammaticalization is that there is no special type of semantic change characteristic of grammaticalization, but rather that it is generally well-known types of semantic change which contribute to the stepwise development typical of grammaticalization processes: "Grammaticalization is only one subclass of change based on expressivity" (Detges & Waltereit 2002: 190). To sum up, the contribution of the grammaticalization research programme in its various forms to the study of meaning change consists mainly in the fact that it initiated substantial cross-linguistic research into possible paths of semantic change and the issue of unidirectionality, which has considerable heuristic value for historical semantics.

6 Meaning as use and pragmatic semantics

The family of theoretical approaches dealt with in this section goes back mainly to works by Wittgenstein and some of his followers on the one hand (e.g. Strawson 1964; Alston 1964; Heringer 1978) and to Grice and his followers on the other. As is well known, Grice was very doubtful as to the usefulness of the precept that one should be careful to identify meaning and use (Grice 1989: 4), so it seems that there is at least a certain reading of Wittgenstein (and Grice), where the Wittgensteinian and the Gricean views on meaning are not easily reconciled. This has to do with their divergent views on the foundational role of rules and established practices on the one side and intentions on the other, which lead to differing perspectives on the analysis of the relation between *Bedeutung* (*Gebrauch*) and *Meinen* in Wittgenstein's picture of meaning and *sentence-meaning* (or *word-meaning*) and *utterer's meaning* in Grice's theory. It is not possible to review here the relevant discussion (e.g. Black 1975; cf. Gloning 1996: 110ff). Suffice it to say that it seems possible to bridge the differences of these views by emphasizing the instrumental aspect of Wittgenstein's view of language and taking into account the fact that Grice in his analysis of "timeless meaning" also accepted not only "established meaning", but also "conventional meaning" with its element of normativity ("correct and incorrect use", Grice 1989: 124ff). Such an integration of views (cf. Meggle 1987; Keller 1998) provides a useful starting point for an empirical theory of meaning and meaning change. For this kind of theory it comes quite naturally to see the historical character of meaning as an essential aspect of meaning and to view uses of linguistic expressions as emerging solutions to communicative and cognitive tasks (cf. Strecker 1987). It is furthermore part of the Gricean heritage to assume that what is meant is often underspecified by what is said.

It is remarkable that both Wittgenstein and Grice at least hinted at the fact that there is an historical dimension to the use of language, Wittgenstein in § 23 of his "Philosophical Investigations" (Wittgenstein 1953), where he emphasized that new types of language games continually arise and old ones disappear (cf. also

Wittgenstein 1975, § 65), and Grice in a passage in "Logic and conversation", where he mentioned that "it may not be impossible for what starts life, so to speak, as a conversational implicature to become conventionalized" (Grice 1989: 39). It is of course true, however, that neither Wittgenstein nor Grice developed a theory of meaning change or of polysemy which could be simply applied to empirical work. This has to do with the context in which their theoretical views were developed. Wittgenstein's insistence on the importance of scrutinizing the multiple uses of words, for example, is not due to a special interest in polysemy as a linguistic phenomenon, but rather as a therapeutical move in conceptual analysis. Therefore, in order to implement the relevant ideas of these philosophers in an empirical theory of meaning change and the methodology of historical semantics one has to spell out in detail many aspects of meaning and meaning change which are only hinted at by these authors.

Such details of theory and methodology include: (i) an explication of the concept of "use" (cf. Heringer 1978; Heringer 1999: 10ff), including the analysis of types and aspects of contexts of use (cf. Fritz 2005: 17ff) and an explication of the relationship between "uses" and collocations of expressions (cf. Heringer 1999: 32ff), (ii) methods for the description of the structures of polysemies (cf. Fritz 1995), (iii) the classification of types of semantic innovations, their functions and resources (cf. Fritz 2006: 36ff; Keller & Kirschbaum 2003, Ch. 4), including the minimal changes in collocations which have generally been neglected by historical semanticists, (iv) corpus-based methods for the description of semantic innovation and meaning change (cf. Fritz 1991, 1997b; Heringer 1999).

The instrumental view of meaning provides powerful instruments, guiding principles and assumptions for historical semantics. Such instruments comprise (i) Grice's theory of implicatures as an instrument for analysing meaning innovation, including the role of "conversational maxims" and the structure of reasonings as hermeneutical devices (that inferences play an important role in meaning change), (ii) the concept of "mutual knowledge" (as a methodological fiction) developed as an extension of Gricean ideas (Schiffer 1972), which is related to such linguistic concepts as "common ground", (iii) Lewis's theory of convention (Lewis 1969), which shows the reasoning involved in a process of conventionalization, a useful instrument for the analysis of the dynamics of conventionalization, (iv) the contextual view of meaning rules embodied in the concept of language games (cf. Wittgenstein 1953, § 23), (v) the assumption that language games and meaning rules are embedded in historical forms of life, (vi) the assumption that in many cases the uses of a word have a family resemblance structure (cf. Wittgenstein 1953, § 66f), (vii) the assumption that among the uses of certain expressions there are more central and more peripheral cases (cf. Wittgenstein

1970: 190), (viii) the assumption that the meaning of natural-language expressions is (usually) open-textured (cf. Wittgenstein 1953, §§ 68–71: 84, 99), (ix) the assumption that there is no division in principle between knowledge of meaning and knowledge of fact (Wittgenstein 1953, §§ 79: 242; Wittgenstein 1975, § 63).

Whereas cognitive theories of meaning change tend to concentrate on the processes of conceptualisation which make an individual's innovation cognitively plausible, a functional and dialogical view also takes into account the fact that innovations are often sparked off und facilitated by the dynamics of local communicative context, that speakers aim at "recipient design" in their (innovative) talk and "work" to ensure uptake, that it is socially and culturally distributed knowledge which, in many cases, is both a condition and a consequence of semantic innovation, and that the reasons for which an innovation is attractive in the first place (e.g. functional benefits like expressive value or cognitive value) also facilitate its acceptance by other speakers and thereby advance its diffusion. Generally speaking, a basically functional and dialogic approach to meaning innovation and meaning change favours an integrative perspective on the resources and the functions of semantic innovations and it also helps to focus on problems which are neglected by other approaches, e.g. the processes of routinization and conventionalization and the paths of diffusion of new uses (cf. Fritz 2005: 49ff). It also shows an affinity to an explanation of meaning change in terms of an invisible hand theory (cf. Keller 1990), in which action-theoretical concepts like intentions and maxims of action loom large.

Examples of the kinds of problems discussed in these frameworks and of the empirical work available include: the historical development of systems of metaphorical and metonymical links (Fritz 1995 on the history of the extreme polysemy of German *scharf*), the complex developments in the semantics of modal verbs (Traugott 1989; Traugott & Dasher 2002; Fritz 1991, 1997a, 1997b), developments in the history of speech act verbs (Traugott & Dasher 2002; Hundsnurscher 2003; Fritz 2005, Ch. 16), the development of evaluative uses of adjectives (Keller & Kirschbaum 2003), the development of various types of uses of conjunctions (causal, conditional, concessive) (Traugott & König 1991), the development of discourse markers and modal particles (e.g. Jucker 1997; Günthner 2003; Hansen 2005; Fritz 2005, Ch. 18), the functional explanation of grammaticalization in terms of unintentional results of expressive discourse techniques (Detges & Waltereit 2002), the description and analysis of invisible-hand processes in the conventionalisation and diffusion of lexical items (Keller & Kirschbaum 2003, Ch. 4), the functional explanation of developments in the structure of vocabulary (Gloning 2003).

A classical example of the Gricean approach to the analysis of an innovation is the description of the evolution of causal connectives from earlier purely temporal connectives (e.g. English *since*, German *weil*) given by various authors (e.g. Traugott & König 1991). This type of development was well known to pre-structuralist linguists and also described in ways broadly similar to modern Griceans (e.g. Paul 1895: 72 on German *weil*). However, the modern analysis achieves a higher degree of explicitness concerning the aspects of communication involved. A connective like *since* (Old English *siþþan*) originally meant 'after', however in certain contexts it seems to have been used to contextually suggest (in addition) a causal relation. Making use of the shared assumption that an event following another might be caused by the prior event and applying principles of relevance and informativity, the speaker could implicate or invite the inference that there was a causal relation between the two events. This could be described as a case of "pragmatic strengthening" (cf. Traugott 1989). When such a conversational implicature became conventionalized, a new variant of use arose, leading to polysemy, as in the case of Modern English *since* (temporal and causal uses). The theory of "invited inference" and "pragmatic strengthening" has also been applied to other types of expressions, e.g. speech act verbs (Traugott & Dasher 2002) and the development of epistemic uses of modal verbs (Traugott 1989; Traugott & Dasher 2002, Ch. 3). As Traugott and Dasher noted, the Gricean analysis covers many cases of what was traditionally subsumed under metonymy, which is not surprising, as metonymy uses shared knowledge concerning inferential ("associative") connections within a given domain. It is also worth noting that the Gricean viewpoint in some cases suggests a non-metaphorical inferential analysis where earlier cognitivist work preferred an explanation in terms of metaphorical extension (cf. Sweetser 1990, Ch. 3). This is the case for a much-discussed topic, viz. the rise of epistemic meaning in modals, where detailed corpus analysis seems to speak against an analysis in terms of metaphor (cf. Traugott 1989 for modals in English, Fritz 1991, 1997a: 94ff for modals in German).

Comparing the approaches presented in this section with the cognitivist approaches mentioned in section 4, one finds deep-going theoretical divergences and also differences in perspective, but also remarkable convergences (cf. Fritz 2011). A fairly fundamental theoretical difference consists in the fact that cognitivists embrace a representationalist view of meaning (words stand for concepts), whereas functionalists tend to favour an instrumentalist view. Related to this we find another divergence: at least from a purist Wittgensteinian position, the definition of meaning as conceptualization would seem to be an elementary category mistake. As for differences in perspective, the basic difference seems to be: Whereas cognitivists will use the analysis of semantic innovation mainly as a window on cognitive processes, functionalists will be primarily interested in the linguistic (pragmatic, rhetorical) practices of meaning innovation and their function in the strategic negotiation of speaker-hearer interaction. They will therefore view types of knowledge, connections between knowledge frames etc. as resources used for meaning innovation, usually showing a somewhat agnostic attitude towards the various types of "backstage cognition" (Fauconnier 1999: 96) assumed in cognitive approaches. On the other hand, cognitivists and functionalists join hands in assuming polysemy as a fundamental fact of linguistic practice and cognitive processes, family-resemblance and prototype structures of polysemous meaning, the central role of metaphor and metonymy in meaning innovation, and the indiscernibility of semantic and encyclopedic knowledge. As for the tendencies of convergence, which have been growing in the last few years, I shall add a few remarks in the concluding section of this article.

I should like to conclude this section by drawing attention to a problem which has, to my knowledge, so far not been seriously tackled by historical semanticists, but which is certainly also a problem for historical semantics and not just for philosophers and historians of science. This is the much-debated question of the relationship between theory change, change of meaning, and change of concepts. One of the central problems discussed in this debate, the problem of "incommensurability of theories", is basically a problem of meaning. In a recent work on this topic, Kuukkanen states that "incommensurability may be taken as the practical difficulty of achieving translation and reaching comprehension in a situation where the same expressions imply radically different assumptions" (Kuukkanen 2006: 10). As Dascal has shown in various writings, there is at the moment an impasse in the philosophy and history of science (cf. Dascal 2000), which has to do with a lack of attention to the actual communicative processes (often) involved in the growth of scientific knowledge. At least partly, the questions if and how communication between opposing parties in a foundational controversy is possible and if in the course of such debates there is a change of meaning of relevant expressions are empirical questions that cannot be answered in the philosopher's armchair, but only by empirical studies, to which historical semantics could certainly contribute. In the case of the famous Phlogiston controversy one could, for instance, show how critical expressions like *air* (*Luft*) or *combustion* (*Verbrennung*) are used by the opposing parties and in which way they are connected to the use of other expressions like *phlogiston* or *oxygen* and to descriptions of the experimental praxis involved in the development of this theoretical field. A case in point is the debate between the German chemist Gren and his opponents in the "Journal der Physik", which ended by Gren's conversion to (a version of) Lavoisier's theory of oxidation. To my mind, the type of semantic theory that would be most adequate to this analytical task is a version of pragmatic semantics.

7 Formal semantics and pragmatics

Trying to write the present section some twenty years ago, one would have probably come to the conclusion that there was nothing to write about. Formal semantics was concerned with rules of inference, matters of compositionality and the proper treatment of quantifiers and logical connectives, but rarely with lexical semantics and certainly not with matters relating to the change of meaning. Now this is in fact not quite true. As far back as Frege's writings from the 1890s onwards we find an awareness that ordinary language is flexible in a way that influences the reliability of formal reasoning or at least implies aspects that might be relevant to logical consequence. Frege noticed that there are individual differences in the use of expressions (e.g. proper names with a different sense ("Sinn") for different persons, Frege 1892/1969: 42), that the denotation of certain expressions is determined by context, that we sometimes make certain presuppositions in using referring expressions, that natural language words are sometimes ambiguous, and that some natural language connectives (like *if—then*, *but* or *although*) have properties which their truth-functional counterparts do not have. In addition to their truth-functional properties the latter connectives serve to give extra hints ("Winke") as to the kind of connection involved (Frege 1918/1966: 37). As Frege also noted, the use of the conditional connective often suggests an additional causal connection, which is however not part of the truth-functional meaning of this connective. In Gricean terms it is a conversational implicature, but conversational implicatures may in time become conventional, as can be shown for many connectives in different languages.

So what we find in Frege's writings is a certain amount of attention to problems relating to semantic and pragmatic aspects of natural language, which are in turn related to questions of historical semantics, i.e. ambiguity, context-dependence, individual differences of use, and implicatures. But, of course, Frege mentioned these things mainly to get them out of the way of his project of producing a well-behaved language for scientific uses. Therefore, for him and for many later logicians and formal semanticists the standard solution to these problems was to suggest that one should "purify ordinary language in various ways" (Montague 1974: 84). Another strategy was to delegate these aspects of natural language use to an additional pragmatic theory, where they could be dealt with, for instance, with the help of Grice's theory of implicatures.

In recent times, this picture of how formal semantics relates to matters of semantic variation and semantic change has obviously changed. Generally speaking, there has been a development towards the integration of dynamic, pragmatic and lexical aspects of meaning into formal semantic or formal pragmatic theories which are relevant to questions of meaning change (cf. article 8 [this volume])

(Eckardt) *Grammaticalization and semantic reanalysis*). Although attempts to capture the dynamics of language change with formal theories have received sceptical comments in the past (cf. Eckardt 2006: 28), recent developments in formal semantics seem to give hope for a fruitful rapprochement. If the use of formal theories in historical semantics should in future contribute to an increase in explicitness, precision and systematicity of semantic analyses, this would certainly be a good thing. Of course, using a formal apparatus does not guarantee rigour in semantics, as Geach ably showed in his criticism of Carnap (Geach 1972).

There are various recent approaches which could be related to questions of meaning change or which have actually tackled such questions, of which I shall mention three. A first family of such approaches are dynamic theories which could be subsumed under the heading of *update semantics/pragmatics*. The common denominator of such approaches is the view that the utterance of a certain expression changes the context, i.e. the common beliefs of the interlocutors, in a specific way (cf. Stalnaker 1978, 2002), from which one can go on to assume that the meaning of an expression could be modelled in terms of its context change potential. In order to model this dynamic aspect of discourse and meaning one has to assume some kind of score-keeping procedure, e.g. "commitment store operations" as in Hamblin's Formal Dialectic (Hamblin 1970: 253, ff) or Lewis's "rules specifying the kinematics of conversational score" (Lewis 1979: 346). This basic idea has been spelt out in different versions, e.g. in Kamp's Discourse Representation Theory (cf. Kamp & Reyle 1993) and Heim's file change semantics (cf. Heim 1983). By using these and similar methods, it is possible to produce semantic models of information growth which can, among other things, deal with the phenomenon of an incremental updating of common ground.

This type of approach could be useful for research in historical semantics in several respects. It could, for instance, give us a clearer picture of the processes involved in the emergence of "common ground" in general (e.g. the concept of mutual knowledge specified in Lewis 1969: 56, or Schiffer 1972) and conventions in particular (cf. Lewis 1969). As new uses of words often emerge against the background of common assumptions, the building-up of common ground is an important aspect of semantic innovation. By using this kind of apparatus one could, for example, model a very frequent type of semantic change which consists in the emergence of new evaluative uses of expressions originally used descriptively. Take a noun like (*young*) *servant*, which serves to refer to persons of a certain social status: If in a given speaker community the assumption becomes common knowledge that such persons frequently show criminal tendencies, this expression can be used to accuse someone of being a criminal, which in time may become a conventional use of the word. This kind of development is frequently found in various languages (cf. Middle High German *buobe* and *schalk*, English *knave* and *varlet*, French *gars*). A similar process permits descriptive adjectives to be used in evaluative function, which is also a very frequent type of meaning change.

A second trend in recent formal semantics and pragmatics is the interest in "systematic polysemy", especially in the various uses of words based on metonymic relations, e.g. uses of expressions denoting institutions like *the university* to refer to the buildings housing this institution or to the members of this institution. Recent analyses of this kind of polysemy include Nunberg (1995), Pustejowsky (1995), Copestake & Briscoe (1996), Blutner (1998) and Peters & Kilgarriff (2000). In historical semantics, awareness of this type of polysemy and its regular character goes back to its very beginnings in the 19th century, so historical semantics has much to offer in terms of historical data for this kind of phenomenon. On the other hand historical semantics could profit from relevant theoretical work and from work on large present-day corpora. Recent work has shown that metonymic sense extension can be considered a productive—or at least semi-productive—process, which is, however, subject to certain restrictions. One can assume that certain groups of words have the same extension potential, which is however not always exhaustively used. It would be very useful to systematically survey the ways in which this extension potential was used in different historical periods and to analyze the factors blocking the productivity of this process, of which some may turn out to be language specific or culture specific.

A third approach, which has fortunately gone beyond the programmatic stage and has produced actual empirical work in the field of historical semantics, is the formal reconstruction of the process of semantic reanalysis (cf. Eckardt 2006 and article 8 [this volume] (Eckardt) *Grammaticalization and semantic reanalysis*). Meaning change under reanalysis is particularly frequent in instances of grammaticalization. Cases in point are the development of the English *going-to* future marker or the development of the German quantifier-like expression *lauter* in the sense of 'only' or 'many' from the earlier adjective *lauter* 'pure'. Eckardt's analyses proceed from the idea that meaning change under reanalysis is essentially a change of the contribution of the respective expressions to the compositional structure of typical sentences. In order to analyze these changes in compositional structure, Eckardt uses techniques of truth-functional semantics, "which is still the semantic paradigm that addresses semantic composition in the most explicit manner" (Eckardt 2006: 235), and combines them with methods of conceptual semantics and pragmatics. This is an ingenious approach which considerably stretches the boundaries of what would traditionally be considered truth-functional semantics. One of the hallmarks of this approach is a high degree of explicitness and precision, which proves extremely useful in the analysis of rather subtle and complicated processes of change. In addition to reaching very interesting empirical results, Eckardt succeeds in demonstrating "that the notions and formalisms in formal semantics can be fruitfully set to work in the investigation of diachronic developments" (Eckardt 2006: 234) and that "the investigation of language change can offer substantial input to synchronic semantic research" (Eckardt 2006: 188).

8 Conclusion

As we have seen, historical semantics is a research area where fundamental problems of semantics tend to surface and which can be seen as a testing ground for theories of meaning and for methodologies of semantic description. A case in point is structural semantics with all its strengths and weaknesses, which brought into focus meaning relations between different expressions in a lexical paradigm, but which had no answers to problems like the nature of metaphor, polysemy and evolutionary processes in general, and which therefore fell into disfavour in the last twenty years. Historical semantics as a field of empirical research always flourished in times when it was a focus of theoretical debate. This is true of the 1890s, of the 1930s, and of the last 25 years. So, with cognitive semantics and pragmatic semantics competing and with formal semantics joining in the recent debate, signs are good for a dynamic development of this field of research.

It is obvious that the direction of interest and the emphasis on certain aspects of meaning change is largely determined by the concept of meaning which individual authors and schools of thought embrace. It is, however, striking to see that in many cases empirical work with corpus data forced researchers to transcend the limitations of scope of their respective theoretical frameworks and take into account aspects of meaning and meaning change which were not really covered by their semantic theory. This is true of most of the schools of historical semantics discussed in this article, and it seems to demonstrate the healthy effect of data-driven work, which potentially also motivates advances in theoretical reflection.

A good example of this effect is the attitude towards semantics and pragmatics as distinct areas of theory. Certain ways of making the demarcation would be completely unplausible for an empirical theory of meaning change from the start, e.g. viewing semantics in terms of truth-conditions and pragmatics as taking charge of the rest. But also the standard demarcation in terms of conventional and conversational aspects of meaning does not fare much better. As most of the dynamic aspects of meaning change, e.g. innovation, selection, and diffusion, are generally considered to fall into the field of pragmatics, historical semantics, as it is practiced today, would have to be seen as a proper subfield of historical pragmatics. The publication policy of a journal like "Historical Pragmatics" bears witness to this view. If, however, semantics is considered to be concerned only with established meanings to the exclusion of contextually determined utterance meaning, we get a somewhat restrictive view of historical semantics, according to which it should concentrate on contrasting the established meanings of certain expressions at time 1 with those at time 2. This is basically the structuralist picture, which leaves out just about everything that is interesting about change of meaning. In view of the fact that routinization and conventionalization are gradual processes one could argue that there is a gradual transition from pragmatic to semantic phenomena. This argument, apart from showing that there is, strictly speaking, no such thing as a semantics-pragmatics interface, would make historical semantics a subject which hovers uneasily between two theoretical fields. So what seems to be needed as a basis for an empirical theory of meaning change is a genuinely dynamic theory of meaning and understanding which encompasses both the rule-based and the inference-based aspects of meaning. From this it does of course not follow that there is no categorial difference between speaker meaning (*Meinen*) and word/sentence meaning (*Bedeutung*), as some cognitive semanticists seem to assume.

Looking to the future development of historical semantics there seem to be at least three areas where progress in theory and methodology could be achieved: (i) the detailed comparison of competing theories of meaning as to their contribution to a theory of meaning change, and the clarification of points of convergence of these theories, (ii) further clarification of basic concepts like "explanation of meaning change", "uses of words", "metonymy", and descriptive categories like "bleaching", "subjectification" etc., (iii) further development of descriptive methodology, especially corpus-methodology, for historical semantics. Of these points I should like to briefly take up the first and the last.

As mentioned in sections 4 and 6 there is a tendency within cognitive linguistics to extend its scope to a "cognitive-functional" view (cf. Tomasello 1998). Within historical semantics this tendency is apparent in publications by Blank and Koch as well as in recent work by Geeraerts and others (e.g. Nerlich & Clarke 2001; Traugott & Dasher 2002), where we find attempts at integration of cognitivist and pragmatic views. Geeraerts explicitly stated that "such a process of convergence—if it will take place at all—could find a focal point in a pragmatic, usage-based perspective to lexical semantics" (Geeraerts 2002: 38f). This is not a trivial project, as there are still fundamental divergences in theoretical outlook between these approaches, e.g. the big divide between representionalist and instrumentalist (functionalist) theories of meaning and the complex corollaries of this divide concerning the status of conceptualization and linguistic meaning etc. It would be a remarkable development indeed, if the methodological needs of historical semantics should pave the way to bridging this theoretical divide. A similar thing could be said for the divide between cognitivist and realist theories of meaning, the latter of which are the prevailing view in formal semantics. In actual empirical work researchers often practice a certain degree of theoretical and methodological opportunism, which furthers fruitful empirical work while leaving basic theoretical questions untouched. Maybe this is a useful application of Austin's principle of letting "sleeping dogmatists lie" (Austin 1970: 75). From a more theoretically-minded perspective, however, one would like to see these foundational questions clarified.

Concerning descriptive methodology, it is worth noting that semantic minimalism, which is the methodological preference of many scholars in theoretical semantics as a means for preserving unity of meaning, is as a rule not favoured by researchers doing empirical work in historical semantics. The precept that one should not multiply senses (beyond necessity), advocated both by structuralists (e.g. Bech 1951) and, more recently, by Griceans (cf. Grice 1989: 47–50), is basically a useful principle in that it forces researchers to differentiate between what a word means and what is conversationally implicated in a certain context. But it also fosters the tendency to explain as implicatures what must be seen as established uses of expressions. This tendency is counterproductive in historical semantics, as in many cases the interesting question is exactly how to differentiate between conversational innovations and well-established uses of an expression. In this situation, corpus data often give very good indications as to which uses (or senses) of an expression can be considered firmly established at a given point in time and which are transient or peripheral. Furthermore, from what research in historical semantics has found in the last few years, both within cognitive and pragmatic frameworks, semantic minimalism seems to give a fundamentally wrong picture of what is going on in change of meaning in many cases. Arguably, the most fruitful approach to the description of meaning change from the semasiological perspective consists in treating semantic evolution as the development through time of sets of uses and their respective internal structures (cf. Geeraerts 1997: 23ff; Fritz 2006: 14ff).

As for corpus methods, corpus-based analysis has traditionally played an important role in historical semantics, because researchers cannot rely on their own linguistic competence in historical studies. Recent developments in corpus technology and corpus methods have strengthened this methodological preference and widened its scope of application. Modern corpus linguistics has, however, not only provided new methods of data generation and data interpretation, but has also inspired reflection on theoretical questions like the relationship between collocations of given expressions and their meaning (cf. Heringer 1999). Large corpora can also help to make visible phenomena which are not easily seen in smaller collections of texts, e.g. gradual changes in the contexts of use of given expressions within a diachronic corpus, which can be interpreted as reflexes of gradual changes of meaning. More sophisticated analyses of gradual change of meaning certainly belong to the desiderata for future empirical research. In semantics, the availability of large amounts of data does, however, not render unnecessary methodological procedures like the contextual interpretation of instances of the use of a word or the inference from distributional facts to semantic descriptions. This is true a fortiori of historical semantics. Such procedures are widely used, but are theoretically not well understood, so here we have another area where further studies are necessary. Generally speaking, the important recent developments in historical semantics have opened new vistas for empirical research, and in so doing have also shown the necessity for further clarification of basic theoretical and methodological issues.

9 References

Aijmer, Karin 1985. The semantic development of "will". In: J. Fisiak (ed.). *Historical Semantics. Historical Word-Formation.* Berlin: de Gruyter, 11–21.
Alston, William P. 1964. *Philosophy of Language.* Englewood Cliffs, NJ: Prentice-Hall.
Austin, John L. 1970. The meaning of a word. In: J.L. Austin. *Philosophical Papers.* Oxford: Oxford University Press, 55–75.
Bech, Gunnar 1951. Grundzüge der semantischen Entwicklungsgeschichte der hochdeutschen Modalverba. *Historisk-Filologiske Meddelelser* (Kongeliske Danske Videnskabernes Selskab) 32(6), 1–28.
Black, Max 1975. Meaning and intention. In: M. Black. *Caveats and Critiques. Philosophical Essays in Language, Logic, and Art.* Ithaca, NY: Cornell University Press, 109–138.
Blank, Andreas 1997. Prinzipien des lexikalischen Bedeutungswandels am Beispiel der romanischen Sprachen. Tübingen: Niemeyer.
Blank, Andreas 2003. Words and concepts in time: Towards diachronic cognitive lexicology. In: R. Eckardt, K. von Heusinger & Ch. Schwarze (eds.). *Words in Time. Diachronic Semantics from Different Points of View.* Berlin: Mouton de Gruyter, 37–65.
Blank, Andreas & Peter Koch 1999. Introduction: Historical semantics and cognition. In: A. Blank & P. Koch (eds.). *Historical Semantics and Cognition.* Berlin: Mouton de Gruyter, 1–14.
Blutner, Reinhard 1998. Lexical pragmatics. *Journal of Semantics* 15, 115–162.
Bréal, Michel 1897/1924. *Essai de sémantique. Science des significations.* Paris. 7th edn. Paris: Hachette, 1924.
Brinton, Laurel J. & Elizabeth C. Traugott 2005. *Lexicalization and Language Change.* Cambridge: Cambridge University Press.
Brugman, Claudia & George Lakoff 1988. Cognitive topology and lexical networks. In: S.L. Small, G. Cottrell & M. Tanenhaus (eds.). *Lexical Ambiguity Resolution: Perspectives from Psycholinguistics, Neuropsychology, and Artificial Intelligence.* San Mateo, CA: Morgan Kaufmann, 477–508.

Bybee, Joan, Revere Perkins & William Pagliuca 1994. *The Evolution of Grammar. Tense, Aspect, and Modality in the Languages of the World*. Chicago, IL: The University of Chicago Press.
Campbell, Lyle 2001. What's wrong with grammaticalization? *Language Sciences* 23, 113–161.
Campbell, Lyle & Richard Janda 2001. Introduction: Conceptions of grammaticalization and their problems. In: L. Campbell (ed.). *Grammaticalization: A critical assessment*. Special issue of *Language Sciences* 23, 93–112.
Copestake, Ann & Ted Briscoe 1996. Semi-productive polysemy and sense extension. In: J. Pustejowsky & B. Boguraev (eds.). *Lexical Semantics. The Problem of Polysemy*. Oxford: Clarendon Press, 15–68.
Coseriu, Eugenio 1964. Pour une sémantique diachronique structurale. *Travaux de Linguistique et de Littérature* 2, 139–186.
Coseriu, Eugenio 1974. *Synchronie, Diachronie und Geschichte. Das Problem des Sprachwandels*. München: Fink.
Darmesteter, Arsène 1887. *La vie des mots étudiée dans leurs significations*. Paris: Delagrave.
Dascal, Marcelo 2000. Controversies and epistemology. In: T.Y. Cao (ed.). *Philosophy of Science. Proceedings of the 20th World Congress of Philosophy*. Philadelphia, PA: Philosophers Index Inc., 159–192.
Detges, Ulrich & Richard Waltereit 2002. Grammaticalization vs. reanalysis: A semantic-pragmatic account of functional change in grammar. *Zeitschrift für Sprachwissenschaft* 21, 151–195.
Diewald, Gabriele 1999. *Modalverben im Deutschen. Grammatikalisierung und Polyfunktionalität*. Tübingen: Niemeyer.
Diewald, Gabriele 2002. A model for relevant types of contexts in grammaticalization. In: I. Wischer & G. Diewald (eds.). *New Reflections on Grammaticalization*. Amsterdam: Benjamins, 103–120.
Eckardt, Regine 2006. *Meaning Change in Grammaticalization. An Enquiry into Semantic Reanalysis*. Oxford: Oxford University Press.
Eckardt, Regine, Klaus von Heusinger & Christoph Schwarze (eds.) 2003. *Words in Time. Diachronic Semantics from Different Points of View*. Berlin: Mouton de Gruyter.
Fauconnier, Mark 1999. Methods and generalizations. In: T. Janssen & G. Redeker (eds.). *Cognitive Linguistics: Foundations, Scope, and Methodology*. Berlin: de Gruyter, 95–128.
Fauconnier, Gilles & Mark Turner 2002. *The Way we Think. Conceptual Blending and the Mind's Hidden Complexities*. New York: Basic Books.
Firth, John Rupert 1957. *Papers in Linguistics 1934–1951*. London: Oxford University Press.
Frege, Gottlob 1892/1969. Über Sinn und Bedeutung. *Zeitschrift für Philosophie und philosophische Kritik* 100, 25–50. Reprinted in: G. Patzig (ed.). *Gottlob Frege: Funktion, Begriff, Bedeutung. Fünf logische Studien*. 3rd edn. Göttingen: Vandenhoeck & Ruprecht, 1969, 40–65.
Frege, Gottlob 1918/1966. Der Gedanke. Eine logische Untersuchung. *Beiträge zur Philosophie des deutschen Idealismus* 1(1) 1918, 58–77. Reprinted in: G. Patzig (ed.). *Gottlob Frege. Logische Untersuchungen*. Göttingen: Vandenhoeck & Ruprecht, 1966, 30–53.
Fritz, Gerd 1991. Deutsche Modalverben 1609: Epistemische Verwendungsweisen. Ein Beitrag zur Bedeutungsgeschichte der Modalverben im Deutschen. *Beiträge zur Geschichte der deutschen Sprache und Literatur* 113, 28–52.
Fritz, Gerd 1995. Metonymische Muster und Metaphernfamilien. Bemerkungen zur Struktur und Geschichte der Verwendungsweisen von *scharf*. In: G. Hindelang, E. Rolf & W. Zillig (eds.). *Der Gebrauch der Sprache. Festschrift für Franz Hundsnurscher zum 60. Geburtstag*. Münster: Lit, 77–107.

Fritz, Gerd 1997a. Historische Semantik der Modalverben. Problemskizze—exemplarische Analysen—Forschungsüberblick. In: G. Fritz & T. Gloning (eds.). *Untersuchungen zur semantischen Entwicklungsgeschichte der Modalverben im Deutschen*. Tübingen: Niemeyer, 1–157.

Fritz, Gerd 1997b. Deutsche Modalverben 1609. Nicht-epistemische Verwendungsweisen. In: G. Fritz & T. Gloning (eds.). *Untersuchungen zur semantischen Entwicklungsgeschichte der Modalverben im Deutschen*. Tübingen: Niemeyer, 249–306.

Fritz, Gerd 1998. Sprachwandel auf der lexikalischen Ebene. In: W. Besch et al. (eds.). *Sprachgeschichte. Ein Handbuch zur Geschichte der deutschen Sprache und ihrer Erforschung* (HSK 2.1). 2nd edn. Berlin: de Gruyter, 860–874.

Fritz, Gerd 2005. *Einführung in die historische Semantik*. Tübingen: Niemeyer.

Fritz, Gerd 2006. *Historische Semantik*. 2nd rev. edn. Stuttgart: Metzler.

Fritz, Gerd 2011. Historische Semantik—einige Schlaglichter. In: J. Riecke (ed.). *Historische Semantik. Perspektiven der Forschung im Dialog der Fachkulturen. Jahrbuch für Germanistische Sprachgeschichte* 2, Berlin: de Gruyter, 1–19.

Geach, Peter T. 1972. On rigour in semantics. In: P.T. Geach. *Logic matters*. Oxford: Blackwell, 198–201.

Geeraerts, Dirk 1997. *Diachronic Prototype Semantics. A Contribution to Historical Lexicology*. Oxford: Clarendon Press.

Geeraerts, Dirk 2002. The theoretical and descriptive development of lexical semantics. In: L. Behrens & D. Zaefferer (eds.). *The Lexicon in Focus: Competition and Convergence in Current Lexicology*. Frankfurt/M.: Peter Lang, 23–42.

Gibbs, Raymond W. 1994. *The Poetics of Mind. Figurative Thought, Language and Understanding*. Cambridge: Cambridge University Press.

Gloning, Thomas 1996. *Bedeutung, Gebrauch und sprachliche Handlung. Ansätze und Probleme einer handlungstheoretischen Semantik aus linguistischer Sicht*. Tübingen: Niemeyer.

Gloning, Thomas 2002. Ausprägungen der Wortfeldtheorie. In: D. A. Cruse et al. (eds.). *Lexikologie—Lexicology. Ein internationales Handbuch zur Natur und Struktur von Wörtern und Wortschätzen* (HSK 21.1). Berlin: de Gruyter, 728–737.

Gloning, Thomas 2003. *Organisation und Entwicklung historischer Wortschätze. Lexikologische Konzeption und exemplarische Untersuchungen zum deutschen Wortschatz um 1600*. Tübingen: Niemeyer.

Grice, H. Paul 1957. Meaning. *The Philosophical Review* 66, 377–388.

Grice, H. Paul 1989. *Studies in the Way of Words*. Cambridge, MA: Harvard University Press.

Günthner, Susanne 2003. Lexical-grammatical variation and development: The use of conjunctions as discourse markers in everyday spoken German. In: R. Eckardt, K. von Heusinger & Ch. Schwarze (eds.). *Words in Time. Diachronic Semantics from Different Points of View*. Berlin: Mouton de Gruyter, 375–403.

Hamblin, Charles L. 1970. *Fallacies*. London: Methuen.

Hansen, Maj-Britt Mosegaard 2005. From prepositional phrase to hesitation marker: The semantic and pragmatic evolution of French 'enfin'. *Journal of Historical Pragmatics* 6, 37–68.

Heim, Irene 1983. File change semantics and the familiarity theory of definiteness. In: R. Bäuerle, Ch. Schwarze & A. von Stechow (eds.). *Meaning, Use, and Interpretation of Language*. Berlin: de Gruyter, 164–190.

Heine, Bernd 2003. On the role of context in grammaticalization. In: I. Wischer & G. Diewald (eds.). *New Reflections on Grammaticalization*. Amsterdam: Benjamins, 83–101.

Heine, Bernd & Tania Kuteva 2002. *World Lexicon of Grammaticalization*. Cambridge: Cambridge University Press.
Heringer, Hans Jürgen 1978. *Practical Semantics. A Study in the Rules of Speech and Action*. The Hague: Mouton.
Heringer, Hans Jürgen 1999. *Das höchste der Gefühle. Empirische Studien zur distributiven Semantik*. Tübingen: Stauffenburg.
Hopper, Paul J. & Elizabeth C. Traugott 2003. *Grammaticalization*. 2nd edn. Cambridge: Cambridge University Press.
Hundsnurscher, Franz 2003. *Sprechen* und *sagen* im Spätmittelalter und in der frühen Neuzeit. Zum Wechsel der Inquit-Formel *er sprach / er sagte*. In: N. Miedema & R. Suntrup (eds.). *Literatur—Geschichte—Literaturgeschichte. Beiträge zur mediävistischen Literaturwissenschaft*. Frankfurt/M.: Peter Lang, 31–52.
Jaberg, Karl 1901. Pejorative Bedeutungsentwicklung im Französischen. *Zeitschrift für Romanische Philologie* 25, 561–601.
Jucker, Andreas H. 1997. The discourse marker *well* in the history of English. *English Language and Linguistics* 1, 91–110.
Kamp, Hans & Uwe Reyle 1993. *From Discourse to Logic*. Dordrecht: Kluwer.
Keller, Rudi 1990. *Sprachwandel*. Tübingen: Francke Verlag.
Keller, Rudi 1998. *A Theory of Linguistic Signs*. Oxford: Oxford University Press.
Keller, Rudi & Ilja Kirschbaum 2003. *Bedeutungswandel. Eine Einführung*. Berlin: de Gruyter.
Koch, Peter 2001. Metonymy: Unity in diversity. *Journal of Historical Pragmatics* 2, 201–244.
Koch, Peter 2003. Historical Romance linguistics and the cognitive turn. *La Corónica. A Journal of Medieval Spanish Language and Literature* 31, 41–55.
Kronasser, Heinz 1952. *Handbuch der Semasiologie. Kurze Einführung in die Geschichte, Probleme und Terminologie der Bedeutungslehre*. Heidelberg: Winter.
Kuukkanen, Jouni-Matti 2006. *Meaning Change in the Context of Thomas S. Kuhn's Philosophy*. Ph.D. dissertation. The University of Edinburgh.
Lakoff, George 1987. *Women, Fire, and Dangerous Things. What Categories Reveal about the Mind*. Chicago, IL: The University of Chicago Press.
Lakoff, George & Mark Johnson 1980. *Metaphors we Live by*. Chicago, IL: The University of Chicago Press.
Langacker, Ronald W. 1988. A view of linguistic semantics. In: B. Rudzka-Ostyn (ed.). *Topics in Cognitive Linguistics*. Amsterdam: Benjamins, 49–90.
Lehrer, Adrienne 1985. The influence of semantic fields on semantic change. In: J. Fisiak (ed.). *Historical Semantics. Historical Word-Formation*. Berlin: de Gruyter, 283–296.
Lewis, David 1969. *Convention: A philosophical study*. Cambridge, MA: Harvard University Press.
Lewis, David 1972. General semantics. In: D. Davidson & G. Harman (eds.). *Semantics of Natural Language*. Dordrecht: Reidel, 169–218
Lewis, David 1979. Scorekeeping in a language game. *Journal of Philosophical Logic* 8, 339–359.
Locke, John 1689/1975. *An Essay Concerning Human Understanding*. London. Ed. by Peter H. Nidditch. Oxford: Oxford University Press, 1975.
Lyons, John 1963. *Structural Semantics. An Analysis of Part of the Vocabulary of Plato*. Oxford: Blackwell.
Lyons, John 1991. Bedeutungstheorien. In: A. von Stechow & D. Wunderlich. *Semantik. Ein internationales Handbuch der zeitgenössischen Forschung* (HSK 6). Berlin: de Gruyter, 1–24.

Meggle, Georg 1987. Pragmatische Semantik im Ausgang von Ludwig Wittgensteins Sprachspielkonzept. In: H. Stachowiak (ed.). *Pragmatik. Handbuch pragmatischen Denkens*. Vol. 2. Hamburg: Meiner, 279–301.
Meillet, Antoine 1905/1965. Comment les mots changent des sens. *Année Sociologique* 9, 1905/1906, 1–38. Reprinted in: A. Meillet, *Linguistique Historique et Linguistique Générale*. Paris: Champion, 1965, 230–271.
Meillet, Antoine 1912/1965. L'évolution des formes grammaticales. *Scientia* (Rivista di scienza) Vol. XII (1912), no. XXVI, 6. Reprinted in: A. Meillet, *Linguistique Historique et Linguistique Générale*. Paris: Champion, 1965, 130–148.
Montague, Richard 1974. *Formal Philosophy. Selected Papers of Richard Montague*. Edited and with an introduction by Richmond H. Thomason. New Haven, CT: Yale University Press.
Nerlich, Brigitte 1992. *Semantic Theories in Europe 1830–1930. From Etymology to Contextuality*. Amsterdam: Benjamins.
Nerlich, Brigitte & David D. Clark 2001. Serial metonymy: A study of reference-based polysemisation. *Journal of Historical Pragmatics* 2, 245–272.
Nunberg, Geoffrey 1995. Transfers of meaning. *Journal of Semantics* 12, 109–132.
Nyrop, Kristoffer 1903. *Das Leben der Wörter*. Autorisierte Übersetzung aus dem Dänischen von Robert Vogt. Leipzig: Avenarius.
Paul, Hermann 1886. *Prinzipien der Sprachgeschichte*. 2nd edn. Halle: Niemeyer.
Paul, Hermann 1895. Über die Aufgaben der wissenschaftlichen Lexikographie mit besonderer Rücksicht auf das deutsche Wörterbuch. *Sitzungsberichte der philosophisch-philologischen und der historischen Classe der Königlich-Bayrischen Akademie der Wissenschaften München* Jahrgang 1894, 53–91.
Peters, Wim & Adam Kilgarriff 2000. Discovering semantic regularity in lexical resources. *International Journal of Lexicography* 13, 287–312.
Porzig, Walter 1934. Wesenhafte Bedeutungsbeziehungen. *Beiträge zur Geschichte der deutschen Sprache und Literatur* 58, 70–97.
Pustejowsky, James 1995. *The Generative Lexicon*. Cambridge, MA: The MIT Press.
Rosch, Eleanor & Carolyn B. Mervis 1975. Family resemblances: Studies in the internal structure of categories. *Cognitive Psychology* 7, 573–605.
de Saussure, Ferdinand 1916/1968. *Cours de linguistique générale*. Paris: Payot. Edition critique par Rudolf Engler. Tome 1. Wiesbaden, 1968.
Schiffer, Stephen 1972. *Meaning*. Oxford: Oxford University Press.
Seiffert, Leslie 1968. *Wortfeldtheorie und Strukturalismus. Studien zum Sprachgebrauch Freidanks*. Stuttgart: Kohlhammer.
Sinha, Chris 1999. Grounding, mapping, and acts of meaning. In: T. Janssen & G. Redeker (eds.). *Cognitive Linguistics: Foundations, Scope, and Methodology*. Berlin: de Gruyter, 223–255.
Sperber, Hans 1923/1965. *Einführung in die Bedeutungslehre*. Bonn. Reprinted: Bonn: Dümmler, 1965.
Stalnaker, Robert C. 1978. Assertion. In: P. Cole (ed.). *Syntax and Semantics 9: Pragmatics*. New York: Academic Press, 315–332.
Stalnaker, Robert 2002. Common ground. *Linguistics & Philosophy* 25, 701–721.
Stanforth, Anthony 1967. *Die Bezeichnungen für „groß", „klein", „viel" und „wenig" im Bereich der Germania*. Marburg: Elwert.
Stern, Gustaf 1931. *Meaning and Change of Meaning. With Special Reference to the English Language*. Göteborg: Elander.

Stöcklein, Johannes 1898. *Bedeutungswandel der Wörter. Seine Entstehung und Entwicklung.* München: Lindauersche Buchhandlung.
Strawson, Peter F. 1964. Identifying reference and truth-values. *Theoria* 30, 96–118.
Strecker, Bruno 1987. *Strategien des kommunikativen Handelns. Zur Grundlegung einer Grammatik der Kommunikation.* Düsseldorf: Schwann.
Sweetser, Eve E. 1990. *From Etymology to Pragmatics. Metaphorical and Cultural Aspects of Semantic Structure.* Cambridge: Cambridge University Press.
Taylor, John R. 1999. Cognitive semantics and structural semantics. In: A. Blank & P. Koch (eds.). *Historical Semantics and Cognition.* Berlin: Mouton de Gruyter, 17–49.
Taylor, John R. 2002. *Cognitive Grammar.* Oxford: Oxford University Press.
Taylor, John, Hubert Cuyckens & René Dirven 2003. Introduction: New directions in cognitive lexical semantic research. In: H. Cuyckens & R. Dirven (eds.). *Cognitive Approaches to Lexical Semantics.* Berlin: de Gruyter, 1–27.
Tellier, André 1962. *Les Verbes Perfecto-Présents et les Auxiliaires de Mode en Anglais Ancien (VIIIe S.–XVIe S.).* Paris: Klincksieck.
Tomasello, Michael 1998. Introduction: A cognitive-functional perspective on language structure. In: M. Tomasello (ed.). *The New Psychology of Language. Cognitive and Functional Approaches to Language Structure.* Mahwah, NJ: Lawrence Erlbaum, vii–xxiii.
Traugott, Elizabeth C. 1989. On the rise of epistemic meanings in English: An example of subjectification in semantic change. *Language* 65, 31–55.
Traugott, Elizabeth C. & Richard B. Dasher 2002. *Regularity in Semantic Change.* Cambridge: Cambridge University Press.
Traugott, Elizabeth C. & Ekkehard König 1991. The semantics-pragmatics of grammaticalization revisited. In: E.C. Traugott & B. Heine (eds.). *Approaches to Grammaticalization. Vol. I. Focus on Theoretical and Methodological Issues.* Amsterdam: Benjamins, 189–218.
Trier, Jost 19931. *Der deutsche Wortschatz im Sinnbezirk des Verstandes. Von den Anfängen bis zum Beginn des 13. Jahrhunderts.* Heidelberg: Winter.
Ullmann, Stephen 1957. *The Principles of Semantics.* 2nd edn. Oxford: Blackwell.
Wegener, Philipp 1885. *Untersuchungen über die Grundfragen des Sprachlebens.* Halle: Niemeyer.
Weisgerber, Leo 1927. Die Bedeutungslehre: Ein Irrweg der Sprachwissenschaft? *Germanisch-Romanische Monatsschrift* 15, 161–183.
Wellander, Erik 1917. *Studien zum Bedeutungswandel im Deutschen.* 3 Bde. Uppsala Universitets Årsskrift 1917, 1923, 1928.
Whitney, William Dwight 1876. *Leben und Wachsthum der Sprache.* Übersetzt von August Leskien. Leipzig: Brockhaus.
Wittgenstein, Ludwig 1953. *Philosophical Investigations.* Translated into English by G.E.M. Anscombe. Oxford: Blackwell.
Wittgenstein, Ludwig 1970. Eine philosophische Betrachtung. In: L. Wittgenstein. *Schriften 5.* Frankfurt/M.: Suhrkamp, 9–282.
Wittgenstein, Ludwig 1975. *On Certainty.* Edited by G.E.M. Anscombe & G.H. von Wright. Translated by D. Paul & G.E.M. Anscombe. Oxford: Blackwell.
Wundt, Wilhelm 1904. *Völkerpsychologie. Eine Untersuchung der Entwicklungsgesetze von Sprache, Mythus und Sitte.* 2 Bde. 2nd edn. Leipzig: Engelmann.

Dirk Geeraerts
6 Cognitive approaches to diachronic semantics

1 Cognitive linguistics and historical semantics —— 147
2 Diachronic prototype semantics —— 149
3 Conceptual metaphors through time —— 157
4 Diachronic onomasiology —— 165
5 Rounding off —— 172
6 References —— 172

Abstract: The emergence of Cognitive Linguistics (an approach to language description that pays specific attention to the crucial role of meaning in the structure and the functioning of language) has led to a renewed interest in mechanisms and processes of meaning change. In this chapter, the impetus for diachronic semantics that comes from Cognitive Linguistics is illustrated on the basis of three important areas of investigation, representing different levels of the semantic organization of the lexicon. First, the investigation of the internal semantic structure of individual expressions has been profoundly influenced by the introduction of prototype-based models of semantic organization. Second, if we zoom in on the links between the senses within such semantic structures, mechanisms like metaphor and metonymy receive new attention. Third, if we zoom out, beyond the level of individual expressions, towards the vocabulary as a whole, we witness a change towards a pragmatic, contextualized conception of onomasiology. The chapter spells out the consequences of these three developments for the diachronic study of meaning.

1 Cognitive linguistics and historical semantics

Cognitive Linguistics is an approach to the analysis of natural language that focuses on language as an instrument for organizing, processing, and conveying information. This implies that the analysis of meaning is of primary importance for linguistic description: in Cognitive Linguistics, the formal structures of language are studied as reflections of general conceptual organization, categorization principles, processing mechanisms, and experiential and cultural influences. Cognitive

---

Dirk Geeraerts, Leuven, Belgium

https://doi.org/10.1515/9783110589825-006

Linguistics originated with a number of Californian linguists in the late 1970s and early 1980s, basically as an attempt to carry further the interest in meaning phenomena that was typical of the so-called Generative Semantics movement within generative linguistics. In contrast with Generative Semantics, however, Cognitive Linguistics is situated entirely outside the generative tradition. Leading figures within Cognitive Linguistics are George Lakoff, Ronald W. Langacker, Leonard Talmy, Charles Fillmore, and Gilles Fauconnier. For recent introductions and basic readings, see Geeraerts (2006), Kristiansen et al. (2006), Evans & Green (2006), Unger-er & Schmid (2006), Geeraerts & Cuyckens (2007), and compare article 1 [Semantics: Theories] (Talmy) *Cognitive Semantics*.

The renewed interest in semantics that drives the development of Cognitive Linguistics opens up interesting perspectives for diachronic semantics (for an exemplary sample of current research, see Winters et al. 2010). Specifically, the way in which the meaning-oriented research programme is elaborated in the context of Cognitive Linguistics links up conceptually with the way in which meaning was studied in the prestructuralist heyday of diachronic semantics, i.e. with the study of meaning change that dominated the scene from roughly 1870 to 1930 and that is represented by researchers like Bréal, Paul, Darmesteter, Nyrop, and (at the end of the relevant period) Carnoy and Stern. For a systematic treatment of the main figures and currents, see Nerlich (1992) and article 9 [Semantics: Foundations, History and Methods] (Nerlich) *Emergence of semantics*.

The link between Cognitive Linguistics and prestructuralist semantics rests on two specific points (compare Geeraerts 2010 for a more extended treatment in the context of the history of lexical semantics). First, the mechanisms of semantic extension, like metaphor and metonymy, that were traditionally studied from the point of view of diachronic meaning change only, reappear in the context of Cognitive Linguistics as synchronic phenomena: as associative links between the different senses of a lexical item or a grammatical construction, or as mechanisms that underlie the synchronic, contextual variability of meaning (compare article 11 [Semantics: Lexical Structures and Adjectives] (Tyler & Takahashi) *Metaphors and metonymies*). Second, both the prestructuralist tradition and Cognitive Linguistics take an integrated approach, i.e. an approach in which language is not considered to be an autonomous system, but rather an aspect of human life that is integrated into cognition and culture at large.

Cognitive Linguistics, however, does more than just pick up the thread of prestructuralist diachronic semantics. Although the study of meaning within Cognitive Linguistics at large is more concerned with the synchronic flexibility of meaning than with semantic change in the historical sense, the cognitive approach introduces a number of novel perspectives and areas for research into diachronic semantics, and these will constitute the focus of the present chapter.

Four specific subjects should be mentioned in this respect: prototype theory, Conceptual Metaphor Theory, cognitive onomasiology, and grammaticalization research. The first three of these topics will be treated in the following pages. For grammaticalization and the related issue of regularity of change (Traugott & Dasher 2002), see articles 6 [this volume] (Fritz) *Theories of meaning change* and 101 (Eckardt) *Grammaticalization and semantic reanalysis*. Each of the three topics is treated in a separate section, the first subsection of which introduces the domain. The second subsection presents an illustrative case study, together with an overview of some of the relevant literature. The third subsection introduces a number of theoretical or methodological issues that need to be further explored. The focus of the chapter will be on meaning changes at word level, but all of the phenomena discussed here can be straightforwardly extrapolated to the semantics of other meaningful linguistic elements, below or above the level of the word.

2 Diachronic prototype semantics

2.1 Introducing prototypicality effects

The prototype model of the internal semantic structure of words (compare Taylor 2003 and article 2 [Semantics: Theories] (Taylor) *Prototype theory*) highlights two structural characteristics: differences of structural weight on the one hand, and fuzziness and flexibility on the other. To illustrate, consider the word *fruit*. This is a polysemous word: next to its basic, everyday reading ('sweet and soft edible part of a plant, containing seeds'), there are various other readings conventionally associated with the word. In a technical sense, for instance ('the seed-bearing part of a plant or tree'), the word also refers to things that lie outside the range of application of the basic reading, such as acorns and pea pods. In an expression like *the fruits of nature*, the meaning is even more general, as the word refers to everything that grows and that can be eaten by people (including, for instance, grains and vegetables). Further, there is a range of figurative readings, including the abstract sense 'the result or outcome of an action' (as in *the fruits of his labour* or *his work bore fruit*), or the somewhat archaic reading 'offspring, progeny' (as in the biblical expressions *the fruit of the womb, the fruit of his loins*).

Each of these readings constitutes a separate sense of *fruit*, but in turn, each sense may be thought of as a set of things in the outside world. The basic sense of *fruit*, for instance, corresponds with a set including apples, oranges, and bananas (and many other types of fruit). If you think of *fruit* in this central sense as a category, the set consists of the members of the category. These members are 'things' only in a broad sense. In the *fruit* example, they happen to be material objects, but in the case of verbs, they could be actions, or situations, or events; in the case of adjectives, they could be properties; and so on. Given this example, we can now describe the two structural characteristics that receive special attention within a prototype-theoretical framework.

Differences of structural weight

Differences in salience involve the fact that not all the elements at a specific level of semantic analysis carry the same structural weight. For instance, the everyday reading of *fruit* occupies a more central position than the archaic reading 'offspring' or the technical reading. Various indications may be adduced for this central position. For one thing, the central reading more readily springs to mind when people think of the category: on being asked what *fruit* means, you are more likely to mention the edible parts of plants than a person's offspring. For another, the 'edible part' reading is more frequent in actual language use.

In addition, the 'edible part' reading is a good starting-point for describing the other readings. It would probably be more easy to understand the expression *the fruit of his labours* (if it is new to you) when you understand the 'edible part' reading than the other way round. The basic reading, in other words, is the center of semantic cohesion in the category; it holds the category together by making the other readings accessible. Three features, in short (psychological salience, relative frequency of use, interpretative advantageousness), may be mentioned as indications for the central position of a particular reading.

Centrality effects are not restricted to the level of senses and readings, however, but may also be invoked at the referential level, i.e. the level where we talk about the members of a category. When prompted, Europeans will more readily name apples and oranges as types of fruit than avocados or pomegranates, and references to apples and oranges are likely to be more frequent in a European context than references to mangos. This does not exclude, moreover, cultural differences among distinct parts of Europe.

The terminology used to describe these differences of structural weight is quite diverse, and the description in the foregoing paragraphs has featured such (intuitively transparent) terms as *salience*, *typicality*, and *centrality*. The most technical term however is *prototypicality*: the central reading of an item or the central subset within the range of a specific reading is the prototype.

Fuzziness and flexibility

How clearly distinguishable are the elements of a semantic description? Consider the question whether the central sense of *fruit* can be delimited in a straightforward fashion. Such a delimitation will take the form of a definition that is general and distinctive: it is general in the sense of naming characteristics that are common to all fruits, and it is distinctive in the sense of being sufficient to distinguish the category 'fruit' (in the relevant sense) from any other category. (If a definition is not distinctive, it is too general: it will cover cases that do not belong in the category to be defined.)

Now, many of the characteristics that one might be inclined to include in a definition of the central reading of *fruit* do not have the required generality: fruits are not necessarily sweet, they do not necessarily contain parts that are immediately recognizable as seeds, they are not necessarily soft. There are, to be sure, a number of features that do have the required generality: all fruits grow above the ground on plants or trees (rather than in the ground); they have to ripen before you can eat them, and if you want to prepare them (rather than eat them raw), you would primarily use sugar, or at least use them in dishes that have a predominantly sweet taste. Taken together, however, these features do not suffice to prevent almonds (and other nuts), or a vegetable like rhubarb (which is usually cooked with sugar), from being wrongly included into the category that is to be defined. We have to conclude, then, that the central sense of *fruit* cannot receive a definition that is both general and distinctive. If we shift the attention to the members of a category, similar effects may be observed: the borderline of categories is not always clearly delineated. For instance, is a coconut or an olive a fruit? Observations such as these lead prototype theory to the conclusion that semantic structures need not necessarily consist of neatly delineated, rigidly defined entities, but that they may rather be characterized by a certain amount of fuzziness and vagueness—a fuzziness and vagueness that entails flexibility: if the criteria for using a word are less stringent than a naive conception of meaning would suggest, there is likely to be a lot of plasticity in meaning.

2.2 Illustration and overview

Following Molina (2000, 2005), the diachronic importance of prototypicality effects may be illustrated by the history of *sore* and *sorrow*. In contemporary English, *sore* essentially refers to a specific type of wound or physical injury, viz. a bruise, a raw place on the body as caused by pressure or friction. In Old English, however, the range of application is much broader. The following Old English quotations from the ninth and tenth century show that, next to the 'wound' reading as represented by (1a), we find references to bodily suffering (1b), to sickness (1c), and to emotional suffering (1d). (Note that the modern form *sore* appears in the older form *sar* in the following quotations, which date from the ninth and tenth century.)

(1) a. *Wið wunda & wið cancor genim þas ilcan wyrte, lege to þam sare. Ne geþafað heo þæt sar furður wexe*
'For wounds and cancer take the same herb, put it on to the sore. Do not allow the sore to increase'
b. *Þisse sylfan wyrte syde to þa sar geliðigað*
'With this same herb, the sore of the teeth calms widely'
c. *Þa þe on sare seoce lagun*
'Those who lay sick in sore'
d. *Mið ðæm mæstam sare his modes*
'With the greatest sore of his spirit'

Given that Old English *sore* thus appears to have a wider range of application than contemporary *sore*, what could have happened? How can we describe the semantic shift from Old English to contemporary English? Let us first have a closer look at the Old English situation. Two features that link up directly with the prototype-theoretical model as described above need to be mentioned.

First, the different meanings in Old English have a different status and a different weight within the cluster of applications. This becomes clear when we have a look at the frequencies of the *sore* quotations that may be found in the Oxford English Dictionary (OED) in the successive centuries: see Fig. 6.1 (simplified from Molina 2000: 99). The roman figures along the top of the figure indicate centuries; the lines indicate the distribution over time of the various readings of *sore*. While the 'bodily suffering' reading appears first and occupies the central position in the initial semantic structure of *sore*, the 'injury, wound' reading takes up a dominant position only much later. What we see, in other words, is an illustration of the first feature of prototypicality as defined: in the semantic structure of words, we have to distinguish central from peripheral instances. In the case of *sore*, the core meaning shifts over time from 'bodily suffering' to 'wound'.

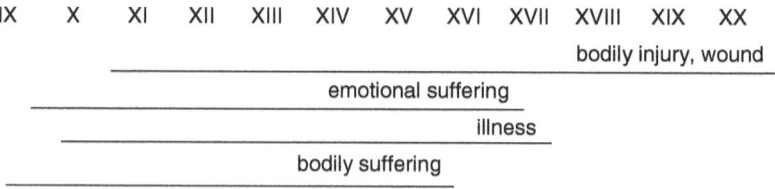

Fig. 6.1: Distribution of SORE meanings over time

But *sore* illustrates the second feature of prototypicality as well. *Sore* and *sorrow* are etymologically unrelated, but the 'emotional suffering' reading of *sore* overlaps with *sorrow*, which exhibits only that meaning. In fact, the frequent co-occurrence of *sore* and *sorrow* in alliterating binominals, as in the Middle English examples (1e)-(1f) below, indicates that both words were readily recognized as (near-)synonyms: in Middle English, the formal closeness and the semantic overlap between the two words seem to converge towards an incipient merger. From the prototype point of view, this specific configuration of *sore* and *sorrow* (in the forms *sorhe* and *sorge* in the quotations) illustrates the absence of rigid borderlines between words.

(1) e. *Ant te unseli swalen sunken to helle, to forswelten i sar & i sorhe eaure*
'And the unhappy souls sink to hell, to die in sore and sorrow ever'
f. *On heorte he hafde sorge & sar*
'On heart he had sorrow and sore'

Summarizing, the initial situation in the semantic history of *sore* is one in which the concept of 'bodily suffering' occupies the centre of the word, with metonymical extensions towards 'illness' and 'wound' on the one hand, and on the other with a metaphorical extension towards 'emotional suffering' that constitutes an overlap, possibly even an incipient merger, with *sorrow*. Fig. 6.2 graphically represents the situation. Solid circles represent meanings of *sore*, the dotted circle that of *sorrow*. The size of the circles identifies the centrality of the meaning: 'bodily suffering' is the core of the *sore* structure. The links with the secondary readings are identified as being metonymical or metaphorical.

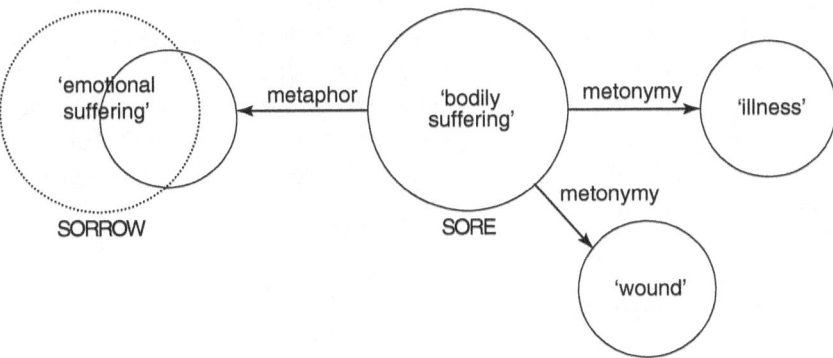

Fig. 6.2: The SORE cluster in Old English

The major force in the transition towards the present-day situation may now be identified: the French loan *pain*, first attested in 1297, takes over the meaning of *sore*. But typically (and this is where the fruitfulness of a prototype-theoretical approach shows up most clearly), it does not substitute *sore* in a wholesale manner, but rather occupies the central area of the meaning of *sore*, leaving only the specialized 'wound' reading with *sore* itself. In terms of the graphical representation of Fig. 6.2, the center of the *sore* cluster is so to speak invaded and occupied by *pain*, and as such, the original cluster dissolves, with only a fraction of the original range staying with *sore*. It should be mentioned that the story told here is a simplified one: it does not involve intriguing questions like the relationship between *pain* and *pine* (an older word for 'suffering', which survives in the verb *to pine* 'to suffer'), or the relationship between the nouns *sore* and *sorrow*, and the adjectives *sore* and *sorry*. Nevertheless, it illustrates how useful it can be to think of semantic structures as clusters of readings organized around prototypical cores.

The prototype structure of semantic change in its various aspects is discussed at length in Geeraerts (1997), a monograph devoted entirely to diachronic prototype semantics. Apart from Molina (2000, 2005), which served as the basis for the illustrations above, it is further acknowledged and exemplified in one form or another in many studies, among them Dirven (1985), Casad (1992), Evans (1992), Dekeyser (1996), Cuyckens (1999), Soares da Silva (1999, 2003), Koivisto-Alanko (2000), Tissari (2003). While these are predominantly lexical studies, the application of the model to the evolution of grammatical rather than lexical categories is illustrated and discussed, among others, by Winters (1989, 1992), Melis (1990), Nikiforidou (1991), Luraghi (1995), de Mulder (2001).

In this context, we should also mention studies that focus on the individual links within the prototype structure: the traditional mechanisms of semantic change. Apart from the theoretical attention for metaphor and metonymy as synchronic phenomena (see article 11 [Semantics: Lexical Structures and Adjectives] (Tyler & Takahashi) *Metaphors and metonymies*), these involve suggestions to revise the traditional classification of semantic changes, such as Grygiel's attempt (2004) to explain the emergence of new meanings on the basis of Fauconnier's blending theory. For a comprehensive treatment of the classification of semantic changes, see Blank (1997).

2.3 Further perspectives

Apart from the further descriptive elaboration of diachronic prototype semantics, two broad areas for further research may be identified. A first topic involves the relationship between the notion of prototype and the concept of stereotype as defined by Putnam (1975). According to Putnam, ordinary language users possess no more than 'stereotypical' knowledge about natural kinds, that is to say, they are aware of a number of salient characteristics, such as the fact that water is a transparent, thirst-quenching, tasteless liquid. The technical definition of *water* as H_2O, on the other hand, is to be located primarily with scientific experts. It is the experts' knowledge that ultimately determines how natural kind terms are to be used. On the one hand, a 'division of linguistic labor' ensures that there are societal experts who know that water is H_2O, that there is a distinction between elms and beech, how to recognize gold from pyrites, and so on. On the other hand, laymen attune their own linguistic usage to that of the expert scientists, technicians, etc. The members of the non-specialized group are not required to have expert knowledge, but if they wish to be considered full-fledged members of the linguistic community, they are supposed to know the 'stereotype' connected with a category. A stereotype is, thus, a socially determined minimum set of data with regard to the extension of a category. Given the similarity between Putnam's stereotypes and the prototypes of Cognitive Linguistics (both consist roughly of the most salient information connected with a category), the division of linguistic labor might be used to rescue a classical view of concepts that contradicts the flexibility signalled by prototypicality. Expert definitions being classical (they specify an essentialist 'hidden structure' for natural kinds), the stereotypical concepts of everyday language users might now be seen as hardly more than a sloppy derivative of those classically defined expert categories. 'True' (expert) definitions would be classical, and stereotypical/prototypical concepts might be dismissed as sociolinguistically secondary phenomena.

However, as a 'sociolinguistic' theory about the social factors that determine how lexical items may be used, the division of linguistic labor theory is not entirely adequate. The primacy of expert definitions would seem to imply that natural language follows the developments and discoveries of science in a strict fashion. In actual fact, however, natural language categorization is not only determined by the state of affairs in the sciences, but also by the communicative and cognitive requirements of the linguistic community in its own right. More generally, if Putnam's view is seen as a theory about the sociolinguistic structure of semantic norms, his hierarchical model (with experts at one end and laymen at the other) is only one among a number of alternatives, some of which (such as the one described by Bartsch 1987) link up closely with a prototypical conception of categorial structure. For further discussion of Putnam's views and semantic change, see Eckardt (2003), Geeraerts (2008) and article 8 [this volume] (Eckardt) *Grammaticalization and semantic reanalysis*.

A second, not unrelated topic for further scrutiny involves the role of prototypicality in an explanatory theory of semantic change. Prototypicality effects may be observed, but to what extent can they be explained, and further, to what extent can they themselves contribute to the explanation of change? These questions are best addressed in a functional theory of semantic change (see Geeraerts 1997 for a more extended treatment). There are, in fact, several functional reasons for having a prototypical conceptual structure of word meanings, and all three are functional requirements that the conceptual system has to fulfil if it is to carry out optimally its task of storing categorial knowledge and making it accessible for cognitive and communicative purposes.

The first of these requirements has been mentioned by Eleanor Rosch (who first drew the attention to prototype effects) herself (see Rosch 1977): it is cognitively advantageous to lump as much information as possible into one's conceptual categories. Making conceptual categories as informatively dense as possible enables one to retrieve the most information with the least effort. Clearly, prototypically organized categories achieve such an informational density, because they are clusters of subconcepts and nuances.

Further, the cognitive system should combine structural stability with flexibility. On the one hand, it should be flexible enough to adapt itself to the everchanging circumstances of the outside world. On the other hand, the categorial system can only work efficiently if it does not change its overall structure any time it has to cope with new circumstances. Again, prototypical categories obviously fulfil the joint requirements of structural stability and flexible adaptability. On the one hand, the development of peripheral nuances within given categories indicates their dynamic ability to deal with changing conditions and changing cognitive requirements. On the other hand, the fact that marginally deviant concepts can be peripherally incorporated into existing categories indicates that the latter have a tendency to maintain themselves as particular entities, thus maintaining the overall structure of the system. Prototypical categories are cognitively efficient because they enable the subject to interpret new data in terms of existing concepts; as expectational patterns with regard to experience, prototypically organized categories maintain themselves by adapting themselves to changing circumstances.

In short, the cognitive system favours prototypical categories because they enable it to fulfil the functional requirements of *informational density*, *structural stability*, and *flexible adaptability* as a pattern of expectations. This functional view of conceptual structure can be further specified in the following way. The flexibility that is inherent in prototypically organized concepts cannot work at random; there have to be a number of principles that restrict the flexible extendibility of concepts. These principles define what is an acceptable extension of a particular concept. The traditional associationist mechanisms of semantic change (such as metaphor and metonymy) have precisely that function; they restrict the set of acceptable conceptual extensions to those changes that are brought about by regular associationist mechanisms such as metaphor and metonymy. In this sense, then, the traditional classificatory categories of historical semantics can in fact be incorporated into a functional classification of the causes of semantic change. But prototypicality itself has a similar restrictive function: the constraint that new meanings be linked to existing ones prevents the semantic flexibility of lexical items from deteriorating into communicatively inefficient arbitrariness.

The implications of prototype theory for the functioning of the human conceptual capacities make it an explanatory basis for diachronic semantics, because the dynamic nature of human thinking is recognized as one of the fundamental structural characteristics of conceptual categories. In this respect, accepting prototype theory is a question of explanatory adequacy rather than descriptive adequacy: prototype theory explains the observed prototypical characteristics of semantic change, because it relates them to general epistemological beliefs about the working of the human conceptual system, beliefs it shares with other cognitive theories. And at the same time, of course, the overall conception of a prototypical organization of conceptual categories can itself be explained on functional grounds.

At the same time, however (and this is where a domain for further research may be identified), the functional motivation behind prototypicality effects is not the only functional principle at work in the association between linguistic forms and meanings. Consider homonymic clashes. Gilliéron's famous example involves the collision of Latin *cattus* ('cat') and *gallus* ('cock') into Gascon *gat* (Gilliéron & Roques 1912). The tension is resolved by replacing *gat* ('cock') by *bigey*, a local equivalent of *vicaire* ('curate'), or by *azan*, the local equivalent of *faisan* ('pheasant'), or by the cognates of Latin *pullus*. The moral of the story is usually taken to be that homonymic ambiguities set off therapeutic diachronic changes towards their resolution. The rationale behind the avoidance of homonymy might be called a principle of formal efficiency, more particularly a 'one form—one meaning' principle: formally disambiguated languages are functionally superior, because they avoid communicative misunderstandings. But a formal kind of efficiency of this type contrasts with the type of efficiency underlying prototypicality effects: in the former case, there is a tendency to reduce polysemy, in the latter, semantic diversity is enhanced. It will have to be determined, then, how exactly the various functional principles interact.

3 Conceptual metaphors through time

3.1 Introducing conceptual metaphors

Suppose that you talk about relationships in the following way.

(2) He is known for his many rapid *conquests*. She *fought* for him, but his mistress *won* out. He *fled* from her *advances*. She *pursued* him relentlessly. He is

slowly *gaining ground* with her. He *won* her hand in marriage. He *overpowered* her. She is *besieged* by suitors. He has to *fend* them off. He *enlisted* the aid of her friends. He made an *ally* of her mother. Theirs is a *misalliance* if I've ever seen one.

All these expressions are related by a common theme: love is war. A source domain (war) is more or less systematically mapped onto a target domain (love). The target domain is understood in terms of the source domain; the conceptual structure that we associate with the source domain (like the recognition that a war involves specific actions like fighting and spying and fleeing and finding allies) is invoked to bring structure to the target domain.

Crucially, this mapping involves not just a single word, but a whole set of lexical items, an entire subfield of the vocabulary. In such cases, Cognitive Linguistics speaks of *conceptual metaphors*: metaphorical mappings that are not restricted to a single item but that overarch an entire subset of the vocabulary. Typically, in Conceptual Metaphor Theory, such supralexical metaphors are identified by a 'target domain is source domain' format: LOVE IS WAR. (For an introduction to contemporary metaphor theory, see Kövecses 2002, and compare article 11 [Semantics: Lexical Structures and Adjectives] (Tyler & Takahashi) *Metaphors and metonymies*.) From a cognitive point of view, such conceptual (rather than lexical) metaphors are extremely interesting, because they may well reveal underlying patterns of thought, basic models that we use to reason about a given topic (like love). From a historical point of view, then, the question arises to what extent such conceptual metaphors for a given target domain change through time: can an analysis of changing conceptual metaphors reveal cultural and historical changes in the way in which a specific domain of human experience is conceptualized?

3.2 Illustration and overview

Following Geeraerts & Grondelaers (1995), let us consider the evolution of anger metaphors in English. Conventionalized phrases such as those in (3) have been subsumed by Lakoff & Kövecses (1987) under the conceptual metaphor ANGER IS HEAT, which is further specified into ANGER IS THE HEAT OF A FLUID IN A CONTAINER when the heat applies to fluids, and into ANGER IS FIRE when the heat is applied to solids.

(3) I had reached the boiling point, She was seething red with rage, He lost his cool, You make my blood boil, He was foaming at the mouth, He's just letting off steam, Don't get hot under the collar, Billy's a hothead, They

were having a heated argument, When I found out, I almost burst a blood vessel, He got red with anger, She was scarlet with rage, I was fuming, When I told him, he just exploded, Smoke was pouring out of his ears, He was breathing fire, Those are inflammatory remarks, That kindled my ire, He was consumed by his anger.

At a lower level of analysis, these and many similar expressions are grouped together under labels such as when the intensity of anger increases, the fluid rises (his pent-up anger *welled up* inside him), intense anger produces steam (I was *fuming*), and when anger becomes too intense, the person explodes (when I told him, he just *exploded*). Next to the basic conceptual metaphor ANGER IS HEAT, less elaborate metaphorical patterns such as ANGER IS INSANITY, ANGER IS AN OPPONENT, ANGER IS A DANGEROUS ANIMAL, and CAUSING ANGER IS TRESPASSING are identified. Lakoff & Kövecses tend to interpret these findings in terms of physiological effects: increased body heat is taken to be a physiological effect of being in a state of anger, and anger is metonymically conceptualized in terms of its physiological effects.

If we now have a look at the following quotations from Shakespeare's *The Taming of the Shrew*, we may easily come to the conclusion that these examples too illustrate the conceptual metaphor ANGER IS HEAT.

(4) Were I not a little pot and soon hot [IV:1:5]

(5) Is she so hot a shrew [IV:1:17]

(6) I tell thee, Kate, 't was burnt and dried away,
and I expressly am forbid to touch it,
for it engenders choler, planteth anger;
and better it were that both of us did fast,
since, of ourselves, ourselves are choleric [IV:1:156]

(7) Grumio: What say you to a neat's foot?
Katherina: 'Tis passing good. I prithee let me have it.
Grumio: I fear it is too choleric a meat.
How say you to a fat tripe finely broil'd?
Katherina: I like it well. Good Grumio, fetch it me.
Grumio: I cannot tell. I fear 'tis choleric.
What say you to a piece of beef and mustard?
Katherina: A dish that I do love to feed upon.
Grumio: Ay, but the mustard is too hot a little [IV:3:25]

But would these older images have the same, allegedly universal physiological basis as the contemporary expressions described by Lakoff & Kövecses? It has been described by various authors (among them Schäfer 1966; Pope 1985) how the psychology of Shakespeare's dramatic characters unmistakenly refers to the theory of humours. The humoral theory, to be precise, is the highly influential doctrine that dominated medical thinking in Western Europe for several centuries.

The foundations of the humoral doctrine were laid by Hippocrates of Kos (*ca.* 460 BC–*ca.* 370 BC). Physiologically, the four humoral fluids regulate the vital processes within the human body; the secretion of the humours underlies the dynamical operation of our anatomy. Psychologically, on the other hand, they define four prototypical temperaments, i.e. a person's character is thought to be determined by the preponderance of one of the four vital fluids in his body. Thus, the *choleric* temperament (given to anger and irascibility) is determined by a preponderance of the yellow bile, while the *melancholic*, gloomy and fearful, suffers from a constitutional excess of black bile. The *phlegmatic* personality is typically placid and unmoved, while the *sanguine* temperament (defined in correlation with blood, the fourth humour) is passionate, optimistic, and brave. The singular combination of physiological and psychological concepts that characterizes the theory of humours also shows up in the fact that a disequilibrium of the fluids does not only characterize constitutional temperaments, but also causes temporary diseases—which are then typically described in bodily, biological terms as well as in psychic terms. For instance, an overproduction of yellow bile may be signalled by the patient's vomiting bile, but also by his dreaming of fire. In the same line, an excess of blood shows up in the redness of the skin and swollen veins, but also in carelessness and a certain degree of recalcitrance. In this sense, the humoral theory is a medical doctrine: it identifies diseases and their symptoms, and defines a therapy. Obviously, the basic therapeutic rule will be to restore the balance of the humours, given that a disturbance of their well-balanced proportion is the basic cause of the pathological situation. The long-lasting popularity of blood-letting, for instance (a standard medical practice that continued well into the 19th century) has its historical origins in the theory of humours.

The connection between yellow bile and fire that was mentioned a moment ago is not accidental. It is part of a systematic correlation between the human, anatomical microcosm and the macrocosm, thought to be built up from four basic elements. Thus, yellow bile, black bile, phlegm, and blood corresponded with fire, earth, water, and air respectively. In the Aristotelian elaboration of the Hippocratic doctrine, these correlating sets of microcosmical and macrocosmical basic elements were defined as combinations of four basic features: cold, warm, wet, and dry. Blood was thought to be warm and wet, phlegm cold and wet, yellow bile warm and dry, and black bile cold and dry.

The classical humoral doctrine received the form in which it was to dominate the Middle Ages in the work of Galen (129–199). He added a dietary pharmacology to the humoral edifice. All plants (and foodstuffs in general) could be characterized by one of four degrees of warmth, cold, wetness, and dryness. Given that diseases are caused by an excess of one of the four humours, and given that these are themselves characterized by the four features just mentioned, the basic therapeutic rule is to put the patient on a diet that will ensure a decrease of the superfluous humour.

In the course of the Middle Ages, the Galenic framework was further developed into a large-scale system of signs and symbols. In a typically medieval analogical way of thinking, widely divergent phenomena (ranging from the ages of man to astrological notions such as the system of the planets and the signs of the zodiac) were fitted into the fourfold schema presented by the medical theory. In Tab. 6.1, an overview is given of a number of those correlations. The humoral edifice began to be undermined as soon as the Renaissance introduced renewed empirical medical investigations, like William Harvey's description of the circulation of the blood in 1628. However, the disappearance of the theory from the medical scene was only very gradual, and it took approximately another three centuries before the last vestiges of the humoral framework were finally removed. The standard view of the historians of medicine is, in fact, that only in the middle of the 19th century did the humoral pathological conception receive its final blow.

Tab. 6.1: A system of humoral correspondences

	phlegm	black bile	yellow bile	blood
characteristic	cold and wet	cold and dry	warm and dry	warm and wet
element	water	earth	fire	air
temperament	phlegmatic	melancholic	choleric	sanguine
organ	brain/bladder	spleen	liver/stomach	heart
color	white	black	yellow	red
taste	salty	sour	bitter	sweet
season	winter	autumn	summer	spring
wind	North	West	South	East
planet	moon	Saturn	Mars	Jupiter
animal	turtle	sparrow	lion	goat

It will be clear by now that the conceptualization of anger in the Shakespeare quotations conforms to the model furnished by the theory of humours: anger is caused by black bile, also named choler (6), the production of which may be stimulated by certain kinds of food (6), (7); while a choleric temperament is a permanent personality trait (6), the main attribute of the choleric personality is hotness (4), (5). The fact that passages such as the ones quoted above can be multiplied from the work of other English Renaissance playwrights like Webster, Marlowe, or Jonson, leads Schäfer (1966) to the conclusion that the humoral conception of physiology and psychology is something of a true fashion in the plays produced when Queen Elizabeth I reigned in England, from 1558 until 1603. He attributes this to the fact that it is only in the middle of the 16th century, after the invention of printing, that the doctrine became known to a wider audience than that of learned men who could read the medical authorities in their Latin and Greek originals. But if this dissemination of the doctrine of humours from the realm of learned knowledge to that of popular belief implies that it is technically a piece of *gesunkenes Kulturgut*, the question arises how far it actually sank. In particular, how deeply did it become entrenched in the language itself?

In Tab. 6.2, we have systematically brought together a number of items and expressions in three European languages (English, French, and Dutch) that can be considered a part of the legacy of the theory of humours.

Tab. 6.2: Lexical relics of the humoral doctrine

	English	**French**	**Dutch**
phlegm	phlegmatic 'calm, cool, apathetic'	avoir un flegme imperturbable 'to be imperturbable'	een valling (dialectal) 'a cold, a running nose' (literally 'a falling', viz. of phlegm)
black bile	spleen 'organ filtering the blood; sadness'	mélancolie 'sadness, moroseness'	zwartgallig 'sad, depressed' (literally 'blackbilious')
yellow bile	bilious 'angry, irascible'	colère 'anger'	z'n gal spuwen 'to vent (literally 'to spit out') one's gall'
blood	full-blooded 'vigorous, hearty, sensual'	avoir du sang dans les veines 'to have spirit, luck'	warmbloedig 'passionate' (literally 'warm-blooded')

If we zoom in on one of the cells of Tab. 6.2, still further examples may be found. According to Roget's Thesaurus, the items listed under (8) all refer to anger or related concepts.

(8) *choler* 'anger', *gall* 'anger', *rouse one's choler* 'to elicit anger', *stir one's bile* 'to elicit anger', *galling,* 'vexing, causing anger', *choleric* 'irascible', *liverish* 'irascible', *splenetic* 'irascible', *hot-blooded* 'irascible', *fiery* 'irascible', *hot-headed* 'irascible'

Given these lexical relics of the humoral doctrine, it will be obvious that the conceptual metaphor ANGER IS THE HEAT OF A FLUID IN A CONTAINER neatly fits into the humoral views: the body is the container of the four cardinal fluids, and anger involves the heating up of specific fluids (either yellow bile as the direct source of ire, or blood, which is not only a humour in itself, but which is also a carrier for the other humours). This means, in other words, that the purely physiological interpretation put forward by Lakoff & Kövecses needs to be interpreted along cultural and historical lines. When we recognize that the medieval physiological-psychological theory of the four humours and the four temperaments has left its traces on our emotional vocabulary, we learn to see the ANGER IS THE HEAT OF A FLUID IN A CONTAINER metaphor as one of those traces. It is then not motivated directly by the physiological effects of anger, as Lakoff & Kövecses suggest, but it is part of the historical (but reinterpreted) legacy of the humoral theory.

Although the interest for a cross-cultural comparison of conceptual metaphors (see Kövecses 2005 for a theoretical view and Sharifian et al. 2008 for an illustration) generally seems to be bigger than that for a historical comparison, a growing number of researchers is undertaking diachronic studies on the ways in which particular conceptual metaphors develop: see Gevaert (2001, 2005), Fabiszak (2002), Tissari (2003), van Hecke (2005), Diller (2007), Trim (2007), Geeraerts & Gevaert (2008), Allan (2008).

3.3 Further perspectives

The 'anger' example shows that an adequate analysis of the motivation behind cultural phenomena in general and language in particular has to take into account the diachronic dimension. Cultural models, i.e. the more or less coherent sets of concepts that cultures use to structure experience and make sense of the world are not reinvented afresh with every new period in the culture's development. Rather, it is by definition part of their cultural nature that they have a historical dimension. It is only by investigating their historical origins and their gradual transformation that their contemporary form can be properly understood.

For Conceptual Metaphor Theory, that means two things. On the one hand, diachronic studies of linguistic conceptualization patterns may shed an interesting light on the development of cultures. On the other hand, it is important not to come to the rash conclusion of the presence of a conceptual metaphor. After all, the humoral doctrine was initially a literal, physiological theory—a wrong one, given our current knowledge of anatomy and physiology, but a literal theory nevertheless, and not just a metaphor. It is only when the original theory as a motivating context disappears that the lexical relics of the humoral doctrine become metaphorical expressions, or even worse, dead metaphors that evoke no specific concept whatsoever. An expression like *full-blooded* may safely be categorized as metaphorical to the extent that the concept 'blood' evokes vigour, strength and dynamism in other expressions of the language as well: *bloodless* and *new blood* are used in contexts in which a link with anatomy and physiology is definitely absent and in which there is no doubt that *blood* as a sign of life is used non-literally. But the Dutch dialect word *valling* no longer evokes the verbal concept *vallen* 'to fall' in any way: it is a semantically empty relic. (The danger of underestimating the importance of dead metaphors was raised early on in the history of Conceptual Metaphor Theory; see Traugott 1985.)

This means that the study of diachronic changes of conceptualization faces a double danger of over-metaphorization. On the one hand, with regard to older stages of the language, we may be tempted to interpret expressions as metaphorical that were taken literally at the time. Unless we are aware of the importance and the scientific status of the humoral theory in the Elisabethan era, we might think that the Shakespearean expressions have the same metaphorical status as *to make one's blood boil* in contemporary English. On the other hand, with regard to the present-day situation, metaphor researchers may be tempted to overstate the presence of live metaphor at the expense of dead metaphors. These dangers can only be overcome if reliable methods can be developed to determine metaphoricity in contrast with literal use. At present no such generally accepted set of criteria exists.

Next to the double-sided problem of literalness, there is another methodological issue that needs to be raised in connection with diachronic metaphor studies. If metaphors are interpreted as a mapping from source concepts to target concepts, then current metaphor studies seem to have a tendency to start from source concepts rather than target concepts. A typical kind of research, for instance, would ask the question to what extent the heart is seen as the seat of the emotions, i.e. to what extent the source concept 'heart' conceptualizes the target concept 'emotion' (see Sharifian et al. 2008). However, the recognition that source concept X conceptualizes target concept Y does not necessarily imply that target concept Y is conceptualized by source concept X, at least not if the latter statement implies that Y is universally or predominantly conceptualized in the light of X. A lot of the research inspired by Conceptual Metaphor Theory, however, seems to rely precisely on such an unwarranted shift of interpretation. Studies on 'the conceptualization of Y in language Z' more often than not content themselves either with focusing on a particular X, or at most with listing various X's that appear in the expression of Y in Z, without asking the critical question what weight these metaphorical expressions carry with regard to each other, and with regard to alternative expressions of Y. Target concept Y may very well be conceptualized by source concept X, but if it is *not only* conceptualized by X, you will want to know exactly what the impact of X is in comparison with the other types of expression.

To illustrate the danger of ignoring the relative salience of alternative expressions, Geeraerts & Gevaert (2008) present a case study that involves *heart* as the seat of feeling and thought in Old English. They show that there is clear evidence that feelings and thoughts are indeed conceptualized as being metaphorically situated in the heart, but at the same time, they point out that this perspective is very much secondary with regard to an alternative, more literal one that involves *mood* rather than *heart*. The apparent necessity to take into account the relative position of competing expressions involves a comparison of the relative weight of the alternatives. Such an approach is known as an *onomasiological* one. But Cognitive Linguistics has more to say about onomasiology, as we shall see in the next section.

4 Diachronic onomasiology

4.1 Introducing diachronic onomasiology

Although it has hardly found its way to the canonical English terminology of linguistics, the distinction between onomasiology and semasiology is a traditional one in Continental structural semantics and the Eastern European tradition of lexicological research. The following quote from Baldinger (1980: 278) illustrates the distinction quite nicely: "Semasiology [. . .] considers the isolated word and the way its meanings are manifested, while onomasiology looks at the designations of a particular concept, that is, at a multiplicity of expressions which form a whole." The distinction between semasiology and onomasiology, then, equals the distinction between *meaning* and *naming*: semasiology takes its starting-point in the word as a form, and charts the meanings that the word can occur with; onomasiology takes its starting-point in a concept, and investigates by which different expressions the concept can be designated, or named.

Now, in order to understand the specific impact of Cognitive Linguistics on onomasiological research, an additional distinction has to be introduced, viz. that between what may roughly be described as the *qualitative* versus the *quantitative* aspects of linguistic semantic structure. The distinction may be introduced by considering semasiological structures first. Qualitative aspects of semasiological structure involve the following questions: which meanings does a word have, and how are they semantically related? The outcome is an investigation into polysemy, and the relationships of metonymy, metaphor etc. that hold between the various readings of an item. Quantitative aspects of lexical structure, on the other hand, involve the question whether all the readings of an item carry the same *structural weight*. The semasiological outcome of a quantitative approach is an investigation into prototypicality effects of various kinds, as will be obvious to anyone who has followed the developments in semasiological research of the last two decades: prototypicality research is basically concerned with differences of structural weight among the members or the subsenses of a lexical item. The qualitative perspective is a much more traditional one in semasiological lexicology than the quantitative one, which was taken up systematically only recently, with the birth and development of prototype theory.

The distinction between qualitative and quantitative aspects of semantic structure can be extrapolated to onomasiology. The qualitative question then takes the following form: what kinds of (semantic) relations hold between the lexical items in a lexicon (or a subset of the lexicon)? The outcome, clearly, is an investigation into various kinds of lexical structuring: field relationships, taxonomies, lexical relations like antonymy and so on. The quantitative question takes the following onomasiological form: are some categories or mechanisms cognitively more salient than others, that is, are there any differences in the probability that one category rather than another will be chosen for designating things out in the world? Are certain lexical categories more obvious names than others?

The terms *qualitative* and *quantitative* as used here are not in all respects adequate, to be sure. Fundamentally, what is at issue here is the distinction between the mere presence of an item within a structure and the structural weight of that item, or, if one wishes, between the *presence* of an item and the *preference* language users may have for that item. The terms *quantitative* and *qualitative* are only used to avoid cumbersome paraphrases expressing this distinction.

The novelty of Cognitive Linguistics in the domain of onomasiology lies mainly on the quantitative side, but we should first say something about the older strands of onomasiological research. A substantial part of onomasiological research is occupied by the study of lexicogenetic mechanisms. *Lexicogenesis* involves the mechanisms for introducing new pairs of word forms and word meanings—all the traditional mechanisms, in other words, like word formation, word creation, borrowing, blending, truncation, ellipsis, folk etymology and others, that introduce new items into the onomasiological inventory of a language. Crucially, semasiological change is a major mechanism of lexicogenesis, i.e. of introducing new pairings of forms and meanings. Now prestructuralist semantics—apart from coining the term *onomasiology* itself (Zauner 1902)—has introduced some of the basic terminology for describing lexicogenetic mechanisms. Although basically concerned with semasiological changes, the major semasiological treatises from Bréal (1897) and Paul (1880) to Stern (1931) and Carnoy (1927) do not restrict themselves to strictly semasiological mechanisms like metaphor and metonymy, but also devote attention to mechanisms of onomasiological change like borrowing or folk etymology (compare Kronasser 1952 and Quadri 1952 for overviews of semasiological and onomasiological research respectively).

Structuralist semantics insists, in the wake of de Saussure himself, on the distinction between semasiology and onomasiology. In the realm of diachronic linguistics, this shows up in Ullmann's classification of semantic changes (1951, 1962), or in Baldinger's argumentation (1964) for studying the interplay between semasiological and onomasiological changes. More importantly, the bulk of (synchronic) structuralist semantics is devoted to the identification and description of different onomasiological structures in the lexicon, such as lexical fields, taxonomical hierarchies, lexical relations like antonymy and synonymy, and syntagmatic relationships (compare Lutzeier 1995).

Both the prestructuralist attention for lexicogenetic mechanisms and the structuralist attention for onomasiological structures in the lexicon are examples of a 'qualitative' approach. Cognitive Linguistics, in contrast, devotes specific attention to quantitative aspects of onomasiology. With regard to the onomasiological structures in the lexicon, the best-known example to date is Berlin and Kay's basic level model (Berlin & Kay 1969; Berlin 1978), which involves the claim that a particular taxonomical level constitutes a preferred, default level of categorization. The basic level in a taxonomy is the level that is (in a given culture) most naturally chosen as the level where categorization takes place; it has, in a sense, more structural weight than the other levels.

But obviously, the basic level approach belongs to synchronic linguistics rather than diachronic onomasiology. For a contribution of Cognitive Linguistics to the latter, we have to turn to the study of lexicogenetic mechanisms.

4.2 Illustration and overview

Cognitive semantics introduces a 'quantitative' perspective into the study of lexicogenetic mechanisms. Within the set of lexicogenetic mechanisms, some could be more salient (i.e. might be used more often) than others. Superficially, this could involve, for instance, an overall preference for borrowing rather than morphological productivity as mechanisms for introducing new words, but from a cognitive semantic perspective, there are other, more subtle questions to ask: do the ways in which novel words and expressions are being coined, reveal specific (and possibly preferred) ways of conceptualizing the onomasiological targets? An example of this type of research (though not specifically situated within a cognitive semantic framework) is Alinei's work (e.g. 1996) into the etymological patterns underlying the European dialects: he argues, for instance, that taboo words in the European dialects may be motivated either by Christian or Islamic motifs, or by pre-Christian, pre-Islamic heathen motifs; the 'quantitative' perspective then involves the question whether one of these motifs is dominant or not. On a broader scale, the etymological research project started by Koch and Blank (Koch 1997; Blank & Koch 1999, 2003), intends to systematically explore motivational preferences in the etymological inventory of the Romance languages. In comparison with much of the metaphor-based research that was introduced in the previous section, the approach put forward by Blank and Koch takes into account all possible pathways of lexicalization (and not just metaphor).

Tab. 6.3: 'Match' in English, French, German, and Spanish

target concept	target form	process/relation	source form
match 'short, slender piece of wood or other material tipped with a chemical substance which produces fire when rubbed on a rough or chemically prepared surface'	English *match*	semantic change / metaphorical similarity	English *match* 'wick'
	French *allumette*	semantic change / taxonomic subordination	French *allumette* 'splinter for the transport of fire'
	German *Streichholz*	compound / metonymy + metonymy	German *streichen* 'to rub' + *Holz* 'wood'
	Spanish *fósforo*	loan + conversion / metonymy	Old Greek *phosphóros* 'fire-bringing'
	Spanish *cerilla*	suffixation / taxonomic subordination	Spanish *cera* 'wax' + *-illa*

Descriptively, the approach takes the form of overviews like that in Tab. 6.3, adapted from Blank (2003). The table charts the different names for the target concept *match* in a number of European languages, as identified in the second row. Each of these names is itself derived from a source form, as may be found in the final row. Source form and target form are related in specific ways, specified in the third row of the table. The relationship involves both a formal process and a semantic relation. The English target form *match*, for instance, is related by a process of semasiological change to the older reading *match* 'wick'. Semantically, the relationship between 'wick' and 'short, slender piece of wood or other material tipped with a chemical substance which produces fire when rubbed on a rough or chemically prepared surface' is one of metaphorical similarity. German *Streichholz*, on the other hand, is related to the verb *streichen* and the noun *Holz* through a process of compounding; semantically, the relationship between target form and source form is metonymical. Needless to say, the source forms may often themselves be further analysed as target forms: *allumette* 'splinter designated to transport fire', for instance, is related by a process of suffixation and a semantic relationship of metonymy to the verb *allumer* 'to light' and the suffix *-ette*.

If sufficient materials of the form illustrated in Tab. 6.3 are available, it will be possible to compare the relative salience of different lexicogenetic mechanisms, not just on the abstract level where, for instance, the importance of metonymy in general would be gauged against the importance of metaphor in general, but more importantly also on a more fine-grained level where the conceptualization of a specific target concept can be investigated: "Combining diachronic lexicology with onomasiology and applying it to more than just one or a few languages allows us to show, in an empirically justified way, which conceptualizations are proper to a single or very few speech communities versus those that can be found universally and thus may match a biological predisposition of perceiving the world. Cognitive onomasiology hence can procure us deeper insight into the way our mind works." (Blank 2003: 44).

Beyond the work of Blank, Koch, and their associates (see e.g. Gévaudan, Koch & Neu 2003; Gévaudan 2007; and compare Grzega 2002), this type of cognitive onomasiology, in spite of its obvious interest, has not yet given rise to a major wave of research.

4.3 Further perspectives

The two descriptions of onomasiology in the Baldinger quotation are not exactly equivalent. On the one hand, studying 'a multiplicity of expressions which form a whole' leads directly to the *traditional, structuralist conception of onomasiology*, i.e. to the study of semantically related expressions (as in lexical field theory, or the study of the lexicon as a relational network of words interconnected by links of a hyponymical, antonymical, synonymous nature etc.). On the other hand, studying 'the designations of a particular concept' opens the way for a *contextualized, pragmatic conception of onomasiology*, involving the actual choices made for a particular name as a designation of a particular concept or a particular referent. This distinction can be further equated with the distinction between an investigation of *structure*, and an investigation of *use*, or between an investigation of *langue* and an investigation of *parole*. The structural conception deals with sets of related expressions, and basically asks the question: what are the relations among the alternative expressions? The pragmatic conception deals with the actual choices made from among a set of related expressions, and basically asks the question: what factors determine the choice for one or the other alternative?

Developing diachronic onomasiology on the level of actual usage, then, should be a major area for further research in historical Cognitive Linguistics. To give an example of the kind of research involved, we may cite some of the factors that have been identified in Geeraerts, Grondelaers & Bakema (1994) and Geeraerts, Grondelaers & Speelman (1999) as determinants of lexical choices. Using corpus-based methods, these studies established that the choice for one lexical item rather than the other as the name for a given referent is determined by the semasiological salience of the referent, i.e. the degree of prototypicality of the referent with regard to the semasiological structure of the category; by the onomasiological entrenchment of the category represented by the expression; and by contextual features of a classical sociolinguistic and geographical nature, involving the competition between different language varieties. While these studies concentrate on synchronic variation and short term lexical changes (see also Tafreschi 2006), other studies starting from cognitive semantic models have been devoted to long term onomasiological changes: Dekeyser (1990, 1995), Kleparski (1997), Geeraerts (1999), Molina (2000).

Pragmatic onomasiology yields an integrated picture of semantic change. To begin with, pragmatic onomasiology combines the study of actual structures with that of latent mechanisms: the *input* for any onomasiological act (the act of naming, the act of choosing a category) is always both the set of already available expressions, and the set of expressions that is virtually available through the presence of lexicogenetic mechanisms. Choosing an expression can in fact take the form of selecting an option that is already there, or of creating a new alternative on the basis of one of the mechanisms.

Further, onomasiological change in the language at large cannot be understood unless we take into account pragmatic onomasiology: changes are always mediated through the onomasiological choices made on the level of *parole*. Words die out because speakers refuse to choose them, and words are added to the lexical inventory of a language because some speakers introduce them and others imitate these speakers; similarly, words change their value within the language because people start using them in different circumstances. Structural change, in other words, is the *output* of processes that are properly studied in the context of pragmatic onomasiology. Also, this pragmatic, *parole*-based perspective automatically takes the form of a sociovariational investigation: in choosing among existing alternatives, the individual language user takes into account their sociolinguistic, non-referential value, and conversely, the expansion of a change over a language community is the cumulative effect of individual choices. In this sense, it is only through an investigation into factors determining these individual choices, that we can get a grasp on the mechanisms behind the invisible hand of lexical change.

The overall picture, then, is given in Fig. 6.3. The boxes to the left and to the right refer to the distinction between an interest in onomasiological structures on the one hand, and an interest in lexicogenetic mechanisms on the other. Within each box, the boldface captions identify the 'qualitative' aspects, whereas the other captions identify the 'quantitative' approaches. The arrows pointing away from the boxes indicate that both boxes constitute input for the processes that play a role at the pragmatic level: an act of naming may draw from the potential provided by the lexicogenetic mechanisms, or it may consist of choosing among alternatives that are already there. The arrows pointing towards the boxes indicate how the pragmatic choices may lead to change. These processes will primarily affect the actual synchronic structures, through the addition or removal of senses or items, shifts in the variational value of expressions, or changes in the salience of certain options. Secondarily (hence the dotted arrow), a change may affect the lexicogenetic mechanisms, for instance when a particular lexicalization pattern becomes more popular.

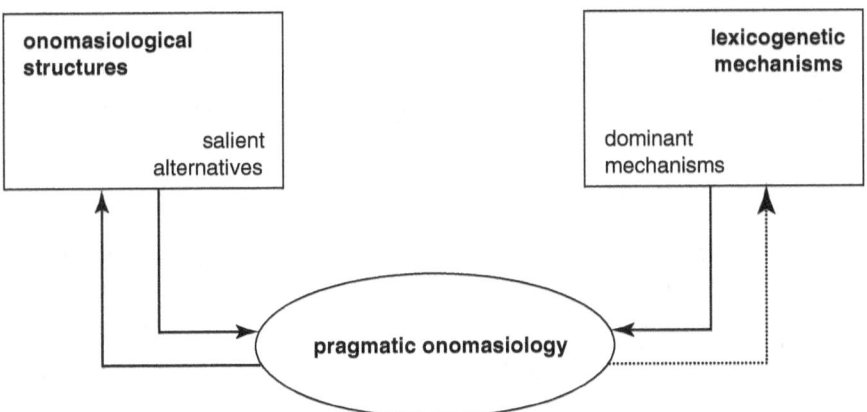

Fig. 6.3: The central position of pragmatic onomasiology

Onomasiological research at the level of *parole*, in other words, is central to the whole onomasiological enterprise; it mediates between what is virtual and what is actual, and it combines the traditional 'qualitative' approaches and the recent 'quantitative' innovations.

5 Rounding off

If the picture drawn in Fig. 6.3 indeed offers a comprehensive view of an integrated model of semantic change, it should be clear that the specific strands of investigation that we have identified as typical for Cognitive Linguistics contribute considerably to filling out the overall model. First, given that the semasiological extension of a given expression is also an onomasiological mechanism for introducing new form/meaning pairs, prototypicality as an architectural feature of semasiological extension sheds new light on one of the major lexicogenetic mechanisms. Second, given that conceptual metaphors and cultural models at large are one specific type of onomasiological structure (they combine various expressions on the basis of an underlying common source/target pattern), the study of historical changes in the dominant conceptualization of a given target reveals how the salience relationship between alternative onomasiological structures may change over time. Third, the comparative study of onomasiological mechanisms may reveal differences of cognitive salience among alternative forms of lexicogenesis. And fourth, the gradual emergence of a *parole*-based form of onomasiological research opens the path to an integration of these various forms of research.

6 References

Alinei, Mario 1996. Aspetti teoretici della motivazione. *Quaderni di Semantica* 17, 7–17.
Allan, Kathryn 2008. *Metaphor and Metonymy: A Diachronic Approach*. Chichester: Wiley-Blackwell.
Baldinger, Kurt 1964. Sémasiologie et onomasiologie. *Revue de Linguistique Romane* 28, 249–272.
Baldinger, Kurt 1980. *Semantic Theory*. Oxford: Basil Blackwell. English translation of: *Teoría semántica. Hacia una semántica moderna*. Madrid: Ediciones Alcalá 1977.
Bartsch, Renate 1987. *Norms of Language. Theoretical and Practical Aspects*. London: Longman.
Berlin, Brent 1978. Ethnobiological classification. In: E. Rosch & B. B. Lloyd (eds.). *Cognition and Categorization*. Hillsdale, NJ: Lawrence Erlbaum, 9–26.
Berlin, Brent & Paul Kay 1969. *Basic Color Terms. Their Universality and Evolution*. Berkeley, CA: University of California Press.

Blank, Andreas 1997. *Prinzipien des lexikalischen Bedeutungswandels am Beispiel der romanischen Sprachen.* Tübingen: Niemeyer.
Blank, Andreas 2003. Words and concepts in time: Towards diachronic cognitive onomasiology. In: R. Eckardt, K. von Heusinger & Ch. Schwarze (eds.). *Words in Time. Diachronic Semantics from Different Points of View.* Berlin: Mouton de Gruyter, 37–65.
Blank, Andreas & Peter Koch 1999. Onomasiologie et étymologie cognitive: L'exemple de la tête. In : M. Vilela & F. Silva (eds.). *Actas do 1º Encontro Internacional de Linguística Cognitiva.* Porto: Faculdade de Letras, 49–72.
Blank, Andreas & Peter Koch (eds.) 2003. *Kognitive romanische Onomasiologie und Semasiologie.* Tübingen: Niemeyer.
Bréal, Michel 1897. *Essai de Sémantique.* Paris: Hachette.
Carnoy, Alfred 1927. *La Science du Mot. Traité de Sémantique.* Leuven: Editions Universitas.
Casad, Eugene 1992. Cognition, history, and cora *yee. Cognitive Linguistics* 3, 151–186.
Cuyckens, Hubert 1999. Historical evidence in prepositional semantics. The case of English *by*. In: G.A.J. Tops, B. Devriendt & S. Geukens (eds.). *Thinking English Grammar: To Honour Xavier Dekeyser.* Leuven: Peeters, 15–32.
Dekeyser, Xavier 1990. The prepositions *with, mid* and *again(st)* in Old and Middle English. A case study of historical lexical semantics. In: D. Geeraerts (ed.). *Diachronic Semantics.* Brussel: Editions de l'Université de Bruxelles, 35–48.
Dekeyser, Xavier 1995. Travel, journey and voyage. An exploration into the realm of Middle English lexico-semantics. *North-Western European Language Evolution* 25, 127–136.
Dekeyser, Xavier 1996. Loss of prototypical meanings in the history of English semantics or semantic redeployment. *Leuvense Bijdragen* 85, 283–291.
Diller, Hans-Jürgen 2007. Medieval "with a mood" and modern "in a mood": Changing a metaphor we live by. *Poetica* 66, 127–140.
Dirven, René 1985. Metaphor as a basic means for extending the lexicon. In: W. Paprotté & R. Dirven (eds.). *The Ubiquity of Metaphor. Metaphor in Language and Thought.* Amsterdam: Benjamins, 85–119.
Eckardt, Regine 2003. Meaning change in conceptual Montague Semantics. In: R. Eckardt, K. von Heusinger & Ch. Schwarze (eds.). *Words in Time. Diachronic Semantics from Different Points of View.* Berlin: Mouton de Gruyter, 225–247.
Evans, Nicholas 1992. Multiple semiotic systems, hyperpolysemy, and the reconstruction of semantic change in Australian languages. In: G. Kellermann & M.D. Morrissey (eds.). *Diachrony within Synchrony: Language, History, and Cognition.* Frankfurt/M.: Peter Lang, 475–508.
Evans, Vyvyan & Melanie Green 2006. *Cognitive Linguistics. An Introduction.* Mahwah, NJ: Lawrence Erlbaum.
Fabiszak, Małgorzata 2002. A semantic analysis of *fear, grief* and *anger* words in Old English. In: J.E. Díaz Vera (ed.). *A Changing World of Words. Studies in English Historical Lexicography, Lexicology and Semantics.* Amsterdam: Rodopi, 255–274.
Geeraerts, Dirk 1997. *Diachronic Prototype Semantics.* Oxford: Clarendon Press.
Geeraerts, Dirk 1999. Vleeshouwers, beenhouwers en slagers. Het WNT als bron voor onomasiologisch onderzoek. *Nederlandse Taalkunde* 4, 34–46.
Geeraerts, Dirk (ed.) 2006. *Cognitive Linguistics: Basic Readings.* Berlin: Mouton de Gruyter.
Geeraerts, Dirk 2008. Prototypes, stereotypes and semantic norms. In: G. Kristiansen & R. Dirven (eds.). *Cognitive Sociolinguistics. Language Variation, Cultural Models, Social Systems.* Berlin: Mouton de Gruyter, 21–44.
Geeraerts, Dirk 2010. *Theories of Lexical Semantics.* Oxford: Oxford University Press.

Geeraerts, Dirk & Hubert Cuyckens (eds.) 2007. *Handbook of Cognitive Linguistics*. Oxford: Oxford University Press.
Geeraerts, Dirk & Caroline Gevaert 2008. Hearts and (angry) minds in Old English. In: F. Sharifian et al. (eds.). *Culture, Body, and Language: Conceptualizations of Internal Body Organs across Cultures and Languages*. Berlin: Mouton de Gruyter, 319–347.
Geeraerts, Dirk & Stefan Grondelaers 1995. Looking back at anger. Cultural traditions and metaphorical patterns. In: J. Taylor & R. E. MacLaury (eds.). *Language and the Cognitive Construal of the World*. Berlin: de Gruyter, 153–180.
Geeraerts, Dirk, Stefan Grondelaers & Peter Bakema 1994. *The Structure of Lexical Variation. Meaning, Naming, and Context*. Berlin: de Gruyter.
Geeraerts, Dirk, Stefan Grondelaers & Dirk Speelman 1999. *Convergentie en Divergentie in de Nederlandse Woordenschat. Een Onderzoek naar Kledingen Voetbaltermen*. Amsterdam: Meertens Instituut.
Gevaert, Caroline 2001. Anger in Old and Middle English: A "hot" topic? *Belgian Essays on Language and Literature*, 89–101.
Gevaert, Caroline 2005. The anger is heat question: Detecting cultural influence on the conceptualization of anger through diachronic corpus analysis. In: N. Delbecque, J. van der Auwera & D. Geeraerts (eds.). *Perspectives on Variation. Sociolinguistic, Historical, Comparative*. Berlin: Mouton de Gruyter, 195–208.
Gévaudan, Paul 2007. *Typologie des lexikalischen Wandels*. Tübingen: Stauffenburg Verlag.
Gévaudan, Paul, Peter Koch & Antonia Neu 2003. Hundert Jahre nach Zauner: Die romanischen Namen der Körperteile im DECOLAR. *Romanistisches Jahrbuch* 54, 1–27.
Gilliéron, Jules & Mario Roques 1912. *Etudes de Géographie Linguistique*. Paris: Champion.
Grygiel, Marcin 2004. Semantic change as a process of conceptual blending. *Annual Review of Cognitive Linguistics* 2, 285–304.
Grzega, Joachim 2002. Some aspects of modern diachronic onomasiology. *Linguistics* 40, 1021–1045.
van Hecke, Pierre 2005. Pastoral metaphors in the Hebrew Bible and its ancient near eastern context. In: R.P. Gordon & J.C. de Moor (eds.). *The Old Testament and Its World*. Leiden: Brill, 200–217.
Kleparski, Grzegorz A. 1997. *Theory and Practice of Historical Semantics: The Case of the Middle English and Early Modern English Synonyms of 'girl / young woman'*. Lublin: The University Press of the Catholic University of Lublin.
Koch, Peter 1997. La diacronica quale campo empirico della semantica cognitiva. In: M. Carapezza, D. Gambarara & F. Lo Piparo (eds.). *Linguaggio e Cognizione. Atti del XXVIII Congresso Internazionale della Società di Linguistica Italiana*. Roma: Bulzoni, 225–246.
Koivisto-Alanko, Päivi 2000. *Abstract Words in Abstract Worlds: Directionality and Prototypical Structure in the Semantic Change in English Nouns of Cognition*. Helsinki: Sociéte Néophilologique.
Kövecses, Zoltan 2002. *Metaphor: A Practical Introduction*. Oxford: Oxford University Press.
Kövecses, Zoltan 2005. *Metaphor in Culture*. Cambridge: Cambridge University Press.
Kristiansen, Gitte et al. (eds.) 2006. *Cognitive Linguistics: Current Applications and Future Perspectives*. Berlin: Mouton de Gruyter.
Kronasser, Heinz 1952. *Handbuch der Semasiologie. Kurze Einführung in die Geschichte, Problematik und Terminologie der Bedeutungslehre*. Heidelberg: Carl Winter Universitätsverlag.

Lakoff, George & Zoltan Kövecses 1987. The cognitive model of anger inherent in American English. In: D. Holland & N. Quinn (eds.). *Cultural Models in Language and Thought*. Cambridge: Cambridge University Press, 195–221.

Luraghi, Silvia 1995. Prototypicality and agenthood in Indo-European. In: H. Andersen (ed.). *Historical Linguistics*. Amsterdam: Benjamins, 254–268.

Lutzeier, Peter Rolf 1995. *Lexikologie. Ein Arbeitsbuch*. Tübingen: Stauffenburg Verlag.

Melis, Ludo 1990. *La voie pronominale. La systématique des tours pronominaux en français moderne*. Paris: Duculot.

Molina, Clara 2000. *Give Sorrow Words*. Ph.D. dissertation. Universidad Complutense, Madrid.

Molina, Clara 2005. On the role of onomasiological profiles in merger discontinuations. In: N. Delbecque, J. van der Auwera & D. Geeraerts (eds.). *Perspectives on Variation*. Berlin: Mouton de Gruyter, 177–194.

de Mulder, Walter 2001. La linguistique diachronique, les études sur la grammaticalisation et la sémantique du prototype: Présentation. *Langue Française* 130, 8–32.

Nerlich, Brigitte 1992. *Semantic Theories in Europe, 1830–1930: From Etymology to Contextuality*. Amsterdam: Benjamins.

Nikiforidou, Kiki 1991. The meanings of the genitive. A case study in semantic structure and semantic change. *Cognitive Linguistics* 2, 149–205.

Paul, Hermann 1880. *Prinzipien der Sprachgeschichte*. Halle: Niemeyer.

Pope, Maurice 1985. Shakespeare's medical imagination. In: S. Wells (ed.). *Shakespeare Survey 38*. Cambridge: Cambridge University Press, 175–186.

Putnam, Hilary 1975. The meaning of 'meaning'. In: K. Gunderson (ed.). *Language, Mind and Knowledge*. Minneapolis, MN: University of Minnesota Press, 131–193.

Quadri, Bruno 1952. *Aufgaben und Methoden der onomasiologischen Forschung. Eine entwicklungsgeschichtliche Darstellung*. Bern: Francke Verlag.

Rosch, Eleanor 1977. Human categorization. In: N. Warren (ed.). *Studies in Cross-cultural Psychology I*. New York: Academic Press, 1–49.

Schäfer, Jürgen 1966. *Wort und Begriff 'Humour' in der elisabethanischen Komödie*. Münster: Aschendorff Verlag.

Sharifian, Farzad et al. (eds.) 2008. *Culture, Body, and Language: Conceptualizations of Internal Body Organs across Cultures and Languages*. Berlin: Mouton de Gruyter.

Soares da Silva, Augusto 1999. *A semântica de Deixar: Uma contribuição para a abordagem cognitiva em semântica lexical* [The semantics of the verb 'deixar': Towards a cognitive approach in lexical semantics]. Braga: Faculdade de Filosofia de Braga, Universidade Catolica Portuguesa.

Soares da Silva, Augusto 2003. Image schemas and category coherence: The case of the Portuguese verb 'deixar'. In: H. Cuyckens, R. Dirven & J. Taylor (eds.). *Cognitive Approaches to Lexical Semantics*. Berlin: Mouton de Gruyter, 281–322.

Stern, Gustaf 1931. *Meaning and Change of Meaning*. Göteborg: Elanders.

Tafreschi, Agnes 2006. *Zur Benennung und Kategorisierung alltäglicher Gegenstände: Onomasiologie, Semasiologie und kognitive Semantik*. Kassel: Kassel University Press.

Taylor, John R. 2003. *Linguistic Categorization*. 3rd edn. Oxford: Oxford University Press.

Tissari, Heli 2003. *LOVEscapes: Changes in Prototypical Senses and Cognitive Metaphors since 1500*. Helsinki: Sociéte Néophilologique.

Traugott, Elisabeth C. 1985. 'Conventional' and 'dead' metaphors revisited. In: W. Paprotté & R. Dirven (eds.). *The Ubiquity of Metaphor*. Amsterdam: Benjamins, 17–56.

Traugott, Elisabeth C. & Richard T. Dasher 2002. *Regularity in Semantic Change*. Cambridge: Cambridge University Press.
Trim, Richard 2007. *Metaphor Networks. The Comparative Evolution of Figurative Language*. London: Palgrave Macmillan.
Ullmann, Stephen 1951. *The Principles of Semantics*. Glasgow: Jackson.
Ullmann, Stephen 1962. *Semantics. An Introduction to the Science of Meaning*. Oxford: Blackwell.
Ungerer, Friedrich & Hans-Jörg Schmid 2006. *An Introduction to Cognitive Linguistics*. 2nd edn. Harlow: Pearson Longman.
Winters, Margaret E. 1989. Diachronic prototype theory: On the evolution of the French subjunctive.
Linguistics 27, 703–730.
Winters, Margaret E. 1992. Schemas and prototypes: Remarks on syntax change. In: G. Kellermann & M.D. Morrissey (eds.). *Diachrony within Synchrony: Language History and Cognition*. Frankfurt/M.: Peter Lang, 265–280.
Winters, Margaret E., Heli Tissari & Kathryn Allan (eds.) 2010. *Historical Cognitive Linguistics*. Berlin: de Gruyter.
Zauner, Adolf 1902. *Die romanischen Namen der Körperteile. Eine onomasiologische Studie*. Doctoral dissertation. Universität Erlangen. Reprinted in: *Romanische Forschungen* 14, 1903, 339–530.

Regine Eckardt
7 Grammaticalization and semantic reanalysis

1 Grammaticalization as a conspiracy of changes —— 177
2 The semantic side to grammaticalization —— 183
3 Semantic reanalysis —— 186
4 More examples —— 194
5 What semantic reanalysis is not —— 200
6 Avoid Pragmatic Overload —— 202
7 Summary —— 205
8 References —— 206

Abstract: The article starts by describing grammaticalization—a kind of language change—on basis of examples and characterizations in earlier literature on language change. I argue that a full understanding of grammaticalization can only be achieved when we take compositional semantics and the syntax-semantics interface into account. The analysis of cases of grammaticalization as cases of semantic reanalysis not only allows to describe more precisely the synchronization of changes in meaning and structure. It also reveals why the resulting new units in language (morphemes, constructions, words) are often 'abstract' and in what sense such changes overwhelmingly but not necessarily are unidirectional. Section 4 offers a detailed account of the semantic reanalysis of German fast$_1$ ('solid, tight') to fast$_2$ ('almost') which illustrates the general principles of sections 2 and 3. After contrasting the present analysis of grammaticalization with earlier proposals in the literature (section 5), section 6 addresses the reasons for semantic reanalysis. I propose that one driving factor is the urge to avoid accommodation of presuppositions which are costly and implausible. This I call the strategy to "Avoid Pragmatic Overload", an interpretive strategy of the hearer.

1 Grammaticalization as a conspiracy of changes

Research in grammaticalization was inspired by the question "where does grammar come from?". While it is almost tautological that any communication

Regine Eckardt, Göttingen, Germany

system requires signals for entities, properties, relations ("content words"), grammatical structures don't seem to be required by signalling systems as such. Nevertheless, practically all natural languages include grammatical structure of surprising complexity. Moreover, there is no correlation between the level of cultural achievements of a society and the level of grammatical complexity of the society's language. These observations suggest that our universal linguistic abilities drive us to collectively enrich signalling systems of content words with grammatical infrastructure. The present article takes a closer look into the semantic processes involved in these developments.

The prototypical instance of language change called 'grammaticalization' is a change where a word with independent content, preferably of one of the main lexical categories A, V or N, develops a new use with a comparatively more dependent, more abstract content, changed word class, typically of a functional nature, e.g. auxiliary, modal, preposition, particle or other functional word or even affix. The development of Latin and French future tense forms is often presented as a typical model case of grammaticalization.

(1) Expression of Future tense: *we will sing*

Pre-Latin	Latin	French
*kanta bʰumos →	canta-bimus	
sing be-2Pl.pres.	sing-2Pl.fut.	
	cantare habemus →	*chante-rons*
	sing have-2Pl.pres.	sing-2Pl.fut.
		allons chanter → ?
		go-2Pl.pres. sing

The semantic link between main verb ('sing') and embedding verb ('be', 'have', 'go') changes during the development. The grammatical status of the latter verb changes (from embedder to auxiliary verb), later also its morphological status (from independent word to affix). While it is usually a larger part of sentences which undergoes restructuring in such developments, it is often possible to spot one participant which is most involved, for instance the verb 'have' in the Latin > French change which turns from embedding verb via auxiliary to inflectional affix. 'Grammaticalization' is often used as if it affected exactly one word, clitic, or syllable. I will frequently talk about *items* as a cover term for 'construction', 'word', 'clitic', 'affix'; firstly because grammaticalization processes are assumed to affect all these parts of speech, and secondly because changes can turn for instance a 'word' into an 'affix', still the object will remain an 'item'.

The first studies in grammaticalization concerned the origin of grammatical structures like case endings, tense and aspect systems, determiners or classifiers. As the field broadened its focus, the need arose to replace the intuitive characterization of an item changing from "something less grammatical" into "something more grammatical" by a more specific characterization. One of the most sophisticated models, and one that is still in use (e.g. Fischer 2007) was developed by Lehmann in (1995/2002). Lehmann proposes three parameters of grammaticalization, each being realised in a syntagmatic and a paradigmatic dimension. The following table of criteria emerges (Lehmann 1995/2002: 110, Tab. 4):

Tab. 7.1: Lehmann's parameters of grammaticalization

	paradigmatic	syntagmatic
weight	integrity	structural scope
cohesion	paradigmaticity	bondedness
variability	paradigmatic variability	syntagmatic variability

Grammaticalization, according to Lehmann, is characterised by an *increase in cohesion* along with a *decrease in weight and variability* from older item to newer item. The system is to be read as a cluster of correlated features rather than a list of necessary and sufficient criteria. Cases of grammaticalization should show sufficiently many, but need not exhibit all of the listed tendencies.

The paradigmatic weight of a sign, or its integrity, measures its distinctness and independence of other signs both in terms of phonology and semantics. Hence both phonological reduction and semantic generalization (see below on bleaching) constitute a loss in integrity, according to Lehmann. The paradigmaticity of a sign reflects the degree to which it functions as part of a paradigm of signs of complementary distribution in certain contexts. Grammaticalization frequently involves a trend for an item to turn into part of a paradigm of fixed semantic and structural function. Paradigmatic variability, finally, concerns the question whether an item can be freely replaced by other signs of the same paradigm, or be left out altogether. A loss in paradigmatic variability means an increase in obligatoriness of a sign in certain contexts.

The syntagmatic weight of a sign, according to Lehmann, is its structural scope. He discusses various examples where either semantic scope or syntactic scope is at stake, the prime cases being former independent items that turn into affixes or clitics. The criterion of *reduced* scope is however easily challenged by all those cases where content words develop into propositional operators (most prominently the modal verbs in English), an observation that was taken up in Tabor & Traugott (1998). Syntagmatic bondedness measures the degree to which an item is dependent on the presence of other signs, or attaches to them in a morphophonologically significant manner. Syntagmatic variability, finally, reflects the degree to which an item has to hold a fixed position or can be freely moved around in the clause.

Lehmann demonstrates that typical traditional case studies in grammaticalization show the predicted kind of shifts in at least *some*, sometimes *most* of the given parameters. He suggests that an instance of language change should be called grammaticalization exactly if it shows enough of increased cohesion or decreased weight and variability, syntagmatically or paradigmatically.

A synopsis of known patterns of change revealed several typological near-universals of grammaticalization. Perhaps the most prominent and controversial is the unidirectionality hypothesis, the observation that the changes at stake tend to adhere to one direction. There are no known cases of inflexion affixes developing into content words, of tense forms being reinstalled as full verbs etc. The universal trends are often summarized in so-called *clines*, a small number of attested possible roads through the major grammatical categories, like the following:

(2) content word > function word > clitic > affix > ø
    verb > preposition > affix > ø

Another observation concerned the fact that even at a more fine-grained level, similar or identical developments can be found repeatedly in different languages. Many languages, for instance, possess future tense forms that are based on a verb of volition/desire (type *will* future), future tenses that rest on the verb *to go*, complementizers based on deictics or the verb *say*, prepositions that derive from nouns for *back* and *front* etc. A very inspiring survey of attested pathways of grammaticalization was compiled by Heine & Kuteva (2002). Observations like these suggested that *grammaticalization* could be an independent mode of language change, subject to its own laws and generalizations, a linguistic process that is driven by autonomous rules that deserve investigation.

The main problem in developing a theory of grammaticalization consists in the fact that no given instance of language change carries the label "grammaticalization" on its sleeve. Hence if some instance of change looks similar to other cases of grammaticalization but contradicted some universal, it is never clear whether this means that the universal was falisified, or that the change was not an instance of grammaticalization in the first place. The emergence of discourse adverbials and other sentence level operators offers a typical battlefield in this debate. We know a wide range of pragmatic and logical markers which derive from content words, often along universal pathways. For instance, the complementizer *while* as well as German *weil* ('because') both derive from the noun *weile* ('time') used as a free genitive (*der Weile*$_{GEN}$ = 'at that time', see König & Traugott 1988, Traugott & König 1991). In terms of semantic development, we see a move from an independent concept to an abstract temporal or causal relation. The scope of the item, however, clearly increases in the development, and its status with respect to paradigmaticity is somewhat unclear— after all, there is no grammatical requirement to use temporal or causal subordinate clauses. So it is unclear whether this change is an instance of grammaticalization or not! Similarly, the content adjective *butan* ('outside') develops into the contrastive conjunction *but* (Merin 1996), and the prepositional phrase *in dede* ('in action', 'in what people do') turns into the discourse marker *indeed* (the Oxford English Dictionary OED offers rich track records of carefully dated uses of *but*, *indeed* and other functional words). Likewise, proximative particles like German *fast* ('almost'), which developed from the adjective *fast* = 'immovable, solid' (like the English adjective *fast* = 'speedy') are hardly part of the core grammatical system and yet, the changes in grammatical category as well as the loss of "concrete" meaning seems to put all these examples close to other instances of grammaticalization. Similarly, discourse particles arise by a change of category as well as a change towards a more abstract meaning while it is dubitable whether they are "more part of the grammar" after the change. As an example, consider the adjective *even/eben* (≈ 'flat', 'smooth') in English and German. In Modern High German, it developed a use as a modal where it serves to add a consoling undertone to the assertion:

(3) *Peter ist ein Junggeselle.* ('Peter is a bachelor'; neutral statement)
 Peter ist eben ein Junggeselle. ('Peter is a bachelor, you can't help it'; justifying or excusingly)

The grammatical category of *eben* changes from adjective to particle (= a typical "elsewhere" category). In its new sense, it does not denote a specific property of Peter (Peter is not a "flat bachelor") but adds a speaker comment aside of the at-issue content of the sentence (Potts 2005). Should this and similar language changes be classed as grammaticalization?

Emergent discourse particles are easy to find and occur in considerable number (Abraham 1991, Brinton 1996, Wegener 2002, Mosegaard Hansen & Rossari 2005 among others). What they share with other instances of grammaticalization is that an item with a comparatively more concrete meaning is reinterpreted to yield a more general, abstract item, accompanied by a change in the grammatical category and new distribution patterns. Unlike in classical grammaticalization, however, the resulting item is *not* part of the core grammar. Discourse particles specifically are clearly outside the range of what is classically considered as 'grammar'. They have to observe only very general syntactic restrictions, they are classically omissible (at least in terms of grammatical requirements), they are usually neglected in grammars as well as grammar theories, they have high scope over the full assertion (Tabor & Traugott 1998), they often do not contribute to the propositional content of the assertion, etc. (cf. also article 15 [Semantics: Sentence and Information Structure] [Zimmermann] *Discourse particles*). So, accepting them as cases of 'grammaticalization' in the sense of Lehmann would evidently lead the Lehmann parameters to collapse.

However, leaving aside the degree of fit to Lehmann's parameters, scholars who work on the emergence of discourse particles repeatedly voice the intuition that particles emerge, like other "grammatical stuff", when words as part of an utterance loose their old sense and are re-assigned a new sense because the speaker apparently seemed to intend to convey just this extra bit of meaning (in the case of *eben*: wanted to console the listener). Different authors have adopted different positions with respect to this challenge. Many just take an agnostic stance (e.g. Fischer & Rosenbach 2000; Mosegaard Hansen & Rossari 2005), allowing for a 'narrow' and a 'wide' sense of grammaticalization. Others, most prominently Traugott, adopt a more interesting strategy. Traugott advocates the more inclusive class of changes (i.e. including the cline towards discourse particles) by postulating *subjectification* as an independent mode of semantic change (Traugott & Dasher 2002). She proposes that this mode of semantic change is shared by both typical instances of grammaticalization (e.g. the development of the English modals, Traugott 1989) and the cline to discourse particles. I will come back to this below.

The problem eventually boils down to the question: Do Lehmann's criteria – or similar lists – have the status of a *definition for grammaticalization* or of an independent *observation about grammaticalization*? In a very balanced special issue of Language Sciences in 2001, the papers Campbell (2001), Janda (2001), Joseph (2001), Newmeyer (2001) and Norde (2001) focus on exactly this question, and convincingly argue that cases of grammaticalization come about by the felicitous conspiracy of independent modes of language change in phonology, mophosyntax, and semantics. Specifically, Newmeyer (2001) offers a rich and well-chosen range of examples that reveal grammaticalization as the epiphenomenal result of semantic changes, structural reanalysis and phonological reduction. I will rest my discussion on this view, and will hence focus on the semantic processes of change that can be observed *predominantly, but not exclusively* in grammaticalization. In spite of the long tradition of research in diachronic linguistics, I think that the nature of semantic change as it accompanies syntactic reanalysis has not been fully understood so far.

The semantic reorganization that is required in grammaticalization essentially operates at the syntax-semantics interface. Grammaticalization entails changes in the syntactic structure of the sentence, and as syntactic structure—as we believe—guides semantic composition, it is to be expected that the compositional structure of the sentence needs to change as well, including the functional structure of the items involved. The investigation of semantic composition, and specifically the functional parts of semantic composition, has been focussed by the so-called "formal" semantic approaches. Truth conditional semantics has developed a level of exactness, explicitness and sophistication in the semantic analysis of meaning composition which has never been reached, as I think can fairly be said, by traditional frameworks of semantic description. I will propose that *semantic reanalysis* is at the heart of most instances of grammaticalization, and I will argue that none of the more traditional modes of meaning change that have been used in the debate captures exactly this process. I will then move on to illustrate semantic reanalysis in different types of language change, including but not restricted to cases of grammaticalization. For example, semantic reanalysis also underlies most changes from adverb to discourse particle, or prepositional phrase to discourse adverbial—so, this approach in some sense follows Traugott's argumentation (Traugott & Dasher 2002), however on the basis of a different mode of change. While Traugott takes subjectification as the driving force in grammaticalization, I will argue that the concept is not necessary to explain the common traits of many instances of structural reanalyses.

2 The semantic side to grammaticalization

Is grammaticalization a gradual process or discrete change? In this debate, authors standardly adopt the following two equations: Structural change = discrete change, and semantic change = gradual change (see for instance Fischer & Rosenbach's 2000 opposition of formal vs. functional approaches to language change in the introduction; Fischer 2007; Hopper & Traugott 1993), in turn concluding that any change that looks gradual must be semantically motivated. I want to challenge the assumption that semantic change be necessarily gradual, and suggest that the impression of "gradual change" is an epiphenomenon of semantic interpretation and pragmatic enrichment.

First note that the meanings of words and sentences of earlier stages are only accessible as part of texts in old documents. We see the surface structure of the data, but we get neither a syntactic nor a semantic analysis (and, apart from translated text, no independent paraphrase). In the investigation of sources, researchers often report an intermediate stage of "gradual shift". Looking into matters in more detail, one finds that some of the utterances that contain the item-under-change seem to favour an analysis in terms of the *old* use of the item. Some of the sentences are plainly synonymous under the older or newer use of the item, and some seem to favour an interpretation in terms of the *new* use although they could still be possibly interpreted in terms of the older stage of the item. (So at the time, without knowledge of future developments, the hearer/reader might just have faced a quirky sentence.)

This gradual approximation of a new stage has been taken as evidence that language change in general be gradual. With the advent of more fine-grained structural descriptions, syntacticians proposed to analyze allegedly gradual shift from one major grammatical stage to another as a series of discrete steps between more finely distinguished grammatical stages. At the level of meaning, however, the terminology in use so far did not allow, nor suggest, similar series of small, descrete steps. Consequently, the claim that changes are gradual iff they are semantic changes is still unchallenged in the community. I think that this equation is severely mistaken.

The first problem seems to be that the difference between sentence meaning and word meaning is severely blurred in the debate. This can lead to the expectation that two sentences with more or less the same "message" on basis of more or less the same words entail that the word meanings be likewise identical, more or less. So, the common meaning of sentences like the following are taken as indication that meaning changes can be ignored.

(4) *Evans did not walk*
     Evans did not walk a step
     Evans did not understand 'a step'

The first two sentences exhibit a minimal pair of negative sentences with and without emphatic component ('*a step*'); the third one shows a fictious extension of the emphatic use of '*a step*' to other contexts. In view of the fact that all three sentences are negations and contain *not*, one might conclude that the word '*a step*' doesn't play a role in the examples at all. This diagnosis has actually been proposed by Haspelmath (1999) who observes:

> One of the most widely discussed aspects of grammaticalization, the fairly dramatic semantic changes, has not been mentioned [in Haspelmath's paper] explicitly at all so far. The reason is that I am not sure that semantic grammaticalization is as central to the process as has generally been assumed. (. . .) For instance, the emphatic negation marker *pas* in older French has lost its pragmatic markedness and has become the normal negation marker, without any semantic changes in the narrow sense having taken place. (Haspelmath 1999: 1062)

This quote suggests that the semantic side of grammaticalization is virtually nonexistent and hence does not pose an interesting object for study at all. While Haspelmath rightly observes that the overall *sentence* meaning of the crucial examples does not change, he fails to acknowledge that the meaning change at the *word level* is considerable. We will see examples later where the meaning of an utterance before and after semantic reanalysis is practically identical even though the meanings of its parts have changed drastically. This observation is, of course, neither new nor surprising, and moreover is the exact analogue to structural reanalysis. The process was described by Langacker (1977: 58) as follows: "change in the structure of an expression or class of expressions that does not involve any immediate or intrinsic modification of its surface manifestation".

Another problem lies in the fact that a concept-based semantic analysis usually fails to represent the functional structure of words, structure that subsequently has to be relegated to constructions (e.g. Traugott 2008). Practically all literature on language change shares this feature. Hence, the terminological frameworks in use simply do not allow to represent many changes at the compositional level, changes that can severely alter the meaning of an item even on the basis of more or less the same conceptual ingredients (see the case study on *fast* in section 4). Isolated articles like von Fintel (1995), Kempson & Cann (2007), Merin (1996), or Zeevat & Karagjosova (2009) pose exceptions to this generalization. Generally, changes that yield functional words need to be described in terms of a semantic framework that can express the meaning of functional words. Concept-based semantic frameworks are notoriously vague at this point, supporting the misconception that semantic changes can not be discrete.

The present article aims at defining and defending the notion of semantic reanalysis. In the next section, I will characterize this process and point out differences to the modes of semantic change that were proposed in the literature, including

1. generalization or bleaching, going back to Paul (1880) and von der Gabelentz (1901)
2. metaphor (most prominently proposed by Heine, Claudi & Hünnemeyer 1991; Bybee, Perkins & Pagliuca 1994; and Sweetser 1990)
3. metonymy (e.g. in Hopper & Traugott 1993), soon made precise as
4. shift from implicature to literal content (with the side effect of strengthening, not predicted by the first two approaches)
5. semantic rearrangement of atoms of meaning, Langacker (1977)
6. subjectification, proposed by Traugott (1989), Traugott & Dasher (2002)

These earlier proposals can be criticised more succinctly once we know what an alternative proposal could look like.

3 Semantic reanalysis

I will start this section by taking a closer look at some examples. The first case concerns the reanalysis of a German adjective *voll* ('full') into the head of a complex determiner phrase that denotes quantities. The following two sentences illustrate the shift, which is one of those cases of grammaticalization that are currently under way (Sahel 2007; Traugott 2008 offers a description of the similar shift of *a lot of* in English). Both uses are part of Modern High German but the one in (6) is newer and derives from the older one in (5).

(5) *Ein Glas voll Weines stand auf dem Tisch.*
     a glass full of-wine stood on the table
(6) *Ein Glas voll Wein muss in die Soße.*
     a glass-full of wine must into the sauce

Simplifying the actual patterns a little bit, the contrast is the following: In (5), the referent of the subject argument is a glas. Reference is also made to wine, but only as part of the AP modification of the glas. The glas is available as discourse referent. The adjective *voll* assigns genetive case to its complement DP (*Weines*), and the adjective phrase modifies the head noun (*Glas*) of the subject DP. In (6), the referent of the subject DP is the wine, whereas no referent is introduced by *Glas*. Both the container noun *(Glas)* as well as the whole DP show nominative case, i.e. receive case by the verb. No genitive case is assigned. For ease of exposition, I will concentrate on these two kinds of use which were brought to my attention by Sahid Sahel.

In the use in (5), the adjective *voll* actually carries a highly complex functional load based on the conceptual core FILL, the relation of some container x being filled with substance or objects y. I will use FILL(x,y) for this binary relation. The adjective phrase *voll* DP_{GEN} arises by combining a complex noun NP with the FILL relation to yield a property. The following lambda term specifies the contribution of *voll* in uses like (5). (Note that the existential quantification over *Wein* is provided by the adjective; alternative formalizations could be envisaged.)

(7) $[[voll_{adj}]] = \lambda Q \lambda x [\exists y (FILL(x, y) \land Q(y))]$

As a consequence, the adjective *voll* can combine with a property Q, leading to the property of being filled with some Q-object or substance (e.g. 'voll Milch').

In the relevant use of (6), *voll* has likewise a complex functional load, but a different one. Now it has to combine with an existential noun phrase that denotes a potential container, like *eine Hand, mehrere Gläser* etc. It moreover has

7 Grammaticalization and semantic reanalysis — 187

to combine with a numeral (*ein, zwei, . . .*) which agrees with the container noun. The result is a generalized quantifier. The lambda term in (8) offers a first approximation.

(8) $[[voll_{measure}]] = \quad \lambda D \lambda P \lambda Q [\exists y (\Diamond[D(\lambda x.\text{FILL}(x, y)] \land P(y) \land Q(y))]$

The rationale behind this semantic building block does not reveal itself easily. It can best be understood if we consider the intended result. Combined with a measure NP (e.g. '*ein Glas*') and a noun that denotes a substance ('*Wein*'), the result should denote a complex NP meaning ('there is wine that could possibly fill a glas, which does *P*'). The combination proceeds as follows:

(8′) a. $[[ein\ Glas]] = \lambda Q. \exists z[\text{GLAS}(z) \land Q(z)]$
 b. $[[ein\ Glas\ voll]] =$
 $\lambda D \lambda P \lambda Q'[\exists y(\Diamond[D(\lambda x.\text{FILL}(x, y)] \land P(y) \land Q'(y)])] (\lambda Q[\exists z(\text{GLAS}(z) \land Q(z))])$
 $= \lambda P \lambda Q'(\exists y[\Diamond[\lambda Q[\exists z(\text{GLAS}(z) \land Q(z))] (\lambda x.\text{FILL}(x, y)] \land P(y) \land Q'(y)])$
 $= \lambda P \lambda Q'(\exists y[\Diamond[\exists z(\text{GLAS}(z) \land \text{FILL}(z, y))] \land P(y) \land Q'(y)])$
 c. *Wein* → $\lambda w.\text{WINE}(w)$
 d. *ein Glas voll Wein* →
 $\lambda P \lambda Q'(\exists y[\Diamond[\exists z(\text{GLAS}(z) \land \text{FILL}(z, y))] \land P(y) \land Q'(y)]) (\lambda w.\text{WINE}(w))$
 $= \lambda Q'(\exists y[\Diamond[\exists z(\text{GLAS}(z) \land \text{FILL}(z, y))] \land \lambda w.\text{WINE}(w) (y) \land Q'(y)])$
 $= \lambda Q'(\exists y[\Diamond[\exists z(\text{GLAS}(z) \land \text{FILL}(z, y))] \land \text{WINE}(y) \land Q'(y)])$

The result denotes the generalized quantifier that holds true of those properties Q′ such that there is something *y* that is wine, that can possibly be filled into one glass, and that has Q′. Note that as a consequence of the modal embedding of the container statement, the resulting semantic representation is still based on our old predicate FILL but we can explain that no real glas is referred to (and hence, no real glas has to be thrown into the sauce in sentence (6)). Let me repeat the old and new representation of *voll* below:

(7) old: $[[voll_{adj}]] = \quad \lambda Q \lambda x[\exists y(\text{FILL}(x, y) \land Q(y))]$
(8) new: $[[voll_{measure}]] = \quad \lambda D \lambda P \lambda Q'[\exists y(\Diamond[D(\lambda x.\text{FILL}(x, y)] \land P(y) \land Q'(y))]$

I think that this example nicely illustrates that the new measure head *voll* still rests on the property of *x* being filled with *y*, but integrates this property with the denotations of its sister constituents in a radically different manner. The full development of classifiers of the N-*voll* type would deserve an investigation in its own right. Interestingly, there are instances of the older meaning with the newer case assignment pattern; i.e (8) could *sloppily* be used to refer to a glas which has the property of being filled with wine. Obviously, many sentences are such that the two readings are practically synonymous. For instance, *Eine Flasche voll Wein stand auf dem Tisch* (A bottleful / bottle full of wine was standing on the table) can only be true if the container is also present; otherwise the wine would not stand but float on the table. I will moreover leave it open whether N-*voll* ('N-full') turns into a complex quantifier at a certain point and looses all internal structure, as orthography may suggest.

Consider once again possible ambiguous uses of *N-voll* as the one above. Observations like these are typically refered to as "gradual meaning change" in the literature. A concept-only semantic analysis would presumanly not see much difference in terms of content at all; the different combinations would perhaps be relegated (without analysis) to constructions. The semantic values in (7) and (8) explicate the combinatorical structure of either item and reveal that the change in meaning is considerable.

In other cases, we do find a real redistribution of conceptual content. The following steps recapitulate the development of *go* + *progressive* + *implicatures* into *going-to* as a future tense. In this case, the reanalysis has to refer to sentence level because I will assume that implicatures arise at the sentence level.

(9) *Emil is going to visit a priest.*

I will start with the semantic analysis of (9) in terms of the older movement reading of *go*.

(10) a. [[*go-*]]
 = $\lambda e \lambda x \text{Go}(x, e)$

 b. [[*to visit a priest*]] = $\lambda e \lambda x \exists e'(\text{GOAL}(e, e') \land \exists y(\text{PRIEST}(y) \land \text{VISIT}(x,y,e'))$

This is the goal-oriented interpretation of the *to* phrase, which provides a relation between people x and events e, e' such that there is some priest y whom x visits in e', and e' is the GOAL of some further event e. (I take a short-cut and will not use a PRO to mediate between matrix subject and the subject of the infintival clause). Next, the two relations can be intersected.

 c. [[*go- to visit a priest*]] =
 $\lambda e \lambda x(\text{Go}(x, e) \land \exists e'(\text{GOAL}(e', e) \land \exists y(\text{PRIEST}(y) \land \text{VISIT}(x, y, e')))$

We can now turn to the integration of the progressive aspect, which I will analyse in Reichenbachian terms as locating the event time $\tau(e)$ around the current reference time R.

d. [[PROGRESSIVE *go- to visit a priest*]] =
   λx(∃e (R ⊂ τ(e) ∧
   Go(x, e) ∧ ∃e'(GOAL(e', e) ∧ ∃y(PRIEST(y) ∧ VISIT(x, y, e')))))

Next, we integrate the tense information.

e. [[PRESENT PROGRESSIVE *go- to visit a priest*]] =
   λx(R = S ∧ ∃e (R ⊂ τ(e) ∧
   Go(x, e) ∧ ∃e'(GOAL(e', e) ∧ ∃y(PRIEST(y) ∧ VISIT(x, y, e')))))

Finally, we will apply this predicate to the subject of the sentence, the denotation of the name *Emil*.

f. [[*Emil* PRESENT PROGRESSIVE *go- to visit a priest*]] = ∃e(R = S ∧ R ⊂ τ(e) ∧
   Go(EMIL,e) ∧ ∃e'(GOAL(e',e) ∧ ∃y(PRIEST(y) ∧ VISIT(EMIL, y, e'))))

The literal content of example (10), represented in (10f), allows the default inference that the planned visit is imminent, assuming some world knowledge about Go and its goals. We can now proceed to the reanalysis process. The first step consists in an inference that hearers might standardly draw when presented with content like (10f). (11) captures the belief that 'seen from now, the proposition that Emil visits a priest will be true soon' or so. A similar step is assumed in most accounts of the development of *going to* future in English. My explication of semantic reanalysis will just make use of this "understood message" in a richer and more elaborate sense, as will become clear presently.

(11) Default inference:
     ∃p(IMMINENT(now, p) ∧ p = ^[∃y∃e'(PRIEST(y) ∧ VISIT(EMIL, y, e'))])

The modal relation IMMINENT is supposed to hold true for those propositions which are bound to become true in the future, as far as we can tell at the time *now*. Interestingly, the inference (11) is not as yet temporally anchored, and hence the proposition in (11) does not lend itself to become the literal content of a sentence. The hearer who has decided to understand (10) as denoting something like (11) will first have to guess a reference time for (11), proceeding to (12). The move from (11) to (12) reflects the difference between a listener who subconsciously reasons "hm, (9) might entail something like (11)" to the listener who believes "hm, the speaker uttered (9) which *literally means something like* (11)—or, rather (12)".

(12) (R = S ∧ ∃p(IMMINENT(R, p) ∧ p = ^[∃y∃e'(PRIEST(y) ∧ VISIT(EMIL, y, e'))])

Now we can reason backwards, trying to build up (12) from the linguistic material in (9), leaving as much unchanged as possible. Hence, we leave the parts in (13) untouched.

(13) a. $[[visit]] = \lambda y \lambda e' \lambda z(\text{VISIT}(z, y, e'))$
 b. $[[a\ priest]] = \lambda Q \exists y(\text{PRIEST}(y) \wedge Q(y))$
 b. $[[Emil]] = \text{Emil}$
 c. $[[\text{PRESENT}]] = (R = S)$

Yet, the derivation of (12) from (9) leaves a semantic chunk that is not as yet provided by any part of the sentence. Luckily, however, we also have a remnant phrase. At this point, the missing link depends on the assumed syntactic structure of the resulting construction. I will assume, conservatively, that the order of combination was still such that the *be going to* chunk is combined with the VP, and only then the subject NP enters the computation.

(14) remnant material ⟺ missing meaning
 $[[be\ going\ to]]$ $\lambda P\, \lambda x[\text{IMMINENT}(R, {}^\wedge P(x))]$

The futurate meaning (14) will take scope over the proposition p which arises by interpreting the root clause; the PRESENT tense takes scope over the constituent in (14). The composition of the parts in (13) and (14) can now proceed in the regular way, and will, as shown in (15), yield exactly the target proposition in (12). (If the reader attempts to do the composition of (13a) and (13b), note that it gives rise to the notorious type mismatch for object quantifiers. Presenting a full semantic derivation of the example would burden the article unnecessarily; for a standard treatment see Heim & Kratzer 1998.)

(15) a. $[[visit\ a\ priest]] =$
 $\lambda z \exists e'\ \exists y(\text{PRIEST}(y) \wedge \text{VISIT}(z, y, e'))$
 b. $[[b\text{-}going\ to\ visit\ a\ priest]] =$
 $\lambda P\, \lambda x[\text{IMMINENT}(R, {}^\wedge P(x))]\ (\lambda z\ \exists e'\ \exists y(\text{PRIEST}(y) \wedge \text{VISIT}(z, y, e')))$
 $= \lambda x[\text{IMMINENT}(R, {}^\wedge \lambda z\ \exists e'\ \exists y(\text{PRIEST}(y) \wedge \text{VISIT}(z, y, e'))(x))]$
 $= \lambda x[\text{IMMINENT}(R, {}^\wedge \exists e'\ \exists y(\text{PRIEST}(y) \wedge \text{VISIT}(x, y, e')))]$
 c. $[[Emil\ b\text{-}going\ to\ visit\ a\ priest]] =$
 $= \lambda x[\text{IMMINENT}(R, {}^\wedge \exists e'\ \exists y(\text{PRIEST}(y) \wedge \text{VISIT}(x, y, e')))]\ (\text{EMIL})$
 $= [\text{IMMINENT}(R, {}^\wedge \exists e'\ \exists y(\text{PRIEST}(y) \wedge \text{VISIT}(\text{EMIL}, y, e')))]$
 d. $[[Emil\ \text{PRESENT}\ b\text{-}going\ to\ visit\ a\ priest]] =$
 $(R = S \wedge [\text{IMMINENT}(R, {}^\wedge \exists e'\ \exists y(\text{PRIEST}(y) \wedge \text{VISIT}(\text{EMIL}, y, e')))])$

The analysis rests on the assumption that the subject has always scope over the future operator. This assumption is corrobated by corpus studies on the early uses of *going to* (see Krug 2000), which show that impersonal subjects, subjects in the scope of the future operator, and expletive subjects do not occur at an early stage (around 1600). The present analysis hence requires that we assume a further generalization of *going to* to a propositional operator for these cases. This illustrates how small discrete steps of change can create the impression of gradual semantic shift.

Taking stock, we find the following changes at the structural and semantic level. At the structural level, the status of the auxiliary *be*, and the gerund *-ing* have changed. In the conservative interpretation in (10), they contribute the progressive aspect. In the reanalysed interpetation in (15), they are part of the phrasal *be going to* construction. The structural status of the particle *to* likewise changed. In the older analysis, it figured as part of the embedded infinitive clause. In the reanalysed interpretation, it is an unanalysed part of the phrasal *be going to* construction. In the present case, hence, there is no continuity in the parts of the sentence such that we could spot one item that carries the change. However, we can—as is often done—at least parallel the meaning of the older *be going* and the newer *be going to* in the given sentences.

(16) $[[be\ going]]_{OLD}$ → $\lambda e \lambda x (R \subset \tau(e) \wedge \text{Go}(x,e))$
    $[[be\ going\ to]]_{NEW}$ → $\lambda P \lambda x [\text{IMMINENT}(R, {}^{\wedge}P(x))]$

Comparing old and new in (16), we can trace all changes that have been proposed in the literature. A simple intransitive turns into an aspectual which relates a proposition (to be built up from VP and the subject) to the time of reference, stating that the proposition is bound to become true, as far as can be said at the reference time **R**.

The crucial observation is that the new meaning did not arise in any way by looking hard at the old meaning in (16), extending it in a metaphoric sense, sensing metonymic relations between walking and futurity, generalizing the notion of walking, or anything the like. $(16)_{NEW}$ arose by attributing a missing chunk of meaning to a suitable chunk of form. This was done in (14), and the motivation for (14) is simply to come from (13) to (15d) in a compositional manner. If you find this spooky, acknowledge that we perform similar tasks in very innocent situations. Suppose that your spouse enters the flat, accompanied by a dark stranger that you have never seen before, and you hear him say (17):

(17) "Meet my old school mate Toni!"

You will infer in this situation that you are supposed to meet the stranger, and the best compositional way to derive this proposition from the sentence in (17) is by assuming that the word *Toni* refers to the dark stranger. What is special about the guessed correspondence in (14), in contrast to (17), is that the intended denotation is not conveyed by an act of ostension (= pointing to things in the world). The denotation in (14) only becomes salient as filling the gap between two other denotations; it's a spandrel, so to speak. The concept TONI, in contrast, could be conveyed without further linguistic knowledge by simple deixis. The intended denotation in (14) is "waiting for a property concept, waiting for an individual concept, attributing former to latter and stating the imminence of the resulting proposition". Such a denotation can *necessarily* only arise after speakers have mastered the art of functional and syntactic composition.

Another advantage of this analysis lies in the fact that it can help to resolve the tension between gradual changes at the surface, and discrete steps of change, as assumed in reanalysis. Old and New denotation in (16) are not similar at all, and the analysis implies that the latter arose in one step, without any gradual intermediate stages. Meaning change in semantic reanalysis is discrete. This does not contradict the justified observation that *sentences* can receive very similar interpretation in the old, and the new analysis (particularly if we count in pragmatic implicatures).

After these examples, I will now turn to a general characterization of semantic reanalysis. Consider an utterance u with speaker S and interpreter H. I will refer to the language system (lexicon, grammar, phonological forms) before utterance u as the "old" language system. The language system of the interpreter H after having parsed u will be an instance of the "new" language system (so we restrict attention to utterances where something changes).

i. The utterance u is uttered, and can be understood, in terms of a structural analysis in terms of the *old language system*. In this interpretation, it will convey some proposition ϕ_{old} as its literal content.

ii. There are several dimensions in which u can transcend this old state. On the semantic side, the utterance u can be understood in the utterance context with a richer or different meaning ϕ_{new}. ϕ_{new} may come about as ϕ_{old} plus implicatures. ϕ_{new} may also come about by interpretative processes outside the core language system, in the extreme case by chance guessing.

On the syntactic side, the hearer may see the possibility for a different structural analysis of the utterance (see the *voll* example). Both changes can co-occur.

iii. The hearer hypothesizes a second possible syntactic/semantic analysis for
    u. All parts of the utterance need to contribute denotations such that the
    regular semantic composition (possibly with a new structural backbone) of
    these parts yields ϕ_{new}.
iv. Most parts of the sentence contribute conservatively in iii., that is according
    to their old lexical entry. Some parts can be attributed a new meaning by the
    interpreter in order to achieve iii. Specifically, the hearer will assume that
    some parts should contribute *those* denotations that are missing in order to
    come to the understood meaning ϕ_{new} in a compositional manner.

These steps pertain to single utterance interpretations. Evidently, the occurrence of just one single situation of this type is not sufficient to make a language change. However, if a suitable number of utterance situations support the hypothesized "new" meanings for old word forms in iv., the new entry is permanently adopted into the lexicon of the speaker community. Note that the described utterance situation is a true turning point. The speaker of *u* is still confidently using the *old language system*. The interpreter derives a hypothetical *new* language system on basis of this utterance. This narrow conception of semantic reanalysis, hence, does *not* rest on creative intentions of the speaker *S* in the above utterance situation.

Another aspect of this analysis is that semantic reanalysis is not necessarily restricted to shifts from content word to grammar. Semantic reanalysis can recruit parts of a sentence for denotations that are considered 'grammar', but the process can equally well couple an item with information about the current discourse moves, information about logical coherence, scalar information, and in rare cases even independent conceptual content. (For instance, novels by A. McCall Smith use a version of English where the adverbial *late* 'former' has turned into an adjective *late* 'dead' with both attributive and predicative use.) The result may be of a kind that suggests a radically different word class for the new item, or only mild changes. I will review more examples below.

It is still open what leads the interpreter *H* to hypothesize a new semantic derivation for the utterance. The mere presence of implicatures can't be sufficient, because we know a wide range of conventionalized implicatures that have resisted semantic reanalysis over long periods. Little can be said about cases of simple error. Many actual instances of semantic reanalysis suggest that the urge to *Avoid Pragmatic Overload* often plays a rôle: Assume that *u* in the old sense ϕ_{old} requires unwarranted presuppositions. The speaker makes his utterance under the assumption that the interpreter will accommodate them. The interpreter may see this possibility but considers the required accommodations implausible. As an interpretive alternative, H hypothesizes a new message ϕ_{new}, leading to reanalysis. A survey of examples suggests that this constellation might typically arise for "fashion words" associated with high status. Fashion words are cognitively salient and tend to be over-used, with the side effect of not always perfectly matching the intended message. It would be a fascinating task to find out whether this kind of "premium access" bears similarity to priming and can block lexical access to other, semantically more appropriate items. Suitable psycholinguistic investigations would lead to a better understanding of the synchronic mental processes that feed language change.

4 More examples

We have seen an example for structure-driven semantic reanalysis at the beginning of section 3. Another nice example is the reanalysis of the participle (genitive) *währendes* into a preposition. The Deutsches Wörterbuch (Grimm 1885–1962, DW) attests the following context of change.

(18) a. währendes Krieges
 lasting$_{GENITIVE}$ war$_{GENITIVE}$ "while the war was lasting"

 b. *während des Krieges*
 during$_{PREP}$ the$_{GENITIVE}$ war$_{GENITIVE}$ "while the war was lasting, during war"

In this case, reanalysis is presumably driven by structural factors. The original (18a) was a free genitive NP in an appositive sense, an increasingly rare construction that has survived only in few fixed collocations in German ([*stehenden Fußes*]$_{GEN}$ "standing foot's " = 'immediately, without even sitting down', [*blutenden Herzens*]$_{GEN}$ "bleeding heart's" = 'with bleeding heart'). The homonymy of *d+es* (genitive affix) and *des* definite article (masc.) offered the basis of a new analysis as a prepositional phrase, at least for nouns of masculine gender.

The earlier participle belongs to the verb *währen* ('go on for a long time', 'continue') Definiteness of the NP (*Krieges*) and temporal co-occurrence (of 'war' and the events in the main clause for (18a)) is part of the meaning of the free genitive appositive, which introduces concomitant circumstances in a general sense.

The newly emerging preposition *während* requires a complement that denotes an event or a time interval, and turns it into a temporal modifier for events (or time frames). The new preposition follows the compositional pattern of other prepositions and therefore allows for more types of argument NPs, e.g. NPs that denote time intervals and even quantified NPs as arguments (e.g. *während der meisten Sitzungen* = 'during most of the sessions' would not have an analogue in the old construction). The new meaning of the PP is also more concise than the denotation of the older appositive, in that unspecific concomitance is replaced by succinct temporal inclusion. For a formal spell-out of the semantic steps, see Eckardt (2011).

Sometimes, metaphoric extension and semantic reanalysis work hand in hand. A recent study by Heine & Miyashita (2006) traces the development of *drohen zu* in German to become a marker of unwelcome-futurate. They distinguish four different current stages, illustrated below.

(19) *Karl droht seinem Chef, ihn zu verklagen.*
    Karl threatens to.his boss him to sue
    'Karl threatens to sue his boss' (volitional)
(20) *Uns droht nun eine Katastrophe.*
    to.us threatens now a disaster
    'A catastrophy is treatening'
(21) *Das Hochwasser droht die Altstadt zu überschwemmen.*
    The flood threatens the old-town to flood
    'The flood threatens to flood the old town.'
(22) *Mein Mann droht krank zu werden.*
    my husband threatens sick to become
    'My husband is about to become sick'

Clearly, the old lexical verb *drohen* ('threaten'), description for a kind of verbal or nonverbal aggression, has been extended to a so-called semi-modal (Eisenberg 1999). I propose that two semantic shifts interact in this case. First, there is clearly a metaphoric component that allows to extend the behavioral concept *threat* to inanimate subjects. When we talk about a "threatening thunderstorm", we conceptualize the black clouds that approach at the horizon as an animate subject which volitionally causes the emotional impression that we feel. To the extent that the metaphor of some animate threatening agent is implausible, hearers will consider the more plausible *new* structural analysis of the clause, one that takes the denoted state of affairs in total as the threat. In terms of syntax, *drohen* is then close to a modal verb (or semi-modal). In terms of meaning, *drohen* denotes a modal of *unwelcome futurate* and takes scope over the rest of the sentence. It is at this point that structural and semantic reanalysis takes place. After the change, sentences like (22) are truely structurally ambiguous. (22) in the old meaning of *drohen* states that my husband—somewhat irrationally—utters a threat to the end that he will volitionally become sick. (22) in the new sense of *drohen* states that there is a state of affairs 'my husband sick' which is presently imminent, and which the speaker does not like. This turns *drohen* into something like an anti-buletic modality. Like all threats, *drohen* leaves it open wether the state of affairs is likely to become true, or just possible. After all, we utter threats in order to influence other peoples' behaviour—the ideal threat is the one that we need not exert.

The old Germanic adjective *fast* in the sense of 'firm', 'solid', 'immovable' has been subject to an interesting development in German. In modern German, its descendant *fast* is an proximity adverb 'almost' (while the umlaut variant *fest* still carries the original sense). The German proximity adverb *fast* derives from the degree comparative *fast* = *hard, very much*, . . . like in English "grip fast" (which, in English, turned into the adjective for *with high speed*, see the extremely comprehensive study by Stern 1921). How can a word that denotes "very much so" turn into a word that means "almost, but not actually"? The authors of DW (Grimm 1885–1962: Vol.3, 1348–1350) offer a very detailed database for the stages of the development.

The old use *fast* in the sense of "tight", "firmly" was used for physical or metaphorical links between things (used c1500–c1700):

(23) a. *sölh pflicht halt fast*
 this duty hold <u>fast</u>
 b. *halt fast den pfluog*
 hold the plough fast / <u>tightly</u>

From this intensifying use with verbs that report maintenance of contact, *fast* was extended to a generalized degree adverb, roughly like *very, much$_{adv}$*. (It is from this point that *fast* in English was reduced again to high degrees of speed for movement verbs).

(24) *dis ler und trost mich* FAST ERQUICKT
 this lesson and consolation <u>revives</u> me <u>very much</u>
(25) *wenn du gleich* FAST *danach* RINGEST, *so erlangest du es doch nicht.*
 even if you <u>struggle</u> for it <u>hard</u>, you will not attain it

It is also in this sense that we find it with participles and adjectives, such that *fast schön* at that time meant 'very beautiful', and *not* like ModHG "almost beautiful".

Interestingly, the DW faithfully reports on examples where "die bedeutung sehr in die von *fere* (= Latin *almost*) ausweich(t)", i.e. where the meaning strongly tends to 'almost' rather than 'very'. The quoted examples offer very nice evidence in which sense the intensifying 'very' sense became shifty.

(26) *weil er fast hundertjerig war*
   he was *very much?/ almost?* hundred years old
(27) *kamen darauf fast um zwo uren*
   (they) arrived there *very much?/ almost?* at two o'clock /*sharp?*
(28) *das fast nicht ein balken vergessen war*
   that *very much?/ almost?* not a single log was forgotten

In the long run, the two different readings were correlated with the stem-umlaut difference and *firmly* was conventionally expressed by *fest* whereas *fast* was reserved for the new meaning *almost*. I will use *fast*$_{deg}$ to refer to the degree adverb, whereas *fast*$_{prox}$ will be used for the proximity adverb.

In order to understand the change that occured in the wake of examples like (26) to (28), let us look at the older meaning of *fast* in the sense of *very much*. Without aiming at a full analysis of modern *very much* or *sehr*, I propose the following representation: *fast*$_{deg}$ can combine with a scaled property P and states that the event/entity talked about is at the high end of the scale.

(29) *fast*$_{deg}$ *hungrig*
   "be hungry to a degree which is high on the scale of possible degrees of hungriness"

It still contrasts with "absolutely" or "extremely", hence it is plausible to allow for higher values on the P scale.

(30) *fast*$_{deg}$ *hungrig*
   "be hungry to a degree which is high on the scale of possible degrees of hungriness, with (possibly) some higher degrees"

Let us assume that the degrees are represented as a linear order <. This leads to the following representation for older *fast*$_{deg}$:

(31) *fast*$_{deg}$
   FAST($\lambda x \lambda s P(s,x)$)
   := $\lambda x \lambda s [P(s,x) \land MOSTy(P(s,y) \rightarrow y<x) \land \exists z(P(y,z) \rightarrow x<z)]$

In prose, *fast*$_{deg}$ takes a property P as its argument, and maps it to that subproperty which comprises those entities which have the property P, and are more *P-ish* than most but not all other entities in terms of the relevant ordering. This is reflected by the use of the ordering relation < which is supposed to cover up for more intricate ways to determine the degree of *P*-ness of a given object *a*. The semantic representation predicts that *fast*$_{deg}$ can only apply to *gradable* properties P. (As an aside, note that the given definition needs to be complemented by a clause which ensures that FAST-P denotes a convex area on the scale. I would like to thank Hans-Martin Gärtner for clarifying discussions, for details see Eckardt 2007.)

The quotes in (26)–(28) and similar ones in the DW have in common that the pragmatic support for the use of *fast*$_{deg}$ in the *very much* sense is lacking. Consider an example like (26). The property of *"being 100 years old"* does not commonly refer to degrees. Degrees can, perhaps, be introduced, like in contexts where different 100 year olds show typical properties of the very old to various degrees. In such a situation, one might state that "Jones is so very much a 100 yearer". The incompatibility between *fast* and the property *be 100 years old* hence is a conceptual one, not one of grammar. However, nothing in the quoted contexts seems to have warranted such a scale. An utterance like (26') in a context without support for a suitable scale creates a *pragmatic overload*.

(26') Er war fast$_{deg}$ 100 Jahre alt.

The speaker might have trusted in the intensifying use of fast$_{deg}$. We can but guess. He might have had the intention to refer to a scale ranging from "*around 100 years*", to "*very close to 100 years*" and culminating in "*exactly 100 years*". This is indeed a scale, and one that would predict that "*very much 100 years old*" in this sense means "*exactly 100 years old*". The use of such a scale would have warranted a conservative use of *fast*$_{deg}$, but one that the contemporary reader (as well as the authors of the DW) did not find very plausible. A pretty insalient scale would have to be accessed in order to get this reading. Instead, listeners hypothesized a pragmatically leaner reading which rests on a new meaning: *fast*$_{prox}$. And in fact, the reanalysis is minimal. In order to see this, we need to consider a semantic representation of the proximal adverbs. In (32), we see a suitable denotation *Almost* for *fast* in its new, 'almost' sense (a detailed discussion is offered in Eckardt 2007; for a fuller record of data in the change of *fast* see Eckardt 2011).

(32) a. *Almost* is an operator that can combine with property concepts of arbitrary arity, including zero (i.e. propositions). The argument will be written as $\lambda \bar{x} \lambda s P(s, \bar{x})$ where $\bar{x}$ is a vector of variables. This reflects that *Almost* can combine with propositions, relations, properties; in other words: the new item is very flexible in semantic composition.
b. The operator *Almost* poses the following presuppositions on its argument and context of use:

a. There is a conceptually salient SUPERPROPERTY of P, Π such that
$\lambda \bar{x} \lambda s P(s,\bar{x}) \subset \lambda \bar{x} \lambda s \Pi(s,\bar{x})$
b. The elements of the superproperty can be compared in terms of a PRE-ORDER <: For any a, b, c and s, s', s" such that $\Pi(s,a)$ and $\Pi(s',b)$ and $\Pi(s",c)$:
transitivity: $<\bar{a},s> < <\bar{b},s'> \wedge <\bar{b},s'> < <c,s"> \rightarrow <\bar{a},s> < <c,s">$
asymmetry: $<\bar{a},s> < <\bar{b},s'> \rightarrow \neg(<\bar{b},s'> < <\bar{a},s>)$
c. The argument taken by *almost* has to cover the maximal part in Π with respect to the order. MAXIMALITY of P: for all $\bar{x}, \bar{y}, s, s'$: $P(s, \bar{x}) \wedge \Pi(s', \bar{y})$ $\rightarrow <\bar{y},s'> \leq <\bar{x},s>$

In prose, ALMOST applies to a property P by making reference to a superproperty of P, like for example $P =$ 'be 100 years old' with superproperty 'be n years old, for some n'. The superproperty here is naturally ordered by n (so, 'be 5 years old' would count less than 'be 10 years old' etc.)

If all these requirements are supported either by world knowledge or contextual background, *almost* can apply and maps P to the property ALMOST(P).

(33) ALMOST ($\lambda \bar{x} \lambda s P(s,\bar{x})$)
  $:= \lambda \bar{x} \lambda s [\text{MOST}<\bar{y},s'>(\Pi(s',\bar{y}) \rightarrow <\bar{y},s'> < <\bar{x},s>) \wedge$
    $\forall <\bar{z},s">(P(s",\bar{z}) \rightarrow <\bar{x},s> < <\bar{z},s">)]$
  'all those x that are high in the superproperty, though they do not reach the maximal P
  region'; in our example 'all those x of high age but below 100'.

The present analysis of *almost* reveals that an intensifier *very* (see (31)) only needs minimal adjustments in meaning in order to turn into the proximal adverb, and it moreover predicts that such adjustments should be made in response to exactly those uses that define the turning point. It turns out that the conceptual core of the item did not change much. Confronted with examples like (26) that lack a scale, hearers addressed a scale on a derived superproperty Π instead of the original property P, and applied just the old denotation of *fast*$_{\text{deg}}$ to that superproperty. (34) reveals that the actual meaning change at the level of the modifier was really minimal.

(34) $fast_{\text{prox}}(P) := fast_{\text{deg}}(\Pi)$

In other words, $fast_{\text{deg}}$ modifies a scalar property P exactly in the same way as $fast_{\text{prox}}$ modifies a derived scalar property Π. It should be noted that ALMOST is *not* the widely used modal analysis that goes back to Sadock (1981). Among other disadvantages of the Sadock analysis, only the operator presented here allows to undersstand the semantic relation to older $fast_{\text{deg}}$.

5 What semantic reanalysis is not

Generalization or bleaching have been proposed to be the driving force in grammaticalization. Is semantic reanalysis the same as *generalization*? I would argue against this identification. Semantic reanalysis *can* lead to an increased range of application for some word. We saw an instance in the case of *drohen* where a property of persons turned into a propositional operator. Other modals show similar developments. Yet, the essence of semantic reanalysis lies in a changed compositional structure of sentences; extensions can, but need not happen. Grammatical meanings have also been claimed to be more abstract than content words, and hence arise by *bleaching*. I suggested in the discussion of the *going to* future that the denotations of grammatical words become salient as spandrels between content word meanings and clause meanings (Givón 2009: 316). This can explicate in which sense these meanings are abstract, without postulating a new type of meaning change. On somewhat different grounds, Traugott (1988) argues that grammaticalization involves enrichments as well as generalizations and hence *bleaching* alone does not suffice.

Metaphor was proposed to be the semantic shift in grammaticalization by Heine, Claudi & Hünnemeyer (1991), Bybee, Perkins & Pagliuca (1994), Sweetser (1990), Stolz (1994) and others. We saw in the case of *drohen* that metaphor can be the first step of a development. However, I proposed that the grammaticalized form follows later, driven by avoidance of pragmatic overload when the original metaphor is used without conceptual support. Other examples of semantic reanalysis clearly show that metaphor need not figure in the process at all, like in the stories of *voll, fast, während, a lot of*, or *selbst, lauter* (Eckardt 2006), the *say*-based futures in Bantu languages (Uche 1996/1997; Botne 1998) and many other cases.

Metonymy was proposed by Traugott, and most detailed in Hopper & Traugott (1993) as the process accompanying grammaticalization. The authors identify the pairing of a certain syntactic structure with a certain *supposed* literal meaning as the true source of grammaticalization. In order to justify the classification as metonymy, the authors count the coupling of form and meaning as an instance of *contiguity*. Contiguity is the term traditionally used for conceptual closeness in metonymic shifts like from container to thing contained, from author to book, from disease to patient, etc. I think that semantic reanalysis differs substantially from metonymy because the two kinds of 'closeness' are distinct. Metonymy rests on contiguity relations between things in the world which hold true independently of language. Containers and the things contained are close concepts, no matter whether we talk about this fact or not. In contrast, semantic reanalysis rests on incidental 'closeness' between words and possible contents. For example, the closeness between the word *go* in the progressive form and the possible content: *imminent future* can only ever arise because people talk. To put it more drastically, a dog can master the contiguity between container and thing contained, but certainly not the contiguity between *going-to* and imminent future. (While I do not deny a dog's understanding for fixed phrases like *we're going to go out for a walk*, there is no evidence so far that dogs possess function words or morphemes.)

Traugott in collaboration with König, Schwenter, Dasher and others (Traugott 1988, 1989; Schwenter & Traugott 2000; Traugott & König 1991; Traugott & Dasher 2002) comes very close to the notion of semantic reanalysis; specifically when Traugott & Dasher (2002) point out that the reclassification of information from implicature to literal content of an utterance is the initiating step in the change. They also can capture the effect of *strengthening*, not predicted by analyses of grammaticalization in terms of generalization / bleaching.

As early as 1977, Langacker made a first attempt at describing semantic reanalysis as *semantic redistribution of atoms of meaning* over the parts of clauses. He discusses the origin of functional morphemes and words in several Indian languages. The approach was fraught by the problem that the relevant "conceptual chunks" that play a role in grammaticalization are arguably not atoms—most of them only become salient as spandrels. This might be the main reason why the proposal, otherwise very much in line with his characterization of structural, morphosyntactic reanalysis was never taken up in later years.

Finally, Traugott in a series of papers proposes *subjectification* as a general mode of meaning change. Subjectification is diagnosed when the speaker, hearer or other aspects of the utterance situation turn into parameters of the message. For instance, in the emergence of epistemic readings for modals, Traugott points out that the modal base refers to the epistemic alternatives of the *speaker*. Hence the utterance (35) is more subjective in that the speaker relates the proposition to her epistemic base whereas (36) boldly asserts the proposition as true in the real world Portner (2009).

(35) *Tom must be Susan's new husband.*
(36) *Tom is Susan's new husband.*

Likewise, items that are reanalysed as discourse markers often convey a propositional attitude of the speaker, like in the following.

(37) *Tom is indeed a genius.*
(38) *Tom ist eigentlich ein angenehmer Mensch.*

Tom is *actually* an agreeable person

I think that these observations involve two interacting factors. One factor is semantic reanalysis, a process where—under suitable circumstances—*any* salient possible denotation can be coupled with an item. This part has nothing to do with a desire to express the subjective. On the other side, however, the numerous instances of emergent discourse particles offer strong evidence that emotional undertones may be *one strong source* for denotations that hearers find salient. Semantic reanalysis is a "denotation recruiting" process, drawing on several sources for new denotations: the new denotation can convey emotional information, or the spandrel consists of temporal information, or the spandrel consists of scalar information, or quantity information, and so on. Against this background, we can describe cases of semantic reanalysis without the need to sense subjectification as a justificational label all over the place (see e.g. the attempts in Visconti 2005 to diagnose subjectification in the emergence of *even* synonyms in Italian).

6 Avoid Pragmatic Overload

In the final section, we will consider the factors in utterance contexts that set reanalysis into motion. What is it that turns a potential change into an actual change? Proposals in recent years mostly are based on "conventionalization" (Lehmann 2002, Diewald 2002, Heine 2002) which, in the absence of a definition, suggests something like the adoption of a habit. This view does not explain why sentences S that were formed according to the rules of an older grammar L_{old} should ever be reanalysed in the first place. Sentence S under the older grammar was very well capable of expressing all the content that the speaker intended to convey. Hence, speakers could have maintained a habit of using certain phrases or constructions without any incentive to reanalyse anything, or "conventionalize" new language uses.

As an alternative to the habit view, I propose that the desire to *Avoid Pragmatic Overload* (APO) can start reanalysis (Eckardt 2009, 2011). In the present section, I will illustrate this proposal with some examples. Consider once again the development of *fast* to a proximity adverb. Examples like (26)–(28) turn up at a time when only the older (intensifying) reading should have been available. They violate the presuppositions of the intensifying adverb in that the modified properties are not gradeable. While unsupported presuppositions in general can be accommodated by the hearer, matters are different in the present case. There is no salient scale for the property of "being 100 years old"; the speaker may have had some kind of scale in mind but whatever it was, it is not generally available. The hearer faces an instance of pragmatic overload. She could hypothesise suitable information and accommodate the unwarranted and unperspicious presuppositions. Alternatively, she can believe that the speaker meant to use the words and phrases of the utterance in a different, novel way. Under this alternative assumption, the hearer will parse a reanalysed version of the original utterance. (To repeat: the changes are still effected by semantic reanalysis, but the hearer undertakes reanalysis as an alternative to a pragmatically overloaded reading.)

Uses of words or constructions that rely on unwarranted presuppositions can be observed in many other instances of change. I will list some examples, pointing out the unwarranted presuppositions without further discussion; for an extensive discussion see the respective references.

The change of *selbst* from intensifier (*-self*) to focus particle (*even*) was antedated by uses like (39). The intensifier presupposes that the associated referent can be conceptualized as the center in a range of peripheral objects. This is what is violated in (39); the bees do not make a good center in a periphery of happy entities, neither the range of alternatives mentioned (wind, field, flowers) nor any other (Opitz 1978; see Eckardt 2007: ch. 6 and Eckardt 2001).

(39) *Bald kömpt der scharpffe Nord gantz vnverhofft gebrauset*
Quer vber Feld daher / pfeifft / heulet / singt vnd sauset /
Vnd nimpt die Lilie mit Vngestümme hin;
Die liebliche Gestalt bricht nichts nicht seinen Sinn.
Das grüne Feld beginnt vmb seine Zier zu trawren /
Die andern Blumen auch muß jhre Schwester tawren /
Die BIENEN *fliegen* SELBST *vor Schmertz vnd Trawrigkeit*
Verjrrt jetzt hin / jetzt her / vnd tragen grosses Leyd.

'(. . .) Soon comes the sharp north (wind) browsing quite unexpectedly / over the field, hissing, howling, singing and whistling / and takes the lily with violence / the lovely figure can not break his mind / The green field begins to mourn for its embellishment / the other flowers likewise must feel sorry for their sister / THE BEES THEMSELVES, FOR GRIEF AND SORROW, FLY ERRING NOW HERE NOW THERE / and carry great mourning.'

We can hence assume that APO motivated the reader to search for another interpretation of the crucial passage.

Another case is offered in Visconti (2005) who dicusses a similar development of Italian *perfino*. The original meaning was 'to-the-end', localizing a given entity at the endpoint of a presupposed temporal, spatial or abstract scale. The item developed a new use in the sense of 'even'. (40) shows the crucial kind of examples at the turning point, quoted in Visconti as the stage between the older, and the 'even' scalar use.

(40) ... *in acqua, in neve, in grandine o pruina: a tutto il ciel s'inclina, perfino a quel che la natura sprezza.* ('Water, snow, hail or frost: To everything bends the sky, even to that which nature despises.') (Visconti 2005: ex. 17)

perfino in its older sense presupposes a scale of things and refers to its end point; however, the listed alternatives in the given example (water, snow, hail, frost) are not plausibly ordered on any motivated scale. In order to supply a scale against which the semantic contribution of *perfino* can be made, hearers seem to have resorted to the scale of likelihood. If we understand *perfino* relative to this scale, the resulting message will be that some referent is located at the endpoint of this scale. In other words, the state of affairs is reported as being the most unlikely among given alternatives—and hence APO leads straight to the *even*-use of *perfino*.

Another range of examples that create pragmatic overload can be found in the development of German *lauter* (*merely*; use around 1500) towards a quasi-determiner 'many/only'. The unwarranted presupposition of *merely* in an example like (41) consists in the claim that *devils* be a minor variant of *saints*.

(41) (...) *die barfuosser haben vil gelts außgeben dem Bapst, das sy den Franciscum iren Abgott auch moechten in des hibsch Register bringen, O ain kostliche eer das gewest wer,*
(...) 'the barefooted friars (= Franciscans) spent much money to the pope that they might also get Franciscus, their idol, into that nice register, O a fine honour this would have been, ... '

sodoch	lautter	Teuffel	solten	darinn	begriffen
as yet	lauter	devils	should	therein	comprised
seyn	und	kain	haylig		
be	and	no	saints		

It is a subtle mismatch, but, as further developments showed, a substantial one. Rather than believing that devils could be conceptualized as fake-saints, the hearers hypothesized an instance of the newer 'many'/'only' use of *lauter*, hence understanding that 'only and many devils' were on the list, instead of the intended but infelicitous 'barely devils, no saints'.

These case studies suggest that the principle to *Avoid Pragmatic Overload* can indeed offer a plausible analysis for the initial phase of change. For instance, the authors of etymological dictionaries frequently offer examples at the turning point between older and newer meaning of a word that seem to fit the *APO* principle very well. A full analysis would need to start from attested older uses, and a tenable semantic/pragmatic analysis of these. Next, the actual uses in the crucial period need to be traced carefully in search for utterances where, to the best of our knowledge, we find that the item was used with unwarranted presuppositions that are moreover hard to accommodate. Driven by the APO principle, the reader may have searched for another plausible interpretation of the utterance, and often it can be seen that only minor supposed changes in structure and meaning yield a result that the hearers at the time must have found more convincing.

It is not an accident that the *Avoid Pragmatic Overload* principle echoes Lightfoot's principle to avoid structural complexity, first formulated in Lightfoot's (1979) reconstruction of the development of the modal system in English and echoed in later work (Lightfoot 1991, 1999, van Gelderen 2004). Lightfoot proposes that children at certain crucial historical stages ignore the older complex syntactic structure of certain constructions in favour of a simpler new structural analysis. This analysis is still one of the most plausible assumptions in syntactic change, in spite of the problems that it raises for verification in historical data. It is assumed to operate during language acquisition, where virtually none is known for historical times. The principle to *Avoid Pragmatic Overload* can be understood as the semantic counterpart of Lightfoot's principle.

7 Summary

The present article took its start from grammaticalization, viewed as a special kind of language change. While the restructuring at the morpho-syntactic level is well-understood in many cases, the nature of the changes at the semantic side has only been tentatively addressed in traditional theories of language change. I argue that a compositional semantic theory is necessary to capture and investigate changes in the semantic composition of phrases and sentences that accompany morpho-syntactic restructuring. I introduced the core mechanisms in semantic reanalysis on basis of an example in section 3. While semantic reanalysis is of good service in analysing prototypical cases of grammaticalization, I argued in section 4 that this mode of change is by no means limited to changes that would classically count as grammaticalization.

I presented more examples (*drohen, während, fast*) which illustrate the range of possibe applications for semantic reanalysis. Section 5 argues why semantic reanalysis is not simply a new word for modes of semantic change that were proposed earlier in the literature. Specifically, I argued that it is different from *generalization, bleaching, metonymy* and *subjectification*. The final section addresses the question of *why* hearers would assume new compositions for old messages of old sentences—innovation seems surprising, given that the older language system must already have been capable of conveying exactly the same messages (by literal content plus entailments) in exactly the old words. I suggest that the point of innovation is often defined by cases where the intended entailments are costly to derive. I call these cases instances of *pragmatic overload*. According to this picture, innovation arises essentially due to hearer's lazyness, or the attempt to *avoid pragmatic overload*.

8 References

Abraham, Werner 1991. The grammaticalization of the German modal particles. In: E. C. Traugott & B. Heine (eds.). *Approaches to Grammaticalization. Vol. 2*. Amsterdam: Benjamins, 331–380.

Botne, Robert 1998. The evolution of future tenses from serial 'say' constructions in central eastern Bantu. *Diachronica* XV.2, 207–230.

Brinton, Laurel 1996. *Pragmatic Markers in English. Grammaticalization and Discourse Function*. Berlin: Mouton de Gruyter.

Bybee, Joan, Revere Perkins & William Pagliuca 1994. *The Evolution of Grammar. Tense, Aspect, and Modality in the Languages of the World*. Chicago, IL: The University of Chicago Press.

Campbell, Lyle 2001. What's wrong with grammaticalization? In: L. Campbell & R. D. Janda (eds.). *Grammaticalization: A critical assessment*. Special issue of *Language Sciences* 23, 113–162.

Diewald, Gabriele 2002. A model for relevant types of contexts in grammaticalization. In: I. Wischer & G. Diewald (eds.). *New Reflections on Grammaticalization*. Amsterdam: Benjamins, 103–120.

Eckardt, Regine 2001. Reanalysing 'selbst'. *Natural Language Semantics* 9, 371–412.

Eckardt, Regine 2006. *Meaning Change in Grammaticalization. An Enquiry into Semantic Reanalysis*. Oxford: Oxford University Press.

Eckardt, Regine 2007. *Almost—A Theory*. Ms. Göttingen, University of Göttingen. http://semanticsarchive.net/Archive/GRmOWZmN/SemanticReanalysis.pdf, June 21, 2011.

Eckardt, Regine 2009. APO: Avoid Pragmatic Overload. In: J. Visconti, M.-B. Mosegard Hansen (eds.). *Current Trends in Diachronic Semantics and Pragmatics*. London: Emerald, 21—42.

Eckardt, Regine 2011. Semantic reanalysis and language change. *Language and Linguistics Compass* 5, 33–46. doi: 10.1111/j.1749–818X.2010.00260.x.

Eisenberg, Peter 1999. *Grundriss der Deutschen Grammatik. Bd. 2: Der Satz*. Stuttgart: Metzler.

von Fintel, Kai 1995. The formal semantics of grammaticalization. In: J. N. Beckman (ed.). *Proceedings of the Annual Meeting of the North East Linguistic Society (= NELS) 25*. Amherst, MA: GLSA, 175–189.

Fischer, Olga 2007. The role of analogy in morphosyntactic change. Plenary lecture given at the *29th Annual Meeting of the Deutsche Gesellschaft für Sprachwissenschaft* (German

Linguistic Society), *Workshop (AG 8): The Role of Variation in Language Evolution*, University of Siegen.
Fischer, Olga & Anette Rosenbach 2000. Introduction. In: O. Fischer, A. Rosenbach & D. Stein (eds.). *Pathways of Change: Grammaticalization in English*. Amsterdam: Benjamins, 1–37.
van Gelderen, Elly 2004. *Grammaticalization as Economy*. Amsterdam: Benjamins.
von der Gabelentz, Georg 1901. *Die Sprachwissenschaft. Ihre Aufgaben, Methoden und bisherigen Ergebnisse*. Tübingen: Narr.
Givón, Talmy 2009. *The Genesis of Syntactic Complexity: Diachrony, Ontongeny, Neuro-Cognition*. Amsterdam: Benjamin.
Grimm, Jacob & Wilhelm Grimm 1885–1962. *Deutsches Wörterbuch*. Leipzig: Schmidt Periodicals. Reprinted: Leipzig: Hirzel, 1985.
Haspelmath, Martin 1999. Why is grammaticalization irreversible? *Linguistics* 37, 1043–1068.
Heim, Irene & Angelika Kratzer 1998. *Semantics in Generative Grammar*. Oxford: Blackwell.
Heine, Bernd 2002. On the role of context in grammaticalization. In: I. Wischer & G. Diewald (eds.). *New Reflections on Grammaticalization*. Amsterdam: Benjamins, 83–102.
Heine, Bernd & Tania Kuteva 2002. *World Lexicon of Grammaticalization*. Cambridge: Cambridge University Press.
Heine, Bernd & Hiroyuki Miyashita 2006. *Accounting for a Functional Category: German 'drohen'*. Ms. Köln, University of Köln.
Heine, Bernd, Ulrike Claudi & Friederike Hünnemeyer 1991. *Grammaticalization: A Conceptual Framework*. Chicago, IL: The University of Chicago Press.
Hopper, Paul & Elizabeth C. Traugott 1993. *Grammaticalization*. Cambridge: Cambridge University Press. 2nd, rev. edn. 2003.
Janda, Richard D. 2001. Beyond "pathways" and "unidirectionality". On the discontinuity of language transmission and the counterability of grammaticalization. In: L. Campbell & R. D. Janda (eds.). *Grammaticalization: A critical assessment*. Special issue of *Language Sciences* 23, 265–340.
Joseph, Brian D. 2001. Is there such a thing as "grammaticalization"? In: L. Campbell & R. D. Janda (eds.). *Grammaticalization: A critical assessment*. Special issue of *Language Sciences* 23, 163–186.
Kempson, Ruth & Ronnie Cann 2007. Dynamic syntax and dialogue modelling: Preliminaries for a dialogue-driven account of syntactic change. In: J. Salmons & S. Dubenion-Smith (eds.). *Historical Linguistics 2005: Selected Papers from the 17th International Congress of Historical Linguistics*. Amsterdam: Benjamins, 73–102.
König, Ekkehard & Elisabeth C. Traugott 1988. Pragmatic strengthening and semantic change: The conventionalizing of conversational implicature. In: W. Hüllen & R. Schulze (eds.). *Understanding the Lexicon: Meaning, Sense and World Knowledge in Lexical Semantics*. Tübingen: Niemeyer, 110–124.
Krug, Manfred G. 2000. *Emerging English Modals: A Corpus-based Study of Grammaticalization*. Berlin: Mouton de Gruyter.
Langacker, Ronald W. 1977. Syntactic reanalysis. In: C. Li (ed.). *Mechanisms of Syntactic Change*. Austin, TX: University of Texas Press, 57–139.
Lehmann, Christian 1995/2002. *Thoughts on Grammaticalization*. München: Lincom. 2nd, rev. edn. Erfurt: University of Erfurt, 2002 (Arbeitspapiere des Seminars für Sprachwissenschaft der Universität Erfurt No. 9).
Lehmann, Christian 2002. New reflections on grammaticalization and lexicalization. In: I. Wischer & G. Diewald (eds.). *New Reflections on Grammaticalization*. Amsterdam: Benjamins, 1–18.

Lightfoot, David 1979. *Principles of Diachronic Syntax*. Cambridge: Cambridge University Press.
Lightfoot, David 1991. *How to Set Parameters: Arguments from Language Change*. Cambridge, MA: The MIT Press.
Lightfoot, David 1999. *The Development of Language: Acquisition, Change, and Evolution*. Oxford: Blackwell.
Merin, Artur 1996. *Formal Semantic Theory and Diachronic Data: A Case Study in Grammaticalization* (Arbeitsbericht des Sonderforschungsbereich 340, No. 75). Stuttgart: Universität Stuttgart.
http://www.semanticsarchive.net/Archive/jhjZDgzY/fstadd.pdf, June 21, 2011.
Mosegaard Hansen, Mai-Britt & Corinne Rossari 2005. The evolution of pragmatic markers. Introduction. *Journal of Historical Pragmatics* 6, 177–187.
Newmeyer, Frederick J. 2001. Deconstructing grammaticalization. In: L. Campbell & R. D. Janda (eds.). *Grammaticalization: A critical assessment*. Special issue of *Language Sciences* 23, 187–230.
Norde, Muriel 2001. Deflexion as a counterdirectional factor in grammatical change. In: L. Campbell & R. D. Janda (eds.). *Grammaticalization: A critical assessment*. Special issue of *Language Sciences* 23, 231–264.
Opitz, Martin 1978. *Gesammelte Werke: Kritische Ausgabe. Bd. II: Die Werke von 1621 bis 1626*. George Schulz-Behrend (ed.). Stuttgart: Anton Hiersemann Verlag.
Paul, Hermann 1880. *Principien der Sprachgeschichte*. Halle: Niemeyer. Reprinted as Studienausgabe of the 8th edition. Tübingen: Niemeyer, 1970.
Portner, Paul 2009. *Modality*. Oxford: Oxford University Press.
Potts, Christopher 2005. *The Logic of Conventional Implicatures*. Oxford: Oxford University Press.
Sadock, Jerrold M. 1981. 'Almost'. In: P. Cole (ed.). *Radical Pragmatics*. New York: Academic Press, 257–271.
Sahel, Said 2007. Das Lexem "voll" als Kasuszuweiser—Kasusvariation aber kein Genitivschwund. Paper presented at the *Norddeutsches Linguistisches Kolloquium*. University of Göttingen.
Schwenter, Scott & Elizabeth C. Traugott 2000. Invoking scalarity: The development of *in fact*. *Journal of Historical Pragmatics* 1, 7–25.
Stern, Gustaf 1921. *Swift, Swiftly, and Their Synonyms. A Contribution to Semantic Analysis and Theory*. Ph.D. dissertation. University of Göteborg. Reprinted: Göteborg, 1921 (Göteborgs Högskolas Årsskrift, Vol. 27).
Stolz, Thomas 1994. *Grammatikalisierung und Metaphorisiserung*. Bochum: Universitätsverlag Brockmeyer.
Sweetser, Eve 1988. Grammaticalization and semantic bleaching. In: S. Axmaker, A. Jaisser & H. Singmaster (eds.). *Proceedings of the 14th Annual Meeting of the Berkeley Linguistics Society (= BLS)*. Berkeley, CA: Berkeley Linguistics Society, 389–405.
Sweetser, Eve 1990. *From Etymology to Pragmatics. Metaphorical and Cultural Aspects of Semantic Structure*. Cambridge: Cambridge University Press.
Tabor, Whitney & Elizabeth C. Traugott 1998. Structural scope expansion and grammaticalization. In: G. Ramat, A. Hopper & P. Hopper (eds.). *The Limits of Grammaticalization*. Amsterdam: Benjamins, 229–272.
Traugott, Elizabeth C. 1988. Pragmatic strengthening and grammaticalization. In: S. Axmaker, A. Jaisser & H. Singmaster (eds.). *Proceedings of the 14th Annual Meeting of the Berkeley Linguistics Society (= BLS)*. Berkeley, CA: Berkeley Linguistics Society, 406–416.

Traugott, Elizabeth C. 1989. On the rise of epistemic meanings in English: An example of subjectification in semantic change. *Language* 57, 33–65.

Traugott, Elizabeth C. 2008. Grammaticalization, constructions and the incremential development of language. In: R. Eckardt, G. Jäger & T. Veenstra, (eds.). *Language Evolution: Cognitive and Cultural Factors*. Berlin: Mouton de Gruyter, 219–252.

Traugott, Elizabeth C. & Richard B. Dasher 2002. *Regularities in Semantic Change*. Cambridge: Cambridge University Press.

Traugott, Elizabeth C. & Ekkehard König 1991. The semantics-pragmatics of grammaticalization revisited. In: E. C. Traugott & B. Heine (eds.). *Approaches to Grammaticalization. Vol. 1*. Amsterdam: Benjamins, 189–218.

Uche, Aaron 1996/1997. Grammaticization of the verb 'say' to future tense in Obolo. *The Journal of West African Languages* 26, 87–94.

Visconti, Jacqueline 2005. On the origins of scalar particles in Italian. *Journal of Historical Pragmatics* 6, 237–261.

Wegener, Heide 2002. The evolution of the German modal particle *denn*. In: I. Wischer & G. Diewald (eds.). *New Reflections on Grammaticalization*. Amsterdam: Benjamins, 379–394.

Zeevat, Henk & Elena Karagjosova 2009. History and grammaticalization of "doch"/ "toch". In: A. Benz & R. Blutner (eds.). *Papers on Pragmasemantics* (ZAS Papers in Linguistics 51). Berlin: ZAS, 135–152.

Lyn Frazier
8 Meaning in psycholinguistics

1   Introduction —— 210
2   Architectural issues and preliminaries —— 211
3   Processing quantifiers —— 215
4   Different types of DPs —— 224
5   Beyond DPs —— 229
6   Conclusions —— 231
7   References —— 232

Abstract: The psycholinguistic study of meaning is beginning to attract considerable interest. In the area of adult language comprehension, experimental methods familiar from the study of syntactic and intonational processing, such as comprehension time studies, have examined issues at the interface of syntax and semantics, such as those involving the processing of quantifier scope, the identification of implicit domain restrictions, and the complexity predictions of various theories of quantifiers. They have also been used to investigate the processing of non-quantificational phrases in discourse contexts, especially anaphoric phrases. 'Visual world' studies now supply evidence about processing language in the presence of rich visual contexts, and event related potential studies provide continuous qualitative measures of ongoing interpretation. Outside the domain of DPs, less processing research has been conducted, with the exception of studies of verb classes, and a handful of studies of aspect, tense, and scalar adjectives. The picture that emerges is one of ongoing interpretation of syntactic structure, constrained by world knowledge and discourse context from the beginning of interpretive processes, with particular attention allocated to focused phrases.

1 Introduction

A psycholinguistic theory of adult semantic processing presumably must be concerned with actual linguistic structures and the mechanisms available for interpreting them. It must include a particular semantic theory, as well as spelling out assumptions about how semantics interfaces with syntax and with other relevant representations, such as a representation of intonation, and a mental

Lyn Frazier, Amherst, MA, USA

https://doi.org/10.1515/9783110589825-008

model representation. One of the core questions in semantics proper is how the meanings of words, and the way they are combined syntactically, determines the meaning of novel phrases and sentences. A theory of semantic processing must say how this is done in 'real time': what commitments are made when, what interpretations are favored, and why, and what counts as context for any given interpretive decision.

This chapter will take up topics in linguistically-guided semantic processing. It will be geared to language comprehension rather than to language production. Production and comprehension impose quite different processing demands and thus it would be dizzying to jump back and forth between the two systems. Further, the chapter will emphasize the processing of different kinds of Determiner Phrases, because this has been the focus of much of the psycholinguistic literature on semantic processing. However, pointers to research on other topics in semantic processing will be presented in Section 5.

Section 2 provides a look at the interplay of semantics with syntax, and to a lesser extent with focus. It is an attempt to orient the reader with respect to important processing findings and with respect to architectural issues concerning the structure of the language comprehension system. Section 3 takes up the processing of quantifiers. What determines their preferred scope? How are restrictions on the domain of quantification identified? Do all quantifiers exhibit the complexity effects expected given Generalized Quantifier Theory? Under what circumstances are pragmatic implicatures generated due to the choice of one particular quantifier from among the various options on an entailment-scale? Section 4 takes up non-quantificational Determiner Phrases (DPs). It looks at 'anaphoric' DPs, DPs with an accommodated referent, the processing of plural DPs, and preferences for collective versus distributive interpretations. Section 5 provides pointers to other processing research, in particular research on verb classes, and Section 6 concludes.

2 Architectural issues and preliminaries

A theory of actual semantic processing should be sufficiently detailed to deliver an account of how an interpretation unfolds over time, and of how semantic processing is related to other kinds of processing, in particular, syntactic processing. In this section, it will be suggested that syntax normally takes the lead in processing, but with several caveats, as will be seen below.

Listeners and readers construct a syntactic analysis of a sentence as the words of the sentence are encountered. Generally the syntactically simplest analysis is pursued or given highest priority, other things being equal, see Frazier (1987), van Gompel et al. (2005). Usually, the syntax seems to lead interpretation (Lipka 2002), but there may be exceptions in the case of highly predictable or stereotypical relations, where expectations based on non-syntactic information may guide or even override the syntax (Kim & Osterhout 2005). For example, in highly circumscribed contexts, eye movements suggest the verb *eat* predicts *cake* and vice versa given a visual world with only one edible object (the cake) and only stereotypical relations expressed in the sentences (Altmann & Kamide 1999).

When utterances are only about a visually present world, (visual) context effects are strong and they may guide ongoing sentence analysis. Imagine a visual world containing a frog on a napkin and an empty napkin, as well as two irrelevant distracter objects. Eberhard et al. (1995) showed that in this one-frog scenario, when instructed to "*Put the frog on the napkin . . . (into the box)*," listeners' eyes quickly moved to the frog-less napkin (the 'false goal'), indicating that they had interpreted the prepositional phrase *on the napkin* as the locative argument of *put*. But if a second frog was also present in the display, false-goal looks were largely eliminated. Presumably this was because the presence of a modifier *on the napkin* was needed in order to pick out the intended referent (or to justify the use of the definite determiner) in the two-frog scenario. The elimination of the looks to the false goal in the two-frog scenario has been taken to suggest that context directs sentence analysis. This is consistent with the referential theory of processing (Crain & Steedman 1985) which emphasizes the importance of referential factors during sentence processing. According to the referential model, referential success, and the avoidance of presupposition failure, is central to online comprehension. The processing system weeds out syntactic analyses on a word-by-word basis if the analysis gives rise to referential failure or to an unsatisfied presupposition, assuming the existence of some alternative syntactic analysis that does not give rise to a violation.

"Semantic coercion" refers to interpretations, or interpretive processes, that are not supported by overt morphology or syntax (see article 10 [Semantics: Lexical Structures and Adjectives] (de Swart) *Mismatches and coercion*). Psycholinguists have examined aspectual coercion, *The frog jumped for an hour*, where *jumped* must be coerced into an iterative activity to combine with a durative phrase (Piñango, Zurif & Jackendoff 1991), and also complement coercion, where an event-taking verb may receive a non-eventive argument, as in *The author began the book*, Traxler et al. (2005). The studies showed an increase in processing times at the point of the trigger (the durative *for*-phrase or the non-eventive nominal *book*.) The timing of coercion effects has been taken as additional evidence that semantic interpretation lags behind syntactic analysis (Piñango et al. 2006). See also Harris et al. (2008) for a study of concealed questions.

It isn't really known at present how the interpretation of a phrase is influenced by its syntactic position. There is, however, some experimental support for Diesing's (1992) mapping hypothesis, which assigns existential interpretations to phrases internal to the VP, but presuppositional interpretations to phrases external to the VP. In English, where subjects are VP external, readers should prefer a presuppositional interpretation of the subject. Given a mini-discourse like *Five ships appeared on the horizon. Three ships sank.*, they should prefer a presuppositional interpretation of *three ships* (i.e., the interpretation where the referent of three ships is a subset of the already introduced five ships). In Frazier et al. (2005), this prediction was confirmed in a written interpretation study. Further, longer reading times were observed when *three ships* was later disambiguated to an existential (three new ships) interpretation than when it was disambiguated to a presuppositional (three of the five ships) interpretation. In English and in German, the preference for a presuppositional interpretation was stronger when the cardinal phrase appeared outside the VP than when it appeared inside the VP. In Korean, it was stronger with a topic marked phrase than with a nominative marked phrase. For similar evidence from Dutch, see Wijnen & Kaan (2006).

Typically only grammatical interpretations of sentences are considered by the processor. However, there are some interesting exceptions. For example, studies of negative polarity items suggest that the processing of sentences with unlicensed polarity items may be facilitated by the presence of a licensor even if the licensor appears in a structural position where it cannot license the polarity item (Drenhaus, Frisch & Saddy 2005). The reason for this 'spurious licensing' effect is not entirely clear and continues to be debated (Xiang, Dillon & Phillips 2009).

The standard assumption in linguistics is that only grammatical interpretations are computed and they are computed by interpreting the constituents and relations present in the syntactic tree. Psycholinguistic evidence fits with this view, but with certain limitations. Ungrammatical analyses or interpretations may play a role in processing when they correspond to a temporary analysis or an analysis considered before the correct analysis was identified. With stereotypical relations or in the presence of a rich visual context, the context may generate expectations before the syntactic analysis is available or even override the actual syntax (possibly because the comprehender assumes the speaker has made a speech error, e.g., in sentences like *"The fox shot the hunter."*).

There is no general agreement about the structure of the language comprehension system. The assumption that a syntactic module exists would explain the speed and automaticity of syntactic processing. However, to accommodate the evidence that semantic interpretation may guide syntactic analysis rather than follow it, one must assume that the syntactic module is defined by its representations, and not by temporal relations or some ordering of modules imposed by the language comprehension system.

Before leaving this section, attention allocation issues should be mentioned. Listeners and readers allocate attention unevenly through a sentence. 'Focus' (see article 10 [Semantics: Sentence and Information Structure] (Hinterwimmer) *Information structure*) plays an important role in guiding attention. Comprehenders process focused information more quickly and deeply than unfocused information whether focus is conveyed intonationally, by the presence of a pitch accent (Cutler & Foss 1977), or semantically, by the nature of a preceding question (Cutler & Fodor 1979). Often unfocused material is not processed deeply. Indeed, it may be processed so shallowly that anomalies in unfocused positions are not detected reliably (see Sturt et al. 2004).

A contrastive focus conveyed by a pitch accent may immediately indicate that a contrast is intended by the speaker, resulting in quick eye-movements to objects that contrast along the relevant dimension. For example, in a visual world study, eye movements were launched to a big blue square, not a big yellow circle, given a display with a small blue square but no small yellow circle, and the instruction "*Touch the BIG . . .*" (see Eberhard et al. 1995).

Intonation probably defines the domains in which interpretation proceeds, as argued by Schafer (1997). Schafer (1997) showed that reanalyzing the meaning of a word takes longer across an intonational phrase boundary than across a phonological phrase boundary, as one would expect if incomplete interpretive processes are finished at the ends of intonational phrases, before proceeding to the analysis of new material. In a similar vein, Hirotani (2004) argues that scopal elements must be bound by operators within the same major phrase as the scopal element, e.g., a bound pronoun and its binder.

There is a vast literature on processing ambiguous words (e.g., *bank*) and a growing literature on processing words with distinct senses (McElree, Frisson & Pickering 2006, Frisson & Frazier 2005). Due to space limitations, no attempt will be made to discuss that literature here. However, one study of lexical processing is particularly relevant. Van Berkum, Hagoort & Brown (1999) investigated whether a word 'meaning' was first integrated into the context provided in the sentence containing the word, and only later was integrated with the larger discourse context, or whether the meaning of a word is immediately related to the larger discourse context. In an Event Related Potential (ERP) study measuring electrical activity at the scalp, van Berkum, Hagoort & Brown found that a word which is not anomalous in its sentence context but which IS anomalous in its larger discourse context yields an N400, a marker of semantic anomaly, within 150 milliseconds of the onset of the anomalous word. This suggests that some aspects of interpretation involve integration of new material into the larger discourse from very early in the interpretive process.

To sum up, the fairly standard assumption that what gets interpreted is an already assigned syntactic representation is supported in part by available evidence. However, given a rich visual context and a task specified in advance of the linguistic input, context can guide both sentence analysis and interpretation. Further, each word of a sentence is not necessarily processed completely (whatever that might mean). Rather interpretation, at least the conscious part of interpretation, is directed largely by focus, which determines the allocation of attentional resources. Prosodic phrases appear to serve as the units of interpretation, with material within the prosodic phrase being more easily related to other material within the same prosodic phrase than to material outside it, at least for purposes of lexical reanalysis (Schafer 1997) and for Logical Form operations (Hirotani 2004). Integration of word meaning into context, however, appears to involve sentence-external discourse context from very soon after the onset of the word.

3 Processing quantifiers

Research on mental models began with Johnson-Laird's pioneering studies of syllogistic reasoning. The idea was that listeners and readers instantiate the relations conveyed by a quantificational sentence using non-linguistic representations of token entities and the relations between them. Errors in syllogistic reasoning result from not instantiating all possibilities in the mental model. Verification times were predicted by the number of different models consistent with the premises, see in particular Johnson-Laird (1977). While these studies are impressive in terms of understanding how people reason with quantifiers, they have several limitations. First, individuals who perform poorly on formal reasoning tasks (e.g., most untrained participants in a Wason task) perform extremely well on the same problem when it is cast in the form of detecting cheaters. This suggests that humans are equipped with reasoning mechanisms that were adaptive in the evolution of the species. Under what circumstances these adaptive reasoning mechanisms come into play rather than formal reasoning mechanisms is largely unknown. Nor is it known how these mechanisms map onto other cognitive processes. Second, the Johnson-Laird type studies of reasoning do not address the issue of how listeners and readers linguistically process quantificational sentences.

Despite their obvious intrinsic interest, no attempt will be made to discuss reasoning studies in this section. Instead, the linguistic processing of quantifiers will take center stage. The following questions will be addressed: How do listeners identify the scope of a quantifier? In cases of ambiguity, do they prefer to interpret a quantifier with scope corresponding to its surface position, or do they prefer to assign it scope with respect to a lower 'reconstructed' position? Are the complexity predictions of Generalized Quantifier Theory confirmed? That is, do quantifiers behave as if they take two arguments? How do comprehenders identify the restrictions on the domain of the quantifier? And, finally, under what circumstances do quantifiers trigger pragmatic implicatures? See article 4 [Semantics: Noun Phrases and Verb Phrases] (Keenan) *Quantifiers* for background on quantifiers.

3.1 Scope

Ioup (1975) pioneered the processing of scopally ambiguous sentences. She argued that individual quantifiers have different inherent propensities for acquiring scope, e.g. *each > every > all*, and she proposed a grammatical function hierarchy specifying, for example, that subjects (and topics) tend to take wide scope. Subsequent research confirms Ioup's basic finding that both the particular quantifier and its position influence preferred scope assignments. Kurtzman & MacDonald (1993) investigated sentences like those in (1) and (2) in a makes-sense judgment task. Participants read the sentences one at a time, and then pressed a button to indicate whether the second sentence was a good continuation of the first sentence. Response times were not informative, but readers did accept the continuation more often when it was consistent with the subject taking wide scope, i.e., (1a) and (2a).

(1) a. Every kid climbed a tree. The trees were full of apples.
    b. Every kid climbed a tree. The tree was full of apples.

(2) a. A kid climbed every tree. The kid was full of energy.
    b. A kid climbed every tree. The kids were full of energy.

In a second experiment, testing passives, the preference for surface scope was weaker than with actives, and the acceptability of continuations compatible with the inverse scope reading was higher for passives than for actives. In subsequent experiments, complex noun phrases were tested, and inverse scope was found to be preferred, for reasons that remain unclear. Kurtzman & MacDonald concluded the processor considers various scope interpretations simultaneously and a variety of factors contribute to the ultimate preference for a particular scope-assignment. Tunstall (1998) noted that one problem interpreting the above results is the fact that the second sentence in (1b) is a perfectly good continuation of the discourse even if the universal quantifier takes wide scope. The wide scope universal reading of *Every kid climbed a tree* permits but does not require multiple instantiation of the referent of the object *a tree*.

Tunstall (1998) reported a variety of comprehension and production experiments on quantifier scope, focusing on the difference between *each* and *every*. She argued for a Surface Scope principle: If Q1 c-commands Q2 at surface structure, then perceivers prefer Q1 to scope over Q2. She assumed that *each* and *every* are both distributive and argued that *each* is used when the speaker is interested in the individuals in the set *each* quantifies over. In one study, changing a situation slightly from one where the members of this set were uniform to one where some property distinguished the individual members of the set from each other (e.g., employees all wear identical clothes versus having salient color differences in their uniforms) determined whether speakers described the situation using *each*, for differentiated situations, or *every*, for undifferentiated situations. The Surface Scope principle lies at the heart of Tunstall's account of processing quantifiers. On her view, perceivers assign surface scope but then alter that scope if the conditions associated with the individual quantifiers are not met, though see also Filik, Paterson & Liversedge (2004).

Anderson (2004) conducted an extensive study of processing quantifier scope in sentences like *Every/an expert climbed a/every cliff*. In a large number of written interpretation and self-paced reading studies, surface scope was preferred to inverse scope. Inverse scope sentences also took longer to process than surface scope sentences even when the sentences were unambiguous or presented with a prior disambiguating context. She attributed the cost of inverse scope to its representational complexity, e.g., the extra structure resulting from the application of quantifier raising.

In one set of studies, she investigated the economy of scope hypothesis (Fox 1995) which claims that quantifier raising (that is not forced by type-shifting considerations) may only be performed when it delivers an interpretation that is semantically distinct from the meaning obtained without quantifier raising. Assuming the existence of a constraint requiring scope parallelism, the economy of scope hypothesis predicts that example (3) is unambiguous for grammatical reasons. *Marta* cannot raise because raising would produce no semantic effect, and parallelism thus requires the first sentence in (3) to have only the surface scope interpretation (with *some student* scoping over *every film*).

(3) Some student loves every Hitchcock film. Marta does too.

Anderson (2004) tested examples like (3) in contexts biased to inverse scope. 67% of the responses indicated participants had assigned the inverse scope interpretation, counter to the predictions of the grammatical economy of scope hypothesis. Anderson concluded that processing factors, the general preference for surface scope, not a grammatical principle such as scope economy, accounts for the preference for the surface scope reading of (3).

It is generally assumed that quantifiers may not take scope outside their immediate clause. But apparent counterexamples to this claim may be found in corpora in so-called 'telescoping' environments (*Every candidate approached the stage. He tooks his diploma and returned to his seat.*). Anderssen (2008) provides an analysis of such examples which involves an implicit generic quantifier, and backs up the analysis with corpus examples and with processing evidence showing that the examples are felicitous primarily in examples with non-accidental properties. (For additional processing evidence on telescoping, see Carminati, Frazier & Rayner 2002.)

3.2 Reconstruction

The studies described in section 3.1 investigated sentences where the quantifier phrase occupied an argument position. Very few studies have examined the processing of quantifers that appear in other positions. Typically such quantifiers may receive scope either in their surface position or in their reconstructed (theta-) position.

Villalta (2003) investigated the processing of *how many*-questions in English and (their counterparts) in French, in contexts supporting both readings. She found that, in contrast to the strong surface scope preference observed for scope ambiguities in studies of quantifiers in argument positions, 'reconstructed scope' (scope determined with respect to the base position of a phrase) was preferred for questions like *How many pieces did every student play?*, and this preference was strong, preferred roughly 80% of the time, in both English and French. Villalta attributed the preference for the reconstructed reading to a delay imposed by not knowing which set in the preceding context was the intended referent for the restrictor. (Note that delayed assignment might explain the absence of an immediate surface scope preference, though presumably something more is needed in order for the delay to result in a commitment to 'reconstructed' scope.) She offered some data from a self-paced reading study as evidence for the delay account, see Villalta for details.

In written questionnaire studies, Bader & Frazier (submitted) investigated German sentences with expected subject-before-object order and unexpected object-before-subject order. They found that an object moved over a universally quantified subject was likely to reconstruct, unless it was potentially specific (e.g., *ein Buch von Chomsky* 'a book by Chomsky' as opposed to *irgendein Buch von Chomsky* 'some book by Chomsky – I don't know or care which'). The particular universal quantifier also mattered: *fast jeder* ('almost every') received the most wide scope (followed by *jeder* ('every'), *fast alle* ('almost all') and *alle* ('all'). Finally, more 'reconstructed' (low) scope was observed for phrases moved to the beginning of the sentence (Spec, CP) than for phrases moved in front of the subject in the middlefield. These results were explained in terms of a Base position preference principle favoring scope assignments with respect to the base position of a phrase (presumably due to a desire to interpret a phrase in just one location with respect to all properties, including thematic role, scope and focus). Base position preference may be offset in the case of specific indefinites by a reluctance to reanalyze a phrase if it has already been interpreted as a variable at the highest level of the discourse representation structure (Kamp & Reyle 1993).

To sum up, the data available to date clearly indicate a preference for surface scope in doubly quantified sentences. However, the surface scope preference observed for sentences with quantifiers in argument positions does not hold generally for sentences in which quantifier phrases have been moved out of those positions, in particular when one quantifier phrase has moved over another to Spec,CP.

3.3 Complexity

Do quantifiers by definition take two arguments (a restrictor and a nuclear scope) as claimed by Generalized Quantifier Theory and, if so, do these semantically predicted arguments guide sentence processing? The question about semantic prediction, in particular, is extremely difficult to ask properly, because of the overlap between syntactic predictions and semantic predictions. In a study cleverly designed to disentangle syntactic and semantic predictions, Arregui (2003) investigated center-embedded sentences missing their middle verb phrase. There exists an interesting linguistic illusion where listeners' immediate reaction is to accept an ungrammatical sentence like: *The man the woman the dog bit on the cruise ship had a beard*, which omits the middle of three required predicates (Gibson & Thomas 1999). Arregui exploited this illusion by placing a quantifier either in a position where, assuming the quantifier takes two arguments, it would predict the existence of the missing verb phrase or in a position where it would predict the existence of one of the overt verb phrases. As expected, sentences containing a quantifier in a position where it predicted the missing verb phrase resulted in significantly lower acceptability ratings than sentences where the quantifier predicted one of the arguments that actually occurred. This suggests that the quantifier does indeed semantically predict two arguments and these semantic predictions influence processing in an observable manner when the corresponding syntactic predictions have been nullified.

Using quantifiers like *everyone* and *no one*, Warren & Gibson (2002) found that sentences with quantifiers were rated as being less complex than their definite description counterparts (more accurately, sentences containing these quantifiers in the most troublesome or demanding positions were rated as less complex than sentences containing definite descriptions in those positions). In later work, reviewed in Section 3.4 below, Warren showed that it is only quantifiers lacking content noun restrictors, such as *everyone* as opposed to *every reporter*, that are processed quickly and rated as being less complex than their definite description counterparts.

In two studies, Martin Hackl and his students have tested complexity predictions of current linguistic theory. Varvoutis & Hackl (2006) found preliminary evidence that quantifiers in object position do show the complexity effect one would expect if they needed to raise from this position for type reasons, i.e., because the internal argument of a verb should be of the semantic type of an entity/referring expression, not a quantifier. Basically they reasoned that a postverbal phrase that could temporarily be analyzed as either the object of the preceding verb or as the subject of another clause should trigger a direct object reading with definite descriptions due to the preference for minimal structure. However, with a quantifier phrase the direct object analysis should not be preferred due to the extra complexity resulting from the need to move a quantifier out of object position to avoid a type mismatch. The reading time predictions of this account were confirmed in a self-paced reading study of sentences like *The nun remembered the/every child (who) was abused and malnourished*.

Hackl & Acland (2006) compared the verification of sentences containing *most* or *more than half*, in a novel self-paced counting study. Participants had to verify sentences containing these quantifiers (*Most dots are black*) by pressing a button that progressively revealed more dots. Despite being semantically equivalent (or nearly equivalent), sentences containing *more than half* took longer to verify than sentences containing *most*. The result is unexpected if only the truth-conditional properties of quantifiers matter. On the other hand, if the denotation of the syntactic constituents of *more than half* are important for determining the interpretation of the expression, then it is not surprising that it is processed in a different manner than *most*.

To date, there have been only a handful of psycholinguistic studies testing the complexity predictions of various theories of quantifiers. The existing studies make it clear that there is great potential for this line of research.

3.4 Domain restriction

The issue of how domain restrictions are identified is central to any theory of semantic processing. Warren (2003) found that reading times in a self-paced reading study were longer for quantifier phrases (*every reporter, no reporter*) than for their definite description counterparts (*the reporter*) except when the quantifier lacked a contentful restrictor (*everyone, everybody, no one*, and surprisingly, *many people*). In a follow-up study the target sentences in (6) followed either a context that provided an antecedent set, as in (4), or one without an antecedent set, as in (5). The presence of an antecedent set speeded reading times on the critical ("x reporter") phrase in the relative clause targets, or after the critical phrase in the complement clause targets, for both the quantifier phrases and the definite descriptions.

(4) Context with an antecedent set: There was a coffee shop next to the offices of the Boston Globe. On Monday, a group of reporters gathered there for lunch.

(5) Context without an antecedent set: There was a coffee shop next to the offices of the Boston Globe. On Monday, people who worked nearby gathered there for lunch.

(6) Targets:
A waiter who {no reporter, every reporter, the reporters} liked very much dropped a tray of drinks. (Relative clause)
A waiter knew that {no reporter, every reporter, the reporters} liked potato salad so he brought out a big bowl of it. (Complement clause)

It is perhaps of interest that the presence of an antecedent set was equally helpful for the different targets (*no, every, the*). One might have expected that a phrase with a referent would benefit more than a phrase without a referent (*no reporter*). The timing of the facilitation effect is also noteworthy. In the more difficult relative clause sentence type, the facilitation effect appeared on the quantifier phrase itself, whereas in the easier complement sentence, it showed up on the following region. If the pattern is reliable and general, it would argue against a system which always integrates the interpretation of the current phrase with preceding discourse before moving on to process new material.

3.5 Pragmatic implicatures

The issue of how and under what circumstances pragmatic (Gricean) implicatures are drawn has begun to receive attention in the adult processing literature. Some studies have investigated enriched meanings of quantifiers (and other scalar terms such as *or* and cardinal numbers). One approach has focused on whether adults make a distinction between what is said and what is implicated. Gibbs & Moise (1997) presented evidence from paraphrase selection studies, where participants read sentences and selected a paraphrase corresponding to what interpretation best matched what its speaker might have said by its use. Even after participating in a tutorial on what is literally said, participants' judgments of what was said was influenced by pragmatics, with over 75% enriched interpretations for cardinals (interpreting *three* as exactly three), quantifiers (interpreting *everyone* as everyone in some group), 'time-distance' implicatures (interpreting *some time* as a long time), and conjunction (interpreting *and* as and then). The results fit with a neo-Gricean view where certain 'generalized' implicatures are computed automatically. See in particular Levinson (2000), also Bezuidenhout & Cutting (2002) for online evidence.

Not all evidence supports automatic computation of implicatures. Noveck & Posada (2003) investigated underinformative sentences (the French counterpart of *Some elephants have trunks*) along with clearly true sentences (*Some houses have bricks*) and false sentences (*Some crows have radios*). In timed visual verification of sentences, twelve participants said false for nearly all underinformative sentences, consistent with automatic computation of the implicature 'some but not all elephants have trunks', but seven participants said true for nearly all underinformative sentences. Further, in the same study, electrical potentials were measured and they showed a steeper N400 for clearly true or clearly false sentences than for the underinformative sentences even for the group of participants that rejected the underinformative sentences. Since the N400 has been taken to be a marker of semantic unpredictability or anomaly, a possible implication might be that the same linguistic processing occurred for the two groups of participants. What may have differed is their non-linguistic evaluation or classification of the input due to their understanding of the verification task itself. The study highlights the difficulty of targeting precisely the question of interest in experimental studies. This problem is especially acute in the case of interpretation which may encompass strictly linguistic 'semantic' processing, pragmatic processing, conceptual processing, and/or evaluation of an utterance as a description of some state of affairs.

Breheny, Katsos & Williams (2005) argued that implicatures are drawn only when they are relevant to context. They tested Greek sentences containing the counterpart to *some* or *only some* in several self-paced reading experiments. In one experiment (Experiment 3), they tested the Greek counterpart of *some* in Upper-bound (7a) and Lower-bound (7b) contexts, as illustrated in (7).

(7) a. Mary asked John whether he intended to host all of his relatives in his tiny apartment. John replied that he intended to host some of his relatives. The rest would stay in a nearby hotel.
   b. Mary was surprised to see John cleaning his apartment and she asked the reason why. John replied that he intended to host some of his relatives. The rest would stay in a nearby hotel.

Reading times were longer on the quantifier (*some of his relatives*) in the inference-supporting Upper-bound context than in the Lower-bound context, and reading times were shorter on the target segment (*the rest*) in the Upper-bound context than in the Lower-bound context. The investigators interpreted the data to show that the inference "some but not all" was generated in the context where it was invited, thereby facilitating interpretation of *the rest* (the complement of some of his relatives), but the implicature was not drawn in the Lower-bound context where it was not invited.

Research on implicatures is likely to explode in the next few years. Several directions for this research are already discernible. One uses on-line processing techniques, such as the visual world paradigm, to address issues about the time course of implicature computation. For example, Huang & Snedeker (2009) find a brief stage of purely semantic processing for *some* (though see also Grodner et al. 2008).

Another line of inquiry investigates the pragmatic conditions under which implicatures arise or don't. For example, Grodner & Sedivy (2011) explore the effects of informing participants that the speaker has "an impairment that caused language and social problems." They argue that conversational implicatures are not generated for utterances that participants are told were produced by an unreliable speaker. In a related vein, Noveck et al. (2007) have argued that autistic individuals do not draw certain implicatures due to deficits involving 'theory of mind.'

A third line of inquiry investigates the effects of the type of grammatical context in which an implicature trigger appears. The existing studies on processing implicatures examine contexts that are non-Downward Entailing. Based on written interpretation studies and self-paced reading studies, Frazier (2008) argues that fewer implicatures are drawn in Downward Entailing (DE) contexts, which license inferences from sets to subsets, than in non-Downward Entailing contexts. This line of inquiry is also likely to be fruitful, because finding a difference between DE contexts and non-DE contexts might support the view that some pragmatic inferences are computed hand-in-hand with the semantic computation (Chierchia 2004 and article 10 [Semantics: Interfaces] (Chierchia, Fox & Spector) *Grammatical view of scalar implicatures*). The results may also bear on the issue of whether certain kinds of inferences, and contexts based on those kinds of inferences or inference patterns, are distinguished because of the ease of computing the inferences, namely, inferences merely involving substitution of one set, a superset or subset, for another (Geurts & van der Silk 2005).

4 Different types of DPs

4.1 Anaphoric DPs

There is a vast literature on the processing of anaphoric phrases. Much of it is consistent with centering-theory, e.g., Grosz (1977), Gordon, Grosz & Gilliam (1993), and related proposals claiming that pronouns are used for reference to prominent constituents (though see among others Wolf, Gibson & Desmet 2004, and especially Kehler et al. 2008, for evidence that discourse coherence structures based on similarity or contrast, or parallel structures, alter preferences). Considerable evidence shows that using a name to refer to a prominent constituent results in long comprehension times, the so-called 'Repeated Name Penalty,' Gordon et al. (1999). Further, a sentence containing a pronoun will take longer to comprehend if its antecedent is a non-topic than a topic (Clifton & Ferreira 1987) and if the antecedent is a part of a constituent rather than the whole constituent (e.g., "*Bill's mother . . . he . . .*" will be read slower than "*Bill's mother . . . she . . .*"), Gordon et al. 1999). In Italian, it has been shown that null pronominals prefer antecedents that occur in the highest preverbal subject position (Carminati 1992), whereas overt pronouns tend to take less prominent antecedents.

Vonk, Hustinx & Simons (1992) have presented evidence suggesting that overspecification of a referent, using a referring expression that is more than is needed (where pro < pronoun < name < definite description), is an indication of a break in the discourse. The hypothesis is interesting because it suggests that the choice of a referring device conveys information to the listener or reader beyond that needed to identify the referent, namely, subtle information about the structure of the discourse. The hypothesis may also explain the 'Repeated Name Penalty' since the short discourses that have been tested typically don't contain multiple episodes that would warrant overspecification when referring to a prominent entity.

Competition between pronouns and demonstratives has been investigated by Brown-Schmidt, Byron & Tanenhaus (2005). In a visual world study where participants' eye movements were recorded as they carried out instructions, the investigators showed that a pronoun will preferentially refer to an already available entity whereas a demonstrative will pick up a composite (the cup on the saucer, given (8)).

(8) Put the cup on the saucer. Now put it (cup)/that (composite) on the tray.

Taken together, the above results strongly suggest that anaphoric phrases are specialized in the sense that the anaphoric device chosen by the speaker to refer to some referent implicitly codes information about the discourse structure and the prominence of the discourse referents it contains.

Whether a phrase is taken to be anaphoric or not may depend on its syntactic position. Kaiser & Trueswell (2004) showed that in Finnish using a scrambled OVS word order (e.g. doctor-saw-nurse) may suffice to quickly pick out a discourse-new entity (an unmentioned nurse), as opposed to an already mentioned entity (nurse), as the referent of the post-verbal subject.

4.2 Accommodated DPs

The presuppositions of a word often are not satisfied before that word is encountered and they must be added to the model ('accommodated') by the listener in response to the presupposition trigger itself. For example, a previously unmentioned entity is often introduced with a definite description even though the familiarity (or uniqueness, or maximality) presupposition of the word *the* is not satisfied. One approach to presupposition accommodation is to invoke the idea of a bridging inference between the current material and prior discourse. Burkhardt tested the German counterpart to the sentences in (9), where a critical definite (*the conductor*) appeared in a context which either explicitly mentioned the corresponding entity, implied the existence of the entity (a 'bridging' context) or did neither. In an Event Related Potential study, Burkhardt (2006) found that already-given DPs elicited a reduced N400 (also found when the descriptive content of a word is highly expected), and that discourse-new DPs elicited a P600 (often found for higher level syntactic and semantic integration processes). Bridged DPs patterned first with given DPs, exhibiting a reduced N400 compared to the new DPs, and then patterned with new DPs, exhibiting a P600.

(9) a. Tobias visited a conductor in Berlin. Given context
    b. Tobias talked to Nina. New context
    c. Tobias visited a concert in Berlin. Bridging context
    Target:
    He said that the conductor was very impressive.

She interpreted the results as showing that, if available, referential dependencies to already given entities are formed (indexed by the N400) and that establishing new discourse referents in a mental model involves extra processing and storage, evidenced by the P600.

Chambers et al. (2002) explored referential domains in a visual world study. Participants were instructed to *Put the cube inside the can*... When there was only one can big enough to hold the cube, looks to the smaller can were very limited. However, when the display contained two cans big enough to hold the cube, there were significantly more looks to the alternative can. The authors concluded that referential decisions are constantly informed by their relevance for the action described by the unfolding utterance. In the present case, the affordance structure of the cans (their potential to serve as the goal of the action described) determined the domain. The smaller can was apparently eliminated from the domain by its affordance structure. Using a similar methodology, Sussman et al. (2006) found evidence for Carlson's (2005) analysis of weak definites (*Emily read the newspaper*), which treats them like bare plurals. In contrast to ordinary definites, with weak definites participants did not avoid looking at pictures containing two newspapers when they heard *the newspaper*, nor were their looking times delayed by the presence of an 'extra' newspaper.

Evans (2005) put forward the "Small world hypothesis" which claims that "In order for a new single entity to be introduced with the definite article, the scope of its frame of reference must be small enough to single that entity out as more relevant than all others of its type. In this way, an entity designated by the definite article must be locally unique within its frame of reference." In support of the Small world hypothesis, Evans showed that 'singling out' examples where the comprehender can zoom-in on a particularly relevant member of a plural set, as in (10a) and (11a), were rated as significantly more natural than their 'no singling out' b-counterparts.

(10) a. Juan drove up to the busy tollbooths. The tolltaker was rude.
b. Juan looked at the busy tollbooths. The tolltaker was rude.

(11) a. Lyla opened the book. The page was ripped.
b. Lyla flipped through the book. The page was ripped.

In a written completion task where participants filled in a determiner, the definite was supplied more often than the indefinite when the context singled out an entity from a larger set even though the entity was not previously mentioned. The Small world hypothesis is important because it suggests that accommodating presuppositions may be viewed not as adding missing propositional knowledge to a model, but rather as instructions about the frame size of the active context or the situation described. The comprehender is implicitly instructed to adjust the size of the contextual frame/situation in such a way that the presupposition is satisfied.

Of course presupposition accommodation must occur for categories other than DPs. Schwarz (2007) presented data from the processing of German *auch* ('*too*') suggesting that readers do not readily accommodate its presupposition. Instead they will perform a very costly syntactic reanalysis to an object before subject analysis of the sentence if doing so will result in satisfying the presupposition. This fits with theories (Abusch 2005) which claim there is a distinction in kind among different presupposition triggers.

Accommodated DPs are not exceptional. If linguistic input is immediately mapped onto world knowledge (Ferguson & Sanford 2008) using presupposition satisfaction as a means to delimit the active frame, as in Evans' proposal, it may be possible to explain how interpretation may proceed so smoothly without explicitly introduced referents for definite descriptions and in the absence of overtly expressed domain restrictions.

4.3 Plurals

The interpretation of plurals is a huge, interesting, and underinvestigated topic. There have been only a few studies of the topic to date. Koh & Clifton (2002) investigated processing plural pronouns lacking syntactically plural antecedents. They showed that group formation was easier with symmetric predicates than with nonsymmetric predicates. Specifically, forming a plural group consisting of the 'subject' and 'object' was easier, as measured by reading times, and more likely, as indicated by fragment completion, when the individual group members were introduced by symmetric verbs (*Tom sang with Jim and Tony. They* . . ., where they = 3 people) than when they were introduced with nonsymmetric verbs (*Tom recognized Jim and Tony. They* . . ., where they = 3 people).

Turning to the opposite situation, 'DP-splitting' is required when one conjunct of a conjoined phrase is the antecedent of a pronoun. Albrecht & Clifton (1998) and Gordon et al. (1999) showed that there were longer reading times for a sentence containing a pronoun in examples where the antecedent was introduced inside a conjoined phrase like "*Stan and Pam* . . . *He* . . ." than in examples where the antecedent was not embedded in a larger phrase, e.g., "*Stan* . . . *He* . . . ." This suggests that discourse referents are initially postulated for the referent of a plural DP but not for DPs embedded inside it.

There is an ongoing debate about whether the plural marker is semantically plural, or whether it only implies a plurality because the speaker didn't use the singular, Sauerland (2003). Sauerland, Anderssen & Yatsushiro (2005) argued for the latter, implicature-based, approach. In addition to linguistic arguments, they presented a reading study in support of their claim. In the critical condition "*Does a dog have tails?*" (vs. the control "*Does a dog have two tails*"), participants were less accurate than for the control (they gave a "no" response only 85% of the time vs. over 95% for the control) and the response times were longer than for the control. A semantic account of plurality would presumably have difficulty explaining these results. On the implicature account, the variability observed in the responses is expected (see the discussion of "underinformative statements" above in section 3.5).

Collective/distributive interpretations have also been investigated. In an eye movement recording study, Frazier, Pacht & Rayner (1999) tested sentences with early or late disambiguation to a collective or distributive interpretation. If an underspecified representation exists which may be further specified to a particular interpretation, then it shouldn't matter whether the disambiguation occurs early or late in the sentence. Assuming an underspecified representation, the processor can simply add the appropriate specification if and when it encounters biasing or disambiguating information. However, if there is an actual ambiguity between two interpretations/readings, then the processor must presumably choose and plausibly it will choose the simpler representation, by hypothesis, the one without a distributive operator. These predictions were tested in an eye movement recording study using sentences like those in (12).

(12) a. Lynne and Patrick saved $1000 each to pay for their honeymoon. (Distributive, late disambiguation)
 b. Lynne and Patrick saved $1000 together to pay for their honeymoon. (Collective, late disambiguation)
 c. Lynne and Patrick each saved $1000 each to pay for their honeymoon. (Distributive, early disambiguation)
 d. Lynne and Patrick together saved $1000 each to pay for their honeymoon. (Collective, early disambiguation)

The results showed reading times were long for just one of the late disambiguation conditions (12a), as expected according to the hypothesis that collective/distributive distinction is a real ambiguity. This showed up as an interaction of ambiguity (early vs. late disambiguation) and interpretation (collective vs. distributive) in first pass reading times, total times, and the number of regressions to already read material. The fact that it was the late disambiguation distributive interpretation that took longest to read suggests that perceivers adopted the collective (or cumulative) interpretation in the absence of evidence and then revised this decision when they later encountered evidence for the distributive interpretation. See also Kaup, Kelter & Habel (2002) for compatible evidence about the preferred interpretation of the plural pronoun *sie* ('they') in German.

The processing of plurals is not understood at present. A small number of interesting investigations have opened up this avenue of inquiry, but firm conclusions are probably not warranted at this time.

5 Beyond DPs

The semantic processing of DPs has been the focus of the discussion in preceding sections. Of course, psycholinguists have also investigated the processing of other types of constituents. A brief pointer to some of this literature follows, starting with verbs, moving on to aspect and tense, and ending with scalar adjectives.

Verbs have been studied from a variety of perspectives. Gennari & Poeppel (2003) compared stative verbs and eventive verbs. They expected eventive verbs to be more complex than stative verbs because they have a causal structure which is lacking in stative verbs. They report a lexical decision experiment and a self-paced reading experiment supporting this complexity prediction.

Unaccusative verbs have been studied by a number of authors (see Friedmann et al. 2008 and references therein). Friedmann et al. (2008), among others, have tested the unaccusativity hypothesis, which claims that the subject of an unaccusative starts out in direct object position. Using cross-modal semantic priming to determine if the subject of an unaccusative verb behaves as if it is reactivated at some point following the verb, Friedmann et al. found significant reactivation effects for unaccusative verbs but not for unergative verbs. The results thus support the unaccusativity hypothesis.

Gennari et al. (2002) studied motion verbs in Spanish and in English. Their aim was to determine whether claimed cross-language differences in the expression of 'path,' typically expressed in a PP in English but inside the verb in Spanish, translate into perceptual differences when native speakers view scenes which are similar in either their path (dragging a board into a room or out of the room) or their manner (dragging a board or carrying it). They found little support for the hypothesis: speakers of Spanish and speakers of English did not differ much in their behavior and the small differences that were found were only present under circumstances where language could be used as a strategy for classifying similar situations. Papafragou, Hulbert & Trueswell (2008) tested a similar hypothesis concerning cross-language differences in how path is expressed and its effect on perception under circumstances where the participants did or did not have to formulate sentences. In the Papafragou, Hulbert & Trueswell study, differences between English speakers and Greek speakers were observed when sentence production routines were engaged, but not otherwise.

Thematic roles have been investigated by numerous researchers. One central question is whether implicit arguments are introduced lexically as a semantic argument or by a conceptually derived inference. Carlson & Tanenhaus (1988), Mauner & Koenig (1999), Mauner, Tanenhaus & Carlson (1995) present evidence for the lexical approach.

Aspect has been approached primarily in terms of 'semantic coercion' (see Section 2 above, also discussion in Bott 2008 and references therein). Complexity effects are observed when the denotation of a constituent requires 'subtractive' coercion, e.g., a *for*-phrase conflicts with an accomplishment, requiring subtraction of the endpoint of an eventuality to obtain an activity, but not reliably with additive coercion (Bott 2008).

There has been surprisingly little attention paid to the processing of tense. One exception is an investigation by Walsh Dickey (2001). Among other things, he presented evidence that the interpretation of tense is delayed until event type (e.g., telicity) information is available. Gennari (2004) examined temporal relations between distinct clauses and showed that reading times were longer when the two clauses had distant non-overlapping references. Finally, to my knowledge, the processing of modality is essentially unexplored territory (with the exception of Dwivedi et al. 2006).

Scalar adjectives have been investigated in visual world studies. Sedivy et al. (1999) showed that context-specific contrast can be used by the listener to identify a referent even before the head noun has been encountered. If two objects contrast with respect to size, for example a short glass and a tall glass, then an instruction to *Pick up the tall* . . . may induce listeners to look at the tall object which has a short counterpart rather than at a tall competitor (tall pitcher) which has no short counterpart (a short pitcher).

Rips & Turnbull (1980) contrasted relative (*small*) and absolute (*six-legged*) adjectives in verification studies. They compared *An insect is small/six-legged* and *An insect is a small animal/six-legged animal*. They expected relative adjectives to be more context dependent than absolute adjectives, and thus predicted a penalty for having the adjective by itself as the predicate only for the relative adjectives, not the absolute adjectives. The results confirmed the prediction.

Frazier, Clifton & Stolterfoht (2008) studied absolute scalar adjectives, such as *clean* and *dirty* using written interpretation studies and eye movement recording. They found support for the current semantic analysis (Kennedy 1999,

Kennedy & McNally 2005, Rotstein & Winter 2004) of absolute scalar adjectives. They also established quantificational variability effects arising in sentences like *The dishes are mostly clean/dirty*, where a proportional reading of the subject *most of the dishes* tends to be reported when *mostly* would otherwise have to modify a minimum standard adjective like *dirty*. They attribute the effect to a clash between the adjective having as a standard any non-zero value and the need of *mostly* to have a determinate value to modify.

The paucity of research in many areas of semantic processing does not seem to be due to in principle problems in pursuing the questions in these areas. Rather these lacunae may have arisen somewhat accidentally due to the lack of collaboration in the past between psycholinguists and semanticists. Psycholinguistic issues and methods and semantic questions have, for the most part, been pursued by distinct researchers in largely non-overlapping communities.

6 Conclusions

The study of linguistically guided semantic processing is in its infancy, but the stage is set for a dramatic growth spurt. Indeed, the mere fact that there exists a literature on semantic processing is evidence of great progress in this area. Ten or fifteen years ago, nearly all experimental work on 'semantic' processing investigated 'semantic' processing in the rather loose sense often used in psychology where the term may refer to any aspect of interpretation, be it semantic, pragmatic, conceptual, or whatever.

There are probably several reasons for the recent progress in the psycholinguistic study of meaning. In part, it may be due to the various methodologies now employed, including visual world studies, which permit rich contexts to be studied, ERP studies, which offer a continuous measure of ongoing processing of an input, and various neuroimaging techniques, which allow questions to be asked about where in the brain certain processes take place (e.g., Pylkkänen & McElree 2007). In part, the recent progress is also due to the better integration of psycholinguistics into linguistics. There are now a few young researchers who are well-trained both in psycholinguistics and in formal semantics. As a result, semantic investigations motivated by linguistic questions are beginning to appear.

This work was supported by NIH Grant HD-18708 to the University of Massachusetts. I am very grateful to Paul Portner for helpful suggestions, and to the semantics graduate students and faculty at the University of Massachusetts for educating me about semantic issues.

7 References

Abusch, Dorit 2005. *Triggering from Alternative Sets and Projection of Pragmatic Presuppositions*. Ms. Ithaca, NY, Cornell University.

Albrecht, Jason & Charles E. Clifton, Jr. 1998. Accessing singular antecedents in conjoined phrases. *Memory & Cognition* 26, 599–610.

Altmann, Gerry & Yuki Kamide 1999. Incremental interpretation at verbs: Restricting the domain of subsequent reference. *Cognition* 73, 247–264.

Anderson, Catherine 2004. *The Structure and Real-time Comprehension of Quantifier Scope Ambiguities*. Ph.D. dissertation. Northwestern University, Evanstone, IL.

Anderssen, Jan 2008. *Topics in Quantification*. Ph.D. dissertation. University of Massachusetts, Amherst, MA.

Arregui, Ana 2003. A study of the semantic predictions of quantificational NPs. In: L. Alonso-Ovalle (ed.). *On Semantic Processing* (University of Massachusetts Occasional Papers in Linguistics, vol. 27). Amherst, MA: GLSA, 28–55.

Bader, Markus & Lyn Frazier Submitted. *Reconstruction, Scope and the Interpretation of Indefinites*.

Bezuidenhout, Anne & J. Cooper Cutting 2002. Literal meaning, minimal propositions, and pragmatic processing. *Journal of Pragmatics* 34, 433–456.

Bott, Oliver 2008. Doing it again and again may be difficult—but it depends on what you are doing. In: N. Abner & J. Bishop (eds.). *Proceedings of the 27th West Coast Conference on Formal Linguistics (= WCCFL 27)*. Somerville, MA: Cascadilla Press, 63–71.

Breheny, Richard, Napoleon Katsos & John Williams 2005. Are generalized scalar implicatures generated by default? An on-line investigation into the role of context in generating pragmatic inferences. *Cognition* 100, 1–30.

Brown-Schmidt, Sarah, Donna Byron & Michael Tanenhaus 2005. Beyond salience: Interpretation of personal and demonstrative pronouns. *Journal of Memory and Language* 53, 292–313.

Burkhardt, Petra 2006. Inferential bridging relations reveal distinct neural mechanisms: Evidence from event-related brain potentials. *Brain & Language* 98, 159–168.

Carlson, Greg 2005. Weak definite NPs. Paper presented at the *36th Annual Meeting of the North Eastern Linguistic Society (= NELS 36)*, University of Massachusetts, Amherst, MA.

Carlson, Greg & Michael Tanenhaus 1988. Thematic roles and language comprehension. In: W. Wilkins (ed.). *Thematic Relations*. New York: Academic Press, 263–288.

Carminati, Maria Nella 1992. *The Processing of Italian Subject Pronouns*. Ph.D. dissertation. University of Massachusetts, Amherst, MA.

Carminati, Maria Nella, Lyn Frazier & Keith Rayner 2002. Bound variables and c-command. *Journal of Semantics* 19, 1–34.

Chambers, Craig G., Michael K. Tanenhaus, Kathleen M. Eberhard, Hana Filip, & Gregory N. Carlson 2002. Circumscribing referential domains during real-time language comprehension. *Journal of Memory and Language* 47, 30–49.

Chierchia, Gennaro 2004. Scalar implicatures, polarity phenomena and the syntax/pragmatics interface. In: A. Belletti (ed.). *Structures and Beyond*. Oxford: Oxford University Press 1, 39–103.

Clifton, Jr., Charles E. & Fernanda Ferreira 1987. Discourse structure and anaphora: Some experimental results. In: M. Coltheart (ed.). *Attention and Performance, vol. 12: The Psychology of Reading*. Hillsdale, NJ: Lawrence Erlbaum Associates, 635–654.

Crain, Stephen & Mark Steedman 1985. On not being led up the garden path: The use of context by the psychological parser. In: D. Dowty, L. Karttunen & A. Zwicky (eds.). *Natural Language Parsing: Psychological, Computational and Theoretical Perspectives*. Cambridge: Cambridge University Press, 320–358.
Cutler, Anne & Jerry A. Fodor 1979. Semantic focus and sentence comprehension. *Cognition* 7, 49–59.
Cutler, Anne & Donald J. Foss 1977. On the role of sentence stress on sentence processing. *Language and Speech* 29, 233–251.
Diesing, Molly 1992. *Indefinites*. Cambridge, MA: The MIT Press.
Drenhaus, Heiner, Stephen Frisch & Douglas Saddy 2005. Processing negative polarity items: When negation comes through the backdoor. In: S. Kepser & M. Reis (eds.). *Linguistic Evidence: Empirical, Theoretical and Computational Perspectives*. Berlin: Mouton de Gruyter, 145–165.
Dwivedi, Veena D., Natalie A. Phillips, Maude Laguë-Beauvais & Shari R. Baum 2006. An electrophysiological investigation of mood, modal context and anaphora. *Brain Research* 1117, 135–153.
Eberhard, Kathleen, Michael Spivey-Knowlton, Julie Sedivy & Michael Tanenhaus 1995. Eye movements as a window into real-time spoken language comprehension in natural contexts. *Journal of Psycholinguistic Research* 24, 409–436.
Evans, William 2005. *Small Worlds of Discourse and the Spectrum of Accommodation*. Ms. Amherst, MA, University of Massachusetts Honors Thesis.
Ferguson, Heather & Anthony Sanford 2008. Anomalies in real and counterfactual worlds: An eye movement investigation. *Journal of Memory and Language* 58, 609–626.
Filik, Ruth, Kevin Paterson & Simon Liversedge 2004. Processing doubly quantified sentences: Evidence from eye movements. *Psychonomic Bulletin & Review* 11, 953–959.
Fox, Danny 1995. Economy and Scope. *Natural Language Semantics* 3, 283–341.
Frazier, Lyn 1987. Sentence Processing: A tutorial review. In: M. Coltheart (ed.). *Attention and Performance, vol. 12: The Psychology of Reading*. Hillsdale, NJ: Lawrence Erlbaum Associates, 559–586.
Frazier, Lyn 2008. Computing scalar implicatures. In: T. Friedman & S. Ito (eds.). *Proceedings of Semantics and Linguistic Theory (= SALT) XVIII*. Ithaca, NY: Cornell University, 319–339.
Frazier, Lyn, Charles E. Clifton, Jr. & Britta Stolterfoht 2008. Scale structure: Processing minimum standard and maximum standard scalar adjectives. *Cognition* 106, 299–324.
Frazier, Lyn, Jeremy Pacht & Keith Rayner 1999. Taking on semantic commitments, II: Collective versus distributive meanings. *Cognition* 70, 87–104.
Frazier, Lyn, Charles E. Clifton, Jr., Keith Rayner, Patricia Deevy, Song Yongh Koh & Markus Bader 2005. Interface problems: Structural constraints on interpretation. *Journal of Psycholinguistic Research* 34, 193–223.
Friedmann, Nama, Ginal Taranto, Lewis Shapiro & David Swinney 2008. The Leaf fell (the Leaf): The online processing of unaccusatives. *Linguistic Inquiry* 39, 355–378.
Frisson, Steven & Lyn Frazier 2005. Carving up word meaning: Portioning and grinding. *Journal of Memory and Language* 53, 277–291.
Gennari, Silvia 2004. Temporal references and temporal relations in sentence comprehension. *Journal of Experimental Psychology: Learning, Memory and Cognition*, 30, 877–890.
Gennari, Silvia & David Poeppel 2003. Processing correlates of lexical semantic complexity. *Cognition* 89, 27–41.

Gennari, Silvia, Steven Sloman, Barbara Malt & W. Tecumseh Fitch 2002. Motion events in language and cognition. *Cognition* 83, 49–79.

Geurts, Bart & Frans van Der Silk 2005. Monotonicity and processing load. *Journal of Semantics* 22, 97–117.

Gibbs, Raymond & Jessica Moise 1997. Understanding what is said. *Cognition* 62, 51–74.

Gibson, Edward, & James Thomas 1999. Memory limitations and structural forgetting: The perception of complex ungrammatical sentences as grammatical. *Language and Cognitive Processes* 14, 225–248.

Gordon, Peter, Barbara Grosz & Laura Gilliam 1993. Pronouns, names and the centering of attention. *Cognitive Science* 17, 311–347.

Gordon, Peter, Randall Hendrick, Kerry Ledoux & Chin Lung Yang 1999. Processing of reference and the structure of language: An analysis of complex noun phrases. *Language and Cognitive Processes* 14, 353–380.

Grodner, Dan & Julie Sedivy 2011. The effect of speaker-specific information on pragmatic inferences. In: E. Gibson & N. Perlmutter (eds.). *The Processing and Acquisition of Reference*. Cambridge, MA: The MIT Press, 239–272.

Grodner, Dan, Natelie Klein, Katie Carbary & Michael K. Tanenhaus 2008. Experimental evidence for rapid interpretation of pragmatic 'some.' Paper presented at the *21st Annual City University of New York Conference on Human Sentence Processing*, University of North Carolina, Chapel Hill, NC.

Grosz, Barbara 1977. *The Representation and Use of Focus in Dialogue and Understanding*. Technical Report 151. Menlo Park, CA: Artificial Intelligence Center, SRI International.

Hackl, Martin & Ben Acland 2006. Investigating verification procedures for quantified statements. Poster presented at the *19th Annual City University of New York Conference on Human Sentence Processing*, CUNY Graduate Center, New York.

Harris, Jesse, Liina Pylkkänen, Brian McElree & Steven Frisson 2008. The cost of question concealment: Evidence from MEG and eye-tracking. *Brain & Language* 107, 44–61.

Hirotani, Mako 2004. *Prosody and LF Interpretation: Processing Japanese Wh-Questions*. Ph.D. dissertation. University of Massachusetts, Amherst, MA.

Huang, Yi Ting & Jesse Snedeker 2009. On-line interpretation of scalar quantifiers: Insight into the semantics-pragmatics interface. *Cognitive Psychology* 41, 491–505.

Ioup, Georgette 1975. *The Treatment of Quantifier Scope in Transformational Grammar*. Ph.D. dissertation. City University of New York, New York

Johnson-Laird, Phillip N. 1977. Reasoning with quantifiers. In: P. N. Johnson-Laird & P. C. Wason (eds.). *Thinking: Readings in Cognitive Science*. Cambridge: Cambridge University Press, 129–142.

Kaiser, Elsi & John Trueswell 2004. The role of discourse context in the processing of a flexible word order language. *Cognition* 94, 113–147.

Kamp, Hans & Uwe Reyle 1993. *From Discourse to Logic*. Dordrecht: Kluwer.

Kaup, Barbara, Stephanie Kelter & Christopher Habel 2002. Representing referents of plural expressions and resolving plural anaphors. *Language and Cognitive Processes* 17, 405–450.

Kehler, Andrew, Laura Kertz, Hannah Rohde & Jeffrey Elman 2008. Coherence and coreference revisited. *Journal of Semantics* 25, 1–44.

Kennedy, Chris 1999. *Projecting the Adjective: The Syntax and Semantics of Gradability and Comparison*. New York: Garland.

Kennedy, Chris & Louise McNally 2005. Scale structure, degree modification, and the semantics of gradable predicates. *Language* 81, 345–381.

Kim, Albert & Lee Osterhout 2005. The independence of combinatory semantic processing: Evidence from ERPs. *Journal of Memory and Language* 52, 205–221.

Koh, Song Yongh & Charles E. Clifton, Jr. 2002. Resolution of the antecedent of a plural pronoun: Ontological categories and predicate symmetry. *Journal of Memory and Language* 46, 830–844.

Kurtzman, Howard & Mary Ellen MacDonald 1993. Resolution of quantifier scope and ambiguities. *Cognition* 48, 243–279.

Levinson, Stephen C. 2000. *Presumptive Meanings: The Theory of Generalized Conversational Implicature*. Cambridge, MA: The MIT Press.

Lipka, Sigrid 2002. Reading sentences with a late closure ambiguity: Does semantic information help? *Language and Cognitive Processes* 17, 271–299.

Mauner, Gail & Jean-Pierre Koenig 1999. Linguistic vs. conceptual sources of implicit agents in sentence comprehension. *Brain & Language* 68, 178–184.

Mauner, Gail, Michael K. Tanenhaus & Greg Carlson 1995. Implicit arguments in sentence processing. *Journal of Memory and Language* 34, 357–382.

McElree, Brian, Steven Frisson & Martin Pickering 2006. Deferred interpretations: Why starting Dickens is taxing but reading Dickens isn't. *Cognitive Science* 30, 181–192.

Noveck, Ira & Andres Posada 2003. Characterizing the time course of an implicature: An evoked potentials study. *Brain & Language* 85, 203–210.

Noveck, Ira, Raphaele Guelminger, Nicolas Georgieff & Nelly Labruyere 2007. What autism can reveal about 'Every . . . not' sentences. *Journal of Semantics* 224, 73–90.

Papafragou, Anna, Justin Hulbert & John Trueswell 2008. Does language guide event perception? Evidence from eye movements. *Cognition* 108, 155–184.

Piñango, Maria, Edgar Zurif & Ray Jackendoff 1991. Real-time processing implications of aspectual coercion at the syntax-semantics interface. *Journal of Psycholinguistic Research* 28, 395–414.

Piñango, Maria Mercedes, Aaron Winnick, Rashad Ullah & Edgar Zurif 2006. Time-course of semantic composition: The case of aspectual coercion. *Journal of Psycholinguistic Research* 35, 233–344.

Pylkkänen, Liina & Brian McElree 2007. An MEG study of silent meaning. *Journal of Cognitive Neuroscience* 19, 1905–1921.

Rips, Lance J. & William Turnbull 1980. How big is big? Relative and absolute properties in memory. *Cognition* 8, 145–174.

Rotstein, Carmen & Yoad Winter 2004. Total adjectives vs. partial adjectives: Scale structure and higher order modifiers. *Natural Language Semantics* 12, 259–288.

Sauerland, Uli 2003. A new semantics for number. In: S Moore & A. Z. Wagner (eds.). *Proceedings of Semantics and Linguistic Theory (= SALT) XIII*. Ithaca, NY: Cornell University, 258–275.

Sauerland, Uli, Jan Anderssen & Katsumo Yatsushiro 2005. The plural is semantically unmarked. In: S. Kepser & M. Reis (eds.). *Linguistic Evidence: Empirical, Theoretical and Computational Issues*. Berlin: Mouton de Gruyter, 413–434.

Schafer, Amy 1997. *Prosodic Parsing: The Role of Prosody in Sentence Comprehension*. Ph.D. dissertation. University of Massachusetts, Amherst, MA.

Schwarz, Florian 2007. Processing presupposed content. *Journal of Semantics* 24, 373–416.

Sedivy, Julie, Michael Tanenhaus, Craig Chambers & Greg Carlson 1999. Achieving incremental semantic interpretation through contextual representation. *Cognition* 71, 109–147.

Sturt, Patrick, Anthony J. Sanford, Andrew Stewart & Eugene Dawydiak 2004. Linguistic focus and good-enough representations: An application of the change-detection paradigm. *Psychonomic Bulletin & Review* 11(5), 882–888.

Sussman, Rachel, Natalie Klein, Gregory N. Carlson & Michael Tanenhaus 2006. Weak definites: Evidence for a new class of definite NP interpretation. Poster presented at the *19th Annual City University of New York Conference on Human Sentence Processing*, CUNY Graduate Center, New York.

Traxler, Matthew, Brian McElree, Rihana Williams & Martin Pickering 2005. Context effects in coercion: Evidence from eye movements. *Journal of Memory and Language* 53, 1–25.

Tunstall, Susanne 1998. *The Interpretation of Quantifiers: Semantics & Processing*. Ph.D. dissertation. University of Massachusetts, Amherst, MA.

van Berkum, Jos, Peter Hagoort & Colin Brown 1999. Semantic integration in sentences and discourse: Evidence from the N400. *Journal of Cognitive Neuroscience* 11, 657–671.

van Gompel, Roger, Martin Pickering, Janie Pearson & Simon Liversedge 2005. Evidence against competition during syntactic ambiguity resolution. *Journal of Memory and Language* 52, 284–307.

Varvoutis, Jason & Martin Hackl 2006. Parsing quantifiers in object position. Paper presented at the *19th Annual City University of New York Conference on Human Sentence Processing*, CUNY Graduate Center, New York.

Villalta, Elizabeth 2003. The role of context in the resolution of quantifier scope ambiguities. *Journal of Semantics* 20, 115–162.

Vonk, Wietske, Lettica G.M.M. Hustinx & Wim H.G. Simons 1992. The use of referential expressions in structuring discourse. *Language and Cognitive Processes* 7, 301–333.

Walsh Dickey, Michael 2001. *The Processing of Tense: Psycholinguistic Studies on the Interpretation of Tense and Temporal Relations*. Dordrecht: Kluwer.

Warren, Tessa 2003. The processing complexity of quantifiers. In: L. Alonso-Ovalle (ed.). *On Semantic Processing* (University of Massachusetts Occasional Papers in Linguistics, vol. 27). Amherst, MA: GLSA, 211–237.

Warren, Tessa & Edward Gibson 2002. The influence of referential processing on sentence complexity. *Cognition* 85, 79–112.

Wijnen, Frank & Edith Kaan 2006. Dynamics of semantic processing: The interpretation of bare quantifiers. *Language and Cognitive Processes* 21, 684–720.

Wolf, Florian, Edward Gibson & Timothy Desmet 2004. Discourse coherence and pronoun resolution. *Language and Cognitive Processes* 19, 665–676.

Xiang, Ming, Brian Dillon & Colin Phillips 2009. Illusory licensing effects across dependency types: ERP evidence. *Brain & Language* 108, 40–55.

Stephen Crain
9 Meaning in first language acquisition

1   Overview of research on the acquisition of semantics —— 237
2   Two solutions to Plato's problem —— 244
3   Disjunction in human languages: A parameter —— 256
4   Disjunction and downward entailing expressions —— 258
5   Loose ends and conclusions —— 266
6   References —— 268

Abstract: Every normal child acquires a language in just a few years. By four or five, children are effectively adults in their abilities to understand novel sentences, to discern entailment relations, and to assess the truth or falsity of endlessly many statements presented to them in conversational contexts. There are two main approaches to explain this remarkable acquisition scenario: one emphasizes the contribution of innate knowledge, and one emphasizes the availability of relevant cues in children's experience. Semantic knowledge is a good testing ground for adjudicating between these alternative approaches, because evidence for principles of interpretation appears to be thin at best. The main focus of this chapter is on children's interpretation of disjunction (e.g., English or). In classical logic, disjunction has truth conditions corresponding to inclusive-or. It is evident from cross-linguistic research that human languages assign the inclusive-or interpretation to disjunction, and it is evident from recent experimental research that this is children's initial interpretation, despite the absence of decisive evidence in children's experience. This invites two conclusions: that disjunction has the same basic meaning in classical logic and in human languages, and that children do not learn what disjunction means from experience; rather, this knowledge is innately specified.

1 Overview of research on the acquisition of semantics

The present chapter describes a series of interwoven linguistic phenomena, all dealing with the interpretation of disjunction (English *or*) in human languages. The main focus is on child language because, as we will see, children can be

---

Stephen Crain, Sydney, Australia

https://doi.org/10.1515/9783110589825-009

more revealing about the interplay of logic and language than adults are. In discussing the interplay of logic and language, we describe research investigating children's interpretation of disjunction across languages, and in sentences where disjunction appears in combination with other logical expressions: negation, focus expressions, and the universal quantifier. This leaves insufficient space to spend on other research findings about the nature of meaning in first language acquisition. To make up for this, the following paragraphs briefly introduce a range of other topics, with suggestions for further reading. Children's first words are predominantly open-class or content words (nouns, verbs, adjectives), rather than closed class or function words (determiners, prepositions, pronouns). So, we begin this survey by discussing the emergence of the open class vocabulary, namely nouns and verbs.

1.1 Nouns and verbs

Even six-month old English-speaking infants show a preference for listening to open class vocabulary items rather than closed class items (Shi & Werker 2001). In languages like English and Italian, nouns dominate the child's first 200 words, then verbs creep in, followed by closed-class function words (e.g., *and*, *or*) and finally closed-class vocabulary items such as prepositions, determiners and pronouns (Dromi 1987; Nelson 1973). To explain the early emergence of nouns, it has been proposed that nouns are more "cognitively dominant" than verbs or closed-class items, and that closed-class items, in particular, derive their meanings from their linguistic environment and represent opaque grammatical constructs (Gentner 1982; Gentner & Boroditsky 2001). The suggestion that child language is "noun friendly" has been challenged, however, in observational studies of children learning other languages, such as Japanese, Korean and Mandarin Chinese (see, e.g., Tardif, Gelman & Xu 1999, for Mandarin Chinese). In these languages, young children apparently produce verbs in higher proportions than nouns, at least as compared to child English and child Italian.

Another issue is the meanings that children initially assign to nouns. It has been suggested in various studies that children interpret words too broadly (*overextend* their meanings) or too narrowly (*underextend* their meanings) as compared to adults. However, experimental assessments of children's overextensions and under-extensions indicate that, in fact, mistaken interpretations are quite rare. Children's non-adult behavior is more likely to occur in their productions than in language understanding, and mistakes are likely to be performance errors in on-line language processing, due to less-than-optimal strategies of lexical retrieval in sentence planning, rather than being due to non-adult semantic representations in children's mental dictionaries (e.g., Clark 2003; Huttenlocher & Smiley 1987). A number of cognitive constraints have been proposed to account for children's early associations of labels to objects (see e.g., Markman 1989). One constraint is called *mutual exclusivity*, which guides children to associate a novel linguistic expression with a novel object, rather than associating it with an object that the child can already name. The source of children's one-to-one mapping of labels onto objects is subject to debate. Some researchers attribute it to word learning, whereas others attribute it to pragmatic knowledge (see Bloom 2000).

Turning next to the acquisition of verb meaning, it has been argued that the multiple sentence structures in which a verb appears provide young children with cues to its meaning (see Gleitman 1990). In child directed speech, mothers use most verbs in several sentence structures (e.g., *He broke the vase. The vase broke.*), and it has been shown experimentally that two-year-olds gain insight into the meanings of verbs by attending to the syntactic frames in which they occur (Naigles 1998). This, in turn, is evidence that 2-year-olds are capable of building syntactic representations for sentences (Guasti 2002).

Another topic in the acquisition of verb meaning is telicity. A verb (or verb phrase) that depicts an action or event as complete is said to be **telic,** whereas one that depicts an action or event as incomplete is said to be **atelic** (see article 9 [Semantics: Noun Phrases and Verb Phrases] (Filip) *Aspectual class and Aktionsart*). Various studies have investigated children's sensitivity to the telic/atelic distinction. English-speaking and Dutch-speaking children's sensitivity to telicity has been demonstrated in a series of studies by van Hout (1998; 2003; 2004). One study showed 3- to 5-year-old children two versions of an event, such as one picture of an elephant that had consumed only part of a bucket of water, and another picture in which the elephant had consumed the entire contents of a bucket of water. Child preferred the picture that depicted the completed event in response to a description using a verb-particle construction, e.g., *The elephant drank up the water*, as compared to one without a particle, e.g., *The elephant drank the water*). Similarly, Wagner & Carey (2003) claim that children as young as three years old mark telicity in English. In one study, children were shown animations in which periods of activity (separated by breaks) lead to a culminating event (*paint a flower, build a house*). Various types of events were presented (creation, destruction, change of state). The events were described using either atelic or telic predicates. Children were then asked to count the events in the animations. Children's strategy for counting events was influenced by the type of predicate that was used. It has also been found that English-speaking children tend to restrict their use of perfective past tense morphology (*-ed*) to telic verbs, and they tend to restrict the use of imperfective progressive (*-ing*) to atelic verbs for the most part (Bloom, Lifter & Hafitz 1980; Shirai & Andersen 1995). Note that adult English does not adhere to these restrictions; verb forms such as *making* and *bumped* are perfectly natural. Thus the observed pattern in child language is not likely to be learned from adult input.

We move now to topics in the acquisition of the closed class vocabulary, beginning with negation.

1.2 Negation

(For background on negation, see article 2 [Semantics: Sentence and Information Structure] (Herburger) *Negation*.) Early work on child language by Klima & Bellugi (1966) charted the course of development of English-speaking children's negative utterances. They found that children typically go through distinct stages, beginning with a stage during which they produce negative statements with a negative expression followed by a proposition (NEG+PROPOSITION), e.g, *No, the sun shining*, or *No, Mommy do it*. The existence of an early 'primitive' stage of negation was questioned by later researchers, but at least some children appear to pass through a stage of 'external' negation, and such utterances have been analysed in several ways. Many examples have been analysed as anaphoric negation, in which the negative element constitutes a rejection of a previous utterance, so *No, the sun shining* means *The sun is not shining* (Bloom 1970). Other examples have been interpreted as the negation of an implicit verb *want* that resides in a higher clause, so *No Mommy do it* means *I don't want Mommy to do it* (de Villiers & de Villiers 1979). According to these accounts of children's early syntactic development, children's utterances with external negation are structurally different from those of an adult speaker, but they are semantically equivalent to the corresponding adult utterances with sentence-internal negation. A detailed syntactic analysis relating children's external negation to adult sentence-internal negation is offered by Déprez & Pierce (1993) (but cf. Stromswold & Zimmermann 2000). Taking a different line, Drozd (1995) argues that children's utterances with 'pre-sentential' negation are adult-like utterances expressing 'metalinguistic exclamatory' negation. On this account, the child is objecting to a previous utterance, so *No, the sun shining* means *Don't say the sun is shining*, cf. *The hell the sun is shining*. When negation appears sentence-internally in children's utterances, they continue to produce certain kinds of non-adult utterances, including ones that contain an uninflected verb, such as *Mary no like cheese* and *Mary not like cheese*. An interesting proposal by Harris & Wexler (1996) is that children who produce such utterances are correctly categorizing the negative element (as a head), but children are at a stage during which Tense or Agreement is optionally omitted. This analysis has been called into question, however, by Thornton & Tesan (2007). These researchers elicited negative sentences from children at the same stage of development, and they recorded a robust sample of negated utterances that are not expected on the Harris and Wexler account, such as *Mary not likes cheese*. Based on such non-adult utterances in which Tense and Agreement are present, Thornton & Tesan (2007) argue that children adopt a UG-compatible analysis of negation, one that categorizes negation in a way that is appropriate for embedded clauses in Mainland Scandinavian languages, but neither for main nor embedded clauses in languages such as English. There have been a number of experimental studies on English-speaking children's interpretation of disjunction (English *or*) in the scope of negation and in the scope of negative quantificational expressions such as *not* and *none of the* (Chierchia et al. 2001; Crain et al. 2002; Crain 2008; Crain, Goro & Thornton 2006; Gualmini et al. 2001; Gualmini & Crain 2002, 2004). These studies have revealed that 4- to 5-year-old English-speaking children are aware of the adult interpretation of disjunction when it appears in the scope of these downward-entailing operators. A representative example is an experiment by Crain et al. (2002) using the Truth Value Judgment Task in the prediction mode (see Crain & Thornton 1998). On a typical trial, sentence (1) was uttered by a (wizard) puppet as a prediction about how events would unfold in a story. It subsequently turned out that the girl who stayed up late received a jewel, but not a dime. The 3- to 5-year-old English-speaking subjects correctly rejected sentences like (1) in experimental contexts such as this. Children's stated reason for rejecting (1) was that the girl who stayed up late had received a jewel. It is evidence that, in children's grammars, (1) entails that the girl would receive neither a dime nor a jewel, i.e., she would not receive a dime *and* she would not receive a jewel. This conjunctive entailment follows only if the disjunction operator *or* is assigned an inclusive-*or* interpretation, as in classical logic.

(1) The girl who stayed up late will *not* get a dime *or* a jewel.

(2) The girl who did*n't* go to bed will get a dime *or* a jewel.

The same children consistently accepted sentences like (2) in the same contexts. In (2), the negative element does not have scope (does not c-command) over the disjunction operator. The fact that sentences like (2) do not engender conjunctive entailments for children demonstrates their knowledge of the structural relation that governs semantic interpretation in children's grammars (see section 5).

1.3 Focus expressions

As we discuss in section 4.1, focus expressions such as English *only* are typically associated with a particular linguistic expression somewhere else in a sentence. The associated expression is called the focus element. More often than not, the focus element receives phonological stress. In addition, sentences with focus operators are felicitous mainly in contexts in which there is a contrast set. The contrast set consists of individuals in the domain of discourse that are taken by the speaker and hearer to be alternatives to the focus element. These individuals should have been introduced into the conversational context before the sentence was produced; their existence is presupposed. Much of the previous literature on the acquisition of the focus operator, *only*, has centred on children's non-adult interpretation of sentences with a focus operator. For example, it has been observed (Crain, Ni & Conway 1994) that some children associate pre-subject *only* with the VP, such that they interpret *Only John speaks Spanish* as meaning that John only speaks Spanish. There are two main accounts of such non-adult behaviour. On one account, children fail to use phonological stress as a cue in identifying the focus element. For a comprehensive review of the relevant literature on the relation between phonological stress and children's semantic interpretation, see Reinhart (2006). On a second account, it is suggested that young children simply lack the ability to compute contrast sets. Following this second line, Paterson et al. (2003) argue that children fail "to mentally represent contrast information", and often can only compute semantic representations using lexical material that is made explicit, and cannot compute representations that include implied information (Paterson et al. 2003: 276–277, 286, 289). In the present chapter, by contrast, we report the findings of studies showing that children are just as facile as adults in computing contrast sets with focus operators like *only*, as long as the contrast set is made salient in the experimental workspace. The finding has been replicated in studies of English, Japanese, and Chinese (Crain, Goro & Minai 2007; Jing, Crain & Hsu 2006; Notley et al. 2009; Zhou & Crain 2009, 2010).

1.4 Universal quantification

Investigations of sentences with the universal quantifier, e.g., English *every*, have led to qualitatively different conclusions about children's linguistic knowledge. One line of research has uncovered systematic non-adult responses by preschool and even school-age children (Inhelder & Piaget 1964; Philip 1995). For example, 5- and 6-year-old children sometimes reject (3) as an accurate description of a picture in which every boy is riding an elephant, but there is an 'extra' elephant that is not being ridden by a boy.

(3) Every boy is riding an elephant.

Children non-adult behaviour in response to questions such as (3) has been called the *symmetrical response* since children appear to demand a one-to-one relation between the set of boys and the set of elephants. To explain the symmetrical response, Philip (1995) advanced an analysis in which the universal quantifier takes scope over both the subject N (boy) and the object N (elephant) in children's grammars. In the grammars of adults, the universal quantifier *every* quantifies over the set denoted by the subject N (boy), but not over the set denoted by the object N (elephant), so the presence of an 'extra' elephant does not render sentences like (3) false for adults. Children's symmetrical responses fail to emerge, however, in certain experimental tasks, such as the truth value judgment task (Crain et al. 1996; Crain & Thornton 1998). The observation that different tasks lead to different behaviours has been the subject of considerable debate. According to one account, children's grammars make two readings available for sentences like (3), including one reading that is not attested in human languages, namely the reading on which a pre-subject universal quantifier takes scope over an object N. The crucial point is that this non-adult reading is prompted in certain tasks, including picture verification tasks, which draw children's attention to the set of individuals denoted by the object N; by contrast, the contention is that other tasks, such as the truth value judgment task, draw children's attention to the set denoted by subject N, thereby increasing the proportion of adult-like interpretations (Gordon 1996; Drozd 2006; Geurts 2003). An alternative account maintains that children's grammars are the same as those of adults, with just the reading on which the restriction of a quantifier is the noun it combines with in the syntax. The reason that children produce non-adult responses in certain tasks, on this account, is that these tasks violate ordinary rules of conversation by asking "a question whose answer is already known by both speakers" (Dehaene 1997: 46). As Guasti (2002) points out, the observation that violations of conversational rules evoke 'errors' from children (and adults) has been found in other research domains, such as in number conservation.

1.5 Polarity sensitivity

(For background, see article 3 [Semantics: Sentence and Information Structure] (Giannakidou) *Polarity items*.) There are only a handful of studies bearing on the development of polarity sensitivity in children, but what little is known is consistent with the conclusion that young children produce and avoid negative polarity items in the same linguistic contexts as adults do (O'Leary & Crain 1994; Thornton 1995; van der Wal 1996). An experiment by O'Leary and Crain is representative. These researchers used a Truth Value Judgment task with an elicitation component. In the task, the puppet, Kermit the Frog, often produced false descriptions of the events that had taken place in the story. Whenever Kermit the Frog failed to accurately state what had happened in a story, children were asked to say 'what really happened'. The experimenter who was manipulating Kermit produced sentences like those in (4) and (5).

(4) Kermit: Every dinosaur found **something** to write with.
    Child: *No, this one didn't find anything to write with.*

(5) Kermit: Only one of the reindeer found **anything** to eat.
    Child: *No, every reindeer found something to eat.*

In the condition illustrated by (4), Kermit's statement had a universal quantifier *every*, which does not tolerate negative polarity items, such as *anything*, in its scope; instead, the (positive polarity) expression *something* was used. Eleven children (mean age 4;10) participated in the study. These children's responses frequently contained the negative polarity item *anything* in linguistic contexts that license it. In another condition, illustrated in (5), Kermit's statement contained the negative polarity item *anything*. However, in correcting Kermit, children consistently used the universal quantifier *every*, so this linguistic context forced children to avoid repeating the negative polarity item *anything*, despite having just heard it used by Kermit. These findings make it clear that children have mastered some, if not all, of the requisite knowledge of downward entailment, which underlies the appropriate use and avoidance of negative polarity items.

Having surveyed some of the literature on the acquisition of the meanings of open and closed class vocabulary items, we now take a detailed look at the investigation of children's interpretation of disjunction in a variety of linguistic contexts, including sentences with negation, ones with the universal quantifier *every*, and ones with the focus operator *only*.

2 Two solutions to Plato's problem

Without special training or carefully sequenced input, every normal child acquires a language in just a few years. By four or five, children have invariably converged on a grammar that is largely equivalent to that of adult speakers in the same linguistic community. Children have effectively become adults in their abilities to understand novel sentences, to discern relations of paraphrase and entailments, and to judge the truth or falsity of endlessly many statements presented in conversational contexts. The alternative approaches to the study of first language acquisition can be traced back to the 'nature versus nurture' debate about how knowledge is acquired in any domain. The debate dates back to Plato's dialogue "The Meno". In this dialogue, the protagonist, Socrates, demonstrates to Meno that a young slave knows more about geometry than he could have learned from experience. By extension, "Plato's Problem" refers to any gap between experience and knowledge.

One solution to Plato's problem views the process of language acquisition on a par with the acquisition of knowledge in all other domains: e.g., social skills, learning to count, learning to read, and so forth. This is a domain-general approach to language development. This 'nurture' approach highlights the availability of relevant cues in the input to children. These cues serve as the basis for the generalizations that children form about language. These generalizations are formed using statistical learning mechanisms including distributional analysis, analogy, cut and paste operations, and the like. The products of these learning algorithms are 'shallow' records which children keep of their linguistic experience. These are piecemeal records of construction types (templates/schemas/constructs) that encode linguistic patterns displayed by the input. Construction types are concatenated sequences of category labels such as *NP, V, neg, INF, P*, etc., drawn from an intuitively simple typology, and are learned solely from positive evidence. (see, e.g., Pullum & Scholz 2002). When children's generalizations extend beyond their experience, the supposition is that this is just an instance of a completely general induction problem that arises for all learning that involves projection beyond one's experience (see, e.g., Cowie 1999). On the experience-dependent approach, child language is expected to match that of adults, more or less, with more frequently attested construction types being learned earlier than less frequently attested ones (e.g., Ambridge & Lieven 2011; Tomasello 2000, 2003).

The alternative view is that the gap between the child's linguistic experience and the knowledge they achieve is filled by innate principles of language. This 'nativist' approach highlights the contributions of human nature to the acquisition of linguistic knowledge. It supposes that children are biologically fitted, as part of the human genome, with a theory of 'Universal Grammar' (e.g., Chomsky 1965, 1975, 1986). Universal Grammar contains the core principles of language, i.e., principles that are manifested in all human languages. In addition, Universal Grammar spells out particular ways in which human languages can vary; these points of variation are called parameters. Taken together, the core principles and parameters of Universal Grammar establish the boundary conditions on what counts as a possible human language. Children navigate within these boundaries in the course of language development. This approach views language learning as the by-product of a task-specific computational mechanism that enables children to rapidly and effortlessly acquire any human language without formal instruction and despite the considerable latitude in experience for different children. Universal linguistic principles are not learned by the computational mechanism, but are implicit in the structure of the mechanism itself. The parameters of Universal Grammar permit children to sometimes "try out" parameter values which generate constructions that are unattested in the local language, but only if such constructions are attested in other human languages (Crain & Pietroski 2001, 2002; Crain & Thornton 1998; Crain 2002).

Both approaches attempt to explain the universal mastery of language by young children. The details of the alternative explanations turn on three factors: (i) the linguistic competence children achieve, (ii) the linguistic input children receive, and (iii) the nonlinguistic capacities of children to form and evaluate generalizations based on their experience. First, let us consider the linguistic competence children achieve.

Children's linguistic competence encompasses a variety of rich and interrelated linguistic generalizations. To illustrate, we will look at some representative generalizations that govern the interpretation of **disjunction** in human languages (e.g., English *or*, Japanese *ka*, Chinese *huozhe*).

One generalization arises in statements in which disjunction appears with negation, as in (6). First, note that example (6) entails both (6a) and (6b). It follows that (6) entails (7), which is simply the conjunction of (6a) and (6b).

(6) *Suzi didn't see Max order sushi or pasta.*
    a. Suzi didn't see Max order sushi.
    b. Suzi didn't see Max order pasta.

(7) Suzi didn't see Max order sushi and Suzi didn't see Max order pasta.

Let us call (7) the *conjunctive entailment* of disjunction in the scope of negation. So, the English statement (6) generates a conjunctive entailment. Remarkably, when (6) is translated into Japanese or Chinese (or any other language, as far as we know), the corresponding statements also generate conjunctive interpretations. So, what is acquired by any particular child who is learning any particular language is just an instance of a generalization that extends across the globe, to all human languages. It is interesting to note that a similar cross-linguistic generalization does not extend to simple negative sentences with disjunction, such as *Max didn't eat sushi or pasta*. In statements of this form, some languages (e.g., English, German) license conjunctive entailments, but others (e.g., Japanese, Chinese) do not. This parametric variation, and what children make of it, is discussed in section 3.

Another generalization about the interpretation of disjunction concerns statements with the universal quantifier, e.g., *every* in English. As (8) shows, when disjunction is in subject phrase of a sentence with *every*, the sentence yields the entailments (8a) and (8b). Therefore, the English statement in (8) makes the conjunctive entailment in (9). And when (8) is translated into Japanese or Chinese (and any other language, as far as we know), the corresponding statements also make conjunctive entailments.

(8) *Every student who took French or Spanish went to the conference.*
 a. Every student who took French went to the conference.
 b. Every student who took Spanish went to the conference.

(9) Every student who took French went to the conference
 and every student who took Spanish went to the conference.

Once more, what is acquired by any particular child in any particular language is just an instance of a broader cross-linguistic generalization.

Children also learn where disjunction does *not* license a conjunctive entailment. Interestingly, when disjunction is in the predicate phrase of a sentence with the universal quantifier, *every*, it no longer generates a conjunctive entailment. This is illustrated in (10), which has been formed from (8) by reversing the contents of the subject phrase and the predicate phrase.

(10) *Every student who went to the conference took French or Spanish.*
 a. # Every student who went to the conference took French.
 b. # Every student who went to the conference took Spanish.

In (10), the predicate phrase (*took French or Spanish*) contains disjunction, but a conjunctive entailment is not licensed, because the relevant entailments in (10a) and (10b) are not valid inferences from (10). Later in this chapter we will see why disjunction is interpreted differently in the subject phrase and in the predicate phrase of sentences with the universal quantifier. For now, suffice it to say that this asymmetry extends to languages around the globe and, again, children are aware at an early age that disjunction does *not* generate a conjunctive entailment in the predicate phrase of sentences with a universal quantifier.

Having provided a sample of the kinds of linguistic generalizations that children achieve, let us now consider the second piece of the acquisition puzzle, the nature of children's abilities to learn. Theories of language learning must be compatible with observations about the cognitive capacities of children to form and evaluate generalizations based on their experience. Children presumably do not (as linguists do) confirm hypothesized principles based on how well principles unify and explain disparate phenomena. Children also do not (as linguists do) confirm hypothesized principles based on both positive and negative evidence, and based on a range of crosslinguistic data.

Nevertheless, perhaps children can extract the relevant generalizations from what adults actually say, in the circumstances in which they say them. Recent research findings have demonstrated children's sensitivity to some statistical and distributional properties of the linguistic input. A study by Read & Schreiber (1982) showed that 7-year-olds are sensitive to structural notions like subject noun phrase, as long as such phrases contain more than one word. Moreover, Saffran, Aslin & Newport (1996) showed that infants can learn to segment speech into "word" boundaries by attending to statistical properties of the input. These researchers demonstrated that 8-month-old children could exploit statistical learning mechanisms to extract information about transitional probabilities from the input. Infants inferred the existence of word boundaries between three-syllable nonsense "words" using some experience-dependent mechanism. Sequences of syllables that crossed a word boundary were not treated as a "word" during the post-test phase, because there was a lower probability for a sequence of syllables to be repeated if it crossed a word boundary than if that sequence was part of a "word". These discoveries are of genuine interest. But there is no evidence that the statistical sensitivities children possess are relevantly like the statistical sensitivities they would need to learn the generalizations about the interpretation of disjunction, such as the fact that "or" is assigned different truth conditions in sentences with the universal quantifier, *every*, depending on its position in sentence structure (as illustrated in examples 8 and 10, above). In the absence of a plausible learning account of the acquisition of the kinds of interpretive phenomena that are exhibited by human languages, many linguists have concluded that there are substantive universal principles of human grammar and that, as a result of human biology, children can only acquire languages that conform to these principles. The development of semantic competence is likely to be especially revealing abut the kinds of principles that are not learned from experience, since there is no realistic database by which children could come to understand principles of interpretation using the familiar mechanisms of learning.

Still, no one doubts that children use experience-dependent learning mechanisms to master some aspects of language. Children who grow up in an English-speaking community learn to speak English; those who grow up in a Basque-speaking community learn to speak Basque. But is it reasonable, therefore, to infer that the linguistic principles that govern the interpretation of disjunction, illustrated in (6)–(10) above, are acquired by children around the globe using statistical learning mechanisms? To answer this question, it is important to know what experience-dependent mechanisms can and cannot do. One kind of experience-based learning mechanism is a connectionist or parallel distributed processing network. Such networks rely on local regularities—i.e., changes in the "connection between one unit and another on the basis of information that is locally available to the connection" (Rumelhart & McClelland 1986: 214). According to Rumelhart & McClelland (1986: 214), such models "provide very simple mechanisms for extracting information from an ensemble of inputs without the aid of sophisticated generalizations or rule-formulating mechanisms." In response, Marcus (1998; 1999) and Smith (1996) have shown that while such mechanisms are capable of extracting information about transitional probabilities, they are ill-suited to learning many other properties of languages. We contend that such mechanisms are ill-suited to learn the semantic principles that govern the interpretation of disjunction in human languages.

Not only are experience-dependent learning mechanisms too weak to learn certain properties of human languages, they are also too strong, in the sense that these mechanisms readily make generalizations about human languages which language-users themselves cannot make. Consider again the Read and Schreiber study. In that study, 7-year-old children were found to be sensitive to structure-dependent aspects of language. Read and Schreiber also showed that 7-year-old children cannot learn structure independent rules, like 'drop the first four words of a sentence'. Similarly, Smith & Tsimpli (1995) showed that adults are unable to learn *structure-independent* rules for question formation. Because experience-dependent learning mechanisms are able to form structure-independent generalizations, these mechanisms are quite unlike human minds.

The third piece of the acquisition puzzle is the linguistic input children receive. A casual (or even intensive) examination of what adults actually say does not reveal the descriptive generalizations we have presented—much less the deeper principles that explain them. For example, we just observed that children come to know about the meanings that speakers' *do not* assign to otherwise well-formed sentences with disjunction. Yet, as far as we know, children are rarely (if ever) informed about the meanings sentences do not have (see Chierchia 2004; Crain 1991; Crain & Pietroski 2001, 2002; Pinker 1990). It is reasonable to suppose that children make use of positive data, sentences in ordinary contexts. However, positive evidence can be misleading. For example, a survey of the input to children (see CHILDES, e.g., the transcripts of Adam or Eve) reveals that the overwhelming majority of adult utterances with disjunction are subject to a scalar implicature of exclusivity or, worse, express mutually exclusive alternatives (e.g., *Was it a big yard or a small yard*?). Moreover, it is highly unlikely, as Chierchia (2004) points out, that English-speaking children are informed that the word for disjunction *or* has a different interpretation when it appears in the subject phrase of a sentence with the universal quantifier, as in (8), than it does when it appears in the predicate phrase, as in (10). And, we will see (section 2.4) that Japanese-speaking children initially interpret negative statements with disjunction (*ka* in Japanese) in the same way as English-speaking children. Japanese-speaking adults, by contrast, assign a different interpretation. This means that Japanese-speaking children cannot be relying on the input as the basis for their initial interpretation of negative statements with disjunction. Despite the sometimes misleading positive data, the lack of negative evidence or information about subtle differences in interpretation, and despite cross-linguistic variation in input to children, all normal children reach the same generalizations about the interpretation of sentences with disjunction, namely that the meaning of disjunction is inclusive-or. We summarize some of the empirical evidence for this conclusion starting in section 2.3.

In this introduction, we have described two main approaches to first language acquisition, one emphasizing the contribution of innate knowledge, and the other emphasizing the availability of experience and children's abilities to extract generalizations from the input. Semantic knowledge is a good test case in adjudicating between these alternative approaches. To illustrate, the chapter will describe, in further detail, some principles governing the interpretation of disjunction in human languages. A second item on the agenda is to assess the contribution of logic to human languages, and to determine what's left over—the specific contingent properties of language that influence logical reasoning, but that do not follow from logic. Although there are some clear differences between classical logic and natural language semantics, there are reasons to suppose that logic and human language share some of the same basic meanings, including the meaning of disjunction, e.g., English *or*. We will examine the interplay of logic and language by studying how children and adults interpret disjunction, across languages.

2.1 Disjunction in classical logic

In classical logic, the disjunction operator ('$\vee$') has the truth conditions associated with inclusive-*or*. Consider a statement of the form ($A \vee B$). Since the disjunction operator has the truth conditions associated with inclusive-or, ($A \vee B$) is true in three cases: if A is true but not B (A, ¬B), if B is true but not A (B, ¬A), and if both A and B are true (A, B). A statement of the form ($A \vee B$) is false only if both A and B are false (¬A, ¬B). The negation of the original statement is true just in those cases in which the original statement is false. Therefore, ¬(A ∨ B) is true in just one case, when both A and B are false (¬A, ¬B). It follows that ¬(A ∨ B) logically entails (¬A ∧ ¬B), where '∧' is logical conjunction. This yields one of De Morgan's laws: ¬(A ∨ B) ⇒ (¬A ∧ ¬B). The critical point is that this law assumes that disjunction is inclusive-*or*.

2.2 Disjunction in human languages

Turning to human languages, one way to examine the interplay of logic and language is to ask whether or not child and adult speakers of human languages assign the inclusive-*or* interpretation to words that express disjunction in human languages (e.g., English *or*; Japanese *ka*; Chinese *huozhe*). It will be instructive to look at statements that correspond to the logical statements we just discussed: (A ∨ B), and ¬(A ∨ B). In both cases, the question is whether or not child and adult speakers judge statements like these, when they are expressed in human languages, to be true in the same circumstances as the corresponding logical statements. If so, then disjunction in human languages is also inclusive-*or*. In particular, we saw that, in the case of classical logic, ¬(A ∨ B) is true only if both A and B are false: (¬A ∧ ¬B). We will call this the 'conjunctive entailment' of disjunction under negation. In recent research, we have adopted the research strategy of identifying linguistic constructions in human languages in which (a) disjunction appears under negation (and other expressions), and which language users judge to have truth conditions corresponding to the conjunctive entailment. This research strategy has proven extremely productive in both cross-linguistic research and in research in child language. We will review some of the main discoveries.

We begin with the human language counterparts to statements of the form (A ∨ B). Suppose you and a friend have just seen Max order some sushi and some pasta. Later you overhear your friend tell someone "Max ordered sushi or pasta." Would you contradict your friend, saying "No, that's wrong, Max ordered sushi *and* pasta."? That's what adult speakers of English would do, but child speakers would not do this. For young children, "Max ordered sushi or pasta" correctly describes the case where Max ordered both. Since classical logic statements of the form A ∨ B include the possibility of both A and B, child speakers of English appear to be more logical than adult speakers. As children grow up, their decisions change about when "or" is appropriate, because their interpretation of "or" clashes with how adult speakers use the term. But the difference in meaning between disjunction in formal logic and in English emerges late in language development.

Much early research on child and adult language reached a different conclusion about children's interpretation of disjunction. The findings from several studies were interpreted as showing that children assign the truth conditions associated with exclusive-*or* (A or B, but not both) to disjunction in human languages. For example, Braine & Rumain (1983: 291) acknowledge the view that "equates *or* with standard logic," yet they ultimately reject this view on the grounds that "coherent judgments of the truth of *or*-statements emerge relatively late and are not universal in adults." The conclusion that children and adults assign the exclusive-*or* interpretation to disjunctive statements is unwarranted, however, because it rests largely on tasks that involve requests to perform actions. For example, in an experiment reported in Braine & Rumain (1981), children were instructed to "pick a red balloon or a blue balloon." The finding was that children generally picked either a red balloon or a blue balloon, but few children picked both—although such 'conjunctive' truth-conditions verify statements with disjunction in classical logic. But this kind of research methodology has limited value in determining the full range of truth conditions that are associated with a linguistic expression. At most, a task in which subjects act out instructions provides evidence that the subjects' grammars allow one interpretation (the one that is acted out), but the findings from such a task cannot be used to infer that other interpretations are not available to them. Children (and adults) may simply favour certain one reading over others in the experimental context. The following section provides ample evidence, from recent research, that children interpret disjunction as inclusive-or, as in classical logic (see Crain 2008; Crain & Khlentzos 2008).

2.3 The implicature of exclusivity

(For background, see article 2 [Semantics: Sentence and Information Structure] (Herburger) *Negation* and article 10 [Semantics: Interfaces] (Chierchia, Fox & Spector) *Grammatical view of scalar implicatures*.) Why do adults understand *or* differently than children do? For adults, simple affirmative sentences of the form *A or B* are subject to an implicature of exclusivity. That is, the use of *or* usually implies 'not both', although it does not entail it. For adults, then, a simple statement of the form *A or B* is pragmatically odd (or infelicitous) as a description of a situation in which both *A* and *B* are true. This is why the use of *or* by adult speakers does not appear to conform to classical logic. But appearances can be deceiving. The implicature of 'exclusivity' stems from the availability of another statement, namely *A and B*, which is more informative. *A and B* is more informative than *A or B*, because *A and B* is true in only one set of circumstances, whereas *A or B* is true in other circumstances as well as in the circumstance in which A and B are both true, namely circumstances in which either A or B is true, but not both. Due to this overlap of truth conditions, the expressions *or* and *and* form a scale, based on information strength, with *and* being more informative (i.e., stronger) than *or*. A pragmatic principle *Be Cooperative* (cf. Grice 1975) entreats speakers to be as informative as possible. Upon hearing someone use the less informative (weaker) term on the scale, *or*, listeners assume that the speaker was being cooperative and they infer that the speaker was not in position to use the stronger term *and*. If listeners believe, in addition, that the speaker is informed about the truth or falsity of the stronger term, then the speaker's selection of the weaker term is taken to imply the negation of the stronger term: *not both A and B*. In short, adult use of *or* is governed by a *scalar implicature* of exclusivity So, adults avoid using *A or B* in situations in which both A and B are clearly true. Consequently, the vast majority of children's experience is consistent with the conclusion that natural language disjunction is exclusive-*or*, not inclusive-*or* (see Crain, Goro & Thornton 2006).

In contrast to adults, children younger than six or seven apparently do not compute scalar implicatures for sentences with *or* (Chierchia et al. 1998; Chierchia et al. 2001; Chierchia et al. 2004; Guasti et al. 2005; Noveck 2001; Papafragou & Musolino 2003). Because of young children's lack of sensitivity to scalar implicatures, considerable evidence has been amassed in favor of the conclusion that young children interpret *or* as the inclusive-*or* of classical logic, both in contexts where adults enforce an implicature of exclusivity, and in contexts where adults interpret *or* as inclusive-*or*. This makes it look as though children are more logical than adults. But the real moral to draw is simply that adults compute scalar implicatures in situations where children do not.

So the basic storyline for disjunction in human languages is as follows. Both children and adults assign the truth conditions of inclusive-*or* to ordinary statements with disjunction. In many contexts, however, some of the truth conditions associated with inclusive-*or* are eliminated due to a scalar implicature of exclusivity. The implicature is well in place for adults. This means that the input to children is most often consistent with an exclusive-*or* reading. The fact that children do not interpret disjunction as exclusive-*or*, despite the input from adults, suggests that the only available meaning for children is the one associated with inclusive-*or*. Why isn't the interpretation associated with exclusive-*or* available to children? One proposal is that children's knowledge that disjunction is inclusive-*or* comes from universal grammar, taking universal grammar to be a theory of the initial state of language acquisition. Universal grammar contains the linguistic principles that all languages share and all language learners draw upon in the course of language development. On this scenario, children 'project' the interpretation of inclusive-*or* onto human language, regardless of the input, rather than 'inferring' the meaning of disjunction on the basis of experience.

2.4 Disjunction in the scope of (non-local) negation

There is further evidence that both children and adults interpret disjunction as inclusive-*or*, as in classical logic. This evidence comes from studies of linguistic constructions in which disjunction appears in negative statements, i.e., the human language counterparts to ¬(A ∨ B) in classical logic. Suppose you and your friend were watching Max order lunch. This time, suppose Max didn't order sushi and he didn't order pasta. Later you overhear your friend tell someone "Max didn't order sushi or pasta." Would you agree with your friend? That's what adult speakers of English would do, and that's what child English-speakers would do. And textbooks of logic would agree. In classical logic ¬(A ∨ B) excludes the possibility of A and the possibility of B. And in English, the statement *Max didn't order sushi or pasta* excludes the possibility that Max ordered sushi and the possibility that Max ordered pasta. So, it looks like English disjunction generates a conjunctive entailment when it appears under local negation, as in one of De Morgan's laws: ¬(A ∨ B) ⇒ (¬A ∧ ¬B). Since this law assumes that disjunction is inclusive-*or*, this is a reason for concluding that English disjunction is inclusive-*or*.

Why aren't English-speakers' judgments influenced by an implicature of exclusivity in interpreting sentences like (11) *Max didn't order sushi or pasta*? To answer this, compare this to (12) *Max didn't order sushi and pasta*, where *or* has been replaced by *and*.

(11) Max didn't order sushi or pasta.

(12) Max didn't order sushi and pasta. (Just pasta. / Just sushi. / In fact, neither one.)

Adults judge (12) to be true in various different circumstances, as indicated by the possible follow up parenthetical comments. By contrast, (11) is judged to be true in only one set of circumstances, where Max ordered neither sushi nor pasta. In fact, (11) is true in a subset of the circumstances that verify (12). So negation reverses the subset/superset relation of truth conditions that hold for statements with *or* and *and* in positive statements. In the scope of negation, the use of *or* makes a stronger statement than the corresponding statement with *and*. Under negation, therefore, there is no implicature of exclusivity for *or*.

There is another distinction to be drawn. In (11), the negation and disjunction operators, *n't* and *or*, appear in the same clause. In (13), negation and disjunction are in different clauses.

(13) Utako didn't see Max eat sushi or pasta.
    a. Utako didn't see Max eat sushi *and* she didn't see him eat pasta
    b. *Utako didn't see Max eat sushi *or* she didn't see him eat pasta

In (13), the clause that contains disjunction, ... *Max eat sushi or pasta*, is embedded in the clause with negation. Semantically, the critical observation is that (13) generates a conjunctive entailment, as indicated in (13a); it does not have the 'disjunctive' truth conditions indicated in (13b). When (13) is translated into Japanese, Chinese, Russian, and so forth, its variants in these other languages also carry conjunctive entailments. Here are further examples from (a) English *or*, (b) Chinese *huozhe*, and (c) Japanese *ka*. In each case, the statement with disjunction generates a conjunctive entailment.

(14) a. *Mary didn't say*   ₛ[*John speaks French or Spanish*]
   b. *Mali meiyou shuo-guo*   ₛ[*Yuehan hui shuo fayu huozhe xibanyayu*]
      Mary not   say-PAST   John   can speak French or   Spanish
   c. *Mary-wa* ₛ   *John-ga   French ka Spanish-wo   hanas-u*]*-to   iwa-nakat-ta*
      Mary-TOP   John-SUBJ French or Spanish-OBJ speak-COMP say-not-PAST

As these examples illustrate, in certain linguistic constructions in which negation appears in a higher clause than the clause that contains disjunction, i.e., *not* ₛ*[A or B]*, the corresponding statements are interpreted as excluding the possibility of both A and B. As the examples in (14) indicate, this phenomena appears in typologically different languages.

Notice that in the Japanese example, (14c), the statement takes a different form; *[A or B]*ₛ *not*, rather than *not* ₛ*[A or B]*. This is because Japanese is verb-final and negation is attached to the verb. Nevertheless, the Japanese example has the same truth conditions as the examples from English and Chinese. It makes no difference that the disjunction operator, *ka*, precedes negation in Japanese, whereas *or* and *huozhe* follow negation in the English and Chinese examples. This shows that the interpretation of disjunction does not depend on linear order; what matters is constituent structure. In any event, we may now derive a candidate for consideration as a linguistic universal:

I. When disjunction appears in a lower clause than negation, it licenses a conjunctive entailment

This principle needs further refinement to exclude so-called intervention effects. For example, if a universal quantifier intervenes between negation and disjunction, it may interfere with the interpretive relationship that would otherwise hold. Nevertheless, in constructions without such interveners, such as (14), speakers of typologically distinct languages interpret disjunction as licensing a conjunctive entailment. And this reinforces the conclusion that disjunction has the truth conditions associated with inclusive-*or* in (perhaps all) human languages.

3 Disjunction in human languages: A parameter

You may be wondering why we didn't derive the universal principle using simple negative sentences such as *Max didn't eat sushi or pasta*, with negation and disjunction in the same clause. After all, this sentence also licenses a conjunctive entailment that Max didn't eat sushi *and* Max didn't eat pasta. The problem is that, if we translate the English into Japanese, Russian, or Chinese, the corresponding sentences do not generate a conjunctive entailment. Example (15) illustrates, in Japanese. Adult speakers of Japanese typically interpret (15) to mean that the pig didn't eat the carrot or didn't eat the pepper. Despite the appearance of the disjunction operator *ka* under local negation in the surface syntax, *ka* is interpreted as if it has scope over negation.

(15) *Butasan-wa ninjin* **ka** *pi'iman-wo tabe-***nakat**-*ta*
 pig-TOP pepper or carrot-ACC eat-NEG-PAST
 Literally: 'The pig didn't eat the pepper or the carrot'
 Meaning: 'The pig didn't eat the pepper *or* the pig didn't eat the carrot'

Pursuing a suggestion by Szabolcsi (2002), Goro (2004) proposed that languages are partitioned into classes by a 'parameter.' According to this parameter, the disjunction operator is a *positive polarity item* (like English *some*) in one class of languages (including Japanese and Russian, among others), but disjunction is not a positive polarity item in another class of languages (including English and German, among others). By definition, a positive polarity item must be interpreted as if it were positioned outside the scope of negation (OR > NEG), rather than in the scope of negation (NEG > OR). The Japanese/Russian setting of the parameter is (OR > NEG), so a paraphrase of (15) would be: *it is a carrot or a pepper that the pig didn't eat*. On this parameter setting, negation does not influence the interpretation of disjunction, so *or* makes a weaker statement than the corresponding statement with *and*. Since *or* and *and* form a scale, with *or* being the weaker term on the scale, the implicature of exclusivity induces Japanese speakers to assume the denial of the stronger term on the scale, resulting in the "not both" reading of *ka* in (15). So Japanese speaking adults interpret (15) to imply that the pig ate either a carrot or a pepper, but not both. On the English/German setting of the parameter (NEG > OR), disjunction is interpreted under negation, so (15) would be paraphrased in English as *the pig didn't eat a carrot or a pepper*. In this case, negation reverses the scale, making *or* stronger than *and*, such that a conjunctive entailment is generated, and no implicature is raised.

Based on considerations of language learnability, Goro (2004) made an intriguing prediction—that young Japanese-speaking children would initially generate a conjunctive entailment in simple negative disjunctive sentences, in contrast to adult speakers of Japanese. The prediction was based on the observation that the two settings of the parameter are in a subset/superset relation. Setting aside the implicature of exclusivity, on the Japanese/Russian setting of the parameter, (15) is (logically) true in three different sets of circumstances: when the pig didn't eat a carrot, but did eat a pepper, when it didn't eat a pepper, but did eat a carrot, and when it didn't eat either one. These are the circumstances associated with the inclusive-*or* interpretation of disjunction when disjunction takes scope over negation (OR > NEG). On the English/German setting of the parameter, negation takes scope over disjunction (NEG > OR). On this setting, (15) is true in just one of set of circumstances, namely ones in which the pig didn't eat either a carrot or a pepper. This parameter setting also invokes the inclusive-*or* interpretation of disjunction. This means that disjunction has the inclusive-*or* interpretation on both settings of the parameter. What changes, according to the setting of the parameter, is the scope relations between disjunction and negation.

Notice that one setting of the parameter (NEG > OR; English/German) makes the statement of (15) true in a subset of the circumstances corresponding to the other setting (OR > NEG; Japanese/Russian). The *semantic subset principle* dictates that, whenever parameter values are in a subset/superset relation, the *language acquisition device* compels children to initially select the subset value (Crain, Ni & Conway 1994). The semantic subset principle anticipates that the subset reading (NEG > OR; English/German) will be children's initial setting (i.e., the default). Based on this line of reasoning, Goro (2004) predicted that children learning Japanese would initially interpret (15) in the same way as English-speaking children and adults. The prediction was confirmed in an experimental investigation of 4- and 5-year-old Japanese-speaking children by Goro & Akiba (2004). They found that young Japanese-speaking children consistently licensed a conjunctive entailment in response to statements like (15). This finding reinforces the conclusion that human languages invoke the inclusive-*or* meaning of disjunction, as in classical logic (Crain, Goro & Thornton 2006).

4 Disjunction and downward entailing expressions

4.1 Disjunction and the universal quantifier

The universal quantifier *every*, and its variants in other languages, are just one of dozens of linguistic expressions that license a conjunctive entailment when disjunction appears in their scope. The group of expressions are known as *downward entailing* operators (again, see article 2 [Semantics: Sentence and Information Structure] (Herburger) *Negation* and article 10 [Semantics: Interfaces] (Chierchia, Fox & Spector) *Grammatical view of scalar implicatures* for background.) An operator is downward entailing if it guarantees the validity of an inference from general statements to more specific statements. The examples in (16) illustrate three expressions that have this defining property of downward entailment, since it is valid to substitute claims about sets (speaking a Romance language) with claims about subsets of the original set (speaking French, speaking Spanish, speaking Italian . . .). Example (16a) shows that the subject phrase of the universal quantifier *every* is downward entailing. Similarly, the antecedent of a conditional statement may be downward entailing, as shown in (16b), and so is the preposition *before*, as illustrated in (16c).

(16) a. Every student who speaks a Romance language likes to travel.
⇒ *every student who speaks French likes to travel*
b. If a student speaks a Romance language, she likes to travel
⇒ *if a student speaks French, she likes to travel*
c. John went to Europe before learning a Romance language.
⇒ *John went to Europe before learning French.*

Another diagnostic of downward entailment is the licensing of certain negative polarity items, such as *ever*, *any* and *at all*. The examples in (17a)–(19a) illustrate that *any* is welcome in the subject phrase (Restrictor) of the universal quantifier *every*, in the antecedent of a conditional statement, and following the preposition *before*. Examples (17b)–(19b) show, however, that *any* is not licensed in the predicate phrase (Nuclear Scope) of the universal quantifier *every*, or in the consequent clause of conditional statements, or following the preposition *after*. Such asymmetries are potentially problematic for language learners.

(17) a. Every linguist who agreed with **any** philosopher is in this room.
b. * Every linguist who is in this room agreed with **any** philosopher.
(18) a. If **any** linguist enters the gym, then Geoff leaves.
b. * If Geoff leaves, then **any** linguist enters the gym.

(19) a. Geoff went to the gym before **any** linguist.
    b. * Geoff went to the gym after **any** linguist.

We have already witnessed another property of downward entailing operators, one that pertains to the interpretation of disjunction. In the scope of a downward entailing operator, disjunction licenses a conjunctive entailment (Boster & Crain 1994; Chierchia 2004; Crain, Gualmini & Pietroski 2005; Crain & Khlentzos 2008). Example (20) shows that *or* generates a conjunctive entailment in the subject phrase (Restrictor) of the universal quantifier *every*; (21) shows that the antecedent of a conditional yields a conjunctive entailment; and (22) shows that a conjunctive entailment is generated by the preposition *before*.

(20) a. Every student who speaks French or Spanish passed the exam.
    b. ⇒ every student who speaks French passed the exam **and**
       every student who speaks Spanish passed the exam

(21) a. If Ted **or** Kyle enters the gym, then Geoff leaves.
    b. ⇒ if Ted enters the gym, then Geoff leaves **and**
       if Kyle enters the gym, then Geoff leaves

(22) a. Geoff went to the gym before Ted **or** Kyle.
    b. ⇒ Geoff went to the gym before Ted **and**
       Geoff went to the gym before Kyle

It is likely that all human languages exhibit the same linguistic behaviour. Example (23) is an example in which the Chinese disjunction operator *huozhe* licenses a conjunctive entailment when it appears in the subject phrase of the universal quantifier *meige*; (24) is the Japanese counterpart to (23).

(23) Meige [hui shuo fayu huozhe xibanyayu de] xuesheng dou
     every can speak French or Spanish DE student DOU
     tongguo-le kaoshi
     pass-Perf exam
     'Every student who speaks French or Spanish passed the exam'

(24) [French *ka* Spanish-wo hanasu] dono gakusei-mo goukakushi-ta
     French or Spanish-ACC speak every student pass-exam-past
     'Every student who speaks French or Spanish passed the exam'

Based on crosslinguistic research, a second linguistic universal can be put forward:

II. Disjunction licenses conjunctive entailments in the scope of downward entailing expressions

By contrast, conjunctive entailments are **not** generated for disjunction when it appears in positions where *any* is not tolerated. To take just one example, a conjunctive entailment is not generated when disjunction is in the predicate phrase of the universal quantifier *every,* as in (25). To see this, notice that (25a) and (25b) are not contradictory, as would be the case if (25a) made a conjunctive entailment. Similarly, there is no conjunctive entailment of *or* when it is in the consequent clause of conditionals, or when it follows the preposition *after.* In all of these linguistic contexts, the disjunction operator *or* carries an implicature of exclusivity.

(25) a. Every student who passed the exam speaks French **or** Spanish.
 b. every student who passed the exam speaks French or Spanish, but no one speaks both languages
 c. * ⇒ every student who passed the exam speaks French **and** every student who passed the exam speaks Spanish

We now turn to the literature on child language. Several studies have investigated the truth conditions children associate with disjunction in the subject phrase and in the predicate phrase of the universal quantifier (e.g., Boster & Crain 1994; Gualmini, Meroni & Crain 2003). Using the Truth Value Judgment task, children were asked to evaluate sentences like those in (26) and (27), produced by a puppet, Kermit the Frog.

(26) Every woman bought eggs or bananas.

(27) Every woman who bought eggs or bananas got a basket.

In one condition, sentences like (26) were presented to children in a context in which some of the women bought eggs, but none of them bought bananas. The child subjects consistently accepted test sentences like (26) in this condition, showing that they assigned a 'disjunctive' interpretation to *or* in the subject phrase of the universal quantifier, *every.* In a second condition, children were presented with sentences like (27) in a context in which women who bought eggs received a basket, but not women who bought bananas. The child subjects consistently rejected the test sentences in this condition. This finding is taken as evidence that children generated a conjunctive entailment for disjunction in the subject phrase of *every.* This asymmetry in children's responses in the two conditions demonstrates their knowledge of the asymmetry in the two grammatical structures associated with the universal quantifier—the subject phrase and the predicate phrase. Taken together, the findings are compelling evidence that children know that the subject phrase of *every* is downward entailing, but not its predicate phrase. In addition, the findings are consistent with the analysis of disjunction according to which (a) disjunction has a basic meaning of inclusive-or, and receives a 'derived' meaning due to a scalar implicature of exclusivity. The findings represent a challenge to the experience-dependent approach to language acquisition. It is conceivable that children could master the facts about the distribution of negative polarity items, such as *any*, based on statistical properties of the input. Even so, children would need to be exceedingly careful record keepers to demarcate the linguistic environments that license such items, to avoid producing them in illicit environments.

A greater challenge is posed by the asymmetry in the interpretation of disjunction *or* in the subject phrase (Restrictor) versus the predicate phrase (Nuclear Scope) of the universal quantifier, since the distinction is one of interpretation, not the distribution, of lexical items (see Chierchia 2004). The problem of record keeping is further escalated in more complex sentences, such as negated universals. Under negation, the interpretations of disjunction in the two arguments of the universal quantifier are reversed, such that *or* yields a conjunctive interpretation in the predicate phrase of *every*, but not in subject phrase. This is a straightforward consequence of the meanings of the relevant logical expressions in first order logic. Again, these facts about the interpretation of sentences with such combinations of logical words (negation, the universal quantifier, and disjunction) are manifested in typologically different languages, such as English, Japanese, and Chinese. To illustrate, examples (20), (23) and (24) were used as evidence that disjunction licences a conjunctive entailment, across languages, when it appears in the subject phrase of a universal quantifier, as for example, in (20) *Every student who speaks French or Spanish passed the exam*. However, when (20) is negated, the conjunctive entailment is no longer licensed, so *Not every student who speaks French or Spanish passed the exam* does not entail that (a) not every student who speaks French passed the exam *and* (b) not every student who speaks Spanish passed the exam. We also saw that disjunction fails to licence a conjunctive entailment when it appears in the predicate phrase of a universal quantifier, as in example (25) *Every student who passed the exam speaks French or Spanish*. Under negation, however, disjunction does generate a conjunctive entailment, so *Not every student who passed the exam speaks French or Spanish* means that some student passed the exam but does not speak either French or Spanish (i.e., the student does not speak French *and* does not speak Spanish). These reversals of entailments follow straightforwardly from first order logic (see Crain & Khlentzos 2008; Crain, Thornton & Khlentzos 2009). They also make the point that the semantic contribution of logical words depends on the linguistic environment; they did not exhibit stable discourse or communicative functions. Unless human children are innately endowed with knowledge about the meanings of logical words, they would have to be excellent record-keepers indeed to master such complex linguistic facts. The next section illustrates another linguistic phenomenon in which the meaning of disjunction is not readily apparent in the input children experience.

4.2 Disjunction in the scope of "only"

Further confirmation that natural language disjunction is inclusive-*or* comes from studies of how speakers of English, Japanese, and Chinese interpret disjunction in sentences with certain focus operators: English *only*, Japanese *dake*; Chinese *zhiyou*. The semantic contribution of such focus operators is quite complex. Consider the statement: *Only Bunny Rabbit ate a carrot or a pepper*. This statement expresses two propositions. Following common parlance, one proposition is called the *presupposition* and the other is called the *assertion* (e.g., Horn 1969; 1996). The presupposition is derived simply by deleting the focus expression from the original sentence; this yields *Bunny Rabbit ate a carrot or a pepper*. For many speakers, there is an implicature of exclusivity ('not both') in the presupposition. The second proposition is the assertion. The assertion concerns individuals that are not mentioned in the sentence. To derive the assertion, the sentence can be further partitioned into (a) a *focus element* and (b) a *contrast set*. Focus expressions such as *only* are typically associated with a particular linguistic expression somewhere in the sentence. This is the focus element. More often than not, the focus element receives phonological stress. In the sentence *Only Bunny Rabbit ate a carrot or a pepper*, the focus element is *Bunny Rabbit*.

The assertion is about a contrast set. The members of the set are individuals in the domain of discourse that are taken by the speaker and hearer to be alternatives to the focus element. These individuals should be available in the conversational context before the sentence was produced; their existence is presupposed. In the present example, the contrast set consists of individuals being contrasted with *Bunny Rabbit*. The sentence would not be felicitous in the absence of this contrast set. The assertion states that the members of the contrast set *lack* the property being attributed to the focus element. In *Only Bunny Rabbit ate a carrot or a pepper*, the assertion is the following claim: *everyone else (being contrasted with Bunny Rabbit) did not eat a carrot or a pepper*. The critical point is that the assertion contains disjunction in the scope of a (local) downward entailing operator, e.g., negation or its semantic equivalent. Because disjunction appears under a downward entailing operator in the assertion, a conjunctive entailment is licensed: *everyone else (being contrasted with Bunny Rabbit) didn't eat a carrot and they didn't eat a pepper*. Japanese sentences with the focus expression *dake* are analysed in the same way, as in (28).

(28) Only Bunny Rabbit ate a carrot or a pepper.
　　　Usagichan-dake-ga ninjin ka piiman-wo taberu-yo.
　　　rabbit-*only*-NOM　carrot*or* green pepper-ACC eat-dec
　　a. *Presupposition*:　Bunny Rabbit ate a carrot or a pepper
　　b. *Assertion*:　　　 Everyone else (being contrasted with Bunny Rabbit) did not eat a carrot or a pepper

The interpretation of *or* by English- and Japanese-speaking children was used to assess their knowledge of the semantics of *only* in a series of experiments by Goro, Minai & Crain (2005, 2006). In one experiment, twenty-one English-speaking children (mean age = 5;0) and twenty Japanese-speaking children (mean age = 5;4) participated. To see if children assign 'disjunctive' truth conditions to *or* in the presupposition of sentences with *only/dake*, the test sentences were presented in a situation in which Bunny Rabbit ate a carrot but not a pepper. The other characters in the story, Winnie the Pooh and Cookie Monster, did not eat a carrot or a pepper. The truth conditions are summarized in (29).

(29) *Condition I*

	Carrot	Pepper
Winnie the Pooh	*	*
Bunny Rabbit	√	*
Cookie Monster	*	*

To see if children generate a conjunctive entailment in the assertion of sentences with *only/dake*, the test sentences were presented (to different children) in the situation represented in (30). As in Condition I, Bunny Rabbit ate a carrot but not a pepper. But in Condition II, Cookie Monster ate a pepper. Because "only" is downward entailing in the assertion, the sentence in (28) is expected to generate a conjunctive entailment—that everyone else (being contrasted with Bunny Rabbit) did not eat a carrot *and* did not eat a pepper. Therefore, children were expected to reject the test sentences Condition II, on the grounds that Cookie Monster ate a pepper.

(30) *Condition II*

	Carrot	Green pepper
Winnie the Pooh	*	*
Bunny Rabbit	√	*
Cookie Monster	*	√

Children responded exactly as predicted. In Condition I, both English-speaking children and Japanese-speaking children accepted the test sentences over 90% of the time. The high acceptance rate in Condition I suggests that children assigned disjunctive (*not both*) truth conditions to *or* in the presupposition. In contrast, the same children rejected the test sentences in Condition II over 90% of the time. (Adult controls accepted Condition I sentences 100% of the time and rejected Condition II sentences 100% of the time in both languages.) The high rejection rate by children in Condition II suggests that they know that the disjunction operator *or* creates conjunctive entailments in the assertion of sentences with *only/ dake*. The findings invite the inference that children have adult-like knowledge about the semantics of *only/dake*, and are able to compute its complex semantic interaction with disjunction. Similar experiments have been conducted with Chinese-speaking children, with the same pattern of results (Jing, Crain & Hsu 2006).

It is likely that sentences with disjunction in the scope of certain focus expressions generate conjunctive entailments in all natural languages, so we can advance a third linguistic universal:

III. Disjunction generates a conjunctive entailment in the assertion of certain focus expressions

Here is an example from Chinese, where the focus expressions is *zhiyou* and the disjunction operator is *huozhe*. Example (31) entails that everyone else (being contrasted with John) does not speak French and does not speak Spanish.

(31) zhiyou Yuanhan hui shuo fayu huozhe xibanyayu
      only   John   can speak French or   Spanish

Recall that in Japanese and Chinese the translation of a simple negative statement with disjunction (e.g., *Max didn't order sushi or pasta*) does not generate a conjunctive entailment (see section 2.4). Rather, adult speakers of these languages judge the corresponding sentences to mean that Ted didn't order sushi *or* Ted didn't order pasta. The same is true for the sentences that constitute the assertion in (28). Example (28) is *Only Bunny Rabbit ate a carrot or a green pepper*. The corresponding assertion is *Everyone else did not eat a carrot or a green pepper*. However, if adult speakers of Chinese or Japanese overtly produce sentences corresponding to the English sentence *Everyone else did not eat a carrot or a green pepper*, these sentences do not have the same meaning as the English sentence. In contrast to the English sentence, the corresponding Japanese sentence (32) and the Chinese sentence (33) do not generate a conjunctive entailment, because these are simple negative statements, with disjunction and negation in the same clause (see section 3). The sentences (32)–(33) mean that everyone else didn't eat a carrot *or* didn't eat a green pepper.

(32) Japanese:
Usagichani gai-no   zen'in-ga   ninjin ka piiman-wo tabe-nakat-ta.
Rabbit   except-GEN everyone-NOM carrot or pepper-ACC eat-NEG-PAST
'Everyone except Bunny Rabbit didn't eat a carrot OR didn't eat a green pepper'

(33) Chinese:
Chule tuzi zhiwai de suoyou dongwu dou meiyou chi huluobo huozhe qingjiao.
Except   rabbit DE every animal   all   not   eat carrot   or   pepper
'Everyone except Bunny Rabbit didn't eat a carrot OR didn't eat a green pepper'

The 'disjunctive' interpretation of (32)–(33) may seem paradoxical because, as we saw, the assertion associated with (28) generates a conjunctive entailment in Japanese and Chinese, just as it does in English. In all three languages, the assertion is the proposition that everybody else did not eat a carrot *and* everybody else did not eat a green pepper. But, making the assertion overt changes its meaning in Chinese and Japanese, cancelling the conjunctive interpretation of disjunction. Consequently, adult speakers of Chinese and Japanese are hard-pressed to overtly instruct children about the meaning of the assertion component of sentences with focus expressions. It also follows from this that evidence for the interpretation of disjunction as inclusive-*or* is even harder to come by for Chinese-speaking children and Japanese-speaking children, as compared to English-speaking children. For English-speaking children, the fact that disjunction generates a conjunctive interpretation under local negation could be used as evidence that disjunction is inclusive-*or*, although negative statements with disjunction are rare in adult speech to children (Crain & Khlentzos 2008). It is striking, therefore, that Japanese-speaking children (and adults) generate a conjunctive entailment for disjunction in the assertion of sentences with *dake*, and Chinese-speaking children (and adults) generate a conjunctive entailment for disjunction in the assertion of sentences with *zhiyou*. The findings from studies of Japanese-speaking children further reinforce the conclusion that disjunction is innately specified as inclusive-*or*. In fact, there is no evidence of an effect of input on the acquisition of disjunction in any language, at any age. Experience-dependent accounts of language acquisition (e.g., Ambridge & Lieven 2011; Goldberg 2003, 2006; Tomasello 2000, 2003) owe us an explanation of this uniformity across languages. Such accounts also owe us an explanation of how the dual interpretations of disjunction arise in sentences with the focus operators like *only/dake/zhiyou*.

5 Loose ends and conclusions

There are two loose ends to tie up. In describing the relation between negation and disjunction, the term "scope" has been used rather loosely. Scope is a structural property that cuts across all of the phenomena we have been discussing. In human languages, scope is defined as c-command. (An expression A c-commands an expression B in a phrase structure diagram if there is a path that extends above A to the first branching node, and then proceeds down to B.) In order for disjunctive statements to license conjunctive entailments, disjunction must appear in the scope (c-command domain) of a 'nearby' downward entailing operator. And in order to license negative polarity items, the downward entailing expression must c-command the position where the negative polarity item is introduced. The general idea can be seen by comparing examples like (34) and (35). Disjunction resides in the scope of the negative expression *not* in (34) but in (35) *not* is embedded in a relative clause (... *who did not go to bed*) so negation fails to have scope over disjunction. This difference in structure results in a difference in interpretation. Example (34) generates a conjunctive entailment, but (35) does not.

(34) The girl who stayed up late did *not* get a dime *or* a jewel.

(35) The girl who did *not* go to bed got a dime *or* a jewel.

A study by Gualmini & Crain (2005) investigated 5-year-old English-speaking children's knowledge that c-command is a structural prerequisite for a conjunctive entailment. On one trial in the study, either sentence (34) or (35) was produced by a (wizard) puppet as a description of a story about two girls who had each lost a tooth. One girl went to sleep, but one girl stayed up to see the tooth fairy. The girl who was asleep received both a dime and a jewel from the tooth fairy, but the girl who had stayed awake was only given a jewel. At the end of the story, some children were presented with sentences (34) and others with (35) as descriptions of what had happened in the story. Children accepted sentences like (34) 87% of the time. By contrast, children rejected sentences like (34) 92% of the time, in the same context, on the grounds that the girl who stayed up late had only received a jewel. It is evident that, in the grammars of these children, (34) licenses a conjunctive entailment—the girl who stayed up did not receive a dime *and* did not receive a jewel. Again, this entailment hinges on disjunction being interpreted as inclusive-*or*.

There is one loose end remaining. The findings reported in this chapter invite the conclusion that children know that natural language disjunction is inclusive-*or*, as in classical logic. This may give the impression that human languages and classical logic go hand in hand in Universal Grammar. While a similar case can be made for conjunction, there are clearly cases, such as material implication, where the correspondence between classical logic and human languages breaks down. And this is just one reason for resisting the conclusion that what is innately specified in the mind/brains of language learners is limited to the conceptual apparatus used in logical reasoning. In fact, there are many specific contingent properties of natural language that are likely candidates for innate specification, but which do not correspond to notions from classical logic. Some of these specific contingent properties of human language are used in the linguistic universals we have proposed. According to these universal principles, disjunctive statements license conjunctive entailments in three linguistic contexts: (a) in the scope of non-local negation, (b) in the assertion of certain focus expressions, and (c) in the scope of downward entailing operators. The first of these contexts invokes a distinction between structures in which disjunction and negation appear in the same clause, and ones in which negation appears in a higher clause than disjunction. If it turns out that aspects of sentence structure (including labelled brackets) are needed to explain when implicatures become engaged or disengaged, as Chierchia has recently proposed, then this would introduce machinery from language that has no counterpart in classical logic. And, as we saw, one class of natural languages exhibits an inverse scope interpretation (rather than the surface scope relations) in structures in which disjunction (a positive polarity item) and negation appear in the same clause. There is nothing like such inverse scope relations in classical logic. The second principle contrasts the interpretation of disjunction in the presupposition and in the assertion of a focus expression. These contrasting meaning components have no counterparts in logic, although one part of the meaning clearly invokes notions from classical logic. Finally, the third principle maintains that the conjunctive entailment of disjunction is licensed by a host of linguistic expressions, namely ones that are downward entailing, and does not arise simply with negation, as in De Morgan's laws. There are no counterparts in logic to many of these downward entailing expressions. There is more to human languages than logic, though logic plays a major role, as we have tried to demonstrate.

6 References

Ambridge, Ben & Elena V. M. Lieven 2011. *Child Language Acquisition: Contrasting Theoretical Approaches*. Cambridge: Cambridge University Press.

Bloom, Lois 1970. *Language Development: Form and Function in Emerging Grammars*. Cambridge, MA: The MIT Press.

Bloom, Paul 2000. *How Children Learn the Meaning of Words*. Cambridge, MA: The MIT Press.

Bloom, Lois, Karin Lifter & Jeremie Hafitz 1980. Semantics of verbs and the development of verb inflection in child language. *Language* 56, 386–412.

Boster, Carole & Stephen Crain 1994. The interaction of *every* and *or* in child language. In: *Proceedings of the Conference on Early Cognition and the Transition to Language*. Austin, TX: University of Texas.

Braine, Martin D.S. & Barbara Rumain 1981. Development of comprehension of "or": Evidence for a sequence of competencies. *Journal of Experimental Child Psychology* 31, 46–70.

Braine, Martin D. S. & Barbara Rumain 1983. Logical reasoning. In: J. Flavell & E. Markman (eds.). *Handbook of Child Psychology, vol. 3: Cognitive Development*. New York: Academic Press, 261–340.

Chierchia, Gennaro 2004. Scalar implicatures, polarity phenomena, and the syntax/pragmatics interface. In: A. Belletti & L. Rizzi (eds.). *Structures and Beyond*. Oxford: Oxford University Press, 39–103.

Chierchia, Gennaro, Stephen Craine, Maria Teresa Guasti & Rosalind Thornton 1998. "Some" and "or": A study of the emergence of Logical Form. In: A. Greenhill et al. (eds.). *Proceedings of the 22th Annual Boston University Conference on Language Development (= BUCLD)*. Somerville, MA: Cascadilla Press, 97–108.

Chierchia, Gennaro, Maria Teresa Guasti, Andrea Gualmini, Luisa Meroni & Stephen Crain 2004. Semantic and pragmatic competence in children and adult's interpretation of 'or'. In: I. Noveck & S. Wilson (eds.). *Experimental Pragmatics*. London: Palgrave Macmillan, 283–300.

Chierchia, Gennaro, Stephen Crain, Maria Teresa Guasti, Andrea Gualmini & Luisa Meroni 2001. The acquisition of disjunction: Evidence for a grammatical view of scalar implicatures. In: A. H.-J. Do, L. Domínguez & A. Johansen (eds.). *Proceedings of the 25th Annual Boston University Conference on Language Development (= BUCLD)*. Somerville, MA: Cascadilla Press, 157–168.

Chomsky, Noam 1965. *Aspects of the Theory of Syntax*. Cambridge, MA: The MIT Press.
Chomsky, Noam 1975. *Reflections on Language*. New York: Pantheon Books.
Chomsky, Noam 1986. *Knowledge of Language: Its Nature, Origin and Use*. New York: Praeger.
Clark, Graham 2003. *Recursion Through Dictionary Definition Space: Concrete Versus Abstract Words*. Ms.
Cowie, Fiona 1999. *What's Within?: Nativism Reconsidered*. New York: Oxford University Press.
Crain, Stephen 1991. Language acquisition in the absence of experience. *Behavioral and Brain Sciences* 4, 597–650.
Crain, Stephen 2002. The continuity assumption. In: I. Lasser (ed.) *The Process of Language Acquisition*. Frankfurt: Peter Lang.
Crain, Stephen 2008. The interpretation of disjunction in Universal Grammar. *Language and Speech* 51, 151–169.
Crain, Stephen & Drew Khlentzos 2008. Is logic innate? *Biolinguistics* 2, 24–56.
Crain, Stephen & Paul Pietroski 2001. Nature, nurture and Universal Grammar. *Linguistics & Philosophy* 24, 139–186.
Crain, Stephen & Paul Pietroski 2002. Why language acquisition is a snap. *Linguistic Review* 19, 163–183.
Crain, Stephen & Rosalind Thornton 1998. *Investigations in Universal Grammar: A Guide to Experiments in the Acquisition of Syntax and Semantics*. Cambridge, MA: The MIT Press.
Crain, Stephen, Takuya Goro & Utako Minai 2007. Hidden units in child language. In: A. Schalley & D. Khlentzos (eds.). *Mental States: Nature, Function and Evolution*. Amsterdam: Benjamins, 275–294.
Crain, Stephen, Takuya Goro & Rosalind Thornton 2006. Language acquisition is language change. *Journal of Psycholinguistic Research* 35, 31–49.
Crain, Stephen, Andrea Gualmini & Paul Pietroski 2005. Brass tacks in linguistic theory: Innate grammatical principles. In: P. Carruthers, S. Laurence & S. Stich (eds.). *The Innate Mind: Structure and Content*. Oxford: Oxford University Press, 175–197.
Crain, Stephen, Weijia Ni & Laura Conway 1994. Learning, parsing, and modularity. In: C. Clifton, L. Frazier & K. Rayner (eds.). *Perspectives on Sentence Processing*. Hillsdale, NJ: Lawrence Erlbaum Associates, 443–467.
Crain, Stephen, Rosalind Thornton, Carole Boster, Laura Conway, Diane Lillo-Martin & Elaine Woodams 1996. Quantification without qualification. *Language Acquisition* 5, 83–153.
Crain, Stephen, Rosalind Thornton & Drew Khlentzos 2009. The case of the missing generalizations. *Cognitive Linguistics* 20, 145–155.
Crain, Stephen, Amanda Gardner, Andrea Gualmini & Beth Rabbin 2002. Children's command of negation. In: Y. Otsu (ed.). *Proceedings of the Third Tokyo Conference on Psycholinguistics*. Tokyo: Hituzi, 71–95.
Dehaene, Stanislas 1997. *The Number Sense: How the Mind Creates Mathematics*. Oxford: Oxford University Press.
Déprez, Viviane & Amy Pierce 1993. Negation and functional projections in early grammar. *Linguistic Inquiry* 24, 25–67.
Dromi, Esther 1987. *Early Lexical Development*. Cambridge: Cambridge University Press.
Drozd, Ken 1995. Child English pre-sentential negation as metalinguistic exclamatory negation. *Journal of Child Language* 22, 583–610.
Drozd, Ken 2006 (ed.). *The Acquisition of Quantification*. Special Issue of *Language Acquisition* 13(3–4).

Gentner, Dedre 1982. Why nouns are learned before verbs: Linguistic relativity versus natural partitioning. In: S. A. Kuczaj (ed.). *Language Development: Language, Thought, and Culture, vol.* 2. Hillsdale, NJ: Lawrence Erlbaum Associates, 301–334.

Gentner, Dedre & Lera Boroditsky 2001. Individuation, relational relativity and early word learning. In: M. Bowerman & S. Levinson (eds.). *Language Acquisition and Conceptual Development.* Cambridge: Cambridge University Press, 215–256.

Geurts, Bart 2003. Quantifying kids. *Language Acquisition* 11, 197–218.

Gleitman, Lila 1990. Structural sources of verb learning. *Language Acquisition* 1, 1–63.

Goldberg, Adele E. 2003. Constructions: A new theoretical approach to language. *Trends in Cognitive Science* 7, 219–224.

Goldberg, Adele E. 2006. *Constructions at Work: The Nature of Generalization in Language.* Oxford: Oxford University Press.

Gordon, Peter 1996. The truth-value judgment task. In: D. McDaniel, C. McKee & H.S. Carins (eds.). *Methods for Assessing Children's Syntax.* Cambridge, MA: The MIT Press, 211–231.

Goro, Takuya 2004. *The Emergence of Universal Grammar in the Emergence of Language: The Acquisition of Japanese Logical Connectives and Positive Polarity.* Ms. College Park, MD, University of Maryland.

Goro, Takuya & Sachie Akiba 2004. The acquisition of disjunction and positive polarity in Japanese. In: V. Chand et al. (eds.). *Proceedings of the 23rd West Coast Conference on Formal Linguistics (= WCCFL).* Somerville, MA: Cascadilla Press, 251–264.

Goro, Takuya, Utako Minai & Stephen Crain 2005. Two disjunctions for the price of *only* one. In: A. Brugos, M. R. Clark-Cotton & S. Ha (eds.). *Proceedings of the 29th Annual Boston University Conference on Language Development (= BUCLD).* Somerville, MA: Cascadilla Press, 228–239.

Goro, Takuya, Utako Minai & Stephen Crain 2006. Bringing out the logic in child language. In: L. Bateman & C. Ussery (eds.). *Proceedings of North Eastern Linguistic Society (= NELS) 35, vol 1.* Amherst, MA: GLSA, 245–256.

Grice, H. Paul 1975. Logic and conversation. In: P. Cole & J. L. Morgan (eds). *Syntax and Semantics 3: Speech Acts.* New York: Academic Press, 41–58.

Gualmini, Andrea & Stephen Crain 2002. Why no child or adult must learn De Morgan's laws. In: B. Skarabela, S. Fisch & A. H.-J. Do (eds.). *Proceedings of the 26th Annual Boston University Conference on Language Development (= BUCLD).* Somerville, MA: Cascadilla Press, 367–378.

Gualmini, Andrea & Stephen Crain 2004. Operator conditioning. In: A. Brugos, L. Micciulla & C.E. Smith (eds.). *Proceedings of the 28th Annual Boston University Conference on Language Development (= BUCLD).* Somerville, MA: Cascadilla Press, 232–243.

Gualmini, Andrea & Stephen Crain 2005. The structure of children's linguistic knowledge. *Linguistic Inquiry* 36, 463–474.

Gualmini, Andrea, Luisa Meroni & Stephen Crain 2003. An asymmetric universal in child language. In: M. Weisgerber (ed.). *Proceedings of Sinn und Bedeutung (= SuB) 7.* Konstanz: University of Konstanz, 136–148.

Gualmini, Andrea, Stephen Crain, Luisa Meroni, Gennaro Chierchia & Maria Teresa Guasti 2001. At the semantics/pragmatics interface in child language. In: R. Hastings, B. Jackson & Z. Zvolenskzky (eds.). *Proceedings of Semantics and Linguistic Theory (= SALT) XI.* Ithaca, NY: Cornell University, 231–247.

Guasti, Maria Teresa 2002. *Language Acquisition: The Growth of Grammar.* Cambridge, MA: The MIT Press.

Guasti, Maria Teresa, Gennaro Chierchia, Stephen Crain, Andrea Gualmini & Luisa Meroni 2002. Children's semantic and pragmatic competence in interaction, In: *Proceedings of Generative Approaches to Language Acquisition (= GALA)*. Lisbon: Associação Portuguesa de Linguística, xiii–xviii.

Guasti, Maria Teresa, Gennaro Chierchia, Stephen Crain, Francesca Foppolo, Andrea Gualmini & Luisa Meroni 2005. Why children and adults sometimes (but not always) compute implicatures. *Language and Cognitive Processes* 20, 667–696.

Harris, Tony & Ken Wexler 1996. The optional-infinitive stage in child English: Evidence from negation. In: H. Clahsen (ed.). *Generative Perspectives on Language Acquisition*. Amsterdam: Benjamins, 1–42.

Horn, Laurence 1969. A presuppositional approach to *only* and *even*. In: R. Binnick et al. (eds.). *Papers form the Fifth Regional Meeting of the Chicago Linguistic Society (= CLS)*. Chicago, IL: Chicago Linguistic Society, 98–107.

Horn, Laurence 1996. Presupposition and implicature. In: S. Lappin (ed.). *Handbook of Contemporary Semantic Theory*. Oxford: Blackwell, 299–319.

Huttenlocher, Janellen & Patricia Smiley 1987. Early word meanings: The case of object names. *Cognitive Psychology* 19, 63–89.

Inhelder, Bärbel & Jean Piaget 1964. *The Early Growth of Logic in the Child*. London: Routledge & Kegan Paul.

Jing, Chunyuan, Stephen Crain & Ching-Fen Hsu 2006. The interpretation of focus in Chinese: Child vs. adult language. In: Y. Otsu (ed.). *Proceedings of the Sixth Tokyo Conference on Psycholinguistics*. Tokyo: Hituzi, 165–190.

Klima, Edward S. & Ursula Bellugi 1966. Syntactic regularities in the speech of children. In: J. Lyons & R. Wales (eds.). *Psycholinguistic Papers*. Edinburgh: Edinburgh University Press, 183–208.

Marcus, Gary F. 1998. Rethinking eliminative connectionism. *Cognitive Psychology* 37, 243–282.

Marcus, Gary F. 1999. Language acquisition in the absence of explicit negative evidence: Can simple recurrent networks obviate the need for domain-specific learning devices? *Cognition* 73, 293–296.

Markman, Ellen M. 1989. *Categorization and Naming in Children: Problems of Induction*. Cambridge, MA: The MIT Press.

Naigles, Letitia 1998. Children use syntax to learn verb meaning. *Journal of Child Language* 17, 357–374.

Nelson, Katherine 1973. *Structure and Strategy in Learning to Talk*. Chicago, IL: The University of Chicago Press.

Notley, Anna, Peng Zhou, Stephen Crain & Rosalind Thornton 2009. Children's interpretation of focus expressions in English and Mandarin. *Language Acquisition* 16, 240–282.

Noveck, Ira 2001. When children are more logical than adults: Investigations of scalar implicature. *Cognition* 78, 165–188.

O'Leary, Carrie & Stephen Crain. 1994. Negative Polarity (a positive result) and Positive Polarity (a negative result). Paper presented at the *18th Annual Boston University Conference on Language Development (= BUCLD)*, Boston University, Boston, MA.

Papafragou, Anna & Julien Musolino 2003. Scalar implicatures: Experiments at the semantics-pragmatics interface. *Cognition* 86, 253–282.

Paterson, Kevin B., Simon P. Liversedge, Caroline Rowland & Ruth Filik 2003. Children's comprehension of sentences with focus particles. *Cognition* 89, 263–294.

Philip, William 1995. *Event Quantification in the Acquisition of Universal Quantification*. Ph.D. dissertation. University of Massachusetts, Amherst, MA.
Pinker, Steven 1990. Language acquisition. In: D. N. Osherson & H. Lasnik (eds.). *An Invitation to Cognitive Science, vol. 1*. Cambridge, MA: The MIT Press, 107–133.
Pullum, Geoffrey K. & Barbara C. Scholz 2002. Empirical assessment of the stimulus poverty argument. *Linguistic Review* 19, 9–50.
Read, Charles & Peter Schreiber 1982. Why short subjects are harder to find than long ones. In: E. Wanner & L. Gleitman (eds.). *Language Acquisition: The State of the Art*. Cambridge: Cambridge University Press, 78–101.
Reinhart, Tanya 2006. *Interface Strategies: Optimal and Costly Computations*. Cambridge, MA: The MIT Press.
Rumelhart, David E. & James L. McClelland 1986. On learning the past tenses of English verbs. In: J. L. McClelland, D. E. Rumelhart & the PDP Research Group (eds.). *Parallel Distributed Processing: Explorations in the Microstructure of Cognition, vol. 2: Psychological and Biological Models*. Cambridge, MA: The MIT Press.
Saffran, Jenny R., Richard N. Aslin & Elissa L. Newport 1996. Statistical learning by 8-month-old infants. *Science* 274, 1926–1928.
Shi, Rushen & Janet F. Werker 2001. Six-month-old infants' preference for lexical over grammatical words. *Psychological Science* 12, 70–75.
Shirai, Yasuhiro & Roger Andersen 1995. The acquisition of tense-aspect morphology: A prototype account. *Language* 71, 743–762.
Smith, Neilson V. 1996. Structural eccentricities. *Glot International* 2, 7–8.
Smith, Neilson V. & Ianthi-Maria Tsimpli 1995. *The Mind of a Savant: Language Learning and Modularity*. Oxford: Blackwell.
Stromswold, Karin J. & Kai Zimmermann 2000. Acquisition of *nein* and *nicht* and the VP-internal subject stage in German. *Language Acquisition* 8, 101–127.
Szabolcsi, Anna 2002. Hungarian disjunctions and positive polarity. In: I. Kenesei & P. Siptar (eds.). *Approaches to Hungarian, vol. 8*. Budapest: Akademiai Kiado, 217–241.
Tardif, Twila, Susan A. Gelman & Fan Xu 1999. Putting the "noun bias" in context: A comparison of Mandarin and English. *Child Development* 70, 620–635.
Thornton, Rosalind 1995. Children's negative questions: A production/comprehension asymmetry. In: J. Fuller, H. Han & D. Parkinson (eds.). *Proceedings of Eastern States Conference on Linguistics*. Ithaca, NY: CLC Publications, 306–317.
Thornton, Rosalind & Graciela Tesan 2007. Categorial acquisition: Parameter setting in Universal Grammar. *Biolinguistics* 1, 49–98.
Tomasello, Michael 2000. First steps toward a usage-based theory of language acquisition. *Cognitive Linguistics* 11, 61–82.
Tomasello, Michael 2003. *Constructing a Language: A Usage-based Theory of Language Acquisition*. Cambridge, MA: Harvard University Press.
de Villiers, Peter A. & Jill G. de Villiers 1979. Form and function in the development of sentence negation. *Papers and Reports on Child Language Development, vol. 17*. Stanford, CA: Department of Linguistics, 56–64.
van Hout, Angeliek 1998. On the role of direct objects and particles in learning telicity in Dutch and English. In: A. Greenhill et al. (eds.). *Proceedings of 22th Boston University Conference on Language Development (= BUCLD)*. Somerville, MA: Cascadilla Press, 397–408.
van Hout, Angeliek 2003. Acquiring telicity cross-lingustically: On the acquisition of telicity entailments associated with transitivity. In: M. Bowerman & P. Brown (eds.). *Crosslinguistic*

Perspectives on Argument Structure: Implications for Learnability. Hillsdale, NJ: Lawrence Erlbaum Associates.

van Hout, Angeliek 2004. Unaccusitivity as telicity checking. In: A. Alexiadou, E. Anagnostopoulou & M. Everaert (eds.). *The Unaccusativity Puzzle. Explorations at the Syntax-Lexicon Interface*. Oxford: Oxford University Press, 60–83.

van der Wal, Sjoukje 1996. *Negative Polarity Items and Negation: Tandem Acquisition*. Wageningen: Grodil.

Wagner, Laura & Susan Carey 2003. Individuation of objects and events: A developmental study. *Cognition* 90, 163–191.

Zhou, Peng & Stephen Crain 2009. Scope assignment in child language: Evidence from the acquisition of Chinese. *Lingua* 19, 973–988.

Zhou, Peng & Stephen Crain 2010. Focus identification in child Mandarin. *Journal of Child Language* 37, 965–1005.

Roumyana Slabakova
10 Meaning in second language acquisition

1 Introduction —— 274
2 Important recent theories of L2A —— 276
3 Assumptions about language architecture and predictions based on them —— 280
4 Two learning situations in the L2A of semantics —— 282
5 Implications and conclusions —— 295
6 References —— 298

Abstract: The article identifies the critical period issue as the fundamental research-generating question in second language acquisition (L2A) theory: namely, is there a critical period after which acquisition of a second language becomes impossible. Recent theoretical answers to this question are presented. A modular view of language architecture suggests that there may be different critical periods for different modules of the grammar and L2A of meaning involves acquiring interpretive mismatches at the L1-L2 syntax-semantics interfaces. In acquiring meaning, learners face two types of learning situations. One situation where the sentence syntax presents less difficulty but different pieces of functional morphology subsume different primitives of meaning is dubbed Simple Syntax—Complex Semantics. Another type of learning situation is exemplified in less frequent, dispreferred or syntactically complex sentences where the sentential semantics offers no mismatch; these are labeled Complex Syntax—Simple Semantics. Two studies representative of these learning situations are reviewed. A third study attests to the superfluousness of explicit instruction with respect to some interpretive properties. Implications of these findings for the critical period issue are discussed. The three representative studies reviewed here and numerous other studies on the L2A of meaning point to no visible barrier to ultimate success in the acquisition of phrasal semantics.

1 Introduction

The outcome of first language acquisition (L1A) is a uniform success: at about five or six years of age, normally developed children fully acquire the grammar of the language that surrounds them (see article 10 [this volume] (Crain) *Meaning in*

Roumyana Slabakova, Iowa City, IA, USA

https://doi.org/10.1515/9783110589825-010

first language acquisition). Adult second language acquisition (L2A), on the other hand, results in varying degrees of success. Failure to acquire the target language grammar is not atypical. This well-known contrast has been amply documented (e.g., Johnson & Newport 1989; Sorace 1993, among many others). Striving to explain this difference in ultimate attainment has been rightfully promoted to the forefront of L2A research and has engendered much debate.

The contrast in ultimate attainment has mostly been associated with age. The Critical Period Hypothesis (CPH) (Penfield & Roberts 1959; Lenneberg 1967) gives a reasonable explanation for the facts of L1 and L2 acquisition. In its most succinct formulation, it states that there is a limited developmental period during which it is possible to learn new languages to normal, native-like levels. Once this window of opportunity has closed, however, the ability to acquire language declines (for some surveys, see Hyltenstam & Abrahamsson 2003; DeKeyser & Larsen-Hall 2005; Birdsong 2005).

It is also relatively well established that failure to engage the "language acquisition device" in children through exposure to meaningful input (due to deprivation or isolation) results in severe linguistic deficits that cannot be overcome by subsequent exposure to language. Cumulatively, these data point to the conclusion that the human brain is particularly adapted for language acquisition during an early period of life and, if this window is not utilized, slight to severe divergence from native norm ensues.

However, as Lenneberg (1967: 176) himself acknowledges, it is not entirely obvious how the CPH relates to L2A, since L2 acquirers already have a native language and the language centers in the brain have been activated in the opportune window. Thus in L2A, it is probably more appropriate to consider age-related effects rather than a critical cut-off point, past which it is impossible to achieve native-like proficiency (see Birdsong 2005 for many explicit arguments in favor of this idea).

The age variable examined in L2A studies is usually the age of first exposure to the L2 (or age of acquisition, AoA). In studies of immigrant populations, this is typically indexed by the learner's age of arrival in the host country. Nowadays, researchers of the CP within L2A fall roughly into two camps: those arguing for the "robustness" of CP effects (DeKeyser 2000; Johnson & Newport 1989; McDonald 2000; Newport 1990) and those who claim that there is no real cut-off point for language acquisition abilities but there are age effects that persist throughout life (Birdsong 2005; Birdsong & Molis 2001; Flege 1999; Hakuta, Bialystok & Wiley 2003).

Another important idea has gained a lot of support recently: there is not just one but multiple critical periods for language acquisition. More specifically, there are differential age-related effects for different parts of grammatical competence.

For example, Eubank & Gregg (1999) proposes that critical or sensitive periods affect various areas of linguistic knowledge differently (i.e., phonology, syntax, lexicon, etc.) and even subcomponents of these modules (e.g., lexical items, inflections, syntactic effects of abstract features). Lee & Schachter (1997) suggests that principles of UG (e.g., binding, subjacency) and parameters have different age-related cut-off points for successful triggering and acquisition. Proposals of this type can be unified under the label Multiple CPH.

In recent years, L2 researchers' efforts have turned to isolating precisely which linguistic modules, submodules, features, or interface areas are affected, how, and why (see more on this in section 2). This chapter addresses the Multiple CPH by promoting the positive side of the argument (in terms of possibility of acquisition). It will demonstrate not what parts of the grammar *are* subject to age-related effects but what is *not* subject to such effects. It is a very common assumption, articulated in, for example, Paradis (2004: 119) that among the language modules are phonology, morphosyntax, and semantics. Semantics should be viewed as comprising two types of linguistic operations on two levels: lexical semantics and phrasal semantics (Jackendoff 2002, among others). The focus here is on acquisition of phrasal semantics, which, similar to the acquisition of the more subtle syntactic properties that purportedly come from UG, does not present insurmountable difficulty to the L2 learner. Behavioral studies of learners of all levels of proficiency support this view. Based on learners' success in acquiring interpretive properties, I argue that there is no critical period for acquisition of phrasal semantics. In order to present a comprehensive picture of L2A, acquisition of semantic properties are compared and contrasted to acquisition of morpho-syntactic properties. The Bottleneck Hypothesis brings these findings together and argues that in certain areas of the grammar, namely, functional morphology, learners can expect to encounter enhanced difficulty, in comparison to other areas such as syntax and phrasal semantics, where they can expect to sail (relatively) free. Lexical entries in the functional lexicon are shown to be *the* bottleneck of L2A, and once their properties are acquired, comprehension of meaning obtains without setbacks.

2 Important recent theories of L2A

An important division in recent accounts of L2A derives from the nature of linguistic properties being acquired, which cuts across modules. Researchers distinguish between acquisition of UG *principles*, purportedly active in all languages, and acquisition of *parameters*, points of variation between languages with highly-restricted, theoretically described values. Since research on acquisition of syntax has been central to the field, that's where the main issues have been debated most extensively. Most theoretical questions in the field have been formulated from a syntactocentric point of view. However, in the last ten or twelve years, there has been a surge of new research involving acquisition of interpretation. Most linguistic properties whose acquisition is discussed in this article are located at the syntax-semantics interface.

Subjacency (a locality constraint on movement) is a linguistic principle tested often in the debate on the CPH. For example, Johnson & Newport (1991) used maturational effects on knowledge of subjacency to support the possibility that adult L2 grammars may be outside the purview of UG, because they allow violations of a language universal and therefore constitute "wild" or unnatural grammars. However, many alternative linguistic explanations for their subjects' grammars can be advanced, making the claim of adult learners' wild grammars difficult to maintain. Later research on principles, notably that of Kanno (1996, 1998) has successfully established that linguistic principles like the Empty Category Principle are active in the grammar of L2 learners, even if their native language does not exhibit the exact same property that the ECP regulates in the L2.

Nevertheless, successful acquisition of universal linguistic principles cannot strongly support the view that L2 learners have continued access to UG in adulthood. It is impossible to know whether their knowledge comes directly from UG or through their native language. For this reason, most of the research addressing the access to UG issue has focused on the acquisition of parameterized properties and in particular, on learning situations where the L1 and the L2 are assumed to have different parametric values.

Several positions on whether or not adult L2 learners "have access to UG" have been articulated. The access to UG metaphor has been accepted to mean that interlanguage grammars are within the hypothesis space of UG, that is, in addition to being regulated by universal principles, they also reveal knowledge of the L2 functional categories, including the L2 values of all formal features. One general position is the Global Impairment view, to borrow a label from White (2003), on which parameter resetting in L2A is fundamentally different from parameter setting in L1A. Proponents of this approach have sought to demonstrate that whenever a cluster of superficially unrelated constructions are ostensibly dependent on a single parameter value, all these constructions appear together in the grammar of children, but not in the grammar of adult L2 learners. That is to say, L2A proceeds construction by construction and is not dependent on underlying parametric choices. Clahsen & Hong (1995) as well as Neeleman & Weerman (1997) make the case for such construction-specific, non-UG-regulated acquisition.

The most recent reincarnation of this view is the Shallow Structure Hypothesis (Clahsen & Felser 2006). The main idea is that in adult native language processing, a lot of the time, language users employ simpler sentence representations that do not utilize the whole spectrum of grammatical mechanisms like movement of NPs, leaving traces at the original and each intermediate position where they land. Instead, language users rely more on lexical, semantic, and pragmatic information to get a fast parse that saves time but also psycholinguistic resources. It has been argued that these "shallower" representations for comprehension are less-detailed than might be necessary, but they are "good enough" most of the time. Townsend & Bever (2001) call such representations "pseudosyntax", a "quick-and-dirty parse", and argue that high frequency templates with the canonical thematic pattern NVN = actor-action-patient play a major role in forming them, as well as the fast recognition of function words. Coming back to L2A, then, Clahsen & Felser (2006) propose that contrary to what happens in native speakers, the shallow processing available to the human processing system is the only type of processing that L2 learners can engage in. However, this is not a claim about processing only, it is a claim about linguistic representations. The supporting evidence comes from studies on the L2A of filler-gap dependencies. One such study is Marinis et al. (2005), who carried out a self-paced reading task on sentences containing long-distance *wh*-dependencies as in (1):

(1) The nurse *who* the doctor argued _____ that the rude patient had angered _____ is refusing to work late.

The native speakers in the Marinis et al. (2005) experiment showed a significant interaction between extraction and phrase type on the crucial segment, indicating that the presence of the intermediate trace (the gap in front of *that* in the example) facilitated the *wh*-phrase integration into the sentence structure. Advanced learners of English with Greek, German, Chinese, or Japanese as native languages did not show such an interaction, thus indicating that they are not sensitive to the intermediate trace. Clahsen & Felser (2006) conclude that advanced L2 learners do not have the same mental representations of long-distance *wh*-questions compared to native speakers, which would constitute a globally impaired grammar.

Another position on the fundamental nature of L2 grammars is the Local Impairment view. In this view, the L2 learners are capable of resetting parameters but under restricted circumstances. The specific claim is that the acquisition of formal features is restricted in some way for L2 learners either because features are permanently "impaired" (Beck 1998), or because L2 learners can only make use of features instantiated in their L1 (Hawkins & Chan 1997; Tsimpli & Roussou

1991). Hawkins & Chan's (1997) Failed Functional Features Hypotheses states that access to new parametric options as instantiated in functional categories and their associated features are no longer available in L2 acquisition after a critical period, but principles of UG still are. L2 learners may be able to map features from functional categories in their L1 to new L2 morpho-phonological material but will not have access to the functional features of the L2. Hence, L2 learners may use the morphology of the target language but with the feature specifications of their L1. Hawkins & Chan show that advanced Chinese learners of English are able to learn Complementizer Phrase (CP) morphology but are unable to reject subjacency violations because their mental representation does not involve *wh*-operator movement triggered by the features [±wh]. In contrast, intermediate Chinese learners were more sensitive to subjacency violations because they were using another operation allowed by their L1. The most recent reincarnation of this view is the Interpretability Hypothesis (Hawkins & Hattori 2006; Tsimpli & Dimitrakopoulou 2007) which makes the claim even more precise: uninterpretable features that are not transferred from the native language cannot be acquired (unlike interpretable features). The evidence in these studies again comes from comprehension of long-distance *wh*-dependencies and knowledge of resumptive pronouns.

Sorace (2003) advances a third hypothesis: Aspects of grammar that require the integration of syntactic knowledge with other types of information (e.g., pragmatic, semantic, prosodic) are more problematic for L2 learners than properties that require only syntactic knowledge. These former properties may present residual difficulties even at the near-native level. In other words, the vulnerability resides at the syntax-semantics or the syntax-pragmatics interface. This proposal implies terminal inability for near-native speakers to retreat from optionality in production or indeterminacy in their comprehension judgments for properties located at the interfaces. Sorace dubs this The Interface Hypothesis. More recently, however, Sorace & Filiaci (2006) offer an interesting specification of these claims. In testing the syntactic and pragmatic knowledge of English-speaking near-native learners of Italian with respect to pronoun–antecedent ambiguity resolution, Sorace & Filiaci find that the syntactic constraints on pronoun antecedents are indeed observed by their participants. What is non-native-like in their performance is processing strategies, more specifically, a processing principle called Position of Antecedent Strategy. Thus under the evidence of more data, Sorace's earlier representational-deficit account has evolved into a processing-load account.

Finally, the most popular view of adult interlanguage grammars is that learners are indeed capable of engaging new functional categories and of acquiring new interpretable and uninterpretable features (Schwartz & Sprouse 1996; Epstein, Flynn & Martohardjono 1996; Lardiere 1998; Prévost & White 2000, see White 2003, particularly chapter 4 for a review). The most cogent argument of this approach is the demonstration that, while L2 learners may omit functional morphology (e.g., past tense *-ed* in English), they acquire the syntactic reflexes (nominative subject, no verb raising, etc) of the respective functional category (in this case, Tense). For these researchers, the correlation between production of morphology and underlying syntactic structure does not necessarily hold. The challenge to this view is explaining the optional suppliance of functional morphology, the use of default forms, as well as the sometimes indeterminate judgments of even advanced L2 learners. Recent attempts to explain this variability, mostly in L2 production, are the Missing Surface Inflection Hypothesis (Prévost & White 2000), the Prosodic Transfer Hypothesis (Goad & White 2004) and the Feature Re-assembly Hypothesis (Lardiere 2008).

3 Assumptions about language architecture and predictions based on them

It is important to review current proposals for the language architecture, with special attention to the syntax–semantics interface, in order to clarify our assumptions on modularity and learning tasks in L2A. The key ideas here are compositionality, a matching procedure between syntactic structure and interpretation, and type-driven interpretive processes. While the content of meaning is the same, different linguistic forms map different natural groupings of meanings. This is particularly clear when we compare grammatical meanings in different languages and how they are assembled in functional morphology. What hosts all the language variation in meaning, then, is the syntax–semantics interface. Thus, linguistic semantics is the study of the interface between conceptual form and linguistic form.

Let us look more closely at the syntax–semantics interface, assuming, for example, the language architecture articulated in Jackendoff (2002). Fairly uncontroversially, syntactic structure needs to be correlated with semantic structure, however, this correlation is not always trivial. The syntactic processor works with objects like syntactic trees, their constituents and relations: DP, VP, uninterpretable features, etc. The semantic processor operates with events and states, agents and patients, individuals and propositions. The operations at the interface are limited precisely to those structures that need to be correlated and they "do not see" other structures and operations (like case-marking) that would have no relevance to the other module.

Semanticists frequently envisage more work being done at the syntax–semantics interface than syntacticians would allow. This is a view that relieves the syntax of much of its complexity. For example, Jackendoff proposes that *wh*-movement, traditionally treated as a syntactic phenomenon, can be dealt with at the interface. The crucial difference, then, between a syntactocentric view like Minimalism and Jackendoff's Parallel Architecture (among other semantic theories) is that, for the latter, there is no operation of sending syntactic structure to the semantic processor like "sending a signal down a wire, or a liquid down a pipe" (Jackendoff 2002: 223). Going from syntactic structure to semantic structure is a computation in its own right, a non-trivial process, and qualitatively different from semantic and syntactic integrative processes.

When more than one language comes into play, this computation gets even more complicated. That is why it is crucial to identify the locus of language variation. The central question for L2 researchers then is: How much of semantic/conceptual structure is part of UG and how much of it may be parameterized? Jackendoff (2002: 417) argues that the basic architecture and contents of conceptual structure are universal and innate, while languages differ in their syntactic strategies for expressing phrasal semantics (see also article 4 [Semantics: Theories] (Jackendoff) *Conceptual Semantics*). Different linguistic forms assemble and map different natural groupings of meanings. There are numerous instances of mismatches at the syntax-semantics interface. For example, while the English past progressive tense signifies an ongoing event in the past, Spanish Imperfect can have both an ongoing and a habitual interpretation. The English simple past tense, on the other hand, has a one-time finished event interpretation and a habitual interpretation while the Spanish Preterite has only the former. Thus, the same semantic primitives (ongoing, habitual, and one-time finished event), arguably part of universal conceptual structure, are distributed over different pieces of functional morphology. (A L2A study of this mismatch, Montrul & Slabakova (2002), is described in section 4.1.) What hosts most of the language variation in meaning, then, is the syntax–semantics interface.

What is involved in learning new meanings as well as new morphosyntactic forms? Within the Minimalist paradigm (Chomsky 1995), meanings and forms are reflected in functional categories with sets of formal features: Complementizer, Tense, Determiner, Aspect are functional categories hosting sets of formal features (e.g., *wh*, case, number, gender, definiteness, ongoing event) and related morphophonological forms (*that*, *-ed*, *-s*, *the*, *-ing*). Features vary as to their strength: strong features often correlate with overt morphology and are checked overtly prior to spell-out, whereas weak features tend to correlate with lack of morphology and are checked after spell-out at the interface (but see Sprouse 1998 for arguments against this claim). Parameter values make up part of lexical entries of functional categories and are encoded in the strengths of associated features (Borer 1984; Chomsky 1995). For language acquisition to take place, children select from a universal inventory of categories and features those relevant to their language and

learn to associate these sets of features with morphemes and certain meanings. Thus, the acquisition of a functional category comprises at least three different types of knowledge:
1) morphological reflexes: target-like usage of inflectional morphology (if any);
2) syntactic reflexes: knowledge of feature strength, which would result in movement prior to or after spell-out, case-marking, etc.; and
3) semantic reflexes: knowledge of the semantic properties of the functional category, or what meanings are computed when the particular functional category is checked.

In the L2 acquisition situation, the task of the L2 learner is to acquire new functional categories, or new features of native functional categories together with their strength, morphological realization, and semantics; or to learn that features already instantiated in her L1 have different strength or meaning in the L2. If building L1 and L2 linguistic representations involves the acquisition of three distinct types of knowledge, then, in principle, these processes can be dissociated in time and/or success of acquisition. What is more, any one of the three types of knowledge (morphological, syntactic, semantic) can constitute evidence for the engagement of a functional category. This is the type of logic employed by studies using acquisition of semantics to address the "access to UG" debate.

To recapitulate our assumptions, linguistic meaning has its own combinatorial structure and is not simply "read off the syntax". The operations at the interface are non-trivial computations. When learning a second language, a speaker may be confronted with different mappings between units of meaning on the conceptual level and units of syntactic structure.

4 Two learning situations in the L2A of semantics

Recent studies on the L2A of interpretive properties have mainly looked at two types of learning tasks. In one type, the syntactic structure presents less difficulty to the learners. Quite often, these studies deal with properties related to truth-conditional meanings of common morphological forms, like the Preterite and Imperfect tenses in Spanish-English interlanguage (Montrul & Slabakova 2002), progressive tenses in Japanese-English interlanguage (Gabriele 2005), bare verb meaning in Bulgarian-English interlanguage (Slabakova 2003). Not surprisingly, native speakers in these experiments show the regular range of accuracy found in studies of L2A (80–90%). The learning challenges lie, however, at the syntax-semantics interface. Learners have to figure out what morphological forms are mapped onto what meanings in the target language, since there is no one-to-one correspondence at the syntax–semantics interface. Somewhat simplistically, I shall dub this learning situation *Simple Syntax– Complex Semantics*. Results at all levels of proficiency from beginner to near-native point to the conclusion that knowledge of this type of semantic mismatch emerges gradually but surely.

In another learning situation, the properties under discussion demonstrate quite complex syntax, in the sense that sentences involve less frequent constructions (double genitives in Dekydtspotter, Sprouse & Anderson 1997; discontinuous constituents in Dekydtspotter & Sprouse 2001; quantifiers at a distance in Dekydtspotter, Sprouse & Thyre 1999/2000; scrambling in Unsworth 2005, etc.). The native speakers in these experiments very often show far lower acceptance rates than we are used to seeing in the L2A literature. In a lot of cases, alternative ways of articulating the same message exist, making the tested constructions dispreferred. (This in itself may explain the fact that learners sometimes have higher rates of acceptance than native speakers.) In most cases, the properties under scrutiny present poverty of the stimulus situations to the learner, in the sense that no positive evidence exists for them in the linguistic input. However, at the syntax–semantics interface, these same properties do not present much difficulty, as there are no mismatches. This situation can be dubbed *Complex Syntax–Simple Semantics*. If learners have acquired the relevant functional lexicon item and have constructed the right sentence representation, the presence or absence of semantic interpretation follows straightforwardly without any more stipulations. In most cases, learners demonstrate that a contrast exists in their grammar between the allowed and the disallowed interpretations. In the next sections, we discuss studies representative of the two learning situations.

4.1 Simple Syntax–Complex Semantics: Acquisition of grammatical aspect (Montrul & Slabakova 2002)

In a series of studies (Montrul & Slabakova 2002, 2003; Slabakova & Montrul 2002, 2003) Montrul and Slabakova investigated acquisition of interpretive properties related to the aspectual functional projection AspP in English-Spanish interlanguage (for background, see article 9 [Semantics: Noun Phrases and Verb Phrases] (Filip) *Aspectual class and Aktionsart*, article 10 [Semantics: Noun Phrases and Verb Phrases] (Portner) *Perfect and progressive*, article 4 [this volume] (Smith) *Tense and aspect*). Montrul & Slabakova's (2002) study was specifically designed to probe the connection between acquisition of inflectional morphology and interpretations related to the aspectual tenses Preterite and Imperfect. As already discussed above, Spanish and English aspectual tenses encode different meanings. While the English past progressive tense signifies an ongoing event in the past, Spanish Imperfect can have both an ongoing and a habitual interpretation. The English simple past tense, on the other hand has a one-time finished event interpretation and a habitual interpretation while The Spanish Preterite has only the former. The examples below illustrate this:

(2) a. Guillermo robaba   en la calle.   (habitual)
       Guillermo rob-IMP in the street
       'Guillermo habitually robbed (people) in the street.'
    b. Guillermo robó   en la calle. (one-time event)
       Guillermo rob-PRET in the street
       'Guillermo robbed (someone) in the street.'

(3) a. Felix robbed (people) in the street.   (habitual)
    b. Felix robbed a person in the street. (one-time event)

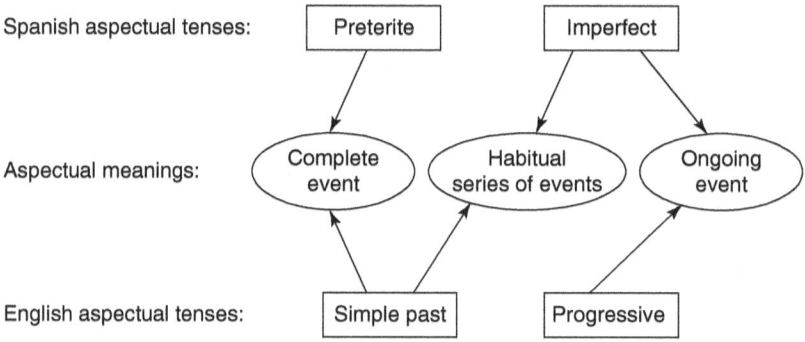

Fig. 10.1: Aspectual tense meanings in English and Spanish

In the diagram in Fig. 10.1, arrows point to meanings that are encoded by the same piece of inflectional morphology. In restructuring her grammar, the learner has to acquire the fact that it is the Imperfect morphology that encodes habituality in Spanish, and not the perfective Preterite morphology. Another acquisition task is noticing that the Imperfective ending is ambiguous between two interpretations, habitual and ongoing, while the Preterite ending only encodes the perfective meaning of a one-time complete event. In this sense, the habitual meaning is now paired with another Imperfective meaning (the ongoing one) and crucially does not depend on the lexical class of the predicate. This situation of course, presents a significant mismatch between syntactic structure and conceptual structure. The pieces of inflectional morphology come from the functional lexicon. The functional projections (e.g., AspP) where features are checked are part of sentence syntax. The aspectual meanings (ongoing event, habitual event, one-time complete event) reside in conceptual structure. But different languages have different form-to-meaning mappings, which are calculated at the syntax–semantics interface.

Montrul & Slabakova (2002) tested 71 adult learners of Spanish. Based on a proficiency task, they were divided into advanced and intermediate learners. Based on a test of inflectional morphology of aspectual tenses, the intermediate learners were further divided into those that demonstrated knowledge of the inflectional morphology and those who did not (a Yes-morphology group and a No-morphology group). The main test instrument was a sentence conjunction judgment task which specifically tested the semantic implications of the Preterite and Imperfect tenses. In this task, subjects were presented with a list of sentences consisting of two coordinated clauses. Some of the combinations were logical while others were contradictory. Subjects had to judge on a scale ranging from -2 (contradiction) to 2 (no contradiction) whether the two clauses made sense together. Following is an example with an accomplishment verb:

(4) Joaquín corría (imperf) la carrera de fórmula 1 pero no participó.
 'Joaquín was going to participate in the Formula One race but he didn't take part in it.'

 –2   –1   0   1   ②

(5) Pedro corrió (pret) la maratón de Barcelona pero no participó.
 'Pedro ran the Barcelona marathon but he didn't take part in it.'

 ⊖   –1   0   1   2

In addition to the described form-to meaning mismatches in the aspectual tense morphology, lexical aspectual classes of verbs are another factor in the acquisition picture. Stative verbs are infelicitous with the progressive in English (*The room was being white) but are fine with the Imperfect in Spanish. Achievements in the Imperfect and in the progressive force aspectual coercion on the predicates, a pragmatic process which provides a context to avoid a clash of semantic features. Coercion shifts the emphasis to the process immediately preceding the change of state, so they can be negated without contradiction: *The Smiths were selling their house but in the end they did not sell it* (see article 10 [Semantics: Lexical Structures and Adjectives] (de Swart) *Mismatches and coercion* and de Swart 1998). That is why the authors look at aspectual classes of verbs separately in Tab. 10.1. Group results show that advanced

Tab. 10.1: Mean rates for acceptable/unacceptable combination of clauses with the different lexical classes (range +2/−2)

Groups	Accomplishments	States	Achievements
Native speakers	1.34 / −.98*	1.56 / −1.5*	1.39 / −1.69*
Advanced	1.23 / −1.1*	.92 / −.9*	.25 / −1.79*
Intermediate yes-morphology	.42 / −.2*	.53 / −.32*	.03 / −.86*
Intermediate no-morphology	.24 / −.24*	.12 / −.25	−.57 / .75 *

Notes: * The contrast between these two means is significant by t-test.

and intermediate learners who scored above 80% accuracy with the morphology test (the yes- morphology group) appear to have acquired the semantic implications associated with Preterite and Imperfect tenses in Spanish. By contrast, those intermediate learners who have not controlled knowledge of the Preterite/Imperfect morpho-phonology (the no-morphology group) are not yet sensitive to the semantic contrast between these tenses, especially with achievement and state predicates. The no-morphology group of intermediate learners even displayed the opposite pattern: they rejected achievements with Imperfect and accepted those with Preterite.

In addition, individual results were calculated with scalar responses converted into absolute values (acquired, has not acquired). Contingency tables based on these values reveal that there is a significant correlation between knowledge of morphology and knowledge of semantics, and that knowledge of morphology necessarily precedes knowledge of semantics in this aspectual domain. The acquisition of the semantic contrast appears to be a gradual development, which eventually reaches complete native-like knowledge in advanced proficiency learners.

A possible criticism that may be addressed to this study is that it looks at learners' recognizing the form and basic meanings of grammatical aspect morphemes (the aspectual tenses). Not only the forms but their aspectual meanings are widely taught and drilled in language classrooms. Thus it is difficult to rule out instruction effects. The study we discuss in section 4.3 was designed to control for such a possibility.

4.2 Complex Syntax—Simple Semantics: *Wh*-quantifiers and tense distinctions (Dekydtspotter & Sprouse 2001)

In this section, we look at a study representative of the second learning situation. Dekydtspotter & Sprouse's (2001) experiment investigates tense-dependent interpretations of discontinuous quantifiers. The semantic knowledge to be acquired involves the speech-time vs. past-time construal of adjectival restrictions of quantifiers. Consider the data in (6).

(6) Qui   de   célèbre fumait   au   bistro dans les   année 60?
    Who   of   famous smoked   at-the bar   in   the   60ies?
    'Which famous person smoked in bars in the 60ies?'

A possible answer to this question may involve a present and a past celebrity. On the other hand, it is impossible to answer the discontinuous interrogative constituent as in (7) with a present celebrity. Only someone who was a celebrity in the past is the appropriate answer.

(7) Qui   fumait   de   célèbre   au   bistro dans les   année 60?
    Who   smoked   of   famous   at-the bar   in   the   60ies?
    'Which famous person smoked in bars in the 60ies?'

The linguistic facts that bring these interpretations forward can be explained by combining language-specific movement for checking of a *wh*-feature, the possibility of left-branch extraction (again, language-specific) and a universal semantic-computational mechanism. When a *wh*-phrase (*qui*) moves to Spec, CP to check a *wh*-feature (pied-piping the rest of the phrase with it, or checking a strong feature) it can optionally take its adjectival restrictions (*de célèbre*) along for the ride, resulting in the structures in (8) and (9).

(8) [$_{CP}$ Qui de célèbre [$_C$ [$_{TP}$ $t_{\text{qui de célèbre}}$ fumait [$_{VP}$ $t_{\text{qui de célèbre}}$ [V' t_{fumait}] au bistro]]]]?
    who of famous   smoked   at-the bar

(9) [$_{CP}$ Qui [$_C$ [$_{IP}$ t_{qui} [$_{I'}$ fumait [$_{VP}$ [t_{qui} de célèbre] [V' t_{fumait}] au bistro]]]]?
    who   smoked   of famous   at-the bar

The authors argue that the relevant aspects of the expression *qui de célèbre* can be interpreted at any of the various steps in the derivation (see also article 5 [Semantics: Sentence and Information Structure] (Krifka) *Questions*). More specifically, the analysis in (8) allows *de célèbre* to be interpreted in CP, in TP, or in VP (assuming local movement). The past tense operator P is located in TP. Thus the continuous interrogative constituent can be interpreted to pertain to either people who are famous at the time of the utterance (without tense restrictions), or to people who were famous at the time when the smoking in bars, the verbal predicate, was taking place. On the other hand, the discontinuous constituent in (9) has the adjectival restriction in VP, under the scope of the past operator, hence one of the two interpretations is missing. The habitual smoking state and the state of being famous have to coincide temporally.

What kind of knowledge must an L2 learner have in order to be aware of both interpretations in the case of continuous *wh*-constituents but only one interpretation in the case of discontinuous ones? First, knowledge of overt *wh*-movement is required. It relies on properties of *wh*-words encoded in the functional lexicon but such knowledge can be transferred from the native language in English-French interlanguage, since both English and French exhibit *wh*-movement to Spec, CP. Secondly, knowledge that discontinuous interrogatives are allowed in French is necessary. This property is not taught in French classrooms (Dekydtspotter & Sprouse 2001: 7) but is given to the participants in the experiment in the form of the test sentences (assuming they believe that the researchers did not trick them into judging ungrammatical sentences). Thirdly, the (not taught) language-specific knowledge that French allows the *wh*-word *qui* 'who' to have an adjectival restriction at all is necessary, while English *who famous* and *who of famous* are not legitimate strings. Most importantly, however, what Dekydtspotter & Sprouse label "the universal deductive procedure" is indispensable for reaching the interpretive knowledge. The authors make a convincing case for the interpretations' not being learnable on the basis of input alone (pairing of linguistic sign with meaningful extralinguistic context) and not transferable from English (Dekydtspotter & Sprouse 2001: 7–10).

The researchers tested 47 intermediate English-native learners of French, who were enrolled in third and fifth semester French classes at a US university and a group of 11 advanced speakers who had spent more than a year at a French-speaking country. Although no independent proficiency measure was administered to those latter learners, it is possible that some of them were at or close to near-native proficiency. There were two control groups tested as well. One control group was made up of 30 native French speakers. The second control group was composed of 47 English-speaking individuals with no exposure to French, who were given literal translations of the test sentences in English (see the glosses of examples 8 and 9). The purpose was to see how the interlanguage group would have performed on the experimental task if they had judged the test sentences based solely on their English intuitions.

The task of the participants was to read a paragraph-length context in English matched with a test sentence in French. After the test sentence, the participants had to answer whether that was the correct answer to the question. Test sentences in the form of question and answer sequences were organized in quadruples, as exemplified below:

(10) Sample stimuli: Context for all 4 items in the quadruple:
Attitudes toward smoking have changed drastically since the 1960s. In the 60s many people would go to bars and smoke every night. For example, Herman the Hermit was a famous rock star in those days and was often seen at bars smoking with Linda Tripp, who was then totally unknown. How times have changed! Now it is Linda Tripp who is famous, and neither of them smokes any more!

Continuous interrogative with past time answer:
Mme Goyette: Qui de célèbre fumait—dans le bistro—pendant les année 60?
Élève+: Herman the Hermit

Continuous interrogative with speech time answer:
Mme Goyette: Qui de célèbre fumait—dans le bistro—pendant les année 60?
Élève: Linda Tripp

Discontinuous interrogative with past time answer:
Mme Goyette: Qui fumait de célèbre—dans le bistro—pendant les année 60?
Élève: Herman the Hermit

Discontinuous interrogative with speech time answer:
Mme Goyette: Qui fumait de célèbre—dans le bistro—pendant les année 60?
Élève: Linda Tripp

Question for respondents on all items: Is this a correct answer to the question?

The results are summarized in Tab. 10.2 (based on Dekydtspotter & Sprouse 2001).

As Tab. 10.2 indicates, past time construals are preferred across the board by natives and learners alike. Speech time construals are in bold with a checkmark after the available one and a hachure after the unavailable one. It is knowledge of the missing interpretation, the speech-time construal with discontinuous constituents, that is crucial in answering the research question of this study. Both learner groups show a statistically significant difference between the available and the unavailable interpretations. In other words, they reliably treat the two constructions differently. The argument would have been even more convincing if the native speakers had exhibited more categorical knowledge of the property. As it is, French natives do not like speech time construals, and do not reliably

Tab. 10.2: Percentage of acceptance of past time and speech time construals with continuous or discontinuous interrogatives

construal	Intermediate (n=47)		Advanced (n=11)		Native French (n=30)	
	past	speech	past	speech	past	speech
continuous interrogatives	90.7	41.2 (√)	79.6	46.6 (√)	88.8	12.5 (√)
discontinuous interrogative	90.7	25 (#)	90.9	15.9 (#)	96.3	5 (#)

distinguish between the two constructions ($t(29) = 1.61$, $p = .119$, with a large SD of 27.46 on the discontinuous constituent meanings and a much smaller SD of 7.76 on the continuous constituent meanings). However, what is important is the behavior of the learners. They are successfully combining the properties related to the French functional lexicon: the availability of *wh*-movement and discontinuous interrogatives, with the universal meaning-calculating algorithm. Note that even not very proficient L2 learners, in this case learners with as little as three semesters of exposure to French, are capable of manifesting knowledge depending on this universal algorithm. In addition, the results of the English control group demonstrate that a pure glossing strategy (mapping word for word the English and French questions) would not lead the French learners to the expected contrast in their L2 knowledge. In judging ungrammatical but interpretable questions such as *Who of famous smoked in bars in the 60ies?*, the English native speakers allowed speech-time construals equally with continuous and discontinuous interrogatives.

One final observation pertaining to this experimental study is in order. I have argued here, together with the researchers themselves, that the interpretive knowledge comes for free, and thus precedes the morphosyntactic knowledge involved in the relevant properties. Why don't we see reliably high percentages of acceptance then? To appreciate the findings, we need to keep in mind that the study examines dispreferred grammatical options. The past-time construal was widely preferred to the speech-time construal by all participants, including the English control group. It is no small achievement, then, on the part of the learners, that even with dispreferred strings or interpretations and under severe poverty of the stimulus, they manage to exhibit the contrasts we expect based on the respective syntactic structures and the universal meaning computation procedure.

4.3 Ruling Out the Effect of Instruction: viewpoint aspect-related interpretations (Slabakova 2003)

The linguistic properties investigated by Slabakova (2003) have to do with viewpoint (grammatical) aspect again. In this sense, they fall into The Simple Syntax—Complex Semantics type of learning situation. It is well known that English differs from German, Romance, and Slavic with respect to the semantics of the present simple tense in that it cannot denote ongoing events.

(11) a. *She eats an apple right now.   #Ongoing event
　　 b. She is eating an apple right now.   Ongoing event
　　 c. She eats an apple (every day).   Habitual series of complete events

Furthermore, the English bare infinitive denotes not only the processual part of an event but includes the completion of that event. English accomplishment and achievement predicates in the infinitive (without any aspectual morphology) have only complete events in their denotations. Sentence (12a) cannot be uttered in a situation where a truck comes along while Mary is crossing the street and it hits her before she can reach the other sidewalk, while (12b) can.

(12) a. I saw Mary cross the street.   completion entailed
　　 b. I saw Mary crossing the street.   no completion entailed

In trying to explain the relationship between the facts illustrated in (11) and (12), many researchers have noticed that English verbal morphology is impoverished (Bennett & Partee 1972/1978; Landman 1992). The experimental study adopts Giorgi & Pianesi's (1997) proposal. English verbs, they argue, are "naked" forms that can express several verbal values, such as the bare infinitive, the first and second person singular, and the first, second and third person, plural. Many English words are even categorially ambiguous in that they can either identify an "object" or an "action," such as *cry, play, drive*, and many others. Giorgi & Pianesi (1997) propose that verbs are disambiguated in English by being marked in the lexicon with the aspectual feature [+perf] (perfective). English eventive verbs acquire categorial features by being associated with the aspectual marker [+perf]. In other words, English (eventive) verbs are inherently perfective and include both the process part of the event and its endpoint. Thus, children acquiring English notice the morphological poverty of English verbs and attach the [+perf] feature to verbal forms, thus distinguishing them from nominals, whose feature specification bundle excludes it. This feature has to be checked in a functional category, say AspP, in the sentential structure. We shall not go into the rest of the analysis here of how the other grammatical aspectual meanings obtain (but see the original study for details).

In Romance, Slavic, and other Germanic languages, on the other hand, all verbal forms have to be inflected for person, number, and tense. Thus, nouns and verbs cannot have the same forms, unlike English, in which zero-derivation abounds. The Bulgarian verb, for example, is associated with typical verbal features as [+V, person, number] and it is recognizable and learnable as a verb because of these features. Nominal inflections are distinguishable from verbal ones. Bulgarian verbs are therefore not associated with a [+perf] feature. Unlike English, Bulgarian has no present progressive tense and the present simple tense is ambiguous between a habitual and an ongoing event or state. This is true of eventive verbs as in (13) below, as well as of stative verbs. Thus, Bulgarian and English exhibit a contrast of viewpoint aspect in present tense forms (see article 9 [Semantics: Noun Phrases and Verb Phrases] (Filip) *Aspectual class and Aktionsart*).

(13) a. Maria sega jade jabəlka.   simultaneous event
     Maria now eat-PRES apple
     'Mary is eating an apple right now.'
   b. Maria jade jabəlka vseki den.   habitual series of events
     Maria eat-PRES apple every day
     'Mary eats an apple every day.'

Because Bulgarian verbs are not marked [+perf] in the lexicon, Bulgarian equivalents to bare infinitives do not entail completion of the event.

(14) Ivan vidja Maria da presi ča ulicata.   no completion entailed
     Ivan saw Maria to cross street-DET
     'John saw Mary crossing the street.'

In the acquisition of English by Bulgarian native speakers, then, the learning task is to notice the trigger of this property: the fact that English inflectional morphology is highly impoverished, lacking many person-number-tense verb endings. The property itself, if Giorgi & Pianesi are correct, is the [+perf] feature that is attached to English eventive verbs in the lexicon. Knowledge of this property will entail knowledge of four different interpretive facts: 1) bare verb forms denote a completed event; 2) present tense has only habitual interpretation; 3) progressive affix needed for ongoing interpretation of eventive verbs; 4) states in the progressive denote temporary states. Even if the four facts above are not related, or not due to the presence or absence of a specific formal feature, the language contrasts remain as syntax–semantics mismatches, and they have to be acquired. Crucially for this study, of the four semantic properties under investigation enumerated above, the second, third, and fourth are introduced, discussed, and drilled in language classrooms. The first one, however, is not explicitly taught.

A hundred and twelve Bulgarian learners of English took part in the experiment, as well as 24 native speaker controls. The learners were typical classroom instructed learners. All participants took a Truth Value Judgment Task with a story in their native language and a test sentence in English. The same story appeared with another test sentence (see below) elsewhere in the test. Here is an example of a test quadruple:

(15) Quadruple testing completed interpretation of English bare forms (the construction is known as "perceptual reports")

Matt had an enormous appetite. He was one of those people who could eat a whole cake at one sitting. But these days he is much more careful what he eats. For example, yesterday he bought a chocolate and vanilla ice cream cake, but ate only half of it after dinner. I know, because I was there with him.

	I observed Matt eat a cake.	True	False
or			
	I observed Matt eating a cake.	True	False

Alicia is a thin person, but she has an astounding capacity for eating big quantities of food. Once when I was at her house, she took a whole ice cream cake out of the freezer and ate it all. I almost got sick, just watching her.

	I watched Alicia eat a cake.	True	False
or			
	I watched Alicia eating a cake.	True	False

Results on the acquisition of all four semantic properties pattern the same way. We focus on the instructed properties first. The less proficient learners are quite accurate in mapping the present simple tense to habitual context (roughly around 80 %), while they are slightly less accurate at recognizing the progressive form semantics (around 65%). This contrast may be due to the fact that the habitual meaning *can* be expressed by the present tense form in their L1, even though it has to be supported by adverbials and/or context. The progressive meaning, on the other hand, is associated with a *different* piece of morphology in the L2, making the process of form–function mapping more problematic. The advanced learners are highly accurate on all three properties taught in classrooms. Thus initial L1 transfer and subsequent morphological acquisition are clearly attested in the data.

Fig. 10.2 presents accuracy on the untaught property: in the perceptual report construction, the bare verb has a completed interpretation. As the figure shows, advanced learners are even more accurate than native speakers in their knowledge that an English bare verb denotes a complete event, and consequently is incompatible with an incomplete event story (see first group of columns). Even more importantly, all learner groups are quite accurate in attributing a complete interpretation to the bare verb, a property that cannot transfer from the L1, as example (14) indicates. Note also that both native speakers and advanced learners prefer to combine complete event stories with a bare verb form, although the *-ing* form is not ungrammatical. In other words, both groups focus on completion in the context of a telic event.

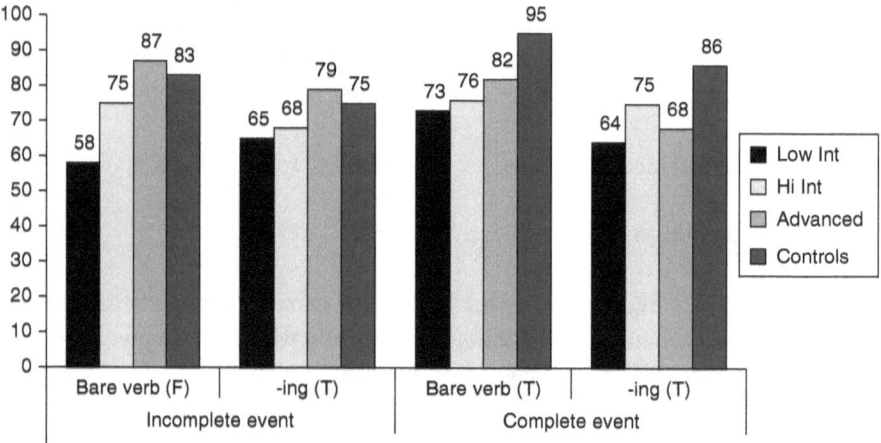

Fig. 10.2: Mean accuracy on bare verbs versus -ing forms in perceptual reports (in percentage)

After establishing that it is *possible* to acquire semantic properties in the second language that are not manifested in the native language, let us now turn to the impact of the instruction variable. Slabakova (2003) reports that extensive scrutiny of the instruction materials and discussions with the instructors ascertained that the present simple and progressive tense meanings are explicitly taught and drilled from the beginning of classroom instruction. On the other hand, the telic interpretation of bare verb forms is not taught, and the Bulgarian teachers are not consciously aware of it. Is it the case that instruction is a significant variable and learners were more accurate on the taught than on untaught properties? The short answer is no. Analysis of variance was performed on the data for each group, with condition as the sole factor. The Low Intermediate Group performed equally accurately on all conditions ($F(2, 93) = 1.71$, $p = .185$), and so did the High Intermediate Group ($F(2, 120) = 2.67$, $p = .07$). The Advanced Group showed a marginally significant difference for condition ($F(2, 114) = 3.11$, $p = .05$), but it is due to the only lower accuracy score (68%) on the -*ing* verb form combined with a telic story. (As mentioned above, this combination is not ungrammatical, it is simply dispreferred.) In general, there seems to be no effect of instruction in Bulgarian learners' acquisition of the semantic properties of English present tenses. The theoretical implication of this finding is that all semantic effects of learning the trigger (English verbs are morphologically impoverished) and the related property ([+perf] feature attached to verbs in the lexicon) appear to be engaged at the same time.

5 Implications and conclusions

The three studies discussed in this article are representative of at least 20 other studies, in a rapidly growing field of inquiry within generative L2A research. Their findings are not at all unique or atypical in that field of research (Dekydtspotter & Sprouse 1997; Dekydtspotter, Sprouse & Thyre 1999/2000; Dekydtspotter, Sprouse & Swanson 2001; Marsden 2004; Unsworth 2005; Gabriele 2005; Ionin, Ko & Wexler 2004; Borgonovo, Bruhn de Garavito & Prévost 2006; for an overview of more studies, see Slabakova 2006, 2008). We will now turn to the implications of the findings we have observed. In section 2 we summarized briefly several influential proposals on whether adult L2A proceeds much like child language acquisition. Within the Global Impairment View, the Shallow Structure Hypothesis argues that adult L2A is fundamentally different from L1A because adult L2 language users do not process long-distance dependencies as native speakers do. One type of evidence that addresses the question of whether or not L2 speakers utilize detailed and complete syntactic representations in their parsing comes from comprehension experiments of the type we have discussed above. Let us take, for example, the correct interpretations of sentences as in (8) and (9) tested in Dekydtspotter & Sprouse (2001).

(8) [$_{CP}$ Qui de célèbre [$_C$ [$_{TP}$ t $_{qui\ de\ célèbre}$ fumait [$_{VP}$ t $_{qui\ de\ célèbre}$ [$_{V'}$ t_{fumait}] au bistro]]]]?
    who of famous   smoked   at-the bar

(9) [$_{CP}$ Qui [$_C$ [$_{IP}$ t $_{qui}$ [$_{I'}$ fumait [$_{VP}$ [t $_{qui}$] de célèbre] [$_{V'}$ t_{fumait}] au bistro]]]]?
    who   smoked   of famous   at-the bar

Recall that (8) allows for a past and present celebrity construal while (9) only allows for a past celebrity construal. In order to recognize these meanings, speakers need to interpret the *wh*-phrase with or without its associate *de célèbre* at each of the intermediate sites. That is, correct interpretation crucially depends on positing and processing intermediate traces. Intermediate as well as advanced learners of French with English as their native language show statistically significant sensitivity to this contrast, correctly choosing speech time construals more often with continuous interrogatives that with discontinuous interrogatives. This result cannot be explained by the Shallow Structure Hypothesis. The proposal assumes that intermediate traces are not needed on the shallow parse, and not processed by L2 speakers, who rely on argument structure assignment and pragmatics in processing. In examples (8) and (9) above, the verbs are the same, therefore learners should have come up with a similar shallow analysis for them. Since the results of Dekydtspotter & Sprouse (2001) are hardly isolated or atypical, I conclude that the Shallow Structure Hypothesis is an eminently testable and sensible proposal, but there is a lot of experimental evidence militating against it.

The second view we introduced, the Local Impairment position, included Hawkins & Chan's (1997) proposal that the acquisition of formal features is subject to some sort of critical period effect and is unavailable to L2 learners, if the features are not transferable from the native grammar. The more recent version of this position claims that only uninterpretable, but not interpretable features, are uniformly unavailable in L2A. For example, Hawkins & Hattori (2006) and Hawkins et al. (2008) look at semantic effects of uninterpretable features regulating *wh*-movement and verb movement, respectively, and find support for their claim. However, White (2003: 127–141) provides many examples of studies demonstrating successful acquisition of new features, new feature strength values, and new functional categories. As it stands, the Local Impairment position makes a further prediction: that the L2A of a new interpretable feature (e.g., tense on T in English for Chinese native speakers) should be possible, while acquiring a new uninterpretable feature (e.g., a strong [wh] feature in English for Chinese native speakers) should be impossible. To my knowledge, such a direct comparison has not been investigated yet.

The third influential proposal explaining L2A we discussed was Sorace's Interface Hypothesis. It is important to point out that a simpler position, namely, "adult and even advanced learners cannot fully acquire properties at linguistic interfaces" is plainly wrong. All of the studies we have enumerated so far directly contradict this simplistic claim. Sorace (2003) rather claims that linguistic properties requiring *integration* of syntactic knowledge with discourse-pragmatic, semantic, or prosodic information, present insurmountable difficulties even to advanced learners. Unfortunately, at this time linguistic theory has not proposed concrete theoretical analyses of how exactly prosodic and pragmatic (discourse-related) information interact with and change syntactic information (but see article 17 [Semantics: Interfaces] (Potts) *Conventional implicature and expressive content*). Thus, it may be the case that these particular types of information, prosodic and discourse information, are difficult for learners to take into account while calculating appropriate usage. What I have shown in this chapter is that learners do not have trouble calculating meaning at the syntax–semantics interface, even in the case of L1–L2 mismatches at this interface. More empirical investigations targeting prosodic and discourse integration into the syntax are needed before the Interface Hypothesis is substantiated. Its theoretical underpinnings also need to be better defined.

Another highly promising area of inquiry that would also pertain to acquisition at the interfaces is the L2A of scalar implicatures (see article 10 [Semantics: Interfaces] (Chierchia, Fox & Spector) *Grammatical view of scalar implicatures* and article 15 [Semantics: Interfaces] (Simons) *Implicature*). The learning situation in the case of scalar implicatures is the following. Since they are supposed to be universal, once the learners know the lexical items for the scales, they should have no problem computing them. Even though pragmatic competence takes time to develop in children, L2 adults should be better than children since they have already developed that competence in their L1. Native language transfer and lexical learning should bring forward native-like pragmatic competence. The first L2 studies probing these questions (Dekydtspotter & Hathorn 2005; Dekydtspotter, Sprouse & Meyer 2005; Slabakova 2010) indicate that this is indeed the case. Both very complex as well as simple interpretive effects are discovered in learners' grammars, observed in a native-like fashion, therefore supporting the claim that L2A is constrained by a universal meaning computation processor. In sum, we have no reason to expect acquisition at the syntax–pragmatics and semantics–pragmatics interfaces to be any less successful than that at the syntax–semantics interface.

Returning to the syntax–semantics interface then, let us reiterate that most current studies on L2A of semantics fall into two major groups: those investigating Simple Syntax—Complex Semantics and those investigating Complex Syntax—Simple Semantics. As exemplified in the Montrul & Slabakova (2002) and Slabakova (2003) studies, in the first learning situation, characterized with an L1–L2 mismatch at the syntax–semantics interface, both initial transfer from the native language and subsequent incremental development reaching native levels are attested. In the second learning situation, illustrated by Dekydtspotter & Sprouse (2001), learners' answers are characterized with lower acceptance rates altogether, but both proficient and less proficient learners demonstrate that they have established the semantic contrast in their interlanguage grammars. Once learners are capable of understanding the test sentences by being able to parse their complex syntax, they have no trouble with the available interpretations, since there is no syntax–semantics mismatch and they have recourse to the universal semantic calculation procedures.

Taken together, these findings point to the conclusion that inflectional morphology encoded in the functional lexicon presents the most formidable challenge to L2 learners. The morphology has to be learned on an item-by-item basis, a process that takes time and is subject to individual differences. The inflectional morphology is either mapped onto new meanings (the first learning situation) or implicated in the calculation of complex syntactic structures (the second learning situation). The different patterns of acquisition in the two situations are explained by the Bottleneck Hypothesis, which claims that morphology is the bottleneck of L2 acquisition. Incremental morphology learning reaching high accuracy levels happens in the first case. Lower morphology accuracy, but with the semantic contrast in place from the beginning, is attested in the second case.

The claims of the Bottleneck Hypothesis (Slabakova 2006, 2008) are partially based on these observed patterns of acquisition. This hypothesis postulates that indeed the functional morphology is the "tight spot" in the acquisition process flow. Morphology is processed by declarative memory, has to be learned by rote, and its forms (or phonological features) present difficulty for L2 learners not only at beginning stages of acquisition but at later stages, too (Lardiere 2008). It is a stumbling block in linguistic production, but it is also crucial in comprehension. Past the figurative bottleneck, application of universal semantic principles continues to flow freely, and target interpretations are achieved.

Looking at the big picture, then, the Critical Period Hypothesis that we discussed in the introduction is not precise enough to predict differential effects for different areas of the grammar. The Multiple Critical Period Hypothesis, postulating such differential effects, is obviously closer to the mark. Within the latter, data from numerous experimental studies investigating two learning situations confirmed that there is no critical period for the acquisition of phrasal semantics.

6 References

Beck, Maria-Luisa 1998. L2 acquisition and obligatory head movement: English-speaking learners of German and the local impairment hypothesis. *Studies in Second Language Acquisition* 20, 311–348.

Bennett, Michael & Barbara Partee 1972/1978. *Toward the Logic of Tense and Aspect in English.* Technical Report, System Development Corporation, Santa Monica, CA. Published with a new appendix: Bloomington, IN: Indiana University Linguistics Club, 1978.

Birdsong, David 2005. Understanding age effects in second language acquisition. In: J. Kroll & A. de Groot (eds.). *Handbook of Bilingualism: Psycholinguistic Perspectives*. Oxford: Oxford University Press, 109–127.

Birdsong, David & Michelle Molis 2001. On the evidence for maturational effects in second language acquisition. *Journal of Memory and Language* 44, 235–249.

Borer, Hagit 1984. *Parametric Syntax*. Dordrecht: Foris.

Borgonovo, Claudia, Joyce Bruhn de Garavito & Philippe Prévost 2006. Is the semantics/syntax interface vulnerable in L2 acquisition? Focus on mood distinctions in relative clauses in L2 Spanish. In: V. Torrens & L. Escobar (eds.). *The Acquisition of Syntax in Romance Languages*. Amsterdam: Benjamins, 353–369.

Chomsky, Noam 1995. *The Minimalist Program*. Cambridge, MA: The MIT Press.

Clahsen, Harald & Claudia Felser 2006. Grammatical processing in language learners. *Applied Psycholinguistics* 27, 3–42.

Clahsen, Harald & Upim Hong 1995. Agreement and null subjects in German L2 development: New evidence from reaction time experiments. *Second Language Research* 11, 57–87.

DeKeyser Robert M. 2000. The robustness of critical period effects in second language acquisition. *Studies in Second Language Acquisition* 22, 499–533.

DeKeyser, Robert & Jennifer Larson-Hall 2005. What does the critical period really mean? In: J. Kroll & A. de Groot (eds.). *Handbook of Bilingualism: Psycholinguistic Perspectives*. Oxford: Oxford University Press, 88–108.

Dekydtspotter, Laurent & Jon Hathorn 2005. *Quelque chose... de remarquable* in English-French acquisition: Mandatory, informationally encapsulated computations in second language interpretation. *Second Language Research* 21, 291–323.

Dekydtspotter, Laurent & Rex Sprouse 2001. Mental design and (second) language epistemology: Adjectival restrictions of *wh*-quantifiers and tense in English-French interlanguage. *Second Language Research* 17, 1–35.

Dekydtspotter, Laurent, Rex Sprouse & Bruce Anderson 1997. The interpretive interface in L2 acquisition: The process-result distinction in English-French interlanguage grammars. *Language Acquisition* 6, 297–332.

Dekydtspotter, Laurent, Rex Sprouse & Thad Meyer 2005. *Was für N* interrogatives and quantifier scope in English-German interpretation. In: L. Dekydtspotter, R. Sprouse & A. Liljestrand (eds.). *Proceedings of the 7th Generative Approaches to Second Language Acquisition Conference (= GASLA 2004)*. Somerville, MA: Cascadilla Press, 86–95.

Dekydtspotter, Laurent, Rex Sprouse & Kimberly A.B. Swanson 2001. Reflexes of the mental architecture in second language acquisition: The interpretation of discontinuous *combien* extractions in English-French interlanguage. *Language Acquisition* 9, 175–227.

Dekydtspotter, Laurent, Rex Sprouse & Rachel Thyre 1999/2000. The interpretation of quantification at a distance in English-French interlanguage: Domain-specificity and second language acquisition. *Language Acquisition* 8, 265–320.

Epstein, Samuel, Suzanne Flynn & Gita Martohardjono 1996. Second language acquisition: Theoretical and experimental issues in contemporary research. *Brain and Behavioral Sciences* 19, 677–758.

Eubank, Lynn & Kevin Gregg 1999. Critical periods and (second) language acquisition: *Divide et impera*. In: D. Birdsong (ed.). *Second Language Acquisition and the Critical Period Hypothesis*. Mahwah, NJ: Lawrence Erlbaum Associates, 65–100.

Flege, James Emil 1999. Age of learning and second language speech. In: D. Birdsong (ed.). *Second Language Acquisition and the Critical Period Hypothesis*. Mahwah, NJ: Lawrence Erlbaum Associates, 101–131.

Gabriele, Alison 2005. *The Acquisition of Aspect in a Second Language: A Bidirectional Study of Learners of English and Japanese*. Ph.D. dissertation. City University of New York, New York.

Giorgi, Alessandra & Fabio Pianesi 1997. *Tense and Aspect: From Semantics to Morphosyntax*. Oxford: Oxford University Press.

Goad, Heather & Lydia White 2004. Ultimate attainment of L2 inflection: Effects of L1 prosodic structure. In: S. Foster-Cohen et al. (eds.). *Eurosla Yearbook, vol. 4*. Amsterdam: Benjamins, 119–145.

Hakuta, Kenji, Ellen Bialystok & Edward Wiley 2003. Critical evidence: A test of the critical-period hypothesis for second-language acquisition. *Psychological Science* 14, 31–38.

Hawkins, Roger & Cecilia Chan 1997. The partial availability of Universal Grammar in second language acquisition: the 'failed functional features hypothesis'. *Second Language Research* 13, 187–226.

Hawkins, Roger & Hajime Hattori 2006. Interpretation of English multiple wh-questions by Japanese speakers: A missing uninterpretable feature account. *Second Language Research* 22, 269–301.

Hawkins, Roger, Gabriella Cassilas, Hajime Hattori, James Hawthorne, Ritta Husted, Cristobal Lozano, Aya Okamoto, Emma Thomas & Kazumi Yamada 2008. The semantic effects of verb raising and its consequences in second language grammars. In: J. Liceras, H. Zobl & H. Goodluck (eds.). *The Role of Features in Second Language Acquisition*. Mahwah, NJ: Lawrence Erlbaum Associates, 328–351.

Hyltenstam, Kenneth & Niclas Abrahamsson 2003. Maturational constraints in SLA. In: C. Doughty & M. Long (eds.). *The Handbook of Second Language Acquisition*. Oxford: Blackwell, 539–588.

Ionin, Tania, Heejeong Ko & Kenneth Wexler 2004. Article semantics in L2 acquisition: The role of specificity. *Language Acquisition* 12, 3–69.

Jackendoff, Ray 2002. *Foundations of Language*. Oxford: Oxford University Press.

Johnson, Jacqueline & Elissa Newport 1989. Critical period effects in second language learning: The influence of maturational state on the acquisition of English as a second language. *Cognitive Psychology* 20, 60–99.

Johnson, Jacqueline & Elissa Newport 1991. Critical period effects on universal properties of language: The status of subjacency in the acquisition of a second language. *Cognition* 39, 215–258.

Kanno, Kazue 1996. The status of a non-parametrized principle in the L2 initial state. *Language Acquistion* 5, 317–335.

Kanno, Kazue 1998. The stability of UG principles in second-language acquisition: Evidence from Japanese. *Linguistics* 36, 1125–1146.

Landman, Fred 1992. The progressive. *Natural Language Semantics* 1, 1–32.

Lardiere, Donna 1998. Dissociating syntax from morphology in a divergent end-state grammar. *Second Language Research* 14, 359–375.

Lardiere, Donna 2008. Feature-assembly in second language acquisition. In: J. Liceras, H. Zobl & H. Goodluck (eds.). *The Role of Features in Second Language Acquisition*. Mahwah, NJ: Lawrence Erlbaum Associates, 106–140.

Lee, Dami & Jacquelyn Schachter 1997. Sensitive period effects in Binding Theory. *Language Acquisition* 6, 333–362.

Lenneberg, Eric 1967. *Biological Foundations of Language.* New York: Wiley.
Marinis, Theodoros, Leah Roberts, Claudia Felser & Harald Clahsen 2005. Gaps in second language processing. *Studies in Second Language Acquisition* 27, 53–78.
Marsden, Heather 2004. *Quantifier Scope in Non-native Japanese: A Comparative Interlanguage Study of Chinese, English and Korean-speaking Learners.* Ph.D. dissertation. University of Durham.
McDonald, Janet L. 2000. Grammaticality judgments in a second language: Influences of age of acquisition and native language. *Applied Psycholinguistics* 21, 395–423.
Montrul, Silvina & Roumyana Slabakova 2002. Acquiring morphosyntactic and semantic properties of preterite and imperfect tenses in L2 Spanish. In: A.-T. Perez-Leroux & J. Liceras (eds.). *The Acquisition of Spanish Morphosyntax: The L1-L2 Connection.* Dordrecht: Kluwer, 113–149.
Montrul, Silvina & Roumyana Slabakova 2003. Competence similarities between native and near-native speakers: An investigation of the preterite/imperfect contrast in Spanish. *Studies in Second Language Acquisition* 25, 351–398.
Neeleman, Ad & Fred Weerman 1997. L1 and L2 word order acquisition. *Language Acquisition* 6, 125–170.
Newport, Elissa 1990. Maturational constraints on language learning. *Cognitive Science* 14, 11–28.
Paradis, Michel 2004. *A Neurolinguistic Theory of Bilingualism.* Amsterdam: Benjamins.
Penfield, Wilder & Larry Roberts 1959. *Speech and Brain Mechanisms.* Princeton, NJ: Princeton University Press.
Prévost, Philippe & Lydia White 2000. Missing surface inflection or impairment in second language acquisition? Evidence from tense and agreement. *Second Language Research* 16, 103–133.
Schwartz, Bonnie & Rex Sprouse 1996. L2 cognitive states and the full transfer/full access model. *Second Language Research* 12, 40–72.
Slabakova, Roumyana 2003. Semantic evidence for functional categories in interlanguage grammars. *Second Language Research* 19, 42–75.
Slabakova, Roumyana 2006. Is there a critical period for semantics? *Second Language Research* 22, 302–338.
Slabakova, Roumyana 2007. Scalar implicatures in L2 acquisition. In: H. Caunt-Nulton, S. Kulatilake & I. Woo (eds.). *Proceedings of the 31st Boston University Conference on Language Development (= BUCLD).* Somerville, MA: Cascadilla Press, 576–584.
Slabakova, Roumyana 2008. *Meaning in the Second Language.* Berlin: Mouton de Gruyter.
Slabakova, Roumyana 2010. Scalar Implicatures in second language acquisition. *Lingua* 120, 2444–2462.
Slabakova, Roumyana & Silvina Montrul 2002. On viewpoint aspect and its L2 acquisition: A UG perspective. In: R. Salaberry & Y. Shirai (eds.). *Tense-Aspect Morphology in L2 Acquisition.* Amsterdam: Benjamins, 363–398.
Slabakova, Roumyana & Silvina Montrul 2003. Genericity and aspect in L2 acquisition. *Language Acquisition* 11, 165–196.
Sorace, Antonella 1993. Incomplete versus divergent representations of unaccusativity in non-native grammars of Italian and French. *Second Language Research* 9, 22–47.
Sorace, Antonella 2003. Near-nativeness. In: C. Doughty & M. Long (eds.). *The Handbook of Second Language Acquisition.* Oxford: Blackwell, 130–151.
Sorace, Antonella & Francesca Filiaci 2006. Anaphora resolution in near-native speakers of Italian. *Second Language Research* 22, 339–368.

Sprouse, Rex 1998. Some notes on the relationship between inflectional morphology and parameter setting in first and second language acquisition. In: M.-L. Beck (ed.). *Morphology and Its Interfaces in Second Language Knowledge*. Amsterdam: Benjamins, 41–67.

de Swart, Henriëtte 1998. Aspect shift and coercion. *Language and Linguistic Theory* 16, 347–385.

Townsend, David J. & Thomas G. Bever 2001. *Sentence Comprehension: The Integration of Habits and Rules*. Cambridge, MA: The MIT Press.

Tsimpli, Ianthi & Anna Roussou 1991. Parameter resetting in L2A? *UCL Working Papers in Linguistics* 3, 149–169.

Tsimpli, Ianthi & Maria Dimitrakopoulou 2007. The Interpretability Hypothesis: Evidence from *wh*-interrogatives in second language acquisition. *Second Language Research* 23, 215–242.

Unsworth, Sharon 2005. *Child L2, Adult L2, Child L1: Differences and Similarities. A Study on the Acquisition of Direct Object Scrambling in Dutch*. Ph.D. dissertation. Utrecht University.

White, Lydia 2003. *Second Language Acquisition and Universal Grammar*. Cambridge: Cambridge University Press.

Stephanie Kelter and Barbara Kaup
11 Conceptual knowledge, categorization, and meaning

1 Introduction —— 303
2 Conceptual knowledge —— 305
3 Theoretical approaches —— 312
4 Issues of debate —— 315
5 Conceptual combination —— 320
6 Relationship between conceptual knowledge and word meanings —— 326
7 Concluding remarks —— 333
8 References —— 335

Abstract: Since Eleanor Rosch's groundbreaking work in the 1970s, conceptual knowledge has become a subject of extensive research in cognitive psychology. This chapter provides an overview of the current state of the art. Research has focused on conceptual knowledge about concrete physical things. The main research questions concern the structure and content of conceptual knowledge and its functions, in particular categorization. Most research is based on the view that conceptual knowledge comprises a set of relatively fixed packets of information, or concepts, which are assumed to correspond to lexical meanings. This view of the relationship between conceptual and lexical-semantic knowledge is discussed towards the end of the chapter.

1 Introduction

The human mind does not have direct access to the world. What is taken as a real situation in the world is the content of a mental representation constructed from sensory data and knowledge stored in long-term memory. Conceptual knowledge plays a pivotal role here, imposing a particular structure on the representation and promoting a conceptualization in terms of entities of particular kinds, possessing certain properties and being related to each other in particular ways. For example, a given dynamic visual input may, by virtue of conceptual knowledge, give rise to

---
Stephanie Kelter, Berlin, Germany
Barbara Kaup, Tübingen, Germany

https://doi.org/10.1515/9783110589825-011

the perception of a structured motion event such as a rabbit jumping into the room. In a similar way, conceptual knowledge also shapes the structure and contents of mental representations in thinking and action planning. It is important to distinguish between conceptual knowledge itself and mental representations constructed at certain points in time that are shaped by conceptual knowledge. The distinction may best be framed in terms of the distinction between long-term memory, which is a permanent store of information, and working memory, where temporary representations are created and manipulated. In working memory, information retrieved from long-term memory is integrated with information from the sensory-motor and emotional systems, and the resulting representations are also heavily influenced by motivational factors and attentional processes. Thus, the mental representation of a situation, event, or individual entity currently perceived or thought of is a representation in working memory. It is shaped by conceptual knowledge but is not part of conceptual knowledge. Conceptual knowledge itself is a component of long-term memory.

Language is a means by which a person can convey information residing in working memory to another person. In doing so, the person needs to carve up the working memory representation and package the intended information in a way which conforms to the linguistic structures of his or her language. For example, to communicate the above mentioned motion event of a rabbit jumping into the room, the various pieces of information, including the entities and the manner and path of motion, must be organized in a particular way. Obviously, the difficulty of the task largely depends on how similar the required structure is to the structure of the given working memory representation, as induced by conceptual knowledge. Many cognitive psychologists assume that conceptual knowledge comprises distinct concepts, each of which corresponds to the meaning of a particular lexical item. If so, carving up working memory representations for the purpose of coding their contents linguistically would be a relatively straightforward process. However, matters are far from settled. As yet few studies have addressed the conceptualization of complex situations or actions and their mapping onto linguistic structures, except in research on the linguistic relativity hypothesis (see Sec. 6) and language development (see, e.g., Snedeker & Gleitman 2004; see also article 13 [this volume] (Landau) *Space in semantics and cognition*). By far the most studies of conceptual knowledge are concerned with concepts of everyday physical things (for research on other noun concepts, see, e.g., Wisniewski 2009 and Papafragou 2005 on substance concepts, and Goldwater, Markman & Stilwell 2011 on relational concepts). Moreover, even for concepts of everyday physical things, the claim that they correspond to lexical meanings is difficult to evaluate. The reason is that research on conceptual knowledge in general simply presupposes that concepts are word meanings, rather than investigating this issue experimentally. Due to this presupposition, it is common practice in empirical studies to employ verbal stimuli to investigate concepts and when using nonverbal tasks, rarely is any effort made to control for internal linguistic processes such as covert naming or priming from preceding or expected linguistic tasks. Thus, for many of the studies on conceptual knowledge it is strictly speaking impossible to decide whether the results do in fact reveal something about conceptual knowledge or rather about lexical semantic knowledge. However, notwithstanding this unfortunate ambiguity, the findings are in any case of interest to semantics.

This chapter provides an overview of research on conceptual knowledge in cognitive psychology. Its focus is on behavioral research (cf. Martin & Caramazza 2003 for neuroscientific research). In Sections 2 to 5 we report empirical findings on the content and structure of conceptual knowledge and outline the different theoretical approaches as well as their major points of contention. In these sections, we adopt the view of concepts as lexical meanings, but in Section 6, we explicitly address the question of how conceptual and lexical-semantic knowledge are related.

The literature on conceptual knowledge is enormous and there are many different foci of research. Our chapter concentrates on research with human adults. Readers interested in conceptual development or concepts in animals are referred to the reviews by Smith & Colunga (2012) and Lazareva & Wasserman (2008), respectively. For reasons of space, we must also ignore research on the impact of conceptual knowledge on inductive reasoning (for a review, see Hayes, Heit & Swendsen 2010) and formal models of categorization (see Pothos & Wills 2011).

2 Conceptual knowledge

2.1 Functions of conceptual knowledge

The most obvious function of conceptual knowledge is to allow for the categorization of things. In fact, this function has traditionally been in the focus of theoretical and empirical research on conceptual knowledge. It is commonly assumed that conceptual knowledge comprises distinct concepts, each of which provides information about a particular category of entities in the world (or more precisely, of entities that people deem as being in the external world). For example, the concept HAMMER may include information about what members of the category {hammers} look like, how they are used, and so on. (We indicate concepts by small caps and sets of entities in the world by curly brackets). A given thing is categorized by examining how well its properties match the information contained in a particular concept, possibly compared with alternative concepts. Theories differ in their assumptions as to the information contained in concepts and categorization decision rules (see Sec. 3 and 4).

A deeper understanding of what conceptual knowledge is good for is gained by considering its influence on representations of things in working memory (cf. Sec. 1). What happens when some part of a scene is recognized as a particular kind of entity, say, as a car? In what way does this use of conceptual knowledge shape the interpretation of the sensory input or, in other words, the mental representation of this part of the scene? Concept theories are not always explicit with respect to this issue but a widespread assumption seems to be that if something is conceptualized as a member of a particular category (e.g., {cars}), then its representation in working memory is essentially a replica of the content of the respective concept. This implies that whenever a person identifies things as a car, the working memory representations of those things are identical in content. Some more recent accounts ascribe greater flexibility to working memory representations. For example, simulation theory (Barsalou 2009) emphasizes that their contents are also influenced by the situational context. On this view, a car may be represented rather differently in working memory depending on whether it is being driven, filled with gas, washed, or bought. In any case, the accounts agree that conceptual knowledge affects representations in working memory in two complementary ways. On the one hand, some pieces of information are suppressed or deleted from the representation, specifically ones that are conceptually irrelevant. This may be considered the *abstraction* function of conceptual knowledge. Instead of representing the given thing in all its details, the representation mainly contains information that characterizes it as a particular kind of entity (in a particular situation). Abstraction is advantageous if not necessary to protect subsequent processing (e.g., thinking, problem solving, action planning) from being influenced by irrelevant information. On the other hand, the representation is supplemented with some pieces of information which stem from conceptual knowledge rather than being given by the stimulus itself. We refer to this as *prediction*. Prediction is a less obvious function of conceptual knowledge than abstraction. Let us therefore consider it in some more detail.

Conceptual knowledge is constantly used for predictions in daily life. When we grasp a hammer, we anticipate its approximate weight, even if we've never seen it before. When we cut an apple we expect it to be white inside. When we see a snowman in a backyard, we assume it to have been built by children. Notice that the predictions considered here are not predictions in the ordinary sense. They may not only concern the future but also the present (e.g., the snowman is made out of snow) and the past (e.g., the snowman was built by children). Furthermore, they may be made unconsciously, and they derive from stored information about past situations rather than from explicitly learned rules. What is the basis for such predictions? Let us assume that in the current situation, there is something possessing the feature A. We further assume that according to the information represented in conceptual knowledge, previous situations with feature A also involved feature C, say, in 70% of the cases. Unless feature C's presence in the current situation is obvious anyhow, this knowledge can be used to estimate that the likelihood of feature C in the current situation is .70. Clearly, using feature A for estimating the likelihood of feature C is pointless if according to prior knowledge, C was present in 70% of *all* past situations (i.e., if according to prior knowledge, the base rate of C is .70). In this case, one could have estimated the likelihood of C to be .70 without considering feature A. However, taking into account feature A *is* advantageous if according to prior knowledge, feature C was more often, or alternatively, less often present in situations containing A than in other situations. More generally speaking, taking into account a given feature A improves the prediction of a yet unobserved feature C, if there is a statistical **association** between the features A and C. Of course, usually more than a single feature A is used to estimate the likelihood of an unobserved feature C, and other features or feature combinations, say B, may modify the association between the features A and C. For example, the likelihood of feature C <breaks when dropped> is high for an object with feature A <cup-shaped> if feature B <made of porcelain> is present but low if feature B' <made of plastic> is present instead.

It should be noted that in the literature on concepts and categorization, one frequently finds the term *correlation* instead of *association*. However, as features are usually considered qualitative properties (i.e., being either present or absent), it is most often the contingency between two features that is at issue. We therefore use the umbrella term *association* to cover both correlation and contingency.

In sum, feature prediction uses information about associations among features in past situations. This information is provided by conceptual knowledge. As we have seen, conceptual knowledge need not be organized into distinct concepts to allow for feature prediction. However, as mentioned, many accounts postulate such an organization. These accounts generally consider categorization a necessary first step for feature prediction. Specifically, a given thing is first assigned to a particular category and then the information contained in the respective concept becomes available (see Murphy & Ross 2010 and Hayes, Heit & Swendsen 2010: 286–287, for a discussion of this issue).

2.2 The content of conceptual knowledge

Our characterization of conceptual knowledge as knowledge about feature associations converges with a view that has been widespread since Rosch's seminal articles (e.g., Rosch 1978; Rosch et al. 1976). On this view, conceptual knowledge has its basis in the correlational structure of the world. Each concept represents a particular bundle of strongly associated features (cf. Sec. 3 for other views). Of course, the features are not features of the world as such but arise from our sensory-motor and emotional systems (e.g., <red>, <sticky>, <ugly>) and higher cognitive processes integrating information from various sources (e.g., <dangerous>, <breakable>, <expensive>).

The relationship between features and concepts is an intricate matter. First, at least many high-level features arise so as to facilitate the discrimination of categories (see Schyns, Goldstone & Thibaut 1998). Thus, rather than being independent building blocks of concepts, features themselves may to some extent depend on required conceptual distinctions. Second, high-level features are probably often configurations of simpler features. From a structural point of view, such features are therefore difficult to distinguish from concepts. Moreover, features may even involve concepts (e.g., <has a pit>, <eats meat>). This entails a significant broadening of the notion of features, and in addition, it introduces a new aspect of conceptual structure, namely that of thematic relations. Let us briefly explain this issue.

In Section 2.2 we deliberately spoke of features *in situations*. People usually do not experience isolated things. Rather they experience things in the context of particular situations and as objects of their own actions. It is likely that associations between the features of a given thing (e.g., a cherry) and features of things frequently encountered in its context (e.g., tree), as well as features of actions frequently performed with the thing (e.g., picking, eating) are encoded. Thus, conceptual knowledge also contains information about so-called thematic relations (e.g., cherry – tree; cherry – eating; hammer – nail; for empirical evidence, see, e.g., Estes, Golonka & Jones 2011). Having a particular thematic relation to other entities can be considered a feature of an entity. Such features are sometimes called *extrinsic* features as opposed to *intrinsic* features, which are true of an entity in isolation (see Barr & Caplan 1987). Thus, for example, the concept CHERRY may include not only the intrinsic features <red> and <round> but also the extrinsic features <grows on trees>, <can be bought on the market>, <can be eaten>. Indeed, many studies have shown that commonalities with respect to extrinsic features increase perceived similarity and affect categorization (for a review, see Estes, Golonka & Jones 2011).

We have emphasized the correlational structure of the world as the basis of conceptual knowledge. However, subjective factors play an important role as well. It is reasonable to assume that the feature associations that get encoded are mainly those that are sufficiently salient and relevant to a person's life. Thus, cultural background, job, and interests may have a significant impact on people's conceptual structure (see, e.g., Medin et al. 2006, and Tanaka & Taylor

1991). It may even be the case that only feature associations construed as causal relations are encoded (see Sec. 4.3 for a discussion). Another important issue is that not all feature associations encoded in conceptual knowledge stem from direct experience; many of them may derive from communication with other people.

2.3 Conceptual hierarchies

Things can often be categorized in various ways. For example, something may be conceptualized as a flute, a component of an orchestra, a gift for a child, a thing to take on a vacation, a recorder, or a musical instrument. Particularly the possibility of identifying things at various levels of specificity (e.g., musical instrument, flute, recorder) has received much attention in research on concepts and categorization. Which level is preferred and why? Before addressing this question, let us consider the conditions for differentiating a concept into more specific concepts.

Establishing concepts at a more specific level of abstraction is not done arbitrarily, but according to certain constraints. For example, most people lack concepts for different types of mountains or ideas. Furthermore, while RED_WINE and WHITE_WINE are well-established concepts, RED_DRESS and WHITE_DRESS are not. Why not? If we take into account that a main function of concepts is feature prediction, the answer is straightforward. A concept such as RED_DRESS would not allow for any predictions other than those inferable from the concept DRESS plus the information that the dress is red. In contrast, the concept RED_WINE allows additional predictions with respect to the taste of the wine, its optimal temperature, and the meals that it goes well with. Such predictions are possible because in the category {wines}, certain colors are associated with certain tastes, optimal temperatures, and appropriate meals. In other words, our conjecture is that a more specific concept is established only if there are feature associations *within* the category specified by the parent concept. The more specific concept then renders it possible to predict new features that cannot be predicted on the basis of the parent concept. It may be interesting to note that according to this view, it is unlikely that the concept BACHELOR only comprises the features listed in the concept MAN (<human>, <male>, <adult>) plus the feature <unmarried>. If conceptually a bachelor were no more than an unmarried man, then the concept would not exist. Rather, the concept captures the association between <unmarried> and certain other features occurring in the category {men}, as for instance, <has to take care of the laundry himself>, <is not responsible for a family>, <is always ready to go to a party>, and so on.

Based on these considerations, it may be supposed that people prefer using concepts at the lowest level, since that allows the most predictions. In their renowned study, Rosch et al. (1976), however, demonstrated that the level that people prefer in conceptual tasks (dubbed the *basic level*) is most often a certain middle level in a taxonomy. For example, people prefer categorizing things as members of {chairs}, {tables}, or {beds} rather than as members of {kitchen chairs} or {pieces of furniture}, and similarly, they prefer using the categories {flutes}, {drums}, {pianos} rather than the subordinate categories (e.g., {recorders}) or the superordinate category {musical instruments}. Many subsequent studies replicated this finding, and in addition provided evidence that basic level superiority is not simply due to the fact that the labels of basic level categories are relatively frequent and short words and are acquired relatively early in childhood (for reviews, see Mervis & Rosch 1981 and Murphy & Lassaline 1997). It should be noted, however, that the basic level is not always privileged. For experts in a domain (e.g., dog experts, bird watchers), the subordinate level is as useful as the basic level in their domain of expertise (e.g., BEAGLE or COLLIE vs. DOG; see Johnson & Mervis 1997; Tanaka & Taylor 1991), and in semantic dementia, the superordinate level appears to be better preserved than the basic level (see Rogers & Patterson 2007).

Why is the basic level usually privileged in conceptual tasks? Important hints come from studies in which participants were asked to list as many features as possible that are shared by the members of a given superordinate, basic, or subordinate category, respectively (e.g., Johnson & Mervis 1997; Rosch et al. 1976; Tanaka & Taylor 1991). Not surprisingly, participants listed more features for categories lower in the hierarchy (e.g., the number of listed features increases from {pieces of furniture} to {chairs} to {kitchen chairs}). Yet, the increase was not constant for each downward move but largest when moving from the superordinate level (e.g., {pieces of furniture}) to the basic level (e.g., {chairs}). The move from the basic to the subordinate level (e.g., {kitchen chairs}) yielded relatively few additional features. This suggests that basic-level categories are much more homogenous than superordinate categories, which is clearly advantageous with regard to category-based feature prediction. In addition, Rosch et al. (1976) found that the members of a basic category (e.g., {chairs}) share relatively few features with the members of other categories at the same level, (e.g., {tables}, {beds}, {cupboards}). In other words, alternative categories at the basic level are particularly clearly differentiated from each other, compared with alternative categories at other levels (e.g., at the subordinate level: {kitchen chairs} vs. {office chairs} vs. {easy chairs}).

On the basis of these findings, Mervis & Rosch (1981) characterized the basic level as the level at which the set of entities of a domain is partitioned in such a way that the categories maximize within-category similarity relative to between-category similarity. Other researchers have also been concerned with the *structural* properties of the partitions at different levels in natural and artificial taxonomies and with possible measures of the utility of partitions (for an overview and a recent proposal, see Gosselin & Schyns 2001).

Another possible explanation of the privileged status of basic-level categories emerges from the consideration that outside of the laboratory, the different kinds of features typically play different roles in conceptual processing. For example, what is typically "given" when perceiving things are salient visual features (e.g., shape, part structure, color, movement), whereas the features that we want to predict are the features that arise over time (e.g., the melting of a snowman), the appropriate motor programs for interacting with the thing, and the features that emerge from this interaction (e.g., the weight of a hammer; the behavior of a rabbit when one approaches it), as well as more abstract features. Thus, concepts should capture the associations between visual features and these latter kinds of features. Superordinate concepts may be largely useless in this regard. Rosch et al. (1976) (see also Jolicoeur, Gluck & Kosslyn 1984; Tanaka & Taylor 1991) found that different superordinate categories (e.g., {vehicles}, {buildings}) can hardly be distinguished on the basis of visual properties; they mainly differ in function (e.g., <used for transport of persons>). In contrast, basic-level categories (e.g., {cars}, {trucks}, {airplanes}) were found to typically differ in salient visual features (shape, part structure) as well as with respect to motor movements for interacting with the things. Thus, identifying a thing as an instance of a particular basic-level concept is probably relatively straightforward and allows predictions as to appropriate interactions. The subordinate level may again be less useful. At this level, the information about the visual features is refined but with respect to action affordances and appropriate motor programs there are no significant differences between the different subordinate categories of the same basic category (e.g., {Rolls Royces} vs. {Mini Coopers}). In other words, categorization at the subordinate level costs more perceptual effort (see, e.g., Collin & McMullen 2005) without providing more information as to how the given thing can be interacted with (clearly, there may be a profit with respect to the prediction of some other features, e.g., <expensive>). Taken together, it is plausible that when perceiving things, the natural "entry point" into conceptual knowledge is at the basic level (Jolicoeur, Gluck & Kosslyn 1984). Let us add, however, that this probably does not apply to all conceptual tasks. For example, in action planning, when pondering about possible means of achieving a particular goal, functional features may come to mind first. Someone who is hungry may think of buying something that can be eaten, and someone planning to go to a dangerous place may think of taking along something for self-defense. Thus, in action planning, the entry point into a taxonomy may often be at the superordinate level.

We end this section with a cautionary remark on the notion of hierarchical relations. The organizational principle of a truly hierarchical classification scheme is that of set inclusion. However, it is questionable whether this principle generally applies to concept-based taxonomies. First, concepts, as we have characterized them, do not provide defining features of the members of a category but features are more or less biased to the assignment of a given entity to a particular category (cf. Sec. 3 and 4). Hence, intransitive categorical decisions may arise. For example, a car seat may be judged to belong to the category {chairs} but not to the category {pieces of furniture} (Hampton 1982; see also Sloman 1998). Second, many of the concepts that are commonly considered superordinate concepts (e.g., CLOTHING, FOOD, JEWELRY) may actually refer to groups or collections of heterogeneous entities, united by spatio-temporal contiguity and function (see Wisniewski, Imai & Casey 1996). If so, then a single item, for example a shirt, can not more be considered an instance of CLOTHING, than a single singer an instance of CHOIR or a single ship an instance of FLEET.

3 Theoretical approaches

Although in the previous section we tried to avoid committing ourselves to a particular concept theory, our presentation was certainly not theory-neutral. This section gives an overview of the theoretical approaches to conceptual knowledge and categorization.

According to the **definitional approach** (or classical approach), a concept defines a category by specifying the features that are singly necessary and jointly sufficient for membership in the category. Few if any cognitive psychologists consider this view adequate for everyday concepts and categories. This is not to deny that in certain kinds of artificial or technical category learning tasks, people may expect the categories to be well-defined and aim at finding a simple rule for discriminating between them (*rule-based categorization*; see Close et al. 2010). However, there are a number of strong theoretical and empirical arguments against the definitional view of everyday concepts (see, e.g., Murphy 2002, chap. 2). Many of them were pointed out by Rosch and her colleagues in a series of seminal articles in the 1970s (for an overview, see Mervis & Rosch 1981). These researchers also proposed an alternative to the definitional view which quickly found many adherents, namely the prototype view (e.g., Rosch & Mervis 1975).

According to the **prototype view,** the different members of a category, rather than all sharing a certain set of features, each match (or resemble) other members in different respects. In other words, they bear a "family resemblance" (Rosch & Mervis 1975). Category membership is a matter of degree; it is a function of an item's similarity to the *prototype* of the category, which is what is represented in the corresponding concept. There are two rather different conceptions of a prototype. According to the first one, it is an assemblage of all possible features, each weighted by its frequency of occurrence in the category (e.g., Rosch & Mervis 1975) or by another measure of its importance for the category (e.g., Hampton 1993). For example, in the prototype for TOMATO, <red> has a greater weight than <green>. According to the second conception, a prototype is a sort of central-tendency instantiation of the category, possessing the features that correspond to the mean or modal value of the category members on each attribute dimension (e.g., Minda & Smith 2011). Notice that neither conception envisages that a prototype captures within-category relations between attribute dimensions or the relative frequency of co-occurrence of certain features in the category (e.g., <red> & <ripe>). Rather, the various attribute dimensions are considered independently of each other. Hence, prototype theories belong to the class of *independent cue theories* (Medin & Schaffer 1978).

The previously mentioned theoretical approaches regard concepts as knowledge structures that – albeit possibly being used as building blocks in other types of knowledge – are in principle independent of other types of knowledge. By contrast, the **theory-based approach** (sometimes referred to as explanation-based or knowledge-based approach) assumes that concepts are embedded in naïve domain-specific theories (e.g., Murphy & Medin 1985). Concepts are "mini-theories" (Rips 1995), specifying categories in terms of causal relationships among features. Category membership is determined by estimating how well the features of a given thing can be explained by the causal mechanisms specified in the concept (e.g., Rehder 2010). One version of the theory-based approach is **psychological essentialism** (e.g., Gelman 2004; Medin & Ortony 1989), according to which people believe that the members of a category share an unchanging property, an essence, that causes category members to have the features they do. The essence of a category may be unknown, in which case the concept contains an "essence placeholder". Notice that psychological essentialism, like the definitional approach, assumes that categories have clear-cut boundaries – every entity either is or is not in a particular category. This does not imply clear-cut categorization judgments. Often a person may be uncertain about the essence of a given thing and needs to rely on features considered diagnostic of essences.

Almost all theories posit that a concept is a sort of summary representation of a category, characterizing the set of category members as a whole. The only exception is the **exemplar approach**, which assumes that a concept represents the individual exemplars of the category that have been encountered in the past (e.g., Medin & Schaffer 1978; Nosofsky 1986; Storms 2004). The "glue" holding together the different exemplars of a category is their common label. A thing with an unknown label is categorized by comparing it with the individual exemplars of the relevant alternative categories and choosing the category for which the observed similarities are largest overall. Exemplar theories imply that people possess implicit knowledge about the co-occurrence of features within categories and that categorization is sensitive to the particular combination of features being true of the given thing.

According to **connectionist models,** conceptual knowledge is encoded in a large network of representational units with weighted connections between them. In distributed models (e.g., McRae 2004; Moss, Tyler & Taylor 2007) the units represent conceptual microfeatures and the weights of the connections reflect the strengths of their associations. When a group of microfeatures becomes activated (e.g., by sensory input), activation is propagated through the network via the connections until eventually a stable pattern of activated units is reached. This pattern is a working memory representation that is shaped by conceptual knowledge. However, the process does not necessarily imply categorization in the usual sense, as distributed connectionist models do not generally assume the conceptual network to be organized into distinct concepts.

A related theory is the **simulation view** of conceptual processing (e.g., Barsalou 2009), which assumes that concepts are bindings of memory traces distributed over modality-specific mental subsystems. Importantly, concepts include information about the situations in which the category's members were encountered. Upon perceiving an entity, its features and the context entail a re-enactment of various memory traces that were formed when similar things were previously encountered in similar situations. The result is a highly situation-specific construal of the given thing as a member of the category.

The various theoretical views are not mutually exclusive. For instance, a prototype model may make the additional assumption that concepts contain information about causal and other relations between features (see Hampton 2006). Furthermore, summary representations and sets-of-exemplars representations are frequently taken as end points of a continuum. Example models include Anderson's (1991) rational model, SUSTAIN (Love, Medin & Gureckis 2004), and the varying abstraction model (Vanpaemel & Storms 2008). Other models assume that people draw on different kinds of knowledge when categorizing items, for instance, on prototypes plus remembered exemplars (e.g., Smith & Minda 2000). Similarly, some researchers emphasize that multiple, neurobiologically distinct memory systems contribute to category learning and categorizing (e.g., Ashby & Maddox 2011).

4 Issues of debate

Many controversies in research on concepts and categorization originate from criticisms of the prototype view. In this section, we address three important issues of debate. In each of them certain implications of the prototype view are compared against those of one or two other theoretical views mentioned in the previous section.

4.1 Is category membership a matter of degree?

Prototype theories assume that category membership is graded. The more similar a given thing is to the prototype the more clearly it is a member of this category. In addition, according to prototype theories, the typicality of an item reflects its degree of category membership. Both these assumptions are questioned by other researchers, in particular by proponents of the definitional and essentialist view. They posit that category membership is all-or-none – a thing is either a full member of a category or it is not a member of the category – and typicality has nothing to do with category membership. Let us first consider the variable of typicality and then turn to the more general question of whether category membership is all-or-none or a matter of degree. Before reviewing the empirical findings, it is important to re-emphasize that in empirical research on conceptual knowledge, the categories and the items to be categorized are often specified linguistically, and this is especially true in this research area. Most of the findings we report in this section are therefore actually findings about knowledge and use of lexical meanings. However, we present them in accordance with the way they are normally interpreted.

It is well-established that members of a category vary in the degree to which they are considered representative or good examples of the category. One particular cat may appear "cattier" than another one. Similarly, a trout or a herring is considered more representative of the category {fish} than a shark or a flounder, for instance. The most common measure of representativeness is typicality. Typicality is operationally defined, namely by responses to questions of the form *How typical is item x of category y?* or *How good an example is item x of category y?* Notice that typicality is a matter of the *relation* between an item and a category. This becomes evident when we consider different levels of a taxonomy. For example, a robin is rated more typical than a chicken if the target category is {birds}, but the opposite is true if the target category is {animals} (see Roth & Mervis 1983).

It should be mentioned that ratings of typicality are not always based on considerations concerning representativeness. Specifically, in domains in which a person has expert knowledge, and with goal-derived categories (e.g., {foods to eat on a diet}), the ratings are mainly determined by how close an item is to the ideal of the category (see, e.g., Barsalou 1985; Lynch, Coley & Medin 2000; for a unified account, see Davis & Love 2010). However, we ignore this "atypical" variant of typicality in the following.

Empirical research has revealed that typicality plays a role in a wide variety of conceptual tasks (for reviews, see Mervis & Rosch 1981 and Smith & Medin 1981, chap. 3), as well as in lexical processing and the pragmatics of certain expressions (see, e.g., Onishi, Murphy & Bock 2008; Rosch, 1978). Most importantly in our context, typicality has been found to be highly correlated with category-membership judgments as well as with measures of feature overlap and other measures of similarity to the prototype (e.g., Hampton 1998; Rosch & Mervis 1975). Proponents of the prototype view consider these findings as evidence that typicality is based on the same underlying variable that category membership is based on, namely similarity to the prototype (see Hampton 2007 for an explication of this assumption). This conclusion is challenged by other researchers (e.g., Armstrong, Gleitman & Gleitman 1983; Kamp & Partee 1995; Osherson & Smith 1997), who argue that for theoretical reasons and in view of certain empirical findings, typicality and category membership need to be distinguished. For example, Armstrong, Gleitman & Gleitman (1983) point out that graded typicality judgments are obtained even for well-defined categories such as {even numbers}. A summary of the main arguments in this debate is given in Hampton's (2007) rejoinder.

Considering the controversial status of typicality ratings, it is reasonable to ask participants directly for judgments of category membership to find out whether category membership is absolute or a matter of degree. The simplest and most frequently used method of obtaining category-membership judgments are Yes-No categorization tasks. Participants are presented with a category name and various items (pictures of objects or verbal labels) and are asked to decide for each item whether or not it is a member of the category. Typically, a gradient of judged category membership is found – some items are categorized as members of the target category by more participants than are others. For example, in a study by McCloskey & Glucksberg (1978), the item *airplane* was categorized as a member of the category *vehicles* by nearly all participants whereas *roller skate* and *parachute* turned out to be "borderline" items, judged as members of the category *vehicles* by barely more than 50% of the participants. Of course, this finding may simply reflect individual differences in the placement of the category boundaries. However, McCloskey & Glucksberg (1978) also found that participants, when presented with the task a second time, sometimes changed their categorization decision, in particular for borderline items. This variability may be attributed to an instability of the criteria for judging category membership or to fluctuations in the content of the representations established in working memory. In any case, the finding suggests that judged category membership is more "fragile" for some items than for others. This however does not yet prove that people believe that category membership is a matter of degree.

To clarify this issue, other experimental paradigms were developed. For example, participants were asked to judge the category membership of items on a scale from "definitely not a member" to "definitely a member", offering the opportunity for expressing degrees of category membership (e.g., *How clearly is an escalator a member of the category 'vehicles'?*) (see, e.g., Barr & Caplan 1987; Diesendruck & Gelman 1999). Furthermore, various meta-cognitive tasks were used. For example, Kalish (1995) presented pairs of statements such as *John says this animal is an elephant* and *Jane says this animal is not an elephant* and asked participants to decide whether this disagreement would in principle be resolvable as only one statement can be true, or whether it would in principle be irresolvable as one can always argue for both sides. Together, the results from these studies (see Estes 2004 and the literature cited therein) suggest that people consider category membership a matter of degree for artifacts (e.g., vehicles, tools), while they are somewhat more inclined to assume absolute membership for many categories of natural kinds (e.g., birds, fruit). It should be added that differences between concepts of artifacts and natural kinds have been revealed in other areas of research as well, but there is as yet no widely accepted answer as to what precisely distinguishes the concepts in these domains (see Margolis & Laurence 2007).

4.2 Summary representations or representations of sets of individual exemplars?

Much research has been devoted to the question of whether concepts provide information about entire categories ("summary representation") or represent individual exemplars of categories. Although the former view is taken by many different theories, the debate is centered between those versions of prototype theory that consider prototypes as central-tendency representations (see Sec. 3) and exemplar theories. The debate led to a flood of categorization studies, mostly using artificial categories (e.g., sets of dot patterns; sets of geometric forms varying in shape, size, and color) that participants first learn in the experiment. Using artificial stimuli has the advantage that the categories can be tailored to the question at hand. To illustrate, let us consider a simple categorization task in which participants assign stimuli to one of two categories, {a} and {b}. According to prototype theory, all that matters is the similarity of the given stimulus S to the prototype of each of the categories (see Minda & Smith 2011). The more similar

S is to one of the prototypes, the more likely it will be categorized as a member of this category. Specifically, if S exactly matches one of the prototypes, say that of category {a}, then the likelihood that it is categorized as a member of category {a} rather than {b} is maximal, even if it is quite similar to some exemplars in the alternative category. According to exemplar accounts, however, what matters is the similarity of S to the individual exemplars of the two categories (see Nosofsky 1986). Even if S is identical to the prototype of one of the categories, it may be categorized as a member of the contrast category, provided it is extremely similar to one or more of the exemplars of this category. By creating artificial categories, variables such as these can be manipulated, while keeping other ones constant. Importantly, whereas in many natural categories the prototype is an abstract entity, which doesn't actually exist, artificial categories can be designed such that the prototype exists in the set of stimuli.

To test the validity of the theories, many studies have investigated the categorization of the prototypes of categories. In a typical experiment, the stimulus material comprises two stimuli constituting the prototypes of two categories (e.g., two different patterns of five dots each) and a number of different "distortions" of the prototypes (e.g., patterns of five dots that slightly differ from the respective prototype with respect to the spatial relations among the dots). In a training phase, participants are presented with a selection of the distortions and are told which category each pattern belongs to. The prototypes themselves are not presented in this phase. In a later transfer phase, participants categorize old distortions (i.e., patterns that were presented during training), new distortions (i.e., patterns that were not presented before), as well as the prototypes of the categories. According to prototype theory, the prototype of a category should be particularly easy to categorize (*prototype-enhancement effect*). Early studies using this prototype-distortion paradigm (e.g., Posner & Keele 1968) confirmed this prediction. However, in those studies, the similarity between the prototype of a given category and the old distortions belonging to the same category was on average higher than the similarity between the new distortions and the old distortions in the same category. For such a situation even exemplar models predict a prototype-enhancement effect (see, e.g., Shin & Nosofsky 1992). More recent studies that tease apart the relevant variables (i.e., similarity to the prototype vs. similarity to other exemplars of the categories) support the predictions of the exemplar view (cf. Nosofsky 2000, but see Minda & Smith 2002).

A possible drawback of artificial categories is that researchers inadvertently create conditions that favor one or the other account. For example, if the experiment involves only a few categories, with a small number of exemplars per category and little "within-category structure", then it isn't surprising that participants tend to encode and remember the individual exemplars. In contrast, if multiple, large and highly structured categories are to be learnt then creating summary representations may be advantageous. Indeed, the results mentioned above that favored exemplar models mostly stemmed from studies that employed only two small categories with little within-category structure. When conditions were less favorable for memorizing individual exemplars, results were more in line with prototype theories than with exemplar models (for an overview, see Minda & Smith 2011). To account for these findings, in recent years various hybrid categorization models have been proposed (see Sec. 3). In addition, increasingly more attention has been devoted to whether the findings generalize to natural language categories (see, e.g., Storms 2004) and to a wider range of category uses (see, e.g., Markman & Ross 2003).

4.3 Relations between features within a category

Rosch (1978) emphasized that conceptual knowledge captures the correlational structure of the world. Surprisingly, however, according to Rosch's and other prototype theories, feature associations *within* categories are not encoded in conceptual knowledge. To illustrate, let us consider the category {spoons} (see Medin & Shoben 1988): Spoons differ from one another with respect to the material they are made of and their size, among other things. For the category {spoons}, these two attribute dimensions are associated: Wooden spoons tend to be relatively large, whereas metal spoons are more often small or medium-sized. Notice that this is a *within-category* relation, which possibly only holds for {spoons}. Across the board, material and size may be unrelated, and in certain other categories there may even be an association in the opposite direction (e.g., in the category {ships}). In any case, according to prototype theories, associations such as these are not captured in a concept. However, other theories do assume that concepts contain information about within-category featural associations. According to exemplar theories, the information about the statistical co-occurrence of features within a category is implicitly coded in the knowledge of the category's exemplars. Connectionist and theory-based accounts both posit explicit representations of feature associations but their assumptions differ in an important respect: Connectionist accounts imply that statistical co-occurrences are encoded; the more often two features are encountered together, the greater the weight of the connection between the respective units (see, e.g., McRae 2004). By contrast, theory-based accounts assume that mainly those feature relations are encoded for which the person has a causal explanation (e.g., Ahn et al. 2002; Murphy & Medin 1985). We will refer to these two kinds of associations as *statistically-based* and *theory-based* associations, respectively.

It is now well-established that, contrary to what prototype theories imply, conceptual knowledge does encode within-category feature associations. Much evidence comes from studies conducted in the theory-based framework. For example, it was found that the status of a feature in the structure of causal relations (supposed to be represented in a concept) affects how much importance is attached to this feature in categorization decisions (*causal status effect*). Furthermore, objects are classified by evaluating whether their features are likely to have been generated by the structure of causal relations that make up the concept (for an overview, see Rehder 2010).

However, these studies have been exclusively concerned with theory-based associations. It remains open whether purely statistically based feature associations are encoded in conceptual knowledge as well, as connectionist and exemplar accounts imply. A study by Ahn et al. (2002) suggests that the associations people are aware of are mostly ones they conceive of as causal relations. However, this conclusion was challenged by McNorgan et al. (2007). Moreover, it must be borne in mind that not all information encoded in conceptual knowledge is necessarily conscious. Indeed, various studies demonstrate that people possess and use knowledge of feature associations that they have probably never consciously thought of and that they may not be able to provide an explanation for (e.g., McNorgan et al. 2007; McRae 2004; Murphy & Ross 2010).

5 Conceptual combination

Conceptual combination is the process by which a complex representation is constructed from two or more concepts. Using almost exclusively linguistic stimuli, research on conceptual combination is effectively concerned with the interpretation of complex linguistic expressions, mainly nominal expressions such as *brown apple*, *sports which are games*, or *mountain bird*. The result of conceptual combination is frequently called a *complex concept*. However, it is important to keep in mind that it is actually a representation in working memory, not a novel long-term memory structure (see Sec. 1). We refer to the result of conceptual combination as a *composite working memory representation* or simply *composite representation*.

After an initial debate about the viability of an extensional analysis of conceptual combination in the early 1980s (e.g., Osherson & Smith 1981), research has focused on intensions, that is, on the properties represented in concepts and in composite representations constructed from them. Consequently, in empirical studies, participants are typically asked to generate or verify properties of the members of a named category or to describe their interpretation of a given stimulus expression in detail.

5.1 Empirical findings and theoretical approaches

An early model of conceptual combination is the Selective Modification Model (Smith et al. 1988), which is concerned with **adjective-noun combinations** (e.g., *brown apple*). Noun concepts (e.g., APPLE) are assumed to have a prototype structure comprising a list of relevant attribute dimensions (e.g., color, shape, taste), with a set of weighted values for each dimension (e.g., <red>, <green>, <brown> for the color dimension in the concept APPLE). To create a composite representation for an adjective-noun phrase such as *brown apple*, the relevant attribute dimension (color) is selected and the weight of the value <brown> is enhanced whereas the weights of the other values are set to zero. With a few additional assumptions, this model accounts for typicality-judgment phenomena observed with adjective-noun phrases. However, the model is limited to adjectives that unambiguously refer to one of the attribute dimensions listed in the noun concept. It cannot deal with multiattribute adjectives (e.g., *shriveled apple* – shape and texture), nor with subsective adjectives (e.g., *good apple* vs. *good coffee*), nor with privative adjectives (e.g., *fake apple*). Several researchers (e.g, Medin & Shoben 1988; Murphy 1988, 1990) take this failure to reflect a more fundamental problem of prototype theories, which, according to their view, severely underestimate the richness of information used in conceptual combination (for another objection, see Connolly et al. 2007). For example, Murphy (1988, 1990) emphasizes that world knowledge plays a pivotal role in conceptual combination, and Medin & Shoben (1988) call attention to the context dependence of adjectives. We shall come back to these arguments in Section 5.2. Since this debate, only few articles addressing adjective-noun combination have been published (e.g., Franks 1995).

Much more research has been devoted to **noun phrases containing a restrictive relative clause** (e.g., *sports which are games*), which are thought to require the conjunction of noun concepts for their interpretation. Research in this field is strongly influenced by Hampton's (1987) Composite Prototype Model, which posits prototype concepts representing property lists, where the properties are weighted according to their importance for the respective concept. A composite representation is formed by merging the properties of the two constituent concepts, assigning new weights to the properties according to certain rules, and performing a consistency checking procedure to ensure that the composite representation does not inherit incompatible properties. This model accounts for a wide range of empirical findings, including concept dominance, non-commutativity, and overextension (see Hampton 1997). There is a phenomenon, however, that must be attributed to processes not captured by the model – the occurrence of *emergent properties*. We discuss this phenomenon in Section 5.2.

The current focus of conceptual-combination research is on (novel and familiar) **noun-noun compounds** (e.g., *mountain book*). There are two different theoretical approaches, the *schema-based* and the *relation-linking* approach. Schema-based theories (e.g., Costello & Keane 2001; Murphy 1988; Wisniewski 1997) posit rich concepts similar to those proposed by the theory-based view (see Sec. 3). Concepts are schema representations with complex internal structure, containing information about possible properties and their interconnections as well as typical functional roles in scenarios (e.g., SPOON: instrument for eating, instrument for stirring), and other thematic relations to other concepts (see Sec. 2.2). According to these theories, a noun-noun compound is interpreted by integrating information from the modifier concept with the head concept. Wisniewski's (1997) Dual-Process Theory may serve as an example. Wisniewski distinguishes between different kinds of interpretations, the two most common ones being *relational interpretations* and *property interpretations*. These interpretations result from different processes. Relational interpretations occur if the modifier and head concept are found to fit different functional roles in a particular scenario. For example, *paint spoon* could be interpreted as a spoon used to stir paint because SPOON can be bound to the instrument role and PAINT to the object role in a stirring scenario. In contrast, property interpretations involve a mapping of one or more properties from the modifier concept onto the head concept. For example, *box clock* may be interpreted as a square clock and *zebra clam* as a striped clam. According to the Dual-Process Theory, property interpretations are the outcome of a process involving a comparison and alignment of the modifier and the head concept. However, recent findings suggest that the salience and diagnosticity of the modifier's properties play a crucial role (see, e.g., Costello & Keane 2001; Estes & Glucksberg 2000).

The relation-linking approach is inspired by traditional linguistic theories of compounding (see article 4 [Semantics: Interfaces] (Olsen) *Semantics of compounds*, Sec. 2) and was introduced into the research on conceptual combination by Gagné & Shoben (1997), see also Gagné & Spalding (2009). According to their theory CARIN (Competition Among Relations in Nominals), a compound noun is interpreted by linking the two constituent concepts via a thematic relation selected from a limited set including 'located', 'made_of', 'about', 'during', and some others. For example, *mountain bird* may be interpreted by selecting the relation 'located' (a bird in the mountains) and *mountain magazine* by selecting the relation 'about' (a magazine about mountains). To find a suitable interpretation, people exploit knowledge about statistical regularities in language use. More specifically, upon encountering a noun in modifier position, knowledge about its past use as a modifier becomes activated and the respective relations then compete for selection. CARIN predicts that, all else being equal, compounds instantiating a relation that has been used frequently with the given modifier are easier to interpret than compounds instantiating a relation less often used with this modifier. Thus, for example, as corpus analyses show that the modifier *mountain* is most often associated with the 'located' relation, *mountain bird* and *mountain tent* should be easier to interpret than *mountain magazine*. Empirical findings correspond to this prediction (e.g., Gagné & Shoben 1997; for left-headed compounds, see Storms & Wisniewski 2005).

It has often been questioned whether the great variety of relationships between nouns in compounds can indeed be reduced to a limited number of categories. However, let us accept this assumption and instead draw attention to CARIN's proposal concerning statistical knowledge. Considering the ample experimental evidence for the exploitation of statistical regularities in language comprehension (see Jurafsky 2003), the claim that people use statistical knowledge in processing compound nouns is no doubt plausible. However, does this knowledge actually concern individual lexical items, as Gagné & Shoben (1997) propose? Maguire, Wisniewski & Storms (2010) have reported that semantically similar words exhibit similar combination patterns in compounds. With the benefit of hindsight, this finding is not surprising. Semantically similar words share many meaning components, and the way words are used in compounds certainly depends to a great deal on certain critical components. For example, the fact that *mountain*, when used as a modifier, is frequently associated with the relation 'located' but not with, say, the relation 'during' is most likely due to the fact that this noun denotes objects conceived as spatially extensive and permanent. Words that likewise denote objects conceived as spatially extensive and permanent (e.g., *valley, sea, city, garden*) can be expected to show the same preference for 'located' over 'during'. More generally speaking, one may assume that certain critical meaning components (or combinations of them) are each associated with a characteristic relation frequency distribution. Thus, the statistical knowledge people use in processing compound nouns may actually concern relation frequencies associated with certain meaning components rather than lexical entries. Unlike Gagné & Shoben's proposal, this revised proposal accounts for the finding that even rare words, which have probably never been encountered in compounds, display clear preferences for certain relations, when used as modifiers (Maguire & Cater 2005).

Certainly, the use of knowledge of statistical regularities can only be a *part* of the interpretation process. It only provides likely candidate relations. The respective interpretations must be worked out and their plausibility must be evaluated in order to eventually settle on one interpretation. CARIN says nothing about these processes. As several researchers (e.g., Storms & Wisniewski 2005) have pointed out, a fully-fledged theory should probably integrate assumptions from

CARIN with those from schema-based theories. The processing of a compound noun may involve a statistic-based activation process (similar to the one assumed by CARIN or the revised proposal) as well as construction and evaluation processes (as proposed by schema-based theories).

As we have seen, research on conceptual combination has been dominated by the prototype view and the theory- or schema-based view. Connectionist theories and simulation theory are only recently becoming involved in the discussion (see, e.g., Levy & Gayler 2004; Wu & Barsalou 2009). The exemplar view, however, faces a particular problem. Its central assumption that a concept is a set of stored exemplars renders it difficult to account for the productivity of conceptual combination. Let us take the concepts STRIPED and APPLE as an example (see Osherson & Smith 1981). How can people form a composite representation out of these concepts if they have never encountered an exemplar of the category {striped apples}? Some authors (e.g., Storms et al. 1993; see also Storms 2004) propose to take representations of subcategories as the stored exemplars of a concept (e.g., PIGEON, CHICKEN, RAVEN are three exemplars of BIRD). However, it is as yet unclear whether this conception of exemplars solves the above-mentioned fundamental problem of the exemplar approach.

5.2 Conceptual compositionality

Psychological research on conceptual combination, in which theories primarily seek to make correct predictions concerning people's interpretations of complex expressions, has devoted relatively little attention to the issue of compositionality (for compositionality in semantics, see article 6 [Semantics: Foundations, History and Methods] (Pagin & Westerståhl) *Compositionality*). Definitions of conceptual compositionality are most often left implicit, but many researchers would probably agree that the composite representations created by means of conceptual combination are compositional to the extent that they are the result of processes that operate on the constituent concepts, guided by syntactic information. According to this definition, any use of information beyond that contained in the constituent concepts counts as non-compositional – even if this information is used in a rule-governed, predictable way. Hence, a non-compositional account of a given phenomenon is not necessarily inferior to a compositional account as far as predictive power is concerned. It should also be borne in mind that composite representations are representations in working memory, constructed in particular situations. Every reasonable theory must therefore acknowledge that at some point in time during the construction of a composite representation, information external to the constituent concepts is used. Of course, whether or not a theory provides a compositional account of a finding is still an important question. Two sets of findings have received particular attention in the discussion, context-dependent property instantiation and emergent properties.

Several researchers have pointed out that properties (even ones named by intersective adjectives) are instantiated differently in composite representations depending on the entities they are applied to (e.g., Medin & Shoben 1988; Murphy 1988; Wisniewski 1997). For example, when *zebra clam* is interpreted as a black-and-white striped clam, the stripes on the clam are probably represented as smaller and thinner than those of a zebra (Wisniewski 1997; see also Wilkenfeld & Ward 2001). Context dependence is often taken as evidence that the properties in a concept are not independent of one another, so that a new property must be accommodated to the particular selection of properties in the head concept (but see Rips 1995 for a more differentiated view). If this is true, then theory-based or schema-based theories are, in principle, able to provide a compositional account, while prototype theories are not, as a prototype concept contains no information about the interrelations among properties (see Sec. 3 and 4.3).

As we mentioned above, conceptual combination sometimes yields emergent properties (or *phrase features*): People consider certain properties true or typical of the composite but not of either of its constituents. For example, Hampton's (1987) participants often listed the property <live in cages> for *pets which are birds* but did not judge this property true of pets nor of birds. Emergent properties have also been observed with other kinds of combinations (e.g., *large spoon* → <wooden>; *beach bicycle* → <equipped with wide tires>) (see, e.g., Hampton 1997; Medin & Shoben 1988; Murphy 1988; Wilkenfeld & Ward 2001). It is widely agreed that there are at least two possible sources of emergent properties. First, they may arise from *extensional feedback*. That is, if the complex expression denotes a category of familiar things (e.g., *large spoons; pets that are also birds*), then people may retrieve familiar instances of this category from long-term memory and "look up" their properties. Notice that according to prototype and theory- or schema-based theories, extensional feedback can only take place *after* the combination of the concepts – the combination process cannot peek at instances of the composite (*no-peeking principle*, Rips 1995). Hence, these theories cannot provide a compositional account of emergent properties arising from extensional feedback. In line with the notion of extensional feedback, empirical studies (e.g., Swinney et al. 2007) have shown that emergent properties become available at a later point in time during the processing of a complex nominal expression than do "inherited" properties. For example, when presented with *peeled apple*, people need more time to access the emergent property <white> than the inherited property <round>.

Second, emergent properties may result from reasoning processes and domain theories. An example is when *helicopter blanket*, interpreted as a cover for a helicopter, is ascribed the emergent property <waterproof> (Wilkenfeld & Ward 2001). Obviously, prototype theories must attribute these properties to reasoning processes taking place after concept combination. In contrast, theory-based approaches may be well-suited to provide a compositional account, by explaining how these properties emerge from reasoning processes that use the mini-theories contained in the concepts. However, as yet there are no systematic studies on this issue.

6 Relationship between conceptual knowledge and word meanings

As we mentioned in the previous sections, many authors assume that conceptual knowledge is organized into distinct packages of information, that is, into concepts, and take concepts to be equivalent to lexical meanings. In the present section, we consider the implications of this equivalence view, and describe possible alternatives. The issue has much in common with the dictionary/encyclopedia debate in linguistics (for an overview, see Peeters 2000; see also article 4 [Semantics: Theories] (Jackendoff) *Conceptual Semantics*, and article 5 [Semantics: Theories] (Lang & Maienborn) *Two-level Semantics*). However, instead of repeating arguments from this debate, we look at the issue from a different perspective, examining whether the equivalence view is compatible with theoretical considerations and empirical findings from research on conceptual knowledge. Accordingly, the focus is on the relationship between concepts and meanings of count nouns. We disregard morphological issues and up until the end we also ignore homonymy, polysemy, and synonymy. Thus, we simply speak of *word meanings* and assume that each of them is associated with exactly one *word form*, and vice versa.

6.1 Equivalence view

The view that concepts are equivalent to the meanings of words comes in two variants (see Fig. 11.1). On the first variant, which seems to be the prevalent one in research on concepts in cognitive psychology, concepts *are* word meanings. On the second variant, concepts and word meanings are stored in different mental subsystems but for each concept there is exactly one word meaning that shares the same informational content and vice versa. This variant is more in line with the traditional notion of a mental lexicon as a mental subsystem clearly separated from non-linguistic long-term memory.

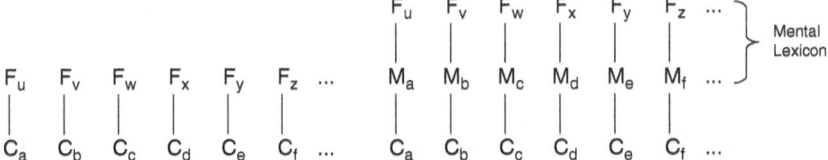

Fig. 11.1: Two variants of the equivalence view. Left: Concepts are word meanings. Right: Concepts and word meanings are distinct but informationally equivalent knowledge structures. C_i = concept, M_i = word meaning, F_i = word form.

One problem with the equivalence view is that it implies that all concepts have a label. Each concept is connected with one particular form, either directly (Variant 1) or indirectly via the corresponding meaning (Variant 2). This entails a very narrow perspective on conceptual knowledge, which disregards concepts in pre-verbal infants and animals (for reviews, see Rakison & Yermolayeva 2010 and Lazareva & Wasserman 2008, respectively) and also a good deal of conceptual knowledge of human adults. Concepts can no doubt be acquired incidentally and without learning labels for them. This has been shown experimentally by studies of unsupervised category learning (e.g., Billman & Knutson 1996) and is also evident in our everyday experience. For example, people often discriminate between several subcategories of things (e.g., different subcategories of trees) without having names for them (see Malt & Sloman 2007: 102), and they possess concepts for which there is no label in their language (e.g., EXTENDING_ONE'S_ELBOWS_TO_THE_SIDE_TO_FEND_OFF_A_SHOVING_NEIGHBOR; see Murphy 2002: 389).

A second important implication of the equivalence view concerns the issue of the universality of the structure of conceptual knowledge. Different languages carve up the world in different ways, and, according to the equivalence view, conceptual distinctions match lexically coded distinctions. Speakers of different languages must therefore be assumed to differ in the structure of their conceptual knowledge. In recent years, there has been a revival of interest in the Sapir-Whorf or linguistic relativity hypothesis, which states that language influences thought (for an overview of current research, see Gleitman & Papafragou 2012). Clearly, this hypothesis goes beyond the equivalence view, which is mute on the factors that give rise to the asserted correspondence between conceptual structures and lexicalization patterns. However, some empirical findings from this research are directly relevant to the issue at hand, demonstrating that, at least in some domains, the structure of conceptual knowledge does *not* vary across speakers of languages that partition the domain in different ways. The domain of motion events may serve as an example. Some languages, including English, typically encode the manner but not the path of motion in motion verbs (e.g., *stroll, creep, run*), while other languages, for example Greek, tend to encode the path rather than the manner (e.g., *anevéno, katevéno* for *to move up to* or *down to*, respectively). The equivalence view predicts analogous differences between English and Greek native speakers on nonverbal conceptual tasks, for example, categorizing visually presented scenes of motion events or judging their similarity. Specifically, English native speakers should pay relatively more attention to the manner than the path of the motions, while Greek native speakers should pay more attention to the path than the manner. Yet, empirical studies have found no difference between English and Greek speakers' performance on such tasks (e.g., Papafragou & Selimis 2010). Dissociations between lexicalization patterns and non-linguistic conceptual performance have also been revealed in the domain of household containers and some other domains (see Malt, Gennari & Imai 2010).

6.2 Free-concepts view

With regard to the first problem mentioned above, an obvious alternative to the equivalence view is to acknowledge that not all concepts have a label. That is, in addition to *lexicalized concepts*, which are directly or indirectly connected with word forms, there are *free concepts*, which lack such connections. Interestingly, this view also allows one to cope with the second problem, concerning the findings from the cross-linguistic studies: People possess a huge repertoire of concepts, which is language-independent (e.g., all people possess concepts of motion events that include manner but no path information as well as concepts that include path but no manner information). A particular subset of concepts, which is language-specific, is lexicalized. The remaining concepts are free concepts. On linguistic tasks, people use lexicalized concepts. On nonverbal tasks, they may use either free or lexicalized concepts, depending on the precise nature of the given task. By these assumptions, the free-concepts view is compatible with virtually every finding concerning the (non)correspondence between the conceptual structures of speakers of different languages, despite the fact that conceptual structures are assumed to be universal.

The free-concepts view appears awkward as it implies that people possess an enormous number of concepts, many of which differ only slightly from each other. Moreover, the proposal that people draw on a particular subset of concepts when using language is not so far from the idea that lexical meanings are knowledge structures of their own. Let us consider this view in more detail.

6.3 Non-equivalence view

A theory postulating only one kind of knowledge structure for both lexical meanings and concepts may be an economical theory. However, whether possessing only one kind of knowledge structure for both lexical meanings and concepts is economical for the human mind is a different matter. Doubts arise when one considers the different functions that language and non-linguistic cognition have to serve. The requirements for successful communication, which is the primary function of language, differ in certain respects from what is useful for object recognition, feature prediction, action planning, and other non-linguistic cognitive tasks. Specifically, since communication is dependent on a common ground, an important constraint for lexical meanings is the shareability of the information they contain. By contrast, the information used in non-linguistic conceptual tasks need not be shared by many people. Thus, concepts may, and even should, include information deriving from a person's individual experience. In addition, lexical meanings, being based on social conventions, are probably relatively stable over time, whereas concepts should be easily malleable in order to be useful across changing life conditions. In sum, it seems reasonable to assume that concepts and lexical meanings are distinct, although related, knowledge structures (for additional arguments, see, e.g., Gleitman & Papafragou 2012; Malt, Gennari & Imai 2010; Vigliocco & Vinson 2007).

One possibility is that concepts and lexical meanings are stored in distinct mental subsystems (as shown on the right side of Fig. 11.1) but are richly connected. Each concept may be linked to more than one meaning, and each meaning to more than one concept. Another possibility, which we consider more plausible, suggests itself when shifting to a finer-grained level of analysis – that is, to the constituents of concepts and lexical meanings. Conceptual and lexical-semantic knowledge may involve a common stock of atomic representations, from which they form their own more complex structures. As we have discussed in Section 3 and 4.2, there are two fundamentally different views of atomic representations in conceptual knowledge – representations of individual exemplars and representations of features (and possibly their interrelations). These two views entail different conceptions of the relationship between conceptual and lexical knowledge, which we outline in the following paragraphs.

Recall that according to the exemplar view, a concept is a set of representations of exemplars encountered in the past. In a framework that we refer to as the **common-stock-of-exemplars framework,** word meanings are assumed to comprise exemplar representations as well. However, concepts and word meanings group the representations according to different principles. A concept is a set of representations of exemplars that are similar according to non-linguistic, conceptual criteria, whereas a word meaning is the set of representations of exemplars that have been associated with this label in the past. The set of exemplar representations constituting a particular meaning may share certain exemplar representations with the set constituting a particular concept. This overlap captures the degree and the respects in which a meaning corresponds to a concept. Note that there are not two separate mental subsystems for concepts and lexical meanings, at least not in the usual sense. Rather, concepts and meanings make use of a common stock of exemplar representations. Nevertheless they are in principle independent of each other, and may for instance gradually change over time in different ways depending on particular individual experiences. Thus, this framework can account for findings concerning the (non)correspondence between lexicalization patterns and nonlinguistic conceptual organization (cf. Malt et al. 1999 for a similar framework). However, whether or not the idea that lexical meanings are sets of stored exemplars stands the test in a wider range of language processing issues has yet to be seen (see also Sec. 5.1). Up until now the exemplar approach has received little attention in psycholinguistic research.

A framework that is easier to align with common psycholinguistic assumptions is what we call the **Common-Stock-of-Features Framework**. The core idea is that both conceptual knowledge and lexical-semantic knowledge involve a common stock of featural atomic representations but combine them into complex structures in a different way. This idea is instantiated in Ursino et al.'s connectionist model (Ursino, Cuppino & Magasso 2010). Instead of describing this sophisticated model in detail, let us point out some interesting aspects on the basis of a raw sketch of a model of this type (see Fig. 11.2). There are a large number of cognitive units representing elementary features which we will refer to as *microfeatures*. They are interconnected by excitatory or inhibitory connections of variable strength, with the strength of a connection reflecting the degree of statistical association or causal relationship between the respective microfeatures. Thus, conceptual knowledge is encoded in the connections among the units. A cluster of relatively strongly interconnected units can be considered a concept, but notice that there are no sharp boundaries between concepts.

The units representing microfeatures are also connected with units outside this network, for instance with units in the sensory, motor, and emotional systems (not indicated in Fig. 11.2). Furthermore, and what is most import to the present issue, with units representing the linguistic form of lexical items. For simplicity, we assume localist form representations, that is, each of these latter units represents a word form as a whole (for distributed word-form representations, see, e.g., Dilkina, McClelland & Plaut 2008). The bundle of connections between microfeatures and a particular word form make up the meaning of the respective word. Note that despite using a common stock of microfeatures, concepts and word meanings are distinct knowledge structures. Conceptual knowledge is encoded in the weights of the connections *among* the microfeatures, whereas lexical-semantic knowledge is encoded in the weights of the connections between microfeatures and forms.

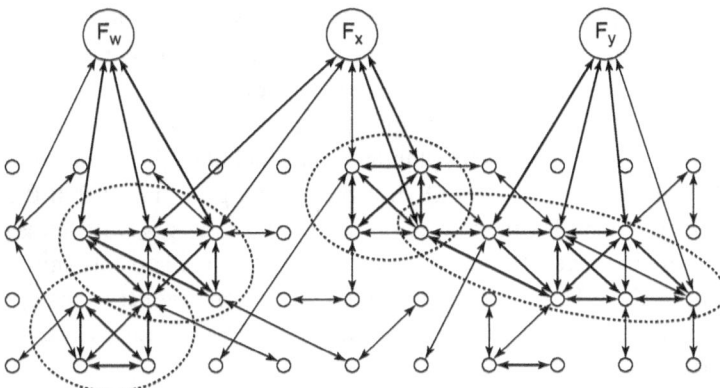

Fig. 11.2: A schematic illustration of a common stock of microfeatures for conceptual and lexical-semantic knowledge. Small circles indicate units representing microfeatures, big circles indicate units representing word forms. Arrows indicate connections, with their thickness representing connection weight (only excitatory connections having substantial weight are depicted). Dotted ellipses indicate clusters of strongly interconnected microfeatures, which may be regarded as concepts.

The cluster of microfeatures constituting a particular concept may overlap to some extent with sets of microfeatures connected to word forms. If there is a large overlap with one of these sets, then the concept may be considered a lexicalized concept. However, even if the overlap is maximal, the concept and the lexical meaning may still differ in their internal structure, since the connections that bind the microfeatures are different in the two cases. In addition, according to our previous considerations regarding specific requirements of communication, it is likely that concepts tend to be richer than the related word meanings. For example, the concept BACHELOR may include microfeatures representing the properties <charming> and <has no children> but possibly these microfeatures are not strongly connected with the form *bachelor*, that is, the meaning of *bachelor* may be lacking these features.

Interestingly, this framework also allows one to distinguish between homonymy (e.g., *bat*: animal / sports equipment) and polysemy (e.g., *opera*: musical drama / building). In general a word form is connected to a set of microfeatures most of which are relatively strongly connected to one another, i.e., which roughly belong to a common lump of features. In the case of homonymy, however, the word form (e.g., *bat*) is connected to different sets of microfeatures with hardly any connections between them. In the case of polysemy, the word form (e.g. *opera*) is connected to units from two or more overlapping feature lumps. The subset of features shared by the lumps captures what the different senses of the polysemous word share (e.g., has to do with music). The remaining units of the different feature lumps are barely connected to one another (cf. Rodd, Gaskell & Marslen-Wilson 2004 for a computational model of this sort).

Languages differ with regard to the composition of the sets of microfeatures that are picked out by words (e.g., a verb of motion may include or lack microfeatures representing the manner of motion). This does not a priori mean that the connections *among* the microfeatures, which make up the concepts, vary across speakers of different languages. Hence, it is possible that there is no correlation between cross-linguistic differences and performance on non-linguistic conceptual tasks. Precise predictions would require more specific assumptions about processing and learning mechanisms.

So far, we have been concerned with long-term memory structures (conceptual knowledge, lexical knowledge). Let us now briefly consider what the common-stock-of-features framework suggests with respect to working memory representations (for the distinction between long-term and working memory, see Sec. 1). Activation is fed into the microfeature network by various systems, including the sensory systems. For example, hearing a sound (e.g., barking) gives rise to the activation of units representing the features of this sound. These units in turn activate or deactivate other units, depending on whether the respective connections are excitatory or inhibitory. This complex process eventually leads to a relatively stable pattern of activated microfeatures, which includes not only microfeatures activated by the sensory input but also microfeatures strongly associated with them. Such a relatively stable pattern of activated microfeatures is what we consider a working memory representation. In our example, the working memory representation resulting from hearing the barking may include many microfeatures representing properties typical of dogs.

As to linguistic input, we assume that hearing or reading a particular word (e.g., "dog") leads to an activation of the corresponding word-form unit. This unit in turn activates the microfeatures to which it is connected and thereby triggers a complex process in the network similar to the one described above. Again, the result is a particular pattern of activated microfeatures. This pattern is the working memory representation of the meaning of the given utterance ("dog"). Note that in this framework, word meanings are not just sets of microfeatures but rather knowledge structures that control the mapping of word forms to microfeatures (and – if we take language production into consideration – the reverse mapping as well).

It should further be noted that working memory representations derived from linguistic input do not differ in principle from ones derived from nonlinguistic input. Thus, although concepts and word meanings are clearly distinct knowledge structures, there is no analogous distinction for working memory representations in the common-stock-of features framework. In fact, it is likely that information from various sources mix in working memory representations. Specifically, working memory representations derived from linguistic input are probably always contaminated by conceptual knowledge, as the microfeatures activated by a word form activate other microfeatures via their connections. This converges with the common belief that the linguistic meaning of a word or sentence underdetermines what listeners construe as the meaning of the utterance. Similarly, representations of nonlinguistic stimuli may be influenced by lexical knowledge, as the microfeature units activated by a nonlinguistic stimulus may feed activation to some word-form units, which in turn may feed activation back to microfeature units (cf. Papafragou & Selimis 2010 and article 13 [this volume] (Landau) *Space in semantics and cognition* for on-line, transient effects of language). Finally, it should be borne in mind that conceptual and linguistic processing always takes place in a particular situation. The sensory-motor and higher cognitive systems constantly feed information into the network concerning the immediate physical environment, social situation, and current goals. Thus, working memory representations, no matter whether constructed for a nonverbal stimulus or an utterance, are always influenced by the situational context (cf. Barsalou 2009).

To summarize, the assumption that concepts are lexical meanings should be abandoned. Minimally, one needs to concede that people possess concepts that do not correspond to lexical meanings. However, it is more plausible that conceptual knowledge and lexical-semantic knowledge are distinct. This does not rule out that they are structurally and functionally closely interwoven with one another. It is even conceivable that conceptual knowledge and lexical-semantic knowledge involve the same set of atomic representations, and only differ in how they combine these atomic representations.

7 Concluding remarks

Research on conceptual knowledge is concerned with a wide spectrum of topics (of which we have addressed but a few). This is of little surprise considering the role of conceptual knowledge in mediating between perception, action, and higher cognitive processes. However, research on conceptual knowledge also reveals considerable heterogeneity of the fundamental views of what concepts essentially are. Do they encode rules of categorization, lists of features of category members, central-tendency information, domain-specific mini-theories, sets of exemplars encountered in the past, or bindings of modality-specific memory traces of past situations? None of these views can be dismissed. Each is supported by some empirical evidence, even though this evidence often comes from a limited type of experimental settings or paradigms. What should we conclude from this? Recent developments in research offer a promising perspective. Researchers are beginning to question some of the traditional tenets that may have hindered the development of an integrative framework for the different notions.

One traditional tenet is that the most important function of conceptual knowledge is to allow for categorization. However, in recent years an increasing number of researchers have recognized that conceptual knowledge serves many different functions besides categorization, including prediction (which we emphasized) and explanation, and that different functions make use of different kinds of information (see, e.g., Barsalou 2009; Markman & Ross 2003). This calls into question another fundamental belief in research on conceptual knowledge, namely that conceptual knowledge comes in discrete packets of information, in concepts. Why should we possess discrete packets of information, accessible in an all-or-none fashion, if, depending on the situation or task at hand, different pieces of these packets become relevant? Wouldn't a large network of knowledge be more plausible, from which the relevant pieces can be selected on the fly and tailored to the particular goals in the current situation? After all, even novel categories can easily be formed if necessary (see, e.g., Barsalou 1985 on *ad hoc* and goal-derived categories). Adopting this view of conceptual knowledge implies that a reframing of research in this domain is necessary. Instead of attempting to characterize the contents of concepts, the objective would be to discover what kinds of information about things is used in different situations (see Malt & Sloman 2007, Murphy & Ross 2010, and Papafragou & Selimis 2010, as examples of this approach). Research may eventually show that the different concept theories apply to different types of situations and tasks.

Intimately connected with the two aforementioned tenets is the assumption that concepts are word meanings. Indeed, a main reason why categorization is traditionally regarded a central function of conceptual knowledge is probably that concepts are taken to be word meanings. Ironically, it is exactly this assumption of a close relationship between conceptual knowledge and language that brought about the unfortunate situation that conceptual research is largely uninteresting for semantics, apart from some basic ideas (see Sec. 1). However, the situation may change as the dominance of the notion of distinct concepts gradually wanes and researchers begin to take a closer look at what pieces of information are drawn from conceptual knowledge in performing a particular task and what the resulting working memory representation is like. Studies of this type, focusing on the conceptualization of things, situations and events in working memory are highly relevant for the question of how conceptually shaped representations are mapped onto linguistic structures and vice versa. They may therefore provide the basis for re-thinking the relationship between conceptual and lexical-semantic knowledge.

We thank Susan Olsen, Paul Portner, and Claudia Maienborn for helpful comments to an earlier version of this article.

8 References

Ahn, Woo-kyoung, Jessecae K. Marsh, Christian C. Luhmann & Kevin Lee 2002. Effect of theory-based feature correlations on typicality judgments. *Memory & Cognition* 30, 107–118.

Anderson, John R. 1991. The adaptive nature of human categorization. *Psychological Review* 98, 409–429.

Armstrong, Sharon L., Lila R. Gleitman & Henry Gleitman 1983. What some concepts might not be. *Cognition* 13, 263–308.

Ashby, F. Gregory & W. Todd Maddox 2011. Human category learning 2.0. *Annals of the New York Academy of Sciences* 1224, 147–161.

Barr, Robin A. & Leslie J. Caplan 1987. Category representations and their implications for category structure. *Memory & Cognition* 15, 397–418.

Barsalou, Lawrence W. 1985. Ideals, central tendency, and frequency of instantiation as determinants of graded structure in categories. *Journal of Experimental Psychology: Learning, Memory, and Cognition* 11, 629–654.

Barsalou, Lawrence W. 2009. Simulation, situated conceptualization, and prediction. *Philosophical Transactions of the Royal Society of London: Biological Sciences* 364, 1281–1289.

Billman, Dorrit & James Knutson 1996. Unsupervised concept learning and value systematicity: A complex whole aids learning the parts. *Journal of Experimental Psychology: Learning, Memory, and Cognition* 22, 458–475.

Close, James, Ulrike Hahn, Carl J. Hodgetts & Emmanuel M. Pothos 2010. Rules and similarity in adult concept learning. In: D. Mareschal, P. C. Quinn & S. E. G. Lea (eds.). *The Making of Human Concepts*. Oxford: Oxford University Press, 29–51.

Collin, Charles A. & Patricia A. McMullen 2005. Subordinate-level categorization relies on high spatial frequencies to a greater degree than basic-level categorization. *Perception & Psychophysics* 67, 354–364.

Connolly, Andrew C., Jerry A. Fodor, Lila R. Gleitman & Henry Gleitman 2007. Why stereotypes don't even make good defaults. *Cognition* 103, 1–22.

Costello, Fintan J. & Mark T. Keane 2001. Testing two theories of conceptual combination: Alignment versus diagnosticity in the comprehension and production of combined concepts. *Journal of Experimental Psychology: Learning, Memory, and Cognition* 27, 255–271.

Davis, Tyler & Bradley C. Love 2010. Memory for category information is idealized through contrast with competing options. *Psychological Science* 21, 234–242.

Diesendruck, Gil & Susan A. Gelman 1999. Domain differences in absolute judgments of category membership: Evidence for an essentialist account of categorization. *Psychonomic Bulletin & Review* 6, 338–346.

Dilkina, Katia, James L. McClelland & David C. Plaut 2008. A single-system account of semantic and lexical deficits in five semantic dementia patients. *Cognitive Neuropsychology* 25, 136–164.

Estes, Zachary 2004. Confidence and gradedness in semantic categorization: Definitely somewhat artifactual, maybe absolutely natural. *Psychonomic Bulletin & Review* 11, 1041–1047.

Estes, Zachary & Sam Glucksberg 2000. Interactive property attribution in concept combination. *Memory & Cognition* 28, 28–34.

Estes, Zachary, Sabrina Golonka & Lara L. Jones 2011. Thematic thinking: The apprehension and consequences of thematic relations. In: B. H. Ross (ed.). *The Psychology of Learning and Motivation, vol. 54*. Amsterdam: Elsevier, 249–294.

Franks, Bradley 1995. Sense generation: A "quasi-classical" approach to concepts and concept combination. *Cognitive Science* 19, 441–505.

Gagné, Christina L. & Edward J. Shoben 1997. Influence of thematic relations on the comprehension of modifier-noun combinations. *Journal of Experimental Psychology: Learning, Memory, and Cognition* 23, 71–87.

Gagné, Christina L. & Thomas L. Spalding 2009. Constituent integration during the processing of compound words: Does it involve the use of relational structures? *Journal of Memory and Language* 60, 20–35.

Gelman, Susan A. 2004. Psychological essentialism in children. *Trends in Cognitive Sciences* 8, 404–409.

Gleitman, Lila R. & Anna Papafragou 2012. New perspectives on language and thought. In: K. J. Holyoak & R. G. Morrison (eds.). *The Cambridge Handbook of Thinking and Reasoning*. Cambridge: Cambridge University Press.

Goldwater, Micah B., Arthur B. Markman & C. Hunt Stilwell 2011. The empirical case for role-governed categories. *Cognition* 118, 359–376.

Gosselin, Frederic & Philippe G. Schyns 2001. Why do we SLIP to the basic level? Computational constraints and their implementation. *Psychological Review* 108, 735–758.

Hampton, James A. 1982. A demonstration of intransitivity in natural categories. *Cognition* 12, 151–164.

Hampton, James A. 1987. Inheritance of attributes in natural concept conjunctions. *Memory & Cognition* 15, 55–71.

Hampton, James A. 1993. Prototype models of concept representation. In: I. van Mechelen et al. (eds.). *Categories and Concepts: Theoretical Views and Inductive Data Analysis*. New York: Academic Press, 67–95.

Hampton, James A. 1997. Conceptual combination. In: K. Lamberts & D. Shanks (eds.). *Knowledge, Concepts, and Categories*. Cambridge, MA: The MIT Press, 133–159.

Hampton, James A. 1998. Similarity-based categorization and fuzziness of natural categories. *Cognition* 65, 137–165.

Hampton, James A. 2006. Concepts as prototypes. In: B. H. Ross (ed.). *The Psychology of Learning and Motivation, vol. 46*. San Diego, CA: Academic Press, 79–113.

Hampton, James A. 2007. Typicality, graded membership, and vagueness. *Cognitive Science* 31, 355–384.

Hayes, Brett K., Evan Heit & Haruka Swendsen 2010. Inductive reasoning. *Wiley Interdisciplinary Reviews: Cognitive Science* 1, 278–292.

Johnson, Kathy E. & Carolyn B. Mervis 1997. Effects of varying levels of expertise on the basic level of categorization. *Journal of Experimental Psychology: General* 126, 248–277.

Jolicoeur, Pierre, Mark A. Gluck & Stephen M. Kosslyn 1984. Pictures and names: Making the connection. *Cognitive Psychology* 16, 243–275.
Jurafsky, Dan 2003. Probabilistic modeling in psycholinguistics: Linguistic comprehension and production. In: R. Bod, J. Hay & S. Jannedy (eds.), *Probabilistic Linguistics*. Cambridge, MA: The MIT Press, 39–95.
Kalish, Charles W. 1995. Essentialism and graded membership in animal and artifact categories. *Memory & Cognition* 23, 335–353.
Kamp, Hans & Barbara Partee 1995. Prototype theory and compositionality. *Cognition* 57, 129–191.
Lazareva, Olga F. & Edward A. Wasserman 2008. Categories and concepts in animals. In: R. Menzel (ed.), *Learning and Memory: A comprehensive Reference, vol. 1: Learning Theory and Behavior*. Oxford: Elsevier, 197–226.
Levy, Simon D. & Ross W. Gayler (eds.) 2004. *Compositional Connectionism in Cognitive Science*. Menlo Park, CA: AAAI Press.
Love, Bradley C., Douglas L. Medin & Todd M. Gureckis 2004. SUSTAIN: A network model of category learning. *Psychological Review* 111, 309–332.
Lynch, Elizabeth B., John D. Coley & Douglas L. Medin 2000. Tall is typical: Central tendency, ideal dimensions, and graded category structure among tree experts and novices. *Memory & Cognition* 28, 41–50.
Maguire, Phil & Arthur W. Cater 2005. Interpreting noun-noun compounds with rare modifiers. In: K. Opwis & I.-K. Penner (eds.), *Proceedings of KogWis05. The German Cognitive Science Conference 2005*. Basel: Schwabe, 131–136.
Maguire, Phil, Edward J. Wisniewski & Gert Storms 2010. A corpus study of semantic patterns in compounding. *Corpus Linguistics and Linguistic Theory* 6, 49–73.
Malt, Barbara C., Silvia Gennari & Mutsumi Imai 2010. Lexicalization patterns and the world-to-word mapping. In: B.C. Malt & P. Wolff (eds.), *Words and the Mind: How Words Capture Human Experience*. Oxford: Oxford University Press, 29–57.
Malt, Barbara C. & Steven A. Sloman 2007. Artifact categorization: The good, the bad, and the ugly. In: E. Margolis & S. Laurence (eds.), *Creations of the Mind: Theories of Artifacts and Their Representation*. Oxford: Oxford University Press, 85–123.
Malt, Barbara C., Steven A. Sloman, Silvia Gennari, Meiyi Shi & Yuan Wang 1999. Knowing versus naming: Similarity and the linguistic categorization of artifacts. *Journal of Memory and Language* 40, 230–262.
Margolis, Eric & Stephen Laurence (eds.) 2007. *Creations of the Mind: Theories of Artifacts and Their Representation*. Oxford: Oxford University Press.
Markman, Arthur B. & Brian H. Ross 2003. Category use and category learning. *Psychological Bulletin* 129, 592–613.
Martin, Alex & Alfonso Caramazza 2003. Neuropsychological and neuroimaging perspectives on conceptual knowledge: An introduction. *Cognitive Neuropsychology* 20, 195–212.
McCloskey, Michael E. & Sam Glucksberg 1978. Natural categories: Well-defined or fuzzy sets? *Memory & Cognition* 6, 462–472.
McNorgan, Chris, Rachel A. Kotack, Deborah C. Meehan & Ken McRae 2007. Feature-feature causal relations and statistical co-occurrences in object concepts. *Memory & Cognition* 35, 418–431.
McRae, Ken 2004. Semantic Memory: Some insights from feature-based connectionist attractor networks. In: B. H. Ross (ed.), *The Psychology of Learning and Motivation, vol. 45*. New York: Academic Press, 41–86.

Medin, Douglas L. & Andrew Ortony 1989. Psychological essentialism. In: S. Vosniadou & A. Ortony (eds.). *Similarity and Analogical Reasoning*. Cambridge: Cambridge University Press, 179–195.

Medin, Douglas L., Norbert O. Ross, Scott Atran, Douglas Cox, John Coley, Julia B. Profitt & Sergey Blok 2006. Folkbiology of freshwater fish. *Cognition* 99, 237–273.

Medin, Douglas L. & Marguerite M. Schaffer 1978. Context theory of classification learning. *Psychological Review* 85, 207–238.

Medin, Douglas L. & Edward J. Shoben 1988. Context and structure in conceptual combination. *Cognitive Psychology* 20, 158–190.

Mervis, Carolyn B. & Eleanor Rosch 1981. Categorization of natural objects. *Annual Review of Psychology* 32, 89–115.

Minda, John Paul & J. David Smith 2002. Comparing prototype-based and exemplar-based accounts of category learning and attentional allocation. *Journal of Experimental Psychology: Learning, Memory, and Cognition* 28, 275–292.

Minda, John Paul & J. David Smith 2011. Prototype models of categorization: Basic formulation, predictions, and limitations. In: E. M. Pothos & A. J. Wills (eds.). *Formal Approaches in Categorization*. Cambridge: Cambridge University Press, 40–64.

Moss, Helen E., Lorraine K. Tyler & Kirsten I. Taylor 2007. Conceptual structure. In: M. G. Gaskell (ed.). *The Oxford Handbook of Psycholinguistics*. Oxford: Oxford University Press, 217–234.

Murphy, Gregory L. 1988. Comprehending complex concepts. *Cognitive Science* 12, 529–562.

Murphy, Gregory L. 1990. Noun phrase interpretation and conceptual combination. *Journal of Memory and Language* 29, 259–288.

Murphy, Gregory L. 2002. *The Big Book of Concepts*. Cambridge, MA: The MIT Press.

Murphy, Gregory L. & Mary E. Lassaline 1997. Hierarchical structure in concepts and the basic level of categorization. In: K. Lamberts & D. Shanks (eds.). *Knowledge, Concepts, and Categories*. Cambridge, MA: The MIT Press, 93–131.

Murphy, Gregory L. & Douglas L. Medin 1985. The role of theories in conceptual coherence. *Psychological Review* 92, 289–316.

Murphy, Gregory L. & Brian H. Ross 2010. Category vs. object knowledge in category-based induction. *Journal of Memory and Language* 63, 1–17.

Nosofsky, Robert M. 1986. Attention, similarity, and the identification-categorization relationship. *Journal of Experimental Psychology: General* 115, 39–57.

Nosofsky, Robert M. 2000. Exemplar representation without generalization? Comment on Smith and Minda's (2000) "Thirty categorization results in search of a model". *Journal of Experimental Psychology: Learning, Memory, and Cognition* 26, 1735–1743.

Onishi, Kristine H., Gregory L. Murphy & Kathryn Bock 2008. Prototypicality in sentence production. *Cognitive Psychology* 56, 103–141.

Osherson, Daniel N. & Edward E. Smith 1981. On the adequacy of prototype theory as a theory of concepts. *Cognition* 9, 35–58.

Osherson, Daniel N. & Edward E. Smith 1997. On typicality and vagueness. *Cognition* 64, 189–206.

Papafragou, Anna 2005. Relations between language and thought: Individuation and the count/mass distinction. In: H. Cohen & C. Lefebvre (eds.). *Handbook of Categorization in Cognitive Science*. Amsterdam: Elsevier, 255–275.

Papafragou, Anna & Stathis Selimis 2010. Event categorisation and language: A cross-linguistic study of motion. *Language and Cognitive Processes* 25, 224–260.

Peeters, Bert (ed.). 2000. *The Lexicon-Encyclopedia Interface*. Amsterdam: Elsevier.
Posner, Michael I. & Steven W. Keele 1968. On the genesis of abstract ideas. *Journal of Experimental Psychology* 77, 353–363.
Pothos, Emmanuel M. & Andy J. Wills (eds.) 2011. *Formal Approaches in Categorization*. Cambridge: Cambridge University Press.
Rakison, David H. & Yevdokiya Yermolayeva 2010. Infant categorization. *Wiley Interdisciplinary Reviews: Cognitive Science* 1, 894–905.
Rehder, Bob 2010. Causal-based classification: A review. In: B. H. Ross (ed.). *The Psychology of Learning and Motivation, vol. 52*. Amsterdam: Elsevier, 39–116.
Rips, Lance J. 1995. The current status of research on concept combination. *Mind & Language* 10, 72–104.
Rodd, Jennifer M., M. Gareth Gaskell & William D. Marslen-Wilson 2004. Modelling the effects of semantic ambiguity in word recognition. *Cognitive Science* 28, 89–104.
Rogers, Timothy T. & Karalyn Patterson 2007. Object categorization: Reversals and explanations of the basic-level advantage. *Journal of Experimental Psychology: General* 136, 451–469.
Rosch, Eleanor 1978. Principles of categorization. In: E. Rosch & B. B. Lloyd (eds.). *Cognition and Categorization*. Hillsdale, NJ: Erlbaum, 27–48.
Rosch, Eleanor & Carolyn B. Mervis 1975. Family resemblances: Studies in the internal structure of categories. *Cognitive Psychology* 7, 573–605.
Rosch, Eleanor, Carolyn B. Mervis, Wayne D. Gray, David M. Johnson & Penny Boyes-Braem 1976. Basic objects in natural categories. *Cognitive Psychology* 8, 382–439.
Roth, Emilie M. & Carolyn B. Mervis 1983. Fuzzy set theory and class inclusion relations in semantic categories. *Journal of Verbal Learning and Verbal Behavior* 22, 509–525.
Schyns, Philippe G., Robert L. Goldstone & Jean-Pierre Thibaut 1998. The development of features in object concepts. *Behavioral and Brain Sciences* 21, 1–54.
Shin, Hyun Jung & Robert M. Nosofsky 1992. Similarity-scaling studies of dot-pattern classification and recognition. *Journal of Experimental Psychology: General* 121, 278–304.
Sloman, Steven A. 1998. Categorical inference is not a tree: The myth of inheritance hierarchies. *Cognitive Psychology* 35, 1–33.
Smith, Edward E. & Douglas L. Medin 1981. *Categories and Concepts*. Cambridge, MA: Harvard University Press.
Smith, Edward E., Daniel N. Osherson, Lance J. Rips & Margaret Keane 1988. Combining prototypes: A selective modification model. *Cognitive Science* 12, 485–527.
Smith, J. David & John Paul Minda 2000. Thirty categorization results in search of a model. *Journal of Experimental Psychology: Learning, Memory, and Cognition* 26, 3–27.
Smith, Linda B. & Eliana Colunga 2012. Developing categories and concepts. In: M. Spivey, M. Joanisse & K. McRae (eds.). *The Cambridge Handbook of Psycholinguistics*. Cambridge: Cambridge University Press.
Snedeker, Jesse & Lila R. Gleitman 2004. Why it is hard to label our concepts. In: D. G. Hall & S. R. Waxman (eds.). *Weaving a Lexicon*. Cambridge, MA: The MIT Press, 257–293.
Storms, Gert 2004. Exemplar models in the study of natural language concepts. In: B. H. Ross (ed.). *The Psychology of Learning and Motivation, vol. 45*. New York: Academic Press, 1–39.
Storms, Gert, Paul de Boeck, Iven van Mechelen & Dirk Geeraerts 1993. Dominance and noncommutativity effects in concept conjunctions: Extensional or intensional basis? *Memory & Cognition* 21, 752–762.
Storms, Gert & Edward J. Wisniewski 2005. Does the order of head noun and modifier explain response times in conceptual combination? *Memory & Cognition* 33, 852–861.

Swinney, David, Tracy Love, Matthew Walenski & Edward E. Smith 2007. Conceptual combination during sentence comprehension. *Psychological Science* 18, 397–400.
Tanaka, James W. & Marjorie Taylor 1991. Object categories and expertise: Is the basic level in the eye of the beholder? *Cognitive Psychology* 23, 457–482.
Ursino, Mauro, Cristiano Cuppino & Elisa Magosso 2010. A computational model of the lexical-semantic system, based on a grounded cognition approach. *Frontiers in Psychology* 1:221. doi: 10.3389/fpsyg.2010.00221.
Vanpaemel, Wolf & Gert Storms 2008. In search of abstraction: The varying abstraction model of categorization. *Psychonomic Bulletin & Review* 15, 732–749.
Vigliocco, Gabriella & David P. Vinson 2007. Semantic representation. In: M. G. Gaskell (ed.). *The Oxford Handbook of Psycholinguistics*. Oxford: Oxford University Press, 195–215.
Wilkenfeld, Merryl J. & Thomas B. Ward 2001. Similarity and emergence in conceptual combination. *Journal of Memory and Language* 45, 21–38.
Wisniewski, Edward J. 1997. When concepts combine. *Psychonomic Bulletin and Review* 4, 167–183.
Wisniewski, Edward J. 2009. On using count nouns, mass nouns, and *pluralia tantum*: What counts? In: F. J. Pelletier (ed.). *Kinds, Things, and Stuff: Mass Terms and Generics*. Oxford: Oxford University Press, 166–191.
Wisniewski, Edward J., Mutsumi Imai & Lyman Casey 1996. On the equivalence of superordinate concepts. *Cognition* 60, 269–298.
Wu, Ling-Ling & Lawrence W. Barsalou 2009. Perceptual simulation in conceptual combination: Evidence from property generation. *Acta Psychologica* 132, 173–189.

Barbara Landau
12 Space in semantics and cognition

1   The geometries engaged by spatial language —— 341
2   Acquisition of spatial language: Empirical evidence for a specialized system? —— 349
3   Effects of spatial language on spatial cognition: Does language influence thought? —— 358
4   Summary —— 361
5   References —— 361

Abstract: Decades of research on the nature, acquisition, and mature use of spatial language reveal three major themes to be discussed in this chapter. First, spatial language is one of several cognitive systems that is specialized, reflecting pressures from the nature of our non-linguistic spatial representation and the nature of language as a symbolic system used for communication. The primitives for spatial language form a closed set and are likely to have evolved in response to these pressures. Second, acquisition involves selection from the set of primitives, partly via learning from input, with the latter subject to the same kind of maturational constraints as are found in phonology, morphology and syntax. Third, although having spatial language greatly increases representational power to express our thoughts, spatial language does not in any direct way change the underlying structure of human spatial thought.

1 The geometries engaged by spatial language

Like all mobile species, humans possess a remarkably powerful capacity to negotiate physical space, moving from place to place in directed fashion, picking up and manipulating objects, attending to the locations of important objects and events, and making inferences about the locations of objects no longer in sight. In addition to these, however, humans possess the capacity to represent their experience of space using formats unavailable to other species: They can talk about space, and they can create external representations of space, such as drawings and maps. These additional functions emerge early in development, with little or no formal tutoring. The ease with which they are carried out invites the naive idea

Barbara Landau, Baltimore, MD, USA

https://doi.org/10.1515/9783110589825-012

that there is a simple and straightforward mapping between our non-linguistic spatial representations (such as those underlying navigation and search) and the spatial representations that are encoded by language.

Several decades of research, however, have revealed that human spatial representational systems are specialized, tailored to the particular kind of function that they carry out. For example, the spatial system underlying our ability to navigate unknown spaces appears to engage representations that include metric properties of space such as angles and distances (Landau, Gleitman & Spelke 1981; Gallistel 1990; Klatzky et al. 1998). The ability to reorient ourselves after disorientation appears to engage representations of space that incorporate geometric descriptions of the environmental layout, but are blind to aspects of the environment that do not contribute to this geometric description (Cheng 1986; Gallistel 1990; Hermer & Spelke 1996). Object recognition and identification engage computations that analyze the stable axial and part structure of objects, and the spatial relationships among them (Biederman 1995; Palmeri & Gauthier 2004; Xu & Singh 2002). Action on objects engages representations that are sensitive to the continually changing relative angles of the arm, wrist, hand, and fingers as they reach, grasp, and manipulate objects (Milner & Goodale 1995). Each of these spatial systems is functionally distinct from the others, engaging different kinds of spatial representations designed to solve different problems. Like each of these specialized systems, spatial language has its own unique computational requirements.

1.1 The closed class and spatial primitives

Most theorists would agree that the central conceptual elements underlying spatial language are those representing objects, places, paths, and motions. Each of these conceptual elements obeys two sets of constraints. First, each must be mapped to some linguistic form. In English and many other languages, objects are mapped to nouns (and/or NPs) and motions are mapped to verbs. Places encode static spatial relationships, and are typically mapped to prepositional phrases in English and often to post-positions or adpositions in other languages. Paths encode trajectories – spatial relationships in which objects move between and among points. These too are encoded by PPs in English and by similar elements in other languages. Talmy (1985) theorized that languages belong to different typologies according to the way that expression of the motion event is partitioned when it is mapped to its lexical and grammatical elements. Spanish and other so-called "verb-framed" languages tend to encode the path element in the verb, e.g. *subir* ('go up'), *bajar* ('go down'), *meter* ('put in'), *poner* ('take out'), often leaving the manner of motion to be encoded separately as an adverb. (This pattern occurs predominantly when the path is bounded; when the path is unbounded, Spanish and other verb framed languages can encode manner in the verb (see Papafragou, Massey & Gleitman 2002, for discussion). In contrast, English and other so-called "satellite-framed" languages tend to encode the path in a PP (e.g. Mary ran *out of the house*), with the main motion and its manner conflated and expressed in verbs such as *run, hop, skip, swim, fly*, etc. As a consequence of this major typological difference, languages like Spanish have more verbs that express different kinds of paths than do languages like English. Talmy's well-known example contrasts the Spanish *La bottela entró la cueva, flotando* with the English *The bottle floated into the cave*, emphasizing the different way that two languages can carve up the same event by assigning different conceptual elements to different forms.

Although this division of labor is important, it is also essential to know that English does have path verbs (e.g. *exit, enter, leave, flee*) and Spanish does have manner of motion verbs (e.g. *bailar*, 'to dance', *caminar*, 'to walk', *saltar*, 'to jump'), so the division of labor is a tendency rather than an absolute rule. Perhaps more important is a deep but often unnoticed similarity across such typologically different languages: Regardless of language type, the kinds of paths that get encoded are quite limited, whereas the manners of motion are quite open. For example, the paths encoded by the some of the most frequent path verbs in Spanish include the same conceptual elements as those encoded by English prepositions. These conceptual elements include directions (up, down, to/towards, away from) and combinations of path with places (into, onto, out of, off of). In fact, the bulk of the path and place terms in English comprise a quite limited set – a closed class, according to Talmy – and the conceptual elements underlying these terms also show up as Path verbs in Spanish and other verb-framed languages. As Talmy (1983) pointed out, the closed class status of these elements – like other elements of grammar – make them especially interesting in any theory of spatial language. They provide a special window into the nature of the spatial-conceptual elements that languages tend to encode, hence a window on this unique aspect of human spatial cognition.

The spatial properties relevant to linguistic encoding of Path and Place are surprisingly distinct from the kinds of spatial properties that are required by many other spatial cognitive systems, consistent with the specialization of spatial language. As noted by linguists such as Talmy (1983), spatial properties that are encoded by the closed class vocabulary of languages typically abstract away from metric properties such as specific angles or distances. The latter are encoded by the open class vocabulary – specifically by the infinite set of number words in combination with number terms (e.g. 3,000 feet above sea level). Landau & Jackendoff (1993) analyzed the set of 85 English prepositions and proposed several sets of properties that capture most of the relevant geometric relationships. They proposed that these properties are the primitive "features" from which all languages select. The idea that features and their combinations can capture the spatial meanings of the closed class vocabulary is consistent with the view of Talmy (1983) and Levinson & Wilkins (2006), among others. It is important to note that Landau & Jackendoff's proposed list of features was *not* a claim that these features correspond to the meanings of English prepositions (cf. Levinson & Wilkins 2006). Rather, the claim is that the primitive features that can be derived from analysis of English prepositions are part of a universal base upon which all languages build their own stock of spatial terms. The variation across languages in the encoding of space (see sections 2 and 3 below) can best be understood as reflecting choices within this universal set of primitives, and/or ways of combining primitives (see also Levinson & Wilkins (2006). The proposed set of primitives could also be viewed as the starting point for the child learner (see section 2 below).

1.2 The spatial primitives for spatial language

The expression of Paths and Places require specifying a relationship between a "figure" object (in Talmy's 1983 terms), a "ground" or "reference" object, and the path or place function, which specifies the spatial relationship between the two. For example, an expression such as "X is on Y" includes the figure (X), the reference object (Y), and the place-function (ON), which specifies the geometric function applied to the reference object. Sentences expressing manner of motion along a path, such as "X ran to Y", could also be viewed as including a figure (X), reference object (Y), and the geometric function (directed path, TO, ending at Y). The spatial content of Path and Place terms is rather restricted (as one would imagine, from their closed class status.) As Talmy (1983) first pointed out, figure objects across languages have remarkably few geometrical requirements. That is, there are few prepositions that require a figure object shaped like a cigar or a cube; rather, most prepositions can combine with figure objects that vary widely in overall shape. With the exception (in English) of terms such as *along* or *through*, which require that the figure object be linear, or execute a linear-path, the figure's exact geometry is often irrelevant. For example, it is natural to say "The ribbon lay *through* the tunnel" (linear object as figure), or "The ball bounced *through* the tunnel" (linear path as figure), but less natural to say "The ball lay *through* the tunnel" (non-linear object as figure). Thus the preposition *through* requires a linear figure object. Prepositions can also select figure objects for quantity, e.g. the terms *throughout* or *all over* require multiple figure objects. But in general, there are few prepositions that require a specific geometry for the figure object.

Talmy's (1985) discussion of Atsugewi shows that the figure object in basic locational expressions *can* require more geometric specification, as this language has roots for locational verbs that include meanings such as 'small, shiny, spherical object to move/be located' and 'runny, icky, material to move/be located'. But even the range shown by this language is limited.

In contrast to the sparse requirements for the figure object, the geometric specification for reference objects is richer, though still far less detail than would be required to recognize or identify the object as a member of some category (see, e.g. Landau & Jackendoff 1993; Landau, Smith & Jones 1998). The geometries that are relevant for reference objects include simple points (as in "near" Y) and lines (x is "along Y") as well as volumes (IN, INSIDE), surfaces (ON), and quantity (the contrast between *between* and *among*, though disappearing in English, is a contrast between two vs. three or more reference objects).

There also exist, in many languages, terms for which the reference object defines a 3-dimensional set of orthogonal axes with an origin that can be centered on a reference object (including one's self) or a place. Depending on the origin of the reference system, different sets of terms are used. For example, English has three sets of terms that engage reference systems. One set engages object-centered reference systems, i.e. those whose origins are the object itself (including one's own body). The axes of this reference system are then used to define six major regions that can be called the top, bottom, front, back, side, left or right of the object. The same axes can be used to define regions extending out in space but surrounding the object, as in above, below, (to the) left and right (or sides), in front of and behind the object. In many languages, including English, the terms that engage the object-based reference system and those that engage the space around the object are morphologically related, e.g. see Levinson (1994) on the use of animal body parts to define locations on and around other objects. For example, although the terms top/bottom only refer to object parts (whereas above/below refer to regions extending outward from the object), the terms left/right can refer to object parts or to the regions surrounding the object, and are distinguished only by combination with *the* for the former (e.g. *the left* of the box) or *to the* for the latter (e.g. *to the left* of the box). Finally, a third set of terms engages earth as the reference system, using terms north, south, east, and west. Speakers of different languages vary in the degree to which they use different sets of terms (such as right/left vs. east/west) to describe relatively small-scale spatial relationships, and a great deal of recent research has addressed the significance of these different tendencies (see Section 3.0, below).

In addition to limitations on the geometric structure of figure and reference objects, languages appear to encode a limited number of spatial relationships (in the closed class set of terms). For example, all languages encode distance, but the closed class set usually encodes relative distance (e.g. near, far, far and out of sight), coarse categorical direction (usually using the six orthogonal axis directions described earlier), and visibility (within view, out of view), and to a certain degree, occlusion. Beyond this, specific angles and distances can be encoded by language, of course, but this tends to occur using phrasal constructions; precise angle and distance depend on expressions from the number system.

Like the geometries relevant for Places, the structures relevant for Paths are limited. Jackendoff's (1983) analysis, building on the work of Fillmore (1971), Gruber (1965), and others, proposes that there are three basic kinds of path. These include TO-paths, which encode the goal or endpoint of the path (by terms such as *to* or *towards* in English), FROM-paths, which encode the origin or starting point of the path (by terms such as *from*) and VIA-paths, which encode the path with reference to an intermediate reference object (term such as *by, via*). These paths – like many place terms – strip away from the specific and detailed geometry of the path, and encode only the beginning, endpoint, and direction of the path. When combined with a Place term, they can encode these as well as some aspects of the reference object geometry; for example, TO-paths ending in a volume (into), or a surface (onto), FROM-paths starting in a volume (out of) or surface (off of). Complex path geometries can be encoded, but they tend to engage open class words such as verbs, e.g. *The receiver zig-zagged/spiralled/twirled/somersaulted across the field*. Like other open class terms, verbs of this sort allow relatively detailed geometric distinctions among path geometries. In contrast, Path and Place terms are part of the closed class, and hence are limited in the kinds of geometry that they can draw on. It is this special status that makes their existence and their acquisition by children so interesting.

1.3 Where do these spatial primitives come from?

Because there is a limited number of spatial primitives, and because they show up across different languages, it is natural to ask about their origin. Like other kinds of grammatical markings – such as aspectual marking – the closed class of spatial terms is linked to important categories of meaning. But the spatial primitives invite a special temptation to look for their origin in systems other than language. One possibility, of course, is that these spatial-semantic primitives have their origins in systems of non-linguistic spatial representation, i.e. that they are not specific to language. Just like the set of phonetic distinctions – universally available to all babies before language learning proceeds – the spatial semantic primitives could be part of the foundation for perceiving and interacting with the spatial world. The explanation for the infant's universal sensitivity to phonetic features usually invokes some initial perceptual space (an attractor space) that is the foundation for learning one's language-specific phonemes. This space need not be specific to humans; indeed there is evidence that chinchillas are sensitive to many of the relevant distinctions (see Kuhl 2000). The analogy for spatial features would be an initial space that – like the space for phonetic features – would have areas of key "salience" that serve as attractors for the categories most important to humans and other species. Such areas might be, for example, the relationship of containment (INSIDE/OUTSIDE), support or attachment (ON/OFF), degree of fit (TIGHT/LOOSE FIT), directions (UP/DOWN or TO/FROM), and so forth.

The attempt to trace the origins of such concepts to non-linguistic spatial systems is not new. Early papers by E. Clark (1973) and H. Clark (1973) speculated that the child's non-linguistic concepts of basic categories such as up/down or containment/support might serve as the foundation for learning spatial terms. Indeed, recent studies have shown that pre-linguistic infants are sensitive to many of spatial properties that later are encoded in spatial terms across different languages. Baillargeon and colleagues have shown that infants are sensitive to many of the spatial relationships that are foundational to languages, for example, the relationships of support, containment, occlusion, etc. (Aguiar & Baillargeon 1998; Baillargeon & Hankosummers 1990; Hespos & Baillargeon 2006). The available conceptual repertoire is broader than that which is needed for learning any particular language, suggesting a set of universal spatial-conceptual distinctions that may later be adopted as relevant semantic features as the child learns his native language. For example, Hespos & Spelke (2004) showed that 5 month-old babies growing up in English speaking households are sensitive to the distinction between "tight fit" and "loose fit". This distinction is encoded by different verbs in the basic vocabulary of Korean speakers, *kkita, nehta, nohta* (Choi 2006); hence babies may learn quite early that it is a semantic feature in their language; in contrast, babies who are learning English may not adopt this as a semantic feature until somewhat later, when they learn verbs such as *insert* that may encode the property of tight fit.

There are several possible ways to think about the origins of these spatially relevant primitives. Mandler (2004) has proposed that these concepts precede language and are the product of a process she calls "perceptual analysis", whereby meaningful units are extracted from the less interpreted perceptual array. She proposes that, as infants come to attend more closely – or examine – objects and their spatial relationships, concepts relevant to the later acquired spatial language are constructed. This view has the benefit that it delivers up conceptual units that will be easily mapped to language; but there is no clear and detailed mechanism for how such "perceptual analysis" occurs.

Another possibility would be to deliver the primitives directly from another existing system, with vision as the most obvious (and well-understood) candidate. One of the most pressing problems within vision science is explaining how rich spatial relationships are computed by the visual system. As an example, Ullman (1984) has beautifully described the great computational difficulty of computing the simple relationship of "inside/outside". Some current solutions involve cognitive operations – "visual routines" – that may be able to compute whether a point is inside or outside of a bounding contour in a relatively automatic way. The deployment of some visual routines – resulting in perception of certain spatial properties appears to require focused attention (Cavanagh, Labianca & Thornton 2001). For example, focused attention is required for the stable binding of property conjunctions, such as color and location. Vision scientists have long thought that a single feature (e.g. color x) can be detected without focused attention: In a display containing a single red line together with multiple green lines, the red line seems to "pop out". But detecting combinations of features (e.g. a red line in a group of red circles and green lines) appears to require focused attention. It is at least tempting to think that the kinds of spatial relationships whose construction requires either visual routines, or focused attention, might provide candidate primitive spatial relationships from which language could draw.

The idea that spatial primitives for language might share their origin with other spatial systems – vision, in particular – is consistent with the theory advanced by Landau & Jackendoff (1993), who proposed that some of the properties of spatial primitives could be traced to the nature of the visual system, in particular, the distinction between "what" and "where" (Ungerleider & Mishkin 1982). Building on Talmy's analysis of the geometric nature of the closed class spatial vocabulary, Landau & Jackendoff argued that the spatial representation of objects draws on two quite different kinds of representation, depending on whether the objects are being named (as category members – "what") or located ("where"). In the former case, the spatial-geometric representation of objects is rather rich, characteristic of the non-linguistic object recognition system. In the latter case, when objects are being located, their spatial-geometric representations are quite coarse, with figures represented as points or lines and reference objects represented as volumes, surfaces, and sets of orthogonal axes centered on an origin. Recent reformulations of the what/where distinction in vision suggest that the "where" system might be better thought of as a "how" system, engaging geometries required for acts such as reaching and grasping; so the mapping between spatial language and these two visual systems is not one to one. Still, the large differences in how objects are represented for the two purposes of naming vs. locating suggest that the visual system has the capacity to represent objects in both of these ways. If the visual system represents objects coarsely in the "where/how" system, but in richer geometric detail in the "what" system, this would correspond to the differences in detail for objects when they play the role of figure and reference object (coarse), compared to their geometric detail when named (highly detailed). Many questions remain, however, about when and how the visual system might compute the coarser representations of object shape required for the roles of figure and ground in spatial expressions. If the computation of coarse object geometries and their related spatial relationships should prove to be an output of visual routines, the latter could supply a crucial link to help us understand the nature and origin of the primitives underlying spatial language. Given the computation of these primitives, languages could then select from them, and children's learning would be occasioned by experience with the relevant contrasts in the linguistic environment around them. Thus, the acquisition of the closed class of spatial terms would be quite analogous to the acquisition of one's native language phonemes.

It should be noted that, even if visual routines can be shown to support the construction of basic spatial relationships, this can only help answer the question of where *spatial* features that are computable by the visual system come from. Some aspects of spatial term meanings are likely to involve force dynamic properties (e.g. Talmy 1988), and it is unclear whether these properties are computable by the visual system, or are solely conceptual in nature. Moreover, analysis of properties computable by vision are not likely to completely explain the extensively generalized use of spatial terms to encode spatial relationships that are much farther removed from visual representations. For example, even so simple a term as *in* can be used to encode full physical enclosure (a ball *in* a tube), partial enclosure (an apple *in* a bowl), or virtual enclosure (the code *in* the computer program). The question of what underlies these generalizations is thorny, and no complete answers exist. However, Herskovits (1986) gives us some purchase by listing the wide range of uses for the basic spatial prepositions in English; Lakoff (1987) and Brugman (1988) emphasize the extensive metaphoric use of spatial terms in English; and Malt et al. (1999) provide some interesting ideas about how basic meanings of words for containers are extended by mechanisms such as convention, pre-emption, and chaining.

2 Acquisition of spatial language: Empirical evidence for a specialized system?

Whatever the origins of the spatial semantic primitives, there are important questions about how these primitives become deployed for the purposes of language. Even supposing that the small set of primitives is available prior to language learning, different sets of features (or different combinations thereof) will be selected by different languages, producing some real differences in the kinds of spatial relationships that are encoded by the basic terms of a language. By analogy with the acquisition of one's native phonemes, one can ask three basic questions: Is there evidence that infants are sensitive to all of the relevant primitives prior to language learning? If so, then what mechanisms produce shaping by the linguistic environment, i.e. how does the child learn which features are selected by his or her language and which are not? Is there any special window of time during which this learning must take place in order to achieve native competence?

2.1 Are infants sensitive to all relevant spatial primitives before learning language?

Recent results suggest that infants are sensitive to many of the spatial categories that later will be encoded in their language. Broad spatial concepts such as containment, support, and occlusion are present even within the first six months of life, although there are also significant developmental changes in the infant's ability to use these concepts across all physical situations (Aguiar & Baillargeon 1998; Baillargeon 1991, 2004; Baillargeon & Hankosummers 1990). Presumably, these concepts will serve as the foundation for the early acquisition and use of spatial terms such as *in* and *on*, which are among the earliest produced and understood (E. Clark 1973; Johnston & Slobin 1979). Infants of 8 and 9 months of age are also sensitive to an independent contrast that has been described as cross-cutting the spatial relationship encoded by English *in* and *on* (Bowerman 1996). This contrast is between tight and loose fit, encoded in Korean by the verb *kkita* compared to *nehta* or *nohta*. Actions in which objects come into tight fit with each other (e.g. a peg put tightly *in* a hole or one lego placed tightly *on* another) are likely to be encoded by speakers of Korean using *kkita* whereas similar actions that do not involve such fit are encoded with other verbs (e.g. a peg put into a wide well or a lego placed on a shelf; see Bowerman 1996). The apparently striking difference in the encoding of such simple spatial events in English and Korean has led to a great deal of research activity designed to determine what the status of "tight" and "loose" fit are in the infant's pre-linguistic conceptualizations. Hespos & Spelke (2004) found that 5 month-olds growing up in English-speaking homes are sensitive to this distinction, even though basic spatial prepositions in English do not encode this degree of fit (tight/loose). McDonough, Choi & Mandler (2003) found that 9 month-olds in both English-speaking and in Korean-speaking homes are sensitive to the tight fit/loose fit distinction. These results suggest that the primitive features corresponding to "containment/enclosure", as well as those corresponding to "tight/loose fit" are both among the primitive features available to infants who must then select among them as they learn their native language. By analogy with the literature on phoneme development, this suggests an available set of primitives, some of which will be selected as children learn their lexicon. The particular set of primitives selected for obligatory lexical encoding may differ over languages, as suggested by Bowerman's (1996) analysis.

Some intriguing results further suggest that there may be asymmetries or marking within primitive features such as "tight/loose fit". Evidence suggests that there may be an asymmetry in the extent to which infants are sensitive to tight vs. loose fit (Casasola 2006; Choi 2006). In Choi's study, English-speaking infants who were familiarized with "tight fit" relationships looked longer at other tight fit relationships than loose fit ones; but infants who were familiarized with loose fit relationships did not look longer at one than the other. A related pattern was recently shown among adults who were asked to make similarity judgments between familiarized events (tight or loose fit) and test events (Norbury, Waxman & Song 2008). When adults were familiarized with tight fit events, they did not view loose fit events as similar; but when they observed loose fit events, they did view tight fit events as similar. These findings suggest there may be a natural marking between the values of the "tight vs. loose fit" feature, or perhaps that loose fit is the default assumption, and tight fit is "special". If so, infants who hear a term applied to a "tight fit" relationship may assume that it does *not* generalize to loose fit, and they would have to learn that it does, through positive evidence of hearing the *same term* applied to, e.g. both tight and loose fit actions. At the same time, infants who hear a term applied to a "loose fit" relationship might assume that it *does* generalize to tight fit (of a particular kind), and would have to learn that it does not, again by hearing a *different* term for the two types of events. Intriguingly, when comparing English to Korean speaking toddlers, Choi (2006) found weakened sensitivity to tight fit among the toddlers learning English, and Choi suggested that they were learning to ignore tight fit as an important semantic distinction in their native language. However, this appealing story is likely to become more complex as we learn more about how the lexicon encodes both tight/loose fit across languages, and how it encodes spatial relationships. For example, Kawachi (2007) has questioned whether the distinction between Korean *kkita* and *nohta/nehta* is really one of "fit", and proposes that *kkita* is actually a manner of motion verb whose distribution is quite different from its counterparts *nohta/nehta*. Clearly, our understanding of how children select semantic features for encoding in language will depend strongly on our understanding of how they work in the target language.

Infants also appear to be sensitive to categories underlying the acquisition of (English) terms *above* vs. *below*, and *left* vs. *right*. In several studies, Quinn

(1994) familiarized 3-month olds to displays in which a dot was displayed either above or below a line. The infants were then tested with displays in which the test dot was equidistant from the original dot at one of two locations: either above or below the same line. Infants looked longer at the dot that was in the contrasting category, relative to the original dot, showing that they are sensitive to differences corresponding to the category above vs. below. The same kind of effect was shown for categories left and right, although at a somewhat later age (Quinn 2004). Although the words for these relationships are not acquired until well into the third year of life, and development of some aspects of their use extends much later, Quinn's evidence shows that the underlying conceptual basis for these axis-based terms is in place prior to learning language. In a sense, this is not surprising, as representation of location within different reference systems is known to be a hard-wired aspect of human representation of space, as well as that of other species (Gallistel 2002).

The acquisition of path terms invites related questions: Are infants sensitive to the relevant primitives for path terms prior to language learning? Following Jackendoff's analysis, the major path types include TO-paths (which encode paths moving to the goal or endpoint), FROM-paths (which encode paths moving from the source or origin) and VIA-paths (which encode paths moving past an intermediate reference object). These can be combined with place primitives, to produce, e.g. terms such as *into* (TO-path ending in a volume), *out of* (FROM-path starting in a volume), *onto* (TO-path ending on a surface), etc. Given that infants are sensitive to properties such as containment and support, the key question is whether they are sensitive to the differences embodied in the three-way distinction among TO-paths, FROM-paths, and VIA-paths. Considerable research has shown that English-speaking children and adults show an asymmetry between TO and FROM paths, with a bias to omit linguistic encoding of FROM-paths when it is a grammatical option (Lakusta & Landau 2005). The same bias has been shown among children learning Japanese (Lakusta et al. 2006) and broader literature suggests that the asymmetry is reflected in children's and adults' non-linguistic representation of events (Lakusta & Landau 2012; Regier & Zheng 2003, 2007), in substitutions of path terms among brain-damage patients (Ihara & Fujita 2000) and among deaf children who have no exposure to a formal linguistic system (Zheng & Goldin-Meadow 2002).

Recent research shows the same asymmetry in pre-linguistic infants. Lakusta et al. (2007) familiarized 12 month-old infants to animate events in which a toy duck moved either along a path to one of two goal objects (e.g. TO-path, ending in box A) or along a path from one of two source objects (e.g. FROM-path, starting at box A). The goal (or source) objects' locations were then switched, and babies were shown events in which they saw the duck move to (a) the same goal/

source (now in a new location), or (b) a new goal/source (now in the old location). Infants looked longer to events in which the duck moved to the new goal or source object, indicating that they were sensitive to which object was the goal (or source) rather than its location. However, infants were only sensitive to the changes in the source object when the source objects themselves were very salient (e.g. bright and highly decorated), suggesting that the infants were less sensitive to changes in source paths than goal paths. Lakusta et al. directly tested this hypothesis by pitting highly salient sources (e.g. a brightly decorated red box) against less salient goals (e.g. a plain red box). Infants were familiarized to events in which the duck moved from the salient source to the less salient goal; they were then tested on events in which the duck moved from a new salient source to the old goal, or the old salient source to a new goal. Infants looked longer when the duck moved to the new goal object, showing that they were more sensitive to (or attended more) to the goal object, and presumably, the TO-path. These findings suggest that pre-linguistic infants are sensitive to the two major path types (TO-paths and FROM-paths) and that the asymmetry observed between the two in language among children and adults is present even prior to language. Combined with the evidence on sensitivity to other primitives underlying place terms in languages, these data suggest that infants may be sensitive to all possible primitives prior to learning language. Future research will be required to determine whether infants are sensitive to other spatial primitives, and whether there is additional evidence of markedness relationships within the set of primitive features.

2.2 How is language learning shaped by input, and is the semantic space altered?

Given the cross-linguistic variation in spatial semantics, it follows that children must learn which primitives are realized in their native language. This means that the semantic space must be shaped in accord with the linguistic environment. A significant amount of learning is accomplished by the time children are two years old. Bowerman (1996) elicited language from children learning English, Dutch, and Korean. The children were shown sets of joining and separating events (e.g. putting together two bristle blocks; removing a hat from a doll, etc.) and were prompted to describe the event to the experimenter, by asking them to "Tell me what to do". The production data showed that children followed some clear universal patterns, but they also showed obvious language-specific effects at even the youngest ages tested (2 to 2–1/2 years of age). For example, regardless of what language was being learned, children never used the same term to apply to events that joined two parts AND events that separated two parts. This suggests that the two opposing directions or results of the events (joining/separation) were likely marked as distinctly different types, leading to marking with different forms. It seems likely that the distinction between separation and joining more generally is a pre-linguistic distinction as well, thus a candidate for a universal spatial-cognitive and semantic distinction.

At the same time, different types of joining and separating acts were distinguished over languages, even for the youngest children. Children learning English grouped together a wide range of joining events under the expressions (put) *on*, including events as diverse as such as putting on a hat, putting two legos together, and putting a ring on a pole. This relatively broad class of events, collapsed under the same expression (verb + on) was similar, though not identical to that of English-speaking adults, who sub-categorized the events by using additional expressions such as *put together* and *join*. The space for children learning Korean differed from that of English-speaking children by including specific verbs encoding the donning of different kinds of clothing; the partitioning was even more finely differentiated among Korean speaking adults, including distinctions of degree of fit and methods of joining. Although the application of spatial expressions to different event types was not as fine-grained among children as among adults, it is clear that even young children learn quite rapidly to activate certain language-specific primitive feature combinations and de-activate others.

A particularly telling comparison is found in Bowerman's (1996) analysis of production for separating events among children learning English vs. Dutch. Children learning English formed two separate categories, labeled by *off* vs. *out*, with the former collapsing events such as "top off pen", "ring off pole", "shoes off", "dress off"; and the latter collapsing event such as "legos out of bag" and "doll out of bathtub". For English speakers, these naturally form two categories of separation, with the latter involving removal from some concave cavity and the former involving removal of various other types. Children learning Dutch collapsed all of these instances under one expression, *uit* (English "out"), thus appearing to violate some presumably "natural" division between the removal from cavity vs. other kinds of removal. Bowerman notes that this is puzzling, until one examines the pattern of production among Dutch speaking adults. They apply *af* (English "off") to the non-clothing exemplars covered by English *off*, but collapse together the removal of clothing with removal from a cavity, under the Dutch term *uit* (English "out"). Bowerman correctly notes that, if universal non-linguistic distinctions are the sole basis for early learning, one might expect Dutch children to ignore this anomaly and sort things the same way as English speaking children (or vice versa, depending on what one thinks is the most natural categorization). Instead, the children appear to discover some meaning that will make some sense of the variety of events that are expressed by *uit*, and end up conjecturing that it covers many different kinds of removal, thus collapsing all three types of removal (tops off pens, shoes off feet, legos out of bag). At some point, they of course notice that there is a further distinction to be made, and add to their lexicon the term *af*, creating two categories from the one. Dutch speaking adults apparently do not consider the two kinds of *uit* to be coherently related to each other; according to Bowerman (1996), they are surprised to reflect on the apparent anomaly, revealing that they likely store the two *uit* meanings separately.

This example reveals the crucial role of linguistic input in the learning process; not surprisingly, since spatial language does vary cross-linguistically, and therefore learning through exposure must be important. What is the mechanism? Landau & Shipley (2001) carried out a study that shows how powerful the role of labeling distribution is in moving the learner towards their specific language. Three year-olds were shown two objects (object A, object E) that were perceptually quite different; however, object E had been produced by a program that morphed object A into the new object E. There were also three intermediate items that had also been created by morphing and represented the states between A and E (B, C, D), thereby creating a set of five objects all related by morphing (A, B, C, D, E). One group of children was told that object A was "a dax", and that object E was also "a dax". A second group of children was told that A was "a dax" and that E was "a rif". All children were then shown the entire series of five objects, one at a time, and asked "Is this a dax?" Children who had heard objects A and E labeled with the same count noun accepted all objects (ends and intervening objects) as members of the dax category. But children who had heard the two objects labeled with different count nouns accepted objects A through E as members of the "dax" category in declining order, with A accepted at 100%, E at close to zero, and objects after C declining sharply in acceptance. Landau & Shipley suggested that children assume that if two objects – no matter how different – are labeled with the same name, they are members of the same category; but if labeled with different names, they must be members of different categories. This principle will allow broader categories to be readily broken down into sub-categories by clear marking with a novel linguistic term. This could be the mechanism whereby children learning Korean separate "removing a hat" from other kinds of removal. It could also be the mechanism whereby children learning Dutch eventually learn to separate the non-cavity removals from the other removal events, once they hear the distinguishing marker. This proposal is consistent with Bowerman's (1996) emphasis on the importance of learning in the acquisition of spatial language, and is similar to proposals emphasizing constraints on word learning more generally (see Bloom 2002).

It is important to note that the strong effects of learning do not in any way obviate the need for a complementary set of universals that will constrain children's conjectures. Universals are needed to explain why children are never observed to collapse joining events with separating events; why they show strong asymmetries in the acquisition of path terms; and why they show evidence of sensitivity to semantic-like elements before learning language at all. The pressing issue is how these universals interact with learning mechanisms to produce native language learning.

2.3 Is there a maturational timetable for learning spatial terms?

The analogy to other areas of language acquisition – especially phoneme acquisition – invites the question of whether there is a maturational timetable under which spatial term learning is optimal. In the case of phonemes, we know that 6 month-old infants are sensitive to all phonemic contrasts that have been tested, whether or not they are part of the native language system that will be learned (Kuhl 2000). By 12 months old, infants are still sensitive to those that are part of their target (native) language system, but not to those that that do not play a role in non-native systems (Saffran, Werker & Werner 2006; Werker & Tees 1999). Adults have difficulty discriminating non-native contrasts (though there are exceptions, see Kuhl 2000 for review), and this global pattern of development is thought to reflect the progressive selection of native language-relevant features and phonemes, with the progressive weakening of sensitivity to non-native phonemes. The same general pattern – early acquisition and selection of native language structure, together with increasing difficulty in learning non-native aspects of structure – has been attested in studies of morphology and syntax (Johnson & Newport 1989). Could the same be true for spatial terms?

On one hand, it seems intuitively plausible that spatial terms might be different from other aspects of language typically considered to be the essence of language structure, such as phonology, morphology, and syntax. After all, spatial terms are somewhat like open class elements in that they appear to have content that is accessible to our larger conceptual systems. Moreover, they seem to encode properties of space that are accessible to us – properties such as containment, support, location along an axis, etc. On the other hand, Talmy (1983, 2000) and others have argued that the closed class set of spatial terms – which I have argued reflect primitives and their combinations – is more like other closed class forms such as tense and aspect than open class terms. If so, the developmental pattern of early shaping and later closure could be similar to phonology, morphology and syntax.

We have already seen that there is evidence for early shaping of the semantic space for predicates of joining and separating (Bowerman 1996; Choi & Bowerman 1991). There is also evidence for early closure of the semantic space. Munnich (2002) and Munnich & Landau (2008) created large sets of static spatial scenes that sampled two kinds of distinctions often found in languages of the world. The first sampled relationships of containment and support, distinguished by English terms *in* and *on*. The second sampled relationships along the vertical axis, distinguished by English terms such as *above/below*, *on/above*, *under/below*, etc. Following the work of Johnson & Newport (1989), Munnich & Landau tested native speakers of Spanish or Korean who had learned English at different ages (ranging from well under 8 to their mid-20's). At the time of test, participants were between 18 and 65 years old, had spent a minimum of 5 years immersed in an English speaking environment, and had all received undergraduate or graduate training at a university in the U.S.

People were given a battery of 80 spatial scenes, and were instructed to describe each using basic spatial terms of English. Half of the battery tapped the obligatory English contrast between *on* and *in* and the other half tapped the obligatory English contrast between *on* and *above*. For example, the *on/in* contrast was tested with pairs of scenes that showed the same objects in a relationship clearly encoded by *on* vs. *in* in English (e.g. pretzels *in* a bag vs. *on* the same bag). These scenes were randomly distributed throughout the battery so that people would not be likely to purposefully contrast opposing pairs. Native Spanish speakers might be expected to have difficulty with the on/in distinction, since Spanish encodes both relationships with a single term *en*, and Korean speakers might be expected to have difficulty with the second distinction, since Korean encodes on/above with the single term *ue ni*.

Results showed clear effects of age of acquisition on production and use of English spatial terms. The overall scores for the basic battery were negatively correlated with age of acquisition, showing that people who had learned English at a later age scored worse than those who had learned it an earlier age. There were no indications, however, that the two native language groups differed on which contrasts they found difficult. The lack of effect could be due to real and general effects of learning at a later age regardless of one's first language, or it could be due to an insufficiently sensitive test battery. To compare these effects with other, well-established effects of age of acquisition on mastery of English morphology and syntax, all participants were also given the morphology and syntax batteries used by Johnson & Newport (1989). Results of this battery replicated the effects found by Johnson & Newport, with Munnich & Landau's second language learners of English showing a negative correlation between performance and age of acquisition. Thus the results of the spatial battery were consistent with those from tests of morphology and syntax, indicating that late learners of English perform worse than early learners.

These results suggest that spatial language – like aspects of language more traditionally considered core aspects of linguistic structure – are subject to effects of age at which the language is learned. The closed class system of spatial terms may be subject to the same biological learning mechanisms as those involved in learning phonology, morphology, and syntax.

3 Effects of spatial language on spatial cognition: Does language influence thought?

Given evidence of substantial cross-linguistic differences in spatial language, it was perhaps inevitable that there should be a resurgence of scientific interest on Whorf's hypothesis. Although Whorf's original hypothesis focused on the coding of time among the Hopi, empirical research has subsequently examined a range of domains including object individuation, number, color, and space – all quite fundamental cognitive categories for which Whorfian effects could radically change cognition. At the point of this writing, there is active investigation of the potential effects of language on thought in each of these domains, with groups of scientists proclaiming victory on each side of the debate. Two main hypotheses have been advanced. One is that learning a particular language radically affects one's non-linguistic "thought" (Levinson 2003; Lucy & Gaskins 2003). A second is that learning *any* language radically affects the nature of non-linguistic thought, primarily by changing computational resources through the use of linguistic format (Carey 2004; Gordon 2004; Spelke 2003). Counter-arguments to both hypotheses can be made, however, on both theoretical and empirical grounds. Theoretically, language can only encode what already exists in thought, hence there can be no permanent effects on the structure of thought caused by learning a particular language (Gleitman et al. 2005; Landau, Dessalegn & Goldberg 2010; Munnich & Landau 2003). Taking spatial reference frames as an example, it is unclear how exposure to language could *cause* people to create the representations needed to use these frames of reference. More likely, the representations are there to begin with, and languages select which of the different kinds of reference frames they will encode. Similarly, learning *any* language must entail being able to represent what is eventually encoded by language.

The empirical evidence for strong Whorfian effects of both types is at present, weak at best. One widely cited set of findings comes from Levinson and colleagues (Levinson 2003; Pederson et al. 1998) and involves the use of different reference frames to encode object locations. Pederson et al. first presented linguistic evidence that languages differ systematically in the frames of reference that speakers prefer to use when encoding small object arrays. Speakers of English, Dutch, and other languages use terms such as *right* and *left*, which engage body-centered and object-centered frames of reference (e.g. the spoon is to my right, or to the left of my coffee cup). Speakers of other languages, including Tzeltal, prefer to use terms that engage a geocentric frame of reference to describe such locations, essentially the equivalent of English speakers saying "the spoon is to the north of me". Given these tendencies, Levinson and colleagues proposed a Whorfian hypothesis: non-linguistic spatial behavior would be strongly affected by the speaker's language. They carried out a set of tasks that were putatively non-linguistic, for example, asking people to observe some animals arranged horizontally in a row in front of the speakers, then asking them to turn 180 degrees and walk to another table, where they were to place the animals in the same spatial relationships as the original array. English and Dutch speakers tended to construct the new array as if they had encoded the original in a body-centered reference system (e.g. same left to right locations, relative to the body) whereas speakers of Tzeltal tended to construct the new array as if they had encoded the original in a geocentric system. Levinson (2003) concluded that the language speakers learned affected their non-linguistic thought.

These findings have been disputed on numerous grounds, and have been subject to both empirical and theoretical scrutiny. Some of the most compelling objections come from Li & Gleitman (2002) who argued that the observed phenomenon could have just as easily been driven by culture and physical environment as by language itself. In several experiments, they showed that English speaking college students could be biased to use either of the reference frames, depending on surrounding cues in the environment, consistent with a large body of literature on animal and human spatial orientation dating back almost a century.

Although these experiments focus on one phenomenon and one aspect of spatial terminology that varies across languages, numerous additional experiments have shown that there are no compelling effects of language that produce long-term, permanent effects on nonlinguistic cognition. The paucity of evidence on these effects, together with the presence of *some* real effects of language on cognitive processing led Landau, Dessalegn & Goldberg (2010) to propose a new hypothesis about the effects of language on cognition. This hypothesis suggests that many (if not all) of the effects claimed to support a Whorfian position are actually the result of momentary interactions between language and non-linguistic processes, whereby language can be seen to drive attention, and thereby modulate the selection of what is to be encoded. Elegant studies in the vision literature show the power of such temporary modulation, with small differences in the onset of linguistic instruction serving to make adults' visual search far more efficient (Spivey et al. 2001). Recent studies show that language can have powerful effects on children's ability to hold in memory combinations of visual features that are otherwise hard to store (Dessalegn & Landau 2008).

Examples of such momentary effects are abundant in the literature. Malt and colleagues (Malt et al. 1999) examined linguistic and non-linguistic categorization of containers by speakers of English, Chinese, and Spanish, and found that their linguistic categorizations were quite different from each other, but their non-linguistic similarity judgments were quite similar to each other. This suggests that there is an underlying similarity space (or spaces) that is non-linguistic, and that language serves to pick out a particular set of relevant properties. Other studies have similarly shown that, even where there are large differences in adults' *linguistic* encoding of motion events (e.g. manner vs. path) or static spatial location (e.g. the obligatory encoding of *on* vs. *above* in English but not Japanese or Korean), non-linguistic differences across speakers are not found (Gennari et al. 2002; Munnich, Landau & Dosher 2001; Papafragou, Massey & Gleitman 2002). Indeed, when people prepare to describe an event, their gaze will be directed to the element of the scene likely to be encoded in the verb of their native language (e.g. manner for English speakers; path for Greek speakers); but when they are merely inspecting the scene without preparing to describe it, eye gazes are no different across speakers of different languages (Papafragou, Hulbert & Trueswell 2008).

Similarly, numerous studies have shown that young children's attention can be driven towards different object properties depending on what syntactic frame is used (e.g. count nouns drive attention to object category and/or the object's shape for artifacts; adjectives drive attention to surface properties; mass nouns drive attention to non-individuated entities, e.g. substances; Landau, Smith & Jones 1998; Smith, Jones & Landau 1996; Waxman & Klibanoff 2000). Lakusta & Landau (2005) found that children have a strong bias to encode events using goal-oriented verbs (i.e. verbs that take TO-path prepositions, such as *give, throw, send*) over source-oriented verbs (e.g. *get, catch, receive*). However, one need only provide a "hint" verb that is source-oriented for children to reverse this tendency, showing that language can serve to drive attention to different aspects of the very same event (see also Fisher et al. 1994).

The idea of momentary effects of language driving change in cognition is consistent with a large body of empirical data, and is reminiscent of an early hypothesis on the effects of cross-linguistic differences on color memory – the idea that encoding in memory might naturally engage language (Kay & Kempton 1984). It accounts for effects observed even in putative nonlinguistic tasks, such as Levinson's, which could readily be accounted for by temporary linguistic encoding. It is consistent with the idea that language can only encode what can already be encoded in non-linguistic representations.

4 Summary

Spatial semantics has long been a touchstone for theories of the relationship between language and cognition. Because we perceive space, move about in space, and think about space, it has often been assumed that the mapping between these systems and spatial language must be relatively simple and direct. However, the past few decades of study have revealed that spatial semantics is remarkably complex in its own right, exhibiting properties that show the necessary reflexes of its relationship to other aspects of spatial cognition but also show special properties that mark its linguistic nature. Discoveries of cross-linguistic differences in the way that space is expressed have raised important questions about the nature of the universal set of primitives and its role in acquisition, the role of learning in selecting from this set, and the maturational constraints that hold for this learning. All of these have opened up new and exciting lines of research that are still in their infancy. The same discoveries have also invited a return to classical questions about the role of language in human thought. Indeed, the study of spatial language is now enjoying a new vigor – well-deserved for its central role in human cognition.

Preparation of this chapter was supported in part by NINDS RO1–050876 and Research Grant# FY-12–04–46 from March of Dimes Birth Defects Foundation

5 References

Aguiar, Andréa & Renée Baillargeon 1998. Eight-and-a-half-month-old infants' reasoning about containment events. *Child Development* 69, 636–653.
Baillargeon, Renée 1991. Reasoning about the height and location of a hidden object in 4.5-month-old infants and 6.5-month-old infants. *Cognition* 38, 13–42.
Baillargeon, Renée 2004. Infants' physical world. *Current Directions in Psychological Science* 13, 89–94.
Baillargeon, Renée & Stephanie Hankosummers 1990. Is the top object adequately supported by the bottom object – young infants understanding of support relations. *Cognitive Development* 5, 29–53.
Biederman, Irving 1995. Visual object recognition. In: S. M. Kosslyn & D. N. Osherson (eds.). *Visual Cognition: An Invitation to Cognitive Science*, vol. 2. 2nd edn. Cambridge, MA: The MIT Press, 121–165.
Bloom, Paul 2002. *How Children Learn the Meanings of Words*. Cambridge, MA: The MIT Press.
Bowerman, Melissa 1996. Learning how to structure space for language: A cross-linguistic perspective. In: P. Bloom et al. (eds.). *Language and Space*. Cambridge, MA: The MIT Press, 385–436.
Brugman, Claudia 1988. *The Story of Over: Polysemy, Semantics and the Structure of the Lexicon*. New York: Garland Press.

Carey, Susan 2004. Bootstrapping and the origin of concepts. *Daedalus* 133, 59–68.
Casasola, Marianella 2006. Can English-learning toddlers acquire and generalize a novel spatial word? *First Language* 26, 187–205.
Cavanagh, Patrick, Angela Labianca & Ian Thornton 2001. Attention-based visual routines: Sprites. *Cognition* 80, 47–60.
Cheng, Ken 1986. A purely geometric module in the rats spatial representation. *Cognition* 23, 149–178.
Choi, Soonja 2006. Influence of language-specific input on spatial cognition: Categories of containment. *First Language* 26, 207–232.
Choi, Soonja & Melissa Bowerman 1991. Learning to express motion events in English and Korean: The influence of language-specific lexicalization patterns. *Cognition* 41, 83–121.
Clark, Eve V. 1973. What's in a word? On the child's acquisition of semantics in his first language. In: T. E. Moore (ed.). *Cognitive Development and the Acquisition of Language*. New York: Academic Press, 65–110.
Clark, Herbert H. 1973. Space, time, semantics, and the child. In: T. E. Moore (ed.). *Cognitive Development and the Acquisition of Language*. New York: Academic Press, 27–64.
Dessalegn, Banchiamlack & Barbara Landau 2008. More than meets the eye: The role of language in binding visual properties. *Psychological Science* 19, 189–195.
Fillmore, Charles J. 1971. *Santa Cruz Lectures on Deixis*. Bloomington, IN: Indiana University Linguistics Club.
Fisher, Cindy, Goffrey Hall, Susan Rakowitz & Lila Gleitman 1994. When it is better to receive than to give: Syntactic and conceptual constraints on vocabulary growth. In: L. Gleitman & B. Landau (eds.). *The Acquisition of the Lexicon*. Cambridge, MA: The MIT Press, 333–375.
Gallistel, Charles 1990. *The Organization of Learning*. Cambridge, MA: The MIT Press.
Gallistel, Charles 2002. Language and spatial frames of reference in mind and brain. *Trends in Cognitive Sciences* 6, 321–322.
Gennari, Silvia, Steven Sloman, Barbara Malt & Tecumseh Fitch 2002. Motion events in language and cognition. *Cognition* 83, 49–79.
Gleitman, Lila, Kimberly Cassidy, Rebecca Nappa, Anna Papafragou & John Trueswell 2005. Hard words. *Language Learning and Development* 1, 23–64.
Gordon, Peter 2004. Numerical cognition without words: Evidence from Amazonia. *Science* 306, 496–499.
Gruber, Jeffrey S. 1965. *Studies in Lexical Relations*. Ph.D. dissertation. MIT, Cambridge, MA.
Hermer, Linda & Elizabeth Spelke 1996. Modularity and development: The case of spatial reorientation. *Cognition* 61, 195–232.
Herskovits, Annette 1986. *Language and Spatial Cognition: An Interdisciplinary Study of the Prepositions in English*. Cambridge: Cambridge University Press.
Hespos, Susan & Renée Baillargeon 2006. Decalage in infants' knowledge about occlusion and containment events: Converging evidence from action tasks. *Cognition* 99, B31–B41.
Hespos, Susan & Elizabeth Spelke 2004. Conceptual precursors to language. *Nature* 430, 452–456.
Ihara, Hiroko & Ikuyo Fujita 2000. A cognitive approach to errors in case marking in Japanese agrammatism: The priority of the goal *-ni* over the source *-kara*. In: A. Foolen (ed.). *Constructions in Cognitive Linguistics: Selected Papers from the Fifth International Cognitive Linguistics Conference*. Amsterdam: Benjamins, 123–140.
Jackendoff, Ray 1983. *Semantics and Cognition*. Cambridge, MA: The MIT Press.

Johnson, Jacqueline & Elissa Newport 1989. Critical period effects in second language learning: The influence of maturational state on the acquisition of English as a second language. *Cognitive Psychology* 21, 60–99.

Johnston, Judith & Dan Slobin 1979. Development of locative expressions in English, Italian, Serbo-Croatian and Turkish. *Journal of Child Language* 6, 529–545.

Kawachi, Kazuhiro 2007. Korean putting verbs do not categorize space contrastively in terms of "tightness of fit". *Lingua* 117, 1801–1820.

Kay, Paul & Willet Kempton 1984. What is the Sapir-Whorf hypothesis? *American Anthropologist* 86, 65–79.

Klatzky, Roberta, Jack Loomis, Andrew Beall, Sarah Chance & Reginald Golledge 1998. Spatial updating of self-position and orientation during real, imagined, and virtual locomotion. *Psychological Science* 9, 293–298.

Kuhl, Patricia 2000. Language, mind, and brain: Experience alters perception. In: M. Gazzaniga (ed.). *The New Cognitive Neurosciences*. 2nd edn. Cambridge, MA: The MIT Press, 99–115.

Lakoff, George 1987. *Women, Fire, and Dangerous Things: What Categories Reveal About the Mind*. Chicago, IL: The University of Chicago Press.

Lakusta, Laura & Barbara Landau 2005. Starting at the end: The importance of goals in spatial language. *Cognition* 96, 1–33.

Lakusta, Laura & Barbara Landau 2012. Language and memory for motion events: Origins of the asymmetry between source and goal paths. *Cognitive Science* 36, 517–544.

Lakusta, Laura, Laura Wagner, Kristen O'Hearn & Barbara Landau 2007. Conceptual foundations of spatial language: Evidence for a goal bias in infants. *Language Learning and Development* 3, 1–19.

Lakusta, Laura, Hanako Yoshida, Barbara Landau & Linda Smith 2006. Cross-linguistic evidence for a Goal/Source asymmetry: The case of Japanese. Poster presented at the *International Conference on Infant Studies*, Kyoto, Japan, June 19–23, 2006.

Landau, Barbara & Ray Jackendoff 1993. "What" and "where" in spatial language and spatial cognition. *Behavioral and Brain Sciences* 16, 217–265.

Landau, Barbara & Elizabeth Shipley 2001. Labelling patterns and object naming. *Developmental Science* 4, 109–118.

Landau, Barbara, Banchiamlack Dessalegn, & Ariel Goldberg 2010. Language and space: Momentary interactions. In: V. Evans, B. Bergen & J. Zinken (eds.). *Language, Cognition and Space: The State of the Art and New Directions*. London: Equinox Publishing, 51–78.

Landau, Barbara, Henry Gleitman & Elizabeth Spelke 1981. Spatial knowledge and geometric representation in a child blind from birth. *Science* 213, 1275–1278.

Landau, Barbara, Linda Smith & Susan Jones 1998. Object perception and object naming in early development. *Trends in Cognitive Science* 2, 19–24.

Levinson, Stephen C. 1994. Vision, shape, and linguistic description: Tzeltal body-part terminology and object description. *Linguistics* 32, 791–855.

Levinson, Stephen C. 2003. Language and mind: Let's get the issues straight! In: D. Gentner & S. Goldin-Meadow (eds.). *Language in Mind: Advances in the Study of Language and Thought*. Cambridge, MA: The MIT Press, 25–46.

Levinson, Stephen C. & David P. Wilkins 2006. The background to the study of the language of space. In: S. C. Levinson & D. P. Wilkins (eds.). *Grammars of Space. Explorations in Cognitive Diversity*. Cambridge: Cambridge University Press.

Li, Peggy & Lila Gleitman 2002. Turning the tables: Language and spatial reasoning. *Cognition* 83, 265–294.
Lucy, John & Suzanne Gaskins 2003. Interaction of language type and referent type in the development of nonverbal classification preferences. In: D. Gentner & S. Goldin- Meadow (eds.). *Language in Mind: Advances in the Study of Language and Thought*. Cambridge, MA: The MIT Press, 465–492.
Malt, Barbara, Steven Sloman, Silvia Gennari, Meiyi Shi & Yuan Wang 1999. Knowing versus naming: Similarity and the linguistic categorization of artifacts. *Journal of Memory and Language* 40, 230–262.
Mandler, Jean 2004. *The Foundations of Mind: Origins of Conceptual Thought*. Oxford: Oxford University Press.
McDonough, Lorraine, Soonja Choi & Jean Mandler 2003. Understanding spatial relations: Flexible infants, lexical adults. *Cognitive Psychology* 46, 229–259.
Milner, David & Melvyn Goodale 1995. *The Visual Brain in Action*. Oxford: Oxford University Press.
Munnich, Ed 2002. *Input and Maturation in the Acquisition of Second Language Spatial Semantics*. Ph.D. dissertation. University of Delaware, Newark, DE.
Munnich, Ed & Barbara Landau 2003. The effects of spatial language on spatial representation: Setting some boundaries. In: D. Gentner & S. Goldin-Meadow (eds.). *Language in Mind: Advances in the Study of Language and Thought*. Cambridge, MA: The MIT Press, 113–155.
Munnich, Ed & Barbara Landau 2008. *Acquisition of Spatial Semantics: A Maturational Timetable?* Ms. Baltimore, MD, Johns Hopkins University.
Munnich, Ed, Barbara Landau & Barbara Anne Dosher 2001. Spatial language and spatial representation: A cross-linguistic comparison. *Cognition* 8, 171–207.
Norbury, Heather, Sandra Waxman & Hyung-Joo Song 2008. Tight and loose are not created equal: An asymmetry underlying the representation of fit in English- and Korean-speakers. *Cognition* 109, 316–325.
Palmeri, Thomas & Isabel Gauthier 2004. Visual object understanding. *Nature Reviews Neuroscience* 5, 291–303.
Papafragou, Anna, Justin Hulbert & John Trueswell 2008. Does language guide event perception? Evidence from eye movements. *Cognition* 108, 155–184.
Papafragou, Anna, Christine Massey & Lila Gleitman 2002. Shake, rattle, 'n' roll: The representation of motion in language and cognition. *Cognition* 84, 189–219.
Pederson, Eric, Eve Danziger, David Wilkins, Stephen C. Levinson, Sotaro Kita & Gunter Senft 1998. Semantic typology and spatial conceptualization. *Language* 74, 557–589.
Quinn, Paul 1994. The categorization of above and below spatial relations by young infants. *Child Development* 65, 58–69.
Quinn, Paul 2004. Spatial representation by young infants: Categorization of spatial relations or sensitivity to a crossing primitive? *Memory & Cognition* 32, 852–861.
Regier, Terry & Mingyu Zheng 2003. An attentional constraint on spatial meaning. In: R. Alterman & D. Kirsh (eds.). *Proceedings of the 25th Annual Conference of the Cognitive Science Society*. Mahwah, NJ: Lawrence Erlbaum, 50.
Regier, Terry, & Mingyu Zheng 2007. Attention to endpoints: A cross-linguistic constraint on spatial meaning. *Cognitive Science* 31, 705–719.
Saffran, Jenny, Janet Werker & Lynne Werner 2006. The infant's auditory world: Hearing, speech, and the beginnings of language. In: D. Kuhn et al. (eds.). *Handbook of Child Psychology, vol. 2*. 6th edn. Hoboken, NJ: Wiley, 58–108.

Smith, Linda, Susan Jones & Barbara Landau 1996. Naming in young children: A dumb attentional mechanism? *Cognition* 60, 143–171.
Spelke, Elizabeth 2003. What makes us smart? Core knowledge and natural language. In: D. Gentner & S. Goldin-Meadow (eds.). *Language in Mind: Advances in the Study of Language and Thought.* Cambridge, MA: The MIT Press, 277–311.
Spivey, Michael, Melinda Tyler, Kathleen Eberhard & Michael Tanenhaus 2001. Linguistically mediated visual search. *Psychological Science* 12, 282–286.
Talmy, Leonard 1983. How language structures space. In: H. Pick & L. Acredolo (eds.). *Spatial Orientation: Theory, Research, and Application.* New York: Plenum Press, 225–282.
Talmy, Leonard 1985. Lexicalization patterns: Semantic structure in lexical forms. In: T. Shopen (ed.). *Language Typology and Syntactic Description, vol. 3: Grammatical Categories and the Lexicon.* Cambridge: Cambridge University Press, 57–149.
Talmy, Leonard 1988. Force dynamics in language and cognition. *Cognitive Science* 12, 49–100.
Talmy, Leonard 2000. *Towards a Cognitive Semantics: Typology and Process in Concept Structuring.* Cambridge, MA: The MIT Press.
Ullman, Shimon 1984. Visual routines. *Cognition* 18, 97–159.
Ungerleider, Leslie & Mortimer Mishkin 1982. Two cortical visual systems. In: D. Ingle, M.A. Goodale & R. Mansfield (eds.). *The Analysis of Visual Behavior.* Cambridge, MA: The MIT Press, 549–586.
Waxman, Sandra & Raquel Klibanoff 2000. The role of comparison in the extension of novel adjectives. *Developmental Psychology* 36, 571–581.
Werker, Janet & Richard Tees 1999. Influences on infant speech processing: Toward a new synthesis. *Annual Review of Psychology* 50, 509–535.
Whorf, Benjamin L. 1956. *Language, Thought, and Reality: Selected Writings of Benjamin Lee Whorf.* Edited and with an introduction by John B. Carroll, Cambridge, MA: The MIT Press.
Xu, Yaoda & Maanish Singh 2002. Early computation of part structure: Evidence from visual search. *Attention, Perception & Psychophysics* 64, 1039–1054.
Zheng, Mingyu & Susan Goldin-Meadow 2002. Thought before language: How deaf and hearing children express motion events across cultures. *Cognition* 2, 145–175.

Manfred Pinkal and Alexander Koller
13 Semantic research in computational linguistics

1 Introduction —— 366
2 Computational semantics in the logical framework —— 368
3 Statistical methods in computational semantics —— 377
4 Current developments —— 389
5 Conclusion —— 399
6 References —— 399

Abstract: Computational semantics is the branch of computational linguistics that is concerned with the development of methods for processing meaning information. Because a computer system that analyzes natural language must be able to deal with arbitrary real-world sentences, computational semantics faces a number of specific challenges related to the coverage of semantic construction procedures, the efficient resolution of ambiguities, and the ability to compute inferences. After initial successes with logic-based methods, the mainstream paradigm in computational semantics today is to let the computer automatically learn from corpora. In this article, we present both approaches, compare them, and discuss some recent initiatives for combining the two.

1 Introduction

In this article, we give an overview of the state of the art in *computational semantics*, i.e. the branch of computational linguistics that deals with the processing of meaning information. The goal of computational linguistics is to develop methods for the automatic analysis and generation of natural language. Ultimately, it aims at creating computer systems that approximate the language skills of an average human speaker. But there are also more immediate and tangible real-world applications, including, for instance, information extraction systems that acquire content for a relational database from large-scale collections of business reports; spoken-language or multimodal interfaces that enable the convenient interaction

---

Manfred Pinkal, Saarbrücken, Germany
Alexander Koller, Potsdam, Germany

https://doi.org/10.1515/9783110589825-013

of users with information systems (e.g., interfaces to healthcare websites or interactive museum guides); or machine translation systems that transfer text or speech input from a source language to a target language. All of these applications require some amount of semantic processing, although not necessarily at a very fine level of detail.

The task of semantic processing can generally be decomposed into two subproblems, namely the problem of computing a formal representation of the meaning of an expression (the *semantic construction* problem) and the task of determining the relation between such formal representations (the *inference* problem). Inference is required, for instance, when a question-answering system determines whether an answer candidate in a document collection actually answers a given question, or when an automatic summarization system must figure out to which extent two sentences describe the same event (and can therefore be compressed into one).

The classical approach to computational semantics uses some form of first-order or higher-order logic for the formal semantic representations and some form of Montague Grammar-style process for semantic construction, and solves the inference problem using programs called *theorem provers*, which can test logic formulas for entailment. This tradition of computational semantics shares its formal and conceptual framework with the mainstream of semantic research in linguistics and the philosophy of language (which we will refer to as "theoretical semantics" in this article). It strongly benefits from the wealth and detail of earlier research in these disciplines.

However, there are a number of challenges that are specific to computational semantics and call for different methods. The aim of computational semantics is to implement human language skills in computer systems – at least partially, in concrete applications. The methods that are used for this must therefore be cast into precisely formalized algorithms. One crucial aspect that drives the development of new approaches is that these algorithms must be *efficient*, even in the face of the massive *ambiguity* that arises in real-world sentences. Second, the computer systems used in computational semantics must be able to process any arbitrary sentence or discourse that can arise in the respective application scenario. The system must have *wide coverage* with respect to semantic construction, and it must also have access to the appropriate large-scale *knowledge bases* that can support the inferences that are necessary for the task at hand. It is hard to achieve all of these goals at once.

The history of computational semantics is defined by attempts to handle these problems, and we will outline some of the most prominent approaches in this article. The classical logic-based approach, which we discuss in Section 2, has made great progress in terms of processing efficiency, but still falls short of practical usability in terms of coverage and performance on the disambiguation task. As a consequence, computational semantics experienced a fundamental paradigm shift around the turn of the century; current mainstream research focuses on statistical models of word and sentence meaning (Section 3). These models have much better coverage, at the expense of the level of detail, precision, and conceptual clarity of the semantic representations. We conclude with an outlook on some novel directions of research, which are aimed at comparing and integrating the worlds of logical and statistical methods (Section 4).

2 Computational semantics in the logical framework

Computational approaches to semantic analysis must deal with two issues. First, they must be able to determine a formal semantic representation for a given input expression; in the case of ambiguity, they also must be able to choose the contextually appropriate reading. This is called the *semantic construction* problem. Second, they must be able to relate different meaning representations to each other to detect equivalence, entailment or inconsistency between different sentences. This is the *inference* problem. Analogous problems occur in natural language generation.

Early research in artificial intelligence (AI) focused on approaches to these problems that were largely disconnected from linguistics. One influential approach was Conceptual Dependency theory (Schank 1975). Semantic representation was done without logic: Word meanings were encoded as graphs made up of a limited number of uninterpreted atomic concepts and relations (partly inspired by Fillmore's (1968) role semantics). From these, sentence representations were constructed by merging smaller graphs into larger ones using a collection of graph rewriting rules. The approach worked to some extent for sentences and texts expressing simple assertive information. However, it did not generalize easily to more complex types of information involving cardinality, quantification, negation, modality, conditional and temporal relations. These were modeled by simply attaching tags to graph edges.

Modern computational semantics started with the use of logics with well-defined model-theoretic interpretations, following the Montagovian revolution in theoretical semantics. This allowed the use of principled inference rules that were justified by soundness and completeness with respect to the model theory. Over the years, a logic-based "standard model" of computational semantics emerged: A semantic representation in first-order or higher-order logic is computed compositionally based on a syntactic analysis, and meaning relations between expressions of language are implemented using standard inference engines for logic. We refer the reader to the textbook by Blackburn & Bos (2005) for details about the standard model. Below, we sketch some of the most important methods in this paradigm.

2.1 Semantic construction

Compositional semantics. In the early 1970s, Richard Montague presented a framework for a strictly compositional interpretation of natural-language sentences in terms of type theory, including a formal treatment of quantifier scope (Montague 1973). His work not only provided the basis for modern semantic theory, but has also had great influence on the development of computational semantics. "Standard model" computational semantics takes it as given that we can assign lambda terms to lexicon entries, combine them by traversing the parse tree bottom-up, and compute lambda terms for larger phrases compositionally out of those for smaller phrases, using functional application and beta reduction. An abbreviated example for the derivation of one reading of the sentence "every man loves a woman" is shown in Fig. 13.1.

Montague's original framework was based on an idiosyncratic version of categorial grammar. Computational linguists mostly used the formalism of *unification grammar*, i.e., phrase-structure grammar extended with feature unification, when they first started developing large-scale grammars in the 1980s. Unification grammars such as LFG (Dalrymple et al. 1995) and HPSG (Pollard & Sag 1994) offered an

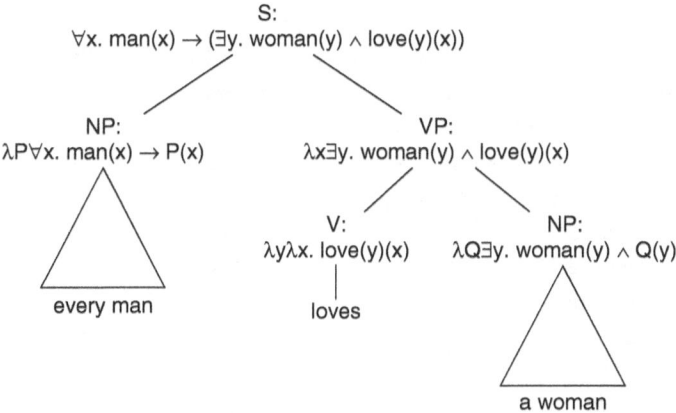

Fig. 13.1: A Montague-style derivation of a semantic representation for the sentence "Every man loves a woman".

elegant and simple way to compute predicate-argument structures by filling the argument positions of a head with the semantic contributions of its complements using unification (see e.g. Pereira & Shieber 1987). These methods were later extended to cover more complex problems in semantic construction (Dalrymple 1999; Copestake, Lascarides & Flickinger 2001).

Dynamic semantics. A number of "non-local" semantic phenomena turned out to be challenging for compositional semantic construction methods. For instance, anaphoric expressions establish coreferential links with antecedents at arbitrarily distant positions in the discourse; ellipsis requires us to copy parts of the antecedent's semantics into the target representation. Furthermore, structural ambiguities, e.g. of quantifier scope, undermine the tidy parallelism of syntactic and semantic structure posited by Montague Grammar.

In order to represent anaphora and, to some extent, ellipsis, the use of Discourse Representation Theory (DRT; Kamp 1981; Kamp & Reyle 1993; see article 11 [Semantics: Theories] (Kamp & Reyle) *Discourse Representation Theory*) has enjoyed much attention in computational semantics. DRT conceives of meaning not in terms of truth conditions, but as context-change potential; in its standard version, it models the anaphoric potential of a text through a set of discourse referents, which are a constitutive part of the semantic representation. Dynamic Predicate Logic (Groenendijk & Stokhof 1991; see article 12 [Semantics: Theories] (Dekker) *Dynamic semantics*) is a closely related formalism that enables a compositional model-theoretic interpretation of anaphora. However, standard DRT employs a top-down, non-compositional algorithm for semantic construction. Computational applications typically combine DRS representations with higher-order logic and lambda abstraction, in order to enable a surface compositional derivation of DRSes, such as Compositional DRT (Muskens 1995) and Lambda-DRT (Kohlhase, Kuschert & Pinkal 1996).

A second issue is that computational applications for processing anaphora cannot skirt the issue of identifying the antecedent of an anaphoric expression in a given text. The possible antecedents are restricted by the hard accessibility constraints of DRT to some degree; they can be narrowed down further by modeling focusing mechanisms based on the global structure of the discourse (Grosz & Sidner 1986; Grosz, Joshi & Weinstein 1995; Asher & Lascarides 2003; see article 14 [Semantics: Sentence and Information Structure] (Geurts) *Accessibility and anaphora* for more on the theoretical aspects). However, these systematic approaches to anaphoric reference leave many cases of referential ambiguity unresolved. The development of methods for *coreference resolution*, which link phrases in a given discourse that refer to the same entity, is an active field of research in computational linguistics (see e.g. Ng 2010; Stede 2011).

Quantifier storage approaches. One non-local aspect of semantic construction that has received particular attention in computational semantics is scope ambiguity. From a perspective of theoretical linguistics, the basic problem of semantic construction for sentences with scope ambiguities was essentially solved by the Quantifier Raising (QR) operation in Montague Grammar. However, QR-based approaches cannot be used effectively in computational semantics because the development of efficient parsing algorithms becomes very complicated, and it is inconvenient to develop large grammars. A second major challenge for a computational treatment of scope is that the number of readings quickly becomes very large as the sentence grows longer, and the algorithm must still remain efficient even when this happens. Algorithms for semantic construction can differ by a huge degree in this respect; recent underspecification-based methods can perform tasks that used to be completely infeasible (requiring years of computation time for one sentence) in milliseconds.

A first step towards removing the reliance on QR was *quantifier storage*, which was first proposed by Cooper (1983) and then refined by Keller (1988). The key idea in Cooper Storage was to replace Montague's treatment of scope ambiguity by a storage technique for quantifiers: Nodes in a (phrase-structure) syntax tree are assigned structured semantic representations, consisting of *content* (a λ-expression of appropriate type) and *quantifier store* (a set of λ-expressions representing noun phrase meanings). As the parse tree is traversed bottom-up, noun phrases may either be applied in situ to form new content; for the example sentence "every man loves a woman," this leads to narrow scope for the object, in essentially the same way as in the Montague-style derivation of Fig. 13.1. Alternatively, we may move the content into the quantifier store at any NP node (as shown at the node for "a woman" in Fig. 13.2) and then retrieve an item from the store and apply it to the content at the sentence node. This enables the non-deterministic derivation of different scope readings of a sentence from a surface-oriented phrase-structure grammar analysis.

A related approach was proposed by Hobbs & Shieber (1987) first, and later generalized to *Quasi-Logical Form* (QLF; Alshawi & Crouch 1992), which became a central part of SRI's Core Language Engine (CLE; Alshawi 1990): During parsing, preliminary semantic representations (QLFs) are built up, which contain the quantifier representations in the argument positions of their main predicate. In a second step, rewrite rules on the QLFs move quantifiers to their appropriate position, leaving a variable behind to bring about proper binding. For the above example, this system would first derive the QLF term love(⟨every, x, man⟩, ⟨some, y, woman⟩), from which it would derive the two readings in Fig. 13.1 and Fig. 13.2 by either scoping ⟨every, x, man⟩ over love first and then ⟨some, y, woman⟩ over the result, or vice versa.

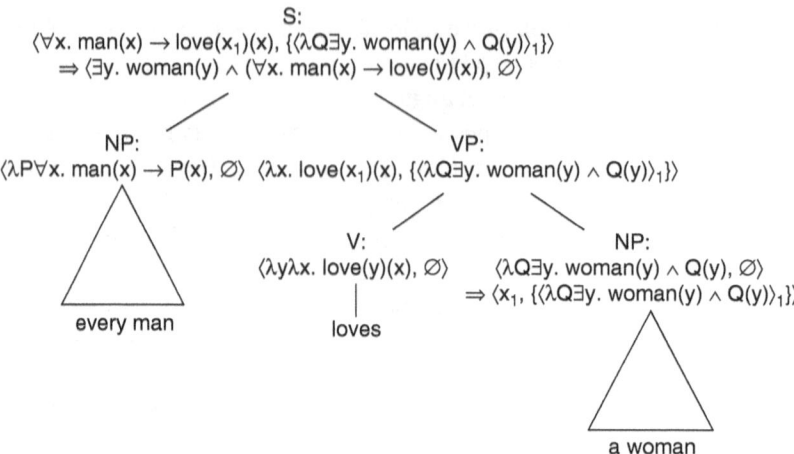

Fig. 13.2: A Cooper Storage derivation for the second reading of the sentence "Every man loves a woman".

Underspecification. As grammars grew larger in order to extend their coverage of free text, a further problem emerged. In a sentence with multiple scope ambiguities, the number of readings can grow exponentially with the number of quantifiers or other scope-bearing operators (such as negations or modal operators) in the sentence. The following sentence from Poesio (1994), which has $(5!)^2 = 14400$ readings in which each quantifier and modal operator takes scope in its own clause alone, illustrates this problem. In practice, the problem is even worse because large-scale grammars tend to make generalizing assumptions (e.g., that all noun phrases take scope) that can cause innocent-looking sentences to be assigned millions of readings.

(1) A politician can fool most voters on most issues most of the time, but no politician can fool every voter on every single issue all of the time.

The standard approach to handling massive ambiguity like this in large-scale grammars today is *underspecification*. Underspecification approaches derive a compact representation of all readings from the syntactic analysis, and proceed to single specific readings only by need, and after irrelevant readings have been filtered out by inferences. Most underspecification approaches that are used in practice specify the parts from which a semantic representation is supposed to be built, plus constraints that govern how the parts may be combined. For instance, the *dominance graph* (Egg, Koller & Niehren 2001; Althaus et al. 2003) for the earlier example sentence "every man loves a woman" is shown in Fig. 13.3a. The parts of this graph may be combined in all possible ways that respect the dotted dominance edges, yielding the two trees in Fig. 13.3b,c. These trees represent the semantic representations that we also derived in Fig. 13.2.

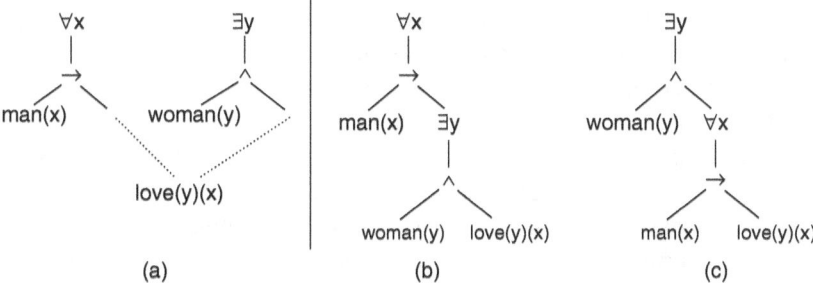

Fig. 13.3: A dominance graph for "every man loves a woman" (a), along with the two trees it describes (b,c).

Most modern large-scale grammars use underspecification in one form or another. HPSG grammars use Minimal Recursion Semantics (MRS, Copestake et al. 2005). The Glue Logic system used by many LFG grammars (Dalrymple 1999) can be seen as an underspecification approach as well; note that some recent LFG grammars also use a simpler rewriting mechanism for semantic construction (Crouch & King 2006). Underspecification-based semantic construction algorithms have also been defined for Tree Adjoining Grammars (Kallmeyer & Romero 2008; Gardent 2003). Hole Semantics (Blackburn & Bos 2005) is a particularly easy-to-understand underspecification formalism. The algorithmic foundations of underspecification have been worked out particularly well for dominance graphs, into which MRS and Hole Semantics can be translated. Dominance graphs also support powerful inference algorithms for efficiently reducing the set of possible readings without even computing them (Koller & Thater 2010). For more information about underspecification, we refer to article 9 [Semantics: Lexical Structures and Adjectives] (Egg) *Semantic underspecification* in this handbook.

One popular grammar formalism in computational linguistics that follows the original Montagovian program more directly is Combinatory Categorial Grammar (Steedman 2000; Bos et al. 2004). CCG is a variant of categorial grammar, with which it shares a very elegant and direct mapping of syntactic to semantic representations. Although this forces CCG into modeling semantic ambiguities as syntactic ambiguities, CCG can still be parsed efficiently by representing both kinds of ambiguity together in a parse chart.

2.2 Inference

The major added value of logic as a representational framework in computational linguistics is its suitability for the development of provably correct *inference procedures*. Because logical deduction is backed by the truth-conditional concept of logical entailment, it is possible to define under what conditions a deduction system is sound and complete, and to develop such systems. This is crucial when we model the processes which people perform when interpreting or producing an utterance – e.g., deriving relevant implicit information from the utterance's semantic interpretation, integrating meaning information into their knowledge, or reducing ambiguity by the exclusion of inconsistent interpretations.

For first-order predicate logic, *theorem provers* – that is, computer programs that test formulas for validity or unsatisfiability – have become efficient enough to support the practical application of deduction systems. Theoretically, first-order logic is undecidable; but theorem provers, which were originally designed for mathematical applications, have nonetheless achieved an impressive average performance on standard tasks. Currently, a variety of highly efficient off-the-shelf theorem provers are available which can be used as general purpose inference engines for natural language processing (Riazanov & Voronkov 2002; Hillenbrand 2003); there are also tools called *model builders* which can test a formula for satisfiability and build satisfying models for them (McCune 1998; Claessen & Sörensson 2003). There has been some research on theorem provers for dynamic logics, such as DRT (van Eijck, Hegueiabehere & O Nuallain 2001; Kohlhase 2000), but these provers have not been engineered as thoroughly as standard first-order provers, and it is more efficient in practice to translate dynamic logic into static logic and use the standard tools (Bos 2001). One example for an end-to-end system of the "standard model", involving semantic construction and the use of first-order theorem provers, is Bos & Markert (2005).

It is known that first-order logic is not expressive *enough* to represent genuinely higher-order or intensional phenomena in natural language, such as embedding under propositional attitudes. Some researchers have directly applied theorem provers for higher-order logic (e.g., Andrews & Brown 2006) to natural-language inference tasks; see e.g. Gardent & Konrad (2000). However, higher-order theorem provers are much less efficient in practice than first-order provers. To compensate for this restriction, computational semantics has a strong tendency towards avoiding higher-order constructs, choosing first-order analyses in the case that semantic theory offers them as an option, and sometimes even using first-order representations to approximate phenomena that would be modeled appropriately with higher-order logic only (e.g. in the "ontological promiscuity" approach (Hobbs 1985); see also Pulman (2007) for a more recent case study).

Conversely, one can explore the use of logics that are *less* expressive than first-order logic in order to maximize efficiency, for restricted tasks and applications. *Description logics* (Baader et al. 2003) are a family of fragments of first-order logic designed to model terminological knowledge and reasoning about the membership of objects in the denotation of concepts, of which the KL-ONE system is an early representative (Brachman & Schmolze 1985). They are supported by very fast reasoning systems (Haarslev & Möller 2001; Tsarkov, Horrocks & Patel-Schneider 2007). Because they offer only restricted types of quantification, however, they have mostly been used for small domains or for specific problem, such as the resolution (Koller et al. 2004) and generation (Areces, Koller & Striegnitz 2008) of referring expressions.

Historically, another fragment of first-order logic that experienced widespread use in computational semantics is *Horn Clause Logic*, which underlies the programming language Prolog. Horn Clause Logic is limited by its inability to express true logical negation, which in Prolog must be approximated as "negation by failure": A negation ¬A is considered as true iff A cannot be proved from the database. Prolog has been widely used in computational linguistics (Pereira & Shieber 1987; Blackburn & Bos 2005) – among other reasons, because it can model the full process of natural-language understanding including parsing, semantic construction, and inference uniformly, by using logical deduction. However, its use has declined due to the availability of fast theorem provers and of NLP software libraries for mainstream programming languages, as well as the growing importance of numeric processing for statistical methods (see Section 3 below).

A final challenge is the modeling of *common-sense reasoning*. Inference steps needed in the process of natural-language understanding may be valid only in the typical case, and thus their results can be overwritten, if more specific contradicting information is added. Knowing that Tweety is a bird allows us to infer that Tweety can fly; adding the information that Tweety is a penguin forces us to revise the derived information. This raises the inference task to another level of difficulty. Standard predicate-logic deduction just adds information, extending the knowledge base in a monotonic way, and has no mechanism for knowledge revision. Several alternative logic frameworks supporting *non-monotonic deduction* have been proposed, most importantly default logic (Reiter 1980), abductive reasoning (Lipton 2001), and auto-epistemic logic (Moore 1985). Of these, default logic (particularly in the context of SDRT, Asher & Lascarides 2003) and abductive reasoning (i.e., reasoning from observations to the best explanation, particularly in the text understanding framework of Hobbs et al. 1993) have become influential in computational semantics.

2.3 Knowledge resources for computational semantics

So far, we have sketched how logic-based semantic representations can be automatically built, and how inferences with these representations can be efficiently computed using theorem provers. To make real use of these systems, we need wide-coverage knowledge bases, which provide us with facts about the meaning of predicates and constants. Consider the following examples:

(2) a. Socrates is a man.
    All men are mortal.
    b. Socrates is mortal.

(3) a. Bill bought a convertible.
    b. Bill bought a car.

(4) a. John went shopping.
    b. Did he bring enough money?

(5) a. Which genetically caused connective tissue disorder has severe symptoms and complications regarding the aorta and skeletal features, and, very characteristically, ophthalmologic subluxation?
    b. Marfan's is created by a defect of the gene that determines the structure of Fibrillin-11. One of the symptoms is displacement of one or both of the eyes' lenses. The most serious complications affect the cardiovascular system, especially heart valves and the aorta.

The range of inferences that we can draw from semantic representations alone without any additional knowledge is very limited. We may be able to do simple syllogistic reasoning as in (2); but the vast majority of intuitively plausible inferences require additional background knowledge. The inference in (3) requires the lexical-semantic information that convertibles are cars; to make sense of the dialogue sequence (4), we must have common-sense knowledge about what happens when people go shopping. The example (5) gives an impression of the complex inferences that a natural-language interface to a medical information system must be able to draw, and of the kind and amount of domain knowledge which is required for this.

Theorem provers support such inferences if they have access to logical knowledge bases which contain this information. Unfortunately, the amount of knowledge which may in principle be relevant for inference is huge, and so hand-crafting comprehensive knowledge bases is a very expensive and cumbersome task. In general, coverage is at present a much harder problem for logic-based inference than efficiency.

Certain types of lexical-semantic knowledge are provided by WordNet (Fellbaum 1998), with impressively wide coverage for English and a variety of other languages (Vossen 2004; Hamp & Feldweg 1997). WordNet distinguishes various *senses* of each word in the lexicon, groups them into *synsets* of synonymous senses, and specifies different semantic relations between these synsets, such as hyponymy (subsumption) and meronymy (part-of). Other resources, such as FrameNet (Baker, Fillmore & Cronin 2003) and VerbNet (Kipper-Schuler 2006) contribute information about described situation type, thematic roles, and alternative syntactic realization patterns for lexical expressions, in particular verbs. For a more detailed discussion of lexical-semantic resources and methods for acquiring lexical-semantic knowledge, see article 16 [this volume] (Frank & Padó) *Semantics in computational lexicons* in this handbook.

However, there are many kinds of knowledge which are not formalized in WordNet and related resources. Examples are script-like information as in the supermarket example above, or stereotypical properties of concepts such as the ability of birds to fly. While it can be debated whether such knowledge should be packaged into the lexicon as components of word meaning or whether it is non-linguistic common-sense knowledge about the world, there is no doubt that such knowledge is necessary for full text understanding; see also article 6 [Semantics: Theories] (Hobbs) *Word meaning and world knowledge*. Because of the magnitude of the task, few attempts have been made to comprehensively axiomatize world knowledge by hand. One notable exception is the Cyc project (Lenat 1995); its aim is to hand-axiomatize enough knowledge that an automated system could then learn more knowledge from natural language text. At the time of writing, Cyc contains five million assertions about several hundreds of thousands of concepts, and has recently become freely available for research purposes as ResearchCyc (Matuszek et al. 2006). Because it aims at massive coverage, Cyc is a rather heavyweight system. It is also optimized for fine-grained reasoning on the conceptual level, rather than for natural-language processing and inference. For instance, Cyc distinguishes between 23 different senses of spatial "in", all of which have different axioms. This degree of ambiguity causes substantial problems for ambiguity resolution, and therefore Cyc can be of only limited use for language-related semantic processing tasks.

3 Statistical methods in computational semantics

The "standard model" we have presented so far enables us to compute logic-based meaning representations, which can be used by theorem provers to draw inferences. This works efficiently and with impressive accuracy, if hand-crafted grammars and knowledge resources are available that cover all information that is required for the interpretation. However, logic-based semantic methods run into a number of fundamental problems:

- Natural language is extremely ambiguous, and understanding of utterances implies *ambiguity resolution:* the determination of a contextually appropriate reading. Underspecification methods enable an efficient representation of semantic ambiguity, but they make no attempt to resolve it. A particular challenge is word-sense disambiguation, because lexical ambiguity comprises a large and extremely heterogenous class of individual phenomena.
- Modeling *inference* for open-domain text understanding with logic requires us to encode a huge amount of *world knowledge* in logic-based knowledge bases, as we have discussed. Such knowledge bases are not available; even large-scale efforts at manual resource creation like WordNet and Cyc have coverage problems.
- Despite the progress in hand-crafting large grammars with semantic information, many free-text sentences cannot be completely analyzed by these grammars: Knowledge-based grammar processing still faces *coverage* problems. Because traditional algorithms for semantic construction can only work on complete parses, no semantic representations can be computed for these sentences. That is, semantic construction procedures are not *robust* to coverage problems.

As a consequence, logic-based methods for computational semantics have not been very successful as part of applications in language technology. In retrospect, this is not entirely surprising. As we know from psycholinguistics, human language use and language learning are not purely categorical processes, but are strongly influenced by statistical expectations. This awareness of preferences speeds up the interpretation process, and in particular enables people to disambiguate expressions effortlessly and in real time. In the nineties, computational linguistics as a whole experienced a "statistical turn". The basic idea behind *statistical* (or, more generally: *data-intensive*) methods is to let a computer system discover statistical regularities in language use in large text corpora (or even the entire Internet), and then exploit them to analyze previously unseen texts or discourses. Because the system learns from data, this approach is also called *machine learning*. The idea was first worked out in the area of automatic speech recognition, and was later applied successfully to syntactic parsing. Today, it is the dominant paradigm in semantic research in computational linguistics as well.

Logic-based and data-intensive approaches are complementary in their strengths and weaknesses. Data-intensive approaches typically take a very shallow view on language from a linguistic point of view. The models they build of natural-language expressions have little to say about issues such as the logical structure of a sentence. They are typically not related to logic, perhaps not even based on a full syntactic parse of the sentence, and the inferences they support are judged to a standard of practical usefulness rather than logical correctness. However, these models can automatically learn information that is implicit in large text corpora, achieving wide coverage with comparatively little human effort. This gives us tools for addressing the coverage problems listed above. Furthermore, the knowledge provided by statistical methods is soft preferential knowledge, in terms of frequencies or probability estimates, which support disambiguation tasks well, and may even be appropriate for modeling defeasible common-sense knowledge.

We assume that a reader of this handbook is less familiar with machine learning techniques than with logic-based approaches. Therefore, the presentation in this section will be more basic than in the rest of the article. We try to give a flavor of statistical methodology, and at the same time provide a short overview of three prominent areas of research in computational semantics: *word-sense disambiguation*, *semantic role labeling*, and the modeling of *semantic relatedness*. These topics and other research in statistical computational linguistics are discussed at greater length in the standard textbooks by Jurafsky & Martin (2008) and Manning & Schütze (1999).

3.1 Word-sense disambiguation: Basics in statistical semantics

Word-sense disambiguation. Lexical ambiguity is pervasive in natural languages, and the determination of the contextually appropriate word meaning, known as *word-sense disambiguation* (WSD), has long been recognized as a hard problem in computational linguistics. Over fifty years ago, Yehoshua Bar-Hillel argued in his famous report on automatic translation (Bar-Hillel 1960) that "a translation machine should not only be supplied with a dictionary but also with a universal encyclopedia". For example, to appropriately translate "the box was in the pen" into another language, a computer program must know about typical sizes and shapes of boxes and pens to conclude that "pen" is used in the "enclosure" sense rather than the "writing implement" sense. Bar-Hillel commented that any attempt to solve this problem with knowledge-based methods was "utterly chimerical and hardly deserves any further discussion".

We can get a first grasp on the problem of WSD from lexical-semantic resources that define an inventory of possible word senses for each word of a language. Two such resources for English are WordNet (Fellbaum 1998) and Roget's Thesaurus

(Chapman 1977). WordNet lists Bar-Hillel's two senses for the noun "pen", along with the senses "correctional institution" and "female swan". English WordNet contains about 29,000 polysemous words, each of these with 3 different senses on average. Neither of these resources contains the information (e.g., box and pen sizes) that is necessary to reliably determine the sense in which a word was used in a given sentence.

Machine learning and WSD. WSD in early large-scale NLP systems was typically done by hand-written rules that were developed specifically for the application and the relevant domain (see e.g. Toma 1977; Hobbs, Jerry R., Douglas E. Appelt et al. 1992; Koch, Küssner & Stede 2000). Early attempts at defining generic rule-based methods for WSD are (Wilks 1975; Hirst & Charniak 1982). The weighted abduction approach by Hobbs et al. (1993) supported a generic, logic-based mechanism for disambiguation, but suffered from efficiency issues and required a large hand-coded knowledge base to work.

By contrast, statistical approaches attempt to solve the WSD problem by automatically learning the choice of the appropriate word sense from text corpora. The fundamental idea of such a machine learning approach is to build a *classifier*, which for each occurrence of a word w in some context c determines the sense s of this occurrence of w. This classifier is automatically learned from observations in a text corpus, in which each occurrence of each word has been manually *annotated* with its sense; one corpus that has been annotated with WordNet senses is the SemCor corpus (Landes, Leacock & Tengi 1998).

Machine learning approaches in which the training data is assumed to be annotated in this way are called *supervised*. The context c is usually approximated by a collection f of *features* that can be automatically extracted from the text. The machine learning system is trained on the annotated training corpus, i.e., it observes the pairs of sense annotations and extracted feature instantiations, for all instances of w, and derives from these data a *statistical model* of the correlation between feature patterns and word senses. The system can then be executed on unseen, unlabeled documents to label each word token automatically with its most plausible word sense, given the feature information extracted from the token's context.

Different approaches to statistical WSD are distinguished by the features they use and the machine learning method. The simplest choice for the features is to use *context words*. For instance, Yarowsky's (1995) system automatically identified the context words *life*, *animal*, and *species* as strong statistical indicators of the biological sense of the target word *plant*, and *manufacturing*, *equipment*, and *employee* as strong indicators of its "factory" sense. To address the disambiguation problem in a systematic way, we might determine the 2000 most frequent content words $w_1, \ldots, w_{2000}$ in the corpus. For any occurrence of a target word w, we could then assign the feature f the value 1 if the context word w_i occurs within a window of n words (for n = 5,10, 30, . . .) before or after w, and 0 otherwise. Approaches to machine learning differ substantially in the exact way in which they make use of the feature information to solve their classification task. For an overview of different approaches to machine learning, see Mitchell (1997), Russell & Norvig (2010), or Witten, Frank & Hall (2011).

Modeling context. The choice of features is a crucial part of designing a successful machine-learning-based WSD system: Since only the information encoded in features is visible to the machine learning system, the design of the feature space entails a decision about the information made available to the disambiguation process. The simplistic view of context as a set of cooccurring content words can be refined by adding more features representing different kinds of information. We can, e.g., include precedence information (does the context word occur to the left or to the right of the target?) or use positional information (does the context word occur as the immediate left and right neighbor of the target instance?). We may enrich the context information with linguistic information provided by available, reasonably efficient and reliable analysis tools: Using lemma and part-of-speech information is standard; adding syntactic information through shallow syntactic parsing is another frequently chosen option.

In principle, it would be desirable to use deeper and more informative context features than this. However, extracting such features tends to be expensive (it may again require large hand-crafted grammar and knowledge resources) or extremely noisy, if it can be done at all. Nevertheless, even the simple context-word approach can capture a remarkable amount of information on different levels of contextual knowledge and their interaction, however. Consider the following example; the common noun *dish* is ambiguous between a "plate" and a "food" sense.

(6) Yesterday night we went to a restaurant; I ordered an expensive dish.

The verb *order* contributes selectional preference information for its object position, and *restaurant* provides relevant topical or situational information. The two pieces of contextual evidence interact in a way that supports a strong prediction of the "food" sense of *dish*. Explicit modeling of the inference process leading to the correct reading would require very specific common-sense knowledge. A simple statistical model is able to predict the effects of this interaction with good results, based on the simple co-occurrence counts of these context words.

Measuring system performance. A machine learning system generalizes from observations without human intervention, and typically only has access to shallow features. The goal in designing such a system is therefore never that it is infallible. Instead, the aim is to balance maximum coverage with making relatively few mistakes. In order to examine the quality of such a system, one *evaluates* it on data for which the correct responses are known. To this end, one splits the manually annotated corpus into two separate portions for training and testing. The machine learning system is trained on the training corpus, and then used to classify every single word in the test corpus. One can, e.g., compute the *accuracy*, i.e., the percentage of word tokens in the test corpus for which the system computed the annotated word sense. This makes it possible to compare the performance of different systems using well-defined measures.

WSD has been an active field of research in computational semantics for the last two decades. An early successful WSD system was presented by Yarowsky (1992). One can get a sense of the current state of the art from the results of the "Coarse-grained English All Words Task" (Navigli, Litkowski & Hargraves 2007), a competition advertised for the SemEval 2007 workshop. This task consists in annotating the words in a given corpus with a coarse-grained sense inventory derived from WordNet. The random baseline, which assigns each word a random sense, achieved an accuracy of about 52% on this task. Because one sense of a word is often strongly predominant, the simple policy of assigning the instances of each word always its globally most frequent sense achieves 79% accuracy on the dataset, which is a much more demanding baseline for WSD systems. On the other hand, the *inter-annotator agreement*, i.e. the percentage of tokens for which the human annotators agreed when creating the SemEval 2007 test data was 94%. This is usually taken to indicate the upper bound for automatic processing. The best-performing WSD system in the 2007 competition reached an accuracy of about 88%, beating the most-frequent-sense baseline significantly. Although the WSD system does not reach human performance yet, it does come rather close. Recent overview articles about WSD are McCarthy (2009) and Navigli (2009).

3.2 Semantic role labeling: The issue of feature design

Semantic roles. WSD algorithms predict atomic meaning representations for lexical items in a text. In order to compute a semantic representation for an entire sentence, we must compose these lexical meaning representations into larger structures. Recent research has focused on the computation of *predicate-argument structures* as the first step in the semantic composition process. This is not a trivial problem, because the syntactic realization of semantic argument positions is subject to considerable variation. The central theoretical concept relating syntactic complements and semantic arguments is that of a *semantic role*. The practical task of computing predicate-argument structures is called *semantic role labeling, SRL*).

The first issue that one needs to address in SRL is what inventory of semantic roles to use. Fillmore (1968) originally proposed a small universal set of *thematic roles*, such as "agent", "patient", "recipient", etc.; see also article 3 [Semantics: Lexical Structures and Adjectives] (Davis) *Thematic roles*. This assumption has turned out to be impractical for wide-coverage lexicons, because it is impossible to map the variation and conceptual wealth of natural-language semantics cleanly to such a small role inventory. For example, in the description of a commercial transaction in (7) does the subject "China Southern" fill the *agent* role (since it pays money to Airbus), or the *recipient* role (since it receives planes from Airbus)?

(7) China Southern buys five A380 planes from Airbus.

FrameNet and PropBank. Research on SRL in computational linguistics therefore tends to use semantic role inventories which do not assume universal semantic roles, either in FrameNet (Fillmore & Baker 2010) or in PropBank style (Palmer, Gildea & Kingsbury 2005).

FrameNet organizes the lexicon into *frames*, which correspond to situation types. The FrameNet database currently contains about 12,000 lexical units, organized into 1,100 frames. Semantic roles (called *frame elements*) are then assumed to be specific to frames. For example, the verbs "replace" and "substitute" (as "exchange" and "switch", and the nouns "replacement" and "substitution") evoke the REPLACING frame; core roles of this frame are *Agent*, *Old*, and *New*. The names of these roles are meaningful only within a given frame. This makes the role concept of FrameNet rather specific and concrete, and makes it possible to annotate role information with high intuitive confidence. Two major corpora that have been annotated with FrameNet data are the Berkeley FrameNet Corpus (Baker, Fillmore & Cronin 2003) and the SALSA Corpus for German (Burchardt et al. 2006). An example that illustrates how different verbs can induce the same predicate-argument structure in FrameNet is shown in (8).

(8) a. [$_{Agent}$ Lufthansa] is replacing$_{REPLACING}$ [$_{Old}$ its 737s] [$_{New}$ with Airbus A320s].

b. [$_{Agent}$ Lufthansa] is substituting$_{REPLACING}$ [$_{New}$ Airbus A320s] [$_{Old}$ for its 737s].

The PropBank approach proposes an even more restricted notion of a semantic role. PropBank assumes specific roles called *arg0, arg1, arg2,* ... for the senses of each verb separately, and thus only relates syntactic alternations of the same predicate to each other. Role label identity between complements of different verbs is not informative, as the examples in (9) illustrate:

(9) a. [$_{Arg0}$ Lufthansa] is *replacing* [$_{Arg1}$ its 737s]
    [$_{Arg2}$ with Airbus A320s].
  b. [$_{Arg0}$ Lufthansa] is *substituting* [$_{Arg1}$ Airbus A320s]
    [$_{Arg3}$ for its 737s].

Of the two approaches, FrameNet is the more ambitious one, in that it supports a more informative encoding of predicate-argument structure than PropBank role labeling. However, annotating a corpus with PropBank roles is easier and can be done much more quickly than for FrameNet. As a consequence, exhaustively annotated corpora are available for several languages; the English PropBank corpus is a version of the Penn Treebank (Marcus, Santorini & Marcinkiewicz 1993) in which the arguments of all verb tokens are annotated with semantic roles.

Semantic role labeling systems. The SRL task for FrameNet or Prop-Bank can be split into two steps. First, because roles are specific to FrameNet frames or PropBank verb senses, we must determine the frame or sense in which a given verb token is being used. This is a WSD task, and is usually handled with WSD methods.

Assuming that each predicate in the sentence has been assigned a frame, the second step is to identify the arguments and determine the semantic roles they fill. The first system that did this successfully was presented by Gildea & Jurafsky (2002) – originally for FrameNet, but the approach has also been adapted for PropBank (see Palmer, Gildea & Kingsbury 2005). It uses a set of features providing information about the target verb, the candidate role-filler phrase, and their mutual relation. Most of the features refer to some kind of syntactic information, which is typically provided by a statistical parser. Features used include the phrase type (e.g., NP, PP, S); the head word of the candidate phrase; the voice of the head verb; the position of the candidate phrase relative to the head verb (left or right); and the path between candidate phrase and head verb, described as a string of non-terminals. Based on this information, the system estimates the probability that the candidate phrase stands in certain role relations to the target predicate, and selects the most probable one for labeling.

Feature design and the sparse data problem. The Gildea & Jurafsky system (as well as more recent approaches to WSD) uses syntactic information, but only looks at a handful of specific features of a syntax tree; much of the available information that the syntax tree contains is hidden from the machine learning system. Even a human annotator would sometimes have difficulties in predicting the correct semantic roles given just this information. If the SRL system assumes that it has full syntactic information anyway, why does it ignore most of it? Couldn't its performance be improved by adding additional features that represent more detailed syntactic information?

This question touches upon a fundamental challenge in using statistical methods, the *sparse data problem*. Every statistical model is trained from a limited set of observations in the corpus, and is expected to make accurate predictions on unseen data. The reliability of these predictions depends greatly on the size of the training corpus and the number of features. If we add features, we increase the number of possible combinations of feature-value pairs, i.e., the size of the *feature space*. For a given size of the training data, this means that certain feature-value combinations will be seen only once or not at all in training, which implies that the estimate of the statistical model becomes too inaccurate to make good predictions. *Smoothing* and *back-off* techniques can improve the performance of systems by assigning some kind of positive probability to combinations that have never or rarely been seen in training. But even these methods ultimately reduce the system's predictions on rare events to educated guesses.

The trade-off between informativity and occurrence frequency is one of the major challenges to statistical NLP. Sensible *feature design*, i.e. selecting a feature set which provides maximal information while keeping the feature space manageable, is a task where combined technical and linguistic expertise is required.

Further reading. For a more detailed introduction to standard SRL, we refer the reader to Jurafsky & Martin (2008). Just as for WSD, a good starting point to get a sense of the state of the art is to look at recent SRL competitions (Carreras & Marquez 2004, 2005; Hajic et al. 2009).

3.3 Semantic relatedness: Minimizing supervision

All data-intensive methods we have described so far are supervised methods: They require manually annotated corpora for training. The sparse data problem we just mentioned arises because annotating a corpus is costly and time-intensive, which limits the size of available corpora (Ng 1997). Conversely, this means that supervised methods can only be used with relatively inexpressive features.

Data expansion methods attempt to work around this problem by partially automating the annotation process. These methods train an initial model on a small amount of manually annotated *seed data*; use this model to identify instances in a large un-annotated corpus whose correct annotation can be predicted with high confidence; add the automatically annotated instances to the corpus; use the extended corpus to retrain the model; and then repeat the entire process in a "bootstrapping cycle". Such *semi-supervised* methods have been quite successful in early WSD systems (Yarowsky 1995), and more recently also for SRL (Fürstenau & Lapata 2009). Another strategy of reducing annotation effort is known as *active learning*: A model is trained on a seed corpus, but it is then used for the identification of low confidence instances. Specifically annotating these low-confidence cases will usually add more relevant information than annotating large numbers of cases that the learning system already "is certain about" (Settles 2009).

Learning from unannotated text. A class of popular approaches take this idea one step further, by requiring no manual annotation of training corpora at all. They are in particular attractive for the acquisition of world knowledge and lexical knowledge, because these tasks require large amounts of training data to achieve thematic coverage. An early representative of this tradition is Hearst (1992), who learned hyponym relations between words by considering occurrences of patterns like "an X such as Y". If this string occurs significantly more frequently than would be expected from the frequencies of X and Y alone, the system infers that Y is a hyponym of X. The approach was later generalized to other semantic relations, e.g. to meronymy (Girju, Badulescu & Moldovan 2006) and certain semantic relations between verbs (Chklovski & Pantel 2004).

Although such pattern-matching approaches sometimes find incorrect pairs (the top Google hit for the above pattern at the time of writing was "a fool such as I"), their great advantage is that they can operate on raw text and require no annotation effort. They can even be used on the entire Web, with certain caveats that are discussed e.g. by Keller, Lapata & Ourioupina (2002), and therefore achieve huge lexical coverage. However, these approaches still require human intervention in the specification of the patterns for which the corpus should be searched. To alleviate the problem, Ravichandran & Hovy (2002) present a bootstrapping approach that can simultaneously learn patterns and instances of the relation.

Distributional models. A more radical approach to the problem of learning knowledge from unannotated corpora is offered by methods which automatically learn from co-occurrence frequencies what expressions are *semantically similar* and do not even require the specification of search patterns. The basic idea, known as the *Distributional Hypothesis*, is that words with similar meaning tend to occur together with the same words. The basic insight can be traced back to the 1950s (Harris 1951). The catchy phrase "You shall know a word by the company it keeps" is due to Firth (1957).

In its basic version, distributional semantics approximates word meaning through counts of context words occurring in the neighborhood of target word instances. Take, as in the WSD example above, the n (e.g., 2000) most frequent content words in a corpus as the set of relevant context words; then count, for

	factory	flower	tree	plant	water	fork
grow	15	147	330	517	106	3
garden	5	200	198	316	118	17
worker	279	0	5	84	18	0
production	102	6	9	130	28	0
wild	3	216	35	96	30	0

Fig. 13.4: Some co-occurrence vectors from the British National Corpus.

each word *w*, how often each of these context words occurred in a context window of *n* before or after each occurrence of *w*. Fig. 13.4 shows the co-occurrence counts for a number of target words (columns), and a selection of context words (rows) obtained from a 10% portion of the British National Corpus (Clear 1993).

The resulting frequency pattern encodes information about the meaning of *w*. According to the Distributional Hypothesis, we can model the semantic similarity between two words by computing the similarity between their cooccurrences with the context words. In the example of Fig. 13.4, the target *flower* co-occurs frequently with the context words *grow* and *garden*, and infrequently with *production* and *worker*. The target word *tree* has a similar distribution, but the target *factory* shows the opposite co-occurrence pattern with these four context words. This is evidence that trees and flowers are more similar to each other than to factories.

Technically, we represent each word *w* as a vector in a high-dimensional vector space, with one dimension for each context word; the value of the vector at a certain dimension *v* is the co-occurrence frequency of *w* with *v*. We define a similarity measure between words based on their respective vector representations. A commonly used measure is the *cosine* of the angle between the two vectors, which can be computed easily from the co-occurrence counts. It assumes the value 1 if the vectors' directions coincide (i.e., the proportions of their context-word frequencies are identical), and 0 if the vectors are orthogonal (i.e., the distributions are maximally dissimilar). In the 5-dimensional word-space of our example, we obtain a high distributional similarity between the targets *tree* and *flower* (cosine of 0.752, representing an angle of about 40°), and a low similarity (cosines of 0.045 and 0.073, respectively, representing angles of about 85°) between either of the two and the target *factory*, as illustrated in Fig. 13.5.

Discussion. Standard distributional models offer only a rough approximation to lexical meaning. Strictly speaking, they do not model semantic similarity in terms of the "likeness" of lexical meaning, but a rather vague notion of "semantic relatedness", which includes synonymy, topical relatedness, and even antonymy

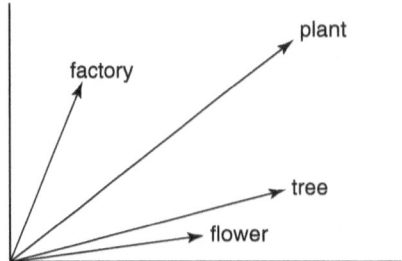

Fig. 13.5: Graphical illustration of co-occurrence vectors.

(Budanitsky & Hirst 2006). This is in part because the notion of context is rather crude. A deeper problem is that textual cooccurrence patterns provide essentially incomplete and indirect information about natural-language meaning, whose primary function is to connect language to the world. We will come back to the issue in Section 4.4.

Nevertheless, distributional approaches to semantics are attractive because they are *fully unsupervised:* They do not require any annotation or other preparatory manual work, in contrast to the supervised and semisupervised methods sketched above. Therefore, one gets wide-coverage models almost for free; the only prerequisite is a text corpus of sufficient size. In particular, distributional models can be easily obtained for languages for which no lexicon resources exist, and adapted to arbitrary genre-specific or domain-specific sub-languages. They have proven practically useful for several language-technology tasks. Examples are word-sense disambiguation (McCarthy & Carroll 2003; Li, Roth & Sporleder 2010; Thater, Fürstenau & Pinkal 2011), word-sense induction (Schütze 1998), information retrieval (Manning, Raghavan & Schütze 2008), and question answering (Dinu 2011).

Contextualization. An obvious flaw of the basic distributional approach is that it counts *words* rather than *word senses*. Because of lexical ambiguity, the distributional pattern of a word is therefore a mixture of the distributional patterns of its individual senses. While ideally each occurrence of *plant* should be either highly similar to *factory* or to *tree*, the model will uniformly assign them a value that is somewhere in between, as indicated by the *plant* arrow in Fig. 13.5.

Dealing with this problem is tricky; adding word-sense information to the corpus is not a real option, since this would throw us back to supervised methods, requiring expensive manual annotation. An approach that has received recent attention is to *contextualize* a target instance, by modifying its meaning with information provided by its actual context words (using algebraic operations on the respective vector representations, such as addition or component-wise multiplication). The effect is that the vector of of an occurrence of *plant* in the context of *water* is "pulled" towards the vector of *tree*, thus modeling a preference for the botanical word sense (Schütze 1998; Mitchell & Lapata 2008; Erk & Pado 2008; Thater, Fürstenau & Pinkal 2010).

Refining distributional similarity measures. The basic approach of distributional similarity modeling has been refined in various ways. Different alternative measures for the association of a target word with the context and for computing similarity between a pair of target words have been proposed. Recent work makes frequent use of "hidden variable" techniques (Dinu & Lapata 2010), which were originally developed for Information Retrieval (Landauer, Foltz & Laham 1998; Schütze 1998). Syntactic information has been added to the model in different ways in order to achieve a finer-grained analysis of distributional similarity, e.g. in the contextualization approaches of Erk & Padó (2008) and Thater, Fürstenau & Pinkal (2010). Lin & Pantel (2001) present an interesting syntax-enriched variant of distributional semantics, which generalizes to *multiword relational patterns*. Their system can discover, for example, that "X solves Y" and "X finds a solution to Y" are paraphrases, based on the fact that the frequency distributions of fillers for the X and Y slots are similar. Work on contextualization and syntactic refinement has initiated a discussion about compositionality in distributional semantics – that is, methods for computing distributional representations for complex expressions from distributional information about individual words (Mitchell & Lapata 2008; Grefenstette & Sadrzadeh 2011).

Unsupervised methods for semantic relatedness are currently a very active field of research, and it will be interesting to see how the area will develop in the future. For a recent detailed overview over the state of the art, see Turney & Pantel (2010).

4 Current developments

We conclude our overview with a discussion of some recent developments in computational semantics. We will look at a general evaluation scheme for computational semantics systems (*textual entailment*, Section 4.1), an approach to shallow logic-based inference that may be a starting point for bringing logic back into broad-coverage computational semantics, *natural logic*, Section 4.2), approaches to the automated learning of wide-coverage semantic construction resources (Section 4.3), and approaches to learning data-intensive models that ground word meaning directly in the real world (Section 4.4). Common to all of these approaches is that they are in their early stages, and there is no telling whether they will be successful in the long run; but they are all promising, active research areas, which may contribute to bringing knowledge-based and data-intensive semantics closer together in the future.

4.1 Textual entailment

As we have argued above, *inference* is the touchstone for computational semantics. It is the capability of supporting inferences that makes semantic processing potentially useful in applications. The performance of a semantic processing method is therefore strongly dependent on its performance in modeling inference. While the evaluation of WSD or SRL systems is straightforward, the question of how to assess a system's performance on the more global task of modeling inference appropriately has long been an open issue in the computational semantics community.

FraCaS. A first step in this direction was the creation of a test suite of inference problems by the FraCaS project in the 1990s (Cooper et al. 1996). Each problem consisted of a premise and a candidate conclusion (phrased as a yes/no question), plus information about their logical relation; systems could then be evaluated by making them decide the logical relation between the sentences and comparing the result against the gold standard. Two of the about 350 examples are shown below:

(10) *P:* ITEL won more orders than APCOM
 Q: Did ITEL win some orders?
 → YES

(11) *P:* Smith believed that ITEL had won the contract in 1992
 H: Had ITEL won the contract in 1992?
 → UNKNOWN

The FraCaS testsuite was hand-crafted to cover challenging semantic phenomena (such as quantifiers, plural, anaphora, temporal reference, and attitudes), while minimizing the impact of problems like syntactic complexity and word-sense ambiguity. This made it a valuable diagnostic tool for semanticists, but it also limited its usefulness for the performance evaluation of semantic processing systems on real-world language data, in which syntactic complexity is uncontrolled and word-sense ambiguity is prevalent.

RTE. A milestone in the development of an organized and realistic evaluation framework for natural-language inference was the *Recognizing Textual Entailment, RTE)* challenge initiated by Ido Dagan and his colleagues in the PASCAL network (Dagan, Glickman & Magnini 2006). The RTE dataset consists of pairs of sentences (a *text* T and a *hypothesis* H) derived from text that naturally occurred in applications such as question answering, information retrieval, and machine translation, plus an annotation specifying whether each sentence pair stands in an "entailment" relation.

In RTE, "entailment" is defined as follows:

> "We say that T entails H if the meaning of H can be inferred from the meaning of T, as would typically be interpreted by people. This somewhat informal definition is based on (and assumes) common human understanding of language as well as common background knowledge." (Dagan, Glickman & Magnini 2006)

For instance, the following sentence pair from the second RTE challenge (Bar-Haim et al. 2006) is in the entailment relation.

(12) *T:* In 1954, in a gesture of friendship to mark the 300th anniversary of Ukrainian union with Russia, Soviet Premier Nikita Khrushchev gave Crimea to Ukraine.
H: Crimea became part of Ukraine in 1954.
→ YES

Crucially, "textual entailment" is not a logical notion; it is a relation between textual objects. The above definition has been criticized for its vagueness and for its insufficient theoretical grounding, in that it blurs the distinction between logical entailment, common-sense inference, presupposition, and conversational implicature (Zaenen, Karttunen & Crouch 2005). However, it was deliberately intended as a specification of a pre-theoretic concept, which is neutral with respect to any particular semantic theory. Determining textual entailment seems to be a quite natural task for people, and is motivated from applications (Manning 2006); one effect of this is that annotators agree quite well on RTE-style entailment judgments (Bos & Markert 2005), whereas agreement on the precise and theoretically well-motivated distinctions tends to be difficult. For instance, it is doubtful whether the following logical reformulation of (12) is logically or analytically sound, given the semantics of the predicates and the sortal information about the argument fillers.

(13) give-to(Khrushchev, Crimea, Ukraine)
$\models$ become-part-of(Crimea, Ukraine)

However, (12) is still a clear case of entailment in the sense of the above definition.

For the RTE challenge, two datasets were created, intended as training and evaluation corpus, respectively. They contained 800 sentence pairs each, annotated with respect to entailment. Participating systems could be tuned on the training corpus, which was made available several weeks in advance. For evaluation, they had to automatically determine for the unseen sentence pairs in the test corpus whether they stand in the entailment relation or not. Performance was measured in terms of accuracy, i.e. the percentage of sentence pairs on which the system's judgment agreed with the annotation in the test corpus. The RTE challenge has established itself as a yearly event, with new datasets every year, and some variation in dataset and evaluation design.

RTE systems. The simplest reasonable baseline system for textual entailment recognition is one which checks for word overlap between T and H: It takes the percentage of words in the second sentence that occur in the first sentence as well as an indicator for entailment, and returns "yes" if this percentage exceeds a certain threshold. Such a system might classify (12) as a positive entailment case because "Crimea", "Ukraine", "in", and "1954" occur both in H and T. A word-overlap system typically gets about 60% of the sentence pairs right, depending on the particular instance of RTE. The accuracy can be increased by combining word overlap with semantic similarity measures (Jijkoun & de Rijke 2005; Glickman, Dagan & Koppel 2005), but the potential for such purely shallow and knowledge-lean improvements seems to be limited.

Pure logic-based systems, located at the other end of the spectrum, have completely failed at the RTE task, which was shown impressively by Bos & Markert (2005). They applied a state-of-the-art logic-based system along the lines of Section 2. Where this system claims entailment for a given sentence pair, its judgment is quite reliable; but because it only claimed entailment for less than 6% of the pairs, it gave far fewer correct answers overall than a simple word-overlap model. This demonstrates the severity of the knowledge bottleneck in logic-based semantics, which we mentioned above.

A standard system architecture that emerged from the experiences in RTE combines syntactic and semantic knowledge with machine learning technology. A typical inventory of knowledge types includes syntactic dependency information contributed by knowledge-based or statistical parsers plus lexical semantic information taken from WordNet or distributional models, potentially complemented by semantic role information (FrameNet, PropBank) and lexical semantic and world knowledge from other sources (e.g., DIRT (Lin & Pantel 2001), VerbOcean (Chklovski & Pantel 2004), or the YAGO knowledge base (Suchanek, Kasneci & Weikum 2008)). This information is used as input to a supervised machine-learning system, which learns to predict the entailment status of a sentence pair from features indicating structural and semantic similarity. Systems enhanced with linguistic knowledge in such ways typically outperform the purely overlap-based systems, but only by a rather modest margin, with an accuracy around 65% (see e.g. Giampiccolo et al. 2007 for an overview).

A notable exception is Hickl & Bensley (2007), a system submitted by an industrial company (LCC) in the RTE-3 Challenge, which achieved 80% accuracy, using a variety of rich resources in a machine learning approach. A second LCC system (Tatu & Moldovan 2007) used a special-purpose theorem prover (Moldovan et al. 2007) and reached a high accuracy as well. Although neither the knowledge repositories nor the details about the method are available to the public, it is likely that the success of these systems stems from language and knowledge resources of various kinds that have been built over years with enormous manpower, accompanied by a consistent optimization of methods based on repeated task-oriented evaluations. This suggests that at the end of the day, the decisive factor in building high-performing systems for entailment checking is not a single theoretical insight or design decision, but rather the availability of huge amounts of information about language and the world. The key difference between the logic-based and machine-learning paradigms is that the latter degrades more gracefully when this information is not sufficiently available.

Discussion. Between 2005 and 2010 a total of about 300 different systems in total were evaluated. This has helped a lot in providing a clear picture of the potential of different methods and resources on the task. However, the RTE Challenges reveal a current state of the art that is not entirely satisfactory. Statistical systems appear to hit a ceiling in modeling inference. This is not just a technical problem: the fundamental shortcoming of purely text-based approaches is that they do not model the truth conditions of the sentences involved, and therefore cannot ground entailment in truth. It is difficult to imagine how a notion of inference for semantically complex sentences can be approximated by a model that does not in some way or another subsume the conceptual framework of logic-based semantics. On the other hand, direct implementations of the logic-based framework do not solve the problem either, because such systems are rendered practically unusable by the lack of formalized knowledge. Resolving this tension remains the central challenge for computational semantics today.

4.2 Natural logic inference

One promising direction of research that might help solve the dilemma is to model truth-based entailment directly in natural language, without resorting to explicit logical representations. The idea is old – indeed, before the introduction of formal logic, it was the only way of analyzing inference –, but was revived and formalized in the 1980s by Johan von Benthem under the heading of *natural logic* (van Benthem 1986; Sanchez-Valencia 1991). Consider the following examples:

(14) a. Last year, John bought a German convertible.
b. Last year, John bought a German car.

To determine the entailment relation between (14a) and (14b), we need not compute the respective logical representations and employ a deduction system. We just need to know that "convertible" is a hyponym of "car". The argument does not apply in general. Replacing "convertible" with "car" in "John didn't buy a convertible" or "John bought two convertibles" has different semantic effects: In the former case, entailment holds in the inverse direction, in the second, the two sentences are logically independent. The differences are due to the different monotonicity properties (in the sense of Barwise & Cooper 1981) of the contexts in which the respective substitutions take place. In addition to knowledge about lexical inclusion relations, we need syntactic information, a mechanism for monotonicity marking, and monotonicity or polarity information for the functor expressions (in the sense of categorial grammar or type theory).

Natural logic and RTE. MacCartney & Manning (2008) and MacCartney (2009) propose a model for textual entailment recognition which is based on natural logic and extends and complements the framework in several aspects. Compared to the original approach of Sanchez-Valencia, they use a refined inventory of semantic relations. Wide-coverage knowledge about lexical semantic relations is obtained from WordNet, with distributional similarity as a fallback. Monotonicity handling includes the polarity analysis of implicative and factive verbs (Nairn, Condoravdi & Karttunen 2006), in addition to the standard operators (negation, determiners, conjunctions, modal expressions) and constructions. Their full model also processes sentence pairs that require multiple substitutions, deletions, or insertions; the global entailment relation between the sentences is computed as the joint entailment effect of the individual edit steps.

Because the preposition "without" introduces a downward monotonic context, the system can thus make the correct, but nontrivial judgment that (15a) and (15b) do not entail each other, based on the edits shown in (16).

(15) a. Some people are happy without a car.
b. Some professors are happy without an expensive convertible.

(16) Some SUBST(people, professors) are happy without an INSERT(expensive) SUBST(car, convertible).

The global entailment relation between the sentences is computed as the joint entailment effect of the single edit steps. Because the preposition "without" is downward monotonic in its internal argument, the system can thus make the correct, but nontrivial judgment that (15a) and (15b) do not entail each other, based on the edits shown in (16).

MacCartney's NATLOG system has been shown to achieve an accuracy of 70% on the FraCaS test suite. This demonstrates that the system can handle logically non-trivial inference problems, although some phenomena, like ellipsis, are outside the system's coverage. On the RTE-3 test set, the system has an accuracy of 59%, which does not exceed the performance achieved by simple word-overlap systems. However, the positive message is that that the natural-logic-based approach is able to avoid the robustness issues that make semantic construction for standard logic-based systems so difficult. Combining NATLOG with the the shallow Stanford RTE system (de Marneffe, Marie-Catherine and Bill MacCartney and Trond Grenager and Daniel Cer and Anna Rafferty and Christopher Manning 2006) increases the accuracy of the shallow system from 60.5% by 4%, which proves that the "deep" inferences captured by the natural-logic-based system are able to complement shallow RTE methods in a substantial way.

Discussion. The natural logic approach does not capture all inferences that a predicate logic approach would. It does not deal with inferences that require multiple premises, and can only relate sentence pairs in which the lexical material is exchanged while the global structure stays the same (e.g., de Morgan's Law is outside its reach). However, the approach does cover many inference patterns that are relevant in natural language, and the overhead for semantic construction and the disambiguation of irrelevant parts of sentences is eliminated, because no translation to logical representation is required.

4.3 Statistical methods in semantic construction

One reason for the low performance of logic-based inference systems in the standard framework of computational semantics is the lack of wide-coverage semantic construction procedures. Natural logic gets around the problem by dispensing with semantic construction altogether. An alternative that has recently been explored is the use of machine learning techniques for the automatic assignment of rich semantic representations.

To get a better idea of the task, it is helpful to consider its relationship to systems for syntactic parsing. The two problems are similar from a high-level perspective, in that both compute structured linguistic representations for natural language expressions. The dominant approach in syntactic parsing is to apply supervised statistical approaches to syntactically annotated corpora, in order to learn grammars and estimate the parameters of a syntactic probability model. For semantic construction, statistical approaches have been much less successful. Even for Semantic Role Labeling, the results are noisier than for syntax. The assignment of complex logical structures as representations for full sentences is harder, due to the fine granularity of the target representations and the difficulty of finding surface features that are indicative of deep semantic phenomena. This makes the specification of annotation guidelines that would allow non-experts to reliably annotate a corpus challenging.

Nevertheless, a considerable amount of research in the past few years has investigated the use of supervised learning in semantic parsers, trained on small domain-specific corpora. Logical annotations are typically obtained by converting the annotations from existing corpora, e.g., the Geo880 corpus (Zelle & Mooney 1996; Tang & Mooney 2000) of 880 geographical queries and the ATIS corpus (Dahl et al. 1994), a corpus of about 5000 spoken queries to a travel planning system. Both of these corpora were originally annotated with database queries that correspond to the natural-language query. When these are converted into lambda terms, examples look as follows:

(17) What states border Texas?
$\lambda x.\text{state}(x) \land \text{borders}(x, \text{texas})$

(18) on may four atlanta to denver delta flight 257
$\lambda x.\text{month}(x, \text{may}) \land \text{day\_number}(x, \text{fourth}) \land \text{from}(x, \text{atlanta}) \land \text{to}(x, \text{denver}) \land \text{airline}(x, \text{delta}) \land \text{flight}(x) \land \text{flight\_number}(x, 257)$

Current approaches for training semantic parsers typically employ methods from statistical machine translation, such as probabilistic synchronous grammars (Chiang 2007). These grammars simultaneously describe a tree for the syntactic representation of the natural-language string and a tree for the semantic representation, i.e. the lambda term. Because the syntactic parses are not explicitly given in the corpora mentioned above, these approaches assume a very permissive syntactic grammar, which allows many ungrammatical analyses of the input expression in addition to the grammatical ones. They then estimate parameters for a probability model that makes the ungrammatical analyses improbable, and maps the grammatical analyses to the correct semantic representations.

One key challenge that research in this area must overcome compared to pure syntactic parsing is that the annotated structures are not syntax trees, but lambda terms, which can be rewritten by $\alpha\beta\eta$-equality. The exact way in which this problem is addressed depends on the grammar formalism that a particular system uses. Wong & Mooney (2007) use a synchronous context-free grammar with an extra mechanism for representing variable binding. Zettlemoyer & Collins (2005) and Kwiatkowski et al. (2010) instead use probabilistic CCG grammars (Steedman 2000), which model the combination of lambda terms directly. The best-performing systems today achieve an accuracy of about 89% exact matches on the Geo880 corpus and still about 82% on the ATIS speech corpus (see Kwiatkowski et al. (2011) for an overview), which demonstrates that the method is feasible in principle. These are very promising numbers, but it is important to keep in mind that these methods have so far been applied only to relatively small corpora from limited domains, and it remains to be seen how well they will scale up.

4.4 Grounded models of meaning

Standard systems of distributional semantics learn meaning information purely from text; but semantics, unlike syntax or morphology, is essentially concerned with the relationship of language with the outside world. Children do not learn what "chair" means by hearing people talk about chairs, but by observing chairs in connection with hearing the word "chair". Certain regularities in the real world are reflected in statistical patterns in texts (chairs are used for sitting, so the word "chair" frequently co-occurs with the word "sit"). But ultimately it is unsurprising that computer systems cannot learn the full semantics of words and sentences, when they are exposed to a much poorer and fundamentally incomplete stimulus.

While the simulation of human meaning acquisition in a full-fledged realistic environment is not feasible, a number of alternative methods have been explored to integrate restricted layers or pieces of extralinguistic information into the learning process. One option is the creation of multimodal corpora consisting of visual material – e.g., pictures or videos – labeled with linguistic descriptions. Large-scale data collections of this kind can be obtained through Internet-based experiments or games; examples are the Google Image Labeler (von Ahn & Dabbish 2004), which lets people annotate pictures with textual descriptions, and the Microsoft Research Video Description Corpus (Chen & Dolan 2011), which was collected by asking people to describe the activities shown in short YouTube videos.

Data of this kind can be used in two ways. First, one may completely disregard the nonlinguistic information, and use picture and video IDs just as indices of the natural-language expressions. This tells the system that the different descriptions of the same picture refer to the same scene: they are proper paraphrase candidates and definitely will not contain contradictory information. A similar effect is obtained by corpora containing parallel texts, which are known to describe the same event. For instance, Titov & Kozhevnikov (2010) use collections of alternative weather forecasts for the same day and region. Their system learns that "cloudy" and "sunny" stand in a different semantic relationship than "cloudy" and "overcast": while both pairs occur in similar linguistic contexts, the former but not the latter are identified as describing two different states of sky cover, because they do not co-occur as descriptions of one world state.

Other approaches have taken the further step of analyzing the contents of the picture or video, typically using methods from computer vision, in order to let the computer system learn an actual mapping of language to extralinguistic objects. For example, Marszalek, Laptev & Schmid (2009) train a machine-learning system to identify instances of activities such as "drinking" in movies. Their training data is the movie itself together with textual descriptions of the current scene collected from subtitles and movie scripts. Learning a mapping between words and the external world is a problem that is frequently considered in cognitive robotics (Gold & Scassellati 2007; Kruijff et al. 2007), where a human user may explicitly teach the robot how to interpret spoken utterances in its environment. This also adds an *interactive* dimension to the process of automated language learning.

The core problem of mapping language to the extralinguistic environment can also be studied in more abstract settings. This has the advantage that the learning system can access the environment more directly. For instance, a system can learn the meaning of expressions referring to actions in a simulated robot soccer game (Chen, Kim & Mooney 2010), and the interpretation of help texts as actions in the Windows GUI, such as clicking buttons or entering text into certain input fields (Branavan et al. 2009). A middle ground is struck by approaches trained on virtual 3D environments (Orkin & Roy 2007; Fleischman & Roy 2005). An instructive account of alternative methods to connect language to real world or virtual reality is given in (Roy & Reiter 2005).

All these approaches to learning meaning representations are necessarily constrained in that they consider only some modalities and some aspects of non-linguistic information. Nevertheless, they form an exciting avenue of future research. From the perspective of semantic theory, they are perhaps most interesting because they open up a new direction in which the use of computers can support research on natural language meaning: as an instrument which connects natural-language expressions with large quantities of data about objects, properties, and events in the real world in a meaningful way.

5 Conclusion

Determining the meaning of a natural-language expression is crucial for many applications in computational linguistics, and computational semantics has long been a very active field of research. An approach to computational semantics that is to be useful for such applications must balance the depth of the linguistic analysis with the ability to compute such analyses reliably with wide coverage, i.e. for arbitrary sentences. Research in computational semantics is characterized by navigating this tension between depth and coverage.

In this article, we have sketched a number of prominent approaches in our field. Direct implementations of logic-based theories of semantics managed to overcome initial efficiency problems and, to some extent, deal with the massive amount of ambiguity that such approaches face in practice. However, making wide-coverage semantic construction robust and acquiring wide-coverage knowledge resources for inferences remain open problems. By contrast, data-intensive approaches have had very impressive successes in extracting useful semantic information from text corpora. But they tend to work with shallower meaning information than logic-based approaches; deeper representations still require a modeling effort by humans. The most promising recent research brings these two paradigms together, and combines them with novel ideas for models of meaning that are grounded in the environment. In our view, this makes the present a very exciting time for research in computational semantics indeed.

Acknowledgments

We gratefully acknowledge Ingo Reich, Caroline Sporleder, Stefan Thater, and Margaret Delap for valuable comments on this article. Several examples are due to Collin Baker, Josef Ruppenhofer, and Gerhard Weikum. Finally, we thank Claudia Maienborn for the infinite patience and cheerfulness with which she handled the perpetually almost-finished state of our manuscript.

6 References

Alshawi, Hiyan (ed.) 1990. *The Core Language Engine*. Cambridge, MA: The MIT Press.
Alshawi, Hiyan & Richard Crouch 1992. Monotonic semantic interpretation. In: H. S. Thompson (ed.). *Proceedings of the 30th Annual Meeting of the Association for Computational Linguistics (= ACL)*. Newark, DE: ACL, 32–39.
Althaus, Ernst, Denys Duchier, Alexander Koller, Kurt Mehlhorn, Joachim Niehren & Sven Thiel 2003. An efficient graph algorithm for dominance constraints. *Journal of Algorithms* 48, 194–219.

Andrews, Peter B. & Chad E. Brown 2006. TPS: A hybrid automatic-interactive system for developing proofs. *Journal of Applied Logic* 4, 367–395.

Areces, Carlos, Alexander Koller & Kristina Striegnitz 2008. Referring expressions as formulas of description logic. In: M. White, C. Nakatsu & D. McDonald (eds.). *Proceedings of the 5th International Natural Language Generation Conference (= INLG)*. Salt Fork, OH: ACL, 42–49.

Asher, Nicholas & Alex Lascarides 2003. *Logics of Conversation*. Cambridge: Cambridge University Press.

Baader, Franz, Diego Calvanese, Deborah McGuiness, Daniele Nardi & Peter Patel-Schneider (eds.) 2003. *The Description Logic Handbook: Theory, Implementation and Applications*. Cambridge: Cambridge University Press.

Baker, Collin, Charles Fillmore & Beau Cronin 2003. The structure of the FrameNet database. *International Journal of Lexicography* 16, 281–296.

Bar-Haim, Roy, Ido Dagan, Bill Dolan, Lisa Ferro, Danilo Giampiccolo, Bernardo Magnini & Idan Szpektor 2006. The second PASCAL Recognising Textual Entailment Challenge. In: B. Magnini & I. Dagan (eds.). *Proceedings of the Second PASCAL Challenges Workshop on Recognising Textual Entailment*. Venice, 1–9.

Bar-Hillel, Yehoshua 1960. The present status of automatic translation of languages. *Advances in Computers* 1, 91–163.

Barwise, Jon & Robin Cooper 1981. Generalized quantifiers and natural language. *Linguistics & Philosophy* 4, 159–219.

Blackburn, Patrick & Johan Bos 2005. *Representation and Inference for Natural Language. A First Course in Computational Semantics*. Stanford, CA: CSLI Publications.

Bos, Johan 2001. DORIS 2001: Underspecification, resolution and inference for Discourse Representation Structures. In: P. Blackburn & M. Kohlhase (eds.). *Proceedings of the Third International Workshop on Inference in Computational Semantics*. Siena, 117–124.

Bos, Johan & Katja Markert 2005. Recognising textual entailment with logical inference. In: *Proceedings of the Human Language Technology Conference and Conference on Empirical Methods in Natural Language Processing (= HLT/EMNLP)*. Vancouver, BC, 628–635.

Bos, Johan, Stephen Clark, Mark Steedman, James Curran & Julia Hockenmaier 2004. Wide-coverage semantic representations from a CCG parser. In: *Proceedings of the 20th International Conference on Computational Linguistics (= COLING)*. Geneva: COLING, 1240–1246.

Brachman, Ronald & James Schmolze 1985. An overview of the KL-ONE knowledge representation system. *Cognitive Science* 9, 171–216.

Branavan, S.R.K., Harr Chen, Luke S. Zettlemoyer & Regina Barzilay 2009. Reinforcement learning for mapping instructions to actions. In: K.-Y. Su et al. (eds.). *Proceedings of the Joint Conference of the 47th Annual Meeting of the Association for Computational Linguistics and the 4th International Joint Conference on Natural Language Processing of the AFNLP (= ACL-IJCNLP)*. Suntec: ACL, 82–90.

Budanitsky, Alexander & Graeme Hirst 2006. Evaluating WordNet-based measures of semantic distance. *Computational Linguistics* 32, 13–47.

Burchardt, Aljoscha, Katrin Erk, Anette Frank, Andrea Kowalski, Sebastian Padó & Manfred Pinkal 2006. The SALSA Corpus: A German corpus resource for lexical semantics. In: N. Calzolari et al. (eds.). *Proceedings of the 5th International Conference on Language Resources and Evaluation (= LREC)*. Genoa: ELRA-ELDA, 969–974.

Carreras, Xavier & Lluis Marquez 2004. Introduction to the CoNLL-2004 shared task: Semantic role labeling. In: H. T. Ng & E. Riloff (eds.). *Proceedings of the Eighth Conference on Computational Natural Language Learning (= CoNLL)*. Boston, MA: ACL, 89–97.

Carreras, Xavier & Lluis Marquez 2005. Introduction to the CoNLL-2005 shared task: Semantic role labeling. In: I. Dagan & D. Gildea (eds.). *Proceedings of the Ninth Conference on Computational Language Learning (= CoNLL)*. Ann Arbor, MI: ACL, 152–164.

Chapman, Robert L. 1977. *Roget's International Thesaurus*. 4th edn. New York: Harper & Row.

Chen, David & Bill Dolan 2011. Building a persistent workforce on Mechanical Turk for multilingual data collection. In: *Proceedings of the 3rd Human Computation Workshop at the 25th Conference on Artificial Intelligence (= AAAI-11)*. San Francisco, CA: AAAI Press. http://www.cs.utexas.edu/users/ai-lab/pubview.php?PubID = 127103. March 29, 2012.

Chen, David L., Joohyun Kim & Raymond J. Mooney 2010. Training a multilingual sportscaster: Using perceptual context to learn language. *Journal of Artificial Intelligence Research* 37, 397–435.

Chiang, David 2007. Hierarchical phrase-based translation. *Computational Linguistics* 33, 201–228.

Chklovski, Timothy & Patrick Pantel 2004. VerbOcean: Mining the Web for fine-grained semantic verb relations. In: D. Lin & D. Wu (eds.). *Proceedings of the Conference on Empirical Methods in Natural Language Processing (= EMNLP)*. Barcelona: ACL, 33–40.

Claessen, Koen & Niklas Sörensson 2003. New techniques that improve MACE-style model finding. In: P. Baumgartner & C. Fermüller (eds.). *Proceedings of the CADE-19 Workshop on Model Computation – Principles, Algorithms, Applications*. Miami, FL, 11–27.

Clear, Jeremy 1993. *The British National Corpus*. Cambridge, MA: The MIT Press.

Cooper, Robin 1983. *Quantification and Syntactic Theory*. Dordrecht: Reidel.

Cooper, Robin, Richard Crouch, Jan van Eijck, Chris Fox, Johan van Genabith, Jan Jaspars, Hans Kamp, David Milward, Manfred Pinkal, Massimo Poesio & Steve Pulman 1996. Using the framework. FraCas project deliverable D-16. Technical Report LRE 62–051. ftp://ftp.cogsci.ed.ac.uk/pub/FRACAS/del16.ps.gz. March 29, 2012.

Copestake, Ann, Alex Lascarides & Dan Flickinger 2001. An algebra for semantic construction in constraint-based grammars. In: *Proceedings of the 39th Annual Meeting of the Association for Computational Linguistics (= ACL)*. Toulouse: ACL, 132–139.

Copestake, Ann, Dan Flickinger, Carl Pollard & Ivan Sag 2005. Minimal Recursion Semantics: An introduction. *Research on Language and Computation* 3, 281–332.

Crouch, Dick & Tracy Holloway King 2006. Semantics via f-structure rewriting. In: M. Butt & T. H. King (eds.). *Proceedings of the LFG06 Conference*. Stanford, CA: CSLI Publications, 145–165.

Dagan, Ido, Oren Glickman & Bernardo Magnini 2006. The PASCAL Recognising Textual Entailment Challenge. In: J. Quiñonero-Candela et al. (eds.). *Machine Learning Challenges*. Heidelberg: Springer, 177–190.

Dahl, Deborah A., Madeleine Bates, Michael Brown, William Fisher, Kate Hunicke-Smith, David Pallett, Christine Pao, Alexander Rudnicky & Elizabeth Shriberg 1994. Expanding the scope of the ATIS task: The ATIS-3 corpus. In: *Proceedings of the ARPA Human Language Technology Workshop*. Plainsboro, NJ: Morgan Kaufmann, 43–48.

Dalrymple, Mary (ed.) 1999. *Semantics and Syntax in Lexical Functional Grammar: The Resource Logic Approach*. Cambridge, MA: The MIT Press.

Dalrymple, Mary, Ronald M. Kaplan, John T. Maxwell & Annie Zaenen (eds.) 1995. *Formal Issues in Lexical-Functional Grammar*. Stanford, CA: CSLI Publications.

Dinu, Georgiana 2011. *Word Meaning in Context: A Probabilistic Model and its Application to Question Answering*. Doctoral dissertation. Saarland University.

Dinu, Georgiana & Mirella Lapata 2010. Topic models for meaning similarity in context. In: *Proceedings of the 23rd International Conference on Computational Linguistics (= COLING)*. Beijing: COLING, 250–258.

Egg, Markus, Alexander Koller & Joachim Niehren 2001. The constraint language for lambda structures. *Logic, Language, and Information* 10, 457–485.
Erk, Katrin & Sebastian Padó 2008. A structured vector space model for word meaning in context. In: M. Lapata & H. T. Ng (eds.). *Proceedings of the Conference on Empirical Methods in Natural Language Processing (= EMNLP)*. Honolulu, HI: ACL, 897–906.
Fellbaum, Christiane (ed.) 1998. *WordNet: An Electronic Lexical Database.* Cambridge, MA: The MIT Press.
Fillmore, Charles J. 1968. Lexical entries for verbs. *Foundations of Language* 4, 373–393.
Fillmore, Charles J. & Collin F. Baker 2010. A frame approach to semantic analysis. In: B. Heine & H. Narrog (eds.). *Oxford Handbook of Linguistic Analysis.* Oxford: Oxford University Press, 313–340.
Firth, John 1957. *Papers in Linguistics 1934–1951.* Oxford: Oxford University Press.
Fleischman, Michael & Deb Roy 2005. Intentional context in situated language learning. In: I. Dagan & D. Gildea (eds.). *Proceedings of the Ninth Conference on Natural Language Learning (= CoNLL)*. Ann Arbor, MI: ACL, 104–111.
Fürstenau, Hagen & Mirella Lapata 2009. Semi-supervised semantic role labeling. In: A. Lascarides, C. Gardent & J. Nivre (eds.). *Proceedings of the 12th Conference of the European Chapter of the Association for Computational Linguistics (= EACL)*. Athens: ACL, 220–228.
Gardent, Claire 2003. Semantic construction in feature-based TAG. In: A. Lascarides, C. Gardent & J. Nivre (eds.). *Proceedings of the 10th Conference of the European Chapter of the Association for Computational Linguistics (= EACL)*. Athens: ACL, 123–130.
Gardent, Claire & Karsten Konrad 2000. Understanding "Each Other". In: *Proceedings of the 1st Meeting of the North American Chapter of the Association for Computational Linguistics (= NAACL)*. Seattle, WA: ACL, 319–326.
Giampiccolo, Danilo, Bernardo Magnini, Ido Dagan & Bill Dolan 2007. The Third PASCAL Recognizing Textual Entailment Challenge. In: S. Sekine et al. (eds.). *Proceedings of the ACL-PASCAL Workshop on Textual Entailment and Paraphrasing.* Prague: ACL, 1–9.
Gildea, Daniel & Daniel Jurafsky 2002. Automatic labeling of semantic roles. *Computational Linguistics* 28, 245–288.
Girju, Roxana, Adriana Badulescu & Dan Moldovan 2006. Automatic discovery of part-whole relations. *Computational Linguistics* 32, 83–135.
Glickman, Oren, Ido Dagan & Moshe Koppel 2005. A probabilistic classification approach for lexical textual entailment. In: M. M. Veloso & S. Kambhampati (eds.). *Proceedings of the 20th National Conference on Artificial Intelligence and the 17th Innovative Applications of Artificial Intelligence Conference (= AAAI-IAAI)*. Pittsburgh, PA: AAAI Press, 1050–1055.
Gold, Kevin & Brian Scassellati 2007. A robot that uses existing vocabulary to infer non-visual word meanings from observation. In: *Proceedings of the 22nd National Conference on Artificial Intelligence (= AAAI)*. Vancouver, BC: AAAI Press, 883–888.
Grefenstette, Edward & Mehrnoosh Sadrzadeh 2011. Experimental support for a categorical compositional distributional model of meaning. In: R. Barzilay & M. Johnson (eds.). *Proceedings of the 2011 Conference on Empirical Methods in Natural Language Processing (= EMNLP)*. Edinburgh: ACL, 1394–1404.
Groenendijk, Jeroen & Martin Stokhof 1991. Dynamic predicate logic. *Linguistics & Philosophy* 14, 39–100.
Grosz, Barbara & Candace Sidner 1986. Attention, intention, and the structure of discourse. *Computational Linguistics* 12, 175–204.
Grosz, Barbara, Aravind Joshi & Scott Weinstein 1995. Centering: A framework for modeling the local coherence of discourse. *Computational Linguistics* 21, 203–225.

Haarslev, Volker & Ralf Möller 2001. Description of the RACER system and its applications. In: C. Goble, R. Möller & P. Patel-Schneider (eds.). *Proceedings of the International Workshop on Description Logics (= DL-2001)*. Stanford, CA, 131–141.

Hajic, Jan, Massimiliano Ciaramita, Richard Johansson, Daisuke Kawahara, Maria Antonia Marti, Lluis Marquez, Adam Meyers, Joakim Nivre, Sebastian Padó, Jan Stepanek, Pavel Stranak, Mihai Surdeanu, Nianwen Xue & Yi Zhang 2009. The CoNLL-2009 shared task: Syntactic and semantic dependencies in multiple languages. In: J. Hajic (ed.). *Proceedings of the Thirteenth Conference on Computational Natural Language Learning (= CoNLL): Shared Task*. Boulder, CO: ACL, 1–18.

Hamp, B. & H. Feldweg 1997. GermaNet – a lexical-semantic net for German. In: P. Vossen et al. (eds.). *Proceedings of the ACL/EACL Workshop on Automatic Information Extraction and Building of Lexical Semantic Resources for NLP Applications*. Somerset, NJ: ACL, 9–15.

Harris, Zellig S. 1951. *Methods in Structural Linguistics*. Chicago, IL: The University of Chicago Press.

Hearst, Marti A. 1992. Automatic acquisition of hyponyms from large text corpora. In: *Proceedings of the 14th Conference on Computational Linguistics (= COLING)*. Nantes: COLING, 539–545.

Hickl, Andrew & Jeremy Bensley 2007. A discourse commitment-based framework for recognizing textual entailment. In: S. Sekine et al. (eds.). *Proceedings of the ACL-PASCAL Workshop on Textual Entailment and Paraphrasing*. Prague: ACL, 171–176.

Hillenbrand, Thomas 2003. CITIUS ALTIUS FORTIUS: Lessons learned from the theorem prover WALDMEISTER. In: I. Dahn & L. Vigneron (eds.). *Proceedings of the 4th International Workshop on First-Order Theorem Proving* (Electronic Notes in Theoretical Computer Science 86.1). 9–21.

Hirst, Graeme & Eugene Charniak 1982. Word sense and case slot disambiguation. In: D. L. Waltz (ed.). *Proceedings of the Second National Conference on Artificial Intelligence (= AAAI)*. Pittsburgh, PA: AAAI Press, 95–98.

Hobbs, Jerry R. 1985. Ontological promiscuity. In: *Proceedings of the 23rd Annual Meeting of the Association for Computational Linguistics (= ACL)*. Chicago, IL: ACL, 61–69.

Hobbs, Jerry R. & Stuart M. Shieber 1987. An algorithm for generating quantifier scopings. *Computational Linguistics* 13, 47–63.

Hobbs, Jerry R., Mark E. Stickel, Douglas E. Appelt & Paul A. Martin 1993. Interpretation as abduction. *Artificial Intelligence* 63, 69–142.

Hobbs, Jerry R., Douglas E. Appelt, John Bear, Mabry Tyson & David Magerman 1992. Robust processing of real-world natural language texts. In: P. Jacobs (ed.). *Text-Based Intelligent Systems: Current Research and Practice in Information Extraction and Retrieval*. Hillsdale, NJ: Lawrence Erlbaum, 13–33.

Jijkoun, Valentin & Maarten de Rijke 2005. Recognizing textual entailment using lexical similarity. In: *Proceedings of the First PASCAL Recognising Textual Entailment Challenge*. Southampton, 73–76.

Jurafsky, Dan & James Martin 2008. *Speech and Language Processing*. 2nd edn. Upper Saddle River, NJ: Prentice Hall.

Kallmeyer, Laura & Maribel Romero 2008. Scope and situation binding in LTAG using semantic unification. *Research on Language and Computation* 6, 3–52.

Kamp, Hans 1981. A theory of truth and semantic representation. In: J. Groenendijk, T. Janssen & M. Stokhof (eds.). *Formal Methods in the Study of Language*. Amsterdam: Mathematical Center, 277–322.

Kamp, Hans & Uwe Reyle 1993. *From Discourse to Logic*. Dordrecht: Kluwer.

Keller, Frank, Maria Lapata & Olga Ourioupina 2002. Using the Web to overcome data sparseness. In: J. Hajic & Y. Matsumoto (eds.). *Proceedings of the Conference on Empirical Methods in Natural Language Processing (= EMNLP)*. Philadelphia, PA: ACL, 230–237.

Keller, William 1988. Nested Cooper storage: The proper treatment of quantification in ordinary noun phrases. In: U. Reyle & C. Rohrer (eds.). *Natural Language Parsing and Linguistic Theories*. Dordrecht: Reidel, 432–447.

Kipper-Schuler, Karin 2006. *VerbNet: A Broad-coverage, Comprehensive Verb Lexicon*. Ph.D. dissertation. University of Pennsylvania, Philadelphia, PA.

Koch, Stephan, Uwe Kössner & Manfred Stede 2000. Contextual disambiguation. In: W. Wahlster (ed.). *Verbmobil: Foundations of Speech-to-speech Translation*. Heidelberg: Springer, 466–480.

Kohlhase, Michael 2000. Model generation for discourse representation theory. In: W. Horn (ed.). *Proceedings of the 14th European Conference on Artificial Intelligence (= ECAI)*. Berlin: IOS Press, 441–445.

Kohlhase, Michael, Susanna Kuschert & Manfred Pinkal 1996. A type-theoretic semantics for λ-DRT. In: P. Dekker & M. Stokhof (eds.). *Proceedings of the 10th Amsterdam Colloquium*. Amsterdam: ILLC, 479498.

Koller, Alexander & Stefan Thater 2010. Computing weakest readings. In: J. Hajic et al. (eds.). *Proceedings of the 48th Annual Meeting of the Association for Computational Linguistics (= ACL)*. Uppsala: ACL, 30–39.

Koller, Alexander, Ralph Debusmann, Malte Gabsdil & Kristina Striegnitz 2004. Put my galakmid coin into the dispenser and kick it: Computational linguistics and theorem proving in a computer game. *Journal of Logic, Language, and Information* 13, 187–206.

Kruijff, Geert-Jan M., Hendrik Zender, Patric Jensfelt & Henrik I. Christensen 2007. Situated dialogue and spatial organization: What, where ... and why? *International Journal of Advanced Robotic Systems* 4, 125–138.

Kwiatkowski, Tom, Luke Zettlemoyer, Sharon Goldwater & Mark Steedman 2010. Inducing probabilistic CCG grammars from logical form with higher-order unification. In: H. Li & L. Marquez (eds.). *Proceedings of the Conference on Empirical Methods in Natural Language Processing (= EMNLP)*. Cambridge, MA: ACL, 1223–1233.

Kwiatkowski, Tom, Luke Zettlemoyer, Sharon Goldwater & Mark Steedman 2011. Lexical generalization in CCG grammar induction for semantic parsing. In: R. Barzilay & M. Johnson (eds.). *Proceedings of the Conference on Empirical Methods in Natural Language Processing (= EMNLP)*. Edinburgh: ACL, 1512–1523.

Landauer, Thomas, Peter Foltz & Darrell Laham 1998. An introduction to latent semantic analysis. *Discourse Processes* 25, 259–284.

Landes, Shari, Claudia Leacock & Randee I. Tengi 1998. Building semantic concordances. In: C. Fellbaum (ed.). *WordNet: An Electronic Lexical Database*. Cambridge, MA: The MIT Press, 199–216.

Lenat, Douglas 1995. CYC: A large-scale investment in knowledge infrastructure. *Communications of the ACM* 38, 33–38.

Li, Linlin, Benjamin Roth & Caroline Sporleder 2010. Topic models for word sense disambiguation and token-based idiom detection. In: J. Hajic et al. (eds.). *Proceedings of the 48th Annual Meeting of the Association for Computational Linguistics (= ACL)*. Uppsala: ACL, 1138–1147.

Lin, Dekang & Patrick Pantel 2001. Discovery of inference rules for question answering. *Natural Language Engineering* 7, 343–360.

Lipton, Peter 2001. *Inference to the Best Explanation*. London: Routledge.

MacCartney, Bill 2009. *Natural Language Inference*. Ph.D. dissertation. Stanford University, Stanford, CA.
MacCartney, Bill & Christopher D. Manning 2008. Modeling semantic containment and exclusion in natural language inference. In: D. Scott & H. Uszkoreit (eds.). *Proceedings of the 22nd International Conference on Computational Linguistics (= COLING)*. Manchester: COLING, 521–528.
Manning, Christopher 2006. *Local Textual Inference: It's Hard to Circumscribe, but You Know It When You See It – and NLP Needs It*. Ms. Stanford, CA, Stanford University.
Manning, Christopher & Hinrich Schütze 1999. *Foundations of Statistical Natural Language Processing*. Cambridge, MA: The MIT Press.
Manning, Christopher, Prabhakar Raghavan & Hinrich Schuützte 2008. *Introduction to Information Retrieval*. Cambridge: Cambridge University Press.
Marcus, Mitchell P., Beatrice Santorini & Mary Ann Marcinkiewicz 1993. Building a large annotated corpus of English: The Penn Treebank. *Computational Linguistics* 19, 313–330.
de Marneffe, Marie-Catherine, Bill MacCartney, Trond Grenager, Daniel Cer, Anna Rafferty & Christopher Manning 2006. Learning to distinguish valid textual entailments. In: B. Magnini & I. Dragan (eds.). *Proceedings of the Second PASCAL Challenges Workshop on Recognizing Textual Entailment*. Venice, 74–79.
Marszalek, Marcin, Ivan Laptev & Cordelia Schmid 2009. Actions in context. In: *Proceedings of the IEEE Computer Society Conference on Computer Vision and Pattern Recognition*. Miami, FL: IEEE, 2929 – 2936.
Matuszek, Cynthia, John Cabral, Michael Witbrock & John DeOliveira 2006. An introduction to the syntax and content of Cyc. In: C. Baral (ed.). *Proceedings of the AAAI Spring Symposium on Formalizing and Compiling Background Knowledge and Its Applications to Knowledge Representation and Question Answering*. Menlo Park, CA: AAAI Press, 44–49.
McCarthy, Diana 2009. Word sense disambiguation: An overview. *Language and Linguistics Compass* 3, 537–558.
McCarthy, Diana & John Carroll 2003. Disambiguating nouns, verbs, and adjectives using automatically acquired selectional preferences. *Computational Linguistics* 29, 639–654.
McCune, William 1998. Automatic proofs and counterexamples for some ortholattice identities. *Information Processing Letters* 65, 285–291.
Mitchell, Jeff & Mirella Lapata 2008. Vector-based models of semantic composition. In: J. D. Moore et al. (eds.). *Proceedings of the 46th Annual Meeting of the Association for Computational Linguistics: Human Language Technologies (= ACL-HLT)*. Columbus, OH: ACL, 236–244.
Mitchell, Tom 1997. *Machine Learning*. New York: McGraw-Hill.
Moldovan, Dan, Christine Clark, Sanda Harabagiu & Daniel Hodges 2007. Cogex: A semantically and contextually enriched logic prover for question answering. *Journal of Applied Logic* 5, 49–69.
Montague, Richard 1973. On the proper treatment of quantification in ordinary English. In: J. Hintikka, J. Moravcsik & P. Suppes (eds.). *Approaches to Natural Language*. Dordrecht: Reidel, 221–242.
Moore, Robert C. 1985. Semantical considerations on nonmonotonic logic. *Artificial Intelligence* 25, 75–94.
Muskens, Reinhard 1995. *Meaning and Partiality*. Stanford, CA: CSLI Publications.
Nairn, Rowan, Cleo Condoravdi & Lauri Karttunen 2006. Computing relative polarity for textual inference. In: J. Bos & A. Koller (eds.). *Proceedings of the Fifth Workshop on Inference in Computational Semantics (= ICoS-5)*. Buxton, 67–76.
Navigli, Roberto 2009. Word sense disambiguation: A survey. *ACM Computing Surveys* 41, 1–69.

Navigli, Roberto, Kenneth C. Litkowski & Orin Hargraves 2007. SemEval 2007 Task 07: Coarse-grained English all-words task. In: E. Agirre, L. Marquez & R. Wicentowski (eds.). *Proceedings of the 4th International Workshop on Semantic Evaluations (= SemEval 2007)*. Prague: ACL, 30–35.

Ng, Hwee Tou 1997. Getting serious about word sense disambiguation. In: *Proceedings of the ACL SIGLEX Workshop on Tagging Text with Lexical Semantics: Why, What, and How?* Washington, DC: ACL, 1–7.

Ng, Vincent 2010. Supervised noun phrase coreference research: The first fifteen years. In: J. Hajic et al. (eds.). *Proceedings of the 48th Annual Meeting of the Association for Computational Linguistics (= ACL)*. Uppsala: ACL, 1396–1411.

Orkin, Jeff & Deb Roy 2007. The Restaurant Game: Learning social behavior and language from thousands of players online. *Journal of Game Development* 3, 39–60.

Palmer, Martha, Daniel Gildea & Paul Kingsbury 2005. The Proposition Bank: An annotated corpus of semantic roles. *Computational Linguistics* 31, 71–105.

Pereira, Fernando C. N. & Stuart M. Shieber 1987. *Prolog and Natural Language Analysis*. Chicago, IL: CSLI Publications.

Poesio, Massimo 1994. Ambiguity, underspecification, and discourse interpretation. In: H. Bunt, R. Muskens & G. Rentier (eds.). *Proceedings of the First International Workshop on Computational Semantics (= IWCS)*. Tilburg: ITK, Tilburg University, 1–10.

Pollard, Carl & Ivan Sag 1994. *Head-driven Phrase Structure Grammar*. Chicago, IL: The University of Chicago Press.

Pulman, Stephen 2007. Formal and computational semantics: A case study. In: J. Geertzen et al. (eds.). *Proceedings of the 7th International Workshop on Computational Semantics (= IWCS)*. Tilburg: ITK, Tilburg University, 181–196.

Ravichandran, Deepak & Eduard Hovy 2002. Learning surface text patterns for a question answering system. In: *Proceedings of the 40th Annual Meeting of the Association for Computational Linguistics (= ACL)*. Philadelphia, PA: ACL, 41–47.

Reiter, Ray 1980. A logic for default reasoning. *Artificial Intelligence* 13, 81–132.

Riazanov, Alexandre & Andrei Voronkov 2002. The design and implementation of VAMPIRE. *AI Communications* 15, 91–110.

Roy, Deb & Ehud Reiter 2005. Connecting language to the world. *Artificial Intelligence* 167, 1–12.

Russell, Stuart & Peter Norvig 2010. *Artificial Intelligence: A Modern Approach*. 3rd edn. Upper Saddle River, NJ: Prentice Hall.

Sanchez-Valencia, Victor 1991. *Studies on Natural Logic and Categorial Grammar*. Ph.D. dissertation. University of Amsterdam.

Schank, Roger C. 1975. *Conceptual Information Processing*. Amsterdam: North-Holland.

Schütze, Hinrich 1998. Automatic word sense discrimination. *Computational Linguistics* 24, 97–123.

Settles, Burr 2009. *Active Learning Literature Survey*. Computer Sciences Technical Report 1648, University of Wisconsin-Madison. http://www.cs.cmu.edu/~bsettles/pub/settles.activelearning.pdf. March 29, 2012.

Stede, Manfred 2011. *Discourse Processing*. San Rafael, CA: Morgan & Claypool.

Steedman, Mark 2000. *The Syntactic Process*. Cambridge, MA: The MIT Press.

Suchanek, Fabian M., Gjergji Kasneci & Gerhard Weikum 2008. YAGO: A large ontology from Wikipedia and WordNet. *Journal of Web Semantics* 6, 203–217.

Tang, Lappoon R. & Raymond J. Mooney 2000. Automated construction of database interfaces: Integrating statistical and relational learning for semantic parsing. In: H. Schütze &

K.-Y. Su (eds.). *Proceedings of the Joint SIGDAT Conference on Empirical Methods in Natural Language Processing and Very Large Corpora.* Hong Kong: ACL, 133–141.

Tatu, Marta & Dan Moldovan 2007. COGEX at RTE 3. In: S. Sekine et al. (eds.). *Proceedings of the ACL-PASCAL Workshop on Textual Entailment and Paraphrasing.* Prague: ACL, 22–27.

Thater, Stefan, Hagen Fürstenau & Manfred Pinkal 2010. Contextualizing semantic representations using syntactically enriched vector models. In: J. Hajic et al. (eds.). *Proceedings of the 48th Annual Meeting of the Association for Computational Linguistics (= ACL).* Uppsala: ACL, 948–957.

Thater, Stefan, Hagen Fürstenau & Manfred Pinkal 2011. Word meaning in context: A simple and effective vector model. In: H. Wang & D. Yarowsky (eds.). *Proceedings of the 5th International Joint Conference on Natural Language Processing (= IJCNLP).* Chiang Mai: Asian Federation of Natural Language Processing, 1134–1143.

Titov, Ivan & Mikhail Kozhevnikov 2010. Bootstrapping semantic analyzers from non-contradictory texts. In: J. Hajic et al. (eds.). *Proceedings of the 48th Annual Meeting of the Association for Computational Linguistics (= ACL).* Uppsala: ACL, 958–967.

Toma, Peter 1977. SYSTRAN as a multilingual machine translation system. In: C. of the European Community (ed.). *Overcoming the Language Barrier. Proceedings of the 3rd European Congress on Information Systems and Networks.* Munich: Verlag Dokumentation, 569–581.

Tsarkov, Dmitry, Ian Horrocks & Peter F. Patel-Schneider 2007. Optimizing terminological reasoning for expressive description logics. *Journal of Automated Reasoning* 39, 277–316.

Turney, Peter & Patrick Pantel 2010. From frequency to meaning: Vector space models of semantics. *Journal of Artificial Intelligence Research* 37, 141–188.

van Benthem, Johan 1986. *Essays in Logical Semantics.* Dordrecht: Reidel.

van Eijck, Jan, Juan Hegueiabehere & Breanndan O Nuallain 2001. Tableau reasoning and programming with dynamic first order logic. *Logic Journal of the IGPL* 9, 411–445.

von Ahn, Luis & Laura Dabbish 2004. Labeling images with a computer game. In: E. Dykstra-Erickson & M. Tscheligi (eds.). *Proceedings of the ACM CHI 2004 Conference on Human Factors in Computing Systems.* New York: ACL, 319–326.

Vossen, Piek 2004. EuroWordNet: A multilingual database of autonomous and language-specific wordnets connected via an Inter-Lingual-Index. *International Journal of Lexicography* 17, 161–173.

Wilks, Yorick 1975. A preferential, pattern seeking semantics for natural language inference. *Artificial Intelligence* 6, 53–74.

Witten, Ian H., Eibe Frank & Mark A. Hall 2011. *Data Mining: Practical Machine Learning Tools and Techniques.* 3rd edn. Amsterdam: Morgan Kaufmann.

Wong, Yuk Wah & Raymond J. Mooney 2007. Learning synchronous grammars for semantic parsing with lambda calculus. In: A. Zaenen & A. van den Bosch (eds.). *Proceedings of the 45th Annual Meeting of the Association for Computational Linguistics (= ACL).* Prague: ACL, 960–967.

Yarowsky, David 1992. Word-sense disambiguation using statistical models of Roget's categories trained on large corpora. In: *Proceedings of the 14th Conference on Computational Linguistics (= COLING).* Nantes: COLING, 454–460.

Yarowsky, David 1995. Unsupervised word sense disambiguation rivaling supervised methods. In: *Proceedings of the 33rd Annual Meeting of the Association for Computational Linguistics (= ACL).* Cambridge, MA: ACL, 189–196.

Zaenen, Annie, Lauri Karttunen & Richard Crouch 2005. Local textual inference: Can it be defined or circumscribed? In: B. Dolan & I. Dagan (eds.). *Proceedings of the ACL Workshop* on *Empirical Modelling of Semantic Equivalence and Entailment at the 43rd Annual Meeting of the Association for Computational Linguistics (= ACL)*. Ann Arbor, MI: ACL, 31–36.

Zelle, John M. & Raymond J. Mooney 1996. Learning to parse database queries using Inductive Logic Programming. In: W. J. Clancey & D. S. Weld (eds.). *Proceedings of the 13th National Conference on Aritificial Intelligence (= AAAI)*. Portland, OR: AAAI Press, 1050–1055.

Zettlemoyer, Luke S. & Michael Collins 2005. Learning to map sentences to logical form: Structured classification with probabilistic categorial grammars. In: *Proceedings of the 21st Conference on Uncertainty in Artificial Intelligence (= UAI)*. Edinburgh: AUAI Press, 658–666.

Graham Katz
14 Semantics in corpus linguistics

1   Introduction —— 409
2   Corpus linguistics and semantics —— 411
3   Theoretical semantics and corpora —— 414
4   Semantic annotation —— 419
5   Distributional semantic models —— 431
6   References —— 434

Abstract: Linguistic corpora are a rich source of data for semantic analysis, and researchers have begun to use these corpora in innovative ways to improve the depth and breadth of semantic theory. Building on a long tradition within classical corpus-linguistics, which has focussed on word meaning and collocation, theoretical and computational linguists have in recent years used large-scale corpora to study a range of semantic phenomena, from negative polarity and adjectival meaning to anaphora and discourse. In addition, corpora have been annotated with sophisticated semantic information about word meaning, semantic role assignment, discourse structure, anaphoric linking and time and event reference, among other things, bringing closer the goal of an integrated semantic interpretation scheme. Large scale distributional analysis has also emerged as an important avenue for lexical investigation.

> You shall know a word by the company it keeps.
> J.R. Firth (1957)

1 Introduction

These are boom times for corpus linguists. Corpus linguistics – the analysis of collected linguistic performance data – has undergone tremendous growth in recent years (Kytö & Lüdeling 2008, 2009), due in large part to the wide availability of vast quantities of electronic text. Most newspapers and other periodicals have electronic editions, and many now appear only in electronic form. Large numbers of books have been digitized and made available in whole or in part (Hart 1990; Vincent 2007). In addition, non-traditional forms of publication such as informational web pages, internet newsgroups, weblogs, public

Graham Katz, Washington, DC, USA

https://doi.org/10.1515/9783110589825-014

chat-rooms, and electronic mailing lists generate oceans of new text in a wide variety of languages and genres on a daily basis (Pimienta, Prado & Blanco 2009).

A vast assortment of text (and recorded spoken language) has been assembled into corpora for linguistic analysis, including large opportunistically assembled collections, such as the English Gigaword corpus (Graff et al. 2007) and the *WaC* Web-Corpora (Baroni et al. 2009), carefully crafted "balanced" corpora, such as the British National Corpus (Aston & Burnard 1998), the Corpus of Contemporary American English (Davies 2009) and the German Reference Corpus (Kupietz & Keibel 2009), and smaller corpora with sophisticated linguistic annotation such as the Penn Treebank (Marcus, Santorini & Marcinkiewicz 1994) and the TIGER Corpus (Brants et al. 2004). In addition, the ubiquity of world-wide-web search-engines such as Google and Bing has effectively put a extremely large, multilingual corpus at the fingertips of virtually every working linguist (Kilgarriff & Grefenstette 2003).

Convenient access to large linguistic corpora is changing not only the way linguists work, but what questions they ask. Questions about subtle patterns of use and about shifts in these patterns are increasingly the focus of attention for linguists of all kinds (as well as for researchers in allied fields; Michel et al. 2011 make fascinating use of a massive multilingual diachronic corpus to track cultural shifts). It is now possible to determine in a few minutes, for example, whether conjoined temporal expressions such as *weeks and months* are typically iconically ordered or not (they are), or whether *going to* has displaced *will* as the premier marker of future reference in English (it hasn't; see Language Log's 2003 series of "Breakfast Experiments"). This shift in focus has brought about a renewed interest in (and debate over) the role of quantitative information in grammatical theory and the relationship between grammar and usage (Bod, Hay & Jannedy 2003; Newmeyer 2003), and with it a new role for corpus-based investigation in the formal study of language (Meurers 2005). In semantics, the availability of corpus data has sparked a renewed focus by theoreticians on lexical semantic issues and on the scope of empirical predictions made by analyses, with an increased appeal made to distributional data and discussion of variation.

While the use of corpus data in semantics research is coming to be more and more common, even to the point of pervading computationally-oriented work, the relationship between corpus-based linguistic analysis and theoretical semantics is tied up in longstanding debates about the nature of linguistic evidence and the goals of linguistic theory. In the next section we will discuss this issue briefly, outline the views of traditional corpus linguists on semantics and discuss the relationship of corpora to linguistic theory in general. We will then turn to a brief discussion of some of the ways in which corpora have been used to further theoretical natural language semantic investigation. In section 4, we turn to semantic annotation of corpora and describe a number of semantic annotation schemes developed by computational linguists. Finally, current work on distributional models of semantics, which characterize word meaning on the basis of statistical properties of its distribution in text, is briefly reviewed.

2 Corpus linguistics and semantics

There is a long tradition of corpus-based language study which has stood in contrast to generative linguistics. Linguists in this tradition, which has been centered in the United Kingdom and traces its origin back to Quirk (1960), have often emphasized that they are primary concerned with the study of "meaning" (Sinclair 2004; Teubert 2005; Stubbs 2009) rather than the study of form or structure. The intuitive, socially-grounded, textual conception of meaning which has been their focus contrasts radically with the referential, truth-conditional tradition of contemporary semantic theory. Facts about truth and entailment, which Cresswell (1982) called the most certain things that we know about meaning, and which constitute the central empirical explananda of contemporary semantic theory, cf. article 1 [Semantics: Foundations, History and Methods] (Maienborn, von Heusinger & Portner) *Meaning in linguistics*, are taken by many corpus-linguists to be outside the acceptable domain of investigation. Instead, meaning is discussed primarily in intertextual terms, with a focus on non-logical lexical relations such as semantic field and collocation. The UCREL lexicon, for example, which was developed in this tradition (Piao et al. 2005), classifies words according thesaurus-style semantic fields (e.g., *Food and Farming, Education*) rather than the logical relations that structure the more classical WordNet lexicon (Fellbaum 1998).

In Teubert's (2005) overview of the goals and methods of corpus linguistics, he emphasizes the primacy of the study of meaning, but he is careful to distinguish the corpus-linguist's view of meaning from that of the "traditional linguist." For the corpus-linguist, he claims, meaning is a paraphrase relation, a relation among words and not a relation between words and the "real world." Meaning for him is also independent of the intentions of the speaker. The meaning of a word is a generalization over its paraphrases: "the meaning of . . . *lemon* is everything that has been said about lemons" (Teubert 2005: 7). It is a property that emerges from the text rather than something that guides its creation. The mechanisms of compositional interpretation are also outside the scope of study. According to Teubert, the corpus linguist "looks at phenomena which cannot be explained by recourse to general rules" (Teubert 2005: 5). Although not all corpus linguists adhere to this perspective, which is more characteristic of the programmatic "corpus driven" view than of the methodological "corpus based" approach (Hardie & McEnery 2010), it does remain a pervasive undercurrent in much corpus-linguistic work, which contrasts starkly with the perspective of contemporary linguistic semantics.

The traditional corpus-linguist is concerned with meaning in much the way a lexicographer is, with a focus on the particular and the lexical. Especially since the publication of the Collins-COBUILD Dictionary, the use of corpora has become central to the working lexicographer (Sinclair 1987; Hanks 2007; Atkins & Rundell 2008). This has lead to a shift in how dictionaries are produced and what they contain. Many publishers now maintain "monitor" corpora, designed specifically for use in updating dictionaries (McEnery, Xiao & Tono 2006). In addition, vast quantities of phrasal information are being compiled in contemporary dictionaries, particularly those designed for non-native speakers of a language, often containing long lists of phrasal patterns for each word, with discussion of meaning variation and examples of use drawn from a wide range of texts (Herbst 1996).

This lexicographic focus on phrasal meaning led John Sinclair, who long championed corpus-based lexicography (Sinclair 1984), to articulate what might be called the corpus-linguists theory of meaning (Sinclair 1996, Sinclair 1998). Noting the range of very particularized meanings associated with phrases in which the singular noun *eye* is used – *turn a blind eye to*, *in the public eye*, *with the naked eye* – Sinclair argued that the unit of meaning is not the word (or lexeme) but an "extended lexical unit" or ELU. Sinclair characterized ELUs in terms of four aspects: COLLOCATION, the relationship between the abstract ELU and the observable word tokens; COLLIGATION, the relationship between the ELU and abstract grammatical categories; SEMANTIC PREFERENCE, the relationship between an ELU and its semantic field; and SEMANTIC PROSODY, what role the ELU is playing in the larger discourse. The phrase *with the naked eye* realizes an ELU in which *naked* and *eye* are collocates. This same ELU is also realized by the phrase *to the naked eye*, and so *with* and *to* are colligates in this ELU. The *naked eye* ELU is a manner adverbial, semantically selecting for visual actions, and is used to imply difficulty, its "semantic prosody."

The central task of semantic corpus investigation, for Sinclair, was to unearth ELUs in text. This kind of work has been significantly aided by the introduction of computational tools for corpus analysis and manipulation, such as automatic concordancers, corpus query systems, key word in context (KWIC) displays and automatic collocation extractors (Garside, Leech & Sampson 1987; Stubbs 2001; Barlow 2004; Cheng, Greaves & Warren 2006). A common technique for this kind of phraseologicial investigation involves simply identifying the most frequent collocates for a given target word and classifying the lexical frames of the collocation pair in intuitive semantic terms. As illustrated in Figure 1, the noun *resemblance* appears in three characteristic phrasal forms with its most frequent collocate *bear*. On Sinclair's view, *bear* and *resemblance* are the central collocates in an ELU that is used to indicate degree of similarity, which has three characteristic phrasal forms:

(1) a. BEAR no *or* little **resemblance** to . . .
 b. BEAR a passing *or* physical **resemblance** to . . .
 c. BEAR a strong *or* striking *or* uncanny **resemblance** to . . .

It is the ELU as a whole that bears meaning, a meaning which, according to Sinclair, is not compositionally determined by the constituting lexical items. On this view, what is traditionally seen as ambiguity is instead a word's (perhaps arbitrary) participation in a number of different extended lexical units. For example, the verb *bear* is not ambiguous; it simply occurs in collocation with *resemblance* as part of the EMU illustrated in (1) and in collocation with *fruit* in a different ELU, this one having a semantic preference for plants (*the tree bore fruit*).

The differences between traditional corpus linguistics and contemporary semantics are well illustrated by contrasting Sinclair's discussion of the verb *budge* with the treatment of such items in the formal semantics literature, cf. article 3 [Semantics: Sentence and Information Structure] (Giannakidou) *Polarity items*. Sinclair characterized this word as part of an Extended Lexical Unit which contains *budge* and an accompanying negative element as collocates. The negative element can be realized by many colligates (e.g. *didn't budge* or *refused to budge*) and occurs "to the left" of *budge* in the phrasal frame. In addition, the *budge* ELU has a semantic preference for grammatical subjects which denote movable entities (literally or figuratively) – such as people or door handles, and the use of the *budge* ELU in a discourse seems

```
            She bore a very strong resemblance to Vera Norman
             campus bore a faint resemblance to a military camp
             Pétain bore some resemblance to the great Turenne
          father bears a passing resemblance to that of the Prince
       proposed so far bear much resemblance to this reality
 performance that has little resemblance to conversational speech
                who bears an amazing resemblance to him.
```

Fig. 14.1: KWIC display of concordance for *resemblance* in the BNC

to imply that there have been attempts at movement that have failed (the semantic prosody). In the contemporary formal semantic tradition, the distribution of *budge* and similar negative polarity items is characterized by the logical properties of the contexts in which they appear. On Ladusaw's (1979) well-known account, for example, *budge* is taken to be licensed when it is in the syntactic scope of downward entailing operators, a class which includes negation, but also the antecedent of a conditional and other non-negative elements. Of course, the notions of scope and entailment which are central to this account are outside the domain of investigation for corpus linguists in the tradition of Teubert and Sinclair.

While the theoretical commitments of traditional or corpus-driven corpus linguists are largely incompatible with those of contemporary semantic theory, the methodology which is employed – large scale investigation of usage data – has entered mainstream semantics, and there are increasingly-many corpus-based analyses of semantic phenomena. It should be noted that the existence of well-designed corpora, annotated with linguistic features such as the parts-of-speech, clausal and sentence boundaries as well as easy-to-use to corpus exploitation software has made this kind of investigation much more widespread (Christ et al. 1999; Bird & Liberman 2001).

3 Theoretical semantics and corpora

In one of the first studies integrating modern corpus methods with semantic theory, Barker (1998) analyzed the English suffix *-ee*, characterzing the relationship between such verb/noun pairs as *stand* and *standee*. Barker used corpus-based quantitative productivity measures (Baayen & Lieber 1991) to show that *-ee* is indeed a productive suffix – and thus that it's analysis must be compositional – and made reference to a large corpus of *-ee* derived nouns, which he compiled, to inform this analysis. The corpus data showed that there are many cases (*amputee*, for example), for which the denotation of the derived *-ee* noun does not appear to be related to the source verb's thematic arguments (e.g., the Agent or Patient of *amputate*). To account for the entire range of data, Barker introduced the more general semantic notion of "episodic linking." (Barker's corpus-based perspective on this phenomenon was taken up more recently on a web-scale by Mühleisen 2010.) Barker's study illustrates important ways in which corpus investigation can inform semantic theory: It can extend the empirical reach of a theory and it can underscore the relevance of certain data to analysis. Barker showed both that a compositional account of *-ee* affixation was needed and that the predictions of prior such analyses were not borne out by the data.

As Partee (1979), points out, theoretical semantics (and theoretical linguistics in general) typically addresses only a selected sample of idealized data. These data are gleaned from the literature, from introspection, from conversation and chance encounter, with an ill-understood idealization process selecting data which are relevant to the theoretical question at hand. This unconstrained, haphazard process has made researchers uncomfortable about its reliability (e.g., Schütze 1996). Corpora can play an important role in moderating this idealization process (Meurers 2005; Pullum 2007) by confronting theoretical claims with a wide range of data. Sæbø (2004) illustrates this by examining the distribution of Free-Choice *any* from a corpus-linguistic perspective. Corpus-based investigation of polarity items and their licensing environments has been an active area of research for a number of years (Hoeksema 1997, Richter, Sailer & Trawiński 2010). Because of the close relationship between the distribution of negative polarity items (NPIs) and their licensing operators, researchers have been able to work in two directions: characterizing the set of licensing operators by observing the distribution of polarity items and specifying the set of NPIs by observing their distribution with known licensers (Soehn, Trawiński & Lichte 2010).

In the context of Free-Choice *any*, Sæbø evaluated the empirical predictions of Kadmon & Landman's (1993) well-known and widely accepted theory and compared it to those of Dayal's (1998) competing approach. On the Kadmon & Landman theory, FC *any* is hypothesized to be a domain-widened version of the generic indefinite, and is taken to be licensed whenever the generic indefinite is. Sæbø discovered that many uses of FC *any* – nearly half the occurrences in his corpus – were in sentences such as (2), in which generic *a* would be infelicitous, however.

(2) Ruth resigned herself to the irony of reading a murder mystery; but, at the moment, Ruth would have read {anything/??a thing} to escape her own imagination.

Such examples had gone unnoticed (or unremarked) by linguists committed to the domain-widening analysis. In addition to unearthing this fact, Sæbø also discovered that nearly every occurrence of FC *any* in his corpus was in the scope of a modal expression (or in an implicitly-modal context). The corpus data, then, would appear to support Dayal's alternative "modal-licensing" theory on which FC *any* must be licensed by a modal operator scoping over it. Sæbø suggests that this investigation is indicative of the role corpus study can play in theoretical semantics, as the corpus provides a readily-available, theory-neutral source of naturalistic data against which a given theory can be tested.

Harris & Potts' (2009) study of appositives illustrates this point further. Potts (2005) had claimed that appositives and expressives are invariably speaker oriented. Counterexamples to this claim had appeared in the literature, and Harris and Potts sought to assess these counterexamples. Assembling a 177 million word corpus, they were able to provide convincing evidence that indeed non-speaker-oriented appositive attribution (as in *Israel says Arad was captured by Dirani, who may have then sold him to Iran*) is a systematic part of the grammar. Harris & Pott's study is notable also because it illustrates a way in which the relationship of corpus-data to linguistic theory has changed as the size of corpora have grown. It was once certainly true that most constructions of theoretical interest, such as the sentence-final non-restrictive relative clauses adjoined to attitude-verb complements that Harris & Potts were investigating, couldn't be expected to occur frequently enough in a corpus for such data to be relevant to theoretical debate. In the early 1 million word Brown Corpus (Francis & Kučera 1982), for example, there are just six sentences of this type, all of them speaker-oriented. As available corpora have grown larger, however, we increasingly find realistic data from corpora used to support theoretical claims in a wide range of studies, taking advantage of what Meurers (2005) called the "rich variation" of corpus data. We are approaching a time, it seems, that corpus-evidence will be available for any construction of interest.

Corpus data isn't always used to test a theory, however, sometimes corpus data are simply used to provide evidence that a semantic observation is actually part of a productive process that deserves analysis. Heycock & Zamparelli (2005), for example, used data from the British National Corpus to show that coordinated nominals such as *friend and colleague* are used productively with both the joint (*she as a friend and colleague*) and the split (*her friend and colleague argued*) interpretation. The existence of many clearly non-idiomatic, split-interpreted coordinated DPs motivated their effort to rethink the the syntax and semantics of coordination, cf. article 4 [Semantics: Sentence and Information Structure] (Zamparelli) *Coordination*.

Corpora are also used to provide evidence for subtle semantic distinctions otherwise hard to support. Kennedy & McNally (2005) used corpus counts in the BNC to argue for a classification of gradable predicates, cf. article 8 [Semantics: Lexical Structures and Adjectives] (Kennedy) *Ambiguity and vagueness*. They show that gradable adjectival participles exhibit a near-complementary distribution with the modifiers *very*, *much* and *well*. Although the contrasts are subtle (compare *much acquainted*, *well acquainted*, and *very acquainted*), the actual distributions are striking, as illustrated in Table 14.1.

Tab. 14.1: Distribution of degree modifiers in the BNC (adopted from Kennedy & McNally (2005))

	WELL	VERY	MUCH
acquainted	56	0	0
protected	58	2	0
documented	213	0	1
edcuated	78	3	0
needed	2	0	211
criticised	0	0	19
praised	1	0	17
appreciated	12	0	124
surprised	0	151	1
worried	0	192	0
frightened	0	92	0
interested	0	335	10

In related work, Sassoon (2010) used corpus data to buttress her claim that ratio modifiers *(twice/half)* do not combine with negative adjectives such as *short*, showing that such expressions as *twice as short* appear dramatically less frequently than do expressions such as *twice as tall*.

In many cases, the range of empirical phenomena becomes much clearer when large amounts of data are brought to bear. For example, one of the puzzles in the literature on the resultative construction has been to account for the pattern of acceptability illustrated (3).

(3) a. wipe the table clean/dry/*dirty/*wet
    b. hammer the metal flat/smooth/*beautiful/*safe/*tubular

Wechsler (2005) made use of Boas' (2000) extensive corpus study of this construction, containing over 6000 occurrences, to explore the semantic properties of adjectives appearing in it. He showed both that the pattern of acceptability illustrated in (3) is reflected in usage data – those adjectives that have been claimed to be ruled out are, indeed, quite rare in this construction – and that the adjectives that do appear in this construction can be characterized as being minimal standard, closed-scale adjectives, in terms of Kennedy & McNallys classification scheme. Because the data for the Kennedy & McNally classification and for acceptability in the resultative construction are both delicate, the weight of lexical evidence emerging from the corpus study was crucial to uncovering this generalization.

Finally there are cases in which hidden aspects of the range of variation that had not been noted previously are revealed through corpus investigation. Beaver, Francez & Levinson (2005), for example, examined the rates of use of different quantifying determiners in canonical (non-existential) sentences and in existential (*there*-subject) sentences, as measured through internet search. Traditional semantic accounts have suggested that there is a clear and categorical distinction between "weak" quantifiers such as *a* and *some* and "strong" quantifiers such as *every* and *most*, cf. article 8 [Semantics: Sentence and Information Structure] (McNally) *Existential sentences*. As illustrated in Figure 14.2, the corpus data reveal a more variegated pattern, however.

While "weak" and "strong" quantifiers are seen to have quite different distributions, it is clear that many more factors influence use than just this contrast.

In each of these cases, usage data has been brought to bear on questions of theoretical interest by examining lexical distribution. To investigate more abstract semantic phenomena, such as anaphoric binding or argument role assignment, requires more than information about raw lexical distribution, however. It requires that corpora be annotated with information about the intended interpretation of a given utterance. This kind of SEMANTIC ANNOTATION has been carried out – in large part by computational linguists – for a range of semantic phenomena, from lexical interpretation to event ordering to anaphora-antecedent relations. In the next section

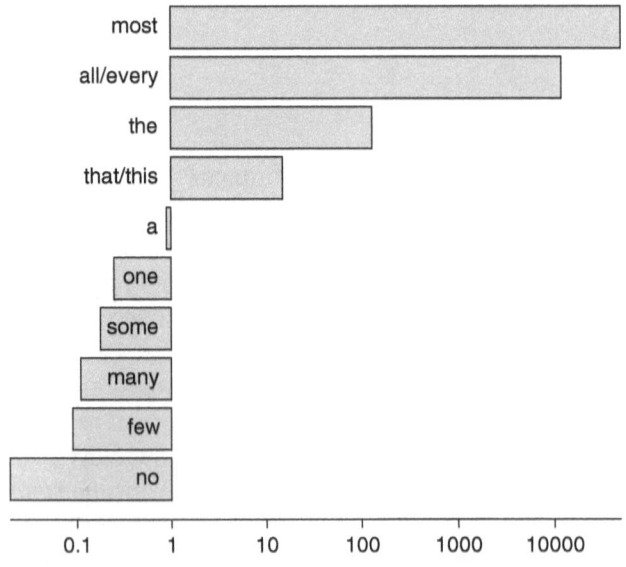

Fig. 14.2: Canonical to existential ratios (log), after Beaver, Francez & Levinson (2005).

we turn to semantic annotation. (It should be noted that the term "semantic annotation" is used in a related way in the context of the SEMANTIC WEB for the annotation of content in internet web-pages, cf. article 17 [this volume] (Buitelaar) *Web Semantics*.)

4 Semantic annotation

Computational linguists have treated semantic annotation as a way of extracting from speakers information about aspects of the interpretation of a text which are of particular interest. Much research in semantic annotation has focussed on three fundamental aspects of meaning: Reference, word meaning, and semantic role assignment. Consider the first two sentences of the Brown corpus:

(4) The Fulton County Grand Jury said Friday an investigation of Atlanta's recent primary election produced "no evidence" that any irregularities took place. The September-October term jury had been charged by Fulton Superior Court Judge Durwood Pye to investigate reports of possible "irregularities" in the hard-fought primary which was won by Mayor-nominate Ivan Allen Jr. (Francis & Kučera 1982)

The task of NAMED ENTITY ANNOTATION involves specifying the objects that the nominal expressions in a text refer to (e.g. determining the referents of *Fulton County*, *Durwood Pye*, and *Friday*), typically by associating the expressions with entities in a database. The task of WORD SENSE ANNOTATION involves specifying the intended meaning for an ambiguous word in context (e.g., the word *charge* here refers to an order and not an accusation). The task of SEMANTIC ROLE LABELING involves specifying what role entities play in the events described (e.g., Pye is the person doing the charging and not the person being charged). Additional types of semantic annotation are: TIME AND EVENT ANNOTATION – specifying the temporal relations that hold among the events described in a text (e.g., the election victory was before the investigation); COREFERENCE ANNOTATION and ANAPHORA ANNOTATION – identifying expressions in a text that co-refer or are referentially dependent (e.g., *Fulton County Grand Jury* and *September-October term jury* corefer); and DISCOURSE ANNOTATION – specifying discourse relations that hold among clauses (e.g., the second sentence in (4) provides background for first).

Semantic annotation tasks can be roughly classified into two types: *language-oriented* annotation and *content-oriented* annotation. Language-oriented annotation involves the association of words and phrases in a corpus with information in a lexical database. Such annotation makes use of a language-particular resource such as a dictionary. Content-oriented annotation involves associating linguistic elements in a corpus with non-linguistic values – time stamps, dollar amounts, or items in a database such as a list of names or gazeteer of places. The most prominent content-oriented annotation schemes are those developed as part of the Translingual Information Detection, Extraction and Summarization (TIDES) program (Cieri & Liberman 2002) and the Automatic Content Extraction (ACE) initiative (Doddington et al. 2004).

4.1 Annotation methodology

Creating a semantically annotated corpus, of whatever sort, involves three subtasks: the design of an annotation scheme (or "annotation language"), the selection of a corpus to be annotated, and the specification of how to apply the annotation scheme to the corpus, in the form of an annotation guideline. For complex annotation tasks such as time and event annotation, the annotation guidelines (and the annotation language) tend to undergo a series of modifications in the face challenges met by annotators in the course of preliminary corpus-annotation. As Zaenen (2006) points out, the intuitive accessibility of many semantic concepts belies the complexity of natural language semantic analysis, and annotation languages and guidelines – particularly those designed by computational linguists with practical goals in mind – often fail to be adequately researched. This often leads to a series of extensive revision in the face of problematic cases. For example in a time and event annotation task, annotators might come across the phrase *September-October term jury* in (4) and wonder how, or even whether, it should be annotated, a question that involves non-trivial considerations about the lexical semantics of the noun *jury*. Or in a coreference task, the question of whether *the hard fought primary* corefers with *Atlanta's recent primary election* might come up. These cases are adjudicated on a case-by-case basis and documented in the annotation guidelines (e.g., "temporal adverbials modifying expressions referring to individuals or groups of individuals need not be annotated"). Annotation guidelines tend to be long documents full of detailed discussion of individual cases and how they were adjudicated; the TimeML annotation guideline (Saurí et al. 2006) is about six times as long as the TimeML specification (Pustejovsky et al. 2003a), for example.

To evaluate the clarity of the annotation guidelines, the difficulty of the annotation task and the quality of the annotators, quantitative measures of INTER-ANNOTATOR AGREEMENT are used. The most common of these is the inter-annotator AGREEMENT RATE, which is computed by comparing multiple independent annotations of the same corpus. High inter-annotator agreement indicates that the annotation task and annotation guidelines are well-chosen and that the annotators can apply them consistently. Inter-annotator agreement rates on semantic annotation tasks vary from under 60% for certain word sense annotation tasks (Ng, Lim & Foo 1999) to nearly 95% for certain semantic role labeling tasks (Palmer, Gildea & Kingsbury 2005). A measure which is more useful for comparing across annotation schemes is the κ coefficient, which Carletta (1996) imported from the field of content analysis (Cohen 1960; Krippendorff 1980). This value measures the degree to which annotators agree beyond what would be expected by chance. A κ value of 0 corresponds to agreement at rates expected by chance. This measure has become the *de facto* standard for measuring inter-annotator agreement (Artstein & Poesio 2008), with values above 0.70 taken to indicate reliable annotation.

Further complexity in measuring inter-annotator agreement arises when annotation is not just simple classification, but where partial agreement is common, as in the case of co-reference annotation (Passonneau 2004), or where there are complex semantic relations among the annotations, as in the case of temporal annotation (Katz & Arosio 2001). For example in a temporal annotation task with annotators specifying the order of events in a texts, consider comparing the annotations in (5).

(5) Ann_1: **before**(a,b), **before**(a,c)
    Ann_2: **before**(a,b), **before**(b,c)

The most straightforward measurement, which counts exact agreement (giving a 50% agreement rate here), fails to take into account the implicit information contained in Ann_2. A measure based on information would seem appropriate, but such measures face challenges in handling inconsistent annotations (as in comparing Ann_2 with Ann'_1: **before**(a,b), **before**(a,c), **before**(c,b)). It is still quite unclear how exactly to measure partial "semantic agreement."

In the next sections we briefly describe a range of semantic annotation schemas. While we don't seek to be exhaustive, the range of schemes discussed provides a snapshot of the current state of the art (see also article 16 [this volume] (Frank & Padó) *Semantics in computational lexicons*). We will first overview some of the major language-oriented semantic annotation schemes and then the major content-oriented schemes.

4.2 Language-oriented annotation

Language-oriented annotation involves associating elements of a linguistic resource – a lexicon, for example – with tokens in a corpus. Miller (1995) identified two strategies for annotation: the "targeted" (or "lexicon-based") approach, and the "sequential" (or "corpus-based") approach. On the targeted approach, lexical entries are primary and the corpus is used as a resource for testing and improvement of the lexicon. On the corpus-based approach, the corpus is primary, and words in the corpus are annotated as they come, with the lexicon serving only as a resource for the annotation. Targeted annotation yields a set of illustrative cases for each entry in the lexical resource without generating a true annotated corpus, while corpus-based annotation yields a fully annotated corpus but might not lead to the creation of a complete lexicon. To mitigate the deficiencies of each strategy, language-oriented annotation efforts have often incorporate some aspects of both.

4.2.1 Word senses annotation

The task of word-sense annotation is illustrated in (6):

(6) a. Next to her was a white haired gentleman wearing a cap_1 and heavy rural looking jacket.
 b. A cap_2 is included to cover the hole not used for mounting.

The ambiguous word *cap* is annotated with a specification of the intended meaning, here the clothing sense in (6a) and the covering sense in (6b). Sense annotation clearly requires that annotators be provided with a sense inventory, a set of senses and sense descriptions for each word. Indeed, the first large-scale word-sense annotation project, the HECTOR lexicon project (Atkins 1992; Glassman et al. 1992), a joint effort of Oxford University Press and DEC, involved the parallel development of an annotated 300,000 word corpus and an inventory of senses covering 500 words. Since the mid-1990s, however, word-sense annotation for English has almost exclusively used WordNet as a sense inventory (Ng & Lee 1996; Landes, Leacock & Tendi 1998; Passonneau et al. 2010).

WordNet, which was conceived of as a "dictionary based on psycholinguistic principles" (Miller et al. 1990), is a sophisticated lexical resource, encoding not only a senses for each word, but a range of semantic relations among these senses (Miller 1995; Fellbaum 1998), such as *synonymy*, *antonymy*, *hyponymy*, and *meronymy*, cf. article 6 [Semantics: Lexical Structures and Adjectives] (Cann) *Sense relations*. Incorporating two decades of incremental improvement WordNet currently encodes semantic information for nearly 150,000 words of English (Miller & Fellbaum 2007). There have been two large-scale sense-annotation projects based directly on WordNet. In the SEMCOR project (Landes, Leacock & Tengi 1998) all the occurrences of nouns, verbs, adjectives and adverbs that appear in a subset of the Brown corpus – in total 234,843 – were annotated with WordNet sense tags. In the DSO project (Ng & Lee 1996), a similar number of tokens taken from a more limited set of the most frequent ambiguous nouns (121) and verbs (70) were annotated.

Word-sense annotation has proved to be surprisingly difficult task (Fellbaum, Grabowski & Landes 1998). Ng, Lim & Foo (1999) compared the annotations in the overlapping parts of the SEMCOR and DSO corpora, finding an interannotator agreement rate of just 57%, with κ values of less than 0.4. One explanation for this difficult is that WordNet encodes finer-grained distinctions than annotators can easily draw (Palmer, Dang & Fellbaum 2007). For example, WordNet distinguishes four physical movement senses of the verb *shake*, distinguishing manners of vibration from tremors to swaying. In a sentence such as *His arm shook*, however, it is hard to know which is intended, or even if the speaker intended to draw a distinction at all. Two factors that have been shown to improve interannotator agreement on word sense tagging are training (Kilgarriff 1999; Passonneau et al. 2010) and targeted crafting of the sense inventory (Ng, Lim & Foo 1999; Palmer, Dang & Fellbaum 2007). It was found that using syntactic criteria such as subcategorization frame to help draw sense distinctions was particularly helpful to annotators.

4.2.2 Semantic role annotation

Semantic role annotation involves specifying for each predicate in a sentence what semantic role its syntactic arguments and adjuncts play (Márquez et al. 2008; Palmer, Gildea & Xue 2010), cf. article 3 [Semantics: Lexical Structures and Adjectives] (Davis) *Thematic roles*. The Proposition Bank, or PropBank (Palmer, Gildea & Kingsbury 2005), and FrameNet (Baker, Fillmore & Cronin 2003) represent the two most prominent such schemes.

PropBank is a set of semantic role annotations for the syntactic arguments and adjuncts of verbal predicates in the syntactically-annotated Penn Treebank corpus. The roles used for annotation are specified in a lexical resource, the Frameset inventory. The set of frames for *open*, given in (7), serves as the basis for the annotation in (8), for example.

(7) Frameset **open.01**, "cause to open"
    Arg0: agent
    Arg1: thing opened
    Arg2: instrument

(8) [$_{Arg0}$ John] opened [$_{Arg1}$ the door] [$_{Arg2}$ with his foot]

In contrast to word-sense annotation, PropBank semantic role annotation is quite reliable (with κ-scores above 0.9). Note that in PropBank each sense of each verb is provided with its own set of semantic roles. VerbNet (Kipper-Schuler 2005) is a related lexical resource which encodes more abstract information about semantic frames. VerbNet frames are associated with classes of verbs, rather than single verbs, and contain generalized semantic roles, such as Agent and Patient. Also related is the NomBank project (Meyers et al. 2004), which has sought to annotate the arguments of nominal predicates, with Framesets constructed to provide direct mapping between roles for verbs in PropBank and roles for derivationally-related nouns in NomBank, so that *John's opening of the door with his foot* would be annotated analogously to (8).

The other major semantic role annotation project is FrameNet (Baker, Fillmore & Cronin 2003; Ruppenhofer et al. 2010). While PropBank is primarily a corpus-annotation effort, FrameNet is primarily a lexical-resource development effort. Building on Fillmore's (1982) insight that much in the semantic representation of a predicate is encoded in the semantic frames that the predicate evokes, cf. article 3 [Semantics: Theories] (Gawron) *Frame Semantics*, the FrameNet lexicon seeks to provide a complete semantic representation of a predicate through the information encoded in the role specifications. In FrameNet, words are associated with sets of very fine-grained semantic roles (called "frames") which are evoked by the word. These specify characteristic aspects of the typical situations described by the word; the verb *fry*, for example, evokes the APPLY_HEAT frame, which has the associated semantic roles COOK, FOOD and HEATING_INSTRUMENT. Other verbs evoking this frame are *bake, poach* and *roast*. These roles are used to annotate sentences by associating the roles with words and phrases, as illustrated in (9).

(9) [COOK Matilde] fried [FOOD the catfish] [HEATING_INSTRUMENT in a heavy iron skillet]

FrameNet roles are associated with rich semantic information. A **Cook** is an agent, likely to be a person, acting intentionally to achieve a goal. FrameNet frames are not limited to encoding information for verbs; semantic frames for nouns, adjectives, adverbs, and prepositions are part of FrameNet. FrameNet, like WordNet, has been developed in a lexicon-driven manner, with annotation of sentences from the BNC used to explore the ranges of meanings associated with individual lexical elements. FrameNet's lexical database of more than 10,000 lexical entries has been used to annotate over 135,000 sentences from the BNC (Ruppenhofer et al. 2010), with inter-annotator agreement reported on both frames and roles to be approximately 90%.

FrameNet-style lexical resources and annotated corpora are under construction for a number of languages, including Italian, German, Japanese, Spanish, and Hebrew (Boas 2009). The SALSA project (Burchardt et al. 2009) is particularly noteworthy, having used a FrameNet-style semantic resource for the annotation of the German TIGER treebank (Brants et al. 2004) in a sequential, corpus-driven way. Since FrameNet is semantically rich, it was largely possible for the SALSA team to use frames developed for English words to annotate German sentences. The Assistance frame, for example, (which is evoked by *help*, *aid*, etc.) was used to annotate the German verb *helfen* as in (10):

(10) [$_{\text{HELPER}}$ Luise] hilft [$_{\text{CO-AGENT}}$ Hans, [$_{\text{GOAL}}$ das Geschirr zu spülen]

Multilingual FrameNet annotation presents a number of interesting opportunities for investigating cross-linguistic similarities and differences in lexicalization patterns and patterns of subcategorization and argument selection (Padó & Lapata 2009).

4.2.3 Discourse and dialog annotation

Researchers interested in discourse and dialog have been involved in the annotation of a variety of semantic/pragmatic relationships that hold among phrases or utterances. One strand of research describes the structure of a text via the DISCOURSE COHERENCE RELATIONS that hold among discourse segments, cf. article 13 [Semantics: Sentence and Information Structure] (Kehler) *Cohesion and coherence*. Another body of work involves the analysis of dialog and the flow of conversation in terms of sequences of DIALOG ACTS or CONVERSATIONAL MOVES (Franck 1979; Traum 2000). Each of these research programs has had an important corpus-based component.

Interpreting connected discourse involves determining how the pieces of a discourse are understood with respect to one another. It is commonly assumed that units of discourse– clauses or sequences of clauses (*discourse segments*) are linked by a small number of discourse-coherence ("rhetorical") relations, cf. article 13 [Semantics: Theories] (Zeevat) *Rhetorical relations*. Corpus-based investigation of these relations has involved the annotation of naturally occurring text with information about which relations hold among what elements in the text. Carlson, Marcu & Okurowski (2001) used Mann & Thompson's (1988) tree-based Rhetorical Structure Theory as the basis for their discourse structure annotation scheme, marking the rhetorical relations between clauses and sets of clauses using a set of 78 relations (e.g., *evidence*, *reason*, *purpose*, *consequence*, *question-answer*, etc.). As illustrated in (11), the annotation involved both specifying the segments to be related (here the discourse segments marked 1, 2 and 3) and specifying the relations among the discourse segments.

(11) [Norfolk is likely to draw down its cash initially]$_1$ [to finance the purchases]$_2$ [and thus forfeit some interest income.]$_3$
   2 is the **purpose** of 1; 3 is a **consequence** of 1–2

This scheme was applied to 385 Wall Street Journal articles from the Penn Treebank. On average there were about 56 discourse segments per article. In a similar task, Wolf & Gibson (2005) used a more parsimonious set of 12 discourse relations-based on Hobbs' (1985) ontology of coherence relations – *cause-effect, condition, violated expectation, elaboration*, etc. – and relaxed the adjacency requirement commonly assumed for discourse relations. Both Carlson, Marcu & Okurowski (2001) and Wolf & Gibson (2005) report very high inter-annotator agreement on the annotation of discourse relations (with κ scores over. 80 reported for both schemes). Wolf & Gibson also report that 12.5% of the discourse relations annotated in their corpus relate non-adjacent segments, indicating significant deviation from the tree-structure commonly assumed for discourse relation structures.

Discourse relations are often signaled overtly by discourse connectives or cue phrases, such as *because, for example, since* or *then*, as in (12), cf. article 15 [Semantics: Sentence and Information Structure] (Zimmermann) *Discourse particles*.

(12) *Since* [the drought reduced U.S. stockpiles], [they have more than enough storage space for their new crop]

Discourse connectives are typically ambiguous – *since*, for example, has both temporal and causal senses. The Penn Discourse Treebank (PDTB) (Miltsakaki et al. 2004; Prasad et al. 2008) is a discourse-connective annotation of the entire Wall Street Journal subpart of the Penn Treebank, in which 40,000 explicit and implicit discourse connectives were annotated using a hierarchical set of discourse-relations sense tags. PDTB annotation involved specifying both the intended relation and the elements related (as suggested in (12)). Overall inter-annotator agreement was reported as quite high for both tasks, with agreement even at the finest grain being over 80%.

Corpus-based analysis has also played a central role in research on multi-agent dialog, and there have been a number of targeted dialog collection projects in which data is collected from pairs or groups of individuals engaged in some sort of goal-oriented cooperative problem solving task. In the HCRC MapTask project, for example, a corpus of 128 wayfinding dialogs was collected, in which pairs of speakers conversed about navigating a fictional domain. These dialogs were then annotated with dialog structure information indicating the type of dialog move for each utterance (Anderson et al. 1991; Carletta et al. 1997), as illustrated in (13).

(13) G: And then, have you got the pirate ship?   **QUERY**
　　 F: Mmhmm.　　　　　　　　　　　　　　**REPLY-YES**
　　 G: Just curve from the point, go right ...

           go down and curve into the right
           til you reach the tip of the pirate ship   **INSTRUCT**
    F: So across the bay?   **CHECK**
    G: Yeah, through the water.   **CLARIFY**

Similarly, in the University of Rochester TRAINS project (Allen 1991) a large number of dialogs involving joint planmaking under partial information were collected and annotated with dialog structure information (Heeman & Allen 1995). This preliminary work led to the creation of the Dialog Act Markup in Several Layers (or DAMSL) standard for dialog move annotation (Core & Allen 1997), which has subsequently been used to annotate the Switchboard telephone conversation corpus (Stolcke et al. 2000), and other corpora.

Elicited dialog corpora have become important resources for the analysis not only of discourse and dialog structure but also of the attentional and indexical aspects of spatial reference and of anaphoric and definite reference (Poesio & Vieira 1998; Eckert & Strube 2000; Coventry, Tenbrink & Bateman 2009). Particularly in the case of anaphoric reference, there is a longstanding research program in both computational linguistics and more traditional discourse analysis making use of corpora to investigate the factors that go into determining the antecedent of an anaphoric expression, as they relate to sentence structure, discourse structure, and a wide range of other factors (Hobbs 1978; Fox 1987; Biber 1992; Lappin & Leass 1994; McEnery 2000).

4.2.4 Anaphora and definite reference

Large-scale annotation of anaphoric relations in corpora was pioneered by Fligelstone (1992) in the context of the Lancaster "grammar factory" (Garside, Leech & McEnery 1997). An annotation schema was developed for specifying referential dependency relations among expressions in texts, as in (14).

(14) On Monday [the company]$_1$ reported higher fourth quarter earnings, raised its$_1$ dividend and announced plans for a 3-for-2 stock split.

The annotation scheme included specification for the annotation of VP anaphora, discourse deixis and ellipsis, as well as a range of other anaphoric phenomena (see also Tutin et al. 2000) for a discussion of the range of anaphoric phenomena).

Corpora annotated with information about anaphoric relations have played an important role in the development and evaluation of cognitive models of anaphoric processing cf. article 14 [Semantics: Sentence and Information Structure]

(Geurts) *Accessibility and anaphora*. Gundel, Hedberg & Zacharski (1993), for example, argue for a universal Givenness hierarchy (IN FOCUS > ACTIVATED > FAMILIAR > UNIQUELY IDENTIFIABLE > REFERENTIAL > TYPE IDENTIFIABLE) on the basis of the annotation of naturally occurring referring expressions in a number of small corpora. They show that each level in the hierarchy is preferentially signaled by a certain type of referring expression. For example, pronominal expressions are primarily used to refer to IN FOCUS elements, demonstratives to refer to FAMILIAR (but not IN FOCUS) elements. Tetreault (2001) used anaphorically-annotated corpus to evaluate a variety of algorithms for resloving anaphoric dependencies, demonstrating the effectiveness of his variant of centering theory. Bosch, Katz & Umbach (2007) show that the differences distribution of antecedents for demonstrative and personal pronouns in corpora reflects preferences in interpretation evident in comprehension experiments.

Corpus-based methodology has also been used to investigate constraints on the use of definite and indefinite expressions cf. article 2 [Semantics: Noun Phrases and Verb Phrases] (Heim) *Definiteness and indefiniteness*. Poesio & Vieira (1998) annotated sentences from the Wall Street Journal corpus, classifying definite expressions according to their use: anaphoric (*a car ... the Chevy*), bridging (*a car ... the tire*), discourse new (*the first person in line*), and broader context (*the king*). Confirming previous corpus work (Fraurud 1990), they found that about half of the definite expressions uses in the corpus were classified as anaphoric, with the other half unrelated to discourse entities mentioned in the text, raising interesting questions for uniqueness and familiarity theories of definiteness.

In order to better study relationships among various types of semantic processes and structures, in recent years there has been a move toward annotation integration. For example Kibrik & Krasavina (2005) integrate anaphoric annotation with annotation of rhetorical structure. Stede (2004) includes rhetorical structure, information structure and anaphoric reference. Particularly noteworthy is the OntoNotes project (Hovy et al. 2006) which combines word-sense annotation, semantic role annotation and anaphoric reference annotation for a variety of text genres. OntoNotes annotation also associates words with elements in a non-linguistic structured ontology of concepts. This is a step towards the kind of annotation we have termed "content oriented," in which linguistic items are associated with non-linguistic elements. In the next section we briefly turn to this type of semantic annotation.

4.3 Content-oriented annotation

Content-oriented corpus annotation originated with the Message Understanding Conferences (MUC-1 through MUC-7) of the early 1990s (Grishman & Sundheim

1996), designed to foster research on the automatic extraction of information from texts. While the early MUC challenges focussed on a few handpicked data-base templates related to specific pieces of information of interest (e.g. naval engagements or terrorist events), starting with MUC-6 more general domain-independent semantic tasks such as named-entity identification and co-reference recognition were introduced. A set of content-annotated corpora were created in this context.

Content-oriented annotation involves the association of linguistic elements in a text with non-linguistic entities, as indicated in (15), for example, where the linguistic elements are "tagged" with referential information.

(15) <ENAMEX TYPE = "CORPORATION" ID = "APL"> Apple computer </ENAMEX>
<TIMEX VAL = "1997-7-9"> today <TIMEX> hired
<ENAMEX TYPE = "PERSON" ID = "Steven Paul Jobs"> Steve Jobs </ENAMEX>

An attribute on an XML tag marks the intended semantic interpretation of the expression tagged. Temporal expressions (TIMEXs) and numerical values are associated with a normalized value in a standardized notation, such as the ISO 8601 standard for temporal and calendrical expressions. Names (ENAMEXs) and other referential expressions are associated with entries in a databases such as a gazetteer (for places), a stock-exchange listing (for corporations) or a bibliographic listing (for authors and books).

For the past decade, the Automatic Content Extraction (ACE) initiative (Doddington et al. 2004) has been developing guidelines for general content-based annotation. The ACE guidelines are intended to support a wide variety of industrial-scale text-content analysis. The current ACE guidelines describe three main types of annotation: Entity Detection and Tracking, Relation Detection and Characterization, and Event Detection and Characterization. Entity detection, the primary task, involves identifying referring expressions in a text and classifying them, as one of the following seven classes: Person, Organization, Location, Facility, Weapon, Vehicle, Geo-Political Entity. As Zaenen (2006) has pointed out, although identifying referents appears to be a straightforward task, in fact significant subtlety is required. Annotators must determine whether there is a reference to the city of New York in the phrase *The New York Times* or to the country of Vietnam in the phrase *the Vietnam Memorial*. They must also determine when expressions such as *the White House* are used metonymically (to refer, for example, to the entire executive branch) and whether terms such as *president* and *teacher* are being used to refer to an individual or a role. These issues become pronounced – as Deemter & Kibble (2000) noted – when annotators are asked to determine coreference.

Co-reference annotation was introduced as part of the MUC-6 program, and has been an important part of content-oriented annotation efforts since then (Hirschman & Chinchor 1997; Passonneau 2004). COREF, as it has come to be known, involves partitioning the set of referring expressions in a text into sets, so called "co-reference chains," which all refer to the same object. The referring elements in (16), might be partitioned into the following coreference chains: {A, D}, {B, E, F, K}, {C, H, I}, {G, J}.

(16) Committee approval of [Gov. Price Daniel]$_a$'s [abandoned property act]$_B$ seemed certain Thursday despite the protests of [Texas bankers]$_C$. [Daniel]$_D$ personally led the fight for [the measure]$_E$ Under committee rules, [it]$_F$ went automatically to a subcommittee for one week. But questions with which [committee members]$_G$ taunted [bankers]$_H$ appearing as [witnesses]$_I$ left little doubt that [they]$_J$ will recommend passage of [it]$_K$

Co-reference annotation raises a number of issues for evaluating inter-annotator agreement, since annotators might disagree with one another both on the number of coreference chains there are (the number of objects under discussion) and which elements belong in the same chain. In (16) for example, annotators might disagree on whether C is part of the {H, I} chain or forms a chain of its own. This question is made difficult because H might be a subset of C or of I (or of both). Deemter & Kibble (2000) cite this kind of partial co-reference as one of the limitations of annotation based only on an intuitive notion of shared reference, arguing for more sophisticated annotation based on the many ways in which terms can be referentially related.

The most complex of the content-oriented annotation tasks is that involving times and events. The most thoroughly worked-out annotation language for time and event annotation is TimeML (Pustejovsky et al. 2005). TimeML is based on the Davidsonian idea that sentences describe events, cf. article 8 [Semantics: Theories] (Maienborn) *Event semantics*, and TimeML is a way of describing event-relations in an annotation language. This is illustrated in (17).

(17) ```
The Berlin wall <EVENT eid = "e1" class = "OCCURRENCE">
fell </EVENT> <TIMEX3 tid = "t1" val = "1989-11-8">
yesterday </TIMEX>.
<TLINK relatedEventID = "e1" relatedTime = "t1"
relType = "IsIncluded"/>
```

This annotation indicates that the text describes an event of the Berlin wall falling that took place within the temporal interval of November 8, 1989. TimeML contains two types of annotation tags. Referential tags such as EVENT and TIMEX3
```

are used to identify temporal expressions and event expressions and to associate them with values and identifiers. Relational tags such as TLINK are used to relate these entities.

In addition to temporal relations, TimeML encodes information about modal and aspectual dependencies using two other linking relations, SLINKs and ALINKs. SLINKs indicate modal relations between events, crucially distinguishing actual from possible events, as illustrated in (18).

(18) ... Boston center <EVENT eid = "e2" class = "I_ACTION"> tries </EVENT>
to <EVENT eid = "e24" class = "OCCURRENCE"> raise </EVENT> TWA 800.
<SLINK relType = "MODAL" eventID = "e22" subordinatedEventID = "e24"/>

ALINKS encode the relationship between events and their aspectual parts, typically relating verbs such as *begin* and *end* to their complements. TimeML was used to annotate 183 news articles to create the 61,000 word TIMEBANK corpus (Pustejovsky et al. 2003b). A similar annotation language for encoding relational and referential information about events and places known as SpatialML has also been developed (Mani et al. 2010).

TimeML, SpatialML and other sophisticated semantic annotation schemes (such as ACE), which are used to represent complex semantic information, have come to resemble true semantic representation languages. This resemblance points toward a potential convergence between research in formal semantics and corpus-based semantic annotation. In fact some have begun to treat semantic annotation as akin to formal semantic representation – Bunt (2007), for example, has argued that semantic annotation languages should be provided with a formal semantic interpretation, sketching such an analysis for TimeML. Formal analysis can play an important role in assuring the adequacy and consistency of the annotation language, assuring that the intuitive semantics associated with the description of the scheme and implicit in the annotation guidelines is reflected in the formal structures of the annotation language and it can underline any such shortcomings (Katz 2007).

5 Distributional semantic models

The DISTRIBUTIONAL HYPOTHESIS that words that appear in similar contexts have similar meanings has a long heritage, going back to Harris (1954) and Firth (1957) in linguistics and to Rubenstein & Goodenough (1965) in computational linguistics. The hypothesis is based on a simple intuition. We observe that *spaghetti* and *linguini* occur in close textual proximity to many of the same words in a corpus (*cook, sauce, Italian*, etc.) or in many of the same documents (*Pasta for Beginners, Eating Italian*, etc.) and this encourages us to conclude that the words are semantically similar. In recent years a very active research program has developed, which explores this hypothesis using modern computational techniques (Schütze 1993; Lund & Burgess 1996; Landauer & Dumais 1997; McDonald 1997; Sahlgren 2006; Padó & Lapata 2007; Erk 2009; Baroni et al. 2010; Baroni & Lenci 2010).

What distinguishes contemporary distributional semantic models (or DSMs) is the scale of the models and the sophisticated quantitative analysis of lexical distribution that is used. Marrying vector-based techniques from the field of information retrieval (Salton, Wong & Yang 1975) with a dimensional analysis of meaning (Osgood, Suci & Tannenbaum 1957), researchers have characterized semantic properties of lexical items in terms of the relationships among the textual contexts in which these items are used. In what have variously been known as "word-space semantics" (Schütze 1997), "vector-space models" (Turney & Pantel 2010), "latent semantic analysis" (Landauer, Foltz & Laham 1998), or, more generally, "distributional semantic models" (Baroni & Lenci 2010), lexical meaning is characterized as a point or a region in a high-dimensional semantic space constructed on the basis of lexical distribution. Semantic relations among words (such as synonymy, antimony and similarity) are computed on the basis of the vectors characterizing the words in this space.

There are two classes of DSMs (Sahlgren 2006): **Syntagmatic** or document-based models (e.g., the *Latent Semantic Analysis* (LSA) modal of Landauer & Dumais 1997), which base semantic similarity on document co-occurrence (e.g., *cook* appears frequently in the same documents as *spaghetti*, so they are similar); and **paradigmatic** or word-based models (e.g., the *Hyperspace Analogue of Language* (HAL) model of Lund & Burgess 1996), which base semantic similarity on similarity of contexts (e.g., *spaghetti* and *linguini* both appear with *cook* and *sauce*, so they are similar). What counts as a document (a news article; a paragraph; a sentence) or a context (a 10 word window; a sentence; a paragraph) is one of the many parameters that characterize a particular DSM model. Other parameters include how the co-occurrence counts are used to construct the semantic vectors and how semantic relations such as similarity are computed on the basis of these vectors.

As an illustration, consider the three document corpus in (19), with each line constituting a document and each sentence being a context domain.

(19) a. He cooks spaghetti. It cooks quickly.
   b. He cooks lingiuni. It cooks slowly.
   c. Both linguini and spaghetti are tasty.

Counting how many times each word appears in each document yields the syntagmatic vector space in (20), for the content words in this corpus.

(20)

	a.	b.	c.
cook	2	2	0
spaghetti	1	0	1
linguini	0	1	1
quickly	1	0	0
slowly	0	1	0
tasty	0	0	1

A common metric for similarity in DSMs is the **cosine** of the angle between the vectors, which normalizes for the number of occurrences of words. The words *cook* and *spaghetti* have a cosine similarity measure of 0.5, while *cook* and *tasty* have a cosine of 0.0, since they do not occur in any of the same documents.

A paradigmatic (word-based) model of the same corpus yields the semantic space in (21), which is generated by counting the number of word co-occurrences in one of the five "contexts" (sentences) that make up the corpus.

(21)

	cook	spaghetti	linguini	quickly	slowly	tasty
cook	0	1	1	1	1	0
spaghetti	1	0	1	0	0	1
linguini	1	1	0	0	0	1
quickly	1	0	0	0	0	0
slowly	1	0	0	0	0	0
tasty	0	1	1	0	0	0

In this semantic space *cook* and *spaghetti* have a cosine similarity of just under 0.3 – they only occur with the same word (*linguini*) once – while *cook* and *tasty* have a cosine of just over 0.7, since they both occur with *spaghetti* and *linguini*. Sahlgren (2006) compares syntagmatic and paradigmatic models over a range of tasks and finds that paradigmatic models are more effective for identifying such semantic relations as synonymy and antonymy, while syntagmatic models are more effective at identifying general semantic association (as between *milk* and *cow*).

Contemporary DSMs are also distinguished by the techniques used to reduce the dimensionality of the very large semantic spaces built out of word-word or word-document co-occurrence counts (ranging in the tens of thousands of dimensions) to lower-dimensionality "semantic" spaces (typically in the hundreds). The most common such technique is singular value decomposition (SVD). Landauer & Dumais (1997) demonstrated the effectiveness of dimensionality reduction by applying such a model to the TOEFL synonym test (for a given a word, which of the provided alternatives is a synonym). Building a paradigmatic model based on a 5-million-word encyclopedia corpus and reducing the high-dimensional word-word co-occurrence vectors to 300 "semantic" dimensions using SVD, they were able to achieve a performance of 64% on the TOEFL test, a score on par with average student performance, by simply having the model choose the answer with highest cosine similarity to the target word. Rapp (2003) improved this result to over 90% with a similar but more sophisticated DSM based on the much larger BNC.

In recent years DSMs have been applied to a number semantic tasks, from predicting semantic similarity judgements (Miller & Charles 1991; McDonald 1997), to distinguishing and disambiguating word-senses (Schütze 1993, 1998), to rating verb-argument plausibility (Erk, Padó & Padó 2010). While distributional semantic research has primarily focussed on modeling word meanings, there have been efforts to integrating compositional interpretetation into such models (Kintsch 2001). Two recent treatments of adjectives-nouns composition are of particular interest (Baroni & Zamparelli 2010; Guevara 2010). Baroni & Zamparelli built a model that involves treating adjectives as as matrices – functions from vectors to vectors that combine with noun meanings to give modified nominal meanings. The adjective *red*, for example, was interpreted as the function that (best) computed the vector for *red box* from the vector for *box*. Guevara, on the other hand, built a model in which both the noun and the modifying adjective were interpreted as vectors, computing the combination *red box* via a general modifier function applied to each of the constituent vectors.

6 References

Allen, James F. 1991. Discourse structure in the TRAINS project. In: P. Price (ed.). *Speech and Language. Proceedings of a Workshop Held at Pacific Grove, CA*. San Mateo, CA: Morgan Kaufman, 325–330.
Anderson, Anne H., Miles Bader, Ellen Gurman Bard, Elizabeth Boyle, Gwyneth Doherty, Simon Garrod, Stephen Isard, Jacqueline Kowtko, Jan McAllister, Jim Miller, Catherine Sotillo, Henry S. Thompson & Regina Weinert 1991. The HCRC map task corpus. *Language and Speech* 34, 351–366.

Artstein, Ron & Massimo Poesio 2008. Inter-coder agreement for computational linguistics. *Computational Linguistics* 34, 555–596.
Aston, Guy & Lou Burnard 1998. *The BNC Handbook. Exploring the British National Corpus with SARA*. Edinburgh: Edinburgh University Press.
Atkins, Sue 1992. Tools for corpus-aided lexicography: The HECTOR project. In: F. Kiefer, G. Kiss & J. Pajsz (eds.). *Papers Presented at the 2nd International Conference on Computational Lexicography and Text Research (= COMPLEX '92)*. Budapest: Hungarian Academy of Sciences, 1–60.
Atkins, Sue & Michael Rundell 2008. *The Oxford Guide to Practical Lexicography*. Oxford: Oxford University Press.
Baayen, R. Harald & Rochelle Lieber 1991. Productivity and English derivation: A corpus-based study. *Linguistics* 29, 801–844.
Baker, Collin F., Charles J. Fillmore & Beau Cronin 2003. The structure of the FrameNet database. *International Journal of Lexicography* 16, 281–296.
Barker, Chris 1998. Episodic -*ee* in English: A thematic role constraint on new word formation. *Language* 74, 695–727.
Barlow, Michael 2004. Software for corpus access and analysis. In: J. M. Sinclair (ed.) *How to Use Corpora in Language Teaching*. Amsterdam: Benjamins, 205–221.
Baroni, Marco & Alessandro Lenci 2010. Distributional memory: A general framework for corpus-based semantics. *Computational Linguistics* 36, 673–721.
Baroni, Marco & Roberto Zamparelli 2010. Nouns are vectors, adjectives are matrices: Representing adjective-noun constructions in semantic space. In: H. Li & L. Márquez (eds.). *Proceedings of the 2010 Conference on Empirical Methods in Natural Language Processing (= EMNLP)*. Cambridge, MA: ACL, 1183–1193.
Baroni, Marco, Silvia Bernardini, Adriano Ferraresi & Eros Zanchetta 2009. The WaCky wide web: A collection of very large linguistically processed web-crawled corpora. *Language Resources and Evaluation* 43, 209–231.
Baroni, Marco, Brian Murphy, Eduard Barbu & Massimo Poesio 2010. Strudel: A corpus-based semantic model based on properties and types. *Cognitive Science* 34, 222–254.
Beaver, David, Itamar Francez & Dmitry Levinson 2005. Bad subject: (non-)canonicality and NP distribution in existentials. In: E. Georgala & J. Howell (eds.). *Proceedings of Semantics and Linguistic Theory (= SALT) XV*. Ithaca, NY: Cornell University, 19–43.
Biber, Douglas 1992. Using computer-based text corpora to analyse the referential strategies of spoken and written texts. In: J. Svartvik (ed.). *Directions in Corpus Linguistics*. Berlin: Mouton de Gruyter, 215–252.
Bird, Steven & Mark Liberman 2001. A formal framework for linguistic annotation. *Speech Communication* 33, 23–60.
Boas, Hans C. 2000. *Resultative Constructions in English and German*. Ph.D. dissertation. University of North Carolina, Chapel Hill, NC.
Boas, Hans C. 2009. *Multilingual FrameNets in Computational Lexicography: Methods and Applications*. Berlin: de Gruyter.
Bod, Rens, Jennifer Hay & Stephanie Jannedy (eds.) 2003. *Probabilistic Linguistics*. Cambridge, MA: The MIT Press.
Bosch, Peter, Graham Katz & Carla Umbach 2007. The non-subject bias of German demonstrative pronouns. In: M. Schwarz-Friesel, M. Consten & M. Knees (eds.). *Anaphors in Text: Cognitive, Formal and Applied Approaches to Anaphoric Reference*. Amsterdam: Benjamins, 145–164.

Brants, Sabine, Stefanie Dipper, Peter Eisenberg, Silvia Hansen-Schirra, Esther König, Wolfgang Lezius, Christian Rohrer, George Smith & Hans Uszkoreit 2004. TIGER: Linguistic interpretation of a German corpus. *Research on Language & Computation* 2, 597–620.

Bunt, Harry 2007. The semantics of semantic annotation. In: H.-R. Chae et al. (eds.). *Proceedings of the 21st Pacific Asia Conference on Language, Information and Computation* (= *PACLIC*). Seoul: Korean Society for Language and Information, 13–28.

Burchardt, Aljoscha, Katrin Erk, Anette Frank, Andrea Kowalski, Sebastian Pad & Manfred Pinkal 2009. Using FrameNet for semantic analysis of German: Annotation, representation and automation. In: H. C. Boas (ed.). *Multilingual FrameNets in Computational Lexicography: Methods and Applications*. Berlin: de Gruyter, 209–244.

Carletta, Jean 1996. Assessing agreement on classification tasks: The kappa statistic. *Computational Linguistics* 22, 249–254.

Carletta, Jean, Stephen Isard, Gwyneth Doherty-Sneddon, Amy Isard, Jacqueline C. Kowtko & Anne H. Anderson 1997. The reliability of a dialogue structure coding scheme. *Computational Linguistics* 23, 13–31.

Carlson, Lynn, Daniel Marcu & Mary Ellen Okurowski 2001. Building a discourse-tagged corpus in the framework of rhetorical structure theory. In: J. van Kuppevelt & R. Smith (eds.). *Proceedings of the Second SIGdial Workshop on Discourse and Dialogue*. Aalborg: ACL, 1–10.

Cheng, Winnie, Chris Greaves & Martin Warren 2006. From n-gram to skipgram to concgram. *International Journal of Corpus Linguistics* 11, 411–433.

Christ, Oliver, Bruno M. Schulze, Anja Hofmann & Esther König 1999. *The IMS Corpus Workbench: Corpus Query Processor (CQP): User's Manual*. Stuttgart: University of Stuttgart.

Cieri, Christopher & Mark Liberman 2002. TIDES language resources: A resource map for translingual information access. In: M. Gonzlez Rodriguez & C. Paz Surez Araujo (eds.). *Proceedings of the Third International Language Resources and Evaluation Conference* (= *LREC*). Las Palmas: European Language Resources Association, 1334–1339.

Cohen, Jacob 1960. A coefficient of agreement for nominal scales. *Educational and Psychological Measurement* 20, 37–46.

Core, Mark G. & James F. Allen 1997. Coding dialogs with the DAMSL annotation scheme. In: D. Traum (ed.). *Working Papers from the AAAI Fall Symposium on Communicative Action in Humans and Machines*. Cambridge, MA: AAAI, 28–35.

Coventry, Kenny R., Thora Tenbrink & John Bateman 2009. *Spatial Language and Dialogue*. Oxford: Oxford University Press.

Cresswell, Maxwell J. 1982. The autonomy of semantics. In: S. Peters & E. Saarinen (eds.). *Processes, Beliefs, and Questions: Essays on Formal Semantics of Natural Language and Natural Language Processing*. Dordrecht: Reidel, 69–86.

Davies, Mark 2009. The 385+ million word corpus of contemporary American English (1990–2008+): Design, architecture, and linguistic insights. *International Journal of Corpus Linguistics* 14, 159–190.

Dayal, Veneeta 1998. Any as inherently modal. *Linguistics & Philosophy* 21, 433–476.

van Deemter, Kees & Rodger Kibble 2000. On coreferring: Coreference in MUC and related annotation schemes. *Computational Linguistics* 26, 629–637.

Doddington, George, Alexis Mitchell, Mark Przybocki, Lance Ramshaw, Stephanie Strassel & Ralph Weischedel 2004. The Automatic Content Extraction (ACE) program: Tasks, data, and evaluation. In: M. T. Lino et al. (eds.). *Proceedings of the Fourth International Language Resources and Evaluation Conference* (= *LREC*). Lisbon: European Language Resources Association, 837–840.

Eckert, Miriam & Michael Strube 2000. Dialogue acts, synchronizing units, and anaphora resolution. *Journal of Semantics* 17, 51–89.
Erk, Katrin 2009. Representing words as regions in vector space. In: S. Stevenson & X. Carreras (eds.). *Proceedings of the Thirteenth Conference on Computational Natural Language Learning (= CoNLL)*. Boulder, CO: ACL, 57–65.
Erk, Katrin, Sebastian Pad & Ulrike Pad 2010. A flexible, corpus-driven model of regular and inverse selectional preferences. *Computational Linguistics* 36, 723–763.
Fellbaum, Christiane (ed.) 1998. *WordNet: An Electronic Lexical Database*. Cambridge, MA: The MIT Press.
Fellbaum, Christiane, Joachim Grabowski & Shari Landes 1998. Performance and confidence in a semantic annotation task. In: Ch. Fellbaum (ed.). *WordNet: An Electronic Lexical Database*. Cambridge, MA: The MIT Press, 218–237.
Fillmore, Charles J. 1982. Frame semantics. In: The Linguistic Society of Korea (ed.). *Linguistics in the Morning Calm*. Seoul: Hanshin, 111–137.
Firth, John R. 1957. *Papers in Linguistics 1934-1951*. Oxford: Oxford University Press.
Fligelstone, Steve 1992. Developing a scheme for annotating text to show anaphoric relations. In: G. Leitner (ed.). *New Directions in English Language Corpora: Methodology, Results, Software Developments*. Berlin: Mouton de Gruyter, 153–170.
Fox, Barbara A. 1987. *Discourse Structure and Anaphora: Written and Conversational English*. Cambridge: Cambridge University Press.
Francis, W. Nelson & Henry Kučera 1982. *Frequency Analysis of English Usage: Lexicon and Grammar*. Boston, MA: Houghton Mifflin.
Franck, Dorothea 1979. Speech act and conversational move. *Journal of Pragmatics* 3, 461–466.
Fraurud, Kari 1990. Definiteness and the processing of noun phrases in natural discourse. *Journal of Semantics* 7, 395–433.
Garside, Roger, Geoffrey Leech & Anthony McEnery (eds.) 1997. *Corpus Annotation: Linguistic Information from Computer Text Corpora*. London: Longman.
Garside, Roger, Geoffrey Leech & Geoffrey Sampson 1987. *The Computational Analysis of English: A Corpus-Based Approach*. London: Longman.
Glassman, Lucille, Dennis Grinberg, Cynthia Hibbard, James Meehan, Loretta Guarino Reid & Mary-Claire van Leunen 1992. Hector: Connecting words with definitions. In: *Screening Words: User Interfaces for Text. Proceedings of the Eighth Annual Conference of the UW Centre for the New OED and Text Research*. Waterloo, ON: University of Waterloo, 37–74.
Graff, David, Junbo Kong, Ke Chen & Kazuaki Maeda 2007. *English Gigaword Third Edition*. Technical Report LDC2007T07. Philadelphia, PA: Linguistic Data Consortium.
Grishman, Ralph & Beth Sundheim 1996. Message understanding conference-6: A brief history. In: *Proceedings of the 16th Conference on Computational Linguistics (= COLING)*. Copenhagen: ACL, 466–471.
Guevara, Emiliano 2010. A regression model of adjective-noun compositionality in distributional semantics. In: R. Basili & M. Pennacchiotti (eds.). *Proceedings of the 2010 Workshop on GEometrical Models of Natural Language Semantics (= GEMS')*. Stroudsburg, PA: ACL, 33–37.
Gundel, Jeanette K., Nancy Hedberg & Ron Zacharski 1993. Cognitive status and the form of referring expressions in discourse. *Language* 69, 274–307.
Hanks, Patrick (ed.) 2007. *Lexicology: Critical Concepts in Linguistics*. Abingdon: Routledge.
Hardie, Andrew & Tony McEnery 2010. On two traditions in corpus linguistics, and what they have in common. *International Journal of Corpus Linguistics* 15, 384–394.

Harris, Jesse & Christopher Potts 2009. Perspective-shifting with appositives and expressives. *Linguistics & Philosophy* 32, 523–552.
Harris, Zellig 1954. Distributional structure. *Word* 10, 146–162.
Hart, Michael S. 1990. Project Gutenberg: Access to electronic texts. *Database* 13, 6–9.
Heeman, Peter A. & James F. Allen 1995. *The Trains Spoken Dialog Corpus*. CD-ROM, Linguistics Data Consortium.
Herbst, Thomas 1996. On the way to the perfect learners' dictionary: A first comparison of OALD5, LDOCE3, COBUILD2 and CIDE. *International Journal of Lexicography* 9, 321–357.
Heycock, Caroline & Roberto Zamparelli 2005. Friends and colleagues: Plurality, coordination, and the structure of DP. *Natural Language Semantics* 13, 201–270.
Hirschman, Lynette & Nancy Chinchor 1997. MUC-7 coreference task definition. In: *Proceedings of the Seventh Message Understanding Conference (= MUC)*. Fairfax, VA: Science Applications International Corporation.
Hobbs, Jerry R. 1978. Resolving pronoun references. *Lingua* 44, 311–338.
Hobbs, Jerry R. 1985. *On the Coherence and Structure of Discourse*. Technical Report CSLI-85–37. Stanford, CA: Center for Study of Language and Information, Stanford University.
Hoeksema, Jack 1997. Corpus study of negative polarity items. *IV–V Jornades de Corpus Linguistics 1996–1997*. Barcelona: IULA, Universitat Pompeu Fabra, 67–86.
Hovy, Eduard, Mitchell Marcus, Martha Palmer, Lance Ramshaw & Ralph Weischedel 2006. OntoNotes: The 90% solution. In: R. C. Moore et al. (eds.). *Proceedings of the Human Language Technology Conference of the North American Chapter of the Association of Computational Linguistics (= HLT-NAACL)*. New York: ACL, 57–60.
Kadmon, Nirit & Fred Landman 1993. Any. *Linguistics & Philosophy* 16, 353–422.
Katz, Graham 2007. Towards a denotational semantics for TimeML. In: G. Katz, J. Pustejovsky & F. Schilder (eds.). *Annotating, Extracting and Reasoning about Time and Events*. Heidelberg: Springer, 88–106.
Katz, Graham & Fabrizio Arosio 2001. The annotation of temporal information in natural language sentences. In: *Proceedings of the Workshop on Temporal and Spatial Information Processing (= TASIP)*. Stroudsburg, PA: ACL, 1–8.
Kennedy, Chris & Louise McNally 2005. Scale structure and the semantic typology of gradable predicates. *Language* 81, 345–381.
Kibrik, Andrej A. & Olga N. Krasavina 2005. A corpus study of referential choice. The role of rhetorical structure. In: *Proceedings of the Dialog-2005 International Conference on Computational Linguistics and Intelligent Technologies*. Moscow: Nauka, 561–569.
Kilgarriff, Adam 1999. 95% replicability for manual word sense tagging. In: *Proceedings of the 9th Conference of the European Chapter of the Association for Computational Linguistics (= EACL)*. Bergen: ACL, 277–278.
Kilgarriff, Adam & Gregory Grefenstette 2003. Introduction to the special issue on the Web as corpus. *Computational Linguistics* 29, 333–347.
Kintsch, Walter 2001. Predication. *Cognitive Science* 25, 173–202.
Kipper-Schuler, Karin 2005. *VerbNet: A Broad-coverage, Comprehensive Verb Lexicon*. Ph.D. dissertation. University of Pennsylvania, Philadelphia, PA.
Krippendorff, Klaus 1980. *Content Analysis: An Introduction to its Methodology*. Beverly Hills, CA: Sage.
Kupietz, Marc & Holger Keibel 2009. The Mannheim German reference corpus as a basis for empirical linguistic research. In: M. Minegishi & Y. Kawaguchi (eds.). *Working Papers*

in Corpus-based Linguistics and Language Education, vol. 3. Tokyo: Tokyo University of Foreign Studies, 53–59.

Kyto, Merja & Anke Lüdeling (eds.) 2008. *Corpus Linguistics: An International Handbook*, vol. 1. Berlin: de Gruyter.

Kyto, Merja & Anke Lüdeling (eds.) 2009. *Corpus Linguistics: An International Handbook*, vol. 2. Berlin: de Gruyter.

Ladusaw, William 1979. *Polarity Sensitivity as Inherent Scope Relations*. Ph.D. dissertation. University of Texas, Austin, TX.

Landauer, Thomas K. & Susan T. Dumais 1997. A solution to Plato's problem: The latent semantic analysis theory of acquisition, induction and representation of knowledge. *Psychological Review* 104, 211–240.

Landauer, Thomas K., Peter W. Foltz & Darrell Laham 1998. Introduction to latent semantic analysis. *Discourse Processes* 25, 259–284.

Landes, Shari, Claudia Leacock & Randee I. Tengi 1998. Building semantic concordances. In: Ch. Fellbaum (ed.). *WordNet: An Electronic Lexical Database*. Cambridge, MA: The MIT Press, 199–216.

Lappin, Shalom & Herbert J. Leass 1994. An algorithm for pronominal anaphora resolution. *Computational Linguistics* 21, 535–561.

Liberman, Mark 2003. *Language Log*. Blog. http://languagelog.ldc.upenn.edu/nll/, December 8, 2011.

Lund, Kevin & Curt Burgess 1996. Producing high-dimensional semantic spaces from lexical co-occurrence. *Behaviour Research Methods* 28, 203–208.

Mani, Inderjeet, Christy Doran, Dave Harris, Janet Hitzeman, Rob Quimby, Justin Richer, Ben Wellner, Scott Mardis & Seamus Clancy 2010. SpatialML: Annotation scheme, resources, and evaluation. *Language Resources and Evaluation* 44, 263–280.

Mann, William C. & Sandra A. Thompson 1988. Rhetorical structure theory: Toward a functional theory of text organization. *Text* 8, 243–281.

Marcus, Mitchell P., Beatrice Santorini & Mary A. Marcinkiewicz 1994. Building a large annotated corpus of English: The Penn Treebank. *Computational Linguistics* 19, 313–330.

Marquez, Lluís, Xavier Carreras, Kenneth C. Litkowski & Suzanne Stevenson 2008. Semantic role labeling: An introduction to the special issue. *Computational Linguistics* 34, 145–159.

McDonald, Scott 1997. A context-based model of semantic similarity. *ACM Transactions on Programming Languages and Systems (TOPLAS)* 15, 795–825.

McEnery, Tony 2000. *Corpus-based and Computational Approaches to Discourse Anaphora*, vol. 3. Amsterdam: Benjamins.

McEnery, Tony, Richard Xiao & Yukio Tono 2006. *Corpus-based Language Studies: An Advanced Resource Book*. London: Routledge.

Meurers, W. Detmar 2005. On the use of electronic corpora for theoretical linguistics. Case studies from the syntax of German. *Lingua* 115, 1619–1639.

Meyers, Adam, Ruth Reeves, Catherine Macleod, Rachel Szekely, Veronika Zielinska, Brian Young & Ralph Grishman 2004. Annotating noun argument structure for NomBank. In: M. T. Lino et al. (eds.). *Proceedings of the Fourth International Conference on Language Resources and Evaluation (= LREC)*. Lisbon: European Language Resources Association, 803–806.

Michel, Jean-Baptiste, Yuan Kui Shen, Aviva Presser Aiden, Adrian Veres, Matthew K. Gray, The Google Books Team, Joseph P. Pickett, Dale Hoiberg, Dan Clancy, Peter Norvig, Jon Orwant, Steven Pinker, Martin A. Nowak & Erez Lieberman Aiden 2011. Quantitative analysis of culture using millions of digitized books. *Science* 331(6014), 176–182.

Miller, George A. 1995. WordNet: A lexical database for English. *Communications of the ACM* 38, 39–41.
Miller, George A. & Walter G. Charles 1991. Contextual correlates of semantic similarity. *Language and Cognitive Processes* 6, 1–28.
Miller, George A. & Christiane Fellbaum 2007. WordNet then and now. *Language Resources and Evaluation* 41, 209–214.
Miller, George A., Richard Beckwith, Christiane Fellbaum, Derek Gross & Katherine Miller 1990. Introduction to WordNet: An on-line lexical database. *International Journal of Lexicography* 3, 235–244.
Miltsakaki, Eleni, Rashmi Prasad, Aravind Joshi & Bonnie Webber 2004. The Penn Discourse TreeBank. In: M. T. Lino et al. (eds.). *Proceedings of the Fourth International Conference on Language Resources and Evaluation (= LREC)*. Lisbon: European Language Resources Association, 1–4.
Mühleisen, Susanne 2010. *Heterogeneity in Word-formation Patterns: A Corpus Based Analysis of Suffixation with -ee and its Productivity in English*. Amsterdam: Benjamins.
Newmeyer, Frederick J. 2003. Grammar is grammar and usage is usage. *Language* 79, 682–707.
Ng, Hwee Tou & Hian Beng Lee 1996. Integrating multiple knowledge sources to disambiguate word sense: An exemplar-based approach. In: A. K. Joshi & M. Palmer (eds.). *Proceedings of the 34th Annual Meeting of the Association for Computational Linguistics (= ACL)*. Santa Cruz, CA: Morgan Kaufmann, 40–47.
Ng, Hwee Tou, Daniel Chung Yong Lim & Shou King Foo 1999. A case study on inter-annotator agreement for word sense disambiguation. In: *SIGLEX'99: Standardizing Lexical Resources*. College Park, MD: University of Maryland, 9–15.
Osgood, Charles E., George Suci & Percy Tannenbaum 1957. *The Measurement of Meaning*. Urbana, IL: The University of Illinois Press.
Padó, Sebastian & Mirella Lapata 2007. Dependency-based construction of semantic space models. *Computational Linguistics* 33, 161–199.
Padó, Sebastian & Mirella Lapata 2009. Cross-lingual annotation projection of semantic roles. *Journal of Artificial Intelligence Research* 36, 307–340.
Palmer, Martha, Hoa Trang Dang & Christiane Fellbaum 2007. Making fine-grained and coarse-grained sense distinctions, both manually and automatically. *Natural Language Engineering* 13, 137–163.
Palmer, Martha, Daniel Gildea & Paul Kingsbury 2005. The proposition bank: An annotated corpus of semantic roles. *Computational Linguistics* 31, 71–106.
Palmer, Martha, Daniel Gildea & Nianwen Xue 2010. *Semantic Role Labeling*. San Rafael, CA: Morgan & Claypool.
Partee, Barbara 1979. Semantics – mathematics or psychology? In: R. Bäuerle, U. Egli & A. von Stechow (eds.). *Semantics from Different Points of View*. Berlin: Springer, 1–14.
Passonneau, Rebecca J. 2004. Computing reliability for coreference annotation. In: M. T. Lino et al. (eds.). *Proceedings of the Fourth International Conference on Language Resources and Evaluation (= LREC)*. Lisbon: European Language Resources Association, 1503–1506.
Passonneau, Rebecca J., Ansaf Salleb-Aouissi, Vikas Bhardwaj & Nancy Ide 2010. Word sense annotation of polysemous words by multiple annotators. In: N. Calzolari et al. (eds.). *Proceedings of the Seventh International Conference on Language Resources and Evaluation (= LREC)*. Valetta: European Language Resources Association, 3244–3249.
Piao, Scott S.L., Dawn Archer, Olga Mudraya, Paul Rayson, Roger Garside, Tony McEnery & Andrew Wilson 2005. A large semantic lexicon for corpus annotation. In: P. Danielsson

& M. Wagenmakers (eds.). *Proceedings of the Third Corpus Linguistics Conference*. Birmingham: University of Birmingham.

Pimienta, Daniel, Daniel Prado & Alvaro Blanco 2009. *Twelve Years of Measuring Linguistic Diversity in the Internet: Balance and Perspectives*. Paris: United Nations Educational, Scientific and Cultural Organization.

Poesio, Massimo & Renata Vieira 1998. A corpus-based investigation of definite description use. *Computational Linguistics* 24, 183–216.

Potts, Christopher 2005. *The Logic of Conventional Implicatures*. Oxford: Oxford University Press.

Prasad, Rashim, Nikhil Dinesh, Alan Lee, Eleni Miltsakaki, Livio Robaldo, Aravind Joshi & Bonnie Webber 2008. The Penn Discourse Treebank 2.0. In: N. Calzolari et al. (eds.). *Proceedings of the Sixth International Conference on Language Resources and Evaluation (= LREC)*. Marrakech: European Language Resources Association, 2961–2968.

Pullum, Geoffrey K. 2007. Ungrammaticality, rarity, and corpus use. *Corpus Linguistics and Linguistic Theory* 3, 33–47.

Pustejovsky, James, Josś Castaño, Robert Ingria, Roser Saurí, Robert Gaizauskas, Andrea Setzer & Graham Katz 2003a. TimeML: Robust specification of event and temporal expression in text. In: H. Bunt, I. van der Sluis & R. Morante (eds.). *Proceedings of the Fifth International Workshop on Computational Semantics (= IWCS)*. Tilburg: Tilburg University, 337–353.

Pustejovsky, James, Patrick Hanks, Roser Saurí, Andrew See, Robert Gaizauskas, Andrea Setzer, Dragomir Radev, Beth Sundheim, David Day, Lisa Ferro & Marcia Lazo 2003b. The TIMEBANK Corpus. In: D. Archer et al. (eds.). *Proceedings of the Second Corpus Linguistics Conference*. Lancaster: Lancaster University, 647–656.

Pustejovsky, James, Robert Ingria, Jose Castaño, Roser Saurí, Jessica Littman, Robert Gaizauskas, Andrea Setzer, Graham Katz & Inderjeet Mani 2005. The specification language TimeML. In: I. Mani, J. Pustejovsky & R. Gaizauskas (eds.). *The Language of Time: A Reader*. Oxford: Oxford University Press, 545–557.

Quirk, Randolph 1960. Towards a description of English usage. *Transactions of the Philological Society* 59, 40–61.

Rapp, Reinhard 2003. Word sense discovery based on sense descriptor dissimilarity. In: *Proceedings of the Ninth Machine Translation Summit*. New Orleans, LA, 315–322.

Richter, Frank, Manfred Sailer & Beata Trawínski 2010. The collection of distributionally idiosyncratic items: An interface between data and theory. In: S. Ptashnyk, E. Hallsteinsdóttir & N. Bubenhofer (eds.). *Korpora, Web und Datenbanken. Computergestützte und korpusbasierte Methoden in der modernen Phraseologie und Lexikographie*. Hohengehren: Schneider Verlag, 247–262.

Rubenstein, Herbert & John B. Goodenough 1965. Contextual correlates of synonymy. *Communications of the ACM* 8, 627–633.

Ruppenhofer, Josef, Michael Ellsworth, Miriam R. L. Petruck, Christopher R. Johnson & Jan Scheczyk 2010. *FrameNet II: Extended Theory and Practice*. Berkeley, CA: International Computer Science Institute.

Sæbø, Kjell Johan 2004. Natural language corpus semantics: The Free Choice controversy. *Nordic Journal of Linguistics* 27, 197–218.

Sahlgren, Magnus 2006. *The Word-space Model: Using Distributional Analysis to Represent Syntagmatic and Paradigmatic Relations between Words in High-dimensional Vector Spaces*. Doctoral dissertation. Stockholm University.

Salton, Gerard, Anita Wong & Chung-Shu Yang 1975. A vector space model for automatic indexing. *Communications of the ACM* 18, 613–620.

Sassoon, Galit 2010. The degree functions of negative adjectives. *Natural Language Semantics* 18, 141–181.
Saurí, Roser, Jessica Littman, Bob Knippen, Robert Gaizauskas, Andrea Setzer & James Pustejovsky 2006. TimeML Annotation Guidelines, Version 1.2.1. http://timeml.org/site/publications/timeMLdocs/annguide_1. 2.1. pdf, February 28, 2012.
Schütze, Carson T. 1996. *The Empirical Base of Linguistics: Grammaticality Judgments and Linguistic Methodology*. Chicago, IL: The University of Chicago Press.
Schütze, Hinrich 1993. Word Space. In: J. D. Cowan, G. Tesauro & J. Alspector (eds.). *Advances in Neural Information Processing Systems, vol. 5*. San Francisco, CA: Morgan Kaufmann, 895–902.
Schütze, Hinrich 1997. *Ambiguity Resolution in Language Learning*. Stanford, CA: CSLI Publications.
Schütze, Hinrich 1998. Automatic word sense discrimination. *Computational Linguistics* 24, 97–124.
Sinclair, John M. 1984. Lexicography as an academic subject. *LEXeter* 83, 3–12.
Sinclair, John M. 1987. *Looking Up: An account of the COBUILD Project in Lexical Computing and the Development of the Collins COBUILD English Language Dictionary*. London: Collins ELT.
Sinclair, John M. 1996. The search for units of meaning. *Textus* 9, 75–106.
Sinclair, John M. 1998. The lexical item. In: E. Weigand (ed.). *Contrastive Lexical Semantics*. Amsterdam: Benjamins. 1–24.
Sinclair, John M. 2004. *Trust the Text*. London: Routledge.
Soehn, Jan-Philipp, Beata Trawinski & Timm Lichte 2010. Spotting, collecting and documenting negative polarity items. *Natural Language and Linguistic Theory* 28, 1–22.
Stede, Manfred 2004. The Potsdam commentary corpus. In: B. Webber & D. K. Byron (eds.). *Proceedings of the 2004 ACL Workshop on Discourse Annotation*. Barcelona: ACL, 96–102.
Stolcke, Andreas, Klaus Ries, Noah Coccaro, Elizabeth Shriberg, Rebecca Bates, Daniel Jurafsky, Paul Taylor, Rachel Martin, Carol Van Ess-Dykema & Marie Meteer 2000. Dialogue act modeling for automatic tagging and recognition of conversational speech. *Computational Linguistics* 26, 339–373.
Stubbs, Michael 2001. *Words and Phrases: Corpus Studies of Lexical Semantics*. Oxford: Blackwell.
Stubbs, Michael 2009. The search for units of meaning: Sinclair on empirical semantics. *Applied Linguistics* 30, 115–137.
Tetreault, Joel R. 2001. A corpus-based evaluation of centering and pronoun resolution. *Computational Linguistics* 27, 507–520.
Teubert, Wolfgang 2005. My version of corpus linguistics. *International Journal of Corpus Linguistics* 10, 1–13.
Traum, David R. 2000. 20 questions on dialogue act taxonomies. *Journal of Semantics* 17, 7–30.
Turney, Peter & Patrick Pantel 2010. From frequency to meaning: Vector space models of semantics. *Journal of Artificial Intelligence Research* 37, 141–188.
Tutin, Agnès, François Trouilleux, Catherine Clouzot, Eric Gaussier, Annie Zaenen, Stéphanie Rayot & Georges Antoniadis 2000. Annotating a large corpus with anaphoric links. In: P. Baker et al. (eds.). *Proceedings of the Discourse Anaphora and Reference Resolution Conference (= DAARC)*. Lancaster: Lancaster University, 28–38.
Vincent, Luc 2007. Google book search: Document understanding on a massive scale. In: *Proceedings of the Ninth International Conference on Document Analysis and Regognition (= ICDAR)*. Curitiba: IEEE Computer Society, 819–823.

Wechsler, Steven 2005. Resultatives under the 'event-argument homomorphism' model of telicity. In: N. Erteschik-Shir & T. Rapoport (eds.). *The Syntax of Aspect*. Oxford: Oxford University Press, 255–273.

Wolf, Florian & Edward Gibson 2005. Representing discourse coherence: A corpus-based study. *Computational Linguistics* 31, 249–288.

Zaenen, Annie 2006. Mark-up barking up the wrong tree. *Computational Linguistics* 32, 577–580.

Anette Frank and Sebastian Padó
15 Semantics in computational lexicons

1 Representation and computation —— 444
2 Building semantic lexicons —— 459
3 Multilingual and cross-lingual aspects —— 465
4 Interfaces and interoperability —— 468
5 Conclusion and outlook —— 470
6 References —— 472

Abstract: This chapter gives an overview of work on the representation of semantic information in lexicon resources for computational natural language processing (NLP). It starts with a broad overview of the history and state of the art of different types of semantic lexicons in Computational Linguistics, and discusses their main use cases. Section 2 is devoted to questions of how to construct semantic lexicons for Computational Linguistics. We discuss diverse modelling principles for semantic lexicons and methods for their construction, ranging from largely manual resource creation to automated methods for learning lexicons from text, semi-structured or unstructured. Section 3 addresses issues related to the cross-lingual and multi-lingual creation of broad-coverage semantic lexicon resources. Section 4 discusses interoperability, i.e., the combination of lexical (and other) resources describing different meaning aspects. Section 5 concludes with an outlook on future research directions.

1 Representation and computation

1.1 Lexicons in computational semantics

The development of semantic lexicons in and for computational semantic processing has been shaped by two complementary aspects of lexical meaning. Since words are combined to form complex phrases that express specific meanings, lexical meaning clearly relates to *structural aspects of meaning* in compositional meaning construction, with phenomena such as argument structure, quantifier

Anette Frank, Heidelberg, Germany
Sebastian Padó, Stuttgart, Germany

or adverbial scope, presupposition projection, or anaphoric reference (cf. article 6 [Semantics: Interfaces] (von Stechow) *Syntax and semantics*). But more importantly, the lexicon plays its primary role in the representation of the *lexical meaning of individual words* that build the basis for constructing complex meanings, and that can serve as a basis for recognising and modelling paraphrases, lexically driven entailments, or creative meaning extensions such as metaphor.

Computational theories of grammar have been studied extensively in the course of the last decades, with a strong focus on formal modelling and efficient computational processing of compositional meaning construction. Particular focus was put on the design of expressive semantic formalisms, ranging from classical predicate logic to dynamic semantic formalisms, and the design of principled meaning construction methods for diverse grammar frameworks (for an overview see Müller 2010). Since all major computational grammar formalisms are *lexicalised*, it is the computational semantic lexicon in conjunction with compositional meaning construction principles that needs to account for structural semantic phenomena. Phenomena that have received particular attention are quantifier and adverbial scope, plural interpretation, temporal reference, or aspectual properties of events (e.g. Dalrymple et al. 1997, Kamp, van Genabith & Reyle 2011). On the level of representations, a rich body of work is concerned with the compact representation of structural and lexical semantic ambiguities (cf. article 9 [Semantics: Lexical Structures and Adjectives] (Egg) *Semantic underspecification*).

The meaning representations obtained from computational semantic grammars are typically interpreted using a model-theoretic setting. However, practical uses of computational semantics crucially rely on information about the *lexical meaning of predicates*. As an example, consider a Question Answering system that has to determine that *James Watt was the first to build a working steam engine* is a relevant answer to the query *Who invented the steam engine?*. There are various ways of representing the required lexical semantic knowledge, but none can be considered complete on its own.

In traditional formal semantics, lexical meaning is defined by way of meaning postulates, again interpreted against a model (Carnap 1947), or else by way of lexical meaning relations such as synonymy, antonymy, hyponymy, etc. (Lyons 1977). The semantics of predicate-argument structures describing events or situations has been characterised using semantic or thematic roles, or protoroles (Fillmore 1976, Dowty 1991). Formal descriptions that define the lexical meaning of predicates have been attempted by way of decompositional analysis (Katz & Fodor 1964). However, agreement on a basic inventory of atomic meaning descriptions has been elusive (Winograd 1978). Most of these approaches to lexical meaning representation have been applied in work on semantic lexicon building for computational grammars at one time or another.

A few proposals also exist for richer semantic characterisations of lexical meaning. Examples include Pustejovsky's generative lexicon that can account for, i.a., the interpretation of metonymy (Pustejovsky 1995), Copestake and Briscoe's work on sense extension (Copestake & Briscoe 1995), or research on the integration of multi-word expressions (Sag et al. 2002). Sharing the concerns of ontological semantics (Nirenburg & Raskin 2004), Cimiano & Reyle (2005) include interfaces to ontological knowledge. Here, the role of ontological knowledge is to provide semantic criteria for ambiguity resolution, and to support inferences on the basis of the derived semantic representations. Finally, substantial research exists on the development of *linking theories* that capture regularities in the syntactic realisation of arguments with specific semantic properties (Bresnan & Zaenen 1990; Grimshaw 1992; Davis & Koenig 2000; Dang, Kipper & Palmer 2000).

All these approaches are mainly concerned with clarifying the formal and computational aspects of representing and processing lexical meaning in computational grammar formalisms, but have not been scaled to large semantic lexicons for broad-coverage, semantically informed NLP systems. Thus, today there exists a good understanding of the mechanisms that are required for the treatment of structural and lexical semantic phenomena in computational grammars – if the information is actually present in the lexicons. The creation of such semantic lexicons – which may involve highly structured representations – is a tight and serious bottleneck.

1.2 Standalone semantic lexicons

The creation of semantic lexicons has been pursued largely independently of computational grammar research. Depending on theoretical assumptions and the intended usage, semantic lexicons are structured according to different aspects of meaning and thus differ considerably in their descriptive devices. Some lexicon accounts characterise the meaning of individual words (or often, their individual *word senses*) by grouping them into *semantic classes* and by defining lexical semantic relations between these classes. Other lexicons try to capture constitutive meaning aspects of lexical items by decomposing their meaning in terms of atomic meaning primitives and define semantic relations between words on the basis of such primitives. Some lexicons, finally, use a combination of these techniques. This section gives an overview of diverse types of semantic lexicons and their modelling principles. We start with lexicons describing the meaning of lexical items in terms of sense definitions, semantic classes, or lexical semantic relations. Argument-taking predicates require in addition semantic descriptions that capture the constitutive meaning relations holding between predicates and their arguments. A number of lexicons is devoted to specific aspects of the meaning of particular word classes (such as nominalisation, factivity, presupposition, or polarity of emotion). Other specialised lexicons focus on the description of the non-compositional semantics of idiomatic expressions, light verbs, or collocations, or relate different modalities. Finally, we address the relation between semantic lexicons and ontologies.

Lexicons modelling inherent lexical meaning

Building on influential work in theoretical lexical semantics, in particular Dowty (1979), Jackendoff (1972), Jackendoff (1985) (cf. article 2 [Semantics: Lexical Structures and Adjectives] (Engelberg) *Frameworks of decomposition*), early attempts to computational lexicon building aimed at providing *inherent meaning descriptions* that can model lexical inferences, the semantic relations between diatheses and paraphrases, or resolve lexical ambiguities in context. Dowty's and Jackendoff's work both aim at inherent, decompositional meaning descriptions in terms of primitive semantic predicates. The aims and scope of decomposition, however, diverge considerably. Dowty's work focuses on explaining systematic meaning relations between diathesis alternations (e.g. inchoative and causative readings of *open* or *close* using primitives like CAUSE and BECOME), and on the ability of these semantic relations to predict the range of possible constructions for different types of predicates. Further aspects concern aspectual properties of verbs. Decomposition is restricted to modelling these grammaticalised categories of lexical meaning, leaving the core lexical semantics of verbs largely unanalysed.

In contrast, Jackendoff's work on Lexical Conceptual Structure (LCS) attempts to capture the lexical meaning of predicates in terms of a set of primitive predicates such as *cause, go* (inspired by physical motion) to define generalisations across predicates (cf. article 4 [Semantics: Lexical Structures and Adjectives] (Levin & Rappaport Hovav) *Lexical Conceptual Structure*).

Figure 15.1 shows an example for the causative use of *break* with an instrument expressed by a *with*-PP. The heart of the lexicon entry is the semantic description (:LCS) which uses figures to denote semantic categories. It defines the meaning of *break* as "an Agent [1] causes the identity of an Experiencer [2] to become a broken Experiencer [2], using an Instrument [20]" ([9] stands for "Predicate", and [19] for "Instrumental Particle"). The lexicon entry also provides global semantic description of the verb's valency in terms of theta roles (:THETA_ROLES) and selectional restrictions (:VAR_SPEC), as well as mappings to other lexical resources such as WordNet (:WN_SENSE), PropBank (:PROPBANK), and Levin classes (:CLASS).

```
:DEF_WORD "break"
:CLASS "45.1.a"
:WN_SENSE (("1.5" 00787971 00201902)
           ("1.6" 00938146 00231588))
:PROPBANK ("arg0 arg1 arg2(with)")
:THETA_ROLES ((1 "_ag_th,instr(with)"))
:LCS (cause (* thing 1)
     (go ident (* thing 2)
         (toward ident (thing 2)
                 (at ident (thing 2) (break+ed 9))))
     ((* with 19) instr (*head*) (thing 20)))
:VAR_SPEC ((1 (animate +)))
```

Fig. 15.1: LCS lexicon entry for transitive *break* with *with*-PP (Dorr et al. 2001)

Dorr (1997) presents automation techniques to develop LCS-based lexicons, linking LCS representations to Levin classes and WordNet, as seen above. This work proves the applicability of LCS descriptions for special aspects of verb meaning (cf. also VerbNet, below), yet the coverage of LCS-based meaning descriptions is restricted, as is their role in large-scale NLP applications. Pustejovsky (1995) describes the generative capacity of lexical meaning from an opposite viewpoint, assuming a minimal core description and a number of principled operations that allow for systematic sense extensions. The theory considers both verb and noun meanings (cf. article 2 [Semantics: Lexical Structures and Adjectives] (Engelberg) *Frameworks of decomposition*), but the treatment of nouns in terms of *Qualia Structure* is most widely known: it describes the *constitutive, formal, telic* and *agentive* functions of nouns that account for systematic meaning extensions. While there is no large resource providing qualia information, the CORELEX resource (Buitelaar 1998) models another part of the generative lexicon, namely the systematic polysemy of nouns.

Lexicons modelling meaning relations

Another structuring principle for semantic lexicons consists in defining semantic classes, i.e. groups of words that are more or less strictly synonyms, and hierarchical semantic relations among them, in terms of super- and subconcepts. This is the inherent structuring principle underlying taxonomies, which allows us to generalise attributes of concepts at some level in the hierarchy to their subconcepts (cf. article 6 [Semantics: Lexical Structures and Adjectives] (Cann) *Sense relations*). To account for the pervasive phenomenon of lexical ambiguity, semantic classes need to be distinguished. This may be achieved by way of formal semantic descriptions of the inherent meaning of predicates (see above). Given the difficulty of this task, however, semantic classes are most often defined by way of glosses or textual sense descriptions, combined with linguistic examples.

Early instances of this type of semantic lexicons are machine-readable dictionaries (MRDs) such as the Longman Dictionary of Contemporary English, LDOCE (Procter 1978). LDOCE provides linguistic codes and classifications for word senses, including glosses that use a controlled vocabulary, thus approximating a decompositional analysis. However, MRDs are mostly aimed at human users and contain informal descriptions, inconsistencies, and implicit information. This makes the extraction of general-purpose lexicons from MRDs difficult (Carroll & Grover 1989).

The most widely used resource that adheres to the above-mentioned structuring principles is WordNet, a resource originally motivated by psycholinguistic considerations, and designed for computational as opposed to human usage (Fellbaum 1998). WordNet's semantic classes, called *synsets*, are defined as groups of *synonymous word senses*. WordNet consists of different hierarchies, one for each major part of speech (noun, verb, adjective, adverb); the main relation between synsets is the *is-a* relation (corresponding to the hyponymy relation between the lexical items in the synsets). Instead of assuming a single top concept, WordNet established 11 top concepts, corresponding to broad conceptual domains (such as entity, event, psychological feature, etc.). Figure 15.2 shows a small excerpt of the WordNet *is-a* hierarchy around the synset for the "automobile" reading of *car*. It shows how WordNet synsets are described with short natural language glosses which are not drawn from a controlled vocabulary, but can nevertheless be viewed as providing a (pre-formal) decompositional analysis. Formalisation of WordNet glosses has been attempted in Mihalcea & Moldovan (2001) by parsing them into logical forms. For many synsets, short example sentences are also available.

Next to hyponymy, WordNet encodes lexical meaning relations such as antonymy, meronymy (part-of relation), entailment, cause, attribute, derivation, etc. These relations provide additional meaning aspects for a given synset, while only indirectly, in terms of their semantic relations to "neighbourhood" concepts (cf. article 6 [Semantics: Lexical Structures and Adjectives] (Cann) *Sense relations*). The synset *car* from Figure 15.2, for example, is meronymically related to over twenty other synsets, such as *car door, air bag,* or *roof*.

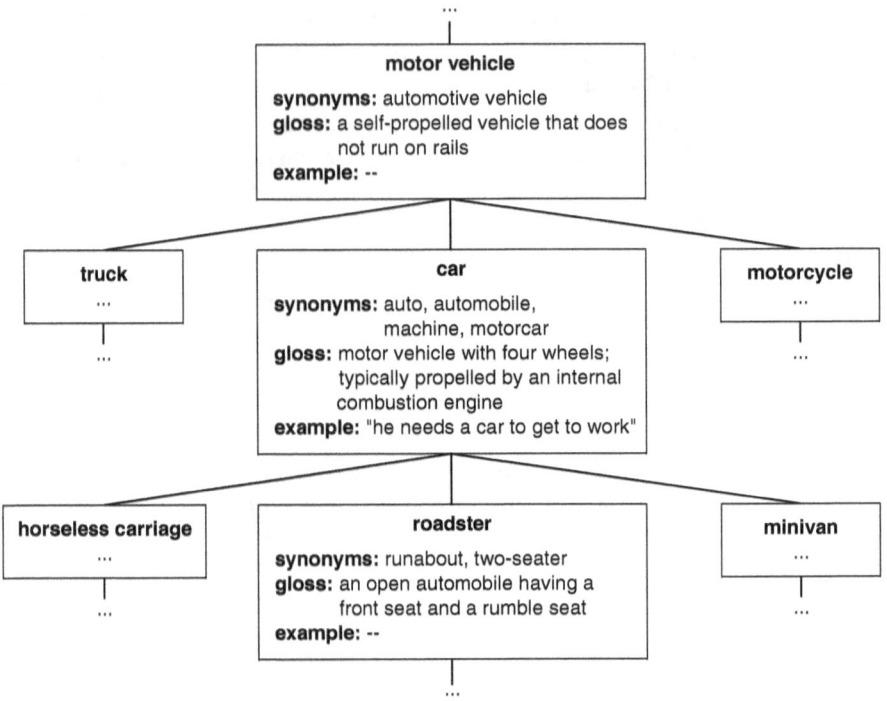

Fig. 15.2: WordNet *is-a* hierarchy centered around the primary sense of *car*

Due to its size (it covers more than 200,000 word senses) and simple structure, WordNet has shown extremely useful in NLP. For example, a wide range of methods exploit its hierarchy to quantify the semantic similarity between words (Budanitsky & Hirst 2006). An unresolved issue, however, is the question of its *granularity*. WordNet uses comparatively fine-grained word senses, which have the potential to convey very specific information. Yet, vagueness and underspecification of lexical meaning in real-world use often make the assignment of a particular sense difficult or impossible (Kilgarriff 1997). Recent work explores strategies to dynamically "group" word senses to find an optimal level of granularity for a given task (Palmer, Dang & Fellbaum 2006; Hovy et al. 2006).

The increased interest in multimodal applications has lead to the development of multimodal lexicons. Borman, Mihalcea & Tarau (2005) have developed a WordNet-based resource, PicNet, that combines linguistic with pictorial representations for concepts. Such knowledge can be used for better video or image retrieval (Popescu & Grefenstette 2008).

Lexicons modelling predicate-argument structure

The characterisation of meaning by way of synonymy, hyponymy and other meaning relations works particularly well for lexical items that refer to entities, as most nouns do. Predicates denoting events or states, such as verbs and deverbal nouns, have a more complex structure in at least two respects: Syntactically, they combine with *arguments*, which requires a semantic characterisation of the arguments in terms of their inherent relation to the event or state (their *semantic role*, such as *agent, patient* or *experiencer*) as well as their linking to surface positions. Also, events and states are often internally structured in terms of aspectual properties. This makes a simple *is-a* hierarchy insufficient to express semantically relevant relations between events and states, for example to draw inferences about the result states of events or the involvement of participants.

A variety of theories exist that characterise the arguments of predicates in terms of thematic or semantic roles, such as AGENT, THEME, LOCATION, etc. (e.g. Gruber 1965, Fillmore 1968, Jackendoff 1972, cf. article 3 [Semantics: Lexical Structures and Adjectives] (Davis) *Thematic roles*). Classifications were intended to capture syntactic and semantic characteristics of the respective arguments and verb classes. Fillmore (1968), for example, argued for a universal set of atomic thematic roles to capture mainly semantic generalisations, and used these to classify verbs according to the case-frames they allow. Jackendoff (1972) defined a small number of thematic roles in terms of primitive semantic predicates in LCS (see above), and established linking principles to map syntactic and semantic arguments (Jackendoff 1990). However, similar to the general problem of decomposition, no agreement could be reached on a complete and universal set of thematic roles. Dowty (1991) introduced a weaker definition of thematic roles, replacing the set of distinct thematic roles with two "proto-roles" (PROTO-AGENT, PROTO-PATIENT) whose semantics are determined through individual entailments holding for a given predicate and argument. Fillmore (1976) later established a radically different view in introducing Frame Semantics, which assumes concept-specific semantic roles of predicate classes, defined in terms of semantic frames and their frame-specific roles. A more syntax-oriented view on the semantics of argument structure emerges from the work of Levin (Levin 1993; Levin & Rappaport Hovav 2005). She establishes semantic verb classes ("Levin classes") on the basis of syntactic argument realisations in diathesis alternations. The underlying assumption is that the ability of a verb to occur in certain syntactic alternations is grounded, or a reflex of underlying semantic properties of verbs.

Out of these traditions, a number of large-scale lexicons have emerged that are based on the syntactico-semantic properties of argument-taking predicates, mainly for verbs and mainly for English. Due to the differences between the underlying theories, they differ considerably in their design decisions and structuring mechanisms (Ellsworth et al. 2004; Merlo & van der Plas 2009). Figure 15.3 shows the entries for transitive *break* in the three most widely used predicate-argument structure based lexicons.

PropBank (Palmer, Gildea & Kingsbury 2005) is a verb lexicon specifying semantic predicate and role annotations on top of the Penn Treebank, a large English treebank with constituent structure annotation (Marcus, Santorini & Marcinkiewicz 1993); NomBank (Meyers et al. 2004) extends the approach to deverbal nouns. PropBank and NomBank annotate coarse-grained word senses called "rolesets" (like *break.01* in Figure 15.3). The semantic roles ("arguments") are given verb-specific mnemonics (like *breaker*). Arg0 and Arg1 correspond to Dowty's proto-agent and proto-patient and thus share meaning across predicates, while arguments with higher numbers are defined in syntactic terms, with limited generalisations. Resources that follow the model of PropBank have been developed for Chinese (Xue 2008) and Korean, although the syntactic nature of PropBank-style roles makes the re-use of English role definitions for other languages difficult.

VerbNet (Kipper-Schuler 2005) represents an extension and refinement of Levin verb classes (Levin 1993). It is thus located directly at the boundary between syntax and semantics. On the syntactic side, the lexicon contains syntactic frames (field Syntax) with selectional restrictions of verb arguments (field Roles). The semantic side is based on intersective Levin classes (Dang et al. 1998), a refinement of Levin's original theory, and defines a hierarchy over verb classes, generally not exceeding a depth of three levels (field Class). It assumes a small set of abstract, semantically motivated thematic roles (field Roles). For selected meaning aspects, VerbNet provides fine-grained definitions in a decompositional style, using conjunctions of semantic predicates to characterise pre- and post-conditions of the event E as well as temporal and aspectual properties (field Semantics).

FrameNet (Fillmore, Johnson & Petruck 2003) is a lexicon in the Frame Semantics paradigm (Fillmore 1976) that groups verbs, nouns, and adjectives into semantic classes (frames) that correspond to abstract situations or events. While a variety of criteria is used in determining frames, most of them tend to be semantic. FrameNet defines semantic roles at the level of individual frames (cf. article 3 [Semantics: Theories] (Gawron) *Frame Semantics* for details). Figure 15.3 shows that *break* is analysed as belonging to the CAUSE_TO_FRAGMENT frame, with definitions of the frame and roles stated in natural language. Some of the semantic roles are further specified in terms of general semantic types such as *Sentient*. The frames are organised into a "frame hierarchy" defined by frame-to-frame relations (*inheritance, subframe, causative-of* etc.) that define hierarchical, but also paradigmatic seman-

PropBank

Roleset	break.01 "break, cause to not be whole"
Verbnet	Class: 1
Roles	Arg0:breaker Arg1:thing broken
	Arg2:instrument Arg3:pieces
Example	[Arg0 John] broke [Arg1 the window] [Arg2 with a rock].

VerbNet

Class	45.1
Roles	Agent [+int_control], Patient [+solid], Instrument [+solid]
Syntax	Agent V Patient {with} Instrument
Example	Tony broke the window with a hammer.
Semantics	cause(Agent,E)
	contact(during(E),Instrument,Patient)
	degradation_material_integrity(result(E),Patient)
	physical_form(result(E),Form,Patient)
	use(during(E),Agent,Instrument)

FrameNet

Frame	Cause_to_fragment
Definition	An Agent suddenly and often violently separates the Whole into two or more smaller Pieces, resulting in the Whole no longer existing.
Roles	Agent: The conscious entity, generally a person, that performs the intentional action that results in the Whole being broken into Pieces.
	Cause: An event which leads to the fragmentation of the Whole.
	Pieces: The fragments of the Whole that result from the Agent's action.
	Whole: The entity which is destroyed by the Agent and that ends up broken into Pieces.
Example	[AGENT He] *ripped up* [WHOLE the letter].
Semantic Types	Agent=Sentient
Inherits From	Transitive_action
Is Causative of	Fragmentation_scenario
Lexical Units	break.v, break_apart.v, break_down.v, break_up.v, chip.v, cleave.v, ...

Fig. 15.3: Lexicon entries for transitive *break* in PropBank, FrameNet, and VerbNet

tic relations, such as successions of events and states in script-like situations. The frame hierarchy also provides mappings between frame-specific semantic roles. Due to its primarily semantics-oriented structuring principles (schematised situations and participant roles), the FrameNet classifications established for English have been successfully transferred to different languages, though not without need for language-specific adjustments in the inventory of frames and roles (Burchardt et al. 2009; Subirats 2009; Ohara et al. 2004).

Due to the differences in their underlying theories, these resources have put different emphases on syntactic vs. semantic structuring principles, and correspondingly achieve different degrees of generalisations in defining and relating semantic classes. PropBank does not specify relations across lexical items on a formal level, although informal characterisations can be read off the free-text descriptions provided for word senses and role labels. VerbNet achieves a higher degree of generalisation by introducing a certain degree of hierarchical structuring. In addition, it provides strong decompositional semantic definitions of verbs, including thematic roles with selectional preferences. In FrameNet, the coarse-grained semantic classes (frames) typically cover a number of predicates and provide only a limited definition in terms of their sets of semantic roles. Additional characterisations and constraints are only available in free text form. Similar to WordNet, it may be possible to gain considerable information from the hierarchical structure that is defined over frames, in terms of frame-to-frame relations, and in fact this network shows potential for use in NLP tasks (Narayanan & Harabagiu 2004). Nevertheless, the FrameNet resource is still far from complete and requires more rigorous formal definition of frames and frame relations.

A largely unexplored area of semantic lexicon building is the design and creation of lexicons for the difficult classes of non-compositional lexical semantic phenomena. Most computational lexicons assume compositionality in the sense that they specify semantic representations only for "atomic" structures (typically, words), as opposed to idiomatic expressions or multiword expressions. Fellbaum et al. (2006) proposes a model for large-scale lexical resource building focusing on idiomatic expressions coupled with textual data. The SALSA project (Burchardt et al. 2009) investigated special annotation schemes and lexicon entry creation for idiomatic expressions and figurative meanings in the Frame Semantics paradigm.

Semantic lexicons, ontologies and world knowledge

There is a close relation between hierarchically structured semantic lexicons such as WordNet and ontologies in that both are organised along the lines of an *is-a* hierarchy. However, there are – at least in theory – two fundamental differences between semantic lexicons and ontologies.

The first distinction lies in the *nature of the objects* that are defined. In semantic lexicons, these are lexical units (words or word senses) of particular languages, while the classes defined in ontologies proper are *concepts* (Gruber 1995) that may or may not be language-independent. This difference becomes obvious once we contrast WordNets for different languages. A comparison of these resources shows that languages can have lexical gaps (cf. the absence of an exact English counterpart to German *Gemütlichkeit*). At the same time, they may lexicalise distinctions that other languages do not (cf. the English distinction between *isolation* and *insulation* both of which translate into German as *Isolation*). Multilingual semantic lexicons must handle such divergences explicitly. In EuroWordNet, this happens via an *inter-lingual index (ILI)* (Vossen 1998).

The second distinction is the *descriptive inventory*. Semantic lexicons categorise lexical items with respect to lexical relations, lexical properties, or predicate-argument structure. In contrast, ontologies provide rigidly defined knowledge-oriented (encyclopedic) relations, attributes and axioms for concepts. For example, the concept *politician* will need to provide typed attributes and relations such as *party*, *period of service*, or *elected by* which are clearly encyclopedic.

In practice, however, the distinction between linguistic meaning and world knowledge is notoriously difficult (Hirst (2004), cf. article 6 [Semantics: Theories] (Hobbs) *Word meaning and world knowledge*). Lexical meaning often closely corresponds to conceptual knowledge. Lexical relations like antonymy, synonymy and also entailment are crucially grounded in ontological categories and properties (such as *dead* vs. *alive*, *bachelor* and *unmarried*), which makes them difficult, if not impossible, to distinguish from ontological concepts and relations. Differences show up in cases of linguistic distinctions that do not have an immediate ontological counterpart, as in linguistically conveyed differences in perspectivisation of one and the same event (e.g. *buy* vs. *sell*). On the other hand, some lexical ontologies, such as WordNet, include semantic relations that are truly ontological, such as *part-of*, which adds to terminological confusion.

While linguistic knowledge is often easier to specify than the potentially open-ended field of ontological information, purely linguistic properties are insufficient for NLP applications that require deeper semantic analysis. On the other hand, the knowledge encoded in ontologies cannot be put to use in NLP applications without relating it to the linguistic realisation of the classes and relations. This may be provided in different ways: by constructing an explicit mapping between a semantic lexicon and an ontology (Niles & Pease 2003); by enriching a semantic lexicon with ontological information (Gangemi, Navigli & Velardi 2003), or through construction of hybrid lexicons that include a linguistic and an ontological level of description, such as OntoSem (Nirenburg & Raskin 2004), or HaGenLex (Hartrumpf, Helbig & Osswald 2003).

Lexicons modelling specific meaning aspects

A number of lexicon resources concentrate on particular meaning aspects. Some focus on linguistic properties like the implicative behaviour of sentence embedding verbs (Nairn, Karttunen & Condoravdi 2006), the evaluative function of lexical items (Esuli & Sebastian 2006; Pang & Lee 2008), or collocation patterns (Spohr & Heid 2006). Others describe the semantics of particular word classes such as prepositions (Saint-Dizier 2006) or nominalisations (Lapata 2002). Yet other lexicons provide information on generic semantic similarity (Lin 1998) or admissible sentence-level paraphrases (Lin & Pantel 2001). These resources vary widely in how structured they are. On one extreme, they may employ complex graph-based structures (Spohr & Heid 2006), or rest upon in-depth linguistic examination, as in the case of Nairn, Karttunen & Condoravdi (2006). On the other end of the spectrum, they are sometimes little more than ranked lists of word pairs (Lin 1998).

1.3 Semantic lexicons in use

From semantic resources to semantic processing. The various types of knowledge that are represented in computational lexicons are potentially beneficial for a wide range of NLP tasks. We will motivate this claim on a small example from Question Answering, where questions and answer candidates can differ on a number of linguistic dimensions. For example, a potential answer to the question *Whom did Peter see?* may be *The man with the moustache was seen by Peter*, i.e., in passive voice. The relationship between active and passive sentences is best modelled by mapping syntactic (surface) argument positions onto their corresponding *semantic roles*, a process known as semantic role labelling or shallow semantic parsing and pioneered by Gildea & Jurafsky (2002). This is a prime application of predicate-argument structure-based lexicons.

A different problem is posed by *Peter saw the man with his binoculars*, a sentence with an attachment ambiguity where it is unclear whether the binoculars modify the object of the seeing event. Such problems can be addressed by forming semantic classes that describe *selectional preferences* for argument positions, such as the instrument of "see" (Resnik 1996). As illustrated above, some lexicons encode conceptual classes, or selectional restrictions for argument positions.

Next, a sentence like *Peter saw the point of Jack's argument* should not be considered relevant even though it shares both predicate and subject with the question. The reason is polysemy: here, the sense of "see" can be paraphrased by "understand" while in the question it is closer to "observe". Selection or assignment of the appropriate word sense in a given context is addressed in the task of *word sense disambiguation* (WSD, Navigli 2009). The by far most widely used sense inventory for this task are the WordNet classes, due to WordNet's high coverage, and the ability to use the detailed hierarchy to guide generalisation. Finally, some answer candidates can only be recognised as relevant through *inference* (Norvig 1987), such as *The man was identified by the eye witness Peter*: Establishing a relation between this sentence and the question requires the knowledge that being an eye witness necessarily requires an act of observation. This relation might be defined in the inherent meaning of the expression in a lexicon, it might be established through a formal inference process, using knowledge from an ontology, or can be modelled through approximate inference methods (see below).

Disambiguation in context. The availability of semantic lexicons and their encoded representations is merely a first step towards their actual use in semantic processing tasks. A serious limitation for their use is that they list the range of possible semantic classes for lexical items, but do not provide specifications as to when these classes are appropriate for a given instance of the lexical item in a specific context. In fact, all applications sketched above crucially depend on *automatic disambiguation* methods that can assign one or more appropriate classes to lexical items in context. Such disambiguation models can be based on a large variety of techniques ranging from knowledge-based or heuristic techniques to statistical models.

Over the last years, robust data-driven methods have been very successful. Such methods can make use of *quantitative information* gained from annotated corpus data which many semantic resource building efforts have produced in parallel with the lexicon resources. The FrameNet database, for example, comes with a large corpus of frame-annotated sentences that were successfully used for training semantic role labelling systems (Gildea & Jurafsky 2002). WordNet provides frequencies of senses through the sense-annotated Semcor corpus (Fellbaum 1998). Data-driven methods for word sense disambiguation are still confronted with serious problems (McCarthy 2009). Due to the highly skewed frequency distribution over senses, supervised models require massive amounts of manual annotations that cannot be achieved on a realistic scale. The performance of unsupervised models, by contrast, is still weak. An alternative to statistical models are knowledge-based methods. The Lesk algorithm (Lesk 1986) and its derivatives compute semantic overlap measures between words in the context of the target word and the words in the sense glosses listed in WordNet for each synset, resulting in a model that is still hard to beat. A promising recent development is the emergence of *knowledge-based* methods that link semantic classes to the vast common-sense knowledge repository Wikipedia, whose articles and link structure can serve as the basis for disambiguation models for the semantic classes without the need for manual annotation (Gabrilovich & Markovitch 2007; Ponzetto & Navigli 2010).

In contrast to independent models for disambiguation, Pustejovsky, Hanks & Rumshisky (2004) propose an integrated *contextual* lexicon model for word senses that associates target entries with syntagmatic patterns of words, so-called *selection contexts*, that determine the assignment of word senses in context.

Approximate semantic processing. Semantic analysis in current practical NLP applications is far from comprehensive. This is due to the scarcity of resources on the one hand, and the complexities of fine-grained semantic analysis on the other. Still, currently available resources have been put to use effectively for a variety of semantic analysis tasks that are known to be highly problematic for computational modelling. A commonly used technique is to approach complex phenomena by considering simplified, and thus more tractable, aspects that are accessible to current semantic processing tools and techniques. A crucial factor in the success of this approach is the large amount of *redundancy* in the text collections most NLP tasks are concerned with. Redundancy lowers the requirements on detail and precision, since relevant linguistic material will usually occur more than once. In consequence, even the simple notion of generic *semantic relatedness* is put to use in many applications. It underlies most Information Retrieval systems, and can inform the resolution of syntactic and semantic ambiguities (Dagan, Lee & Pereira 1999; Resnik 1999; Lapata 2002).

With regard to drawing inferences from text, the textual inference framework (Dagan et al. 2009) has risen to prominence. In textual inference, entailment relations between sentences are not defined through a theory of meaning, but rather established by annotator judgments, with the effect of decoupling phenomenon and processing paradigm. A number of approaches have been applied to textual inference, including full-fledged logical inference. However, most approaches are approximate, relying on the partial information present in current semantic lexicons. WordNet, for example, can be used to add hyponym and hyperonym information to analyses; FrameNet and VerbNet can be used to retrieve similar predicates, and to some extent also information about result states (Burchardt et al. 2007).

Limitations and prospects of current semantic lexicons. The amount of semantic knowledge encoded in today's semantic lexicons is still limited. As a result, more involved inference problems still remain outside the reach of lexicon-driven approaches. This holds even for the currently most advanced "deep" semantic NLP systems that include large-scale meaning construction and inference machinery, such as Bos (2009). For example, the rejection of the standard interpretation of *Peter and Mary got married* in the context of *Peter married Susan, and Mary married John* requires knowledge about the incompatibility of multiple synchronous marriages. One direction of research towards richer semantic resources and processing is the acquisition of such knowledge from corpora, either unstructured text or pre-structured texts from Wikipedia (see Section 2.3.). Another one is the enrichment of semantic representations by building interfaces to manually crafted ontologies such as Cyc or SUMO (Niles & Pease 2003); however, the task of defining flexible interfaces between the lexical and the ontological level is still a challenge (see Section 4.).

2 Building semantic lexicons

Computational lexical semantics has achieved a major break-through in large-scale lexical resource building within the last decade, as evidenced by the resources presented in Section 1. At the same time, current methods are still insufficient to meet the need for deeper analysis, both for general and specialised domains, and, prominently, the need for multilingual resources.

2.1 Strategies for building semantic lexicons

The two main strategies for manual lexicon creation can be seen as opposing poles on a continuum. On one end of the spectrum lie manual resource creation efforts that do not use corpus data at all, relying exclusively on linguistic insight. Great care must be taken not to overlook relevant phenomena, and to achieve a good balance of lexical instances in terms of frequency of occurrence and representativeness of senses.

The other pole is formed by strict corpus-driven lexicon development. This method annotates a corpus from which the lexicon is later extracted. Advantages of this approach include the grounding of the lexicon data in naturally occurring instances, which ensures good coverage of phenomena, and the ability to read quantitative tendencies off the annotations. On the downside, corpus annotation often faces massive redundancy for frequent phenomena. Also, annotation introduces overhead, notably in the effort necessary to guarantee consistency and informativity. Particularly problematic are the ambiguity and vagueness inherent in many semantic phenomena such as word sense (Kilgarriff 1997). Finally, lexicon extraction is confronted with the problem of characterising phenomena across multiple linguistic levels, which requires well-designed interfaces (see Section 4.). In practice, the most feasible strategy for the manual creation of a semantic lexicon is often a compromise. This might involve direct manual creation of the resource that is nevertheless guided by systematic sighting and frequency analysis of the data to encourage high coverage and representativeness. A variety of corpus analysis tools support empirically guided lexicon building through quantitative analysis and linguistically informed search on large corpora: the CQP workbench (Christ et al. 1999), Sketch Engine (Kilgarriff et al. 2004) or the Linguist's Search engine (Resnik & Elkiss 2005). Exemplary corpus annotation can serve to validate analysis decisions and provide data for corpus-driven models.

2.2 Conservative methods for data-driven lexicon creation

Traditional lexicon construction, whether introspective or corpus-driven, proceeds manually and is a long and expensive process. The creation of many semantic lexicons that are in general use, such as WordNet, was only feasible because these resources concentrated on a small set of semantic relations. However, manual lexicon creation strategies can be complemented with semi-automatic methods aimed at extending the coverate of existing lexicon resources. These methods take advantage of corpus-based lexical semantic processing methods and range from simple to challenging.

A pressing need that is comparatively simple to address is an increase in coverage to previously unknown lexical items. In *supersense tagging* (Ciaramita & Johnson 2003; Curran 2005) unknown words (usually nouns) are sense-tagged according to a small number of broad WordNet classes. Pennacchiotti & Pantel (2006) build sense vectors characterising synsets that can be used to find the closest WordNet synset for unknown words, bringing together large-scale extraction and integration of semantic relations.

A more challenging goal is the structural extension of a semantic lexicon, which involves shaping new semantic classes or senses, their insertion into the existing lexical hierarchy, and the induction of semantic relations. Fully automated induction of semantic classes, semantic relations, and full ontologies (see below), is still in its infancy. Hence, practical resource creation often reverts to more controlled, semi-automatic methods. For VerbNet, e.g., Korhonen & Briscoe (2004) automatically acquire new Levin classes using corpus-based methods. The integration of this information into the VerbNet hierarchy still requires manual definition of novel semantic classes and predicates, as well as local modifications of the VerbNet hierarchy (Kipper et al. 2006).

2.3 Automatic acquisition of semantic lexicons and knowledge bases

Fully automatic methods try to reduce human effort as completely as possible. As is evident from the previous discussion, completely automatic acquisition is only possible either for coarse-grained classes or by tuning methods to individual relations.

Most such approaches rely on (unannotated) corpora, which are now available for many languages, domains, and genres, often by harvesting from the web. Semantic relations can be gathered from unanalysed corpora by collecting co-occurrence information about words or word pairs, following Harris' (1968) observation that semantically related words tend to occur in similar contexts. Variation in the specification of contexts gives rise to a range of approaches. *Pattern-based* methods use lexico-syntactic templates to identify contexts (typically a small number) that identify individual relations (Hearst 1992). The upper part of Figure 15.4 illustrates this idea for hyponymy relations. In contrast, *distributional* methods record the co-occurrence of individual words with their surrounding context words (e.g., all words within a context window or within a syntactic relationship). Pairwise similarities between the vector representations (e.g., cosine similarity) can then be interpreted as general semantic relatedness (Schütze 1993); see the lower part of Figure 15.4.

Learning semantic classes

Automatic approaches typically start with the induction of semantic classes or senses, i.e., sets of words with similar semantic properties. Unsupervised approaches to this task almost invariably use *clustering* techniques that group words with similar distributional representations into classes (Hindle 1990; Lin 1998; Pantel & Lin 2002). Further examples are Schulte im Walde (2006), who induces verb classes for German purely on the basis of distributional information, and Green, Dorr & Resnik (2004), who induce word classes that are similar in nature to frame-semantic classes by combining evidence from two dictionaries. Prescher, Riezler & Rooth (2000) cluster verb-object pairs to obtain semantic classes. Grenager & Manning (2006) use a structured probabilistic model to induce equivalence classes of arguments across diathesis alternations that resemble PropBank roles.

A major drawback of unsupervised learning methods is that they are incompatible with pre-structuring the domain of semantic classes. This problem is addressed by semi-supervised *bootstrapping approaches*. Here, a small number of initial "seeds" is used to bias the induction of classes towards a desired class

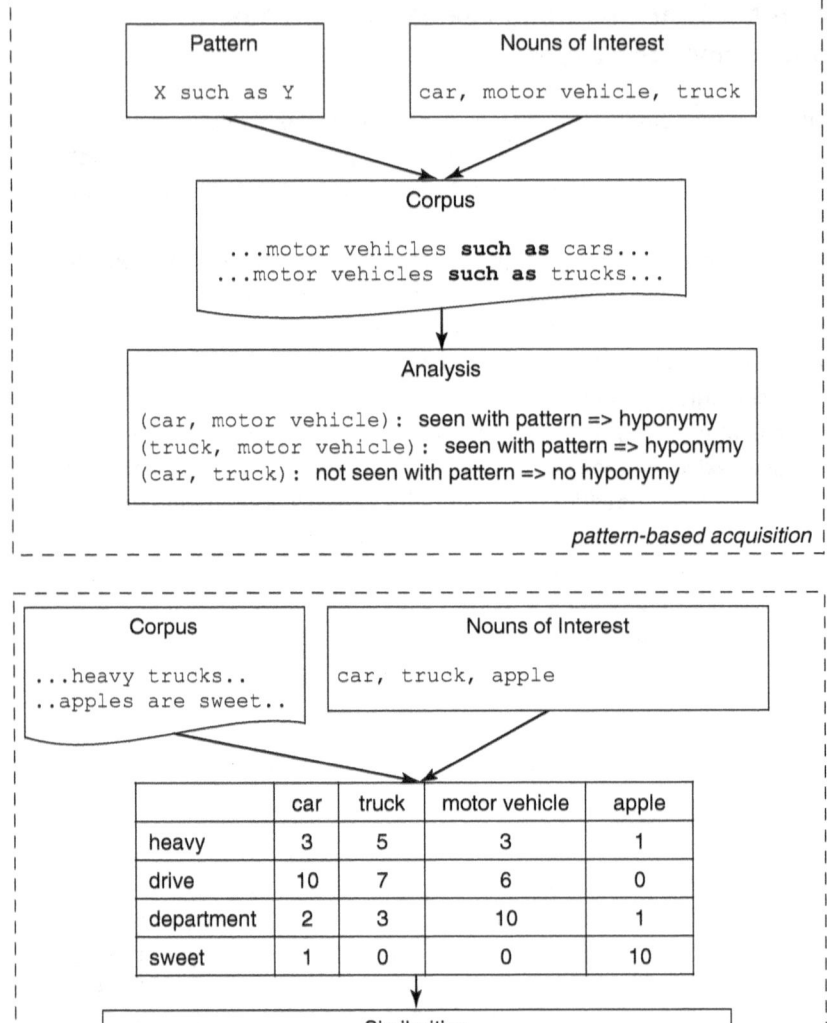

Fig. 15.4: Automatic acquisition of lexical information from corpora

structure. Riloff & Jones (1999), Thelen & Riloff (2002) run a pattern-based bootstrapping process to induce semantic classes such as *building*, *human*, *event*, or *weapon*. A major issue in bootstrapping is the acquisition of bad patterns or items, which can "poison" the bootstrapping process. This is usually avoided by confidence-based filtering. In the verbal domain, Miyao & Tsujii (2009) develop a probabilistic supervised model that classifies unseen verbs into the full inventory of VerbNet classes, relying on features extracted from unannotated corpora.

Beyond the level of individual words, surface-oriented acquisition methods may be used to acquire sets of phrases or sentences with similar meanings ("to work for" ⇔ "to be employed by"). This task is called *paraphrase acquisition* and can be based on comparable and parallel corpora (Barzilay & Lee 2003; Bannard & Callison-Burch 2005).

The main challenge in learning semantic classes is the large number of different criteria by which items can be grouped. This is indicated by the large number of classifications proposed in the literature (cf. Section 1.). Consequently, there is no unique "correct" classification, which exposes evaluation against any fixed gold standard to criticism.

Learning semantic relations

We now consider the induction of (binary) semantic relations holding between words or semantic classes, the so-called *relation extraction* task. Traditionally, the focus is on nominal relations such as synonymy, hyponymy/hyperonymy (*is-a*) and meronymy (*part-of*) – the relations also found in WordNet. In the pattern-based tradition, Hearst (1992) has used simple surface patterns to induce *is-a* relations. Girju, Badulescu & Moldovan (2006) use a similar approach for meronymy induction. Ruiz-Casado, Alfonseca & Castells (2005) learn extraction patterns and acquire new lexical relations for enriching WordNet using Wikipedia. A recent development is a broader focus on other lexical relations, such as *causation* in work by Pantel & Pennacchiotti (2006). They also use the lexical relations they induce to extend WordNet. Fine-grained relation extraction (Agichtein & Gravano 2000) and classification (Girju et al. 2009) tends to target increasingly encyclopedic relations such as *content-container*, *part-whole*, and thus approaches the domain of ontology learning (see below).

A related task is the *acquisition of inference rules*, which identifies pairs of words where the second follows from the first ("to snore" ⇒ "to sleep"). Such inference rules can be acquired not only on the lexical level, but also for multi-word expressions and phrases (Lin & Pantel 2001; Pantel et al. 2007; Pekar 2008).

Turney & Littman (2005) go beyond the search for individual relations. They develop models to determine the semantic similarity holding between pairs of relation tuples, e.g. *mason:stone – carpenter:wood*. This task extends identification of semantic relations to the task of recognising analogies; it requires representations not only of word meaning, but also of relations between words.

Learning and populating ontologies

Techniques for inducing full-fledged ontologies integrate relation learning with class learning, the two tasks described above. It typically begins with the induction of concepts, which may be instantiated with lexical items. The classes are subsequently structured on the basis of semantic relations. These are initially taxonomic, but are subsequently extended by relational and encyclopedic knowledge.

One possibility is to extend the clustering-based methods for inducing semantic classes described above to induce hierarchical structure (Caraballo 1999). Cimiano, Hotho & Staab (2005) refine this technique by using formal concept analysis, employing predicate-argument relations as contexts. Unfortunately, the induction of hierarchies with clustering techniques multiplies the problems encountered in analysing and evaluating clustering-induced semantic classes. A promising new development is the injection of global consistency constraints into ontology learning, e.g. by enforcing the transitivity of hyponymy (Snow, Jurafsky & Ng 2006).

Knowledge can also be drawn from other sources. Traditionally, this meant machine-readable dictionaries (Nichols et al. 2006). In the last years, the huge growth of Wikipedia has led to a flurry of work on this resource. Ponzetto & Strube (2007) convert the category structure of Wikipedia into a large *is-a* hierarchy. Ruiz-Casado, Alfonseca & Castells (2005) use Wikipedia as a resource for learning patterns for semantic relations and extend WordNet with newly acquired relation instances. Suchanek, Kasneci & Weikum (2008) construct a large-scale ontology that combines WordNet and Wikipedia. Its taxonomy backbone is formed by WordNet and enriched with facts derived from Wikipedia. While these approaches are able to derive large-scale and high-quality ontological resources (when evaluated against other ontologies, or human judgements), they rely on the existence and correctness of such resources as well as the compatibility of their structuring principles with the target ontology.

Learning semantic knowledge from corpora or structured resources such as Wikipedia currently seems to be the most promising way to solve the acquisition bottleneck. It is, however, inherently restricted to the type of knowledge that is directly or indirectly recoverable from textual or semi-structured resources. General world knowledge remains difficult to acquire from text, as it is often too basic to be conveyed explicitly, even in encyclopedic sources such as Wikipedia.

3 Multilingual and cross-lingual aspects

The development of comprehensive criteria for semantic classification presents itself as a new challenge for each language. Therefore it seems attractive to start from a monolingual model developed for a given language when developing resources for a new language. However, the structure of a monolingual semantic lexicon is not guaranteed to fit other languages, due to conceptual and lexical differences (cf. article 13 [Semantics: Foundations, History and Methods] (Matthewson) *Methods in cross-linguistic semantics*). In what follows, we discuss strategies for building semantic lexicons for a growing set of languages, and for dealing with cross-linguistic differences in practice.

3.1 Manual multilingual resource development

While some languages (notably English) are fairly well researched, few resources exist for many smaller languages. An important research question is therefore how existing resources in *source* languages (SL) like English can be re-used for efficient development of new *target* languages (TL). Ideally, criteria or even concrete annotation guidelines of the SL can be directly transferred to the TL. This presupposes that the criteria used to structure the SL resource are (at least largely) consistently applicable to other languages. For example, adopting Levin verb classes as structuring principle for a multilingual classification requires that all languages show similar verbal diathesis alternations.

Retaining a tight correspondence between categories and relations across different languages is desirable for another reason: If such correspondences are possible, the design principles evidently capture cross-lingual generalisations. In lexicography, such correspondences allow the study of cross-lingual similarities and differences of lexicalisation patterns (Boas 2005). In NLP, they can be directly exploited for cross-lingual processing, e.g. by translating queries through WordNet synsets or FrameNet classes that relate lexical items across several languages.

The best-known example of parallel lexicon development is WordNet, which has become available for a large number of languages through the EuroWordNet project (Vossen 1998) and the Global WordNet association. Another example is FrameNet, counterparts of which are available or under development for Spanish (Subirats 2009), German (Burchardt et al. 2006), and Japanese (Ohara et al. 2004). PropBank resources are available for Chinese and Korean.

However, the correspondences are rarely, if ever, perfect. There are two strategies how to deal with divergences. EuroWordNet exemplifies *flexible cor-*

respondence. WordNet categories (synsets) are lexical, and therefore tied strongly to individual languages. In EuroWordNet, therefore, resource development in individual languages was largely independent. However, all languages map their synsets onto a so-called "inter-lingual index" (ILI), an unstructured set of language-independent synsets. Specifically, there is an ILI synset for each synset in any of the EuroWordNet languages. However, the links between ILI synsets and synsets of individual languages are not necessarily equivalence (synonymy) links (Peters et al. 1998). For example, the Dutch distinction between "hoofd" (human head) and "kop" (animal head) is mirrored in the existence of two distinct ILI synsets. These ILI synsets are linked to a single English "head" synset by way of a *hypernymy* link. In this manner, the ILI accommodates structural differences between the individual WordNets.

In contrast, work on FrameNets for new TLs attempts to retain *direct correspondence*, since the categories under consideration, schematised situations, lend themselves more readily to cross-lingual generalisation. Consequently, the structure of FrameNet was used as an initial starting point for most other projects, which restricts the work for new TLs to the assignment of lexical items to predefined frames and the collection of examples. Problems arise from FrameNet's assumption that frames are evoked lexically. Figure 15.5 shows an example of a cross-lingual difference in the granularity of lexicalisation. In English FrameNet, the distinction between *driving* a vehicle (as a driver) and *riding* a vehicle

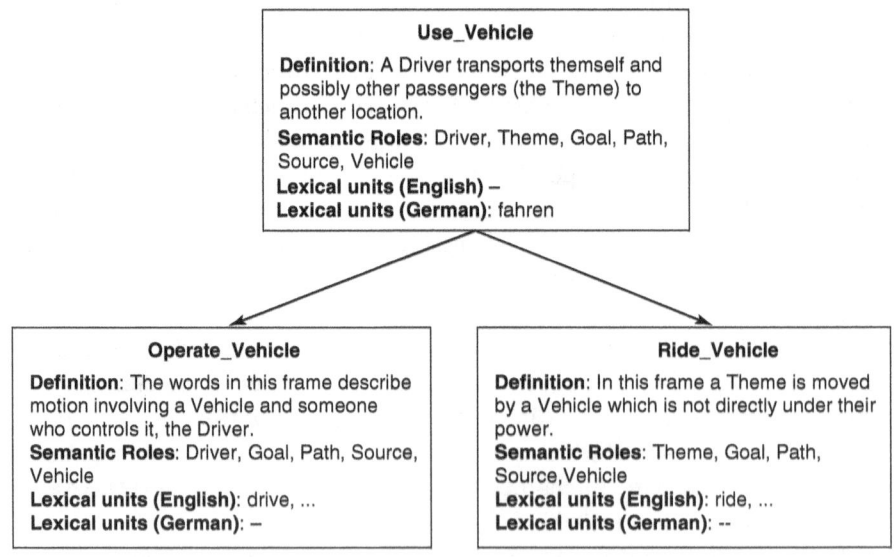

Fig. 15.5: Example for a cross-lingual divergence (German/English) in FrameNet

(as passenger) was codified in the form of two frames: Operate_Vehicle and Ride_Vehicle. In German, however, this distinction is not clearly lexicalised: the verb *fahren* can express both situations and cannot be assigned straightforwardly to one of the two frames. This situation was resolved by introducing a common superframe, Use_Vehicle.

More difficult to amend are general differences in argument realisation patterns between languages (such as differences in the argument incorporation of motion verbs between Romance and Germanic languages). Since in such cases establishing direct correspondence has undesirable consequences, the multilingual FrameNet initiative has decided to revert to an ILI-like flexible mapping when necessary.

3.2 Cross-lingual resource acquisition

For many languages, manual resource development is not an option at all. Thus, current research investigates techniques for cross-lingual resource induction to automate this process as completely as possible.

A first straightforward method is to use an existing *bilingual dictionary* to "translate" a SL resource into a TL resource. This method does not have any linguistic context at its disposal, other than the information encoded in the dictionary. Therefore, it requires (i) a high degree of correspondence on the lexical level between the two languages, and (ii) high-quality sense disambiguation for the selection of appropriate translation pairs from the dictionary. Fung & Chen (2004) construct a Chinese frame-semantic predicate classification by mapping English FrameNet entries onto Chinese using two bilingual dictionaries, with a subsequent monolingual disambiguation step, and obtain a high accuracy. While bilingual dictionaries developed for human users are often inconsistent and lack quantitative information, they can also be induced from corpora and used to induce selectional preference information for TLs (Peirsman & Padó 2010).

A second method is the use of *parallel corpora* in a three-step method called *annotation projection* (Yarowsky, Ngai & Wicentowski 2001). In Step 1, the SL side of a parallel corpus is labeled automatically, using the available SL resources. In Step 2, the SL annotations are transferred to the TL, on the basis of automatically induced word alignments. In Step 3, the TL annotations can serve as input either for lexicon creation, as described in Section 2.3., or as training data for new TL labelers. As Resnik (2004) observes, projection can be understood as reducing an unsupervised setting to a supervised setting, in which the TL labels are provided by the SL via word alignment. The validity of the TL labels relies on the so-called "direct correspondence assumption" (Hwa et al. 2002) – namely, that the semantic annotation of a source expression is also valid for its translation in the parallel corpus. This is an issue in particular for structural annotations, such as dependency relations or morphological information, but can be alleviated with filtering. A factor that can greatly affect the quality of target annotations are errors in the word alignments underlying projection. Here, a useful strategy is the exploitation of data redundancy and robust learning methods (Spreyer & Kuhn 2009). Annotation projection has been applied to various semantic phenomena, such as word sense (Bentivogli & Pianta 2005), frame-semantic information (Padó & Lapata 2009), temporal annotation (Spreyer & Frank 2008), or Information Extraction (Riloff, Schafer & Yarowsky 2002).

4 Interfaces and interoperability

The most widely used semantic lexicons in computational semantics concentrate on some well-defined aspect of meaning. For practical purposes, it is therefore often necessary to combine information from several resources. The three most common scenarios are linking semantic lexicons to other levels of description such as syntax or ontologies; the combination of different semantic lexicons; and the combination of general-vocabulary lexicons with domain-specific ones. While these tasks share a number of concerns, such as the compatibility of design principles and granularity issues, each of them poses its own specific challenges.

Interfaces to morphosyntax. Using a semantic lexicon for tagging free text with classes or senses usually involves part-of-speech tagging and lemmatisation. Morphological analysis may be required for specific semantic properties, for example tense and aspect for temporal analysis. This step can exploit a large body of work on standardisation (e.g. of tagsets), and divergences between the encodings used in the underlying processors and the coding scheme of a given semantic lexicon are usually easy to resolve. More intricate is the definition of interfaces between syntactic structure and semantic roles in predicate-argument structures. Both symbolic (rule-based) and statistical (feature-driven) interfaces to semantic lexicons need to associate syntactic structures obtained from parsing with their corresponding semantic roles (i.e., linking properties). Currently available parsers deliver constituent- or dependency-based structures, using a wide spectrum of categories and structure-building principles. Therefore, explicit mappings need to be defined between parser output and the syntactic representation used in the lexicon. Here, omission or misclassification of syntactic properties can constitute a serious obstacle for the use of semantic lexicons. Problems of this kind have been addressed in the extraction of lexical resources from PropBank and German FrameNet lexicons from annotated corpora (Babko-Malaya et al. 2006; Burchardt et al. 2008).

Interfaces to other semantic lexicons. The coverage of lexical semantic resources that exist for English today is impressive, but when processing free text we are still likely to encounter gaps. This is particularly true for lexicons encoding predicate-argument structure, whose deeper descriptions usually suffer from limited coverage.

This situation has engendered considerable interest in combining and integrating semantic lexicons. Most of the work pursued fully automatic strategies. For example, SemLink (Loper, Yi & Palmer 2007) provides a mapping between VerbNet, PropBank and FrameNet. Often, interest in the mappings is motivated by a particular application: Crouch & King's (2005) Unified Lexicon maps natural language onto a knowledge representation; the goal of Giuglea & Moschitti (2006) and Shi & Mihalcea (2005) is more robust semantic role assignment.

Current approaches rely almost exclusively on simple heuristics to establish inter-resource mappings, such as overlap in verbs between classes, or agreement of verbs on selectional preferences. While the resulting mappings are beneficial for practical purposes, these heuristics cannot deal well with fundamental design differences between resources (such as granularity or the focus on syntactic vs. semantic criteria). Such design differences can be bridged by detailed analysis (Čulo et al. 2008), but appears to be outside the scope of automatic methods.

Interfaces to ontologies. As discussed earlier, semantic lexicons need to be distinguished from ontological resources. Many NLP tasks, however, can benefit from the inclusion of a formal ontology, e.g. as a basis for inference, or as a repository for automatically acquired factual knowledge, as in Information Extraction or Question Answering tasks (Huang et al. 2010).

An explicit mapping has been manually defined between the English WordNet and the SUMO ontology (Niles & Pease 2003). Mismatches in granularity are covered by explicitly marking non-isomorphic correspondences. A method developed in Spohr (2008) makes it possible to extend this mapping automatically to other languages in EuroWordNet.

Among the largest horizontally and vertically connected resources is the Omega ontology (Philpot, Hovy & Pantel 2010). It integrates the WordNet, VerbNet, FrameNet and LCS lexical resources with a number of upper model ontologies (Hovy et al. 2006). In view of the special needs of NLP applications and given the problems encountered in the alignment of independently developed resources, the OntoNotes project (Pradhan et al. 2007) now undertakes a large *integrated multi-level corpus annotation project* as a basis for corpus-based semantic processing: annotations cover word sense, predicate-argument structure, ontology linking and co-reference relations and are tailored to allow rapid but reliable annotation practice with semi-automatic support for validation.

Interfaces between general and domain-specific resources. The development of NLP applications (e.g., for the natural or social sciences) can involve the creation of domain-specific lexical semantic resources, such as lexicons of medical procedures (Fellbaum, Hahn & Smith 2006) or soccer terms (Schmidt 2006). A major challenge lies in the integration of these specific lexicons with existing generic linguistic resources. Particularly striking are changes in syntactic and semantic properties that can affect general vocabulary items when used in a special domain. Verbs, for example, can show exceptional subcategorisation properties and meanings (e.g. the German *verwandeln (to convert)* with exceptional intransitive use in a soccer context for the special meaning "to turn into a goal"). Similar problems arise at other levels: the use of ontologies requires techniques for interfacing general and domain-specific ontologies. The problem of matching and aligning ontologies automatically is the subject of intensive research in Web Semantics (see article 17 [this volume] (Buitelaar) *Web Semantics*).

Thus, domain-specific texts require adapted models for parsing, ambiguity resolution as well as special handling in semantic lexicons and their mapping to ontologies. On the other hand, closed domains can also facilitate tasks such as the heuristic selection of word sense (Koeling, McCarthy & Carroll 2005).

Community efforts for standardisation and interoperability. In response to such problems, techniques for supporting the standardisation of language resources have been discussed and developed for a considerable time, as in the EAGLES initiative. With developing W3C standards, advanced representation models are being proposed to achieve interoperability across different representation frameworks for language resources (Francopoulo et al. 2006). Recent community efforts work towards ISO-standards for language resources (e.g. in LIRICS). Large community projects are developing resource infrastructures to support interoperability and exchange of resources at a large scale (e.g. CLARIN, FLaReNet; see Calzolari 2008). These projects provide a solid *formal* base for data exchange; agreement on standards for the represented *content* remains a more difficult endeavour.

5 Conclusion and outlook

Natural language processing has seen tremendous achievements in the last decade through the development of a range of large-scale lexical semantic resources. As we have shown, most theoretical frameworks for describing the meaning of words have found their way into lexicon resources, to different degrees and in various combinations.

The creation of WordNet, despite its limitations, can be considered a success story that has engendered stimulating research and advances in semantic processing, comparable to the effect that the Penn Treebank had in the area of syntactic processing. A key role for its feasibility and success was its concentration on a simple relational model of lexical meaning. This allowed rapid development to a sizable resource and offers flexible means for deployment in practical semantic NLP tasks. Its intuitive structure also prepared the ground for developing a multilingual EuroWordNet in a linguistically motivated and computationally transparent architecture. The practical use of such resources is greatly enhanced by the parallel creation of annotated corpora as a basis for induction of automatic annotation and disambiguation components.

Virtually all recent major resource creation efforts, such as FrameNet, PropBank and VerbNet, have adopted the methodological aspects of WordNet and its follow-up projects: (i) concentration on the encoding of a coherent, focused aspect of lexical meaning; (ii) empirical grounding, by using data-driven acquisition methods and providing annotated data for corpus-based learning, and (iii) horizontal multilingual extension, building on experiences gained in 'pilot' languages.

Still, the enormous efforts required for creating more complex lexicons such as VerbNet and FrameNet clearly show that the semantic resource acquisition bottleneck is far from being solved. And while some may still nourish hopes that one day 'the' ultimate, unified semantic theory of the lexicon will be reached, only the tip of the iceberg formed by semantic phenomena has been uncovered.

Largely unexplored is in particular the area of non-compositional lexical semantic phenomena (idioms and support constructions, metaphors) and to what extent they can be integrated with existing semantic lexicons. The situation is similar for the acquisition and integration of lexicons for specific domains. Another issue are fine-grained meaning differences, which are especially important for language generation tasks. These are far from being covered by today's semantic descriptive inventories (Inkpen & Hirst 2006).

Today, we observe three major research directions: (i) the rapid creation of multilingual semantic resources using cross-lingual techniques, capitalising on carefully built existing monolingual resources, (ii) the automated induction of semantic knowledge in monolingual settings, through corpus-based induction methods, and (iii) the integration of complementary semantic lexicons and annotated corpora, both horizontally and vertically, into coherent and interoperable resources.

Statistical, data-driven induction of semantic knowledge is a promising step towards the automation of semantic knowledge acquisition. This area of research is novel and comparatively unexplored, and its methods are faced with the core problems of semantics, in particular the structuring of the semantic space into classes and relations and the identification of salient meaning components. These are challenging decisions even for humans; in addition, corpus-based methods reach their limits when it comes to uncovering deeper aspects of semantic knowledge that cannot be derived from surface phenomena and quantitative analysis. As a result, automatic resource induction is typically used in a semi-automatic fashion that integrates human judgements.

In view of these limitations, novel forms of semantic resource acquisition are being explored that build on collaboratively, human-built resources, folksonomies such as Wikipedia, or specially designed annotation tasks (cf. article 17 [this volume] (Buitelaar) *Web Semantics*). Structured and unstructured information from Wikipedia can be used for harvesting semantic resources, from taxonomies to ontological attributes and relations. However, Wikipedia's focus is on encyclopedic information rather than lexical semantic information. A new trend builds non-expert contributions for targeted types of knowledge: translation, semantic tagging, etc., using game-like scenarios or Amazon's Mechanical Turk platform.

The move to corpus-based techniques has led to a big momentum and growth in lexical semantic resource building, and approximate methods for using them are well established in natural language processing. But the need for accurate semantic processing persists. More accurate semantic analysis will be needed for tasks that require high precision and that cannot exploit data redundancy. Examples are applications in the areas of knowledge-based natural language understanding and human-machine interaction.

We thank Rainer Osswald and Alexander Koller for comments and Antonina Werthmann for editorial support.

6 References

Agichtein, Eugene & Luis Gravano 2000. Snowball: Extracting relations from large plain-text collections. In: *Proceedings of the 5th ACM International Conference on Digital Libraries*. San Antonio, TX: ACM, 85–94.

Babko-Malaya, Olga, Ann Bies, Ann Taylor, Szuting Yi, Martha Palmer, Mitch Marcus, Seth Kulick & Libin Shen 2006. Issues in synchronizing the English Treebank and PropBank. In: *Proceedings of the Workshop on Frontiers in Linguistically Annotated Corpora 2006*. Sydney: ACL, 70–77.

Bannard, Colin & Chris Callison-Burch 2005. Paraphrasing with bilingual parallel corpora. In: K. Knight, H. T. Ng & K. Oflazer (eds.). *Proceedings of the 43rd Annual Meeting of the Association for Computational Linguistics (= ACL)*. Ann Arbor, MI: ACL, 597–604.

Barzilay, Regina & Lillian Lee 2003. Learning to paraphrase: An unsupervised approach using multiple-sequence alignment. In: *Proceedings of the Human Language Technology*

Conference of the North American Chapter of the Association for Computational Linguistics (= HLT-NAACL). Edmonton, AB: ACL, 16–23.
Bentivogli, Luisa & Emanuele Pianta 2005. Exploiting parallel texts in the creation of multilingual semantically annotated resources: The MultiSemCor Corpus. *Journal of Natural Language Engineering* 11, 247–261.
Boas, Hans 2005. Semantic frames as interlingual representations for multilingual lexical databases. *International Journal of Lexicography* 18, 445–478.
Borman, Andy, Rada Mihalcea & Paul Tarau 2005. PicNet: Augmenting semantic resources with pictorial representations. In: *Proceedings of the AAAI Spring Symposium on Knowledge Collection from Volunteer Contributors (= KCVC)*. Stanford, CA, 1–7.
Bos, Johan 2009. Applying automated deduction to natural language understanding. *Journal of Applied Logic* 1, 100–112.
Bresnan, Joan & Annie Zaenen 1990. Deep unaccusativity in LFG. In: K. Dziwirek, P. Farrell & E. Meijas-Bikandi (eds.). *Grammatical Relations. A Cross-Theoretical Perspective*. Stanford, CA: CSLI Publications, 45–57.
Budanitsky, Alexander & Graeme Hirst 2006. Evaluating WordNet-based measures of semantic distance. *Computational Linguistics* 32, 13–47.
Buitelaar, Paul 1998. CoreLex: An ontology of systematic polysemous classes. In: N. Guarino (ed.). *Proceedings of the 1st International Conference on Formal Ontology in Information Systems (= FOIS)*. Trento: IOS Press, 221–235.
Burchardt, Aljoscha, Katrin Erk, Anette Frank, Andrea Kowalski, Sebastian Padó & Manfred Pinkal 2009. Using FrameNet for the semantic analysis of German: Annotation, representation, and automation. In: H. C. Boas (ed.). *Multilingual FrameNets – Practice and Applications*. Berlin: Mouton de Gruyter, 209–244.
Burchardt, Aljoscha, Katrin Erk, Anette Frank, Sebastian Padó & Manfred Pinkal 2006. The SALSA Corpus: A German corpus resource for lexical semantics. In: N. Calzolari et al. (eds.). *Proceedings of the 5th International Conference on Language Resources and Evaluation (= LREC)*. Genoa: ELRA-ELDA, 969–974.
Burchardt, Aljoscha, Sebastian Padó, Dennis Spohr, Anette Frank & Ulrich Heid 2008. Constructing integrated corpus and lexicon models for multi-layer annotations in OWL DL. *Linguistic Issues in Language Technology* 1, 1–33.
Burchardt, Aljoscha, Nils Reiter, Stefan Thater & Anette Frank 2007. Semantic approach to textual entailment: System evaluation and task analysis. In: *Proceedings of the 3rd ACL-PASCAL Workshop on Textual Entailment*. Prague: ACL, 10–15.
Calzolari, Nicoletta 2008. Approaches towards a 'Lexical Web': The role of interoperability. In: *Proceedings of the 1st International Conference on Global Interoperability for Language Resources (= ICGL)*. Hong Kong, 34–42.
Caraballo, Sharon A. 1999. Automatic construction of a hypernym-labeled noun hierarchy from text. In: *Proceedings of the 37th Annual Meeting of the Association for Computational Linguistics (= ACL)*. College Park, MD: ACL, 120–126.
Carnap, Rudolf 1947. *Meaning and Necessity: A Study in Semantics and Modal Logic*. Chicago, IL: University of Chicago Press.
Carroll, John & Claire Grover 1989. The derivation of a large computational lexicon for English from LDOCE. In: B. Boguraev & T. Briscoe (eds.). *Computational Lexicography for Natural Language Processing*. New York: Longman, 117–133.
Christ, Oliver, Bruno M. Schulze, Anja Hofmann & Esther König 1999. *Corpus Query Processor (CQP). User's Manual*. Stuttgart: IMS, University of Stuttgart.

Ciaramita, Massimiliano & Mark Johnson 2003. Supersense tagging of unknown nouns in WordNet. In: *Proceedings of the Conference on Empirical Methods in Natural Language Processing (= EMNLP)*. Sapporo, 168–175.

Cimiano, Philipp, Andreas Hotho & Steffen Staab 2005. Learning concept hierarchies from text corpora using formal concept analysis. *Journal of Artificial Intelligence Research* 24, 305–339.

Cimiano, Philipp & Uwe Reyle 2005. Talking about trees, scope and concepts. In: H. Bunt, J. Geertzen & E. Thijsse (eds.). *Proceedings of the 6th International Workshop on Computational Semantics (= IWCS)*. Tilburg: ITK, Tilburg University, 90–102.

Copestake, Ann & Ted Briscoe 1995. Semi-productive polysemy and sense extension. *Journal of Semantics* 12, 15–67.

Crouch, Dick & Tracy H. King 2005. Unifying lexical resources. In: *Proceedings of the Interdisciplinary Workshop on the Identification and Representation of Verb Features and Verb Classes*. Saarbrücken, 32–37.

Culo, Oliver, Katrin Erk, Sebastian Padó & Sabine Schulte im Walde 2008. Comparing and combining semantic verb classifications. *Journal of Language Resources and Evaluation* 42, 265–291.

Curran, James R. 2005. Supersense tagging of unknown nouns using semantic similarity. In: *Proceedings of the 43rd Annual Meeting of the Association for Computational Linguistics (= ACL)*. Ann Arbor, MI: ACL, 26–33.

Dagan, Ido, Bill Dolan, Bernardo Magnini & Dan Roth 2009. Recognizing textual entailment: Rational, evaluation and approaches. *Natural Language Engineering* 15, i–xvii.

Dagan, Ido, Lillian Lee & Fernando C. N. Pereira 1999. Similarity-based models of word cooccurrence probabilities. *Machine Learning* 34, 34–69.

Dalrymple, Mary, John Lamping, Fernando Pereira & Vijay Saraswat 1997. Quantifiers, anaphora, and intensionality. *Journal of Logic, Language and Information* 6, 219–273.

Dang, Hoa T., Karin Kipper & Martha Palmer 2000. Integrating compostional semantics into a verb lexicon. In: *Proceedings of the 18th International Conference on Computational Linguistics (= COLING)*. Saarbrücken: Morgan Kaufmann, 1011–1015.

Dang, Hoa T., Karin Kipper, Martha Palmer & Joseph Rosenzweig 1998. Investigating regular sense extensions based on intersective Levin classes. In: *Proceedings of the 17th International Conference on Computational Linguistics (= COLING)*. Montreal: Morgan Kaufmann, 293–299.

Davis, Anthony & Jean-Pierre Koenig 2000. Linking as constraints on word classes in a hierarchical lexicon. *Language* 76, 56–91.

Dorr, Bonnie 1997. Large-scale dictionary construction for foreign language tutoring and interlingual machine translation. *Journal of Machine Translation* 12, 271–322.

Dorr, Bonnie J., Mari Olsen, Nizar Habash & Scott Thomas 2001. *LCS Verb Database*. College Park, MD: University of Maryland.

Dowty, David 1979. *Word Meaning and Montague Grammar. The Semantics of Verbs and Times in Generative Semantics and in Montague's PTQ*. Dordrecht: Springer.

Dowty, David 1991. Thematic proto-roles and argument selection. *Language* 67, 547–619.

Ellsworth, Michael, Katrin Erk, Paul Kingsbury & Sebastian Padó 2004. PropBank, SALSA and FrameNet: How design determines product. In: C. Fillmore et al. (eds.). *Proceedings of the Workshop on Building Lexical Resources From Semantically Annotated Corpora*. Lisbon, 17–23.

Esuli, Andrea & Fabrizio Sebastian 2006. SentiWordNet: A publicly available lexical resource for opinion mining. In: N. Calzolari et al. (eds.). *Proceedings of the 5th International Conference on Language Resources and Evaluation (= LREC)*. Genoa: ELRA-ELDA, 417–422.

Fellbaum, Christane, Udo Hahn & Barry Smith 2006. Towards new information resources for public health – from WordNet to MedicalWordNet. *Journal of Biomedical Informatics* 39, 321–332.
Fellbaum, Christiane (ed.) 1998. *WordNet: An Electronic Lexical Database*. Cambridge, MA: The MIT Press.
Fellbaum, Christiane, Alexander Geyken, Axel Herold, Fabian Koerner & Gerald Neumann 2006. Corpus-based studies of German idioms and light verbs. *International Journal of Lexicography* 19, 349–360.
Fillmore, Charles J. 1968. The case for case. In: E. Bach & R. T. Harms (eds.). *Universals in Linguistic Theory*. New York: Holt, Rinehart & Winston, 1–88.
Fillmore, Charles J. 1976. Frame semantics and the nature of language. *Annals of the New York Academy of Sciences* 280, 20–32.
Fillmore, Charles J., Christopher R. Johnson & Miriam R.L. Petruck 2003. Background to FrameNet. *International Journal of Lexicography* 16, 235–250.
Francopoulo, Gil, Monte George, Nicoletta Calzolari, Monica Monachini, Nuria Bel, Mandy Pet & Claudia Soria 2006. Lexical Markup Framework (LMF). In: N. Calzolari et al. (eds.). *Proceedings of the 5th International Conference on Language Resources and Evaluation (= LREC)*. Genoa: ELRA-ELDA, 233–236.
Fung, Pascale & Benfeng Chen 2004. BiFrameNet: Bilingual frame semantics resources construction by cross-lingual induction. In: *Proceedings of the 20th International Conference on Computational Linguistics (= COLING)*. Geneva, 931–935.
Gabrilovich, Evgeniy & Shaul Markovitch 2007. Computing semantic relatedness using Wikipedia-based explicit semantic analysis. In: M. M. Veloso (ed.). *Proceedings of the 20th International Joint Conference on Artificial Intelligence (= IJCAI)*. Hyderabad, 1606–1611.
Gangemi, Aldo, Roberto Navigli & Paola Velardi 2003. The OntoWordNet Project: Extension and axiomatization of conceptual relations in WordNet. In: R. Meersman & Z. Tari (eds.). *Proceedings of On The Move to Meaningful Internet Systems (= OTM)*. Heidelberg: Springer, 820–838.
Gildea, Daniel & Daniel Jurafsky 2002. Automatic labeling of semantic roles. *Computational Linguistics* 28, 245–288.
Girju, Roxana, Adriana Badulescu & Dan Moldovan 2006. Automatic discovery of part-whole relations. *Computational Linguistics* 32, 83–135.
Girju, Roxana, Preslav Nakov, Vivi Nastase, Stan Szpakowicz, Peter Turney & Deniz Yuret 2009. Classification of semantic relations between nominals. *Language Resources and Evaluation* 43, 105–121.
Giuglea, Ana-Maria & Alessandro Moschitti 2006. Semantic role labeling via FrameNet, VerbNet and PropBank. In: *Proceedings of the 21st International Conference on Computational Linguistics and 44th Annual Meeting of the Association for Computational Linguistics (= ACL)*. Sydney: ACL, 929–936.
Green, Rebecca, Bonnie Dorr & Philip Resnik 2004. Inducing frame semantic verb classes from WordNet and LDOCE. In: *Proceedings of the 42nd Annual Meeting on Association for Computational Linguistics (= ACL)*. Barcelona: ACL, 375–382.
Grenager, Trond & Christopher D. Manning 2006. Unsupervised discovery of a statistical verb lexicon. In: D. Jurafsky & E. Gaussier (eds.). *Proceedings of the Conference on Empirical Methods in Natural Language Processing (= EMNLP)*. Sydney: ACL, 1–8.
Grimshaw, Jane 1992. *Argument Structure*. Cambridge, MA: The MIT Press.
Gruber, Jeffrey S. 1965. *Studies in Lexical Relations*. Ph.D. dissertation. MIT, Cambridge, MA.

Gruber, Thomas R. 1995. Toward principles for the design of ontologies used for knowledge sharing. *International Journal of Human-Computer Studies* 43, 907–928.
Harris, Zellig S. 1968. *Mathematical Structures of Language*. New York: Interscience Publications.
Hartrumpf, Sven, Hermann Helbig & Rainer Osswald 2003. The semantically based computer lexicon HaGenLex – structure and technological environment. *Traitement Automatique des Langues* 44, 81–105.
Hearst, Marti 1992. Automatic acquisition of hyponyms from large text corpora. In: *Proceedings of the Fourteenth International Conference on Computational Linguistics (= COLING)*. Nantes, 539–545.
Hindle, Donald 1990. Noun classification from predicate-argument structures. In: *Proceedings of the 28th Annual Meeting of the Association for Computational Linguistics (= ACL)*. Pittsburgh, PA: ACL, 268–275
Hirst, Graeme 2004. Ontology and the lexicon. In: S. Staab & R. Studer (eds.). *Handbook on Ontologies*. Heidelberg: Springer, 209–229.
Hovy, Eduard, Mitchell Marcus, Martha Palmer, Lance Ramshaw & Ralph Weischedel 2006. Onto Notes: The 90% solution. In: *Proceedings of the Human Language Technology Conference of the North American Chapter of the Association for Computational Linguistics (= HLT-NAACL)*. New York: ACL, 57–60.
Huang, Chu-ren, Nicoletta Calzolari, Aldo Gangemi & Alessandro Lenci (eds.) 2010. *Ontology and the Lexicon: A Natural Language Processing Perspective*. Cambridge: Cambridge University Press.
Hwa, Rebecca, Philip Resnik, Amy Weinberg & Okan Kolak 2002. Evaluating translational correspondance using annotation projection. In: *Proceedings of the 40th Annual Meeting of the Association for Computational Linguistics (= ACL)*. Philadelphia, PA: ACL, 392–399.
Inkpen, Diana & Graeme Hirst 2006. Building and using a lexical knowledge-base of near-synonym differences. *Computational Linguistics* 32, 223–262.
Jackendoff, Ray 1972. *Semantic Interpretation in Generative Grammar*. Cambridge, MA: The MIT Press.
Jackendoff, Ray 1985. *Semantics and Cognition*. Cambridge, MA: The MIT Press.
Jackendoff, Ray 1990. *Semantic Structures*. Cambridge, MA: The MIT Press.
Kamp, Hans, Josef van Genabith & Uwe Reyle 2011. Discourse Representation Theory. In: D. M. Gabbay & F. Guenthner (eds.). *Handbook of Philosophical Logic, Vol. 15*. 2nd edn. Dordrecht: Springer, 125–394.
Katz, Jerrold J. & Jerry A. Fodor 1964. The structure of a semantic theory. In: J. J. Katz & J. A. Fodor (eds.). *The Structure of Language: Readings in the Philosophy of Language*. Englewood Cliffs, NJ: Prentice-Hall, 479–518. Originally published in *Language* 39, 1963, 170–210.
Kilgarriff, Adam 1997. I don't believe in word senses. *Computers and the Humanities* 31, 91–113.
Kilgarriff, Adam, Pavel Rychly, Pavel Smrz & David Tugwell 2004. The Sketch Engine. In: *Proceedings of the 11th EURALEX International Congress*. Lorient, 105–116.
Kipper, Karin, Anna Korhonen, Neville Ryant & Martha Palmer 2006. Extending VerbNet with novel verb classes. In: N. Calzolari et al. (eds.). *Proceedings of the 5th International Conference on Language Resources and Evaluation (= LREC)*. Genoa: ELRA-ELDA, 1027–1032.
Kipper-Schuler, Karin 2005. *VerbNet: A Broad-Coverage, Comprehensive Verb Lexicon*. Ph.D. dissertation. University of Pennsylvania, Philadelphia, PA.

Koeling, Rob, Diana McCarthy & John Carroll 2005. Domain-specific sense distributions and predominant sense acquisition. In: *Proceedings of the Human Language Technology Conference and Conference on Empirical Methods in Natural Language Processing (= HLT/EMNLP)*. Vancouver, BC, 419–426.

Korhonen, Anna & Ted Briscoe 2004. Extended lexical-semantic classification of English verbs. In: *Proceedings of the HLT/NAACL Workshop on Computational Lexical Semantics*. Boston, MA: ACL, 38–45.

Lapata, Mirella 2002. The disambiguation of nominalisations. *Computational Linguistics* 28, 357–388.

Lesk, Michael 1986. Automatic sense disambiguation using machine readable dictionaries: How to tell a pine cone from an ice cream cone. In: V. DeBuys (ed.). *Proceedings of the 5th Annual International Conference on Systems Documentation (= SIGDOC)*. Toronto, 24–26.

Levin, Beth 1993. *English Verb Classes and Alternations*. Chicago, IL: The University of Chicago Press.

Levin, Beth & Malka Rappaport Hovav 2005. *Argument Realization*. Cambridge: Cambridge University Press.

Lin, Dekang 1998. Automatic retrieval and clustering of similar words. In: *Proceedings of the 17th International Conference on Computational Linguistics (= COLING)*. Montreal: Morgan Kaufmann, 768–774.

Lin, Dekang & Patrick Pantel 2001. Discovery of inference rules for question answering. *Journal of Natural Language Engineering* 7, 343–360.

Loper, Edward, Szu-Ting Yi & Martha Palmer 2007. Combining lexical resources: Mapping between PropBank and VerbNet. In: J. Geertzen et al. (eds.). *Proceedings of the 7th International Workshop on Computational Semantics (= IWCS)*. Tilburg: ITK, Tilburg University, 118–129.

Lyons, John 1977. *Semantics*. Cambridge: Cambridge University Press.

Marcus, Mitchell P., Beatrice Santorini & Mary Ann Marcinkiewicz 1993. Building a large annotated corpus of English: The Penn Treebank. *Computational Linguistics* 19, 313–330.

McCarthy, Diana 2009. Word sense disambiguation: An overview. *Linguistics and Language Compass* 3, 537–558.

Merlo, Paola & Lonneke van der Plas 2009. Abstraction and generalisation in semantic role labels: PropBank, VerbNet or both? In: *Proceedings of the 47th Annual Meeting of the Association of Computational Linguistics and the 4th International Joint Conference on Natural Language Processing of the AFNLP (= ACL/AFNLP)*. Singapore: ACL, 288–296.

Meyers, Adam, Ruth Reeves, Catherine Macleod, Rachel Szekely, Veronika Zielinska, Brian Young & Ralph Grishman 2004. Annotating noun argument structure for NomBank. In: *Proceedings of the 4th International Conference on Language Resources and Evaluation (= LREC)*. Lisbon, 803–806.

Mihalcea, Rada & Dan Moldovan 2001. eXtended WordNet: Progress report. In: *Proceedings of the NAACL Workshop on WordNet and Other Lexical Resources*. Pittsburgh, PA: ACL, 95–100.

Miyao, Yusuke & Jun'ichi Tsujii 2009. Supervised learning of a probabilistic lexicon of verb semantic classes. In: *Proceedings of the Conference on Empirical Methods in Natural Language Processing (= EMNLP)*. Singapore: ACL, 1328–1337.

Müller, Stefan 2010. *Grammatiktheorie*. Tübingen: Stauffenburg.

Nairn, Rowan, Lauri Karttunen & Cleo Condoravdi 2006. Computing relative polarity for textual inference. In: J. Bos & A. Koller (eds.). *Proceedings of the Conference on Inference in Computational Semantics (= ICoS)*. Buxton, 67–78.

Narayanan, Srini & Sanda Harabagiu 2004. Question answering based on semantic structures. In: *Proceedings of the 20th International Conference on Computational Linguistics (= COLING)*. Geneva, 693–701.

Navigli, Roberto 2009. Word sense disambiguation: A survey. *ACM Computing Surveys* 41, 1–69.

Nichols, Eric, Francis Bond, Takaaki Tanaka, Sanae Fujita & Daniel Flickinger 2006. Robust ontology acquisition from multiple sources. In: *Proceedings of the 2nd Workshop on Ontology Learning and Population: Bridging the Gap between Text and Knowledge*. Sydney, 10–17.

Niles, Ian & Adam Pease 2003. Linking lexicons and ontologies: Mapping WordNet to the suggested upper merged ontology. In: H. R. Arabnia (ed.). *Proceedings of the International Conference on Information and Knowledge Engineering (= IKE)*. Las Vegas, NV: CSREA Press, 412–416.

Nirenburg, Sergei & Victor Raskin 2004. *Ontological Semantics*. Cambridge, MA: The MIT Press.

Norvig, Peter 1987. Inference in text understanding. In: *Proceedings of the Sixth National Conference on Artificial Intelligence (= AAAI)*. Seattle, WA: AAAI Press, 561–565.

Ohara, Kyoko H., Seiko Fujii, Toshio Ohori, Ryoko Suzuki, Hiroaki Saito & Shun Ishizaki 2004. The Japanese FrameNet Project: An introduction. In: *Proceedings of the LREC Workshop on Building Lexical Resources from Semantically Annotated Corpora*. Lisbon 1, 9–11.

Padó, Sebastian & Mirella Lapata 2009. Cross-lingual annotation projection of semantic roles. *Journal of Artificial Intelligence Research* 36, 307–340.

Palmer, Martha, Hoa T. Dang & Christiane Fellbaum 2006. Making fine-grained and coarse-grained sense distinctions both manually and automatically. *Journal of Natural Language Engineering* 13, 137–163.

Palmer, Martha, Dan Gildea & Paul Kingsbury 2005. The proposition bank: An annotated corpus of semantic roles. *Computational Linguistics* 31, 71–106.

Pang, Bo & Lillian Lee 2008. Opinion mining and sentiment analysis. *Foundations and Trends in Information Retrieval* 2, 1–135.

Pantel, Patrick, Rahul Bhagat, Bonaventura Coppola, Timothy Chklovski & Eduard Hovy 2007. ISP: Learning inferential selectional preferences. In: C. L. Sidner et al. (eds.). *Proceedings of the Conference of the North American Chapter of the Association for Computational Linguistics (= HLT-NAACL)*. Rochester, NY: ACL, 564–571.

Pantel, Patrick & Dekang Lin 2002. Discovering word senses from text. In: *Proceedings of the 8th ACM SIGKDD International Conference on Knowledge Discovery and Data Mining (= KDD)*. Edmonton, AB: ACM, 613–619.

Pantel, Patrick & Marco Pennacchiotti 2006. Espresso: Leveraging generic patterns for automatically harvesting semantic relations. In: *Proceedings of the 21st International Conference on Computational Linguistics (= COLING) and the 44th Annual Meeting of the Association for Computational Linguistics (= ACL)*. Sydney: ACL, 113–120.

Peirsman, Yves & Sebastian Padó 2010. Cross-lingual induction of selectional preferences with bilingual vector spaces. In: *Proceedings of the Human Language Technology Conference of the North American Chapter of the Association of Computational Linguistics (= HLT-NAACL)*. Los Angeles, CA: ACL, 921–929.

Pekar, Viktor 2008. Discovery of event entailment knowledge from text corpora. *Computer Speech & Language* 22, 1–16.

Pennacchiotti, Marco & Patrick Pantel 2006. Ontologizing semantic relations. In: *Proceedings of the 21st International Conference on Computational Linguistics (= COLING) and the 44th*

Annual Meeting of the Association for Computational Linguistics (= ACL). Sydney: ACL, 793–800.

Peters, Wim, Piek Vossen, Pedro Diez-Ortas & Geert Adriaens 1998. Cross-linguistic alignment of WordNets with an inter-lingual-index. *Computers and the Humanities* 32, 221–251.

Philpot, Andrew, Eduard Hovy & Patrick Pantel 2010. The Omega Ontology. In: C.-r. Huang et al. (eds.). *Ontology and the Lexicon: A Natural Language Processing Perspective.* Cambridge: Cambridge University Press, 309–322.

Ponzetto, Simone Paolo & Roberto Navigli 2010. Knowledge-rich Word Sense Disambiguation Rivaling Supervised System. In: *Proceedings of the 48th Annual Meeting of the Association for Computational Linguistics (= ACL).* Uppsala: ACL, 1522–1531.

Ponzetto, Simone Paolo & Michael Strube 2007. Deriving a large scale taxonomy from Wikipedia. In: *Proceedings of the 22nd National Conference on Artificial Intelligence (= AAAI).* Vancouver, BC: AAAI Press, 1440–1445.

Popescu, Adrian & Gregory Grefenstette 2008. A conceptual approach to Web Image Retrieval. In: N. Calzolari et al. (eds.). *Proceedings of the 6th International Conference on Language Resources and Evaluation (= LREC).* Marrakech: ELRA, 28–30.

Pradhan, Sameer, Eduard Hovy, Mitchell Marcus, Martha Palmer, Lance Ramshaw & Ralph Weischedel 2007. OntoNotes: A unified relational semantic representation. In: *Proceedings of the 1st IEEE International Conference on Semantic Computing (= ICSC).* Irvine, CA: IEEE Computer Society, 517–526.

Prescher, Detlef, Stefan Riezler & Mats Rooth 2000. Using a probabilistic class-based lexicon for lexical ambiguity resolution. In: *Proceedings of the 18th International Conference on Computational Linguistics (= COLING).* Saarbrücken: Morgan Kaufmann, 649–655.

Procter, Paul (ed.) 1978. *Longman Dictionary of Contemporary English.* New York: Longman.

Pustejovsky, James 1995. *The Generative Lexicon.* Cambridge, MA: The MIT Press.

Pustejovsky, James, Patrick Hanks & Anna Rumshisky 2004. Automated induction of sense in context. In: *Proceedings of the 20th International Conference on Computational Linguistics (= COLING).* Geneva, 924–930.

Resnik, Philip 1996. Selectional constraints: An information-theoretic model and its computational realization. *Cognition* 61, 127–159.

Resnik, Philip 1999. Semantic similarity in a taxonomy: An information-based measure and its application to problems of ambiguity in natural language. *Journal of Artificial Intelligence Research* 11, 95–130.

Resnik, Philip 2004. Exploiting hidden meanings: Using bilingual text for monolingual annotation. In: *Proceedings of the 5th International Conference on Intelligent Text Processing and Computational Linguistics (= CICLing).* Seoul: Springer, 283–299.

Resnik, Philip & Aaron Elkiss 2005. The linguist's search engine: An overview. In: *Proceedings of the 43rd Annual Meeting of the Association for Computational Linguistics (= ACL).* Ann Arbor, MI: ACL, 33–36.

Riloff, Ellen & Rosie Jones 1999. Learning dictionaries for information extraction by multi-level bootstrapping. In: *Proceedings of the 16th National Conference on Artificial Intelligence (= AAAI) and the 11th Conference on Innovative Applications of Artificial Intelligence (= IAAI).* Menlo Park, CA: AAAI, 474–479.

Riloff, Ellen, Charles Schafer & David Yarowsky 2002. Inducing information extraction systems for new languages via cross-language projection. In: *Proceedings of the 19th International Conference on Computational Linguistics (= COLING).* Taipei, 828–834.

Ruiz-Casado, Maria, Enrique Alfonseca & Pablo Castells 2005. Automatic assignment of Wikipedia encyclopedic entries to WordNet synsets. In: P. S. Szczepaniak & A. Niewiadomski (eds.). *Advances in Web Intelligence.* Heidelberg: Springer, 380–386.

Sag, Ivan, Timothy Baldwin, Francis Bond, Ann Copestake & Dan Flickinger 2002. Multiword expressions: A pain in the neck for NLP. In: A. F. Gelbukh (ed.). *Proceedings of the 3rd International Conference on Intelligent Text Processing and Computational Linguistics (= CICLing).* Mexico City: Springer, 1–15.

Saint-Dizier, Patrick 2006. PrepNet: A multilingual lexical description of prepositions. In: N. Calzolari et al. (eds.). *Proceedings of the 5th International Conference on Language Resources and Evaluation (= LREC).* Genoa: ELRA-ELDA, 877–885.

Schmidt, Thomas 2006. Interfacing lexical and ontological information in a multilingual soccer FrameNet. In: *Proceedings of the 2nd Workshop on Interfacing Ontologies and Lexical Resources for Semantic Web Technologies.* Genoa, 75–81.

Schulte im Walde, Sabine 2006. Experiments on the automatic induction of German semantic verb classes. *Computational Linguistics* 32, 159–194.

Schütze, Hinrich 1993. Word space. In: S. J. Hanson, J. D. Cowan & C. L. Giles (eds.). *Advances in Neural Information Processing Systems, vol. 5.* San Francisco, CA: Morgan Kaufmann, 895–902.

Shi, Lei & Rada Mihalcea 2005. Putting pieces together: Combining FrameNet, VerbNet and WordNet for robust semantic parsing. In: A. F. Gelbukh (ed.). *Proceedings of the 6th International Conference on Intelligent Text Processing and Computational Linguistics (= CICLing).* Mexico City: Springer, 100–111.

Snow, Rion, Daniel Jurafsky & Andrew Y. Ng 2006. Semantic taxonomy induction from heterogenous evidence. In: *Proceedings of the 21st International Conference on Computational Linguistics (= COLING) and the 44th Annual Meeting of the Association for Computational Linguistics (= ACL).* Sydney: ACL, 801–808.

Spohr, Dennis 2008. A general methodology for mapping EuroWordNets to the Suggested Upper Merged Ontology. In: N. Calzolari et al. (eds.). *Proceedings of the 6th International Conference on Language Resources and Evaluation (= LREC).* Marrakech: ELRA, 65–72.

Spohr, Dennis & Ulrich Heid 2006. Modelling monolingual and bilingual collocation dictionaries in description logics. In: *Proceedings of the Workshop on Multiword Expressions in a Multilingual Context.* Trentohy, 65–72.

Spreyer, Kathrin & Anette Frank 2008. Projection-based acquisition of a temporal labeller. In: *Proceedings of the 3rd International Joint Conference on Natural Language Processing (= IJCNLP).* Hyderabad, 489–496.

Spreyer, Kathrin & Jonas Kuhn 2009. Data-driven dependency parsing of new languages using incomplete and noisy training data. In: S. Stevenson & X. Carreras (eds.). *Proceedings of the Thirteenth Conference on Computational Natural Language Learning (= CoNLL).* Boulder, CO: ACL, 12–20.

Subirats, Carlos 2009. Spanish FrameNet: A frame-semantic analysis of the Spanish lexicon. In: H. C. Boas (ed.). *Multilingual FrameNets in Computational Lexicography: Methods and Applications.* Berlin: Mouton de Gruyter, 135–162.

Suchanek, Fabian M., Gjergji Kasneci & Gerhard Weikum 2008. YAGO: A large ontology from Wikipedia and WordNet. *Journal of Web Semantics* 6, 203–217.

Thelen, Michael & Ellen Riloff 2002. A bootstrapping method for learning semantic lexicons using extraction pattern contexts. In: *Proceedings of the Conference on Empirical Methods in Natural Language Processing (= EMNLP).* Philadelphia, PA: ACL, 214–221.

Turney, Peter D. & Michael L. Littman 2005. Corpus-based learning of analogies and semantic relations. *Machine Learning* 60, 251–278.
Vossen, Piek (ed.) 1998. *EuroWordNet: A Multilingual Database with Lexical Semantic Networks*. Dordrecht: Kluwer.
Winograd, Terry 1978. On primitives, prototypes, and other semantic anomalies. In: D. L. Waltz (ed.). *Proceedings of the Workshop on Theoretical Issues in Natural Language Processing (= TINLAP)*. Urbana-Champaign, IL: ACL, 25–32.
Xue, Nianwen 2008. Labeling Chinese predicates with semantic roles. *Computational Linguistics* 34, 225–255.
Yarowsky, David, Grace Ngai & Roger Wicentowski 2001. Inducing multilingual text analysis tools via robust projection across aligned corpora. In: *Proceedings of the 1st International Conference on Human Language Technology Research (= HLT)*. San Diego, CA, 161–168.

Paul Buitelaar
16 Web semantics

1 Introduction —— 482
2 The Semantic Web —— 483
3 Explicit web semantics —— 487
4 Implicit web semantics —— 494
5 Conclusions —— 496
6 References —— 496

Abstract: This article presents an overview of web semantics, i.e., the use and study of semantics in the context of the Web. We differentiate between explicit web semantics, building on Semantic Web standards for web-based knowledge representation (ontologies) and reasoning, and implicit web semantics, building on text and link mining from web resources.

1 Introduction

This article presents an overview of the emerging field of *web semantics*, divided into *explicit* and *implicit* web semantics.

Explicit web semantics is discussed in the context of the Semantic Web, which is fundamentally based on the formal interpretation of web objects (documents, databases, images, etc.) according to an ontology. Web objects are therefore provided with knowledge markup, i.e., semantically annotated with formally defined ontology classes and/or relations, on the basis of which ontology instances can be extracted. Knowledge markup of textual data relies on information extraction based on shallow or deep linguistic analysis.

Implicit web semantics originates from the analysis of information that is available in web objects in combination with the connecting structures of these web objects. This work uses methods based on data mining (i.e., text and web mining) to explore the network of web links and natural language references between documents (and other web objects) and to derive some level of semantic interpretation from this, e.g., by grouping or otherwise relating documents,

Paul Buitelaar, Galway, Ireland

https://doi.org/10.1515/9783110589825-016

extracted terms, or named entities. Work on web mining has been boosted recently by the emerging infrastructure of user defined tags as developing in the context of blogs, wikis and web communities.

2 The Semantic Web

The Semantic Web is a vision of a future version of the World Wide Web, in which all web-based knowledge is encoded in an explicit, formal way to allow for increasingly intelligent and therefore autonomous artificial agents as discussed by Berners-Lee, Hendler & Lassila (2001).

The Semantic Web idea implies the definition of formal, web-based ontologies to express the knowledge that is understood by humans as well as agents, and knowledge markup of web documents and databases according to these ontologies.

It is to be expected that over the next decade the knowledge structures of many application domains will be formally encoded in web-based ontologies, which will have a considerable impact on the sharing and use of expert knowledge within a wider community.

2.1 Realizing the Semantic Web

The Semantic Web has its origins in the application of knowledge representation languages to the annotation of web documents with semantic metadata. One of the earliest approaches to this is SHOE (Simple HTML Ontology Extensions) as described by Heflin, Hendler & Luke (1999).

SHOE is a knowledge representation language designed specifically for the web, which means that it "exists in a distributed environment with little central control" and therefore "treats assertions as claims being made by specific instances instead of facts to gather and intern as generally-recognized truth".

This is also an important aspect of the Semantic Web in general. In contrast to much of the previous work on Artificial Intelligence, the Semantic Web deals with an object of study that is very large, describes an 'open world' and is inherently dynamic.

Another aspect of the SHOE language that has been taken up in further development of the Semantic Web concerns syntax. As HTML and XML were already established languages on the Web, the syntax of SHOE was defined first in HTML and soon after in XML.

SHOE was a forerunner of the currently predominant Semantic Web representation languages RDF (Resource Description Framework – see http://www.w3.org/RDF/) and OWL (Web Ontology Language – see http://www.w3.org/TR/owl-ref/). OWL in particular allows for the definition of full ontologies – formal representation of entity classes, relationships between them and rules and axioms that guide what kind of assertions can be made and inferences drawn – as well as ontology instances that can be defined over web objects according to indicated ontologies.

The standardization of RDF and OWL allows for an easy exchange of web-based ontologies and instance collections as a growing number of tools become available for analyzing, indexing and otherwise handling such data, which eventually may lead to a realization of the Semantic Web vision of full and automatic access to all available knowledge.

Ontologies and how they are used in representing the meaning of web objects will be explained in more detail in the next section. For now it is important to note that ontologies as well as instances, i.e., individual assertions, are web objects themselves and therefore have a unique identity according to the URI (Uniform Resource Identifier) protocol that guides the Internet as a whole and also the Semantic Web.

URIs are therefore also at the basis of the so-called *semantic web layer cake* of increasingly more powerful representation layers that need to be developed and installed in order to realize the Semantic Web – see Fig. 16.1 below.

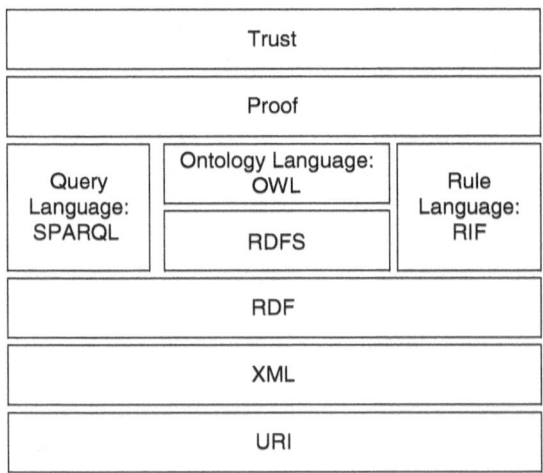

Fig. 16.1: Semantic web layer cake

These layers involve the definition of entity classes and relations using RDF or OWL (based on URIs and XML), of rules and axioms using the rule language RIF and of queries using the query language SPARQL.

On top of this the Semantic Web needs to have a layer of 'proof' and 'trust' by which assertions can be formally verified and traced to their originators.

2.2 Current status of the Semantic Web

The Semantic Web can be viewed from different directions: as a research project that aims at adding semantics to the web, as a set of Internet standards that implement the layers of the Semantic web layer cake, or as the accumulation of actual Semantic Web objects, i.e., web-based ontologies and ontology instances.

In fact it is probably most instructive to look at the Semantic Web from the last point of view, i.e., in terms of its size. For this purpose we can for instance consult the semantic web search engine Swoogle, which keeps track of RDF and OWL web documents that are being published on the Internet – see Ding et al. (2004) and the Swoogle website at http://swoogle.umbc.edu/.

Currently (February 2008), Swoogle reports to have collected almost 2,5 million of such documents, out of which however about half were valid RDF or OWL documents. Perhaps more interestingly however, Swoogle also reports that from these 1 million documents a total number of about 580 million separate simple facts could be extracted, each of which takes the form of a so-called *triple* between a *subject*, a *predicate* and an *object* to which the subject is connected.

For instance, the fact that there is a web document with URL http://www.dfki.de that describes DFKI which is located in Saarbrücken can be defined by three triples over the abstract node resource-1 as *subject*:
- 'URL' as *predicate* with string 'http://www.dfki.de' as *object*
- 'name' as *predicate* with string 'DFKI GmbH' as *object*
- 'location' as *predicate* with string 'Saarbrücken' as *object*

Another source of information on the number of ontologies that have been published on and can be accessed from the Semantic Web is OntoSelect, an ontology library that collects, analyzes and organizes ontologies that have been published on the Internet – see Buitelaar, Eigner & Declerck (2004), Buitelaar & Eigner (2008) and the OntoSelect website at http://olp.dfki.de/OntoSelect/.

OntoSelect allows browsing of currently (February 2008) over 1600 ontologies according to size (number of classes, properties), representation format (DAML,

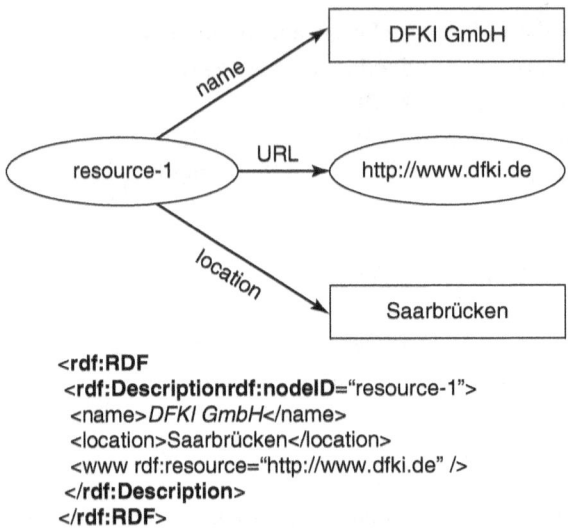

Fig. 16.2: Example of RDF triples

RDFS, OWL-Lite/DL/Full), connectedness (score over the number of included and referring ontologies) and human languages used for class and property labels.

The distribution of human languages across ontologies on the web is given in Tab. 16.1 below. The advance of English over other languages is not surprising as most ontologies still originate from English speaking countries although some start to appear with labels also in other languages, primarily German, French, Spanish and Portuguese.

In summary, the Semantic Web is still in an early stage but already a large number of formally defined facts (ontology instances) and models (ontologies) for interpreting these facts are available online.

Tab. 16.1: Distribution of languages across ontologies on the web (based on OntoSelect)

Language	Percentage of Ontologies with Labels in this Language
English	71.0 %
German	11.5 %
French	6.0 %
Spanish	3.7 %
Portuguese	3.2 %
other	4.6 %

3 Explicit web semantics

The vision of the Semantic Web is to turn the current Web of documents and data into a Web of formally defined knowledge – see for instance Berners-Lee, Hendler & Lassila (2001), Fensel et al. (2002). Ontologies play a central role in this vision and we will therefore consider them in more detail in this section. In particular, we will discuss the knowledge representation languages that have been proposed for defining web-based ontologies, the development and evolution of ontologies and the link between ontologies and the lexicon.

An ontology is an explicit, formal specification of a shared conceptualization of a domain of interest as defined by Gruber (1994), where "formal" implies that the ontology should be machine-readable and "shared" that it is accepted by a group or community. Further, it should be restricted to a given domain of interest and therefore model concepts and relations that are relevant to a particular task or application domain.

Ontologies formalize the intensional aspects of a domain, whereas the extensional part is provided by a knowledge base that contains assertions about instances of concepts and relations as defined by the ontology.

3.1 Knowledge representation for ontologies

The history of web-based knowledge representation languages can be outlined as follows – based on Horrocks & Patel-Schneider (2003).

RDFS was first proposed as an XML-based knowledge representation language with which web-based ontologies could be defined. With RDFS one can define classes and properties (binary relations), range and domain constraints (on properties), and subclass and sub-property (subsumption) relations. RDFS is, however, limited in expressive power. For example, with RDFS it is not possible to define if properties are functional or transitive or to describe classes in terms of the properties of their individuals.

Such limitations led to the development of further, more expressive web-based knowledge representation languages such as OIL (Fensel et al. 2000, 2001), and two languages based on the Darpa Agent Markup Language (DAML _ see Hendler & McGuinness 2000): DAMLONT (McGuinness et al. 2002) and DAML+OIL (Horrocks 2002). DAML+OIL was subsequently used as a basis for the W3C web ontology language OWL.

OWL uses the same syntax as RDF (and RDFS), e.g., *rdfs:subClassOf* to assert sub-class relationships. OWL-specific classes and properties, expressed as combinations of RDF syntactic constructs, are used to extend RDFS functionality, e.g., the *owl:complement Of* property is used to add class complementation.

The semantics of OWL is based on Description Logic (Baader et al. 2002; Horrocks, Patel-Schneider & van Harmelen 2003), whereas the semantics of RDFS are given by a non-standard model theory, where individuals, classes and properties are all elements in the domain, property elements have extensions which are binary relations on the domain, and class extensions are only implicitly defined by the extension of the *rdf:type* property.

OWL is a layered language with three versions: Lite, DL and Full.

OWL Full uses all of the OWL language primitives and is syntactically and semantically upward-compatible with RDF/S. It is however undecidable and therefore does not allow for complete (or efficient) reasoning support.

OWL DL (Description Logic) is a sublanguage of OWL Full that restricts application of the constructors from OWL and RDFS. Therefore it corresponds to a well studied description logic that permits efficient reasoning support. On the other hand we lose however full compatibility with RDF/S.

OWL Lite even further restricts OWL DL to a subset of language constructors, e.g., excluding enumerated classes, disjointness statements, and arbitrary cardinality. The advantage would be that it is easier to understand and implement, although it is much less expressive than OWL Full or OWL DL.

An overview of knowledge representation constructs in RDFS and the three OWL versions can be summarized as follows:

OWL Light
    (sub)classes, individuals
    (sub)properties, domain, range   ⎫ **RDF Schema**
    conjunction   ⎭
    (in)equality
    cardinality 0/1
    datatypes
    inverse, transitive, symmetric
    hasValue
    someValuesFrom
    allValuesFrom

OWL DL
    Negation
    Disjunction
    Full Cardinality
    Enumerated types

OWL Full
    Allow meta-classes etc

Fig. 16.3: Language constructs in RDFS and OWL

3.2 Ontology development

Ontology development is primarily concerned with the definition of classes and class properties, which may include relations between classes. (In OWL this distinction can be expressed by use of *owl:dataProperty* for the former vs. *owl:objectProperty* for the latter.) An ontology thus consists of classes that are organized by way of a taxonomy backbone (is-a relation) and other, non-hierarchical relations. Constraints on classes and relations between classes can be expressed through general and domain-specific axioms. Finally, in order to derive facts that are not explicitly encoded by the ontology but could be derived from it, an ontology may include also (domain-specific) rules that allow for such derivations.

Ontology development can be supported by ontology editing tools, of which Protégé (http://protege.stanford.edu/) is the most well known – see for instance Noy et al. (2001). Protégé provides graphical support for the definition of classes, properties and instances and includes a number of so-called PlugIns for visualization, consistency checking and other applications. Importantly, Protégé also includes a Plug-In for the editing of OWL-based ontologies – see Knublauch et al (2004). Other tools for ontology development exist but most of these are commercial whereas Protégé is freely available for research purposes.

3.3 Ontology learning

Ontologies define the semantics of a particular domain at a particular point of time and in a particular context. However, as domains change over time and can be viewed differently depending on application, ontologies need to evolve as well, as for instance with ontologies that model the rapidly developing biomedical domain. For this purpose a number of researchers have started developing *ontology learning* methods for the automatic extraction of ontological knowledge from data, primarily from text – see for instance Maedche (2002), Gomez-Perez & Manzano-Macho (2003), Shamsfard & Barforoush (2003), Buitelaar, Cimiano & Magnini (2005), Buitelaar & Cimiano (2008).

A large collection of methods for ontology learning from text have developed over recent years as witnessed by the growing number of publications in this area. Unfortunately, there is not much consensus within the ontology learning community on the exact task they are concerned with, which makes a comparison of approaches difficult. In order to estimate the state-of-the-art in ontology learning Buitelaar, Cimiano & Magnini (2005), Cimiano (2006) established an overview of the subtasks that together constitute the complex task of ontology development (either manual or with any level of automatic support).

Tab. 16.2: Ontology learning layer cake

Axioms & Rules	$\forall x, y$ (suffer From $(x,y) \rightarrow$ ill (x))
Relations	cure (domain:Doctor, range:Disease)
Concept Taxonomy	is_a (Doctor, Person)
Concepts	Disease:=<I, E, L>
Synonyms	{disease, illness}
Terms	disease, illness, hospital

Ontology development is primarily concerned with the definition of concepts and relations between them, but connected to this also knowledge about the symbols that are used to refer to them. In our case this implies the acquisition of linguistic knowledge about the terms that are used to refer to a specific concept in text and possible synonyms of these terms.

An ontology further consists of a taxonomy backbone (is-a relation) and other, non-hierarchical relations. Finally, in order to derive also facts that are not explicitly encoded by the ontology but could be derived from it, also rules should be defined (and if possible acquired) that allow for such derivations.

All of these aspects of ontology development can be organized in a layer cake of increasingly complex subtasks, as illustrated in Fig. 16.4 below. The example shows the defined knowledge for the concept *disease* and related concepts, i.e., the terms that can be used to refer to or associated with *disease* – also for languages different than English, the taxonomic relation of the concept *doctor* with *person*, a non-hierarchical relation between *doctor* and *disease*, and a rule that can be defined over the *person* and *disease* concepts.

3.4 Ontology selection

As the Semantic Web continues to grow in terms of developed and published ontologies, it will become much easier to *find* rather than *construct* an appropriate ontology for a particular application. On the other hand, as more and more ontologies become available to choose from it is correspondingly hard to find the best ontology.

Until very recently the solution to this problem was supposed to be handled by foundational ontology libraries as discussed by van Heijst, Schreiber & Wielinga (1997). However, in recent years web-based services like SWOOGLE and OntoSelect have been developed that enable a more data-driven approach to ontology search and retrieval. An important aspect of these services is the ranking of retrieved ontologies relative to a query keyword, or in the case of OntoSelect, a query document.

A web-based ontology, defined in RDFS or OWL, is in many respects just another web document that can be indexed, stored and retrieved. On the other hand, an ontology is a highly structured document with possibly explicit semantic links to other ontologies that are to be addressed by specific measures, e.g., Alani, Brewster & Shadbolt (2006) describe the following measures: "Class Match" (coverage of ontology class names occurring also as search terms in the ontology selection search query), "Density" (the number of links between classes, indicating the depth of knowledge represented by the ontology), "Semantic Similarity" (a measure of similarity between the link structures around classes) and "Betweenness" (a measure of the number of links that go through each class). These last two measures are based on the assumption that ontologies are well-structured with equal semantic balance throughout all constitutive parts, which unfortunately is only seldom the case.

Another set of measures or rather criteria for ontology ranking and selection has been proposed by Sabou, Lopez & Motta (2006). The focus here is more on the application of ranked/selected ontologies and therefore includes such criteria as "Modularization" (Can retrieved ontologies be split up in useful modules?), "Returning ontology combinations" (Can retrieved ontologies be used in combination?) and "Dealing with instances" (Do retrieved ontologies include instances as well as classes/properties?) next to more standard measures such as coverage.

3.5 Ontologies and the lexicon

A lexicon represents different interpretations of words with senses. A sense represents the semantics of a word, very much like a class definition in an ontology. In fact, semantic lexicons such as WordNet are semi-formalized dictionaries that group words into classes (i.e., synsets or senses) for which we can give formal definitions. In this way, semantic lexicons are the reverse of ontologies in that they assign one or more classes (i.e., senses) to a given word, whereas ontologies assign labels (i.e., words or more complex terms) to a given class.

Given these assumptions we may thus view the collection of ontologies on the Semantic Web as a large, distributed semantic lexicon, in which we can look up the meaning of words, just as in a regular dictionary. Consider for instance the meaning of *director* as provided by the following two ontologies.

In the AgentCities ontology a *director* is of class "Role" that somebody can assume. Unfortunately, the ontology provides no additional information on what constitutes a "Role", but simply assigns it as a super-class to the "Director" class as well as to the "Actor" and "Playwright" classes. From this information we may infer something about the meaning of *director*, namely that it is something similar to being an *actor* and a *playwright* but not much more.

(1)   <daml:Class rdf:ID = "Director">
    <rdfs:label>Director</rdfs:label>
    <rdfs:subClassOf>
        <daml:Class rdf:about = "#Role"/>
    </rdfs:subClassOf>
    </daml:Class>

A more informative definition for a different sense of *director* is provided by the University Benchmark ontology, which defines *director* of class "Director" with super-class "Person" that has the property "headOf" with a value of class "Program". As the ontology further defines the class "Program" as a sub-class of "Organization", we may infer that *director* in this sense of the word refers to a *person* who is the *head of* a specific type of *organization*, i.e., a *program*.

(2)   <owl:Class rdf:ID = "Director">
    <rdfs:label>director</rdfs:label>
    <owl:intersectionOf
    rdf:parseType = "Collection">
    <owl:Class rdf:about = "#Person"/>
    <owl:Restriction>
    <owl:onProperty
    rdf:resource = "#headOf"/>
    <owl:someValuesFrom>
        <owl:Class rdf:about = "#Program"/>
        </owl:someValuesFrom>
    </owl:Restriction>
    </owl:intersectionOf>
    </owl:Class>

However, to allow for the application of ontologies in natural language processing (NLP) applications such as semantic annotation and ontology-based information extraction (see below), a richer linguistic representation is needed of domain terms, their synonyms and multilingual variants. Currently, such information is mostly missing, or represented only in an impoverished way (using RDFS Label).

To allow for a richer representation of linguistic information in a domain ontology, Buitelaar, Sintek & Kiesel (2006) developed a lexicon model for ontologies,

LingInfo, which was further developed by Buitelaar, Cimiano, Haase & Sintek (2009) into LexInfo (see http://lexinfo.net/), a principled and formal model for associating linguistic information to ontology elements (classes, properties) with respect to any level of linguistic description and expressivity. The main characteristic of LexInfo is that it allows for a declarative representation of linguistic information on ontology elements, such that this information is reusable across ontology-based NLP systems.

The current situation is that one needs to establish this information anew for each ontology-based NLP system and for each ontology that such a system supports. This is clearly undesirable as it does not allow for a distribution of effort. Instead, a clear modularization of tasks, i.e., separating the creation of lexica from their usage in a particular ontology-based NLP system, would allow for the creation and sharing of lexicons independent of but usable with different ontologies. To realize this vision, LexInfo provides a declarative model for representing such an "ontology-lexicon".

3.6 Ontology-based information extraction

Semantic annotation or 'knowledge markup' of textual data is based on the employment of task- and domain-specific ontologies, thesauri or other semantic resources for enriching this *data* with semantic *metadata* that annotate text segments (names, terms, sentences, paragraphs, images, etc.) with their semantic interpretation.

If knowledge markup is based on a formally defined ontology that describes a knowledge base model, the markup process in effect extracts information from available data to populate a knowledge base of facts (named entities, concepts, events) according to the ontology, a process that is also referred to as 'ontology population'.

The current state-of-the-art in knowledge markup is still largely based on manual data processing, in which domain experts manually tag documents or sections of documents with ontology classes – for an overview see Handschuh & Staab (2003). Alternatively, a knowledge markup system may employ language technology and machine learning tools for the automatic mapping of text segments to ontology classes.

The knowledge markup process in effect will extract information from the textual data to generate a knowledge base of facts as defined by the corresponding ontology. Information extraction consists of a number of steps that will incrementally build on the recognition of basic semantic units and semantic relations between them.

An important first step is named-entity recognition, which is mostly restricted to a small set of non-interrelated and non-formally represented entity classes, e.g., "person", "location", "date", "organization". However, especially in technical domains much larger sets of entity classes are used based on domain ontologies, as used for instance by Reidsma et al. (2003) in sports video annotation, Rebholz-Schuhmann & Kirsch (2004) in the biomedical field, Saggion et al. (2007) in business intelligence.

A related step is the identification of relevant concepts in the text. For this purpose, terms that are indicators for such concepts need to be extracted and semantically classified, i.e., mapped to ontology classes that define the concepts. Semantic tagging has been mostly implemented by use of Wordnet for English or of wordnets for other languages. However, for knowledge markup in technical domains, terms are to be tagged primarily with ontology classes from relevant ontologies as indicated above.

A final step is the identification of events, which may involve several concepts and/or named-entities and which are expressed by relations between them. In traditional information extraction, events have been mostly defined by so-called 'templates': a small number of relations between relevant concepts and/or named-entities that are to be filled by analysis of available data (see Cowie & Wilks 2000).

Obviously, if such templates are expressed in a formally defined knowledge representation and markup language such as RDFS or OWL, they roughly correspond to an ontologically defined class with its properties. This brings together the information extraction tradition – see e.g., Cowie & Lehnert (1996) – with the knowledge representation and reasoning traditions – see e.g., Sowa (2000), both of which will play an increasingly important role in the future of web semantics and in the study of linguistic meaning in general.

4 Implicit web semantics

Ontologies and ontology-based information extraction as discussed in the previous sections are based on the formal and explicit definition of meaning, e.g., by use of RDFS or OWL.

Other routes in web semantics are however taken as well, i.e., by:
- User-defined semantics: annotation of data with keywords without formal definition
- Emergent semantics: induction of recurring patterns across large data sets of linked web data

4.1 User-defined semantics

With the advent of so-called 'Web 2.0' sites, allowing web users to publish their pictures, videos, stories, etc. on the web, these users started to annotate their published items with keywords, mostly by free association. Over time, such keywords were referred to as tags and the process as 'collaborative tagging', 'social tagging' or 'folksonomy' (coined by van der Wal 2004) to highlight the connection of this non-expert or 'folk-based' indexing with taxonomies as used by indexing experts.

Another route in user defined semantics is the collaborative compilation of dictionary and encyclopedia entries as done in the context of Wikipedia (http://www.wikipedia.org/), Wiktionary (http://www.wiktionary.org/) and similar initiatives. Such resources provide a wealth of open-access (lexical) semantic information that can be exploited in NLP applications – see for instance Strube & Ponzetto (2006) who derive a large-scale taxonomy from Wikipedia that they then use to compute semantic similarities between words, e.g., for use in word sense disambiguation and co-reference resolution.

4.2 Emergent semantics

Probably the furthest removed from traditional study of linguistic meaning is the idea of *emergent semantics*, which is based on the induction of recurring patterns across large data sets. An example of such patterns is the analysis of so-called 'social networks' between (web) users based on the data they produce and access (see for instance Wassermann & Faust 1994).

Social network analysis is based on web mining, i.e., the analysis of which web document is connected to which others, assigning weights to heavily used connections and thereby bringing in the web user. Web mining in turn is based on the use of data mining methods as developed originally for finding regularly occurring patterns in databases.

Through a combination of web mining with NLP, in particular text classification and information extraction, social network analysis systems are now able to derive not only networks of web users but also of concepts as used in web documents.

This opens the way to so-called 'emergent semantics', i.e., the definition of meaning based on (web) use, i.e., words and expressions in general deriving their meaning from the way they are actually used instead of their meaning being defined a priori, e.g., through senses in a lexicon – see for instance Mika (2007) who gives this example: "The term ontology is associated [in Web forums], among others, with

HTML, XML and databases, concepts not directly related to the understanding of ontologies in the Semantic Web community."

Finally, a combination of explicit and implicit web semantics can be found in work on Semantic Web mining, which explores the connecting structures of formally interpreted web objects – see for instance Berendt et al. 2002.

5 Conclusions

In this article we presented an overview of the use and study of semantics in the context of the Web. Web semantics is a growing field that will have important implications for the study of semantics in general and linguistic semantics in particular, as more and more parts of our lives (work, study, entertainment, etc.), and therefore also our use of language, are taking place on the Web. It will therefore be of importance to start a serious integration of web semantic research into mainstream linguistic semantic study.

This work has been supported by the European Union FP7 program under grant number 248458 for the Monnet project and by the Science Foundation Ireland under Grant No. SFI/08/CE/I1380 for the project Lion-2.

6 References

Alani Harith, Christopher Brewster & Nigel Shadbolt 2006. Ranking ontologies with AKTiveRank. In: I. Cruz et al. (eds.). *Proceedings of the International Semantic Web Conference (= ISWC) 5*. Berlin: Springer, 1–15.

Baader, Franz, Diego Calvanese, Deborah McGuinness, Daniele Nardi & Peter Patel-Schneider (eds.) 2002. *The Description Logic Handbook*. Cambridge: Cambridge University Press.

Berners-Lee, Tim, James Hendler & Ora Lassila 2001. The semantic web: A new form of web content that is meaningful to computers will unleash a revolution of new possibilities. *Scientific American* 284(5), 34–43.

Berendt, Bettina, Andreas Hotho & Gerd Stumme 2002. Towards semantic web mining. In: I. Harrocks & J. Hendler (eds.). *Proceedings of the First International Semantic Web Conference (= ISWC2002)*. Berlin: Springer, 264–278.

Buitelaar, Paul, Thomas Eigner & Thierry Declerck 2004. OntoSelect: A dynamic ontology library with support for ontology selection. Paper presented at the Demo Session at the *International Semantic Web Conference (= ISWC) 3*, Hiroshima, Japan, November 7–11, 2004.

Buitelaar, Paul, Philipp Cimiano & Bernardo Magnini (eds.) 2005. *Ontology Learning from Text: Methods, Evaluation and Applications Frontiers in Artificial Intelligence and Applications Series, vol. 123*. Amsterdam: IOS Press.

Buitelaar, Paul, Michael Sintek & Malte Kiesel 2006. A multilingual/multimedia lexicon model for ontologies. In: Y. Sure & J. Domingue (eds.). *Proceedings of the European Semantic Web Conference (= ESWC) 3*. Berlin: Springer, 502–513.

Buitelaar, Paul & Philipp Cimiano (eds.) 2008. *Ontology Learning and Population: Bridging the Gap between Text and Knowledge Frontiers in Artificial Intelligence and Applications Series, vol. 167*. Amsterdam: IOS Press.

Buitelaar, Paul & Thomas Eigner 2008. Ontology search with the OntoSelect ontology library. In: N. Calzolari et al. (eds.). *Proceedings of the International Conference on Language Resources and Evaluation (= LREC) 6*. Paris: European Language Resources Association, 1030–1033.

Buitelaar, Paul, Philipp Cimiano, Peter Haase & Malte Sintek 2009. Towards linguistically grounded ontologies. In: L. Aroyo et al. (eds.). *Proceedings of the European Semantic Web Conference (= ESWC) 6*. Berlin: Springer: 111–125.

Cowie, Jim & Wendy Lehnert 1996. Information extraction. *Communications of the ACM 39*, 80–91.

Cowie, Jim & Yorick Wilks 2000. Information extraction. In: R. Dale, H. Moisl & H. Somers (eds.). *Handbook of Natural Language Processing*. New York: Marcel Dekker Publishing, 241–260.

Ding, Li, Tim Finin, Anupam Joshi, Rong Pan, R. Scott Cost, Yun Peng, Pavan Reddivari, Vishal C. Doshi & Joel Sachs 2004. Swoogle: A search and metadata engine for the semantic web. In: D. A. Grossman et al. (eds.). *Proceedings of the ACM Conference on Information and Knowledge Management (= CIKM) 13*. New York: ACM Publishing, 652–659.

Fensel, Dieter, Wolfgang Wahlster, Henry Lieberman & James Hendler 2002. *Spinning the Semantic Web: Bringing the World Wide Web to Its Full Potential*. Cambridge, MA: The MIT Press.

Fensel, Dieter, Ian Horrocks, Frank van Harmelen, Stefan Decker, Michael Erdmann, Michel C. A. Klein 2000. OIL in a nutshell. In: R. Dieng & Olivier Corby (eds.). *Proceedings of the European Workshop on Knowledge Acquisition, Modeling and Management (= EKAW) 12*. Berlin: Springer, 1–16.

Fensel, Dieter, Frank van Harmelen, Ian Horrocks, Deborah L. McGuinness, Peter F. Patel-Schneider 2001. OIL: An ontology infrastructure for the semantic web. *IEEE Intelligent Systems 16*, 38–45.

Gómez-Pérez, Asunción & David Manzano-Macho 2003. *A Survey of Ontology Learning Methods and Techniques*. Technical Report. Madrid, Universidad Politecnica de Madrid, http://www.sti-innsbruck.at/fileadmin/documents/deliverables/Ontoweb/D1.5.pdf, February 6, 2011.

Gruber, Thomas R. 1994. Towards principles for the design of ontologies used for knowledge sharing. *International Journal of Human-Computer Studies 43*, 907–928.

Handschuh, Siegfried & Steffen Staab (eds.) 2003. *Annotation for the Semantic Web. Frontiers in Artificial Intelligence and Applications Series, vol. 96*. Amsterdam: IOS Press.

Heflin, Jeff, James Hendler & Sean Luke 1999. *SHOE: A Knowledge Representation Language for Internet Applications*. Technical Report CS-TR-4078 (UMIACS TR-99-71). College Park, MD, Department of Computer Science/University of Maryland, http://www.cs.umd.edu/Library/TRs/CS-TR-4078/CS-TR-4078.abs, February 6, 2011.

van Heijst, Gertjan, Guus Schreiber & Bob J. Wielinga 1997. Using explicit ontologies in KBS development. *International Journal of Human-Computer Studies 45*, 183–292.

Hendler, James & Deborah L. McGuinness 2000. The DARPA AgentMarkup language. *IEEE Intelligent Systems 15*, 67–73.

Horrocks, Ian 2002. DAML+OIL: A reason-able web ontology language. In: *Proceedings of the International Conference on Extending Database Technology (= EDBT) 8*. Berlin: Springer, 2–13.

Horrocks, Ian & Peter F. Patel-Schneider 2003. Three theses of representation in the semantic web. In: *Proceedings of the International World Wide Web Conference (= WWW 2003) 12*. New York: ACM Publishing, 39–47.

Horrocks, Ian, Peter F. Patel-Schneider & Frank van Harmelen 2003. From SHIQ and RDF to OWL: The making of a web ontology language. *Journal of Web Semantics* 1, 7–26.

Knublauch, Holger, Ray W. Fergerson, Natalya Fridman Noy & Mark A. Musen 2004. The protégé OWL plugin: An open development environment for semantic web applications. In: S. A. McIlraith, D. Plexousakis & F. van Harmelen (eds.). *Proceedings of the International Semantic Web Conference (= ISWC) 3*. Berlin: Springer, 229–243.

McGuinness, Deborah L., Richard Fikes, Lynn A. Stein & James Hendler 2002. DAML-ONT: An ontology language for the semantic web. *IEEE Intelligent Systems* 17, 72–80.

Maedche, Alexander 2002. *Ontology Learning for the Semantic Web*. Dordrecht: Kluwer.

Mika, Peter 2007. Ontologies are us: A unified model of social networks and semantics. *Journal of Web Semantics* 5, 5–15.

Noy, Natalya F., Michael Sintek, Stefan Decker, Monica Crubézy, Ray W. Fergerson & Mark A. Musen 2001. Creating semantic web contents with Protégé-2000. *IEEE Intelligent Systems* 16, 60–71.

Rebholz-Schuhmann, Dietrich & Harald Kirsch 2004. Extraction of biomedical facts – a modular web server at the EBI (Whatizit). Paper presented at the *Healthcare Digital Libraries Workshop (= HDL) 2004*, University of Bath, UK, September 16, 2004.

Reidsma, Dennis, Jan Kuper, Thierry Declerck, Horacio Saggion & Hamish Cunningham 2003. Cross document ontology based information extraction for multimedia retrieval. Paper presented at the *International Conference on Conceptual Structures (= ICCS) 11*. Dresden, Germany, July 21–25, 2003.

Sabou, Marta, Vanessa Lopez & Enrico Motta 2006. Ontology selection on the real semantic web: How to cover the Queens Birthday Dinner? In: St. Staab & V. Svátek (eds.). *Proceedings of the International Conference on Knowledge Engineering and Knowledge Management (= EKAW) 15*. Berlin: Springer, 96–111.

Saggion, Horacio, Adam Funk, Diana Maynard & Kalina Bontcheva 2006. Ontology-based information extraction for business applications. In: K. Aberer et al. (eds.). *Proceedings of the International Semantic Web Conference (= ISWC) 6*. Berlin: Springer, 843–856.

Shamsfard, Mehrnoush & Ahmad A. Barforoush 2003. Learning ontologies from natural language texts. *International Journal of Human-Computer Studies* 60, 17–63.

Sowa, John F. 2000. *Knowledge Representation: Logical, Philosophical and Computational Foundations*. Pacific Grove, CA: Brookes/Cole Publishing.

Strube, Michael & Simon P. Ponzetto 2006. WikiRelate! Computing semantic relatedness using wikipedia. In: A. Cohn (ed.). *Proceedings of the National Conference on Artificial Intelligence (= AAAI) 21, vol. 2*. Boston, MA: AAAI Press, 1419–1424.

van der Wal, Thomas 2004. Folksonomy. http://vanderwal.net/folksonomy.html, February 6, 2011.

Wasserman, Stanley & Katherine Faust 1994. *Social Networks Analysis: Methods and Applications*. Cambridge: Cambridge University Press.

Kurt Eberle
17 Semantic issues in machine translation

1 Introduction —— 499
2 Machine Translation architectures —— 506
3 Transfer of underspecified representations —— 519
4 Flat, underspecified rule-based MT and current empirical MT trends —— 526
5 Conclusion —— 528
6 References —— 529

Abstract: There has been research in Machine Translation for half a century. In this article we sketch the role that semantic knowledge and semantic analysis of words, sentences and texts have played in the different architectures that have been suggested for translating texts automatically. We sketch the reasons for making use of semantics in Machine Translation, the problems that arise from using it, the shape tradeoffs could take for minimizing the cost of semantic analysis and maximizing its impact on translation quality and how linguistic analysis and semantic representation could be combined with data-driven approaches and why this should be done.

1 Introduction

The challenge of Machine Translation (MT) is to translate texts written in a source language A into texts written in a target language B such that the result is a syntactically and semantically well-formed, pragmatically coherent text of the target language and such that the meaning of the target text equals the meaning of the source text. Normally it is assumed that the most natural translation unit be the sentence – or, when required, another expression that the text structure presents as a unit by means of markup information and punctuation, as, for example, a headline, an item in a table, an enumeration, a caption etc.

We neglect the corresponding task of segmenting the text into such units, we skip also other preprocessing tasks like deformatting and spell checking etc. and concentrate on the task of translating unformatted sentences or otherwise syntactically coherent expressions. Also we will not talk about speech and the problems connected to speech translation and the solutions suggested to solve them.

Kurt Eberle, Heidelberg, Germany

1.1 Ambiguity

Most sentences, expressions and words are ambiguous when taken in isolation (cf. article 8 [Semantics: Lexical Structures and Adjectives] (Kennedy) *Ambiguity and vagueness: 'Most linguistic utterances display "interpretive uncertainty",'*) and, because of this, can obtain different translations in different contexts.

Nearly since the beginnings of Machine Translation, it has become clear that ambiguity of words and structures is one of the hardest problems for translating texts automatically: German *Engländer* means *Brit* or *Englishman* or otherwise *monkey wrench* and we know what is meant and know how to correctly translate the word only if we have additional information, like *ein fünfzigjähriger verheirateter Engländer / a fifty years old married Brit* or *ein Engländer für 5-Zoll-Rohre / a monkey wrench for 5 inch tubes* which allows to *disambiguate* the contribution of the word.

Correspondingly, when translating a structurally ambiguous expression one usually must know from context which reading is meant, as when translating *nice mice and cats* into French where one has to know whether the adjectival modification refers to the left conjunct of the coordination or to the coordination as a whole (*des souris gentilles et des chats / des souris et des chats gentils*)

Normally the reader isn't aware of such ambiguities (lexical or structural) because he or she resolves them unconciously using background knowledge about the topic or new knowledge from the text. For Machine Translation disambiguation is a big challenge.

1.2 Disambiguation

Many cases of ambiguity can be resolved by exploiting diverging syntagmatic properties of the associated readings.

1.2.1 Syntactic analysis filter

The importance of syntactic filtering is often illustrated by a paraphrase of Zenon's paradox:

(1) *Time flies like an arrow.*

The words *time, flies* and *like* are multiply ambiguous. There are $2 \times 2 \times 2 = 8$ possibilities of assigning part of speech tags to them ($time_N$ or $time_V$, fly_N or fly_V, $like_{Prep}$ or $like_V$).

When translating into languages that represent the different readings with respect to gender, number, tense and mode by different forms more than English does there are even up to 128 possiblities of assigning forms (for example in German there are 6 word forms for *time:* Zeit, messe, misst, miss, messen, messt etc.). However when the sentence undergoes syntactic analysis there are only three readings left, the Zenon meaning, a reading where a number of representatives of the species *time flies* have a feeling of *liking an arrow,* and an imperative reading where *flies* are *timed like an arrow.* Further filtering is left to pragmatics or semantics.

1.2.2 Semantic analysis filter

Local semantic information can help to disambiguate further, as in the following:

(2) Mary Stuart heiratete einen Engländer.
    Mary Stuart married an Englishman.

The verb *heiraten / to marry* represents an event type which relates to persons. Therefore in (2) *Engländer* obviously designates a person, not a tool (and must be translated by *Englishman* therefore, not by *monkey wrench* or *wrench* - it will not be translated by *British* or *Brit* neither in this case, but this is for detailed historical knowledge which is far beyond linguistic knowledge).

Formally, this type of knowledge can be exploited by assigning semantic *selectional restrictions* to the arguments of the subcategorization frames of the words in the lexicon and by relating the different translations of the arguments to corresponding different semantic specifications (for *'selectional'* or *'selection restriction'* see also article 1 [Semantics: Lexical Structures and Adjectives] (Bierwisch) *Semantic features and primes*). For example, we may assume that the verb *heiraten* is assigned the subcategorization [subj(n):PERSON, obj(n):PERSON] that the noun *Engländer* is assigned the semantic type disjunction PERSON | INSTR plus transfer information stipulating, among other things, that *Engländer* is translated by *Englishman,* if it can be inferred from context that the word designates a PERSON. Given this knowledge we learn from (2) that *Engländer* is a PERSON and must be translated correspondingly.

Disambiguating semantic information may also flow in reversed order in predicate-argument-structures: from argument to syntactic head. German *einstellen* has several meanings. If the direct object is a person it is used in the sense of *to hire,* if it is a payment, it obtains a temporal meaning in the sense of *to suspend* (and must be translated correspondingly in both cases). Of course, several such semantic restrictions may interact.

1.2.3 Selectional restrictions and preferences

Semantic selectional constraints aren't always that precise as in the case of *heiraten* and *einstellen* and its roles. Consider the 'age measuring' adjective *fünfzigjährig / fifty years old* of the introductory example. When applied to *Engländer* it prefers the corresponding reading as HUMAN being, but doesn't reject the TOOL reading completely. Given the attributed age, there is a bias towards the person reading only, probably because it is more natural to characterize persons by age than tools. However, in order to be able to characterize persons the adjective must relate to an appropriate value (a *150 Jahre alter Engländer* is much less likely to refer to a person than an *Engländer* that has 40, 50 or 60 years). This means that not every lexical item that has arguments requires clear-cut restrictions for them or a subset of them, sometimes such restrictions only result from further modifications and sometimes they give hints about preferences only.

1.2.4 Metaphoric use and metonymic variation

It complicates matters that metaphoric use and metonymy aren't rare phenomena, at least when considering literary and newspaper texts (see also article 11 [Semantics: Lexical Structures and Adjectives] (Tyler & Takahashi) *Metaphors and metonymies*: 'Metaphor and metonymy are now understood to be ubiquitous aspects of language'). In a farce or cartoon, for example, there might by machines and tools playing the role of persons such that a sentence like *Der gute Engländer lag traurig auf seinem Lager in der Werkstatt* would have to be translated by something like *Good monkey wrench lied sadly on his bed in the workshop* and would sound quite natural in this context. This means that, given an appropriate global context, semantic relations may change such that semantic conclusions may be suspended that otherwise could be drawn from local constraints as provided by selectional restrictions. (The ontological incompatibility between tools and persons may be suspended for example, such that in a corresponding story about anthropomorphic animated objects the tool reading doesn't provide a clash).

Computing parameters from a text that can reliably guide the interpretation of the text and its passages (informing about the domain an assertion is about and whether it is used literally or as a metaphor etc.) is obviously a rather ambitious task.

1.3 Ambiguity-preserving translation

Machine Translation is not identical to text understanding. It presupposes text understanding to some extent, but there are cases where it can do without resolving ambiguities which from the standpoint of the recipient's interest should be resolved. This is no contradiction. It only says that Machine Translation may trust the assumption that similar ambiguities in source and target text (which correspond to each other) can be disambiguated by similar means and in a similar way if the context of these ambiguities is translated without loss of information.

For example, *Drucker* in German is ambiguous. It may refer to a *print worker* or a *printing device*. Generally, this difference is relevant and the context must be such that it provides information that enables the reader to resolve the ambiguity. Otherwise the text containing the word is not *felicitous* in the sense of the Gricean maxims (cf. article 15 [Semantics: Interfaces] (Simons) *Implicature* 2.2; also 17 [Semantics: Interfaces] (Potts) *Conventional implicature and expressive content*). English *printer* is ambiguous in exactly the same way and it will be disambiguated in the same way as its source counterpart, provided there is corresponding disambiguating information in the source text and provided this information is translated adequately. In this case *printer* is a perfect translation and better than *print device* or *printing worker* which may obtain a flavor of overspecification in the presence of the described context information.

Ambiguity-preserving translation has been advocated for in Kay (1980, 1997), Kay, Gawron & Norwig (1994) among others.

Note that even text understanding doesn't presuppose for a text to be felicitous that every ambiguity must be resolved (and that the context contains enough disambiguating information for this purpose). If the corresponding term or structure doesn't refer to a central topic, message or referent of the text the unresolved information may be completely sufficient. Often, sentences with scope ambiguities are examples of this. In *all politicians talked to a number of experts* the subject may take scope over the object – so that every politician talked to his own group of experts – or the other way around – where there is just one (specific) group of experts the politicians all talk to. For many purposes of using such sentences however, it doesn't matter which scope relation holds; cf. also articles 4 [Semantics: Noun Phrases and Verb Phrases] (Keenan) *Quantifiers* and 1 [Semantics: Sentence and Information Structure] (Szabolcsi) *Scope and binding*.

Ambiguity-preserving translation presupposes that the target language provides lexical or structural forms that are similarly ambiguous as the forms of the source language that are to be translated. With respect to corresponding transfer systems it additionally suggests that the representation formalisms used provide means for *underspecification* of information (cf. article 9 [Semantics: Lexical Structures and Adjectives] (Egg) *Semantic underspecification*).

Availability of ambiguity-preserving transfer equivalents doesn't mean that the corresponding term or structure remains undisambiguated throughout the entire process of translating the sentence or text. It might be disambiguated implicitly by contextual constraints like the mentioned selection restrictions mentioned above. However, disambiguation might have to be carried out explicitly also (where 'explicitly' means that there have to be applied inference rules beyond unification in semantic composition), in order to assure necessary information flow and consistency with regard to other elements in the text (see also article 9 [Semantics: Interfaces] (Kay & Michaelis) *Constructional meaning*). It is important to realize that expressions presenting corresponding translation tasks neither necessarily precede the considered term nor are located in close vicinity of it. Good examples are presented by texts with pronouns as in the following. A simple example:

(3) *Joan bemerkte den Drucker. Sie ging auf ihn zu.*
    Joan noticed the printer. She approached it / him.

In the German sentence of (3), the correct translation of *ihn* into English (by *it* or *him* depends on knowing what *Drucker* stands for, a person or a machine: *Drucker* is the *antecedent* of the pronoun and therefore it should provide the ontological information needed for translating the pronoun correctly. However, here, the noun is ambiguous, it doesn't provide sufficient justification for any of the alternative translations. At best, it can be said that things are interleaved: If *Drucker* is a person, *ihn* must be translated by *him*, otherwise by *it*. But that's not all: If *ihn* is translated by *him*, *Drucker* should be understood as a person and correspondingly with *it*. This means that deciding about the translation of the pronoun causes a decision about the reading of the antecedent even if this decision could be omitted when considering the task of translating the antecedent sentence taken in isolation. In some contexts this 'backwards'-dependency can be exploited for further disambiguation as in the following:

(4) *Kürzlich erst hatte sie den Drucker eingestellt.*
    a. *Jetzt kündigte er schon wieder.*
    b. *Jetzt war er schon wieder defekt.*

   It was only recently that she had hired/adjusted the printer.
    a. *Now he already dismissed.*
    b. *Now it already was defective again.*

In (4a) the selectional restriction provided by *kündigen / dismiss* to its subject indicates that *er* must designate a person. Because of the anaphoric link, *Drucker* must designate the same person. Therefore, *einstellen* must be translated by *to hire*, not by *to adjust*. In (4b) the same flow of information requires *einstellen* to be translated by *to adjust*. Note that in this example it is information from later sentences which is needed to disambiguate terms in previous sentences and to translate them correctly.

We keep from this that an answer to the question asking for the depth of semantic analysis of terms and structures that is appropriate in order to translate a text correctly depends on the language into which it is to be translated and the structural and lexical properties of this language in comparison with the source language, in particular on whether it provides similarly ambiguous terms and structures for the items in question. However, it depends also on whether such disambiguation is needed by separate translation tasks given by terms and structures figuring somewhere else in the text, before or after the item considered. This means that high quality translation in principle cannot be carried out by sequentially running through the text and translating simultaneously. From an epistemological point of view translation presupposes understanding the purpose of the text, understanding the situation at which the text aims, having the necessary background knowledge available, and, on the basis of this, being able to understand the text to a certain degree and having the competence to decide if a (local) ambiguity in the text may remain unresolved in translation or not.

High quality translation in this sense is provided by none of the systems that have been developed so far.

Topics

In the next section, we will give a brief tour d'horizon about what types of architecture have been developed since the beginnings of MT and what kinds of solutions have been presented to the problems mentioned.

During the last decades it has become a common insight that computing detailed semantic representations is very costly and tends to be a kind of overkill, as we have tried to illustrate above. Therefore, shallow semantic representations of various shapes have been suggested as the domain (and range) of translation, seen as a function from representations onto representations. We have tried to illustrate also that such representations must allow gradual disambiguation in order to provide the knowledge needed for the resolution of translation difficulties (which may be *long distance* -transfer- *dependencies*) on a case-by-case basis.

In section 3 we show how a formalism of this type fits in a typical transfer architecture and what the advantages are when compared to other approaches.

In section 4 we will report about current approaches to *hybrid* architectures mixing different translation methods and we will try to show how promising it is in particular to incorporate statistically gained information to semantics-based transfer systems which use underspecified representations.

The overview will end with a short concluding summary and outlook in section 5.

2 Machine Translation architectures

2.1 A brief history of the classical MT architectures

2.1.1 The beginnings

Typically, the beginnings of MT are identified with Warren Weavers initiatives in 1947 and 1949 stimulating renowned thinkers and scientists of that time to think about the possibilities of translating texts automatically. Significantly enough, in his famous memorandum entitled *translation* (cf. Weaver 2003), Weaver (Claude Shannon's co-founder of information theory) addressed ambiguity as the main problem of MT and suggested to use recent knowledge about decryption and about formal languages together with knowledge from context for solving this problem and as an architectural basis for MT as such. Immediate cause of Weaver's initiatives was the increased need for translations that institutions like UNESCO showed and the growing number of such international institutions and also current and foreseeable international conflicts with foreseeable translation needs.

Weaver's credo was to understand translation as a process of decoding an encrypted message. It had a lot of influence on the discussions at those days. There had been recent success in decryption. An outstanding result was the deciphering of the code of the German *enigma* cipher machine in the Second World War.

The first phase of MT guided by this philosophy lead to a first demonstration of a prototype at IBM headquartiers in 1954, where 49 simple Russian sentences could be processed. This demonstration was a big success and triggered comfortable funding during the following years (cf. Hutchins 1995).

2.1.2 The knowledge bottleneck

The Georgetown demonstrator translated word by word. In order to deal with ambiguities it was augmented by morphological and very sparse syntactic analysis taking into account a small number of neighbors of the word to be translated: alltogether it made use of a totality of 6 syntactic rules!

This somehow naive, over-enthusiastic attitude of the beginnings was at the basis of uncautiously trying to solve the translation problem by brute-force methods in the following. The trend was to trust more in calculating capacity than on linguistic research. (Note Loomis' characteristic statement *I instinctively trust the electronics boys more than I do the semanticists*, cf. Hutchins 1997).

In the early and mid sixties the disappointment of the investors, having spent about 20 Mio $ in the *first generation* systems of the Georgetown type without commercially usable results replaced enthusiasm. The famous Alpac report (of the **A**utomatic **L**anguage **P**rocessing **A**dvisory **C**ommitee installed in 1964) by the US National Academy of Sciences came to the conclusion, in 1966, that *we do not have useful machine translation* and that MT is and will be commercially unattractive. With respect to funding: *linguistics should be supported as science, and should not be judged by any immediate or foreseeable contribution to practical translation* (cf. Pierce et al. 1966).

This statement stopped research on MT for a number of years. It is responsible however also for that MT could try a more realistic second start with a much more adult attitude, being aware that much more linguistics would be needed in order to tackle the problem seriously. The first person to see this and the first who did full-time work from a linguistic perspective on MT was Yehoshua Bar-Hillel at MIT who, in 1952, organized the first International Conference on Machine Translation. In the late fifties/early sixties he came to the conclusion that FAHQT, i.e. *fully automatic high quality translation* could not be possible for principle reasons. He argued that position (in Bar-Hillel 1960) with an example which became famous in the sequel, the following:

(5) *Little John was looking for his toy box. Finally, he found it.*
    The box was in the pen. John was very happy.

Pen is either an enclosure, typically in the context of agriculture, or a writing utensil. In (5) it is used in the first sense with a more specific interpretation as *playpen*. In order therefore to translate *pen* into a language which brings out the difference (as in German *Laufstall* vs. *Schreiber*), the pronouns have to be resolved correctly, the box has to be identified as the toy box of the first sentence and what is more: a lot of *world knowledge* must be available according to which we know that in situations with toy boxes playpens are often found also (and less often enclosures for animals) and that boxes normally fit better into enclosures than into writing tools. Since, in principle, we need inferences like these in all domains texts can be about, MT necessitates complete knowledge about the world in order to disambiguate the terms and structures.

This is a very strong argument and at the basis of the criticism expressed against MT architectures with explicit, predefined rules governing text analysis and translation (so-called *rule-based* Machine Translation (RBMT)).

2.1.3 The Vauquois triangle

Bernard Vauquois, renowned pioneer of MT research integrated the architectural suggestions that have been suggested as responses to the challenges in the

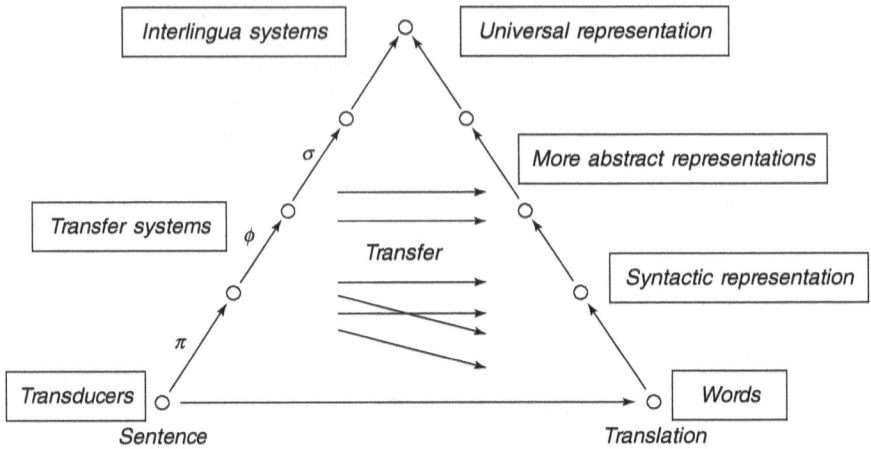

Fig. 17.1: Conventional RBMT architectures

seventies and eighties, after ALPAC and a period of meditation, in a graphical illustration (cf. Vauquois 1975). Because it compares the architectures by a triangular structure, it is called the *Vauquois triangle*. Meanwhile, it is used in nearly every introduction to MT.

Fig. 17.1 adds some detailing illustrations to Vauquois' comparison. In essence it compares the relevant features of *direct translation* to those of *transfer systems* and *interlingua systems*, where *direct translation* means word-to-word translation as realizable via transducers. It characterizes the so-called *first generation* systems which have been developed in the sequel of the Georgetown demonstration. *Transfer systems* analyze the input into some abstract representation, *transfer* it to some representation of the target and generate a target translation from this latter representation. *Interlingua systems* analyze the input into a representation which is universal in the sense that all sentences that are translations from each other share this representation as common content abstracting away from all language specific elements and as 'blueprint' they are generated from. The development of transfer and interlingua systems mark the so-called *second generation* of MT.

The first and second generation systems of the Vauquois triangle do not yet address statistical methods of the so-called *third generation* of MT.

2.1.4 Direct translation

Most commercial initiatives stuck to the direct translation option, whereas most academic research centers investigated the transfer and interlingua option, which caused communication between commercial development and academic research to run dry step by step in the following time (there have been exceptions of course). This trend held for many years and it is only by the late eighties and the nineties that communication began to reincrease. Since the growing success of statistical MT it has become even intense (viz. Google translation).

Commercial systems which developed from first generation prototypes or architectures and survived are *SYSTRAN* (which offers the free online service *Babelfish*) and *LOGOS* (cf. Stoll 1986, Trabulsi 1989, Drouin 1989).

A striking feature of direct translation systems is that they are generally fast and robust, at least when compared to (rule-based) systems of later generations. This is due to the fact that, grosso modo, there is no time-consuming computation of abstract representations and complicated disambiguation operations; analysis settles for some sparse mapping to morphological base forms (*lemmatizing*) such that the translation process nearly exclusively consists of looking up words and expressions and their translations in bilingual dictionaries and combining the results into the target sentence, according to target surface rules. Since there is nearly no information available from compositional processes and generalizations the dictionaries carry most of the translation information and contain huge sets of descriptions of particular cases, considering a lot of syntagmas as a kind of multiwords.

2.1.5 Transfer systems

The arrows added to the Vauquois triangle in Fig. 17.1 indicate that there are many different subtypes of the transfer architecture. A system might use one or more levels of analysis. Analysis might mean syntactic, semantic, syntactico-semantic analysis or something else. Transfer can relate source representations to target representations of the same representation level. It can relate representations of different levels also and it can generate target strings from source representations avoiding construction of intermediate structures which could be interpreted as analyses of the target grammar.

EUROTRA, for example, used 4 layers of analysis: morphological structure (tokens), configurational structure (syntax), relational structure (dependency/predicate-argument structure) and interface structure (predicate-argument-structure with interlingual elements). *Translators* and *generators* mapped the representations of these layers to each other. Transfer was defined for the level of interface structure. EUROTRA was initiated by the European Community and aimed at modular translation systems for all EC languages (cf. Durand et al. 1991, Copeland et al. 1991). The project was very influential throughout the eighties and triggered a lot of research in neighboring domains also. (With respect to its basic settings EUROTRA owes a lot to the earlier ARIANE system (cf. Vauquois & Boitet 1985) of the *Groupe d'Etudes pour la Traduction Automatique* (GETA), which was established by Bernard Vauquois.)

Similarly symmetric with respect to source and target representations are the systems of the *ParTrans* project of the Palo Alto Research Center (Parc –a Xerox institution). ParTrans uses the results of the ParGram project which spells out grammars for many languages in the framework of *Lexical Functional Grammar* (LFG) (cf. Kaplan & Bresnan 1982 to LFG, Butt et al. 2002 to ParGram, Riezler & Maxwell 2006, Frank 1999 to ParTrans). ParTrans can be seen as a successor of the EUROTRA approach. Its representation formalisms are much more general (*syntactic c-, functional f- und semantic s-structure*), with more principle-based mappings. It uses elegant unification principles in order to compute composition and the values of the mapping functions. (In fig. 17.1 π, φ and σ relate to the corresponding projections of the LFG approach). Often, such symmetrical approaches aim at reversibility of the components as well (as LFG does).

In contrast, there are systems which compute the target string from the source representation without computing target language specific representations first and then generating the target string from them. (This transition is mostly realized via language pair-specific rewriting rules). Examples of commercial systems that follow this asymmetric architecture are METAL (*MEchanical Translation and Analysis of Language*, mainly developed by Siemens in the eighties) and IBM's LMT *logic based Machine Translation* (cf. Bennett & Slocum 1988, McCord 1989a, 1989b). (This is true for at least some periods of their development history; both systems or successors of them respectively are still on the market under different names – a successor of METAL among others as Langenscheidt's *T1* and successors of LMT in IBM's *web sphere translation server*, linguatec's *Personal Translator* and Lingenio's *translate*).

2.1.6 Interlingua systems

Interlingua approaches are similarly multi-facetted. There are approaches that aim at universal conceptual structure. An example is the *UNITRAN* system (cf. Dorr 1993, 1994) which translates on the basis of *lexical conceptual structures* (LCS) (cf. Jackendoff 1983, 1990 and article 4 [Semantics: Theories] (Jackendoff) *Conceptual Semantics*, also articles 4 [Semantics: Lexical Structures and Adjectives] (Levin & Rappaport Hovav) *Lexical Conceptual Structure*, 1 [Semantics: Theories] (Talmy) *Cognitive Semantics*, and 5 [Semantics: Theories] (Lang & Maienborn) *Two-level Semantics*).

However, the term *interlingua* doesn't exclusively label universal semantic representations or *logical form*. There are weaker interpretations which settle for representations of source and target sentences only which are not necessarily identical but use isomorphic predicate-argument structures only, with language-specific lexemes. In this case, a minimal step of transfer replacing source lemmas by corresponding target lemmas remains. The academic prototype of the *Linguistic Research Center* (LRC) at the university of Texas in Austin that METAL had been developed from later used this type of structurally isomorphic transfer. It was developed during the seventies. Other examples of this specific variant of interlingua are presented by early translation architectures of GETA in Grenoble (cf. Bennett & Slocum 1988, Vauquois 1975, Slocum 1988).

Finally, there are suggestions which are not interested in the option of logical inference at all, but only in reducing the combinatory complexity which is connected to the transfer setting: Whereas a transfer approach for translating n languages into each other needs n×(n−1) transfer components (which are completely different in the worst case), a corresponding system that does all translations via the same interlingua does not need specific transfer components at all. Instead it needs n components for mapping the input to interlingua representations and another n components to generate the target sentences from such representations. If the interlingua used is not an expressive semantic representation language but just a representative of the n languages considered, analysis doesn't need to be more detailed and generation not more complex than in the transfer case. The approach can even be optimized by designing a kind of translation *esperanto* which approximates the words and structures of the languages considered in order to minimize the differences. In later GETA suggestions this language, called *pivot* language, is a kind of simplified and generalized English, called *unified networking language* (cf. Sérasset & Boitet 2000). (UNL is at the basis of the large international UNL-initiative (put forward among others by Vauquois's successor at GETA, Christian Boitet), aiming at translation between many languages and different languages (including Asian languages), cf. Hong & Streiter 1999. There have been other such approaches also, with other pivots (for example the DLT system (*Distributed Language Translation*) developed at the BSO software company, Utrecht in the late eighties, which used a variant of ESPERANTO, cf. Sadler 1989).

2.1.7 Translation mismatches

Structural differences between source and target representation can be classified into different types of *translation mismatches* (cf. Kameyama, Ochitani & Peters 1991 for the notion, also Dorr 1994). Mismatches help to justify the usefulness of different layers of analysis further.

Typically, next to lexical divergences and gaps there are structural mismatches which, grosso modo, can be classified by three types of changes:
- *Thematic divergence and scrambling*
- Thematic roles are exchanged for each other (cf. Dorr 1990, Hutchins & Somers 1992); the order of constituents changes.
- *Deletion and insertion of structure*
- Words and structures aren't translated (*deletion*) or there are elements in the target without immediate equivalent in the source (*insertion*).
- *Head switching*
- Syntactic head and argument(s) are exchanged for each other.

For example, translation with morphological *contraction* is a phenomenon of deletion of structure (and the retranslation an example of insertion). It is easily resolved at the level of (morpho-)syntactic analysis:

(6) *Er schreibt* [**an die** *Angestellten*]*pp* ↔ *Il écrit* [**aux** *employés*]*pp*
↔ *He writes* [**to the** *employees*]*pp*.

At the level of syntactic analysis, the three-token PP-complement in German and English and the corresponding two-token complement in French are identically represented as instances of the type $[\text{Prep } [\text{DET}_{def} \text{ N}]_{NP}]$.
Similarly, (non-lexicalized) *compounds* may obtain isomorphic analyses.

(7) *Zufallswort* ↔ *random word*
$[NCOMPOUND\ N]_N$

Differences in constituent order disappear at the level of functional analysis (e.g. at the level of LFG's *f-structure*) and consequently for all more abstract representations which are assigned to this level (e.g. semantic representations). Also, structural differences which are due to idiosyncratic tense, modal or negation information disappear if the corresponding information is represented via specific feature values (as in LFG's f-structure) or interpretations of such values in terms of modal and temporal statements of a uniform semantic representation language (as in *Discourse Representation Theory* or *Situation Semantics* etc.; cf. articles 9 [Semantics: Theories] (Ginzburg) *Situation Semantics and NL ontology*, 10 [Semantics: Theories] (Ginzburg) *Situation Semantics*, 11 [Semantics: Theories] (Kamp & Reyle) *Discourse Representation Theory*, 12 [Semantics: Theories] (Dekker) *Dynamic semantics*, and 13 [Semantics: Theories] (Zeevat) *Rhetorical relations*). Thematic divergence is just a matter of renaming attributes or thematic roles.

(8) gives an illustrateing example, (9) presents the corresponding structurally isomorphic f-structures (modulo lexical material and attribute labeling):

(8) *Peter würde der Wein nicht gefallen*
    Peter n'aimerait pas le vin.
    Peter wouldn't like the wine.

(9) $\begin{bmatrix} \text{PRED:} & \text{"}gefallen\langle(\uparrow SUBJ)(\uparrow OBJ)\rangle\text{"} \\ \text{SUBJ:} & [\text{PRED: "}wein\text{"}] \\ \text{OBJ:} & [\text{PRED: "}peter\text{"}] \\ \text{NEG:} & + \\ \text{TENSE:} & COND \end{bmatrix} \begin{bmatrix} \text{PRED:} & \text{"}aimer\langle(\uparrow SUBJ)(\uparrow OBJ)\rangle\text{"} \\ \text{SUBJ:} & [\text{PRED: "}peter\text{"}] \\ \text{OBJ:} & [\text{PRED: "}vin\text{"}] \\ \text{NEG:} & + \\ \text{TENSE:} & COND \end{bmatrix}$

$\begin{bmatrix} \text{PRED:} & \text{"}like\langle(\uparrow SUBJ)(\uparrow OBJ)\rangle\text{"} \\ \text{SUBJ:} & [\text{PRED: "}peter\text{"}] \\ \text{OBJ:} & [\text{PRED: "}wine\text{"}] \\ \text{NEG:} & + \\ \text{TENSE:} & COND \end{bmatrix}$

Head switching is a type of translation mismatch which is often taken as an argument for spelling out transfer at the level of semantic representation. Head switching means that a syntactic head and (some of) its arguments or an adjunct exchange there positions for each other in the target. Example:

(10) *Peter raucht gerne.*
     Peter likes to smoke.

In (10) the head of the German sentence, *raucht*, is translated as a complement of the head of the English sentence which in turn is the translation of *gerne* which is an adjunct of *raucht* in the source sentence. Conceptually, both, the adverb *gerne* and the verb *like* are modal operators (which take a property as argument and relate a second, individual, argument to it). Therefore it is very natural to assign both sentences structurally isomorphic semantic representations as in the follwing:

(11) *gerne(peter,λx.(rauchen(x)))*
     like(peter,λx.(smoke(x)))

However, it depends on the depth of analysis which is aimed at by the semantic formalism and its representations whether the divergence is abstracted away at the semantic level or not. Different perspectives have been taken to that in the past when defining transfer and interlingua architectures using semantic representations.

2.2 The role of semantic representation in different traditional MT architecture types

Throughout second generation MT a number of transfer and interlingua systems have been developed which use semantic representations. We mentioned EUROTRA (using a fourth representation layer called *interface structure*) and ParTrans' LFG translation where it is possible to assign semantic representations to f-structures by means of a projection σ. These *s-structures* can be used as an additional level of transfer on the one hand, or as a means for providing semantic information on the other, which can guide the construction of f-structures (by semantic selectional restrictions for example).

In the LFG-type transfer architecture semantic information is *co-described* to lexical items and grammar rules in the same way as functional and transfer information is. This is an advantage over EUROTRA-type approaches with specific (directional rewriting) *translators* between the representation layers, as all types of information (configurational, functional, semantic, transfer information) can flow together in the LFG typical path equations which constrain the possibilities of understanding and simultaneously translating a sentence. Instead, in the EUROTRA-type architecture, information from earlier processing stages (lower layers in analysis and higher layers in generation) aren't available anymore. Both approaches are similar however in that they do not require representations of particular semantic theories.

At least in principle, such architectures accept representations of any compositional language for semantic representation. Different semantic frameworks have been proposed and used: *Montague semantics* (cf. Dowty, Walland & Peters 1981) has been used in Philipps' Rosetta system (cf. Landsbergen 1982, 1987a, 1987b). *Situation semantics* has been proposed for MT in Kameyama, Ochitani & Peters (1991). *Quasi logical forms* (QLF) are used in the *Bilingual Conversation Interpreter* (BCI) (cf. Alshawi 1992). Discourse representation structure and underspecified versions of DRT have been used in various systems designed in the nineties (Barnett et al. 1991, Emele et al. 2000, Eberle 2002).

There is an important difference between transfer and interlingua architectures with regard to semantic representation: In transfer approaches semantic representations may use language specific predicates and structuring principles; in interlingua approaches (in the narrow sense), semantic representations should be neutral in this respect. They must express the semantic information that sentences of at least two languages that are translated into each other have in common. In principle, they must represent the semantic features that all sentences which are translations of each other have in common, including translations from structurally very different languages. Epistemologically this presupposes the assumption of a universal conceptual structure of the human way of thought that can be found beyond any language specific encoding. The mentioned *Lexical Conceptual Structure* (LCS) is an approach to spell out a corresponding conceptual language and UNIFORM is a MT system that uses it. In LCS (and corresponding conceptual approaches) events and states are broken down into basic action and state types. For example, for both sentences of (10) one might obtain something like (12) as a common representation:

(12) $\left[State\ BE \left[\begin{bmatrix} Thing\ x \\ PositionAT \begin{bmatrix} Thing\ x \\ Event\ SMOKE\ ([Thing\ x]) \end{bmatrix} \\ Manner\ LIKINGLY \end{bmatrix} \right] \right]$

It is of course much more difficult to generate translations from such representations than from representations which are closer to surface structure. In UNITRAN, the problem is alleviated by parameters assigned to the representations which inform about whether a specific argument or structure has to be realized syntactically and how.

Typically, conceptual representations do not model ambiguities, but stand for readings of the sentences. This means that analyzing sentences into such representations presupposes more effort with respect to disambiguation. Generally, the more representations use deep (fundamental) semantic predicates and relations the more the system is faced with disambiguation – or the more features for underspecification are needed if unmotivated disambiguation shall be avoided.

The first option (of disambiguated deep representations) is taken by so-called *Knowledge based Machine Translation* (KBMT, cf. Nirenburg et al. 1992). The basic idea is to provide a large amount of *world knowledge* and to use it for disambiguation when computing the deep interlingua representations of the sentences and texts, in order to be able to solve ambiguity problems as posed by Bar Hillel's problem (example (5), where *event frame knowledge* must be available and used to conclude that *pen* must be interpreted as a *playpen* in the reported situation; cf. also article 3 [Semantics: Theories] (Gawron) *Frame Semantics*). Because of this perspective, the main topics of KBMT are knowledge representation, design and properties of corresponding languages, tractability, and inference algorithms. Typically, information is represented in *frames* using languages which develop from AI languages like KL-One and from feature logic research. In order to be usable in practice, it is obvious that representation and translation must be restricted to specific domains. *Kant* and the later *Mikrokosmos* are renowned KBMT-systems (cf. Carbonell, Mitamura & Nyberg 1992, Onyshkevych & Nirenburg 1995, Nirenburg et al. 1996).

The second option (shallow representation) was a main focus of the *Verbmobil project* (which started in 1994 and ended in 2002, cf. Wahlster 2000). Verbmobil produced a number of (transfer) systems which made use of underspecified structures: different versions of systems on the basis of *minimal recursion semantics* and *underspecified* DRT (cf. Flickinger, Copestake & Sag 2000, Emele et al. 2000). We do not go into detail with them here. Instead, we will sketch the analysis and lexicon formalism of a transfer system that incorporates many features of these systems on the basis of a specific underspecification formalism in the next section. We will discuss the different pros and cons of the differences there.

There are a number of varieties of the more classical interlingua and transfer architectures using semantic representations which we also cannot go into here: *Lexicalist* MT (*LexMT*) focuses on minimizing problems from structural mismatches by defining transfer as a relation between sets of source and target lexeme representations, including representations of multiwords and idioms, where the set of source representations covers the source sentence and where the target sentence is generated from the corresponding set of target lexeme representations using syntagmatic constraints assigned to the representations (constraints with regard to logical type, semantic selectional restrictions, agreement etc.; cf. Whitelock 1992). Kuhn & Heid (1994) combine the codescription approach of LFG (which defines target structures by sets of equations) with semantic interlingua and spell it out in a HPSG setting. There are numerous other combinations. We come back to some of them sporadically in the following sections.

2.3 Trends in current MT research and development

Since the late eighties there have been suggestions for *Statistical Machine Translation* (SMT). The name of one of the first systems, *CANDIDE*, alludes to the underlying epistemological attitude: No a priori knowledge about language and translation is used. The IBM approach which led to the CANDIDE system (which has become classical meanwhile) draws heavily on the experiences made with statistical speech processing and applied corresponding methods to translation. It stipulates the translation of a sentence f_1^J (consisting of words $f_1, \ldots, f_J$) to be that sentence of the target language $ê_1^I$ (consisting of words $e_1, \ldots, e_I$) that has the highest probability given f_1^J. The corresponding maximization uses Bayes's theorem:

$$ê_1^I = \underset{e_1^I}{\operatorname{argmax}} \{P(e_1^I) \times P(f_1^J | e_1^I)\}$$

This approach is referred to as *noisy channel* or *source-channel* approach (cf. Brown et al. 1990, Brown et al. 1992, Brown et al. 1993). (The use of *e* and *f* for sentences and words in the formula alludes to the language pair English-French which was -and still is- a popular field of examination, as the *Hansard corpus* makes large amounts of corresponding parallel texts available electronically; the *Hansard corpus* consists of the transcripts of the Canadian parliament debates with translations into English or French, depending on the original contribution.) It bases upon two probability models: the *language model* of the target language, $P(e_1^I)$, and the *translation model*, $P(f_1^J|e_1^I)$. Often, the translation model uses information from two further submodels: the (bilingual) *lexicon model* (which determines the probability of a source word sw to be translated into a target word *tw* in a context c – which, generally, is a n-gram) and the (word) *alignment model* which weights the positioning of translations of words (or expressions) in the target sentence. The models are trained using mono- and bilingual corpora.

In order to give a better account of various types of information which constrain translation and generation, it has been suggested in the sequel to use maximum entropy models instead, which provide the possibility to add weighted random variables or *feature functions* to the probability model as seems appropriate to the researcher with regard to modeling the data (cf. Och & Ney 2002). According to the maximum entropy approach search of the best translation e_1^I of a sentence f_1^J is steered by the following maximization (where h_m are feature functions and λ_m their weights):

$$\hat{e}_1^I = \underset{e_1^I}{\operatorname{argmax}}\left\{\sum_{m=1}^{M} \lambda_m h_m(e_1^I, f_1^J)\right\}$$

This model, which subsumes the source channel model as a specific case, dominates the current discussion in SMT. There are various suggestions for feature functions, in particular suggestions which relate to linguistic knowledge. Another issue for improving the quality of SMT is to modify the data the models apply to. If knowledge about multiwords, collocational expressions and idioms is available, the model is better based upon sets of words instead of single words. If morphological knowledge is available it can be based on basic forms, instead of inflected words, etc. There are suggestions for computing the corresponding knowledge automatically from (monolingual) corpora using statistical methods.

There is a third strand of approaching the translation problem: *example-based Machine Translation* (EBMT). EBMT has its roots in so-called *Machine aided human translation* (MAHT) and is a sophistication of the *translation memory* technique. Translation memories store translations of sentences of the human translator in easily searchable databases such that he or she can very efficiently access and use them for later translation tasks.

Most commercially available translation memories investigate texts to be translated and prepare them in such a way that the human translator is prompted for translations of sentences only if they haven't been found in the memory. If there are relatively similar sentences in the memory he or she will be provided with the corresponding translations as templates for the new translation. This idea has been put forward by going below the sentence level and storing translations of parts of sentences and their translations – *examples* – and understanding sentence translation as the task of finding an optimal cover of the source sentence by source parts of examples and to put together the target parts in a reasonable way. (Generally, a cover is *optimal* if the parts have to be cut only minimally in order to provide a partition of the sentence). EBMT was pioneered by Nagao and colleagues in the Japanese government project for MT in the late eighties, by Furuse and Iide, and by IBM's Japanese MT group among others (cf. Nagao, Tsujii & Nakamura 1988, Furuse & Iida 1994, Maruyama & Watanabe 1992, Watanabe & Takeda 1998). Today there are a number of groups investigating EBMT, among others a very productive one at DCU (cf. Gough & Way 2004).

Of course, similarities between the different approaches have been noticed. They are exploited in *hybrid* approaches to Machine Translation, which dominate the current discussion in the literature, independently of the specific emphasis the contributions take. For instance, EBMT's *examples* may obtain more structural interpretations which relate them closer to *expressions* in the conventional sense of the term and which allow a more compositional picture of the construction of translations from examples (cf. Chiang (2005). *Phrasal* SMT uses syntactic knowledge in SMT (cf. Quirk, Menezes & Cherry 2006). Of coure, this easily combines with the structured understanding of EBMT examples mentioned before.

The notorious *sparse data problem* of SMT is tried to be weakened by generalizing the data using abstractions of the specific form the sentences take, as sketched further above, and by using similarity knowledge from monolingual corpora in order to improve the bilingual lexicon models (cf. Callison-Burch, Koehn & Osborne 2006 for an example).

SMT, EBMT and the search for hybrid improvements mark the *third generation* of MT development. There is not yet a fourth. (For a general overview to MT history and architectures, compare Hutchins 1986, 2001, Hutchins & Somers 1992, Trujillo 1992 to an early concise comparison of the interlingua and transfer approaches cf. Boitet 1988, to an overview giving a more detailed account of third generation MT cf. Jurafski & Martin 2000, Manning & Schütze.)

3 Transfer of underspecified representations

Many traditional academic transfer systems use large transfer components which specify most of the difficult translation mismatches such that the bilingual lexicon proper (if there is one) contains relatively simple word-to-word statements only. From a commercial point of view this is disadvantageous. It means that relatively complicated programming code has to be maintained and extended continuously by programmers who are also lexicographers or conversely. This is expensive. Therefore many commercial systems have relatively simple transfer components and use huge dictionaries which enumerate many individual translation cases instead of configuring them by using generally applicable mapping rules.

Optimizing on both approaches means to provide a lean transfer component which ignores language specific and language pair specific knowledge and which is hence easy to maintain – and it means to provide a simple but expressive lexicon formalism which allows the lexicographer to define complex declarative transfer relations and to use and define corresponding templates without programming.

A prerequisite is that the representations that transfer applies to firstly abstract away from all types of information which can be inferred by language specific generation rules and, secondly, avoid detailing the meaning beyond the lexical and structural interpretation that is justified by the knowledge of the syntax-semantics interface, at least, as long as there are no requirements from transfer for more precise interpretations. We mean that the level of underspecified semantic representation fits best with these requirements.

3.1 Underspecified source and target representations

In order to illustrate what can be dealt with on the basis of underspecified semantic transfer and how and at which cost this happens, we make use of *flat underspecified discourse representation theory* (*FUDRT* and its representation structures (*FUDRSs*). FUDRT developed from an implementation of Reyle's *underspecified discourse representation theory* (*UDRT;* cf. Reyle 1993) which aimed at extending the theory from representation and interpretation of scope ambiguities to various other ambiguities in order to allow representations of a broad language fragment for practical purposes (cf. Eberle 1997, 2004). It has been used outside research for semantic representation in the MT products *Personal Translator* and *translate* (cf. Eberle 2002).

We concentrate on the structural ambiguity illustrated in sentence (13). It is expressed by different translation alternatives which relate to the different possibilities of disambiguation.

(13) *Lucie zeigte den Film ihrer Familie.*
　　a. *Lucie showed the film of her family.*
　　b. *Lucie showed the film to her family.*

The function of the NP in (13) *ihrer Familie* and the argument it relates to are not clear from the context the sentence provides. It can be understood as a genitive NP modifying *dem Film the film* (*the film of her family*) or as a dative NP providing an (optional) dative argument of *zeigen to show* (*to show to her family*). (13) is an example of an *attachment ambiguity* combined to a *functional ambiguity* (also called *label ambiguity*, cf. article 9 [Semantics: Lexical Structures and Adjectives] (Egg) *Semantic underspecification*).

In FUDRT, when compositionally building up the semantic representation of the sentence, complements and adjuncts aren't applied to their arguments. Instead they are written to the *functor set* of the basic representation (of the noun, verb, etc.). Additionally, there is a *set of conditions* (possibly empty) which captures constraints about the type and order of application as provided by syntactic or other contextual constraints. For (13) a corresponding analysis system computes the following:

(14)
$$1e_{t,\ akt(het),\ mtv(-,\ PAST,\ a)} : \begin{bmatrix} e \\ zeigen(e) \\ agent(e,x) \\ patient(e,y) \\ t \subseteq e \end{bmatrix} \begin{Bmatrix} subj{:}1_{x@HUM}{:}\underline{Lucie}(x),\ obj{:}12_{x@ARTEFACT}{:}\underline{der}(\underline{film}(y)), \\ Func{:}1_{3_{z@HUMCOLL}}{:}\underline{ihr}(familie(z)) \\ \{(Func=gen \wedge first(l2,l3)) \vee Func=dat\} \end{Bmatrix}$$

(14) consists of a verb representation and three functors originating from the three NPs. The function of two of them is clear: They are subject and object of the verb and fill the corresponding thematic roles of the verb representation. The contribution of the third is not yet determined: Either its functional type, *Func*, is dative and it is to be applied as such to the verb representation (simultaneously carrying out the corresponding thematic linking) or it is *genitive* and it is to be applied to the direct object. This alternative is captured by the disjunctive statement in the set of constraints.

FUDRSs use *labels* for structures. The constraint *first*(l_2, l_3) uses this. It means that the representation labeled by l_3 is to be applied to the one labeled by l_2. (The convention is that l_i refers to representation L_i). In contrast to ordering statements like $l_n \leq l_m$ which mean that L_n is to be applied to an argument representation before L_m is, $first(l_n,l_m)$-statements, type-theoretically, mean that the type of L_m is raised such that it can apply to L_n and that this application precedes applications involving L_n. Practically, this is executed by moving the functor L_m to the functor set of L_n (and from this position into functor sets of more deeply embedded functors in later steps of specification, where moving is guided by restrictions from the syntax-semantics interface). Using *first*-statements, attachment ambiguities can be represented satisfactorily.

With respect to L_1 and L_2, there is no order of application given yet in (14). Note that in this representation corresponding specifications are superfluous, as applying subject before object gives the same result as object before subject in this case. However, if subject and object introduce quantified representations, the alternatives that $\{l_1 \leq 1/8\}$ and $\{l_2 \leq l_1\}$ express, represent the two scope readings one gets in this case. This means: FUDRT representations can capture scope ambiguities also. '≤'-statements have been used since the very first outlining of UDRT.

Functors are functions from basic representations into FUDRSs (i.e. the results of applying them to representations show in essence the same tripartite structure as the depicted sentence representation – consisting of a basic representation, a functor set and a set of application conditions). Complex sentences can also be represented this way. Representations allow for (partial) disambiguation by (partial) application of functors in accordance with the constraints of the respective set of conditions.

Underlining as in *Lucie* marks an underspecified lexical structure (which stands for a function onto more precise interpretations the evaluation of which is connected to constraints specified in tle lexicon).

Decorations are used to inform about the referential *discourse referent(s)* (*DRF*) provided by the corresponding structures and their type properties. In (14) it says among other things that the sentence event is of *heterogeneous Aktionsart* and that its location time t has to be located in the contextual *past*. Decorations can also be used for adding pragmatic information to the representations: annotations about the type of speech act, about style and register used. (If recognizable by the system from text information!). In current LMT-implementations, information structure is represented in terms of relations between labels (identifying corresponding substructures of the sentence). We skip explanations about the details of the representations and the complete inventory of the formalism.

Using modern parsing and construction methods (chunk parsing, semantic construction from parse forests etc. cf. Abney 1991, Schiehlen 1996, Schmid & Schulte im Walde 2000), such underspecified semantic representations can be computed efficiently.

3.2 Transfer module

The transfer module constructs a target FUDRS from a source FUDRS. It is guided by the recursive translation function τ. By default, τ defines the translation of a structured representation to be a structured representation consisting of the translation of the basic representation and of the set of translations of the elements of the functor set. The set of application conditions is preserved, modulo renaming of application relations. This default translation is based on default translations of the grammatical relations, τ_r, and on the translations of the basic representations which stem from lexical entries, τ_n (n for lexical *node*). τ normally takes the following shape therefore (AC for *application constraints*):

$$\tau\left(\text{BasicRep} \begin{Bmatrix} \text{rel}_1: \text{Functor}_1, \\ \vdots \\ \text{rel}_n: \text{Functor}_n \end{Bmatrix} \text{AC}\right) := \tau_n(\text{BasicRep}) \begin{Bmatrix} \tau_r(\text{rel}_1):\tau(\text{Functor}_1), \\ \vdots \\ \tau_r(\text{rel}_n):\tau(\text{Functor}_n) \end{Bmatrix} \tau_r(\text{AC})$$

Recursive transfer strategies like this have been suggested by Zajac (1989, 1990), Dorna et al. (1994) and others, typically for different kinds of typed feature structures (expressing syntactic, functional, semantic knowledge or mixtures of such knowledge, as in HPSG).

Note that τ_r, just like the lexical τ_n, is language pair specific: It translates German dass-sentences into English that-clauses (and French and Spanish que-sentences); ob-sentences into whether- (and si-)sentences; prepositional complements and adjuncts into prepositional phrases headed by the typical translations of the source prepositions etc.

Given this algorithm, (14) is translated into an FUDRS with isomorphic structure modulo adjustments as described. These default translations can be specified or overridden however by specific definitions from the lexicon. We sketch examples in the next section.

3.3 Features of a lexicon formalism

The bilingual lexicon provides translations of the words. It defines the contextual circumstances under which specific translations of words are to be preferred. According to the stipulations above, it treats all kinds of translation mismatches mentioned in the introduction, except for those which are a matter of source analysis and target generation: In the FUDR transfer setting these are mismatches relating to different word order, different tense systems, different pragmatic conventions etc. (This means computing target tense forms and corresponding auxiliary structures from compact tense information (mtv-terms), putting pragmatic information into words, ordering words at surface etc. are tasks of generation and have nothing to do with transfer in this architecture). The transfer setting is *lexicalist* in the sense that it stores all knowledge which is specific to the language pair in the bilingual lexicon.

The lexicon formalism described in the following adapts a suggestion of Bernth (1992), McCord & Bernth (1998) for *Logic based Machine Translation* to the case of flat underspecified semantic representation and extends it by a number of instructions.(Both formalisms are used in commercial Machine translation systems, in *Personal Translator* and in *translate*, cf. Eberle 2001). It provides a number of τ-*instructions* which can be combined in order to describe amendments to the default translation. There are *local* and *global* τ-instructions. Local τ-instructions describe specific requirements with respect to the functor set of a representation (they are about the *local domain* of a word or structure). Global τ-instructions are about elements in the wider context of the representation, i.e. about representations which use it as a functor or as a substructure of a functor.

Local τ-instructions define changes of three types: The role a functor plays with regard to the basic representation can be changed (instruction type T_1); a functor can be suppressed (type T_2) or a new one introduced (type T_3). T_1, T_2 and T_3 allow to specify all cases of incorporation and thematic divergence, as have been illustrated in section 2.1.7. For instance, (8) (*Peter würde der Wein nicht gefallen. – Peter wouldn't like the wine.*) is sufficiently described in the lexicon by the following entry of *gefallen* using a T_1-instruction:

(15) • gefallen [subj(n),iobj1(n)]
  τ: like [obj(n),subj(n)]

(15) relates to uses of *gefallen* that have an indirect object (the affix '1' makes the grammatical role it is assigned to obligatory). T_1 makes use of the convention of the lexicon formalism that the arguments of the source and target frame relate to each other from right to left.

According to (15) therefore, the indirect object of the source representation is required to be the subject of the target representation and the source subject the target object.

A position 'e' in the target frame means that the corresponding functor of the source representation is suppressed; that is, a T_2 statement. T_3 introduces new arguments by adding *item(NEW-REL,DESCRIPTION)-terms* to the target frame, where

NEW_REL describes the new relation and where *DESCRIPTION* is a recursively defined expression built from target words, semantic types, pointers to the lexicon etc., describing the new argument (for example *item(comp(p([in – str acc]))*, *[flasche,det(e,pl)]*), with respect to a translation *to bottle – in Flaschen abfüllen*).

Global τ-instructions can erase, modify or replace adjunct representations and also substructures of the wider context of the word representation such that, in principle, each part of the sentence representation can be addressed and manipulated from the perspective of each word (which is assigned a labeled structure). These global τ-instructions do this by identifying substructures via corresponding paths in the source representation and defining what is to be done with these structures in the target.

Transfer by τ-instructions is very similar to LFG's *correspondence-based transfer* (cf. Kaplan et al. 1989). Basically, in both approaches, transfer is described by path equations which are assigned (*co-described*) to the entries of the monolingual source lexicon. (The stipulations of (15) correspond to the set of constraints {↑ PRED = "gefallen⟨(↑SUBJ)(↑ sc OBJ2)⟩", (τ ↑) = "like⟨(τ ↑SUBJ)τ ↑OBJ)⟩", τ(↑ SUBJ) = (τ ↑ OBJ), τ(↑ OBJ2) = (τ ↑ SUBJ)} in LFG notation).

However, here, in contrast to the setting of Kaplan et al. (1989) for LFG transfer, descriptions relate to flat semantics representations, not to f-structures, and statements can be made about substructures from outside the local domain of the word in the sentence representation. (For example, restructuring of the sentence can be triggered and controlled from the position of verb arguments and adjuncts). This is made possible as the internal representation of the FUDRS is not recursive but is realized as flat lists of information items (This is similar to transfer architectures used in the Verbmobil project mentioned in section 2.2.).

In Eberle (2001) it is shown that the τ–instruction mechanism is powerful enough to treat head switching in the lexicon, even cases of embedded head switching. As this is a notoriously difficult problem discussed at various places in the literature, which to our opinion cannot be treated satisfactorily in the lexicon for the level of syntactic or functional structure, this is a strong argument in favor of the described semantics based transfer architecture (compare Sadler & Thompson 1991, Butt 1994, Dorna et al. 1998). We come back to this problem in the next section.

3.4 Dynamic evaluation

Frequently, lexical transfer statements are connected to specific contextual conditions. Assume that the VP of example (13) *einen Film zeigen* is translated into *passer un film* in French if there is no indirect object and into *présenter un film* if there is one. This can be represented in the MT lexicon as follows:

- $_{\text{zeigen}}$ [subj(n),obj(n),iobj(n)]
  c: d(obj):FILM &$\vdash_D$ d(iobj):e
(16) T: passer

  c: d(obj):FILM & $\vdash_D$ d(iobj):f
  T: présenter

Here, c stands for *condition*. *d* means *down* and relates a structured representation to one of its functors; *d(obj)* to a functor whose role is *obj*, etc. *e* means that the corresponding structure is *empty*, i.e. that the corresponding path does not exist. *f* means filled. FILM says that the corresponding structure is of type FILM. On the basis of the representation (14) neither *d(iobj):e* nor *d(iobj):f* can be entailed. However, in a model of the representation one of both holds. Transfer forces a decision in this case. Which one of the two solutions is more appropriate or more likely depends on default or statistics knowledge available to the system. The operator $\vdash_D$ distinguishes weaker default assumptions from 'hard' inferences. Of course, in order to keep things consistent there must be bookkeeping of these decisions. A minimal account of that is that the source representation is specified according to the assumption chosen by transfer. For (14) this means to specify the representation to (14.dat) or (14.gen).

As the translation of (13) into English makes use of different prepositions, there must be a corresponding evaluation trigger in the German-English transfer component, even if there is no difference concerning the translation of the verb, as in (13). This could also be integrated in the lexicon similarly to the case of the French verb. However, as the different translations are instances of general regularities in this case (per default German genitive is translated by an English *of*-phrase and dative by a *to*-phrase, independently of the structures modified), it is more efficient to handle this case in the general transfer component. Note that this doesn't mean to specify particular translations there, but to integrate a corresponding disambiguation trigger, as it is clear that transfer into English always must disambiguate the type of structural ambiguity represented by (13) because of the case representation mismatch between German and English.

Other such disambiguation triggers must be provided for the resolution of (certain) pronouns (see examples (3 and 4). In the system that we sketch here the algorithm of Lappin & McCord (1990) and Lappin & Leass (1994) is used. This is a classical resolution algorithm (and a kind of standard for all successors). It is tailored for slot grammar analyses but can be used for other syntactic analyses also.

It ignores semantic knowledge and is based on syntactic constraints using (handcrafted) weighting of structural configurations for computing rankings. It has been improved significantly by exploiting semantic knowledge from selectional restrictions – mainly with respect to possessive pronouns- and accessibility constraints (compare Eberle 2003). There are other analytic procedures and there are purely statistical methods also (for an overview compare Mitkov 1999, 2002, for a statistical approach Ge, Hale & Charniak 1998). We do not go into detail with this topic here.

As many disambiguations of ambiguous words are interrelated – where the resolution of referential terms is an important example, but not the only one -, maintaining overall consistency is a hard problem for Machine Translation. If, less ambitiously, one aims at more local consistency only (of paragraphs, instead of texts) and if one uses weak definitions of consistency only, the problem is significantly reduced however. This is what one is forced to do in practice. This means, keeping translation consistent is a matter of approximation.

4 Flat, underspecified rule-based MT and current empirical MT trends

During the last decade there has been significantly growing interest to combine features from different types of Machine Translation. In (2.3.) we basically saw three trends towards hybrid systems. Combining EBMT and SMT enables going (far) beyond the word level with defining statistical translation models. Monolingual collocational information helps to circumvent the sparse data problem. Incorporating analytic (linguistic) knowledge into SMT serves the same goal (because statistics can be defined at the level of basic forms instead of inflected forms; in general for more abstract and therefore more frequent elements as are available by linguistic classification and abstraction).

Provided cautious syntactic and semantic representations as advocated for in this overview, a fourth issue seems viable and promising: a rule-based core system with declarative analysis grammar and semantic construction, with transfer on the basis of flat semantic representations and with decision procedures where the 'difficult' decisions are founded on statistically gained knowledge from corpora.

Essentially, we see three types of knowledge which can help to make more justified decisions: selectional restrictions, preferences in the presence of structural ambiguities, operational criteria for lexical disambiguation and choice of transfer equivalents. A prerequesite for extracting reliable information of these types from corpora is that the available corpora are sufficiently *balanced* and sufficiently large.

4.1 Learning selectional restrictions

There are two ways in which knowledge about (semantic) selectional restrictions of subcategorized complements contribute to translation quality: Firstly, it can help to disambiguate ambiguous complements (which may be pronouns) and, conversely, it can help to disambiguate ambiguous syntactic heads by using the semantic relation they define in the opposite direction (compare section 1.2.2.). Secondly, it can contribute to structural disambiguation – if there are different possibilities for identifying the argument of a syntactic head (in the presence of coordinations for example). However, as has been discussed in section 1.2.3., there are a number of phenomena which suggest to model semantic selectional restrictions not as hard rules, but as default rules or to assign them context dependent weights. A prerequisite of learning selectional restrictions from corpora is to have a hierarchy of semantic types available and a corresponding classification of the lexicon. If there is an analysis system available which disposes of correspondingly structured lexical information, a maximum-likelihood approach is natural. An example is the suggestion of Bernth & McCord (2003) for slot grammar analysis: corpus sentences are parsed and the results are used to estimate the distribution of semantic types with respect to the frames as assigned to the words in the lexicon. If there is no a priori information about semantic classes such information can be built – and typically is built – from freely available lexical knowledge resources like WordNet (Fellbaum 1998; for an overview compare Schulte im Walde 2008). Provided a semantic typing of (part of) the lexicon a number of data driven extensions of the semantic knowledge (which can support disambiguation for Machine Translation) suggest themselves: Frame distribution patters can be used to compute semantic typing of syntactic heads, in particular of verbs from corpora (cf. e.g. Schulte im Walde et al. 2008), and, more generally, to extract semantic collocations and contribute to *word sense disambiguation* in general (cf. Yarowsky 2000, Manning & Schütze 1999). Integrating bootstrapping methods, available knowledge about semantic classes as such and classification can be used to complete the lexical knowledge in this respect.

4.2 Learning structural preferences

A lot of erroneous translations are caused by structural misinterpretations; either directly, because the target language provides different structures for the alternatives, or indirectly, because effects from selectional constraints may change. A notorious structural problem is PP attachment. Hindle & Rooth (1993) is an early attempt to improve analysis in this respect by statistical information. It has become very influential in the sequel and is at the basis of a number of extensions and improvements (cf. Volk 2001). As with other phenomena results become more meaningful and reliable if semantic types are considered instead of words when computing probabilities for structural alternatives (cf. Stetina & Nagao 1997). As sketched in the previous paragraph, using (partly) informed systems for analysis in a bootstrapping approach seems very promising to compile preference knowledge for many kinds of structural ambiguities.

4.3 Learning contextual restrictions of transfer equivalents

A third strand of bootstrapping the translation system relates to translation proper. It is known that the use of *cognates* improves statistical word alignment significantly (cf. Simard, Foster & Isabelle 1992). This finding is widely used in modern hybrid systems, mixing EBMT and SMT, in order to learn new reliable equivalences – between simple words or between multi word expressions or structures (cf. Kondrak, Marcu & Knight 2003, Ma et al. 2008). From the perspective of human readable dictionaries it is not sufficient however to have probabilities available for transfer equivalences (as such or connected to word n-grams). The human user wishes operational conditions describing the structural circumstances under which a particular translation is preferred. This is identical to the needs of a RBMT system. A hybrid system built from a RBMT system needs both: exact structural conditions (as in example (16) above) labelled by a probability value which makes the system much more flexible and robust, in the presence of stylistic variation, metonomy, etc. Eberle & Rapp (2008) describes an approach for extracting such knowledge for a LMT system with underspecified semantic representation. Such approaches use the analyses of both source and target sentence in sentence aligned parallel corpora and the existing knowledge about transfer equivalents to extract new transfer relations with conditions to be abstracted from the given context (using semantic types) by testing significance against the sentences in the corpus.

5 Conclusion

Ambiguity is the hardest problem for high quality Machine Translation. Most ambiguities are semantic ambiguities. Classical rule-based systems are overcharged with taking into account all relevant meanings in the lexicon and disambiguating the correct meaning of words and structures in the sentence in order to compute correct translations. Statistics based systems and, more generally, data driven systems are confronted with sparse parallel data for many phenomena and language pairs and with insufficiently balanced corpora. Hybrid systems are promising as they may minimize the disadvantages of the contrasting approaches and optimize the advantages. Doing translation at the level of underspecified semantic representation with semantically typed lexical elements seems promising too. It avoids expensive disambiguation as far as possible. It widely abstracts away from syntactic and other formal language specific idiosyncrasies, in particular with regard to defining and using contextual clues for choosing translation equivalents. A direct consequence of this is that the remaining need for disambiguation in analysis and transfer relates to a wide extent to relations between semantic classes, not to relations between words. Such knowledge can be extracted from corpora by statistical methods if these corpora are annotated by corresponding classifications before. This can be carried out using the system and its resources. Such abstract relational knowledge is much more reliable in principle than knowledge on the basis of words, because corresponding evaluations refer to types of sentences and words, not to tokens and reduce the sparse data problem significantly therefore.

We venture therefore the statement that rule-based Machine Translation will survive and semantics will be a prospective feature of it, provided there is used a modular architecture with lean declarative analysis and transfer components and interfaces for integration of statistics information as obtainable from corpora which are annotated by categorial and semantic evaluations of the sentences, where annotation is carried out with the help of the MT system itself.

6 References

Abney, Steve 1991. Parsing by chunks. In: R. Berwick, S. Abney & C. Tenny (eds.). *Principle-Based Parsing*. Dordrecht: Kluwer, 257–278.

Alshawi, Hiyan 1992. *The Core Language Engine*. Cambridge, MA: The MIT Press.

Bar-Hillel, Yehoshua 1960. The present status of automatic translation of language. In: F. L. Alt (ed.). *Advances in Computers*. New York: Academic Press, 91–141. Reprinted in:
S. Nirenburg, H. Somers & Y. Wilcks (eds). *Readings in Machine Translation*. Cambridge, MA: The MIT Press, 2003, 45–76.

Barnett, James, Inderjeet Mani, Elaine Rich, C. Aone, Kevin Knight & J.C. Martinez 1991. Capturing language specific semantic distinctions in interlingua-based mt. In: *Proceedings of MT Summit III*. Washington, DC, 25–32.

Bennett, Winfield S. & Jonathan Slocum 1988. Metal: The lrc machine translation system. In: J. Slocum (ed.) *Machine Translation Systems*. Cambridge: Cambridge University Press, 111–140.

Bernth, Arendse 1992. *The LMT-book*. Ms. Heidelberg, IBM Deutschland Informationssysteme GmbH Scientific Center, Institute for Logic and Linguistics.

Bernth, Arendse & Michael McCord 2003. A hybrid approach to deriving selectional preferences. In: *Proceedings of MT Summit IX*. New Orleans, LA, 9–15.

Boitet, Christian 1988. Pros and cons of the pivot and transfer approaches. In: D. Maxwell, K. Schubert & T. Witkam (eds.). *New Directions in Machine Translation*. Dordrecht: Foris, 93–106. Reprinted in: S. Nirenburg, H. Somers & Y. Wilcks (eds). *Readings in Machine Translation*. Cambridge, MA: The MIT Press, 2003, 273–280.

Brown, Peter F., John Cocke, Stephen A. Della Pietra, Vincent J. Della Pietra, Robert L. Mercer Fredrick Jelinek & Paul S. Roossin 1990. A statistical approach to machine translation. *Computational Linguistics* 16, 79–85.

Brown, Peter F., Stephen A. Della Pietra, Vincent J. Della Pietra, John D. Lafferty & Robert L. Mercer 1992. Analysis, statistical transfer, and synthesis in machine translation. In: *Proceedings of the 4th International Conference on Theoretical and Methodological Issues in Machine Translation*. Montreal, 83–100.

Brown, Peter F., Stephen A. Della Pietra, Vincent J. Della Pietra & Robert L. Mercer 1993. The mathematics of statistical machine translation: Parameter estimation. *Computational Linguistics* 19, 263–311.

Butt, Miriam 1994. Machine translation and complex predicates. In: G. Görz (ed.). *Konvens '92*. Heidelberg: Springer, 62–71.

Butt, Miriam, Helge Dyvik, Tracy Holloway King, Hiroshi Masuichi & Christian Rohrer 2002. The parallel grammar project. In: *Proceedings of COLING-2002 Workshop on Grammar Engineering and Evaluation*. Taipei, 1–7.

Callison-Burch, Chris, Philipp Koehn & Miles Osborne 2006. Improved statistical machine translation using paraphrases. In: R.C. Moore et al. (eds.). *Proceedings of the Main Conference on Human Language Technology Conference of the North American Chapter of the Association of Computational Linguistics (= HLT-NAACL) 2006*. New York: ACL, 17–24.

Carbonell, Jaime, Teruko Mitamura & Eric H. Nyberg 1992. The KANT perspective: A critique of pure transfer (and pure interlingua, pure statistics, . . . In: *Proceeedings of the 4th International Conference on Theoretical and Methodological Issues in Machine Translation (= TMI '92)*. Montréal, 225–235.

Chiang, David 2005. A hierarchical phrase-based model for statistical machine translation. In: *Proceedings of the 43rd Annual Meeting of the Association for Computational Linguistics (= ACL)*. New York: ACL, 263–270.

Copeland, Charles, Jacques Durand, Steven Krauwer & Bente Maegaard (eds.) 1991. *The Eurotra Formal Specifications. Studies in Machine Translation and Natural Language Processing*. Technical Report, vol. 2. Brussels, Office for Official Publications of the Commission of the European Community.

Dorna, Michael, Kurt Eberle, Martin Emele & C.J. Rupp 1994. *Semantik-orientierter rekursiver Transfer in HPSG am Beispiel des Referenzdialogs* (Verbmobil-Report 39). Stuttgart: IMS, University of Stuttgart.

Dorna, Michael, Anette Frank, Josef van Genabith & Martin Emele 1998. Syntactic and semantic transfer with f-structures. In: *Proceedings of the 36th Annual Meeting of the Association of Computational Linguistics (= ACL/COLING 98)*. Montreal: ACL, 341–347.

Dorr, Bonnie 1990. Solving thematic divergences in machine translation. In: *Proceedings of the 28th Annual Conference of the Association for Computational Linguistics (= ACL)*. Pittsburgh, PA: ACL, 127–134.

Dorr, Bonnie 1993. *Machine Translation: A View from the Lexicon*. Cambridge, MA: The MIT Press.
Dorr, Bonnie 1994. Machine translation divergences: A formal description and proposed solution. *Computational Linguistics* 20, 597–633.
Dowty, David R., R. Walland & P.S. Peters 1981. *Introduction to Montague Semantics*. Dordrecht: Reidel.
Drouin, Normand 1989. Le système logos. In: A. Abbou (ed.). *La traduction assistée par ordinateur: Perspectives technologiques, industrielles et économiques envisageables à l'horizon 1990*. Paris: Editions Daicadif, 35–40.
Durand, Jacques, Paul Bennett, Valerio Allegranza, Frank van Eynde, Lee Humphreys, Paul Schmidt & Erich Steiner 1991. The eurotra linguistic specifications: An overview. *Machine Translation* 6, 103–147.
Eberle, Kurt 1997. *Flat Underspecified Representation and Its Meaning for a Fragment of German* (Arbeitspapiere des Sonderforschungsbereichs 340 *Sprachtheoretische Grundlagen für die Computerlinguistik* 120). Stuttgart: University of Stuttgart.
Eberle, Kurt 2001. FUDR-based MT, head switching and the lexicon. In: *Proceedings of the 8th Machine Translation Summit*. Santiago de Compostela.
Eberle, Kurt 2002. Tense and aspect information in a FUDR-based German French Machine Translation System. In: H. Kamp & U. Reyle (eds.). *How We Say WHEN It Happens. Contributions to the Theory of Temporal Reference in Natural Language*. Tübingen: Niemeyer, 97–148.
Eberle, Kurt 2003. Anaphernresolution in flach analysierten Texten für Recherche und Übersetzung. In: U. Seewald-Heeg (ed.). *Sprachtechnologie für die multilinguale Kommunikation. Textproduktion, Recherche, Übersetzung, Lokalisierung*. Sankt Augustin: Gardez!-Verlag, 216–232.
Eberle, Kurt 2004. *Flat Underspecified Representation and Its Meaning for a Fragment of German*. Habilitationsschrift. University of Stuttgart.
Eberle, Kurt & Reinhard Rapp 2008. Rapid construction of explicative dictionaries using hybrid machine translation. In: A. Storrer et al. (eds.). *Text Resources and Lexical Knowledge: Selected Papers from the 9th Conference on Natural Language Processing (= KONVENS)*. Berlin: de Gruyter, 159–174.
Emele, Martin C., Michael Dorna, Anke Lüdeling, Heike Zinsmeister & Christian Rohrer 2000. Semantic-based transfer. In: W. Wahlster (ed.). *Verbmobil: Foundations of Speech-to-Speech Translation*. Heidelberg: Springer, 359–376.
Fellbaum, Christiane (ed.) 1998. *WordNet – An Electronic Lexical Database*. Cambridge, MA: The MIT Press.
Flickinger, Dan, Ann Copestake & Ivan A. Sag 2000. HPSG analysis of English. In: W. Wahlster (ed.). *Verbmobil: Foundations of Speech-to-Speech Translation*. Heidelberg: Springer, 359–376.
Frank, Anette 1999. From parallel grammar development towards machine translation – a project overview. In: *Proceedings of the 7th Machine Translation Summit. MT in the Great Translation Era*. Singapore, 134–142.
Furuse, Osamu & Hitoshi Iida 1994. Constituent boundary parsing for example-based machine translation. In: *Proceedings of the 15th International Conference on Computational Linguistics (= COLING-94)*. Kyoto, 105–111.
Ge, Niyu, John Hale & Eugene Charniak 1998. A statistical approach to anaphora resolution. In: *Proceedings of the Sixth Workshop on Very Large Corpora (COLING-ACL98)*. Montreal: ACL, 161–170.

Gough, Nano & Andy Way 2004. Example-based controlled translation. In: *Proceedings of the Ninth Workshop of the European Association for Machine Translation* (= *EAMT-04*). Valetta, 73–81.

Hindle, Donald & Mats Rooth 1993. Structural ambiguity and lexical relations. *Computational Linguistics* 1, 103–120.

Hong, Munpyo & Oliver Streiter 1999. Overcoming the language barriers in the web: The unl-approach. In: J. Gippert & P. Olivier (eds.) *Multilinguale Corpora. Codierung, Strukturierung, Analyse*. Prague: Enigma, 253–262.

Hutchins, W. John 1986. *Machine Translation: Past, Present, Future*. Chichester: Ellis Horwood.

Hutchins, W. John 1995. Machine translation: A brief history. In: E.F.K. Koerner & R.E. Asher (eds.). *Concise History of the Language Sciences. From the Sumerians to the Cognitivists*. Oxford: Pergamon Press, 431–445.

Hutchins, W. John 1997. From first conception to first demonstration: The nascent years of machine translation, 1947–1954 a chronology. *Machine Translation* 12, 195–252.

Hutchins, W. John 2001. Machine translation over fifty years. *Histoire, Epistemologie, Langage* 23, 7–31.

Hutchins, W. John & Harold Somers (eds.) 1992. *An Introduction to Machine Translation*. London: Academic Press.

Jackendoff, Ray 1983. *Semantics and Cognition*. Cambridge, MA: The MIT Press.

Jackendoff, Ray 1990. *Semantic Structures*. Cambridge, MA: The MIT Press.

Jurafsky, Daniel & James H. Martin (eds.) 2000. *Speech and Language Processing: An Introduction to Natural Language Processing, Computational Linguistics, and Speech Recognition*. Upper Saddle River, NJ: Prentice Hall.

Kameyama, Megumi, Ryo Ochitani & Stanley Peters 1991. Resolving translation mismatches with information flow. In: *Proceedings of the 29th Annual Meeting of the Association for Computational Linguistics* (= *ACL*). Berkeley, CA: ACL, 193–200.

Kaplan, Ronald & Joan Bresnan 1982. Lexical functional grammar: A formal system for grammatical representation. In: J. Bresnan (ed.). *The Mental Representation of Grammatical Relations*. Cambridge, MA: The MIT Press.

Kaplan, Ronald, Klaus Netter, Jürgen Wedekind & Annie Zaenen 1989. Translation by structural correspondences. In: *Proceedings of the 4th Annual Meeting of the European Chapter of the Association for Computational Linguistics* (= *E-ACL*). Manchester: ACL, 272–281.

Kay, Martin 1980. The proper place of men and machines in language translation. Working paper. Palo Alto, CA, Xerox PARC. Reprinted in: *Machine Translation* 12, 1997, 3–23.

Kay, Martin 1997. It's still the proper place. *Machine Translation* 12, 35–38.

Kay, Martin, Jean Mark Gawron & Peter Norwig 1994. *VERBMOBIL: A Translation System for Face-to-Face Dialog*. Stanford, CA: CSLI Publications.

Kondrak, Grzegorz, Daniel Marcu & Kevin Knight 2003. Cognates can improve statistical translation models. In: *Proceedings of the Human Language Technology and North American Association for Computational Linguistics Conference* (= *HLT-NAACL*). Edmonton, AB: ACL, 46–48.

Kuhn, Jonas & Ulrich Heid 1994. Treating structural differences in an hpsg-based approach to interlingual machine translation. In: P. Bosch & Ch. Habel (eds.). *Kognitive Grundlagen für interlinguabasierte Übersetzung*. Heidelberg: ILL, 11–36.

Landsbergen, Jan 1982. Machine translation based on logical Montague grammars. In: *Proceedings of the Ninth International Conference on Computational* (= *COLING*). Prague: Academia, 175–181.

Landsbergen, Jan 1987a. Isomorphic grammars and their use in the rosetta translation system. In: M. King (ed.). *Machine Translation Today: The State of the Art. Proceedings of the Third Lugano Tutorial*. Edinburgh: Edinburgh University Press, 351–372.

Landsbergen, Jan 1987b. Montague grammar and machine translation. In: P. Whitelock et al. (eds.). *Linguistic Theory and Computer Applications*. London: Academic Press, 113–147.

Lappin, Shalom & Herbert Leass 1994. An algorithm for pronominal anaphora resolution. *Computational Linguistics* 20, 535–561.

Lappin, Shalom & Michael McCord 1990. A syntactic filter on pronominal anaphora in slot grammar. In: *Proceedings of the 28th Annual Meeting of the Association for Computational Linguistics (= ACL)*. Pittsburgh, PA: ACL, 135–142.

Ma, Yanjun, Sylwia Ozdowska, Yanli Sun & Andy Way 2008. Improving word alignment using syntactic dependencies. In: *Proceedings of the Second ACL Workshop on Syntax and Structure in Statistical Translation (SSST-2)*. Columbus, OH: ACL, 69–77.

Manning, Christopher D. & Hinrich Schütze 1999. *Foundations of Statistical Natural Language Processing*. Cambridge, MA: The MIT Press.

Maruyama, Hiroshi & Hideo Watanabe 1992. Tree cover search algorithm for example-based translation. In: *Proceedings of the 4th International Conference on Theoretical and Methodological Issues in Machine Translation (= TMI)*. Montréal, 173–184.

McCord, Michael 1989a. Design of LMT. A prolog-based machine translation system. *Computational Linguistics* 15, 33–52.

McCord, Michael 1989b. A new version of the machine translation system LMT. *Literary and Linguistic Computing* 4, 218–299.

McCord, Michael & Arendse Bernth 1998. The lmt transformational system. In: D. Farwell, L. Gerber & E. Hovy (eds.). *Machine Translation and the Information Soup. Proceedings of the 3rd Conference of the Association for Machine Translation in the Americas (= AMTA)*. Heidelberg: Springer, 344–355.

Mitkov, Ruslan 1999. *Anaphora Resolution: The State of the Art*. Working paper. Wolverhampton, University of Wolverhampton.

Mitkov, Ruslan 2002. Automatic anaphora resolution: Limits, impediments, and ways forward. In: E. Ranchod & N.J. Mamede (eds.). *Advances in Natural Language Processing. Third International Conference (= PorTAL)*. Faro, 3–4.

Nagao, Makoto, Junichi Tsujii & Junichi Nakamura 1988. The Japanese government project for machine translation. In: J. Slocum (ed.). *Machine Translation Systems*. Cambridge: Cambridge University Press, 141–186.

Nirenburg, Sergej, Jaime Carbonell, Masaru Tomita & Kenneth Goodman 1992. *Machine Translation: A Knowledge Based Approach*. San Mateo, CA: Morgan Kaufman.

Nirenburg, Sergej, Stephen Beale, Kavi Mahesh, Boyan Onyshkevych, Victor Raskin, Evelyne Viegas, Yorick Wilks & Remi Zajac 1996. Lexicons in the mikrokosmos project. In: *Proceedings of the Society for Artificial Intelligence and Simulated Behavior (= AISB) Workshop on Multilinguality in the Lexicon*. Brighton, 26–33.

Och, Franz Josef & Hermann Ney 2002. Discriminative training and maximum entropy models for statistical machine translation. In: *Proceedings of the 40th Annual Meeting of the Association for Computational Linguistics (= ACL)*. Philadelphia, PA: ACL, 295–302.

Onyshkevych, Boyan & Sergej Nirenburg 1995. A lexicon for knowledge-based mt. *Machine Translation* 10, 5–57.

Pierce, John R., John B. Caroll, Eric P. Hamp, David G. Hays, Charles F. Hockett, Anthony G. Oettinger & Alan J. Perlis 1966. *Language and Machines: Computers in Translation and*

Linguistics. ("ALPAC-report"). Report 416. Washington, DC, National Academy of Sciences Publication.

Quirk, Chris, Arul Menezes & Colin Cherry 2006. Dependency treelet translation: Syntactically informed phrasal SMT. In: *Proceedings of the 43rd Annual Meeting of the Association for Computational Linguistics (= ACL)*. New York: ACL, 271–279.

Reyle, Uwe 1993. Dealing with ambiguities by underspecification: Construction, representation, and deduction. *Journal of Semantics* 10, 123–179.

Riezler, Stefan & John Maxwell 2006. Grammatical machine translation. In: *Proceedings of the 43rd Annual Meeting of the Association for Computational Linguistics (= ACL)*. New York: ACL, 248–255.

Sadler, Louisa & Henry S. Thompson 1991. Structural non-correspondence in translation. In: *Proceedings of the 5th Conference of the European Chapter of the Association for Computational Linguistics (= E-ACL)*. Berlin: ACL, 293–298.

Sadler, Victor 1989. *Working with Analogical Semantics: Disambiguation Techniques in DLT*. Dordrecht: Foris.

Schiehlen, Michael 1996. Semantic construction from parse forests. In: *Proceedings of the 16th International Conference on Computational Linguistics (= COLING)*. Copenhagen: Center for Sprogteknologi, 907–912.

Schmid, Helmut & Sabine Schulte im Walde 2000. Robust German noun chunking with a probabilistic context-free grammar. In: *Proceedings of the 18th International Conference on Computational Linguistics (= COLING)*. Saarbrücken, 726–732.

Schulte im Walde, Sabine 2008. The induction of verb frames and verb classes from corpora. In: A. Lüdeling & Merja Kytö (eds.). *Corpus Linguistics. An International Handbook*. Berlin: de Gruyter, 952–972.

Schulte im Walde, Sabine, Christian Hying, Christian Scheible & Helmut Schmid 2008. Combining em training and the mdl principle for an automatic verb classification incorporating selectional preferences. In: *Proceedings of the 46th Annual Meeting of the Association for Computational Linguistics (= ACL)*. Columbus, OH: ACL, 496–504.

Serasset, Gilles & Christian Boitet 2000. On unl as the future "html of the linguistic content" & the reuse of existing nlp components in unl-related applications with the example of a unl-french deconverter. In: *Proceedings of the 18th International Conference on Computational Linguistics (= COLING)*. Saarbrücken, 768–774.

Simard, Michel, George F. Foster & Pierre Isabelle 1992. Using cognates to align sentences in bilingual corpora. In: *Proceeedings of the 4th International Conference on Theoretical and Methodological Issues in Machine Translation (= TMI)*. Montreal, 67–81.

Slocum, Jonathan 1988. *Machine Translation Systems*. Cambridge: Cambridge University Press.

Stetina, Jiri & Makoto Nagao 1997. Corpus based pp attachment ambiguity resolution with a semantic dictionary. In J. Zhou & K. Church (eds.). *Proceedings of the 5th Workshop on Very Large Corpora*. Kong Kong, 66–80.

Stoll, Cay-Holger 1986. The systran system. In: T. C. Gerhardt (ed.). *Proceedings of the 1st International Conference on State of the Art in Machine Translation in America, Asia and Europe*. Saarbrücken: IAI/Eurotra-D, 3–19.

Trabulsi, Shadi 1989. Le système systran. In: A. Abbou (ed.). *La traduction assistée par ordinateur: Perspectives technologiques, industrielles et économiques envisageables à l'horizon 1990*. Paris: Editions Daicadif, 15–34.

Trujillo, Arturo 1992. *Translation Engines: Techniques for Machine Translation*. Heidelberg: Springer.

Vauquois, Bernard 1975. *La Traduction Automatique á Grenoble*. Paris: Dunod.
Vauquois, Bernard & Christian Boitet 1985. Automated translation at Grenoble University. *Computational Linguistics* 11, 28–36.
Volk, Martin 2001. *The Automatic Resolution of Prepositional Phrase Attachment Ambiguities in German*. Habilitationsschrift. University of Zürich.
Wahlster, Wolfgang (ed.) 2000. *Verbmobil: Foundations of Speech-to-Speech Translation*. Heidelberg: Springer.
Watanabe, Hideo & Koichi Takeda 1998. A pattern-based machine translation system extended by example-based processing. In: *Proceedings of the Sixth Workshop on Very Large Corpora (COLING-ACL98)*. Montreal: ACL, 1369–1373.
Weaver, Warren 2003. Translation. In: S. Nirenburg, H. Somers & Y. Wilks (eds.). *Readings in Machine Translation*. Cambridge, MA: The MIT Press, 363–394. Reprint.
Whitelock, Pete 1992. Shake-and-bake-translation. In: *Proceedings of the 14th International Conference on Computational Linguistics (= COLING)*. Nantes, 784–791.
Yarowsky, David 2000. Word sense disambiguation. In: R. Dale, H. Moisl & H. Somers (eds.). *Handbook of Natural Language Processing*. New York: Dekker, 629–654.
Zajac, Rémi 1989. A transfer model using a typed feature structure rewriting system with inheritance. In: *Proceedings of the 27th Annual Meeting of the Association for Computational Linguistics (= ACL)*. Vancouver: ACL, 1–6.
Zajac, Rémi 1990. A relational approach to translation. In: *Proceedings of the 3rd International Conference on Theoretical and Methodological Issues in Machine Translation (= TMI)*. Montreal, 235–254.

Index

absolute universals 1, 4, 5, 9
– of meaning 4, 5
accommodated DPs 211, 225–227
acquisition 237–268, 274–298, 349–358, 461–468, 536
– of semantics 237–244, 274–286, 293, 297, 471, 472
(Acquisition of) interpretable features 276, 279, 296
acquisition of spatial language 102, 349–358
ambiguity 228, 371, 377, 390, 500–505, 520
anaphora and definite reference 427, 428
anaphoric DPs 211, 224, 225
aspect 18, 48, 58–68, 84–88, 179, 229, 281, 283, 291, 356
aspectual systems 58–68, 87, 88
aspectual viewpoints 58, 64–68, 81–84, 87, 88, 291, 292
attention allocation 214
Avoid Pragmatic Overload 177, 193, 200–206

bare verb interpretation (perceptual reports) 293, 294
Bottleneck Hypothesis 276, 298

categorization 16, 108, 124, 147, 155, 167, 303–320, 333, 334, 354, 360, 423, 425, 470, 501
change of meaning 113–117, 120, 121, 125, 134, 135, 139–141
Cinque's cartography 3, 16, 17
coercion 59, 60, 63, 64, 87, 212, 230, 285
cognitive linguistics 94, 114, 123–126, 139, 147–149, 155, 158, 165–172
cognitive psychology 303, 305, 326
cognitive semantics 113–115, 123–126, 138, 148, 167, 510
common noun denotations 9, 19
complexity 178, 205, 210, 211, 216–220, 229, 230, 281, 390, 420, 421, 511
complex syntax–simple semantics 274, 283, 286–290, 297
composition 137, 183, 192, 193, 198, 205, 382, 504

computational linguistics 366–399, 427, 432, 444
computational semantics 366–399, 444–446, 468
concepts 11, 31, 132, 160, 164, 165, 168, 169, 192, 198, 303–335, 368, 377, 455, 487
conceptual combination 320–326, 343
conceptual compositionality 324–326
conceptual hierarchies 309–312
conceptual knowledge and word meanings 326–333
conceptual metaphors 157–165, 168, 172
conceptual taxonomies 310–312, 449, 490
content-oriented annotation 419–421, 428–431
corpora 100, 137, 140, 156, 218, 342, 366, 378–386, 396–399, 409–418, 422–429, 459–471, 505, 516–518, 523–529
(corpus-based) lexical acquisition 462, 471, 472
corpus-based methods 131, 140, 170, 414, 428, 460, 472
corpus linguistics 140, 409–414
count environments 32–36, 49
count/mass distinction 14, 29–54
count nouns 14, 22, 29–53, 326, 355, 360
count versus mass 46–53
Critical Period Hypothesis 275–277, 298
cross-categorial classifications 10, 11
(cross-lingual) semantic classification 465–468

diachronic onomasiology 165–172
diachronic prototype semantics 149–157
diachronic semantics 94, 115, 119–123, 147, 148, 157
diachronic structural semantics 119–123
disambiguation 228, 368, 378–381, 388, 395, 457, 458, 467, 471, 495, 500, 504, 505, 509, 515, 520, 521, 525–529
discourse and dialog annotation 425–427
Discourse Representation Structure 61, 71–74, 219, 370, 514, 519–524
– flat underspecified 519–524
– underspecified 519

Discourse Representation Theory 71–74, 136, 370, 374, 375, 512–516, 519–521
disjunction 237, 238, 241, 244–268, 501
– in human languages 237, 246–253, 256, 257, 266–268
distributional semantics 121, 386, 389, 397
domain restriction 210, 221, 227
dynamic semantics 370, 512

effability 4
English simple and progressive (aspectual) tenses 283, 284, 292
events 20, 57–67, 72, 73, 81–87, 96, 107–109, 133, 188, 194, 212, 239, 281–285, 291–294, 304, 351–355, 360, 419, 430, 431, 451
event structure 58, 83, 84, 87
eventualities 15, 20, 64, 84
exemplars 314, 317–319, 324, 329, 333, 354

fictive motion 96, 97, 108
first language acquisition 237–268, 274, 275
FrameNet 377, 383, 384, 392, 423–425, 452–454, 457, 458, 465–471
functional/lexical categories 10, 16, 19, 24, 154, 166, 178, 277, 279, 281, 282, 296
function words 180, 201, 238, 278

generalization 2, 38–46, 53, 119, 185, 200, 245–250
grammaticalization 115, 126–132, 136, 137, 149, 155, 177–186, 200, 201, 205
grammatical meaning 129, 200, 280
grounded models of meaning 397–399

historical semantics 113–127, 130–141, 147–149, 156
historical semasiology 115–119

ideational theory of meaning 115–119, 124
implicational universal 4
implicature of exclusivity 249, 252–257, 260–262
incremental themes and telicity 61, 62
inference 71, 80–84, 133, 189, 223, 224, 367, 368, 373–377, 390–395, 457, 458, 463
information extraction 366, 468, 469, 482, 492–495

Interface Hypothesis 279, 296, 297
Interlingua 508–518
Interpretability Hypothesis 279

knowledge-based methods 377–380, 457, 458, 472, 482
knowledge representation 469, 482, 483, 487, 488, 494, 515

language acquisition 102, 205, 237, 238, 245, 250, 253, 257, 261, 266, 274, 275, 281, 295, 356
language architecture 274, 280
language learning 246, 248, 346, 350–353, 356, 378, 398
Levin classes 447, 448, 451, 452, 460
Lexical Conceptual Structure 447, 448, 451, 469, 510, 515
lexical resources 422–424, 447, 454, 459, 469
lexical-semantic relations 114, 120, 166, 167, 303, 335, 377, 394, 411, 445–449, 455, 460–464, 472, 502
lexical semantics 1, 14, 23, 113, 115, 135, 139, 148, 276, 420, 447, 459
localism 93–96
locative 86, 94–99, 212

Machine translation
    ambiguity-preserving 502–505
    direct 509, 527
    example-based (EBMT) 517, 518, 526, 528
    hybrid 505, 518, 526–529
    knowledge-based (KBMT) 499–501, 506, 515
    rule-based (RBMT) 507–509, 526–529
    statistical (SMT) 396, 516–518, 526–528
mass nouns 14, 29–33, 36, 37, 42–51, 360
meaning change 94, 113–141, 147–149, 183–185, 188, 192, 199–201
– theories of 94, 113–141, 149
metaphor 94, 96, 107, 116, 118, 122–128, 133–134, 138, 147–149, 154–169, 185, 195, 200, 277, 445, 502
metonymy 118, 122, 125, 126, 133, 134, 139, 147, 148, 154, 156, 166–169, 185, 200, 206, 446, 502

motion events 92, 96, 97, 107, 304, 327, 328, 342, 360
multiple critical periods 275

natural language processing (NLP) 374, 375, 380, 385, 444–450, 454–459, 465, 469–472, 492–495
natural logic inference 393–395
number 13, 14, 29–46, 50, 53, 292, 430, 485, 489
– morphology 30–33, 36, 39, 44–51
– neutral nouns 32–38, 40–46, 53
numeral classifiers 29–47, 51–53

ontology 6, 426, 428, 455, 457, 463, 464, 469, 470, 482–495, 512
– learning 463, 464, 489, 490
– lexicon 491–493
– search 490
OWL 484–491, 494

Plato's problem 244–256
plural noun 29, 37, 38, 41–46, 54
polysemy 52, 113–115, 118, 122–125, 131–134, 137, 138, 157, 166, 326, 331, 448, 457
present perfect 72–75
processing quantifiers 211, 215–224
properties and predicatives 18–20
propositions 8, 15, 18, 22, 84, 189, 198, 262, 280
prototypes 124, 155, 314, 317, 318, 509
prototype semantics 149–157
psycholinguistics 97, 210, 231, 378

quasi logical form 371, 514

reference frames 92, 101–109, 358, 359
referential theory of processing 212
relationship between concepts and lexical meanings 303, 326, 329, 330
Resource Description Framework 484–488, 491–494

Sanches-Greenberg-Slobin generalization 29, 30, 38–46, 53
scalar implicatures 223, 249, 252, 253, 258, 261, 297

second language acquisition 274, 275
selectional properties of determiners 36–38
selectional restrictions 447, 452, 456, 501–504, 514, 516, 526, 527
semantic
– annotation 411, 418–431, 468, 492, 493
– change 113, 115, 118, 122–130, 135, 136, 148, 154–157, 167–172, 182–185, 206
– coercion 212, 230
– lexicon 444–449, 454–461, 465, 468–471, 491
– lexicon and ontology 455, 469, 470, 491, 493
– processing 210, 211, 221, 223, 229, 231, 367, 377, 390, 444, 456–460, 470–472
– reanalysis 137, 177–206
– reflexes of formal features 281
– role annotation 423–425, 428
– role labeling 379, 382–385, 396, 419, 421
Semantic Web 419, 482–487, 490, 491, 496
Shallow Structure Hypothesis 278, 295, 296
Simple Syntax–Complex Semantics 283–286, 291, 297
simple syntax–complex semantics 274, 283–286, 291, 297
social networks 495
space 7, 68, 92–109, 341–361
Spanish aspectual tenses 283–286
spatial
– cognition 343, 358–361
– deixis 103, 104
– expression 92–100, 103, 349, 354
– language 93–96, 102, 341–349, 355, 358–361
– language on spatial cognition 358–360
– primitives 342–350, 353
– relations 92–99, 107, 108, 318, 342–351, 359
states 20, 57–63, 73, 82–87, 94, 95, 280, 286, 451, 515
statistical methods 368, 375–379, 385, 395, 508, 517, 526, 529
subjectification 139, 182–185, 201, 202, 206
syntactic categories and semantic types 1, 5, 7–9, 16, 21, 22

syntax-semantics mismatch 274, 281, 283, 293, 297, 298

telicity 60–62, 230, 239
tense 17, 18, 57–88, 95, 179, 180, 189, 210, 229, 241, 280–296, 356, 468, 501, 512, 513, 523
tense and aspect in discourse 84–87
tenseless languages 57, 70, 71, 79–87
tenses in dependent clauses 75, 76
textual entailment 389–394
topology 100, 101
transfer system 503, 505, 508, 509, 516, 519
translation mismatch 511, 513, 519, 522
types and categories 7–23
typology 9, 92, 104, 245

underspecification 371–373, 378, 445, 450, 503, 515, 516, 520

underspecified representations 228, 505, 519–526
universals 1–9, 24, 25, 38, 126, 180, 261, 267, 356
universal types 1, 6

Vauquois triangle 509–511
viewpoint aspect-related interpretations 291–295

web mining 482, 483, 495, 496
web semantics 482–496
Wh-quantifiers and tense interpretation 286
WordNet 376–382, 392, 394, 411, 422–424, 447–450, 454–460, 463–466, 469, 471, 491, 494, 527
word-sense disambiguation 378–382, 388

www.ingramcontent.com/pod-product-compliance
Lightning Source LLC
Chambersburg PA
CBHW031539300426
44111CB00006BA/111